THEATER

NEW, UPDATED EDITION

HARRY N. ABRAMS, INC., PUBLISHERS

IN AMERICA

MARY C. HENDERSON

250 YEARS OF PLAYS, PLAYERS, AND PRODUCTIONS

*This book is dedicated to three women
who have made all the difference in my life:
my sister Christine M. Wilson and my
friends Nelle Smither and Mary Dana*

Project Director: *Margaret L. Kaplan*
Editor: *Ellyn Childs Allison*
Designer: *Judith Michael*
Photo Editor: *John K. Crowley*

Endpapers:
*The 1985–86 theatrical season was considerably enlivened
by* The Mystery of Edwin Drood, *which producer
Joseph Papp transferred from the Delacorte Theater in
Central Park to a Broadway playhouse.*

Page 1:
*Jessica Tandy gave a memorable performance as Blanche
DuBois in Tennessee Williams's* A Streetcar Named
Desire *(1947). Her costume was designed by Lucinda
Ballard.*

Pages 2 and 3:
Patricia Zipprodt designed the costumes for Chicago
*(1975). Shown here are her drawings for the male
chorus.*

Pages 4 and 5:
Jo Mielziner's setting for Death of a Salesman *(1949)
became one of the legendary scenic conceptions of
twentieth-century American stagecraft. Note the sense of
claustrophobia evoked by the tall buildings leaning toward
the house. The sets were built by Nolan Brothers and
painted by the Triangle Scenic Studios.*

NEW, UPDATED EDITION 1996

Library of Congress Cataloging-in-Publication Data
Henderson, Mary C., 1928–
Theater in America : 250 years of plays, players,
and productions / Mary C. Henderson. — New,
updated ed.
p.   cm.
Includes bibliographical references and index.
ISBN 0-8109-3884-7 (clothbound)
1. Theater—United States—History.   I. Title.
PN2221.H38   1996
792'.0973—dc20   95-38148

Illustrations copyright © 1986 Harry N. Abrams, Inc.
New, updated edition © 1996 Harry N. Abrams, Inc.
Published in 1996 by Harry N. Abrams, Incorporated,
New York
A Times Mirror Company
Printed and bound in Japan

PREFACE AND ACKNOWLEDGMENTS

WHEN America was discovered, Europe was in the midst of the second great efflorescence of cultural activity in history: the Renaissance. When America was settled, the second great era of dramatic activity in the West was drawing to a close: the age of Shakespeare, Lope de Vega, and Molière. Seemingly untouched by these momentous events, the colonials at first went about their business of establishing home and village, farm and business, and creed and church. When they had finished these labors, they were ready to open their lives to more earthly delights. Overwhelmingly English-speaking, they permitted the strolling players from their homeland to set up makeshift theaters and put on English plays. With the rise of the Republic at the end of the eighteenth century, theater and drama began a two-hundred-year process of becoming uniquely American.

My book, then, is about the Americanization of drama and theater. More important, it is a chronicle of artistic collaboration. At its best and worst, theater is art by committee. As each member of the committee became conscious of his mission, as each sought to elevate his own position, as each was himself shaped by the unfolding drama of American history, as each prepared the way for his successors, it was inevitable that the creative collaboration would result in something that was both kin to its English and European prototypes and a reflection of the evolving and kinetic American society. Tough, yet romantic at heart, skillful with their hands, fortunate in their material advantages, the American theatrical collaborators invented a vital, unpredictable, often explosive tradition. From Royall Tyler to Neil Simon, from Thomas Godfrey to Eugene O'Neill, from *Evangeline* to *Hair*, from Charlotte Cushman to Geraldine Page, from William Dunlap to Joseph Papp, the course of American theater has never run smooth, but it has never suffered the curse of dullness. It is my hope that I have captured the fun and fury of the process.

The progress of this book from its genesis in my mind many years ago to its actual appearance in print was given the greatest assist by the John Simon Guggenheim Foundation, which awarded me a fellowship so that I could devote an entire year to research and writing. My friend Brooks MacNamara was responsible for recommending me and encouraging me along the way. Without the understanding and support of Joseph Veach Noble, director of the Museum of the City of New York and my employer, I could not have accepted the gift of time afforded by the Guggenheim grant.

To my former colleagues at the Theatre Collection of the Museum of the City of New York, Wendy Warnken and MaryAnn Smith, I owe thanks for their unflagging help and expert knowledge. Nor can I forget the assistance of Maxwell Silverman as I researched my chapter on theater architecture, or the cheerful response that Camille Croce Dee, David Diamond, Kimberly Fink, Stuart Solloway, and Bob Taylor made to my many frantic calls for help in finding the penultimate fact or the perfect illustration.

I especially wish to cite with appreciation the contributions of Richard Stoddard to my chapter on designers. But for his boundless knowledge, his bottomless files, and his extraordinary patience, I doubt that I could have made the chapter as complete as it is.

I give unending thanks to my friends and colleagues at the Billy Rose Theatre Collection of the New York Public Library at Lincoln Center, who include chief of the Performing Arts Research Center Thor Wood, curator Dorothy Swerdlove, Richard Lynch, Donald Fowle, Dr. Roderick Bladel, David Bartholomew, Olive Wong, Edward Sager, Christine Karatnytsky, Daniel Patri, Rosalie Spar, Babs Craven, and Heidi Stock—all of whom I called upon for a multitude of materials. I also thank the paging staff, particularly Louis Paul and Guy Colas, and my friends at the photocopying machines, Donald Madison and Felipe Taveras.

In my travels around the country, I was aided in my research by many colleagues (most of whom I count among my friends). They include Dr. Jeanne Newlin and Martha Mahard of the Harvard Theatre Collection; Dr. William Crain and Paul Bailey of the Hoblitzelle Theatre Arts Library at the University of Texas at Austin; Dr. David Schoonover at the Beinecke Library of Yale University; Brigitte Kueppers of the Shubert Archive in New York; Sally Pavetti and Lois MacDonald of the Eugene O'Neill Theater Center in New London, Connecticut; Geraldine Duclow of the Theatre Collection of the Philadelphia Free Library; Mary Ann Jensen of the Theatre Collection at Princeton University; Louis Rachow of the Booth-Hampden Library of The Players, New York; Mary Ashe of the San Francisco Public Library; the staff of the Southwest Texas Collection at Texas Tech University, Lubbock; and the staff of the Manuscripts and Prints Divisions of the Library of Congress in the James Madison Building.

Golden nuggets of information emerged from discussions with Lucinda Ballard Dietz, Peggy Elson, the late John Krapp, Abe Feder, Robin Wagner, Peggy Clark, Tal Russell, Tharon Musser, Howard Bay, Craig Morrison, Hugh Hardy, Jane Moss, Vera Roberts, William T. Leonard, Bill Orton, Edith Meiser, Stanley Green, Sylvia Herscher, Julia Hansen, and the late Albert Sielke, and with Jim Furlong and Julianne Boyd of the Society of Stage Directors and Choreographers. Help in other ways was forthcoming from Arthur Birsh, Harvey Sabinson, Donald Seawell, Rivka Katvan, Martha Swope, Robert Vose, Clifford Ashby, Louis Botto, Paul Stiga, Susan McTigue, and Suzi DiRosa. To all whom I have named and to those who remain unnamed, I give my heartfelt thanks.

My final words of gratitude belong to Margaret Kaplan, Executive Editor of Harry N. Abrams, Inc., for her unflagging faith in my text and to the able and dedicated team she chose to work with me in producing this book, editor Ellyn Allison, picture editor John Crowley, and designer Judith Michael.

New York, 1986

S ince *Theater in America* appeared a decade ago, certain trends are becoming solidified, and they herald a new age for the American theater. The most important of these has been the dethroning of Broadway as the final, indeed the *only*, arbiter of what constitutes good live entertainment, the kind that traditionally was exported to audiences in the provinces after a healthy run in New York. True, New York continues to send road companies of its biggest hits to theaters and performing-arts centers around the country, but it just as often *imports* productions from the active professional regional theaters far away from the bright lights of Broadway. Although Broadwayites are reluctant to admit it, New York's function as purveyor of theatrical goods to the rest of the country has been usurped by the important regionals. Playwrights increasingly offer their works to the regionals, win national awards for the best of them, and often settle down with one company to ensure for themselves and the host group a flow of their dramatic output.

In the course of the past decade, new names have appeared on the theatrical horizon but none has achieved the kind of instant recognition enjoyed by stars, dramatists, composers, and even directors in earlier times. The effects of electronic entertainment on theater will continue to be felt for generations to come, but even as live performing shrinks to a shred of what it was at the beginning of the twentieth century, it refuses to be snuffed out at the end of the century. What lies ahead is more of the perpetual struggle, but theater in America will survive, waiting for the appearance of a new Eugene O'Neill to lift it into the dramatic stratosphere once again.

The past decade has taken its toll on familiar theatrical figures. The index of this book, revised to 1995, provides the death dates of producers, playwrights, directors, choreographers, actors, designers, and architects who have passed into history. Sadly but predictably, the list contains the names of many whose careers were cut short by the scourge of AIDS.

The original seven chapters of the book remain untouched, except for the correction of errors. The new eighth chapter examines the past, present, and future of theater in America as I see it today and introduces names and faces that promise to loom large in the twenty-first century. There is also an updated chronology and an added bibliographical section for the new chapter.

In preparing the updating of this book, I am grateful to Peter and Lynn Feller of Feller Precision, Neil Mazzella of Hudson Scenic Studio, Tom Janus of Vari-Lite, and Wayne Sapper of King Display for giving generously of their time in explaining the recent technical developments in stagecraft. Without the inspiration of Eldon Elder, Tony Walton, and Betsy and Ming Cho Lee over many, many years, I would never have caught the passion for the contributions of scene designers to play production. I thank, too, Gerald Schoenfeld and his ever faithful assistant Betty Spitz for kindnesses too many to enumerate. Thanks go to Susan Lee and Amy Fleischer of the League of American Theatres and Producers for their help in giving me updates on the new commercial theaters in America and to Jim O'Quinn of *American Stage* for doing the same for the regional theaters. To Eileen Darby and to Martha Swope, I want to say that it would be impossible to illustrate my books without their magnificent and enduring contributions to theatrical photography.

The response from the press departments of the various regional theaters that I contacted was heartening. I pay tribute to Patty Eaton of the San José Repertory Theatre in California, David Schiavone of Steppenwolf Theatre Company in Chicago, Melanie Brenner of the Kravis Center in West Palm Beach, and Bethany Gladhill of Theatre de la Jeune Lune in Minneapolis for promptly sending information and photographs.

I cannot close this list without expressing special gratitude to certain people at the New York Performing Arts Library at Lincoln Center: to Bob Taylor, Curator of the Billy Rose Theatre Collection, for making my life as a researcher in his precincts a joyful rather than an arduous experience; to Richard N. Buck for the many great and small favors which are known only to the two of us; and to Julius Crockwell for making my endless commuting to New York a less than harrowing experience.

Without the friendship and support of Jean Porter, who, among other things, read and reread my manuscripts before I entrusted them to my editor, I am not sure that I could have survived yet another rite of passage to publication.

Congers, New York, 1995

CONTENTS

PRODUCERS

THE IMAGE of a theatrical producer in the public mind is a composite derived from the gossip columns of the tabloids or popular magazines and a movie, *The Producers*, written and produced by Mel Brooks several years ago. The main character, played by Zero Mostel, was portrayed as an oily, smooth-talking, unprincipled, oversexed, money-grubbing scoundrel who delighted in mulcting old ladies of their money to subsidize his questionable theatrical ventures. Mostel's office furniture inevitably included a casting couch, on which his lecherous activities were conducted, and a telephone, on which he conducted everything else. The movie tended to fortify the idea that while everyone else may lose money in the theater, the producer will always walk away with a tidy sum and then move on to his next venture, employing the same unsavory but effective tactics.

Although this stereotype has come to be accepted by average theatergoers as somewhat closer to truth than fiction, they would be hard pressed to name quickly more than one or two active producers. Broadway's Herman Levin went a step further: "If you stopped a thousand people on any well-traveled corner in New York and asked them to name three theatrical producers, I doubt that you'd get a single name—barring a couple of well-publicized people who are better known for what they have done outside the theater than in it." Two hundred years before Levin made this observation, "Candidus," an anonymous commentator upon the London theatrical scene, drily remarked: "The manager [producer] is much more dealt with; let him be ever so assiduous to please the town, he acquires but little praise. The whole consideration of the public is engrossed by the authors or actors, whose labours contribute to their entertainment; whilst the manager, to whom they are in some measure indebted for both, is overlooked as unworthy of notice."

From the myriad autobiographies and biographies of once famous theatrical managers and producers, it is possible to construct a simple psychological profile of these quickly forgotten animators of theatrical art. Each was stung early in life (sometimes in childhood) by the theatrical bug; most tried performing and writing plays, but gave it up or combined it eventually with their managerial duties; all ultimately sought control over the entire collaborative effort, in exchange for which they would give up sleep and any semblance of normal life; and every one of them believed fervently that he (or she) could make it pay, all the while disclaiming any overriding interest in amassing a fortune. Several of them achieved a kind of stardom, sometimes because they appeared onstage or wrote plays, more often because they became identified with a certain standard of production or a specific type of play. Audiences flocked to see the latest Frohman or Belasco or Ziegfeld productions in the early years of the twentieth century as they had patronized the theaters run by Burton, Mitchell, and Daly in the previous century—precisely because they could predict what they were going to see and could anticipate their delight. Whether the name of a producer can sell tickets today is doubtful, although Harold Prince, Alexander Cohen, and David Merrick—and those aspiring to follow them—devoutly pursue this goal.

All the manager-producers down through time have attested to the difficulties of their profession. Just a few years ago, Cheryl Crawford began the chronicle of her years in the theater with the words: "Grubby, it's all so grubby. Who says the theatre is glamorous? I want to go home, I want to go to sleep." She then described her endless day—and her life—as a producer, ending with the inevitable statement that she would not have been happy doing anything else. Her universal plaint echoes through history in the words and lives of all those who came before her. John

Hodgkinson, her counterpart in the late eighteenth century, spoke for them all when he listed his duties:

I had the various Tempers, Rivalships and Ambitions of thirty or forty People to encounter and please. I kept all the Accounts; I made all Disbursements, and was made, in all Money Transactions, solely responsible. My professional Labours were extreme, and I never finished them for the Evening that I did not attend to make the State of each Night's Receipts. Nay, instead of enjoying my comfortable Hour of social Intercourse with my Family, on my Arrival Home, I had a Check Account to take, and to make the regular Entries in my Books. I wrote and corrected every Play-Bill for the Printer. I planned and copied every Scene-Plot for the Carpenter. I attended every Rehearsal, to give Directions. I went through a varied and extensive Line of Characters on the Stage. I found principally my own Wardrobe for them; and my Salary, for all this, was twenty Dollars per Week, paid only when we performed!

Yet, for all his (or her) toil and self-sacrifice, the stereotype has always persisted in the public mind and in the press. "No occupation," wrote a nineteenth-century critic, "appears to be so fascinating as theatrical management or to require so little preparation, intelligence or capital." Despite his eternally bad press, the main ingredient of the producer's diet is hope, and the common trait of the fellowship is optimism.

Because he initiated theatrical activity in this country, the history of the producer—known as the manager for several centuries—is also the history of the theater in America. When the actor-manager arrived on the scene in the mid-eighteenth century, he brought with him the English system based on a limited number of actors and actresses versed in a repertory of current and classic plays (mainly Shakespeare's), rudimentary scenery for all of the plays in the repertory, and a financial organization in which each of the members held shares in the company and received remuneration according to the number held. At the head of this structure was the manager, who was, more often than not, also the leading man of the troupe.

So little is known of the history of the earliest troupes in the colonies that they can claim only the smallest historical niche, as pioneers. When Lewis Hallam and his company landed in Williamsburg, Virginia, in 1752, professional theater in America began in earnest. At the head of the Company of Comedians from London, Hallam acted the leading comedy roles for the troupe. His wife was the leading lady, and his children were also members of the company. Ten adult actors and actresses rounded out the troupe.

The New World created special difficulties for the first managers. Hallam was burdened with the extra chore of overcoming opposition from the pulpit and the financial community. The church was unalterably opposed to playacting as a dissolute and blasphemous profession, and businessmen considered actors irresponsible mountebanks who failed to pay their debts. Only by leading an exemplary life himself and paying his bills was the manager able to pull his company through each barrage of attack. However, when Hallam left Williamsburg in 1753 he was forced to mortgage his theater there in order to make good the debts of several of his actors. Unfortunately, the actors never paid up, and the manager lost his playhouse. This event, in one form or another, was destined to be repeated time and again during the next hundred years. The manager's lot was not an easy one.

After a rigorous two years on the American mainland, in which he added New York and Philadelphia to his itinerary, Hallam sailed to Jamaica in 1754 and died the

The American artist Henry Inman painted this portrait of Edmund Simpson. For most of his career, Simpson was associated with the Park Theatre, first as an actor, then as co-manager with Stephen Price. He died in 1848, shortly before his beloved Park burned to the ground.

At first with John Hodgkinson, then alone, manager William Dunlap struggled valiantly to make a financial success of the Park Theatre in New York, even committing his limited personal fortune to the effort. Although he was forced in 1805 to retreat a bankrupt, he retained ties to the theater until his death, in 1839.

George Frederick Cooke was the first English actor to appear as a guest star at Stephen Price's Park Theatre. Alcoholism made him undependable in performance. He died here in 1812, and his body was later removed to the cemetery of St. Paul's Chapel on lower Broadway, where his countryman Edmund Kean had a monument placed over his grave in 1820.

following year of yellow fever. His place at the head of the troupe and the Hallam household was taken by David Douglass, who married Hallam's widow and assembled a company for another foray in the colonies. Douglass deserves the lion's share of credit for establishing theater in North America. From 1758, the year of their return, to 1774, when the troupe discreetly disappeared on the eve of the American Revolution, Douglass compounded the good will created by his predecessor and expanded theatrical activities. He built theaters in Philadelphia, New York, Charleston, and Providence and coaxed audiences for his presentations into existence.

But Douglass seems always to have swum against the tide of popular opinion—religious, political, or both—and only managed to keep his head above water through a series of imaginative measures. He gave benefits for the poor, to whom he donated the receipts of a particular evening; he soothed religious sensibilities by postponing performances if they fell on holy days; he became a Freemason for respectability's sake; in 1763 he changed the name of his troupe to American Company of Comedians to downplay their English origins; he went to great lengths to insure the comfort of his audience; he advertised his plays as "moral dialogues" whenever he crossed the border into New England; and he appears to have paid his bills and acted the gentleman at all times. Only occasionally did a crack appear in his managerial armor. Once, when the Reverend George Whitefield, the fire-and-brimstone Methodist preacher, was raging against the theater from his Philadelphia pulpit, an exasperated Douglass scheduled a performance of *The Minor*, Samuel Foote's satire on Methodism. The performance was quietly dropped at the request of the governor of the colony.

The Continental Congress closed the theaters in 1774. Douglass returned to Jamaica early in 1775, having singlehandedly laid the foundations for the explosion of theatrical activity in the nineteenth century by creating the climate in which the dramatic arts could grow and prosper. In his retirement he was appointed printer to the king, founded a newspaper, and was eventually appointed Master of the Revels, magistrate, and a member of the Council. During the course of all these activities, he was able to accumulate a fortune of twenty-five thousand pounds sterling, and when he died in 1789, he was described as a "gentleman." Although no actual portrait of the first great producer of the American stage has survived, what he accomplished establishes him clearly as a determined, sensible, hardworking, dedicated, and honorable professional.

When Douglass's stepson, Lewis Hallam the Younger, returned to Philadelphia in 1785, he had with him the remnants of the old American Company, augmented by recruits from England. Since the old Southwark Theatre built by Douglass was still in existence and still owned by his family, he quietly slipped into it and tentatively reintroduced dramatic activity in the city. After a few months, the troupe went to New York and reopened the old John Street Theatre, also built by Douglass, where they were joined by fresh recruits from Jamaica and England. Although the first public response was not altogether approving, and though official sanction was not immediately forthcoming, the actors were permitted to resume their activities. In the course of time, the troupe under Hallam and his successors settled down in New York and built the Park Theatre, in 1798. Meanwhile, theaters with companies attached to them sprang up in other cities.

By the early years of the nineteenth century, the American stock company settled in a theater of its own looked much more like its English counterpart than the band of theatrical nomads of the late eighteenth century. The manager, either singly or in partnership with another actor, continued to control both the artistic and the financial ends of the company. He would act his particular "line of business" (stock of parts), conduct rehearsals, supervise the construction of scenery and the selection of costumes, pick the plays, hire and fire the actors, pay the bills, balance the budget, and function as the publicity director. His chief concern was keeping the actors in his employ from defecting to other troupes. When he wrote his memoirs, in 1854, William Wood, co-manager of the Chestnut Street Theatre in Philadelphia, could recall "scarcely a single instance . . . of a persevering manager dying in comfortable circumstances." For more than half a century the stock company dominated the American stage. By 1825 sixty theaters had come into existence, twenty of them with permanent companies; by 1860 there were more than fifty stock companies in America, and the larger cities, including such bastions of conservatism as Boston, had more than one resident company. The most significant transformation within the system was that actors were paid salaries rather than a portion of the company's profits. By 1800 the citizens of the new towns along the dusty trails to the West could expect to receive a makeshift theater as soon as there were enough of them to support one. Many of the companies traveling in the hinterlands were composed of a few professionals and a bevy of amateurs. Eventually the best of the amateurs ripened into professional actors, and out of their ranks came managers to spread the theater still farther west.

Until 1816 plays were performed only three times a week: on Mondays, Wednesdays, and Fridays. Then the managers of the Park Theatre in New York expanded their schedule to six performances a week, but never on Sunday, and other companies followed suit. There was a nightly change of bill, for the long-running play was still decades away. Under a competent manager, the stock company was a workable and compact organization, but it was to receive its first mortal blow from Stephen Price of the Park Theatre, architect of the star system in America.

When Price took over the Park in 1808, it had passed through a troubled decade. Internal rivalries between old and new members, overspending, and falling box-office revenues threatened its very existence. William Dunlap, who had become manager almost by default, declared personal bankruptcy in 1805, after trying desperately to keep the theater afloat. At first, Price shared control of the Park with a transplanted English actor, Thomas Abthorpe Cooper, but took over as sole manager in 1815. A lawyer by profession, Price was shrewd and manipulative, with more than a touch of the autocrat (Washington Irving dubbed him "King Stephen").

Price's first coup was to import a fading, alcoholic English star, George Frederick Cooke, to play at the Park and other theaters. When Cooke was good, he was very, very good; when he was drunk, he was wretched. Since his appearances sparked interest in the Park and enriched the theater's (and Price's) coffers, the manager sped to England to line up other English stars to appear at the Park and then to travel to other important theaters in America. His greatest stroke was to secure Edmund Kean for guest appearances in 1820 and 1825. As Price began to spend more and more time in England, he entrusted the day-to-day management of the theater to Edmund Simpson, an actor with the company, who was by all reports a decent, direct, and hardworking professional. Simpson received a quarter share in the partnership and spent the rest of his life associated with the Park.

Price's policy of sending in the stars worked, and the theater prospered for some years, but not without invidious consequences. Not only were the actors in the standing company demoralized by being reduced to second-class status, but the public began to show its discontent with the regular repertory by staying away in between star engagements. Price's policies displeased at least one of the owners of the theater, John Beekman, who traveled to Philadelphia in 1821 to try to entice William Wood to take over the Park. By 1840, when Price died, the star system was firmly entrenched in American theater and the stock company was beginning its slow slide to extinction.

Neither actor nor playwright, Stephen Price was not the typical nineteenth-century theater manager. In a period of domination by the star, it was both logical and prudent for talented and energetic actors to guide their own destinies and fortunes by becoming the center of their own producing companies. With the decline of the Park Theatre as the premier playhouse in New York, the void was quickly filled by three stock companies in rapid succession. The first, William Mitchell's Olympic Theatre company, bravely took the stage in 1839, in the midst of one of the worst financial recessions in history, triggered by the Panic of 1837. Mitchell's little playhouse,

The autocratic methods of Stephen Price did not endear him either to the actors of his company or to the public, but he kept the Park Theatre afloat from 1815 to his death, in 1840, by importing English stars.

A typical eighteenth-century manager, John Hodgkinson was saddled with a multitude of responsibilities. An actor first and foremost, he also ran the companies and theaters of the John Street and Park playhouses in New York.

"HUGH TREVOR," IN *ALL FOR HER.*

"CHARLES MARLOW," IN *SHE STOOPS TO CONQUER.*

"HUGH CHALCOTE," IN *OURS.*

"DON FELIX," IN *THE WONDER.*

"ADONIS EVERGREEN," IN *MY AWFUL DAD.*

"ELIOT GREY," IN *ROSEDALE.*

"JOHN GARTH," IN *JOHN GARTH.*

"LEON DEL MAR," IN THE *VETERAN.*

LESTER WALLACK AND HIS MOST CELEBRATED IMPERSONATIONS.—From Photographs by Sarony and Pach Brothers.—[See Page 355.]

located on Broadway between Howard and Grand streets, appealed to businessmen, intellectuals, newsboys, and everyone else who wanted to laugh away the grim recession and the increasing pressures of urban life. Admission to the all-male "pit," or orchestra, was 12½ cents, and the program consisted of low comedy and burlesques. (In the nineteenth century, "burlesque" meant a parody of a current or well-known play. At Mitchell's the popular melodrama *Zampa, the Red Corsair*, for example, became *Sam Parr, with His Red Coarse Hair*; the opera *Norma* emerged as *Mrs. Normer*; and even the immortal *Hamlet* came in for a drubbing.) The actor-manager, a low comedian, was the star of the company, but Billy Mitchell did not fail to gather around him many talented actors. He was particularly adept in his selection of brilliant young actresses, whom he encouraged and nurtured until they became the darlings of the pit. Mitchell also introduced homegrown skits and plays based on the life of the city.

In 1850 Mitchell's light was extinguished by William E. Burton, another low comedian, who came from managing a successful stock company at the Arch Street Theatre in Philadelphia to run a little opera house on Chambers Street. It took Burton two years to put Mitchell out of business, by presenting the same kind of farces and burlesques that were appearing on the Olympic Theatre boards. Hiring actor-playwright John Brougham was the key to Burton's success. "Genial John" was an Irish comedian and a prolific writer with an absurd sense of the comic, and before he left to manage his own company (unsuccessfully), he put Burton's on the map. Burton himself was a large, broad-faced farceur, who appears to have been a master of the double take and blank stare. He worked three "vehicle" plays to death, but they were popular favorites and guaranteed a full house and overflowing cash box. When the public taste became surfeited after many years of this kind of fare, Burton switched to the old, standard English comedies, adaptations of Dickens for the stage, and tasteful Shakespearean productions. In 1856 he followed the fashionable uptown and reopened in a theater farther along Broadway. But his vogue had passed and he gave up management two years later.

Burton furthered the career of John Lester (Wallack), the son of James William Wallack, a first-rate actor who had been brought to New York by Stephen Price in 1818. Remaining in America, he established his own company in 1852 at the Lyceum Theatre, taking over after the departure of John Brougham. J. W. Wallack, with Lester as the leading man, mounted meticulous productions in which ensemble acting, correct costuming, and appropriate scenery were emphasized. It was a perfect English company transplanted in New York. In 1861 the Wallacks, too, followed the uptown movement and opened their most famous theater on the corner of Thirteenth Street and Broadway, where Lester, using his true surname, became de facto manager in

Thomas Wignell achieved popular acclaim as a rapscallion Irish servant in The Poor Soldier *(1785) and* Darby's Return *(1790), becoming one of George Washington's favorite performers. In 1792 he founded his own theater on Chestnut Street in Philadelphia, and it outshone its rivals in New York. Here is Wignell as Darby, in a likeness taken by William Dunlap about 1795.*

place of his ailing father. During their best years, the Wallacks dominated New York's theatrical scene. They attracted a fashionable, well-dressed audience; they never allowed the quality of their productions to vary; and they insisted on a well-trained, disciplined corps of actors and actresses, many of whom "graduated" to become stars in their own right. Commenting on Wallack's, "with some slight feeling of wounded pride," an English traveler in New York observed "that dramas, comedies and burlesques, English in their birth and origin, treating of English homes and scenes, are more carefully mounted and more perfectly put upon the stage in a New York theatre than in houses where they were originally produced."

The production of his own play *Rosedale* in 1863 proved Lester Wallack's undoing. Rather than keep it in repertory, he presented it in an extended run of 125 performances. Eventually his regular audience, feeling the want of their weekly trip to Wallack's, turned elsewhere for their entertainment. In 1882 Lester moved uptown again, this time to Broadway and Thirtieth Street, but the old lure and luster of the name had long since departed. New managers, new actors, new plays, and a new system of production had arisen to challenge the old order. In poor health and financially strained, Lester Wallack retired in 1887 and the following year was honored with an all-star benefit performance of *Hamlet*, headed by Edwin Booth, at the Metropolitan Opera House.

When the nineteenth century began, Philadelphia—not New York or Boston—had the finest stock company in the country. It was run by Thomas Wignell, a cousin of the Hallams, who had joined the old Douglass company on the eve of the Revolutionary War and later became a popular performer in Hallam the Younger's troupe, a favorite of George Washington's. Disenchanted by strife within the company, Wignell eventually defected to try his luck in Philadelphia with his own theater and company. In partnership with Alexander Reinagle, a conductor and musician, in 1792 Wignell traveled to London to recruit actors while a new theater in Chestnut Street was being built for him. An epidemic of yellow fever delayed the opening and a subsequent wave of the disease depressed his audiences and put him in grave financial straits, despite the excellence of his actors and his productions. When Wignell died, in 1803, the charge of running the company fell upon his widow, Ann Merry, a first-rate actress but no manager. She transferred the responsibility to the elder William Warren, whom she later married. In 1809 William B. Wood became Warren's partner, and together, as actors and managers, they stewarded the company through sixteen years of performances, during which time they endured "our great calamity by fire [the theater burned down and had to be rebuilt], the depression by the war, slight occasional losses by languid engagements or the accidents inevitable with all theatres," and other perils. They divided the labors, kept banker's books, paid all their bills, met their payrolls, hired a fine company of actors, and did "a regular, safe, steady business." In recollecting his career, Wood observed that "a well managed theatre is as good a source of fortune as any other profession." Then as now, however, the producer's career had its ups and downs. Wood and Warren parted company. Warren continued as sole manager of the Chestnut Street, only to lose it to his creditors two years later. Wood retired from the stage some twenty years later, while Warren ended his days as a tavernkeeper in Baltimore.

The old stock-company system made its last stand against a new order of play production in Boston. In 1841 Moses and David Kimball opened the Boston Museum and Gallery of Fine Arts, which contained not only mummies, wax figures, specimens, paintings, and curiosities of all sorts, but a "lecture-room," featuring morally uplifting or intellectually instructive entertainments—all for a twenty-five-cent admission fee. The entertainments soon began to veer toward the dramatic, and in 1843 Moses Kimball installed a regular stock company. A year later *The Drunkard*, a play by W. H. Smith depicting the evils of alcohol, enjoyed a run of one hundred performances. The Kimballs, holding a tiger by the tail, in 1846 invested about a quarter of a million dollars in a new, bigger and better museum, which contained a conventional theater. For nearly fifty years, their stock company remained in Boston,

adjusting to changing theatrical conditions but hanging on despite competition from other theaters and from the emerging "combination" and touring companies.

Sensitive to the conservatism of Boston, Kimball and his managers made sure that nothing coarse or vulgar appeared onstage, earning for their auditorium the name of "the deacon's theater." This image of respectability was reinforced by the Kimballs' policy of no performances on Saturday or Sunday (to compensate for the loss of revenue two matinees a week were introduced in the 1860s). And, of course, those who would have felt uneasy going to a theater felt no compunction in going to a "museum." During its fifty-year existence, the quality of the Boston Museum productions was generally high, especially during the peak years of the 1860s. The Kimballs and their managers, by providing competently acted and well-mounted productions and by exercising good financial management, succeeded in propping up a system that had outlived its time, until 1893, when the company was abandoned.

Women were not excluded from the ranks of managers. Two of them, Laura Keene in New York and Louisa (Mrs. John) Drew, of the Arch Street Theatre of Philadelphia, were in the grand tradition of Madame Vestris, the English actress-manager who took over London's Olympic Theatre and, among other things, reformed and streamlined theatrical management. Laura Keene had been an actress for Vestris at the Olympic in London and had worked for J. W. Wallack. In 1856, surrounded by a strong company of actors, she moved into a new, beautifully appointed playhouse on Broadway just below Bleecker Street. Her productions were polished and elegant, exhibiting the benefits of carefully conducted rehearsals and excellent costumes and scenery. Nicknamed "the Duchess," she was the star of her company, refusing to surrender to the prevalent arrangement of booking the visiting or local star for hastily organized productions.

During the season of 1858–59, Joseph Jefferson III, who would undertake his most

famous role as Rip Van Winkle some years later, urged her to produce Tom Taylor's *Our American Cousin* because there was a meaty part in it for himself. She agreed, and the play became the success of her career. Jefferson recalled, "As the treasury began to fill, Miss Keene began to twinkle with little brilliants; gradually her splendor increased, until at the end of three months she was ablaze with diamonds." *Our American Cousin* achieved lasting notoriety when Keene's company played it in Washington at Ford's Theatre on the night Abraham Lincoln was assassinated. In 1863 Keene closed her theater in the face of overwhelming competition from Wallack's and spent the last years of her life as a touring star.

Louisa Drew could be described as the most famous grandmother in the American theater, but that would not do justice to her long and brilliant career. Born of theatrical parents, she was taken by her mother to America in 1827 as an infant prodigy. Child performers regularly strode the stage in adult roles during that era, and little Louisa Lane toured the country to great acclaim. In 1850, after establishing herself as an accomplished adult actress and divorcing two or three husbands, she married actor John Drew, by whom she had three children, one of whom became the mother of John, Lionel, and Ethel Barrymore.

In 1861 Mrs. Drew took over the Arch Street Theatre in Philadelphia and installed a stock company, which became renowned for the quality of its actors, several of whom later became stars. After a rocky beginning, Mrs. Drew settled down to eight years of good fortune, but, following the example of all the other theaters in the city, she abandoned her stock company and turned her theater into a "combination" house, booking single, long-running shows and traveling attractions. In an autobiographical sketch she mourned, "It never did so well as before. The public seemed to miss the old favorites and not care for the new ones." In 1892 she gave up her lease and at the age of seventy-two went back on the road, before finally retiring.

The history of the nineteenth-century theatrical manager in America would be incomplete without a chronicle of the hardy band that opened up the West to bring Shakespeare to fledgling towns and cities. With their companies of actors they took to wagons and riverboats, enduring natural calamities; setting up stages in courthouses, breweries, hotel ballrooms, old salthouses, dance halls, and whatever else was available; running out of money on the way; and turning to other occupations until they had enough for another stake, knowing all the time that there was an audience of entertainment-starved settlers in the vast reaches of the American continent and being sustained by that knowledge.

In 1800 there were no theaters west of the Alleghenies, but by 1850 every major town and city of the Midwest had at least one, and several had two or more; moreover, the Gold Rush of 1849 had sped the rudiments of civilization, theaters included, to the booming California towns.

As early as 1808, Luke Usher, a Kentucky innkeeper, built a theater for the amateur Thespian Society in Lexington and launched full-scale productions. Before long, strolling professional players joined the amateurs and the company began a circuit of Kentucky towns. In 1815 Samuel Drake, an acquaintance of Usher's son, Noble Luke Usher, who had assumed the management of the theater in Louisville, agreed to take over the Kentucky circuit at Usher's suggestion. As Drake lived in upper New York State, he prudently sent out a young apprentice actor, Noah M. Ludlow, to act as advance man.

Drake, his five children (all actors), and five other players set out from Albany, New York, carrying scenery, props, costumes, stage equipment, and personal belongings, on the long trek to Kentucky. On their way they stopped in small towns, playing one-night stands in makeshift theaters. Arriving by wagon in Olean, New York, they picked up a flat-bottomed boat to float to Pittsburgh, two hundred miles downstream, where they found a theater of sorts abandoned by a previous troupe. After a journey of seven months Drake and his party finally reached their destination. For the next two seasons, they played the Kentucky towns.

In 1817 Ludlow decided to strike out on his own and gathered a few actors to form the high-sounding but short-lived American Theatrical Commonwealth Company to take the drama to Nashville, Tennessee, whose citizens had never seen a professional stage performance. Frontier acting troupes like Ludlow's were fluid and loosely organized. Only the hardiest actors survived the rigors of the theatrical campaigns to open up the West. The rugged life notwithstanding, Ludlow died at ninety-one, having spent most of his life on the frontier, as a manager and player. In 1835 a young actor, Sol Smith, threw in his lot with Ludlow and for eighteen years the two shared the management of theaters in New Orleans, Mobile, and St. Louis. In the end, the partners fell out over money and politics (Ludlow supported the South, while Smith remained a loyal Yankee), and each wrote a book about his adventures with hardly a reference to the other.

One of Ludlow's best stories involved swashbuckling Lieutenant Sam Houston. In 1818, grounded in Nashville, Ludlow took over the management of an amateur dramatic company, one of whose members was Houston. As a lark, Ludlow cast him as a drunken porter in a farce, but Houston felt he was miscast. "Look here, Ludlow, if the people hiss me to-night, I'll shoot you to-morrow." Ludlow acquiesced and predicted the novice would receive more applause than anyone else in the play. At the conclusion of Houston's scene, the manager heard "such a roar of applause as made me fear that the seats would give way and come down with a grand crash." Though Ludlow insisted he had never seen the part performed as well by a professional, Houston abandoned his promising career on the stage after this lone triumph.

Although they were the most successful theatrical entrepreneurs of the frontier, Ludlow and Smith were not without competition. James H. Caldwell, an English-born comedian, made his American debut as an actor in 1816 and as a manager a year later, in Washington, D.C. After establishing a small circuit of theaters in neighboring Virginia, in 1820 he decided to take his troupe to New Orleans, where theatrical activity, albeit in the French language, was well rooted. Two years earlier, Ludlow and his American Theatrical Commonwealth Company had played an entire sixteen-week season there, departing with a net profit of $3,000. But it was Caldwell who improved standards of production, employed a first-rate orchestra, built handsome theaters, and introduced stars and grand opera during his dominance over theatrical activity—which ended in 1840, when Ludlow and Smith returned to the city to mount a strong challenge. When he died, in 1863, Caldwell was a respected and well-to-do member of the business community, having introduced gaslight not merely to the theater but to his adopted city.

To the north, the state of Illinois created a long-effective barrier to the spread of the theater by establishing a heavy license fee, which the barnstorming troupes could not afford. In 1837, however, two managers, Isherwood and MacKenzie, were able to scrape together the funds to buy a license and establish a crude theater in Chicago, in the dining room of the Sauganash Hotel. The venture proved so successful that they converted the upper floor of a different building into the Chicago Theatre. Competition rushed in to share their success and in 1847 a conventional playhouse was erected, under the management of J. B. Rice, who spread his interests into politics as well, becoming mayor of Chicago and its congressman. In 1848 he hired a talented low comedian named James H. McVicker for his company. A popular performer of "Yankee" characters, McVicker built a splendid theater in 1857, named it for himself, and installed an excellent company that withstood challenges from other managers and companies for nearly forty years. McVicker's was consumed in the great Chicago fire of 1871 and was rebuilt the following year, burned down again in 1892, rose again, and was still standing at the venerable proprietor's death in 1896. A canny manager as well as successful performer, McVicker was largely responsible for establishing Chicago as the dominant theatrical center of the Midwest.

Alexander MacKenzie, who had been a partner in the Sauganash Hotel venture, in 1838 wrote to his nephew Joseph Jefferson II, urging him to journey from New York to help introduce the citizens of what was then northwest territory to the theater.

A popular actor, James H. McVicker dominated theatrical activity in Chicago for nearly forty years. He also served as Edwin Booth's manager for a short period and was Booth's father-in-law, but the relationship between the two men deteriorated as a result of what McVicker considered improper treatment of the mentally disturbed Mary Booth. He is depicted here as the Gravedigger in act 5 of Hamlet.

The rivers of America's vast interior afforded a convenient route to outpost towns. Not the first itinerant frontier players to seek out remote audiences by boat, the Chapman family went a step further and converted their craft into a theater, with living quarters for the troupe.

After packing up his family and assembling a few actors, Jefferson and his newly formed troupe barnstormed their way to Chicago. After completing a respectable stint there, MacKenzie and Jefferson took to the road to play the burgeoning towns along the upper Mississippi. When they reached Springfield, Illinois, they invested the receipts from their profitable tour in a playhouse that would attract the custom of the crowds present at the convening of the state legislature. The theater was quickly and simply erected, but the managers were stunned by the enactment of a local ordinance levying a stiff license tax, which they could not pay. Joseph Jefferson III, the young son of the manager, described the incident in his autobiography:

In the midst of their trouble a young lawyer called on the managers. He had heard of the injustice, and offered, if they would place the matter in his hands, to have the license taken off, declaring that he only desired to see fair play, and would accept no fee whether he failed or succeeded. The case was brought up before the council. The young lawyer began his harangue. He handled the subject with tact, skill and humor, tracing the history of the drama from the time when Thespis acted in a cart to the stage of to-day. He illustrated his speech with a number of anecdotes, and kept the council in a roar of laughter; his good humor prevailed, and the exorbitant tax was taken off.

The name of the young lawyer was Abraham Lincoln.

In 1849 a sometime horse-and-buggy driver from New York City made his way to California and opened a hotel and gambling saloon in San Francisco. The citizens had plenty of money and little to do but gamble, so Tom Maguire decided to build a theater over his saloon and call it the Jenny Lind. (Though the Swedish Nightingale never came close to California during her 1850–52 tour with P. T. Barnum, her name was a household word from coast to coast during those years.) Unlike his principal competitor in town, the actor, playwright, and manager D. G. "Doc" Robinson, Maguire had absolutely no experience in managing theaters and was thought to be illiterate. But by hiring playwrights as skillful as David Belasco and James A. Herne, by building bigger and better theaters, and by turning to account a genius for showmanship, Maguire rose to become the premier theatrical magnate in California. He systematically accumulated a chain of theaters in San Francisco and inland California and employed talent scouts in New York and Australia, which was then about as reachable by sea as New York was by land. By the 1870s, at the height of his career, Maguire ran a circuit for traveling shows illuminated by stars of the magnitude of Edwin Booth, the Wallacks, the Keans, Adah Isaacs Menken (the reigning sexpot), and important foreign actors, too. He stabilized ticket prices and promoted every kind of entertainment, from minstrel show to grand opera. His overextended empire came crashing down in 1882, when he lost the Baldwin Theatre, the linchpin in his theatrical chain, and a few years later Maguire returned to New York to live in obscurity and poverty until his death in 1896.

One of the most romantic chapters in the history of nineteenth-century theatrical management was written on the great rivers of America. In 1827 William Chapman, a Covent Garden actor, joined the exodus to the new Republic with his numerous family in tow. They found work in New York and Philadelphia, but rather than remain in the East and see his clan disperse, William hit upon a novel way to keep his family together. Hearing of the money to be made in the wilderness, he took his all-Chapman troupe by land to Pittsburgh, where he had a flat-bottomed boat, 100 feet long by 16 feet wide, built to serve as home and theater. The stage was at one end of the structure, the pit in the middle, and the gallery (or balcony, for the use of blacks exclusively) at the opposite end. The price for a seat on the hard, backless, cushionless benches was the same for all except children and blacks, who paid half price. During the trip downriver the usual admission price of fifty cents was adjusted to whatever the traffic would bear: "a peck of potatoes or yams, two gallons of fruit, a side of bacon."

The Chapmans, nine strong, plus a riverman and another actor, pushed off from Pittsburgh in *The Floating Theatre* in 1831, stopping at hundreds of landings

Augustin Daly treasured his memories of boyhood visits to Burton's and Wallack's theaters. They inspired him to create an acting company that would play in perfect unison in a theater of his own. Here is Daly about 1882, surrounded by his loyal, if somewhat overtaxed, company of players. Seated (left to right): James Lewis, George Clarke, Mrs. George Gilbert, Ada Rehan, John Drew, Daly, Charles Fisher, and Virginia Dreher. Standing: John Moore, William Gilbert, Charles Leclerq, and May Fielding.

to play their repertory of Shakespeare and melodramas, followed by monologues, impersonations, sketches, songs, and dances by one or more of the company. The star of the troupe was Caroline Chapman, one of William's daughters, who later became a popular performer in New York. For five years, the family floated down the Mississippi and poled up its tributaries, finally landing in New Orleans, where the boat was sold for firewood. The clan then traveled back to Pittsburgh, and the entire process was repeated. In 1836 prosperity enabled the Chapmans to buy a small steamboat equipped with a stage 20 feet wide by 6 feet deep and to hire additional actors. Steam power allowed them to make the return trip by boat instead of by the arduous overland route and to reach settlements unapproachable by raft.

Although the Chapmans experienced a number of mishaps, William guided them for many years without loss of limb or life. He died on board his ship in 1841, involved in plans to build a bigger steamboat. *Chapman's Floating Palace* was indeed completed the following year, and Sara Chapman, William's widow, managed the amphibious company until 1847, when she sold out to Sol Smith and retired in comfort. Smith's career as a showboat manager was short-lived. The day after he took over the boat, it collided with a heavier steamer and split in half. He and his company swam to shore and he took to the river no more.

The Chapmans' success, of course, encouraged numerous imitators. In the 1840s and 1850s, the American rivers were alive with showboats of varying size and quality, offering every kind of entertainment, both proper and improper. Even some large cities had a showboat, though it is doubtful that any of these floating urban theaters ever left their moorings. In 1845 a large man-of-war was converted into a showboat, dubbed *Temple of the Muses*, and docked at the foot of Canal Street in New York City. The enterprise continued for a month before closing down. Showboating, interrupted by the Civil War, sprang to life again after 1864 with bigger and better boats and equally enterprising managers. The postwar era was celebrated by Edna Ferber in *Show Boat*, and her book was later turned into a musical that became a classic of the American stage.

The careers of the last great theater managers of the nineteenth century, Augustin Daly and A. M. Palmer, represent, paradoxically, the apotheosis of the old system and the genesis of the new. Growing up in the 1850s, Daly had the good fortune to witness the great productions at Burton's and Wallack's. At twenty-one, he got a job as a reporter on the *New York Sunday Courier* and, lucky again, inherited the post of drama critic a few weeks afterward. Sensing that the only way to break into the world of the theater was by creating his own opportunities, he began writing plays, usually with a specific performer in mind, to whom he would send the manuscript. Despite numerous rejections he continued writing, until in 1862 Kate Bateman, a popular actress of the time, accepted his *Leah, the Forsaken*. Both profited from the play's success, and Daly began to sell other plays to leading performers, receiving the ultimate compliment of having Matilda Heron, Adah Isaacs Menken, and Laura Keene all request dramas from him. As a playwright and critic he had the entree to the theater he had long sought, for Daly never failed to keep a steady eye on what he had envisioned for himself.

He began his managerial career with a loan from his father-in-law, John Duff, a successful manager himself, and in 1869 took over the Fifth Avenue Theatre. During the next six months, he produced twenty-one plays and achieved his first hit, *Frou-Frou*, in 1870. Daly enjoyed great prosperity for the next six years, surviving the recession of 1873 and the loss of his first theater by fire. He went on to establish two other playhouses, both named Fifth Avenue Theatre, though, like the first, neither was located on that famous street. By career's end, he had taken over several other theaters in New York and one in London and had sent his company of both well-known and unknown actors and actresses to France for engagements in Paris.

Daly became the paradigm of the old-time manager. He accomplished all of the arduous tasks about which, nearly a century before, the English actor-manager John Hodgkinson had complained so testily, but Daly did them all with great zest, though he eventually came to have little life of his own outside the theater. He ruled his companies autocratically but created possibly the finest dramatic corps on the English-speaking stage of his time, even daring comparison with British productions by establishing a theater in London bearing his own name. Daly was his own playwright, trainer of actors, director, financial manager, publicity director, and supervisor of scenery and lighting. He even tried to extend his control over the private lives of his staff, telling them how to behave when they left his theater. There were many defections but there were also, wonder of wonders, plenty of actors who preferred to suffer his methods in order to remain associated with what was considered by all—even Daly's critics—a temple of high theatrical art.

Daly's prodigious energy—his average working day lasted about sixteen hours—enabled him to perform the duties of producer and director, roles which at the turn of the new century would be divided between two people. Like a modern director, he controlled every aspect of a production and, more important, imposed his own point of view on the play and shaped the actors' performances according to his own vision. Although he had begun his career in the theater by writing vehicles for a star, as head of his company he refused, at first, to give star status to anyone. He did not hesitate to cut and alter scripts, even Shakespeare's, if he thought he could make a play more effective. To his credit, he tried to get the best writers in America to author plays for him. Mark Twain, who collaborated with Bret Harte on *Ah Sin* at Daly's urging, wryly described in a curtain speech the director's participation in the effort: "I never saw a play that was so

A. M. Palmer, the son of a parson and by profession a lawyer, stumbled into the theater world through his business acumen. His appearance there signaled the arrival of the producer in the modern sense of the word and a break with the actor-manager tradition. Palmer extended the profitability of such hits as Augustus Thomas's Alabama (1891) by sending them out on the road. Copies of this poster by the Strobridge Lithographing Company were run off in quantity and warehoused, awaiting orders giving the name of a theater, dates, and any other pertinent information to be inserted at the bottom of a certain quantity of sheets.

Agnes Ethel transferred her loyalties from Augustin Daly to A. M. Palmer, who in 1873 was astute enough to allow her to be billed at his Union Square Theatre as the star of Frou-Frou—*something that his rival had never permitted. The play, adapted from the French original by Henri Meilhac and Ludovic Halévy, was a vehicle for many nineteenth-century actresses, including Sarah Bernhardt.*

The rapaciousness of the new breed of American producer was not lost on the cartoonists of the age. Here, in an original cartoon, Oliver Herford shows the "angels" of the American theater, producers Augustus Pitou and Abe Erlanger, watching benevolently as the Big Bad Wolf offers promise of a national theater to the innocent public, the gullible Little Red Riding Hood.

much improved by being cut down; and I believe it would have been one of the very best plays in the world if his strength had held out so that he could cut out the whole of it."

Despite his many talents, Daly was not a theorist or an intellectualizer of his methods. His contribution was in establishing a model for the person who was to control the artistic fortunes of the theater in the twentieth century: the director. Daly accomplished this by sweeping away most of the conventions of the past and beginning with a fresh eye. He brought no point of view to the theater except his own, and although many others imitated his technique, none could produce a mirror image of Daly's productions.

What Augustin Daly did to elevate and define the manager's role as artistic overseer, A. M. Palmer did to transform the manager's function as animator of dramatic activity. Entering the theater in 1874 with no training, no preparation, no burning desire to direct, write, or act, and with only a layman's perception of the stage from the audience, Palmer, through sheer managerial instinct and talent, rose to be Daly's principal competition and carved himself a place in history as the nontheatrical theater man and the prototype for the twentieth-century producer. At first tentatively, then with more and more assurance, Palmer made the decisions that turned him into a first-rate professional. He had a knack for finding plays that appealed to audiences; he hired the best actors to fill the roles, frequently raiding the companies of Daly, Wallack, and Edwin Booth to do it; he appointed men who would handle all of the details of production capably; he employed the finest scene painters and technicians that he could find; he paid his employees more than they could get working for anyone else; and he knew how to balance the books. He was smart enough to retreat when he had to and was direct in his dealings. Many of Palmer's transactions were sealed with a handshake rather than a contract, so unimpeachable was his word.

Although he relied heavily on English and French plays, mostly melodramas, he also gave opportunities to American playwrights such as Bronson Howard, William Gillette, and Augustus Thomas. His directors included Dion Boucicault, Steele MacKaye, and David Belasco; his companies listed on their rosters Maurice Barrymore, Agnes Ethel, James O'Neill, Kate Claxton, Clara Morris, Charles R. Thorne, and many other performers of the first rank. When he had a long-running success, he sent the members of the company who had been idled by it on the road to Chicago or San Francisco, where they starred at the best theaters in town. When the era of the combination company and the touring or "duplicate" companies arrived, he switched over to the new system and abandoned the stock company. He advertised heavily and published souvenir programs for each of his successes. Palmer had enough of the gambler in him to make and lose several fortunes, and his life in the theater, if nothing else, typifies the extremes a producer's career can reach. At the end of Palmer's life, Charles Frohman, who exemplified the new breed of producers, employed him out of charity. He died a bankrupt in 1905.

Both Daly and Palmer inadvertently contributed to the demise of the old stock-company system by abandoning frequent changes of bill when a play caught the public's fancy for several weeks or months. Like other serious theater managers of the day, they were aware of the money that could be made from an entertainment that continued to attract audiences for months; moreover, after its initial run, a hit show could be sent on intact to first-class playhouses in all of the major cities, providing additional revenue for the manager. Several of the cannier Eastern managers took credit for the creation of the combination company, whose performers, scenery, costumes, and technical personnel had been assembled for a *single* play. Spinning off a successful play that still held the stage in New York were duplicate companies, sent out to perform the same material in the provinces, "Direct from New York."

Without stock companies, managers throughout the country who owned or leased their playhouses were forced to book combination and duplicate companies to keep their theaters operative. With a diminished managerial role, they were forced to write, telegraph, or travel to New York to line up engagements for each upcoming theatrical season, which lasted from September to June of the following year. The managers of the principal or first-class houses in each city arrived en masse during the off-season months in Union Square, the hub of New York's theater world during the last quarter of the nineteenth century, to book the best of the new productions.

It occurred to several of them that since the railroad had shortened distances between cities, a theater cooperative or "circuit" would induce the New York producers to give them firm bookings and a better deal. Independent producers meanwhile had discovered that if they put themselves in the hands of a clearinghouse or "booking agent," they could be assured of a well-planned route (without inefficient "jumps" between far-flung engagements) and a fully occupied season. It was then but a short step to the amalgamation of theaters in chains along the railway lines under the control of one man or office and to the gradual assumption of the producer's role by the booking agent in assembling companies to tour. All of this made sense, mirroring as it did the empire-building activities of the great captains of industry, who were in those same years struggling to control the production of goods from the moment of manufacture until the moment of sale.

By the 1890s the times were ripe for the construction of a theatrical trust. The scenario for it was written, of course, in New York. If myth is to be believed, the first act began in the restaurant of the Holland House Hotel on August 31, 1896. Despite marked differences in temperament and appearance, the six men composing the dramatis personae had several characteristics in common. They were Jews. They or members of their families were recent emigrants to the country. They had known extreme poverty at some point in their lives and had started out humbly in their rise to the top. And they had come into the theater from the "front of the house," the business end. Each had learned about the theater and its operations as an "advance man"—a producer's agent and the prototype of the press agent rolled into one. An advance man preceded a touring show on the road and performed such tasks as discussing details of the physical production with the theater owner, making arrangements for housing the company, advertising the show locally, pasting up posters, spreading "paper" (free tickets) in return for favors, and casting a more than casual eye on local box-office procedures so that his employer's share of the receipts was not (unduly) shaved. Advance men were extremely important cogs in the touring-company machine, and the quality of their performance frequently spelled the difference between profit and loss on the tours.

Finally, all six men had come to know the others simply because, at some point in their peripatetic careers, their paths had crossed. By dessert at the Holland House, Abraham Lincoln Erlanger, Charles Frohman, Al Hayman, Marc Klaw, Samuel Nixon (né Nirdlinger), and Fred Zimmerman had created what came to be known as the Theatrical Syndicate, a simple and effective trust that controlled both the product (the show) and the market outlet (the theater). Klaw and Erlanger were to handle the bookings, while Hayman and Frohman were to oversee the finances. The preamble to the Syndicate agreement reads like a proposition for the establishment of a public service. Envisioned was a new order in which everybody—managers, producers, stars, acting companies, and even audiences—would benefit. The ruinous practices of the prevailing system would be exorcised. Gone would be the theater managers' nefarious practice of booking two or three productions for the same period to insure that at least one would arrive safely in their playhouses. Gone would be the last-minute cancellations, the railroad misroutings, the strandings of entire companies when the managers and producers could not meet their bills. Gone would be the shoestring producer and the fly-by-night manager. And gone would be the inept, badly produced show. Reason and organization would prevail, as it had in the great industry trusts headed by John D. Rockefeller and Andrew Carnegie. Surprisingly, Messrs. Klaw, Erlanger, Frohman, Hayman, Nixon, and Zimmerman among them controlled only thirty-three theaters outright; their assets consisted of their office furniture and a few mortgaged pieces of real estate; and their own productions amounted to a small fraction of the hundreds that were sent out on the road every fall. They built their trust because they got there first and had the nerve, pluck, and imagination to follow

The frequent transatlantic crossings of Charles Frohman were to prove his undoing. The greatest theater mogul of his time, member of the infamous Theatrical Syndicate, the roly-poly C. F. was on the Lusitania when it was sunk in 1915 by the Germans.

The Shubert brothers' first hit on Broadway opened on June 2, 1902. It was an imported English musical comedy about an English stockbroker who marries his typist and takes her to the Orient. The star, Thomas Q. Seabrooke, is here shown as Mr. Pineapple, the stockbroker, embracing two of Sam Shubert's "oriental" chorus girls. The show made a fortune for the young entrepreneurs. The nonsensical plot was interspersed with songs, several of which became immensely popular.

their vision through. Together they sought fulfillment of a sharp hunger for recognition in an America that mistrusted Jews; they sought an outlet for their prodigious energy and natural business acumen in a field not then attractive to Protestant patricians of industry and finance. Finally, they were lured not merely by the prospect of large profits, which was more than counterbalanced by the recognition of risks intrinsic in the theater business, but also by an attraction to the world of make-believe that can never be adequately explained. Many years later, at the negotiating table during the Actors' Equity strike of 1960, an exchange took place between the producers and members of the actors' union that sheds some light on the psyche of the theatrical businessman, or at least on his perception of himself. The lawyer for the union, Herman E. Cooper, asked: " 'What is a producer? What is a producer?' . . . in a voice rising in sarcasm. And then he answered himself: 'A producer is a businessman with artistic pretensions.' " Kermit Bloomgarden, who was representing the producers on the other side of the table, "rose to his feet, shaking in anger. 'I resent Mr. Cooper's statement and the narrowness behind it. What is a producer? What is a producer? A producer is an *artist with business pretensions!*' "

The first act of our romance of the Syndicate was concerned with the evolution and development of the "plot." The second act must deal with the counterstrophe of complications that ensued when the theater world became conscious of what had happened at the notorious Holland House luncheon. First to react were the stars, who found themselves frozen out of first-class theaters if they refused to sign with the Syndicate. Many of them fought the trust in the beginning but later came to terms with it. The Joan of Arc of the opposition was Mrs. Fiske, leading actress of her day, whose war against the Syndicate lasted twelve years, until it accepted *her* terms. Her husband, Harrison Grey Fiske, publisher of the *New York Dramatic Mirror*, put additional muscle in his wife's campaign by attacking the enemy in print. He even managed to unearth an alleged copy of the original Syndicate contract and on March 26, 1898, published it on the front page of his popular weekly.

Like all major trusts of the time, the Syndicate enticed quarry into its net with promises of higher profits and better salaries for everyone. Once in control, it could dictate terms most favorable to the trust. If a theater owner was truculent, the Syndicate would buy, build, or lease another theater in his town, provide it with superior productions, and reduce ticket prices until their competitor was on his knees. The Syndicate never lost money, even when the theater for which it booked a show operated at a loss, because it took its percentage from the gross receipts at the box office.

When the monopoly began to flex its muscles, it immediately received an overwhelmingly hostile press. Editorials were written all over the country condemning the men of the Syndicate and many were tinged with anti-Semitism. Even President Theodore Roosevelt showed his displeasure by appearing at a performance by the great Scottish vaudevillian Sir Harry Lauder in a non-Syndicate theater. But the success of the Syndicate was enormous, and a wall of banknotes protected its directors from attack. For a brief moment they entertained the idea of establishing a world syndicate, and in fact did book some of their productions in Europe on a limited basis. It was on behalf of one of his transatlantic negotiations that Charles Frohman found himself on the ill-fated *Lusitania* in 1915.

The courts were not sympathetic to the opponents of the Syndicate. In 1907 the state of New York instituted a suit against the trust for "criminal conspiracy in restraint of trade." After hearing a long litany of Syndicate abuses, Judge Otto Rosalsky dismissed the case with this curious decision: "In light of the lexicographer's definition of trade, commerce, play, entertainment and theatre, . . . it seems to me that plays and entertainments of the stage are not articles or useful commodities of common use, and that the business of owning theatres, and producing plays therein, is not trade, and that, therefore, the defendants did not commit acts injurious to trade or commerce." For the moment, the theater was still regarded as art and not commerce. Show business continued a little longer as no business.

After Charles Frohman elevated Ethel Barrymore (above right) to stardom in Captain Jinks of the Horse Marines *(1901), the actress was featured in many of his productions. On the wall of her dressing room (above left), to the right of the mirror, hangs a photograph of herself in Frohman's* Carrots *(1902).*

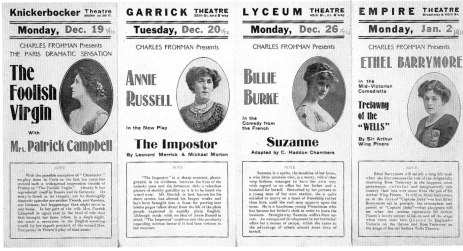

Knickerbocker Theatre	GARRICK THEATRE 35th St. and B'way	LYCEUM THEATRE 45th St., nr. B'way	EMPIRE THEATRE Broadway & 40th St.
Monday, Dec. 19 1910	**Tuesday, Dec. 20** 1910	**Monday, Dec. 26** 1910	**Monday, Jan. 2** 1911
CHARLES FROHMAN Presents THE PARIS DRAMATIC SENSATION	CHARLES FROHMAN Presents	CHARLES FROHMAN Presents	CHARLES FROHMAN Presents
The Foolish Virgin With **Mrs. Patrick Campbell**	**ANNIE RUSSELL** In the New Play **The Impostor** By Leonard Merrick & Michael Morton	**BILLIE BURKE** In the Comedy from the French **Suzanne** Adapted by C. Haddon Chambers	**ETHEL BARRYMORE** In the Mid-Victorian Comedietta **Trelawny of the "WELLS"** By Sir Arthur Wing Pinero

"Charles Frohman Presents" was the magic phrase to catch an audience, as the copywriter of the advertising piece seen at left understood. In 1910 Frohman presented the public with four stars in four popular successes.

Though San Francisco–born William A. Brady believed that the American public wanted youth, beauty, and sentiment on the stage and tried to give it to them, he nevertheless altered course several times during his fifty-five-year stint as a producer to present something different—notably, Elmer Rice's Street Scene, *in 1929. He made Helen Hayes a star in his revival of J. M. Barrie's* What Every Woman Knows *in 1926 and went on to produce a number of successful revivals. His enduring hit was the tear-jerker* Way Down East, *by Lottie Blair Parker, which he first produced in 1898. Pictured is the pink-satin souvenir program issued on the occasion of the 375th performance, on March 27, 1900.*

The final act of this drama of the Syndicate should have been a confrontation between the forces of right, led by Mrs. Fiske and her allies, and the "heavy," represented by the bald and paunchy Abe Erlanger. A climax of this sort was in the making when Mrs. Fiske, David Belasco, and other independent managers attempted to merge about thirty theaters in a circuit for their own and other productions, at rates that would undercut the Syndicate. Their error was to accept the aid of the Shubert brothers, who eventually turned the opportunity to their own advantage, whereupon the alliance collapsed.

The Syndicate died a natural business death. The original agreement called for the members to renew their pact at five-year intervals, which they did until 1916. Although badly shaken by the death of Charles Frohman, the trust survived under the management of Klaw and Erlanger. Seriously drained by the inroads of the Shuberts, it still managed to hang on to a large piece of the action. What the Syndicate could not withstand was the encroachment of the booming film industry. In December 1900, a banner year for the Syndicate, there were 392 touring companies on the road in America. In 1915, the year of D. W. Griffith's landmark movie *The Birth of a Nation*, the number of traveling shows had dropped to 95. With the advent of the talking motion picture, the number fell even further. The Crash of 1929 and the Depression just about wiped out "the road." During the early 1930s, there were fewer than 25 companies touring the country, and most of them were playing shows that had completed their Broadway runs. Hayman died in 1917, Zimmerman in 1925, Erlanger in 1930, and Nixon in 1931. By the time of Klaw's death, in 1936, the Syndicate had become just a memory.

Souvenir Programme...

Academy of Music, N. Y.
TUESDAY EVENING, MARCH 27, 1900.

375th
Performance in New York City.

Wm. A. Brady's
Special Production

WAY DOWN EAST

by LOTTIE BLAIR PARKER.
Elaborated by JOSEPH R. GRISMER.

CAST OF CHARACTERS.

ANNA MOORE	PHŒBE DAVIES
SQUIRE AMASSA BARTLETT	ODELL WILLIAMS
LOUISA BARTLETT, his wife	SARA STEVENS
DAVID BARTLETT, their son	HOWARD KYLE
KATE BREWSTER, their niece	MABEL STRICKLAND
PROF. STERLING, their summer boarder	GEORGE BACKUS
HI HOLLER, their chore boy	FELIX HANEY
LENNOX SANDERSON, the city man	WILL T. ELLWANGER
MARTHA PERKINS, the gossip	ELLA HUGH WOOD
RUBE WHIPPLE, the town constable	FRANK BELL
SETH HOLCOMB	JOHN H. BUNNY
DR. WIGGINS	J. H. DAVIES
ZEKE, the tenor	EDWIN W. HOFF
SAM, the basso. The village choir	GLOVER WARE
CYNTHIA, the soprano	LOUISE BECKMAN
AMELIA, the alto	JANE FORREST
DORCAS	ALICE RADCLIFF
PRISCILLA	CORA E. CALKINS
HANK	BENJ. ACKERMAN
EBEN	R. A. HILLIARD
JAKE	HEWEY DAME
BETSY	LOUISE LEHMAN

SYNOPSIS.

ACT I—Door yard of Squire Bartlett's farm in Summer.

ACT II—A winter evening, eight months later, in the "settin" room of the Squire's house.

ACT III—Kitchen of the same, next evening.

ACT IV—A maple sugar shed in a New Hampshire forest, early next morning.

C. D. McCaull .... Representative

The Shubert brothers, now part of American theatrical legend, were the canniest of the early twentieth-century producers. After winning skirmishes with the Theatrical Syndicate, they went on to consolidate an empire by controlling in the best tradition of trust-building the "product" from inception to distribution to the public. Sam S. Shubert posed in a studio for this portrait.

The elegant Daniel Frohman, who seemed the quintessential Broadwayite (although he was born, in 1851, in Sandusky, Ohio), worked his way up through the ranks as advance man for a touring minstrel show and then as a New York manager. He eventually assembled his own company at his own theater, the first Lyceum, on Fourth Avenue. He joined the theatrical exodus to Longacre (later Times) Square, and there in 1903 built the second Lyceum, shown here, which was designed as a self-contained theatrical plant, with offices, workrooms, rental units and areas to build, paint, and store scenery, as well as a stage, dressing rooms, and rehearsal space. In 1974 it became the first theater in New York to be designated a landmark. Frohman later disbanded his company and leased his house to other producers, but lived in an apartment in the theater he built until shortly before his death, in 1940.

Of the six founders, Charles Frohman was the only genuine producer, for he had carried dramatic entertainments from script to performance. For about twenty years he dominated the American stage. Before he went down on the *Lusitania*, he had introduced more than five hundred plays, and the stars under his management encompassed some of the biggest names on the American and British stages. He owned or controlled eight theaters in New York, three in Boston, two in Chicago, three in London, and one in Paris. At offices in the Empire Theatre building on Broadway he employed a full-time staff consisting of a general manager, a stage director of legitimate drama, a stage director for musicals, and several musical conductors, costumers, carpenters, electricians, scene painters, and property masters. He might have as many as eight productions in rehearsal at once and as many as thirty to forty different productions playing in his own theaters and throughout the Syndicate's empire. At the height of his career, Frohman reportedly had a payroll of some $35 million annually. He staged Shaw and Shakespeare, Wilde and Pinero, Americans Augustus Thomas and William Gillette, French comedies, and even Isadora Duncan in a dance concert. He was also the principal producer of J. M. Barrie's plays. One of his greatest successes was *Peter Pan*, which the English actor-manager Sir Herbert Tree once described to Frohman as "four acts all about fairies, children and Indians, running through the most incoherent story you ever listened to; and what do you suppose—the last act is to be set on top of trees!" As he was swept off the decks of the *Lusitania*, Frohman paraphrased a line from the play: "Why fear death? It is the most beautiful adventure of life."

The meteoric rise of the Shubert brothers to preeminence of power in twentieth-century American theater is the stuff of which legends are made. The information on their early lives is both scant and often contradictory, a state of confusion that they deliberately encouraged. Probably born in the 1870s in Lithuania or Poland, they were brought to America in 1882 as refugees from the czarist pogroms by their father, David, who had fled the year before. Of his six children, Lee (or Levi) was the oldest son, Sam perhaps a year younger than he, and Jacob about a year younger than Sam. The family name underwent several Americanizations before becoming Shubert. Sam was the first to become involved with the theater, appearing for a week as a child supernumerary in a Belasco production at the Wieting Opera House in Syracuse, New York, where the family had settled. He then became a program boy for the Grand Opera House and began a swift ascent in the business until he became treasurer of the Wieting Opera House, at the age of fifteen. As Sam moved up the ladder, he pulled his brothers behind, for one or the other of them would take the job he had just vacated. By making and consolidating contacts, Sam acquired a circuit of theaters in Syracuse, Utica, and Rochester, but his goal was always New York. Before long, Sam got his wish, taking over the lease of the Herald Square Theatre in New York in 1900. Within the next few years, he produced a hit—a spectacle called *A Chinese Honeymoon*—and acquired two more theaters in New York, one in Chicago, and others in Kansas City and St. Louis. Meanwhile, he sent for his brother Lee, who was to be partner in all of his activities. (Brother Jacob was temporarily left behind to manage the Shuberts' upstate New York interests.) But in 1905, Sam's career and life came to an end outside of Harrisburg, Pennsylvania, when a train in which he was traveling was sideswiped by a freight car carrying dynamite.

After much soul-searching, Lee Shubert decided to carry on where his brother had left off. In just five years, he and Sam had acquired thirteen theaters, including one in London, had produced fifteen shows, and had secured the services of performers who, like Lillian Russell, refused to work for the Syndicate. Lee decided he was ready to take on Klaw, Erlanger, and Frohman. Six months after his brother's death, he created a *cause célèbre* by signing Sarah Bernhardt for a tour of America and then finding himself frozen out of the first-class theaters in the major and minor cities. Using the press to help fight his battle, Lee issued a shower of publicity releases exposing Erlanger's unsavory tactics, and he emerged in the public eye, as he intended, a prince of justice and democracy. The Divine Sarah played in city halls, second-class houses, and tents throughout the country in what became a triumphant, celebrated, and highly profitable tour.

Lee brought his brother Jacob, known simply as J. J., into the organization as a full partner, but the move was prompted by necessity and the philosophy that in business blood is always thicker than water. For the rest of their days, the brothers talked as little as possible to each other, though Lee grew to respect J. J.'s ability to produce money-making girly shows and mindless musicals. By 1914 the brothers controlled 350 theaters from coast to coast and had sponsored nearly 150 productions, including plays by Shaw, Maeterlinck, Ibsen, Shakespeare, and Sheridan, as well as witless comedies, noisy spectacles, and tasteless revues. Besides Russell and Bernhardt, they had presented Mrs. Fiske, Sothern and Marlowe, Alla Nazimova, Weber and Fields, Ethel Barrymore, Henry Miller, Mrs. Leslie Carter, and DeWolfe Hopper.

Inevitably, they reached a rapprochement with the Syndicate when competition had begun to produce fewer and fewer benefits for each organization. When the popularity of movies and of lower-priced vaudeville had grown significantly, the Shuberts sat down with their sworn enemies and systematically closed theaters in every city. They retained the lion's share of theaters in New York City, however, and plunged more deeply into production there. By the 1920s they had overtaken Klaw and Erlanger to become the uncontested masters of the American theater. Their empire, a house of cards, consisted of hundreds of small corporations under the general umbrella of the Shubert Theatrical Corporation. It came tumbling down when the full effect of the stock-market crash struck the country. In the early 1930s the Shuberts lost money so quickly that they had to submit to receivership and public auction.

Instead of retiring to a life of ease on the fortunes they had accumulated, the brothers leaped back into the fray, buying back their own theaters, forming the Select Theatres Corporation, and disposing of unprofitable properties. They continued to produce, though on a limited scale, and to control the booking arrangements for all of their theaters.

In 1950 the federal government launched a suit against the Shuberts under the provision of the antitrust laws, and in 1956, by a consent decree, the corporation was forced to divest itself of a portion of its substantial theatrical holdings in New York, Boston, Philadelphia, Chicago, Cincinnati, and Detroit and to dispose of its booking arm. The federal government had succeeded where no one else had in breaking the hold of the Shuberts over the American theater.

Since 1972 The Shubert Organization has been efficiently and profitably managed by Gerald Schoenfeld and Bernard B. Jacobs, who had served as legal counsel to the corporation. In recent years, The Shubert Organization has cautiously begun to depart from its principal business of renting theaters and to invest money in productions both in and out of its own theaters as an act of faith in keeping live entertainment afloat in a country and a culture dominated by television.

At the close of the nineteenth century, the theater in America had a new face and a new animus. The Syndicate had proved beyond the shadow of a doubt that there was money to be made in entertainment once the husk of the old stock company was shucked and the seedling of the new system was allowed to flourish. In 1895 the *New York Sun* described, with some oversimplification, a group of a dozen men who worked "without pecuniary risk, without the cares or responsibilities of management, without acting, without traveling and with, perhaps, not more than ten or twelve weeks of actual work in a season. They are the play producers or play realizers and their functions are practically new in the field of theatricals." These men had astutely realized what would soon become manifestly apparent to many: that the way to theatrical fortune was through the front office or box office and not the stage door, and furthermore that the key to securing it was what the *Sun* reporter described as avoidance of personal "pecuniary risk." In earlier years even the most successful theater managers could expect occasionally to go bankrupt because they used their own or their families' money as capital. By the end of the nineteenth century,

In 1914 Charles B. Dillingham scored a double coup with Watch Your Step. He persuaded the dancers Irene and Vernon Castle (seen here) to appear on Broadway for him and he gave Irving Berlin the opportunity to compose an entire score for the first time. The result was a triumph for all four: producer, stars, and composer. Dillingham, one of Ziegfeld's principal competitors, might have acted the New York producer in a Hollywood movie. An elegant, moustached Broadway boulevardier, he wore pink shirts, lived at the Astor Hotel, and charmed all he met. Once established, he took on risky ventures and sometimes won the gamble. The Shuberts had been unable to fill the cavernous Hippodrome Theatre on Sixth Avenue, but for eight seasons beginning in 1915 Dillingham and his production staff successfully presented oversized revues with such short, catchy titles as Cheer Up, Happy Days, Good Times, and Better Times. In 1916 he brought Anna Pavlova over from Russia to dance The Sleeping Beauty in the Hippodrome, and when she complained that the sound of water splashing in the fountains onstage unnerved her, he promised to substitute "soft" water, which would not make as much noise. Bankrupted by the Crash, he managed to retrieve his fortunes and continued to produce until 1934, the year of his death.

Oliver Morosco began his career with a hit in 1911, The Bird of Paradise, and surpassed it the following year with Peg o' My Heart, which brought fame and fortune to him and stardom to Laurette Taylor. This Sarony Studio portrait of the winsome actress appeared on the cover of The Theatre magazine in June 1914. Morosco had started in show business as an acrobat in California and borrowed the name Morosco from the man for whom he worked. During his career, he made and lost several fortunes, finally went bankrupt in 1923, and turned his attention to movies.

The Theatre Magazine Co.

Florenz Ziegfeld, Jr., brought the revue to such heights that his name is indelibly associated with it. Under his hand, this traditional potpourri of production numbers became extravagantly produced entertainment, with gorgeous showgirls magnificently costumed, brilliant stand-up comics, gifted singers and dancers, and the best show tunes of the time. Although Ziegfeld was as mercurial as he was autocratic, everybody wanted to work for him and the most talented eventually did. From 1907 until 1931, Ziegfeld presented editions of his Follies, each one more lavish than the last. It was once said of Broadway producers generally that money in their hands was as water in a sieve—a statement that applies to Ziegfeld as to no one else. Djuna Barnes's wonderfully vicious caricature of Ziegfeld reflects the disapprobation of his methods felt by much of the theatrical community.

theaters were built, productions were mounted, and shows were toured on money borrowed from outsiders who hoped for a fair or better return on their investment.

Events beyond the world of the theater had made the theater attractive to investors. In the late nineteenth century, the population of the United States swelled enormously as millions of immigrants from Europe flooded through the eastern seaboard gates. The railroad now stretched from coast to coast, and towns and cities sprang up in its wake. After the recession caused by the Panic of 1893 had subsided, the country basked in a new wave of prosperity, and people were hungry for entertainment. When Klaw and Erlanger and the Shuberts blessed their backers with handsome profits, many grew eager to share the world of beautiful actresses and champagne parties and to make a little money on the side. These investors, or stockholders, or backers, or "angels," as they have been variously called, were expected to be neither seen nor heard, but in fact they frequently made themselves visible and vocal. Many years later, producer Arthur Hopkins lamented, "It was once said that every man knows two businesses, his own and show business."

Between 1900 and 1930 the group of twelve men referred to by the Sun grew in number. With a few exceptions, all these producers operated in the same way. They

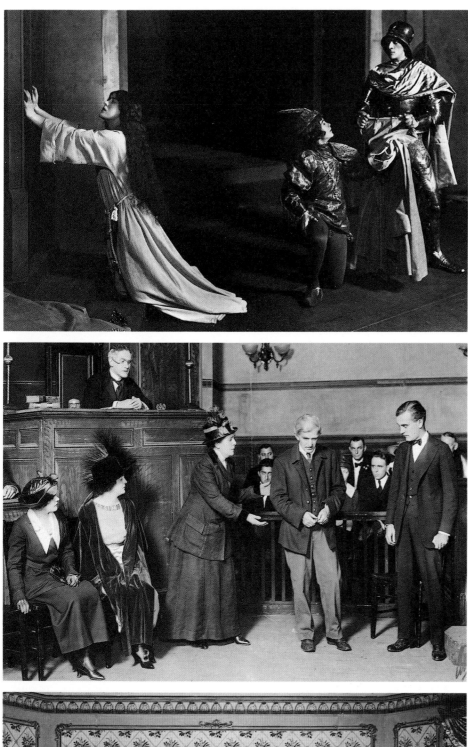

Harvard-educated Winthrop Ames, born in 1870 of a long line of Yankee industrialists and railroad builders, nurtured a passionate interest in the theater. His ambition was to create the perfect playhouse, in which would be incorporated all of his ideas about production, from the operation of the box office to the last nail hammered into the scenery. It almost looked as if his wish would be fulfilled in 1909, when he was invited to direct the fortunes of an enterprise called the New Theatre, an impressive house to rival European state-supported institutions, which was to be subsidized by the wealthy for the benefit of the public. After many false starts, in 1910 Ames found a critical and popular success in Sister Beatrice, a "miracle play" by Maurice Maeterlinck, starring Edith Wynn Matthison in the title role. It was the tale of a nun who falls in love with a prince (Pedro de Cordoba), forsakes her order, and goes out into the world. The Virgin Mary takes the priestess's place but disappears when Sister Beatrice returns, disillusioned and world-weary, to die. It was the kind of play that appealed to Ames. Shown are the stars and the page, Master Russell Reid. For two seasons, Ames struggled against all the inherent handicaps of a misdesigned theater and a misguided purpose, but then withdrew into private production. He built the tiny Little Theatre on West Forty-fourth Street and, with the Shuberts, the Booth Theatre on West Forty-fifth Street. Before retiring to his country home, Ames produced serious, thoughtful plays that appealed to him and his loyal, if somewhat elitist, following.

In act 2 of Lightnin' (1918), "Ma" Jones attempts to divorce the shiftless but irresistible "Lightnin' " Bill Jones so that she can control their house, which lies partly in California and partly in Nevada. To the rescue comes Bill's young lawyer friend, who foils the attempt. In the box is Thomas Maclarnie, as the Judge; at center stage are Jessie Pringle and Frank Bacon, as the Joneses; and at right is Ralph Morgan, as the lawyer. Producer John Golden laid the foundations of his fortune with this comic melodrama. After 1,291 performances on Broadway, the cast and company led a parade from the theater to Pennsylvania Station, cheered on their way by 100,000 well-wishers. Golden's forte became the use of publicity and public events to maintain interest in his productions. After his death, the fortune he had accumulated was used to establish the John Golden Foundation, which supports many worthwhile theatrical activities.

Gilbert Miller, the son of actor-manager Henry Miller and actress Bijou Heron, was not born in the proverbial theatrical trunk, simply because his famous parents were too rich and important for that. After trying to discourage him from a life in the theater, his father hired him as company manager and launched his front-office career. Gilbert Miller's productions appeared for the next thirty-five years, both on Broadway and in the theaters of London's West End, where he was equally at home. After he became established, Miller backed his shows with his own money and preferred English or European plays "Americanized" for Broadway audiences. His formula for success was to use established stars, playwrights, and designers and to leave little to chance. One of his most memorable hits was Laurence Housman's Victoria Regina, which starred Helen Hayes as the English monarch and Vincent Price as her consort. It was staged in 1935 by Miller against Rex Whistler's stunning sets.

Julian Eltinge was launched on his career as the most successful female impersonator on the American stage by producer A. H. Woods in a series of plays beginning in 1911 with The Fascinating Widow. Woods, who called man and woman "Sweetheart," often generated plays by coming up with a title and then finding someone to write a drama around it. He popularized melodramas of a bygone era like Bertha, the Sewing Machine Girl (1907) and strayed from the genre only in the case of Eltinge. Although Woods never fully regained his pre-Depression status, he continued to produce until 1943.

The Guardsman, starring Lynn Fontanne and Alfred Lunt, lifted the sagging fortunes of the Theatre Guild in 1924. The Mexican artist Miguel Covarrubias sketched this impression of the famous pair and their co-star Helen Westley.

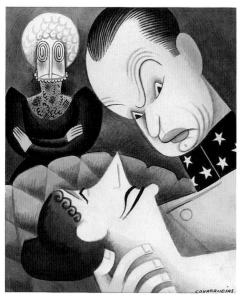

found a play—"a property"—which they optioned from a playwright; raised the money to produce it; rented a theater; hired a cast (preferably with a star), a director, designers, and technicians; ordered the construction of sets and costumes; put the play in rehearsal; and waited for opening night. If they had a hit—audiences for a hundred performances—they could send the production on tour; if the show had the potential for an even longer run in New York, they could assemble duplicate companies and book the production through the Syndicate or the Shuberts or the handful of stubborn independent theater managers for tours throughout the country. The backers would be paid off and then share in the profits. If, however, the play was not a success, the producer would have the sets and costumes carted to a warehouse or sold to someone else, and the investors would be left with a memory of the opening-night party. With a few modifications and, certainly, an overwhelming diminution in activity, the American theater continues to operate in much the same way today. By 1900 the center of the industry was New York City, and so it has remained.

The producers whose careers were forged during the prosperous years between 1900 and 1930 were born in the late nineteenth century. Most survived in their chosen profession until the advent of the Depression. Amazingly, a few weathered that cataclysmic event and retired into happy and well-feathered obscurity. Most, however, went broke and died in unhappy and impoverished obscurity. Except for the few who left heirs in the business, the names of these men and women died with them, for the general public remembers the producers who flourished half a century ago no more clearly than it does their counterparts today. The most important producers of the era stayed in the business for at least twenty years; some had careers that extended through five decades. Since most of them would have agreed that there were better ways of making a living, the explanation for their tenacity lies in their dedication, amounting almost to a fanaticism, to the hurly-burly of show business.

The producers of the early twentieth century could and did take chances on unknown playwrights and players, but they wished to remain solvent and, by and large, played it safe and gave the public what they thought it wanted. Since gauging public taste is ever imprecise, hundreds of productions poured onto Broadway during the peak years of the 1920s and almost as many hundreds swiftly departed. Light romantic comedies and frothy musical comedies, overproduced spectacles and modern melodramas, chic revues and star vehicles, all considered safe fare, overwhelmed the small number of classical revivals and serious message plays. With the American stage tightly controlled by the Syndicate first, the Shuberts second, and the professional producers third, a revolt against the mediocrity and uniformity of the typical Broadway show was inevitable. The "little-theater" movement, launched so spectacularly in Europe in the 1880s, finally reached America and stimulated the formation of groups whose posture was anti-Broadway and noisily experimental.

In 1914 a small party of earnest and intelligent men and women met in Greenwich Village, then center of the bohemian colony in New York, to discuss how they could introduce a theater that would reflect the exciting new trends in European stagecraft. They parceled out tasks, sent letters to potential subscribers, rented the Bandbox Theatre on the East Side of New York, outside the theater district, and began producing plays, written mainly by themselves. The disruptions of World War I forced the group to disband, but an idea had been established that would not die. In 1919 three of the original company met again and organized the Theatre Guild, which they envisioned as a small, independent organization, free of the constraints of commerce. The board of directors included Lawrence Langner, Rollo Peters, Philip Moeller, Helen Freeman, Helen Westley, Justus Sheffield, and Lee Simonson. Maurice Wertheim, who had helped the group financially, was asked to join, and Theresa Helburn assisted the board as play reader and adviser.

With the ardor of the righteous and the vigor of their youth, they began a crusade to cleanse the American theater of provincialism and to shake it into the twentieth century. They took over the Garrick Theatre on West Thirty-fifth Street, where audiences had once rocked to the earthy comedy of Edward Harrigan and later sat spellbound by the serious drama of Richard Mansfield. Jacinto Benavente's *The Bonds of Interest*, their initial offering, was not a success either critically or popularly, but their next play, *John Ferguson*, by the Irish playwright St. John Ervine, profited from an unanticipated circumstance, the actors' strike of 1919, when Broadway was closed down by performers who refused to work without a contract. Because of its liberal stance, the Theatre Guild cheerfully accepted the terms of the actors, and *John Ferguson* became almost the only show in town. When the Guild's offerings—almost all of them realistic or symbolic plays from Europe—had attracted enough critical acclaim and a growing list of subscribers, the board built a playhouse within the theater district and opened it to great fanfare in 1925.

In due course, the Guild became a victim of its own success. The tiny budgets of its early days swelled into the great budgets of Broadway; its production-by-committee, with its free-for-all, intrafamily skirmishes, was replaced by a streamlined organization, headed by Lawrence Langner and Theresa Helburn; and its centralized dynamism was dissipated when the board began to cultivate subscription audiences outside New York with road-company performances of their successful plays. As it prospered, the Guild also grew more conservative. The closely knit company of actors, directors, and designers that had assembled as a community of artists was diluted by outsiders and weakened by defections to mainline Broadway and to Hollywood. Before its glory years were over, however, the Guild had given the American theater *Porgy and Bess* and *Oklahoma!*; had premiered many of Shaw's plays and introduced other European plays no commercial producer would touch; had presented works by the mature O'Neill and the nascent Saroyan; had made stars of many actors and the careers of even more; and had reached out to millions throughout the country through its "Theatre Guild on the Air" in the 1940s and its television productions in the 1950s. With most of the founding members long since dead, it now continues principally as a clearinghouse for subscribers to theatrical attractions in New York and in the major American cities, though from time to time its name is associated with a production. Its everlasting and monumental achievement was in elevating the taste of American audiences and in creating a climate that stimulated the professional producer into taking chances on new American voices struggling to be heard.

In 1938—not a particularly auspicious year for embarking on risky theatrical ventures—five playwrights, challenging the hegemony of the Theatre Guild, formed a cooperative known as the Playwrights' Company. All of them had had plays staged by Guild and other producers and as a result of their experiences sought to exercise as much artistic control as possible over their own work. Maxwell Anderson spoke for all when he wrote of their reasons for forming the company: "We wanted to work with craftsmen whose work we respected, and whose advice was always worth considering because it came out of long experience in the craftsmanship of playwriting. We wanted, in essence, to create a local habitation pleasant enough to put an end to our migratory careers, and it seemed to us that fellow playwrights, with common problems, common aims, and a common enthusiasm, ought to be able to build such a structure, even in the shifting cloud of achievement and dissolution known as the American theatre." Maxwell Anderson, Robert E. Sherwood, Sidney Howard, Elmer Rice, and S. N. Behrman were, then as now, names to conjure with. John F. Wharton, the theatrical attorney, and Roger L. Stevens, a new and ambitious producer, joined the group, as did Kurt Weill and Robert Anderson at later dates.

For the next twenty-two years the association of playwrights did precisely what they had set out to do, and along the way they won audiences and awards; presented seventy-odd plays, both hits and flops; endured internal dissension and frustrations; survived death and defections; and wrote a solid chapter in the history of the American theater.

World War II brought many changes to Broadway. The country's energies were concentrated on foreign hostilities and the city was filled with servicemen seeking entertainment. Established producers presented escapist comedies (*Life with Father*), upbeat war plays (*Winged Victory*), and sturdy revivals of the classics. But there were

In the Follies of 1910, staged at the Jardin de Paris, a roof playhouse atop the New York Theatre on Broadway, producer Florenz Ziegfeld introduced Fanny Brice as a legitimate entertainer. "Lovie Joe" was almost cut out of the show by backer Abe Erlanger. On opening night, she sang eight encores—and the song remained in the show.

Henry W. Savage came to New York from Boston, where he had managed the Castle Square Theatre into prosperity. In 1900 he imported to America Franz Lehár's The Merry Widow and then a successful series of light operas, all in the same general style. As this newspaper cartoon indicates, Savage ran a prosperous real-estate business in addition to his theatrical activities. Impatient with small talk, he installed in his office a carved Japanese chair for guests that was so uncomfortable no one could sit in it for very long, thus insuring that the business at hand was usually accomplished with great dispatch.

A reporter for the New York Clipper and Variety in his early years, Herman Shumlin became a producer in the late 1920s and survived the Depression, wars, and catastrophic changes on Broadway to remain active in his profession until his death, in 1979. During the 1930s, one of his readers, Lillian Hellman, handed him her own play. It was The Children's Hour. In 1934 Shumlin produced it and went on to present four other Hellman dramas. Shown here is a scene from The Children's Hour, a play that shocked audiences with its theme of latent lesbianism in a private school—heady stuff for the time. On the left, a teacher of elocution (Alice McDermott) stands facing the teacher (Ann Revere) who at play's end confesses her love for another woman and ends her life in suicide. Two schoolgirls, played by Elizabeth Seckel (standing) and Eugenia Rawls, look on.

Right below:
An interest in theater developed during her college days propelled Cheryl Crawford to New York, where she found a job with the Theatre Guild. Dissatisfied with the Guild's growing conservatism, in 1931 she founded the Group Theatre with Harold Clurman and Lee Strasberg, also Guild apostates. After she left the Group to work independently, she became noted for her productions of unusual plays, including four of Tennessee Williams's vintage works, innovative musicals, and revivals of significant modern European dramas. Shown here are Maureen Stapleton and Eli Wallach in Crawford's 1951 production of Williams's The Rose Tattoo, which catapulted both actors to stardom.

In 1944 producer Brock Pemberton found himself a hit, Harvey, starring the actor Frank Fay, who is shown here seated in front of his portrait with the giant white rabbit who is his unseen companion in the play. Pemberton, fresh from the drama desk of the New York Times, had served his apprenticeship under Arthur Hopkins, the renowned producer-director. As a fledgling producer, Pemberton had not one but two successes in his first year. The second, Miss Lulu Bett, by Zona Gale, won the Pulitzer Prize for drama in 1921. At first, Pemberton directed as well as produced his plays but later became associated with Antoinette Perry, who thereafter staged all of his productions, including Harvey, another Pulitzer Prize winner. Pemberton's string of successes included many comedies written by American playwrights.

intimations even before the war ended that Broadway would never be what it once was. Movies had siphoned off the audience that purchased balcony seats, and infant television looked ominously as though it might make further inroads. Indeed, in the immediate postwar years urban dwellers melted away to the suburbs, and most were loath to drive into New York City for anything less than a smash hit on Broadway or a touring smash hit in cities west of the Hudson. Theaters fell under the wrecker's ball on Broadway, in the side streets emanating from it, and across the land. There was no longer a new play by Sherwood, Rice, and O'Neill every season, and fresh and promising talents were finding the rewards of television irresistible. The old producers

were dying off, had gone broke, or had lost their taste for battle. The new producers wore conservative business suits and had degrees and backgrounds in law, accounting, or business.

Yet, though they lacked the showmanship of their elders, this younger generation of professionals was just as committed and hardworking. The best of them served apprenticeships with other producers and built on that training by adding their special point of view. One of the most successful of today's producers, Morton Gottlieb, once said that a necessary attribute for a producer is masochism, an ability to accept rejection and survive failure. Although many producers consider theirs a creative job within the dramatic collaboration, one of them, Elizabeth McCann, stated categorically, "There is not a producer alive who makes a really creative contribution to a play. The most important thing for the producer is to make these people [director, writer, actors, and technicians] feel so free and so open that they can admit mistakes and try again."

With the cost of mounting productions on Broadway escalating to a figure of anyone's prediction, there are few plays or musicals today that are not developed and run by committee. David Merrick is the last of the breed to risk his own money, and Alexander Cohen and Hal Prince will perhaps be the last to risk having their names appear alone before the title on the playbill—the reasoning being that there is safety in numbers. The credits page in a theatrical program, already top-heavy with producers, today also lists the names of the general manager, who runs the show on a day-to-day basis, press agents, accountants, advertising agencies, and other support personnel—all of whom used to be part of the team of early twentieth-century producers like Charles Frohman or Winthrop Ames. A theatrical production today supports a whole army of functionaries.

Today, producers operate under the eye of the law. In New York the watchdog is the Bureau of Securities and Public Financing of the Attorney-General's Office of the State of New York. To correct age-old abuses of the profession, the New York state legislature in 1964 set up laws requiring producers to submit legal contracts, known as limited partnership agreements, to the attorney general if they planned to solicit funds

Rodgers and Hammerstein's Oklahoma! *(1943) is today considered the Theatre Guild's most important musical achievement. In this scene at the Skidmore ranch party, most of the principals are onstage: Front row (left to right): Celeste Holm (fifth from left), Lee Dixon, Betty Garde, Ralph Riggs, Owen Martin, and Alfred Drake. Behind Martin is Joan Roberts.*

In 1940 producer Gilbert Miller joined forces with the Theatre Guild to present Helen Hayes and Maurice Evans in Twelfth Night. *This charming poster was designed by Witold Gordon.*

Kermit Bloomgarden's triumphant production (with Walter Fried) of Arthur Miller's Death of a Salesman (1949) was probably the high-water mark of his distinguished career. Shown here are the four principals: Mildred Dunnock, Arthur Kennedy, Cameron Mitchell, and Lee J. Cobb. Bloomgarden learned "the business" as an accountant working for theatrical clients. His first venture was not a success, but in 1945 he produced a racial problem play, Deep Are the Roots, that set a pattern for his future presentations. He remained committed to plays of serious intent and to a playwright's theater. Always considering himself a commercial producer, he believed in spreading the risks so that each investor need not lose a fortune if a production failed.

Jean Dalrymple came to the theater through vaudeville, where she had written and performed sketches for the once dominant Keith-Orpheum circuit. She then worked briefly for John Golden, before setting up her own office as a manager and publicist. In 1943 she volunteered to handle the publicity for the fledgling City Center of Music and Drama in the Mecca Temple in New York, which was to present entertainment that everyone could afford. In 1953 Dalrymple took over the New York City Theatre Company, the dramatic wing of the Center, and guided its fortunes for fifteen years. Her policy was to give fresh showings to the popular successes of Broadway in short runs and with the original stars, if possible. She revived the Leonard Bernstein, Betty Comden, and Adolph Green musical Wonderful Town three times, each time with a different star. In the 1967 edition, Elaine Stritch appeared in the leading role. She is seen here in the show-stopping "Conga" number. When the Theatre Company was dissolved, Dalrymple returned to Broadway as an independent producer.

Master of the grand gesture, Alexander Cohen co-produced King Lear in 1950, at the height of the McCarthy era, and cast every part with a player listed in Red Channels. In this photograph of the production (left to right) are Norman Lloyd, Martin Gabel, Louis Calhern, and Wesley Addy. Like David Merrick, Cohen launched himself with singleness of purpose into show business and became, like Merrick too, a producer-showman in the old mold. At the head of an organization that has branched out into television, he counts among his major achievements productions like Harold Pinter's The Homecoming and Chekhov's Ivanov, which had little chance of becoming commercial Broadway successes. He is one of the last of the current generation of Broadway producers to take significant risks.

In the office of producer Emanuel Azenberg, there hangs a needlepoint sign, "Do Not Invest in Show Business." More than a piece of whimsy, it reflects Azenberg's profound ambivalence toward his calling. His ascent from summer-stock actor to independent producer has left him bloody but unbowed by battles between Greed and Ego, personified by rapacious unions, theater owners, and agents on one side and by temperamental, difficult creative artists on the other. In recent years, he has contributed a "profit-pool" formula to foster sanity on Broadway and to turn plays like "MASTER HAROLD" . . . and the Boys (1982) and The Real Thing (1984), which might have been financial failures, into marginal or outright successes. Pictured here is a scene from Azenberg's most recent Broadway offering, Neil Simon's Biloxi Blues (1984), which has needed no buttressing. Left to right: Matthew Broderick, Brian Tarantina, Matt Mulhern, Alan Ruck (standing), and Barry Miller (on bunk).

Although he has made occasional forays into legitimate or "straight" theater, Harold Prince prefers the musical. Broadway's sometime wunderkind became a producer at twenty-six so that he could hire himself as a director. Since 1954 he has fashioned a string of musicals, all bearing the Hal Prince stamp. From The Pajama Game to Grind, they tend to run against the current of whatever is popular on Broadway. Because they are daring, they are not often imitated. Prince can take special pleasure in the knowledge that his musicals are always anticipated for their fresh themes, their technical innovations, and their theatrical iconoclasm. One of Prince's most stunning productions was Cabaret (1966), a musicalized version of John Van Druten's I Am a Camera, based on Christopher Isherwood's Berlin Stories. Outstanding in the role of the master of ceremonies of the Kit Kat Klub in decadent prewar Berlin was Joel Grey, seen here inviting all to the evening's festivities with the song "Willkommen."

For the most part, the career of Joseph Papp belongs to a chapter on the theater that exists beyond Broadway, but since the success of his recent productions of A Chorus Line (1975), The Pirates of Penzance (1981), and The Mystery of Edwin Drood (1985) he stands with one foot firmly planted off Broadway and the other somewhat tentatively, even reluctantly, on Broadway. His heart and his spirit lie in the New York Public Theater, a few miles south of the theater district, but his pragmatic sense prods him into exploiting the benefits of Broadway exposure. He expects to lose money downtown and to make it uptown, so that downtown can survive. He is a shrewd organizer and has created an appealing public image of a theatrical Don Quixote tilting at the windmills of Broadway's establishment. He finds talent and develops it in his Off-Broadway organization, then brings the best of it into the bright white light of the theater district. Here he stands, surveying the Delacorte Theater as it looked in its early years. Today, after substantial rebuilding, it has become a permanent institution in New York's Central Park.

from the public at large. Since that date, each investor must be given a prospectus of the production and told in sobering language approximately what chances he has for recouping his investment and making any profit. The producer must provide investors with audited statements and live up to the terms of a signed agreement. The breezy "Let's put on a show" of yesteryear has been superseded by a formal legal preliminary, the establishment of a small temporary corporation, enduring for the life of the production, which spells out the responsibilities of the producer in detail.

The age of the union has coincided, not surprisingly, with the era of big business, and the theater has not been exempt from labor's claims. Before the end of the nineteenth century, producers began forming associations to combat the first collectives that sprang into existence to protect performers and backstage personnel. Unfortunately, the organizations had difficulty agreeing with each other and grouped and regrouped until they were forced by the actors' strike of 1919 to make common

cause. Out of the struggle emerged the Producing Managers' Association (PMA), which, with Actors' Equity Association, signed the first American labor-management contract. When in 1924 Lee Shubert and a few other producers became dissatisfied with the PMA, they pulled out to form the Managers' Protective Association, which in 1930 eventually evolved into the League of New York Theatres and Producers and in 1985 changed its name again to League of American Theatres and Producers (LATP). LATP members are active producers and owners of theatrical real estate throughout the country. They use the organization as bargaining agent with all the theatrical unions and empower it to monitor members' activities. Membership is voluntary, and most producers feel it is desirable. Concerned with the health of the theater industry, the organization in recent years has promoted economical and efficient procedures in play production and has kept a watchful eye on the audiences for live entertainment, commissioning studies and making suggestions to its members on how to attract and maintain a steady flow of theatergoers.

Over the years the course of the producer has been neither true nor smooth, and his role as theatrical collaborator eludes exact definition. One thing is certain: without his attachment to a hundred or so pages of playscript, there would be no live theater in America. Without his boundless optimism, without his gambling ardor, without his daring enterprise, theater would have to return to the cart of Thespis and wait for someone like him to come and pull it to the people.

Opposite:
For a time in the 1970s, David Merrick deserted Broadway to try his hand at movie production, but he returned in 1980 with a musical derived from a movie, 42nd Street. Evoking the lush movie musicals of the 1930s, choreographer Gower Champion devised spectacular dance numbers for the show, reverting to precision-tap and cinematic-dance formations.

David Merrick, who has described himself as the "A & P merchant of the Muses," briefly outdid Charles Frohman in having eight shows running at once on Broadway. A St. Louis lawyer, Merrick learned production at the feet of Herman Shumlin and then struck out on his own. This most successful producer in recent Broadway memory has raised theatrical press-agentry to a high art, commissioning his publicists to come up with stunts to insure his shows free and copious newspaper coverage. His formula for production is to take a star, a top-flight director, a play or musical derived from a previously successful incarnation, put them all together, support the enterprise with his own money, and mount a dazzling publicity campaign to turn the show into a hit. I Do! I Do!, produced by Merrick in 1966, had all the ingredients for success: music by Harvey Schmidt, book and lyrics by Tom Jones (with Jan de Hartog's comedy The Fourposter as the foundation), direction and choreography by Gower Champion, and the perennial stars Robert Preston and Mary Martin, who had the stage to themselves throughout the show. They are seen here in an antic moment during the musical.

PLAYWRIGHTS

EUGENE O'NEILL

FÖR HANS AV KRAFT, ÄRLIGHET OCH STARK
KÄNSLA SAMT SJÄLVSTÄNDIG TRAGISK
UPPFATTNING PRÄGLADE DRAMATIK.

STOCKHOLM DEN 10 DECEMBER 1936.

SVENSKA AKADEMIEN

HAR VID SAMMANTRÄDE DEN 19 NOVEMBER 1936
I ENLIGHET MED FÖRESKRIFTEN I
ALFRED NOBELS
TESTAMENTE AV DEN 27 NOVEMBER 1895
BESLUTAT ÖVERLÄMNA
1936 ÅRS NOBELPRIS I LITTERATUR TILL

The Nobel Prize for literature was awarded to Eugene O'Neill in 1936, the first and only time an American dramatist has been so honored.

EUGENE O'Neill received the Nobel Prize for literature in 1936. In a graceful speech of acceptance, printed in the *New York Times*, he noted that the award was a symbol of European recognition of the coming of age of the American theater, honoring not only his work but the work of all of his colleagues in America. "For my plays," he continued,

are merely, through luck of time and circumstances, the most widely known examples of the work done by American playwrights in the years since the World War—work that has finally made modern American drama in its finest aspects an achievement of which Americans can be justly proud, worthy at last to claim kinship with the modern drama of Europe, from which our original inspiration so surely derives.

Although the plays of Eugene O'Neill have slipped in and out of public and critical favor, they have endured. Indeed, for most of the theater-conscious public throughout the world, O'Neill's name is synonymous with American theater.

The German poet Goethe once wrestled with the question: "What are the conditions that produce a great classical national author?" He concluded that such a writer must be born in a commonwealth that has become a happy, unified nation. The writer must respect his countrymen and be a patriot. He must have a sense of history and he must rest his own creations upon the contributions of his predecessors, whatever their imperfections. He must, finally, possess the genius to intuit a great theme and shape it into a polished literary work. Whether O'Neill is America's greatest national author depends on whether his works can be considered literature, but certainly the time of his appearance and the breadth of his genius meet the most stringent of Goethe's conditions, and time has only raised in our estimation the quality of his total body of work.

O'Neill was assuredly as much the product of his country—its history, its aspirations, and its literary impulses—as Shakespeare, Molière, Ibsen, and Shaw were of theirs. That he chose to be a playwright, given his nativity, is understandable. America's history has been and continues to be a great unfolding drama, and its events, the characteristics of its people, the diversity and wonder of its environment, and its ideals are the stuff of drama. If we allow that O'Neill most perfectly caught the temper of his country, the sound of its language, and the common denominator of the ambitions of its citizens and shaped them into the artistic form in which all were best expressed, it should in fairness be said that his predecessors had been groping in their own way toward the same goal. Rightly, his successors consider the quest not complete and have built in their own ways upon his discoveries. It took 150 years to produce an O'Neill, and the explanation for this lies in theatrical history—always evolving, restless and straining, full of real and spectral barriers, rising and falling within the larger picture of American civilization.

American theatrical history did not, of course, begin when the first groups of dissident Englishmen (and a sprinkling of Continental Europeans) stepped ashore in the New World, though their arrival coincided with the greatest efflorescence of drama the world has ever known. The hardy souls who sailed out to the vast continent across the Atlantic were at the spiritual antipodes of the groundlings who were swarming into the Globe to watch Shakespeare and Jonson: they were sober, hardworking, and strong of purpose and mind, and considered revels of any sort impious. In New England theatrical entertainments were soon proscribed by law, and sanctions against them did not come tumbling down until the Republic was established.

During the first fifty years of the eighteenth century, with prosperity quickening in the small, bustling cities, both North and South, an air of sophistication crept into the lives of the American colonials. With more money to spend and more leisure time, they were drawn outside of their homes into worldly pursuits. By the second half of the century, the atmosphere had sufficiently changed to encourage English acting troupes to try their luck in the New World. That entrepreneurial wizard David Douglass permanently cracked the colonial ice as he and his troupe ranged up and down the eastern seaboard from Rhode Island to Virginia, building theaters and selling their theatrical wares. Their repertory consisted of Shakespeare's plays, rounded out with Restoration comedies and tragedies and eighteenth-century dramas. In 1774, just before he ended his sixteen-year sojourn in the colonies, Douglass presented Oliver Goldsmith's *She Stoops to Conquer*, only a few months after it had been introduced on the London stage.

By Douglass's time, life in America was being further enriched by the establishment of newspapers and journals, by the founding of colleges, by the appearance of bookstores, and by the accumulation of private libraries by some of the wealthier citizens. The turn toward intellectual pursuits meant a turn away from the obsessive religious strictures of the previous generations of colonials. With the exception of Boston, the towns and cities of America now enjoyed a more relaxed, more cosmopolitan existence than had ever been known before. The Puritan work ethic had had unpredictable results. The wages of hard work is hard money, and money brought comfort and leisure and a desire to expand and improve not merely present existence but that of future generations as well. Sending the children to school or to England for the finishing touches became the standard goals of prospering families.

America was still very much an English colony culturally, and so it was to remain for at least another century. Everything was based on English models and judged by English standards. As long as the colonials fixed their gaze eastward, they felt no communal urge to establish a native culture or to free themselves intellectually. They were certainly not inspired to write plays based on their experience in the New World. Only one American whose work Douglass considered producing attempted a local theme—that of the pirate Blackbeard's buried treasure—but the pseudonymous Andrew Barton's *The Disappointment* was never shown because Douglass thought it "unfit for the stage." After he withdrew *The Disappointment* from production, however, Douglass immediately announced that *The Prince of Parthia*, "A Tragedy written by the late ingenious Mr. Thomas Godfrey," would be substituted. Not a word appeared in the press concerning the event, nor apparently was it commented upon in the letters or journals of the author's fellow Philadelphians. The play opened and closed on the same night, April 24, 1767. The production was put together on short notice and may have been badly played or poorly rehearsed, but that was not uncommon for first performances of plays. More significant is the fact that Douglass dropped it from his repertory entirely, having tipped his hat in the cause of growing American nationalism.

The drama, centering upon the intrigues and rivalries of Artabanus, ruler of the ancient kingdom of Parthia, his queen, and his three sons, leans heavily on *Macbeth, King Lear, Hamlet, Romeo and Juliet,* and *Julius Caesar* for both its plot and its poetic language. Derivative but seriously intended, *The Prince of Parthia* does reflect the sound education of its young author, who wrote it at twenty-three and died two years before it was presented. Certainly, Godfrey meant his play to be performed, not to be read politely at home as closet drama. He used the best models he could find in the

Eugene O'Neill aged rapidly during his last years, but age is not in evidence in this skillfully lighted photographic portrait by Ben Pinchot, of about 1940.

The actor George "Yankee" Hill found his life's role in a character originally created by Royall Tyler. Hill commissioned plays so that he could continue to play Jonathan under different names.

English language and, had he lived, he might have matured into a playwright. His tragedy can be considered neither better nor worse than many contemporary English plays that have also quietly slipped into oblivion.

No other play by an American author was produced on the American stage until 1787, twenty years later, although during the Revolutionary War several pamphleteers used the dramatic form. They never intended their plays to be acted, but used dramatic dialogue to express their fervent sentiments. Virtually unreadable today, these plays are interesting in that they show how literary Americans enacted the great political and military events of the times upon stages of their own imagination.

By the beginning of the Civil War, America could boast such native writers as James Fenimore Cooper, Ralph Waldo Emerson, Henry Thoreau, Henry Wadsworth Longfellow, Edgar Allan Poe, and Walt Whitman—to name the most outstanding— but no playwright of comparable stature. Each of these writers represented a unique voice, but no single voice could hope to encompass East and West, North and South, federalist and populist, city and country, native and new immigrant. Because American society during the nineteenth century was a constantly moving stream fed by random currents, it was impossible to gather it into a dramatic whole, to select from it universally recognizable scenes, and to give its characters national dimension— in short, to present a national theme. The best that the early playwrights could hope to do was express American character in certain types, and this they did splendidly. They created the stage Yankee, the Indian, the frontiersman, the riverboatman, the boy of the city streets, the immigrant, and the cowboy. These types were first introduced as minor characters, but they proved so popular that soon whole plays were fashioned around them. As an inadvertent benefit, they helped to gain acceptance for American actors, who could play them more convincingly than their English colleagues.

Anyone bent on a literary career in the nineteenth century could expect less profit from plays than from any other form of writing, and indeed a number of early playwrights eventually turned to crafting novels. Playwrights fared very badly at the hands of both managers and stars. Managers were usually English, and they preferred to import a tried and proven London play than to risk producing an untested American one. In those lax precopyright days, American as well as English plays were plagiarized with impunity, and even when an American script was purchased, the playwright stood to make very little if the manager chose to drop his work from the repertory. Many dramas were never published (probably deservedly), and those that were appeared in the bookstores several years after the stage production, when they had lost their bloom. Occasionally a celebrated actor such as Edwin Forrest, James H. Hackett, or Laura Keene sponsored a playwriting contest. Though the stars stood to make thousands of dollars on successful plays, the authors seldom received more than the few hundred dollars originally offered as a prize.

The citizens of the new industrial democracies wanted plays brought to their own level, and the best writers on either side of the Atlantic were not attracted to the modes of drama most popular during the nineteenth century: the farce and the melodrama. The French devised the melodrama, the Germans sentimentalized it, the English stole and Anglicized it, and the Americans got it twice and thrice warmed over. Even Shakespeare, still a favorite, was "improved" along the lines dictated by popular taste in versions by Nahum Tate, Colley Cibber, and David Garrick, who were not above waking Juliet before the death of Romeo and sparing Cordelia's life so that she might marry Edgar.

The essentials of melodrama were defined by the first of its greatest practitioners, the French playwright Guilbert de Pixerécourt: "a villain, an unhappy virtuous woman, a good man who becomes her protector, and the comic character, who helps the good man rescue the heroine." To these he might have added the mystery in the life of one or more of the characters, which was generally revealed to the audience long before the people onstage found it out. To keep the public from becoming tired of the threadbare plots of the "mellers," as they popularly came to be called, playwrights and managers added novelty and spectacle to the proceedings. Live animals were brought on stage, and scene painters and stage carpenters were kept busy creating special effects to titillate the insatiable public. Melodrama created its own special universe. Heroines remained unblemished at the final curtain and villains received their just rewards. No wonder that serious writers shied away from the pat and transparent world of the melodrama.

Stern Congregationalists, Calvinists, and Quakers presented a formidable front throughout the first half of the nineteenth century, and since they were among the most prominent citizens of the large eastern cities, their influence was strong and unwavering. The prejudice of the Protestant churches against the theater made some authors reluctant to write for it. Harriet Beecher Stowe might never have had to write another word had she prepared or authorized her own version of *Uncle Tom's Cabin* for the stage, but she considered the theater anathema and allowed others to reap extraordinary profits from her original creation.

The men and women who in the face of all these deterrents persisted in writing for the theater before the last quarter of the nineteenth century could neither make a living from it nor expect to achieve the public recognition that their colleagues in England enjoyed. Often, to add insult to injury, their very names were omitted from a playbill in deference to the star. So until 1875, the history of American playwrights is the history of their plays or, more specifically, the plays that made it on the stage. Yet if their names have not endured, if even their most successful plays have vanished from every place but the college classroom, they represent the foundation upon which the modern American theater was built and their spirit lives on in the creations of their twentieth-century counterparts. From Royall Tyler to Philip Barry, from Ann Cora Mowatt to Rachel Crothers, from Robert Montgomery Bird to Arthur Miller, from James A. Herne to Eugene O'Neill, there are strong threads of continuity.

With the line "And so, Charlotte, you really think the pocket-hoop unbecoming," the first professionally produced American comedy was launched on the stage of the John Street Theatre. Its author was Royall Tyler, a thirty-year-old Harvard-educated lawyer and army officer, who was on military duty when he reached New York in March 1787. In little more than a month, his play *The Contrast* was on the boards and it created a great stir. Not only was it successful in New York, it was played in Baltimore, Philadelphia, and Boston and revived again and again, mostly by nonprofessional groups, into modern times. In 1972 it was transformed into a musical and presented in an Off-Broadway theater. Light and satiric, the play is typically eighteenth-century in construction and spirit, and although it may have been written in a few weeks, it shows that Tyler was familiar with the dramas of his day. Its model was probably Sheridan's *The School for Scandal*, but the characters and point of view are thoroughly American.

As the first scene opens, Charlotte and Letitia, two girls of good birth and upbringing, are gossiping and comparing notes about fashions. They discuss the impending marriage of Maria Vanrough, a serious young lady, who is averse but resigned to her father's wish that she marry Billy Dimple, an affected man-about-town, who has been educated abroad. In the next act, Charlotte's brother, Colonel Manly, a veteran of the Revolutionary War, appears and reveals himself to be (of course) a sober, patriotic young man. His valet, Jonathan, who declares himself Manly's "waiter," not his servant, and a "true blue son of liberty," is also established as one of nature's noblemen.

Introduced in the third act, Dimple is disclosed (to the audience) as a gambler deeply in debt, who is plotting, despite his engagement, to marry Letitia for her money and make Charlotte his mistress. Meanwhile, Maria accidentally meets Manly and falls in love with him, as does he with her. Dimple is found out by Letitia as he churlishly attempts to seduce Charlotte. Maria's father breaks off the engagement, leaving Manly and Maria free to marry.

Since Tyler himself belonged to an upper-class family of the kind he described in the play and had sowed some wild oats in his youth, *The Contrast* has the ring of truth. Although the principals are prigs, the secondary characters are interesting, charming, and believable. To all the qualities that modern audiences consider quaint Tyler's public responded immediately: the fervent patriotism; the celebration of the distinctively American character, no matter how rough its edges; and the sentimental notion that love will find a way. All would be recurrent themes in American drama during the next century.

The most popular character in the play was Jonathan, cleverly acted by Thomas Wignell, Tyler's inspiration for the role. Though not an original invention of Tyler's, Jonathan represents an important stage in the metamorphosis of the Yankee character in dramatic literature, to which each age, including our own, has added refinements and adjustments. Characterized by independence, love of country, superficial naiveté concealing an uncanny ability to outmaneuver his city brothers and, of course, a down-east New England accent, Tyler's Jonathan inspired a host of imitations on the stage. Two nineteenth-century American actors, James H. Hackett and George "Yankee" Hill, made Jonathan a lifetime career, commissioning plays around him for apparently insatiable audiences. Playwrights after Tyler found a multitude of fanciful names for him: Solomon Swap, Solon Shingle, Industrious Doolittle, Melodious Migrate, Jebediah Homebred, and Jonathan Ploughboy. Each actor varied his costume, but it usually included the striped pants, fancy waistcoat, long-tailed jacket, and top hat that in a later and more stylized evocation became the costume for Uncle Sam.

For his livelihood Tyler returned to the profession of law. Though he continued to write during most of his life and produced a few more plays, he never had a success to equal *The Contrast*. Since there is an unwritten law that a success of any sort deserves imitation, several authors wrote plays very like it. In describing the dramatis personae of his *The Modest Soldier; or, Love in New York*, William Dunlap admitted quite frankly his debt to Tyler: "A Yankee servant, a travelled American, an officer in the late revolutionary army, a fop, such as fops then were in New York, an old gentleman and his two daughters, one of course lively and the other serious." In 1787, recently returned from London, where he had been sent to study portrait painting but had instead been entranced by the theater, Dunlap submitted *The Modest Soldier* to Lewis Hallam and John Henry, the managers of the John Street Theatre, who accepted it but never put it into production. Puzzled at first, Dunlap soon discovered a theatrical verity: a play must always have important parts for the principal players of a company. In his second comedy, *The Father; or, American Shandyism*, he took care to include parts that would please John Henry and his wife. *The Father*, which leaned heavily for inspiration on Laurence Sterne's novel *Tristram Shandy*, was the first of twenty-five original plays by Dunlap that were produced in New York. This considerable output by no means accurately reflects the prodigious energies of its author. In 1796 Dunlap bought into the management of the John Street Theatre, became sole manager, opened the Park Theatre, and struggled to keep it afloat, while continuing to write his own plays and to translate twenty-six others from French and German.

In 1798 his adaptation of *The Stranger* from a garbled version of August von Kotzebue's original play provided a brief reprieve for the tottering Park Theatre. Its theme touched not only Dunlap's audiences but many others to come, and, though no published version has survived, it remained a stock piece throughout the nineteenth century. In sentimentality it was surpassed only by the somewhat similar *East Lynne*, a play adapted in 1863 from a novel by Mrs. Henry Wood, which later supplanted Dunlap's piece in the affections of audiences. *The Stranger* recounts the tale of a recluse who resides on an estate that is looked after by an equally reclusive housekeeper. The woman, years before, had run away with her lover, abandoning her husband and children and finding out too late that her lover was a scoundrel. The man, meanwhile, retreated from society because his wife, years ago, deserted him for another. When the two inevitably meet, they recognize each other. She sees her children and repents her misdeeds, whereupon the family is reunited and the curtain falls. Although Dunlap must have been aware of the meretriciousness of Kotzebue's plays, he also knew that they had the power to move audiences and kept on adapting them for the American theater. During rehearsals for *The Stranger*, he wrote in his diary, "Some of the scenes cannot be played or heard without tears."

The play most often cited by critics as Dunlap's best was also his least popular. *André*, based on the story of a British spy captured by the Revolutionary army, was an original creation. In Dunlap's recounting of the incident, Major André is a noble man who expects to pay for his military crime but begs to be shot as a soldier, not hanged as a spy. An American officer, Colonel Bland, whom André befriended while the young man was a British prisoner, pleads in vain for his life and becomes so angry that he tears the American cockade off his helmet in front of his general—presumably Washington—before storming away. Bland eventually repents his deed, and André is taken off to be executed. The play is strongly patriotic and very subtly antiwar, but audiences were disturbed by Bland's brief insubordination. (At the second performance, Dunlap wisely omitted this scene.) The play lasted only three performances, but Dunlap reworked parts of it into another play, *The Glory of Columbia—Her Yeomanry!*, for a Fourth of July performance in 1803. The second version, ringingly patriotic, proved to be much more popular and was revived frequently.

Although *André* is a decent play that can stand comparison with any English drama written in that mostly barren era in the theater, Dunlap's other plays have rightly passed into oblivion. Dunlap's influence in the theater was effectively over by 1805, when he was forced into bankruptcy after dedicating his personal resources to save the Park. However, he deserves a permanent place in its history, not for what he wrote but for what he represented. He brought status to the role of the playwright and could not help but stimulate other native talents. Through his translations, Dunlap introduced French and German plays to audiences not merely in New York but throughout the country. His name and his work are forgotten now in the theater— although they live on in the fine arts, where he made a more lasting contribution— but his forceful presence in the theater just as the new American Republic was forming most assuredly advanced the cause of drama in its formative stages.

While Dunlap was striving against overwhelming odds to sustain the Park in New York, the theater that Thomas Wignell had built on Chestnut Street in Philadelphia was beginning to prosper. After Wignell's death, in 1803, the new managers, William Warren and William Wood, made it the most influential playhouse in America, and as a consequence Philadelphia became the country's most important center of theatrical activity until New York assumed preeminence, about 1825. The presence of a strong acting company and enlightened management within an attractive theater proved to be a stimulus to local writers. A Philadelphia school of playwrights arose and for a while exported successful plays to other cities. Several writers, notably James Nelson Barker, were vocal in their support of American plays on American themes and practiced what they preached.

Barker, a politician and a civil servant, authored ten plays, three of which became solid successes. Written in 1806 at the behest of Warren, his first produced play, *Tears and Smiles*, was yet another imitation of *The Contrast*, complete with New England character, Nathan Yank. His more original second effort, based on the legend of Captain John Smith and Pocahontas, was the first play about American Indians to be publicly performed. *The Indian Princess* also had the dubious distinction of being pirated for the London stage. *Superstition*, Barker's most interesting drama by far, was set in colonial New England in 1675. This somber tale of evil committed in the name of righteousness was produced at the Chestnut Street Theatre in 1824 and published two years later. Offended that he and his church have not received sufficient respect from Isabella Fitzroy and her son Charles, the Reverend Ravensworth determines to take his revenge. Outside the village, Charles, who is in love with Ravensworth's daughter Mary, meets the Unknown, a recluse who was involved in the plot to murder King Charles I and is, unbeknownst to all, the father of Isabella. Ravensworth charges Isabella and her son with sorcery before a judge and, when he is not believed, accuses Charles of the "contemplated rape and murder" of Mary. After the young man has been led away to execution, an English visitor, Sir Reginald

This frontispiece to the published edition of Royall Tyler's successful comedy The Contrast also gives a suggestion of the staging. The original cast in 1787 included (left to right) John Henry as Colonel Manly, Mrs. Owen Morris as Charlotte, Thomas Wignell as Jonathan, Joseph Harper as Dimple's servant Jessamy, and the younger Lewis Hallam as Dimple.

Born in 1801 in Massachusetts, John Augustus Stone became an actor of character roles and, despite his youth, played old men on stages in Boston, New York, and Philadelphia. Since these roles were minor and paid minimally, Stone also wrote ten plays, of which Metamora; or, the Last of the Wampanoags (1829) *was the most successful.*

Egerton, arrives with a pardon for the Unknown, who promptly identifies his daughter and grandson. Charles's body is brought in, Mary goes mad and dies, and Isabella collapses dead at his bier. The destructive malice of Ravensworth is triumphant.

In *Superstition* Barker relied upon the stock melodramatic devices of coincidence, the mysterious stranger, and hidden identities, but his theme, the unhappy consequences of religious fanaticism, was courageously chosen, recalling as it did a black chapter in American history. In some striking ways it is the spiritual ancestor of *The Crucible*, whose author, Arthur Miller, also found in the history of witch-hunting a parable for his own times.

Four years before *Superstition* was produced, a statement appeared in the *Edinburgh Review* that enraged the growing circle of American writers and citizens who, like Barker, were calling for a national literature free of European dominance. "In the four quarters of the globe," wrote Sidney Smith, "who reads an American book? Or goes to an American play? Or looks at an American picture or statue?" One hundred years would pass before American plays were acted in theaters in the four quarters of the globe, though some, like poor Barker's, were passed off as the work of English writers and successfully produced in London.

Declining the role of pioneer, John Howard Payne, a contemporary of Barker's, preferred to make his mark in England. Born in New York City in 1791, Payne was a precocious lad who, against his family's objections, decided to go on the stage when still in his early teens. He published a theatrical newspaper, *The Thespian Mirror*, when he was fourteen, wrote a play when he was fifteen, and made his acting debut when he was seventeen. In 1813 his friends raised enough money to send him abroad to study. Although he never denied his citizenship, Payne was not to return to America until 1832. His plays were acted first in London, then usually in New York. On several of these, Payne collaborated with Washington Irving, though Irving preferred to suppress his name. As prolific as Dunlap, Payne was also a borrower of plots, and he preferred exotic settings to American backgrounds. His most effective play, *Brutus*, a romantic tragedy based on Roman history, was a favorite with Edmund Kean, who starred in it from opening night at Drury Lane in 1818 throughout his long career. *Brutus* was equally popular in America as a vehicle for American stars.

One of Payne's most successful works was *Clari; or, The Maid of Milan*. Usually referred to as an opera, it was, in fact, a three-act play with music provided by Sir Henry Bishop (an "operatic" plot, which concerns the abduction of a pure peasant maiden from her parents' humble cottage by a rich and powerful duke, may have been responsible for the misconception). Its general silliness is redeemed only by the relatively sprightly dialogue and the music. The principal song, "Home, Sweet Home," with music based on a Sicilian vesper, has the distinction of being the first "hit" song from a musical on the American stage. The New York production of *Clari* followed the London production by only a few months, in 1823, and like other American performances of his plays produced no royalties for the author. Despite his exertions as an actor and a playwright, Payne, like his American predecessors, could not make a career of the theater. In 1842 he became a foreign officer in Tunis for the American government and spent most of his remaining years there.

Fame and money continued to elude American playwrights, but their desire to create a distinctly American school of drama was unflagging. In 1828 the rising young star Edwin Forrest advertised that he would pay $500 for the "best tragedy, in five acts, of which the hero, or principal character, shall be an aboriginal of this country." Of the fourteen plays submitted, the one chosen by a select committee that included William Cullen Bryant was *Metamora; or, The Last of the Wampanoags*, by John Augustus Stone. Unfortunately, the author did not share in the great profits reaped from it by Forrest and, despondent over his poor health and money worries, Stone ended his life by throwing himself in the Schuylkill River in Philadelphia. Forrest placed an impressive tombstone on his grave.

Stone's knowledge of Indians was undoubtedly drawn from stories and plays rather than from profound study of aboriginal history. As Mark Twain would remark of

James Fenimore Cooper's Indians, Stone's subjects came from "an extinct tribe which never existed." *Metamora* contains two simultaneous plots, one concerned with the love story of two colonists in seventeenth-century New England, Oceana and Walter, and the other with the last and futile stand of Metamora and his tribe against the English. Oceana, saved from a menacing panther by an arrow seemingly sped from nowhere, describes her rescuer to Walter as "the grandest model of a mighty man." The mighty man is, of course, Metamora, noblest savage of them all and chief of the Wampanoags. The Indian is full of integrity and high-sounding sentiments, whereas the English are depicted as treacherous and opportunistic. At the end of Stone's play, surrounded by English soldiers, Metamora stabs his wife so that she will be no white man's slave and asks for death. He dies cursing the white man. Oceana and Walter, meanwhile, have been happily united.

Metamora became Forrest's personal and eternal triumph. After his debut in the melodrama, at the Park Theatre in 1829, he toured the country with it, played it in England, and made thousands, perhaps hundreds of thousands, of dollars from it. His contests were also responsible for revealing the talents of Robert Montgomery Bird, who wrote two plays that the actor kept in his repertory for many years. Between 1830 and 1834, Bird won four of Forrest's prizes, but his playwriting career ended abruptly after a falling out over money with the star. He turned to other forms of authorship and other endeavors but sustained more than a trace of bitterness in his heart against Forrest until the day he died.

Bird's principal contribution to Forrest's repertory was *The Gladiator*, a big, sprawling romantic tragedy about the uprising of the gladiator Spartacus against the Romans. The well-known plot offered a larger-than-life part for Forrest and was filled with great speeches about the evils of tyranny and the worth of the common man. Forrest kept the play in his repertory from 1831 until the end of his active career, and after his death it was revived, less successfully, by other actors. After Forrest took it to London in 1836, Bird received the signal tribute of being elected an honorary member of the Dramatic Authors' Society.

Bird's plays were in the mainstream of dramatic writing in his period, and they compare favorably with work produced by Victor Hugo and Alexandre Dumas in France. They also represent a giant step forward in literary sophistication. Unfortunately for Bird, he hitched his wagon to a greedy star and his experiences with Forrest only proved again that playwriting as a profession in America was a form of literary peonage. Even after Bird's death, when his son asked Forrest's permission to publish his father's work, the actor tersely replied that the plays were *his* property.

Despite the many hazards of the profession, writers continued to pour out plays for the burgeoning theater in America. They wrote about Indians, events in American history, famous Americans, Yankees, city life, and life in the wilderness. Many of these plays are produced from time to time for their antiquarian value, and from these usually amateur performances—even more from study of the occasional published script—it is easy to detect a slow and steady progress in craftsmanship during the nineteenth century. Though they were still relying upon foreign models, American playwrights were beginning to respond perceptively to the impulses of developing American society.

In 1917 critic George Jean Nathan cogently observed that American playwrights could not produce a comedy of manners, English style, because they could not present an image of what American society is not. All that they can write, he said, are comedies of bad manners. In a sense, Anna Cora Mowatt (née Ogden) did just that in *Fashion*, her tart critique of American society produced in 1845. She herself had been born into the affluent class (in 1819) and enjoyed the privileges of education and a gentle life, but her play shows that she was aware of the corrupting influences of money, especially new money, in the society around her. She tells us that in a supposedly classless America, money creates its own class, which indulges itself in bad manners and wrong values, abandoning native American honesty and good sense.

The play's principal attraction is in its striking types. The Tiffanys have worked

The 1840s comedy Fashion *was Anna Cora Mowatt's great triumph and her legacy, but during her own day she was better known as an actress. Here she appears as Rosalind in* As You Like It.

their way up into a big house in New York, good clothes, and pretensions. Mrs. Tiffany has a black footman and a French maid, she sprinkles her speech with mispronounced French words, she invites the "right" people to her house, and she is determined to marry off her daughter Seraphina to a titled suitor. Mr. Tiffany has paid for his wife's extravagances by means of improper business practices, and his confidential clerk threatens to expose him unless Seraphina becomes his wife. Seraphina is an empty-headed flirt who is happy to fall in with her mother's plans. The Tiffanys are in contrast to their rough friend from the country, Adam Trueman, to the sensible governess Gertrude (who is discovered to be Trueman's granddaughter and heiress), and to Colonel Howard, the direct stage descendant of Tyler's Colonel Manly. After they have all been put at cross purposes through the machinations of Count Jolimatre, alias the French chef Gustave Treadmill, it is Adam Trueman who sets everyone on the right course. At the final curtain Trueman says of Americans in general: "But we have kings, princes, and nobles in abundance—of Nature's stamp, if not of Fashion's—we have honest men, warm-hearted and brave, and we have women—gentle, fair and true, to whom no title could add nobility."

Fashion was reviewed for the *Broadway Journal* by Edgar Allan Poe, who sought for realism on the stage in an age that was not ready for it. He pronounced it artificial, though very good by comparison with most American dramas. Later he revised his criticism and wrote more warmly of Mrs. Mowatt's play, but his first comments were, in fact, justified. Although *Fashion* is fresh and charming and has genuinely funny moments, it also reflects all of the prevalent dramatic conventions. Despite Poe's reservations, *Fashion* became a hit and was acted in cities throughout America and in London. Mrs. Mowatt wrote a few more plays, but was better known as an actress than a playwright in her own age.

Mrs. Mowatt's contemporary Benjamin A. Baker focused his attention on the lowest rungs of the New York social ladder in *A Glance at New York*, which opened at the Olympic Theatre in 1848 and found an enthusiastic and ready-made audience in the newsboys, bootblacks, apprentices, and stevedores who were the regular habitués of the gallery. Baker served as prompter at Mitchell's theater during its entire existence, but was also an actor and a playwright. For his own benefit performance in 1848, he created a piece entitled *Mose*, in which the actor Frank Chanfrau strutted around the stage as a fireboy—to the delight of the audience. An institution gone the way of the horse-drawn carriage, the nineteenth-century urban fire company was responsible for putting out fires within a city ward. The firehouse became a social club and eventually a political base of action for the boys and men who were the volunteers. They frequently adopted a signature haircut and a special costume. The Olympic was often crowded with fireboys from the Bowery to the "silk stocking" districts and, of course, they went wild over Mose.

At Chanfrau's urging, Baker expanded the skit into *A Glance at New York*, which is little more than a succession of short scenes of street life and city types, moving from the steamboat landing at the foot of New York City through various streets to a saloon, Loafer's Paradise, also in lower Manhattan. A visitor newly arrived from Albany, George Parsells, is immediately set upon by confidence men and during the course of the play is systematically relieved of his watch and his money before he is finally taken in hand by his friend Harry Gordon. They meet the irrepressible Mose, who takes them to a saloon in search of a fight, vowing, "if I don't have a muss soon I'll spile." A fire breaks out and Mose, who rhapsodizes about his company's engine ("I love that machine better than my dinner"), gets an opportunity to pull it across the stage.

Chanfrau made Mose so popular that Baker wrote several sequels for him, sending Mose to France and even China. Other playwrights placed Mose in Boston, Philadelphia, and California. Following in the footsteps of Forrest, Chanfrau became indelibly associated with the character he had brought to life onstage and made vast amounts of money. Baker gained no more from his creation than had Stone and Bird from theirs. The street tough, with his swagger and city argot, became a perennial character in American dramatic literature, to Sidney Kingsley's *Dead End* and beyond, and more recently in the movies and television.

In 1852 *Uncle Tom's Cabin*, a novel written by a northern abolitionist housewife, Harriet Beecher Stowe—the daughter of a Calvinist minister, wife to another, and sister to six others—took the country by storm and eventually found readers in the four corners of the globe. Set both north and south of the Mason-Dixon line, the book contained three distinct plots and had a wealth of characters. Although it was melodramatic and sentimental, it possessed a rich humanity.

Recognizing its dramatic possibilities, several playwrights soon turned the book, or parts of it, into melodrama. The most successful theatrical adaptation was made by a member of a company housed in the Troy Museum, an imitation of P. T. Barnum's famous American Museum in New York City. George C. Howard, leading man and manager of the upstate New York troupe, had a precocious four-year-old daughter, Cordelia, who had captivated Troy Museum audiences as an "infant prodigy" (in that age Americans doted on child actors). Howard was looking for a theater piece that would enable him to capitalize on his daughter's popularity. Mrs. Stowe's novel was on everyone's lips, and someone suggested that it might be dramatized so that Cordelia could play Little Eva. Howard approached his cousin George L. Aiken, an actor in the company and a would-be playwright. For forty dollars and a gold watch, Aiken made a four-act play out of the part of the novel in which Little Eva figured prominently. A short time later, he wrote a four-act sequel, which carried Uncle Tom to his death on Simon Legree's plantation. Eventually the two plays were combined in

In his play of 1848, A Glance at New York, Benjamin A. Baker launched the long career of Mose, the fireboy, on the American stage. Thirty years later, the playwright said in an interview that he had not based Mose on a living person; however, his inspiration was always thought to be Mose Humphreys, an actual street tough. Frank Chanfrau, all swagger and bravado, played Baker's immortal Mose in stovepipe hat, red shirt, and black breeches.

The most famous of the dramatized versions of Uncle Tom's Cabin was created as a vehicle for Cordelia Howard, the child star of the Troy Museum company, in 1852. Though Little Eva is always thought of as a character with long golden curls, Cordelia Howard was actually dark-haired. Her portrait was painted by Alvan Fisher in 1853.

a six-act drama with thirty scenes and eight tableaux. Beginning in the fall of 1852, it ran at the Troy Museum for one hundred performances which, to use Howard's comparison, was like a seven-year run in New York.

Howard took Aiken's play to New York and to instant success, and he and his family continued to troupe with it for the next thirty-five years. Though its initial attraction was little Cordelia as Eva, its triumphant character was Uncle Tom. Never before had there been a stage Negro like him. For many years, the black man had been portrayed onstage as a lazy, shifty, ungrammatical servant and was exploited for his comic possibilities. During the evolution of the minstrel show, musical and dancing talents were added to his comic portrait, but no one had ever attempted a serious treatment, on the supposition that it would not be accepted by audiences. The early dramatizations of *Uncle Tom's Cabin* changed all that, and the impact of the play was incalculable. Not only did it travel like wildfire throughout the United States (with, of course, the exception of the South), it jumped the ocean and became, if imaginable, even more popular in England and Europe. The number of productions fell off somewhat during the Civil War, but *Uncle Tom's Cabin* played on and was revived in the postwar years to become a national institution and a theatrical industry called "Tomming." In 1900 there were five hundred troupes performing it on the road, and in 1931, after *Theatre Arts Monthly* published an article entitled "Uncle Tom Is Dead," letters poured in to report that the show was alive, well, and playing in cities and towns throughout the country.

Since 1852 the play has undergone a multitude of transformations. It has been musicalized, minstrelized, filmed, broadcast, telecast, excerpted, and choreographed. Little Eva has been played by a host of actresses, including Shirley Temple. In the hands of Mrs. Howard, Judy Garland, and many others, Topsy, the black elf, has elicited both tears and laughter from audiences for nearly a century and a half. Uncle Tom's original character was almost totally obliterated in the worst and cheapest dramatizations. Somewhere in tents set among the cornfields he lost his dignity and his persona and became the servile, obedient, sycophantic black man who gave the term "Uncle Tom" its terrible taint. The play continued to represent both the best and worst of American society long after the novel had disappeared from the family library. There is no adequate explanation for its durability. Perhaps in the absence of an American mythology it has slipped in to fill the gap. Whatever the reasons, no other play before or since has had such a special life on the American stage, and its reverberations have continued to be felt in the work of such twentieth-century playwrights as Tennessee Williams.

Like *Uncle Tom's Cabin*, George Henry Boker's *Francesca da Rimini* has been perdurable. Though never a hit, it cannot accurately be described as a *succès d'estime* either, for that term carries the connotation of popular failure, which *Francesca* never quite was. Boker, born in 1823, the scion of a long line of gentleman-authors, wrote well and was appreciated in his own day but did not achieve great fame or popularity. He wrote ten plays, of which six were produced, four remained in manuscript, and only one, *Francesca*, had any kind of afterlife. Most were set in remote times and in foreign places. His one-time advice to a friend was "Get out of your age as far as you can."

Francesca da Rimini was an original reworking of a story in the fifth canto of Dante's *Inferno* and in Boccaccio. In Boker's hands it became a very human drama of three basically good people caught in the toils of circumstances not of their own creation. The marriage of Francesca of Ravenna and Lanciotto of Rimini was designed to put an end to hostilities between the two powerful families. Lanciotto, a hunchback, is accepted as a husband by Francesca, but she is unable to conceal her physical revulsion. The plot is complicated by her attraction to Lanciotto's brother Paolo, and his to her. There is great love between the brothers and Paolo tries hard to subdue his passion. In a masterful scene of mutual seduction, Paolo and Francesca are drawn into each other's arms during their reading of the tale of Guinevere and Lancelot. When they are betrayed by Lanciotto's fool, Pepe, who has spied on them, Lanciotto is

In the third important production of George Henry Boker's Francesca da Rimini, *Otis Skinner (center) played the hunchback Lanciotto, while Aubrey Boucicault acted the role of his brother and rival, Paolo (1901).*

compelled to kill the lovers for the sake of his honor, but then in agony falls dead upon their bodies.

The play is written in blank verse, which with supple grace moves the plot along to its inevitable tragic end. In 1855, more than two years after it was written, *Francesca da Rimini* was first produced at the Broadway Theatre with the star E. L. Davenport as Lanciotto. It ran for eight performances in New York, four in Philadelphia, and then was heard of no more until the star Lawrence Barrett took an interest in it, revised it with the help of the critic William Winter, and produced it in New York in 1882. This time the play ran for nine weeks, after which Barrett made it part of his repertory for a number of years. It continued to be played after Barrett's death and was given another significant production by Otis Skinner in 1901. Skinner had played Paolo in Barrett's production but took the role of Lanciotto for his own presentation. Whenever it was produced, the play always received the plaudits of the critics and the respectful attention of the audience.

Boker was a wealthy man, but he resented the lack of control that playwrights in America had over their own works. He struck as hard a bargain as he could with Barrett over the revival of *Francesca da Rimini*, but what he received in royalties was still less than the star's or manager's share of the receipts. In the 1850s, Boker and Dion Boucicault led a fight to push through Congress a copyright law to protect the playwright. It was the first step in a long fight to redress the wrongs suffered by playwrights for nearly one hundred years. Originally, America had adopted the English system of paying the author the net receipts of the third night's performance—if there was a third night. After a play was introduced, there was little the playwright could do to protect his own work except to withhold it from publication. Once it was published, with or without the permission of the author, it came into the public domain willy-nilly. In 1790 Congress passed a copyright law that protected books, maps, and charts for a period of fourteen years with an option to renew copyright for fourteen more in the case of a living author. In 1831 musical

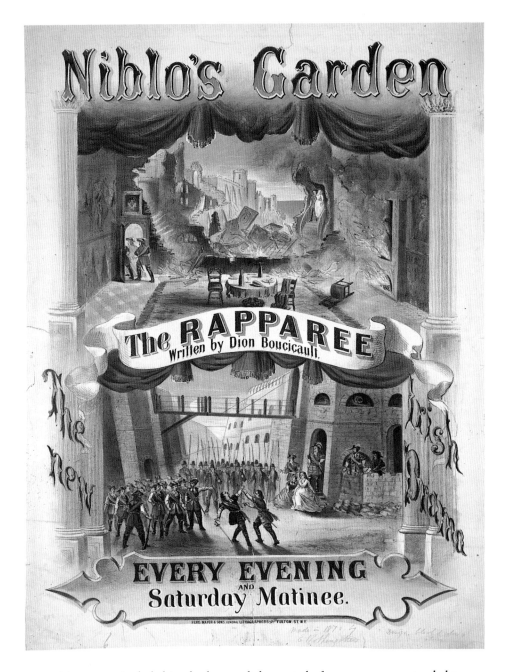

Dion Boucicault mined a rich lode of Irish characters and Irish life during his prolific career, and he always found a ready audience for his plays. The Rapparee, about an Irish mercenary soldier, opened at Niblo's Garden theater in 1870 and was advertised by this poster, which tempted the public with a selection of scenes from the play.

compositions were included in the law, and the period of coverage was extended to twenty-eight years with a twenty-eight-year period of renewal. In 1856 Congress passed the landmark law that gave the author of a play "along with the sole right to print and publish the said composition, the sole right also to act, perform, or represent the same." The protection it offered proved illusory, for only the title of a work was to be filed. Not until 1870, through the efforts of the Librarian of Congress to increase the acquisitions of the nation's library, was it made a requirement to deposit two official copies of the work there.

Boucicault was already an established playwright when he came to America in 1853, for the first time. He was a prolific writer and skillful adapter of plays, stories, and novels. A keenly stagewise man, he turned out melodramas and comedies, in his own words, "as a hen lays eggs," and often directed them and starred in the roles he devised for himself. Born in Ireland in 1822, he never lost his Irish brogue, and, in addition to sojourns in America, he lived and worked in England, France, Ireland, and Australia. His best-known play, *The Octoroon* (1859), left its mark on the American scene because it lightly touched on the hitherto unexplored issue of miscegenation.

Augustin Daly, the foremost director-manager of his day, was as prolific a writer as Boucicault, rivaling him also in the rapidity with which he turned novels into dramas and "naturalized" foreign plays. One of his earliest, most effective, and most original dramas was *Horizon*, produced in New York in 1871. The play begins in New York in the stately house of a grande dame with the fine old New York name of Van Dorp. It then travels to a western settlement, Rogue's Rest, which is on the verge of becoming a respectable community. Then it moves out into the vast territory near Fort Jackson on the Big Run River, dotted with wilderness settlements named Dog's Ears, All Gone, and Hollo Bill, then into the fort, and finally into Indian country. No one character dominates the action. Daly depicted the West as a catchall for many kinds of Americans, a place where people go to find new identities as well as fortunes, or simply for reasons as vaguely formulated as the Widow Mullins's: "Did iver ye go anywhere you didn't see the Irish?" Daly's Indians are not Metamora's descendants, but so crafty and corrupted that one of the characters declares, "When the noble savage was in his native state, he went for the hair of your head. Now he's in the midst of civilization, and he goes for the money in your pocket." But many of *Horizon*'s colorful characters are equally reprobate: a comic Negro who pretends to work while he does nothing; a Heathen Chinee who "steals the bread out of honest men's mouths"; and a shady Washington politician, who has arrived to exploit a questionable land grant of twenty thousand acres for the railroad. For the most interesting character in the play, Daly may have owed his inspiration to Bret Harte. John Loder, loner and outcast, the man who moves on when civilization begins to crowd him, who gambles and drinks hard, who has no truck with Indians or soldiers, and who carries everlastingly with him the aura of a romantic past and the specter of a brief future, foreshadows the laconic, quick-on-the-draw cowboy drifters of the twentieth-century Western.

The plot involves sensational battles between Indians and whites; the love story of a young West Point officer and Med, the long-lost daughter of Mrs. Van Dorp, who just happens to be in Rogue's Rest; and the several adventures and gradual enlightenment of the politician and his English companion, an amusing character who feels invulnerable to everything because he is protected by the British flag. The tale is contrived and melodramatic, but Daly's characterizations more than compensate for its literary deficiencies. His realistic picture of the West and unsentimentalized portrait of the American Indian were superior to any that had yet been presented onstage.

Many years after its brief run, the noted New York manager A. M. Palmer told Daly's brother: "*Horizon* was the best American play I have ever seen; more than that, it was the best play your brother ever wrote; and it was the least appreciated by the public." *Horizon* is rarely cited as one of the earliest pieces of frontier literature, and Daly never received credit for his contribution to the character of the western adventure, later honed to perfection in the movies. The fame that did not go to Daly's play went instead to Frank Murdoch's *Davy Crockett*, which appeared the following year and became a great success, with the actor Frank Mayo in the lead part. The play, which Mayo starred in for many years, created the myth of the frontiersman and launched him into eternal life on the stage, screen, and television.

After the Civil War, the idea of a national culture took on renewed meaning and importance, but its creation was delayed by new tides of immigrants, who cut fresh facets into an already many-sided society. Eventually, the newly assimilated Americans saw themselves portrayed onstage. Like Baker's street-wise Mose, they appeared at first as comic types. No playwright mined this vein of social satire to better effect than Edward Harrigan.

Harrigan began his career as a singer of comic Irish songs in a concert hall in San Francisco in 1867. During the next few years he made his way east, picked up a partner in the brilliant young comic performer Tony Hart, wrote sketches and songs for their special talents, and was carried inevitably to New York. Harrigan's most successful creation was "The Mulligan Guard," first a sketch, then a series of plays that drew its inspiration from the local rifle companies, which had become an institution in New York City after the Civil War. Manned mostly by immigrants who were refused admittance into the local units of the National Guard, the rifle companies offered an excuse for the butchers and bakers and candlestick makers to

Actor and dramatist Dion Boucicault was pleased by the notion that he resembled William Shakespeare in his old age.

Frontiersman Davy Crockett, subject of a play by Frank Murdoch, was played exhaustively by actor Frank Mayo, beginning in 1872.

HOYT'S
A TRIP TO CHINATOWN

FROM
HOYT'S THEATRE
NEW YORK

HOYT & McKEE
PROPRIETORS.

THE BELLE OF THE BALL.

Charles Hoyt's most popular play, A Trip to Chinatown, *contained action, singing and dancing, and not much plot, as is suggested by this poster for the show, which opened in 1891.*

Opposite:
The noisy street life of the Lower East Side furnished inspiration for the plays of Edward Harrigan, who enriched the American theater with unforgettable types of old New York. With his partner, Tony Hart (who usually played a wench), Harrigan performed in his own phenomenally successful "Mulligan Guard" shows. The assorted characters popularized by Harrigan and Hart are gathered together in this newspaper collage.

don uniforms, shoot at targets, march on Sundays, and wind down their activities with a good deal of drinking and boisterous camaraderie at the local saloons. These clublike institutions did not replace the fire companies but were often an adjunct of them.

The adventures and misadventures of Harrigan's company, composed of Dan Mulligan and his cronies, were carried through seven plays, all written between 1878 and 1881. The plots were grandly farcical and interspersed with songs, some of which lived on long after the Mulligan Guard was a theatrical memory. Harrigan's characters were the immigrant population of the Lower East Side of New York. They were Irish, German, Italian, Jewish, and black, and they spoke the English language of the new arrival who has not given up the accents of his native speech. In an appreciation of Harrigan, the American author and playwright William Dean Howells compared his work to the comedies of manners of the Venetian playwright Goldoni. Claiming Harrigan brought native American drama a step closer to realization, Howells analyzed the potential and the limit of his art. "Mr. Harrigan accurately realizes in his scenes what he realizes in his persons; that is, the actual life of this city. He cannot give it all; he can only give phases of it; and he has preferred to give its Irish-American phases in their rich and amusing variety, and some of its African and Teutonic phases. It is what we call low life, though whether it is essentially lower than fashionable life is another question." Harrigan's very human characters were followed from event to event in much the same way that television situation comedies unfold the lives of three or four central characters. His plots were an excuse to get the Mulligans together with the Lochmullers and the other denizens of the neighborhood.

Harrigan's contemporary Charles Hoyt satirized other aspects of the "actual life" that Howells considered an open field in the late nineteenth century. Like many others, he plunged into a theatrical career from the springboard of journalism, as a writer and critic for the *Boston Post*. He wrote his first play almost as a lark and discovered that dramatic writing suited him. His productive life lasted from 1883 to 1899, and during that decade and a half he produced eighteen pieces—seventeen farces and one comic operetta—only two of which were out-and-out failures. His success made him a millionaire at thirty.

An acute observer of human character and foibles, by his own admission Hoyt was no reformer. He enjoyed poking fun at the ridiculous and deflating the pompous. He created types, not people, and like the Elizabethans named them according to their principal "humors": the hypocrite Kneeland Pray; the hypochondriac Welland Strong; the undertaker Christian Berriel; the man-about-town Rashleigh Gay; the surgeon Mark Tombes; and so forth. Hoyt's first major success, A *Trip to Chinatown*, could have been subtitled "*or, How They Never Got There*." Pure farce, it ran for 657 performances after opening in 1891. Such songs as "The Bowery," "Reuben, Reuben, I've Been Thinking," and "After the Ball"—none of which had anything to do with the action—were a great part of the success of the show. His later plays were satires. In A *Temperance Town*, he gibed at the prohibition movement; in A *Milk White Flag*, he made fun of the home-guard militiamen; in A *Contented Woman*, he amused himself at the expense of the woman-suffrage movement; and in A *Parlor Match*, he ridiculed spiritualism and treasure-hunters. (The title of all but one of his plays begins with "A"; after the failure of *The Maid and the Moonshiner*, he stuck with the indefinite article.)

The theatrical success that came so readily to Harrigan and Hoyt eluded William Dean Howells, though he became a leading novelist and critic of his time, a poet and an essayist, and the most respected American man of letters in the late nineteenth century. From childhood onward, Howells loved the theater and went whenever he could. Between 1874 and 1911 he wrote thirty-six plays: short and full-length comedies, adaptations, a libretto, verse plays, and dramatizations of his novels. Eleven of them reached the stage, but the rest appeared only in the *Atlantic Monthly* and *Harper's Monthly*. Howells's handicap was not that he confined himself to writing about the aristocratic society of Boston's Back Bay—for he understood Harrigan's work

JOHN QUEEN.

WILLIAM WEST.

DAVE BRAHAM, THE FAMOUS COMPOSER.

HARRIGAN & HART, IN "THE BLUE AND THE GRAY."

QUILTER & GOLDRICH.

THE ORIGINAL MULLIGAN GUARDS,
TONY HART.   MORGAN BENSON.   EDWARD HARRIGAN.

EMMA POLLOCK, THE ORIGINAL "MAGGIE MURPHY."

ADA LEWIS, ORIGINAL "TOUGH GIRL."

MART HANLEY, MANAGER.

HARRIGAN & HART, IN "YOU SPOKE ME."

HARRIGAN & HART, "LITTLE FRAUD."

EDWARD HARRIGAN, IN "REILLY and the 400."

EDWARD HARRIGAN as PETE, AND HIS DAUGHTER, MISS ADELAIDE HARRIGAN.

EDWARD HARRIGAN, 1875.

TONY HART, 1875.

TONY HART, IN "MULLIGAN GUARD PICNIC."

EDWARD HARRIGAN, IN HIS FAVORITE CHARACTER, "DAN MULLIGAN."

"THE GALLANT 69TH," TONY HART, CAPTAIN, (IN CENTER.)

"THE REGULAR ARMY O,"
Ed Harrigan, Tommy Ryan, Mike Bradley, Ben Diamond, Johnny Wild, Tony Hart.

THEATRE COMIQUE 514 Broadway, New York.

DAN COLLIER, IN "UNDER COVER."

EDWARD HARRIGAN, HIS LAST PHOTO.

JOHNNY WILD,

ANNIE YEAMANS, AS CORDELIA MULLIGAN.

EDWARD HARRIGAN, AS THE MAJOR GILFEATHER.

HARRIGAN & HART, IN COTTON.

HARRY FISHER,

BILLY GRAY.

FROM THE ALBERT DAVIS COLLECTION

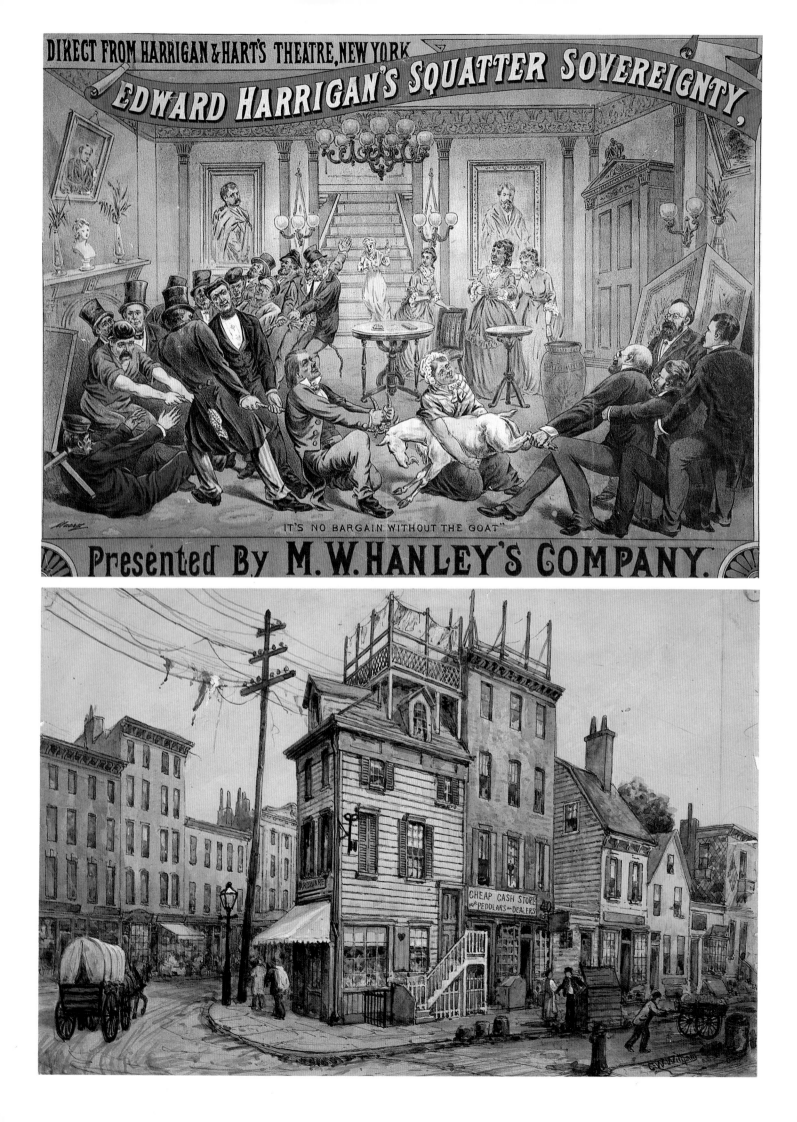

and was capable of doing for the upper echelons of American society what Harrigan had done for the lower—but rather that his best works are one-act plays, and there was no market on the commercial stage for what most managers considered dramatic trifles. These tiny masterpieces, which show his gifts for brilliant repartee, amusing all-too-human situations, and deftly constructed characters, were doomed to a life on the printed page. Howells concerned himself with men and women who lived by rules of etiquette, who had money and prestige, and who entertained at tea and engaged in literate conversation, but he put them into realistic situations, making them react to inconsequential events such as a mouse in the room, a supposed mugging, a stuck elevator, or unexpected guests at a dinner party, and wrestle with the eccentricities of the newfangled telephone, phonograph, Pullman car, and bicycle. He pitted woman against man in the game of love and gave the victory to woman. His plays were clever and charming. Even George Bernard Shaw admired his work and deplored the lack of imagination that banished it from the stage. After searching out a production of Howells's *The Garroters* in London, Shaw wrote: "The little piece showed, as might have been expected, that with three weeks' practice the American novelist could write the heads off the poor bunglers to whom our managers generally appeal when they want a small bit of work to amuse the people who come at eight." Howells often anticipated Shaw as well as such American playwrights as Clyde Fitch, Philip Barry, and S. N. Behrman.

In his novels and criticism, Howells took his place in the vanguard of the movement toward realism. He and a fellow critic, Hamlin Garland, deplored what the latter called "the low level of imitative English sensationalism and sterile sexualism" in American plays of their day. Both became champions of James A. Herne, who has been described by his biographer John Perry as the American Ibsen. Herne began his life in the theater as a stock-company actor and, like most players with ambition, he graduated into stage management. In 1888 he first attracted the critics with a play entitled *Drifting Apart*, a temperance drama, which has not survived. Instead of depicting the mandatory road to ruin with redemption in the last act, Herne presented a dream sequence of chilling realism and then returned the hero to the real world in the final act of his play. Although audiences were not ready to accept changes in the dramatic conventions, critics like Garland were. Herne was probably unaware of the existence of Ibsen and the European realists until Garland introduced him to their somber works and completed his education. In 1891, largely through the efforts of Garland, Herne presented his *Margaret Fleming* in Boston's Chickering Hall, which they hoped would become the Théâtre Libre of America. A. M. Palmer became interested in the play and moved it to New York, but it was not a success and never found its audience.

Early in *Margaret Fleming*, the hero, Philip, is revealed as a rather lax small-town businessman, whose past has included womanizing and hard drinking. We learn, too, that his wife, Margaret, who has recently given birth to their child, has glaucoma and will lose her sight if she is subjected to undue stress. Philip receives the news that one of his former mistresses has delivered his baby and lies near death. Though he does not know it, the girl's sister is employed in his household. She tells Margaret the sad tale and asks her to visit the young mother, who is dying. Margaret is touched and agrees. Arriving at the deathbed, she learns that her husband is the father of the child. The shock of the discovery blinds Margaret, but not before she has seen Philip's child. In a scene that was deplored by both critics and public, Margaret begins to unbutton her blouse in order to nurse the hungry motherless baby as the curtain falls on the second act. In the final scene, Margaret agrees to take Philip back, but not into her bed. When he begins to protest, she asks him, "Suppose—I— had been unfaithful to you?" She tells Philip that he may hope for her forgiveness but assures him that the old Margaret is dead: "The truth killed her."

When the play was reviewed in New York, the *Times* critic Edward A. Dithmar called it "realistic in everything. We see human beings as they are. There are no soliloquies. The meditations of the characters are not spoken aloud. The author has

The career of James A. Herne combined acting, playwriting, and managing in almost equal parts. Here he is shown in 1891 as Joe Fletcher, the one comic character in Margaret Fleming, *his own most important play.*

Opposite above:
"*Direct from New York*" emblazoned across posters in the late nineteenth century caught the eye of theater patrons and lured them into playhouses across America. The "melee" scene from Edward Harrigan's Squatter Sovereignty *depicted on this poster for the road company gave people an idea of what to expect.*

Opposite below:
Edward Harrigan's designer Charles Witham created this New York street scene as a backdrop for Waddy Googan, *which was introduced at Harrigan's Park Theatre in 1888.*

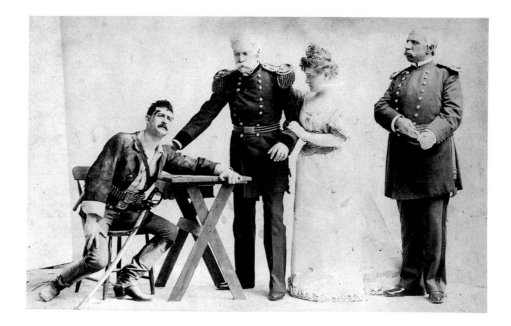

steered clear of all the old conventions of the drama. The personages come and go naturally. It is easy to be natural in making a play without stirring climaxes and forcible dramatic situations." Yet he also described it as "the quintessence of the commonplace. Its language is the colloquial English of the shops and the streets and the kitchen fire-place. Its personages are the everyday nonentities that some folks like to forget when they go to the theatre." Howells and Garland praised the play for the very reasons Dithmar found fault with it. But in the final analysis Howells considered *Margaret Fleming* an epoch-marking rather than an epoch-making play because it found no imitators. After World War I, the play did work its "silent potentiality," as Herne predicted, on a generation of playwrights, among them O'Neill, Elmer Rice, and Sidney Howard, who were to shake off formularized plots and stock characters and to consider the relationships between the sexes, the double standard, and the substantial issues of their time with honesty and compassion.

Like most of the American playwrights who preceded him, Herne could not make a living from his plays and continued to act and manage until illness forced his retirement. Producers still looked to England and France for material and, citing the risks involved in producing American works, they dodged the issue of giving a native-born writer a larger percentage of the receipts if his play turned out to be a hit. As late as 1892, the playwright Charles Klein had to haggle for a fifty-dollar advance and royalties of fifty dollars a week on a play that had turned out to be a substantial success. The playwright's only recourse was to negotiate a better deal for himself with each succeeding production. At the end of the nineteenth century, when the American theater was monopolized by the Syndicate, playwrights had to fight fire with fire and Bronson Howard was the first at the ramparts. He neither acted nor managed, but after struggling for more than twenty years to secure ever more favorable arrangements with producers, he earned the considerable sum of $40,000 on his plays for the year 1894.

Born in Detroit in 1842, when that city was considered far-western, Howard saw his first play produced there. Its success drew him to New York in 1865. In 1870 Augustin Daly, at the beginning of his own successful career, presented Howard's first important play, *Saratoga*, which ran for more than one hundred performances. It caught the eye of an English producer, who brought it out as *Brighton* in England. Since Howard was a slow and painstaking dramatist, he produced only twenty-seven plays in a career that spanned thirty-six years. Sixteen were produced in New York, the last in 1899, but only one of his plays, *Shenandoah*, a large-scale melodrama of the Civil War, is remembered today. Yet during the last three decades of the nineteenth century, Howard was the most important and admired playwright in America.

Although this astute man of the theater was aware of the contemporary currents of realism in American and European literature, he took as the model for his plays about

American life the dramas of a previous generation. He wrote what he called "satisfactory" plays—by which he meant that he was giving audiences what they wanted: plays that punished wrongdoers and the misguided. He glorified the freedom of the new American woman but brought her to the altar in the end. He warned against materialism and the worship of European aristocracy, but these were less than courageous positions. He wrote, too, with an eye to the box office as he shaped characters with particular actors in mind.

Thus, Howard's importance in history does not rest on his dramatic contributions. The success of his plays, their acceptance in England, and the willingness of producers to come to terms with him brought new status to all American theatrical writers and turned their occupation into a profession. No longer would a playwright's name be lost in the small print on the program. In 1891 Howard founded the American Dramatists' Club. At first it was a purely social group, but later, as the Society of American Dramatists and Composers, it advanced the cause of playrights on all fronts. In 1897, Howard and his colleagues lobbied for new copyright protection and succeeded in having legislation enacted which made it a crime to present an unauthorized production of a dramatic work.

When Bronson Howard began his career, the American theater was dominated by English and French plays and adaptations of foreign novels. By 1900 the tables were turned and American writers were crowding out their overseas competitors. Mark Twain, Bret Harte, Thomas Bailey Aldrich, and Henry James are just a few of the better-known novelists who wrote plays. Many others lived to see their prose works turned into dramas. Movies were still a curiosity, and the American public was insatiable for live entertainment. Hundreds of shows were sent out from New York every year. It was the best of times to be a playwright, and anyone who could write a play had a chance to see it produced. Although a few good plays emerged from the constant churning of the theatrical machine, most of them were, as Bronson Howard put it with a jot of cynicism, "dramatic trash," without which "neither theatre nor the profession of acting would exist." Plays of every type and description, from the machine-made "ten-twent-thirt" melodramas (cheaply produced plays that the public paid ten cents to thirty cents to see) to the impeccably produced Belasco drama, were offered to theatergoers at all levels of the economic scale. Mecca was New York and Broadway, and writers who aspired to the stage turned their faces and their feet in that direction.

Two of the most interesting playwrights who emerged before World War I died in their forties, at the peak of their careers. Otherwise they had nothing at all in common. Born in Indiana in 1869, William Vaughn Moody considered Chicago his home, although he made trips abroad, spent periods of his life in New York and Boston, and traveled through the West for his health and for relaxation. Except for a modest income from his publications (he was also a poet and scholar) and the royalties from his one successful play, he lived on the salary of a teacher. His entire dramatic output consisted of a verse trilogy and two prose plays. Born in 1865, Clyde Fitch was an easterner, a boulevardier inclined to English-cut suits and purple cravats, and at the turn of the century the most successful playwright on Broadway, almost as well known in Europe as in America. His name was attached to sixty-two plays, of which thirty-six were original and the others adaptations of European successes and dramatizations of novels. Fitch was one of the most talented directors of his time, frequently overseeing the design of his productions down to the last detail. Actors and actresses besieged him with requests for plays and, although he denied it, he tailored some of his pieces for Ethel Barrymore, Clara Bloodgood, Olga Nethersole, Richard Mansfield, and Maxine Elliott, all of whom had great box-office pull in their day. With as many as ten plays running simultaneously on Broadway, on tour throughout America, and on the English and Continental stages as well, Fitch could boast the greatest success story to date in the history of the American theater.

Both Fitch and Moody tried to write about American life as they saw it. Fitch never forgot that his mission was to entertain and never got very far under the surface

Theatergoers came to anticipate lavish detail in the settings and costumes for Clyde Fitch's plays. This Byron Studio photograph shows a scene from The Climbers *(1901), about life in the upper brackets of American society.*

of his subjects, yet he genuinely tried for a kind of psychological realism. In an arresting scene in *The Climbers*, the character Richard Sterling must confess to his wife that he has gambled with and lost her aunt's money. He hesitates because he does not want to see her disappointment and his own guilt reflected in her eyes. His best friend turns off the lights so that he can make his confession in the darkened room. Maude Adams complained to Fitch that his characters were all neurotics, but aberrant behavior was precisely what interested him and riveted his audiences.

The Climbers, a most interesting play that opened in 1901, begins with a funeral and closes with a suicide and introduces an array of characters, most of whom could have become monstrous if Fitch had not saved them through his benevolent touch. They are for the most part status seekers: a widow more concerned about the social position of the people who attended her late husband's funeral than his death; men of business who speculate recklessly with other people's money; and men and women who marry for all the wrong reasons. When Richard Sterling commits suicide at the end of the play, he washes down the pills with a glass of champagne. *The Climbers* is an indictment of what Fitch obviously found unattractive in American society: the emphasis on acquiring wealth through whatever means and the false sense of worth that wealth confers on people. Like Fitch's other plays, it is "satisfactory" in Howard's sense. It pleased audiences because by the final curtain Fitch had reaffirmed the moral order in the world of the play.

Moody's play *The Great Divide* has an unforgettable opening scene. Alone in a cabin in the Arizona desert, a young New England girl, Ruth Jordan, is beset by drifters. They intend to rape her, but she singles out one of them, Stephen Ghent, and promises to marry him if he will save her from the other two. She makes good her promise, helps him to become wealthy by investing him with a sense of purpose, and then leaves him when she cannot live with her feeling of bondage. Back in New England, she gives birth to his baby and withdraws from life. Stephen follows her and

One of the stars of The Black Crook, a smash hit of 1866 with a cheerfully convoluted book by Charles Barras, was the ballerina Marie Bonfanti, here shown on the cover of music from the long-running, epoch-marking show.

In the second act of William Vaughn Moody's The Great Divide (1904), Margaret Anglin as Ruth returns to her husband, Stephen Ghent, the chain of gold nuggets with which he had previously "bought" her from her attackers. Henry Miller plays Stephen.

secretly saves her family from bankruptcy. When Ruth discovers what he has done, she reexamines her feelings and decides to take up her life with her husband and their son.

Moody used the play to explore the spiritual difference between the America of the East and the America of the West. A true New Englander, Ruth represses all that is free and passionate within herself through self-denial. Stephen, on the other hand, represents the free spirit, the lawlessness, the thoughtlessness of the natural man. Only when each can surrender that part of the self that divides them can they become reconciled. Underlying the story of two individuals is the larger drama of two types of Americans with separate, yet entwined, histories and ways of life, each of whom must make concessions to the other for the sake of the unified nation. Moody's play is powerful on the superficial level, but because it goes further, to examine the strong counter tides in American life, it was uncommon in its time and is of interest today.

In 1905, the year before *The Great Divide* was produced, a young Harvard professor proposed to give a one-semester course in playwriting entitled "English 47: The Technique of the Drama." The instructor, George Pierce Baker, at first intended the course for undergraduates, but he eventually expanded and redesigned it for graduates. By 1912 he had succeeded in enriching it with a laboratory theater and, as the "47 Workshop," it became a school not only for playwrights but for actors, designers, and directors as well. One of Baker's first successful "graduates" was Edward Sheldon, whose first play, about a Salvation Army girl's love for a drunkard, caught the

The Cohans—George M. and Jerry, his father—enjoy a sprightly moment in George Washington, Jr., written, composed, and produced by the legendary G.M.C. in 1906 at New York's Herald Square Theatre.

Put on their mettle by the success of the musical revues imported during the 1870s from England and the Continent, American writers and composers quickly began to write their own opéras bouffes. Henry Wadsworth Longfellow's Evangeline in musical form became a hit at Niblo's Garden theater in 1874. Illustrated here is the sheet music for a popular tune from the show. The cover artist caught the tongue-in-cheek flavor of Edward E. Rice's score and J. Cheever Goodwin's lyrics.

attention of the great American dramatic star Mrs. Fiske and became a hit in 1908 as *Salvation Nell*. Although Baker's own taste was conservative, and although he emphasized the techniques of the modern European masters, he was a great encourager of his students, and the workshop became a magnet for serious young writers. The list of Baker's students who made good reads like a Who's Who of the American Theater for the first half of the twentieth century. In 1914, without academic credentials, O'Neill begged for admission to the course, writing Baker that he wanted to be "an artist or nothing." O'Neill did not return for a second year with Baker, but in 1935, at the time of Baker's death, the playwright paid tribute to his "intelligent encouragement."

In 1924, his building having been commandeered by an unenlightened administration, Baker left Harvard for Yale University, which promised him a full curriculum in the next year and a playhouse (the gift of Edward Harkness) later. With the inauguration of the new theater, in 1926, the Yale School of Drama became preeminent in the teaching of the dramatic arts. Largely in emulation of Baker's pioneering endeavors, most of the major universities in the United States had instituted courses in playwriting by 1920, and the university campus theater continues to figure significantly in the development of new playwrights.

During the late nineteenth century, all forms of musical theater grew in popularity. Long before the time of John Howard Payne, American plays were embellished with music or, more specifically, with interspersed songs. During most of the nineteenth century, musicians entertained from the pit before the show began and between the acts and provided mood music at important moments during the unfolding of a melodrama (a convention that David Belasco preserved in his productions during the early years of the new century). In 1866, when Charles M. Barras's *The Black Crook* took New York by storm, audiences were treated to a rich pastiche of music and ballet and story and scenic spectacle interwoven in one glorious entertainment, and they were enthusiastic enough to keep it going for sixteen months at Niblo's Garden in New York and for forty years in revivals. What made *The Black Crook* unique was the linear story line that distinguished it from such musical entertainments as the minstrel or the variety (vaudeville) show. It provided a gossamer thread on which to hang the songs—and the ballets. No one took the elaborate, Faustian plot very seriously, and everyone went to see the girls, girls, girls in their buff tights.

The course of the American musical theater was influenced by each new importation from abroad. Lydia Thompson and her British blondes arrived in 1868 with their English "burlesques," or travesties on current plays, novels, and fashions, which had convulsed audiences at home but did very little to amuse Americans. They flocked to see Thompson's shows—not to laugh at the peculiarly English humor but to watch her girls cavort and to catch a dirty innuendo now and again. American writers and composers imitated popular foreign revues like Thompson's, but the lesson of *The Black Crook* was not forgotten: songs and dances and scenery do not a musical make. Someone or something had to provide a raison d'être for the show before the enterprise could get off the ground. For the rest of its history, the American musical developed around better and better "books," as the story came to be called.

In 1874 Edward E. Rice and J. Cheever Goodwin set out to create an American opéra bouffe and chose Longfellow's *Evangeline* as their improbable subject. Rice wrote the entire score—a first in the evolution of the musical—and Goodwin wrote the book. A modest production that was slipped into Niblo's Garden in New York in 1874 scored such a success that bigger and better productions followed, and the show became a perennial favorite during the next thirty years.

Jacques Offenbach's comic operettas arrived in America in the late 1860s, followed by Johann Strauss's Viennese variety in the 1870s, but even their popularity was topped by the rage for Gilbert and Sullivan's operettas. These imported delights were supplemented by such homegrown fare as the Harrigan and Hoyt shows. There was no dearth of musical entertainment on the stages of America in the last decades of the nineteenth century.

One writer who absorbed all of the changing currents in the musical theater and transformed them into a string of American hits was Harry B. Smith. His prodigious career spanned five decades. From the age of nine, when he was taken to see Lydia Thompson, to his retirement from the stage in 1932, Smith wrote more than a hundred books for pantomimes, burlesques, and operettas in the French, German, Viennese, and Gilbert and Sullivan styles. In 1890 he secured for himself a permanent place in the annals of American musical theater with his book for *Robin Hood*, written with the composer Reginald De Koven, the first comic opera by Americans to be presented on the American stage. Smith also provided books for Victor Herbert and Sigmund Romberg, to name two of the most famous of his collaborators, all of whom regarded him as a master craftsman. Smith sought his inspiration from literary classics (*Don Quixote*), established plays (*Cyrano de Bergerac*), and English and Scottish legends. He wrote sketches for the *Ziegfeld Follies* and vehicles for Ziegfeld's wife, Anna Held, from 1899 to 1912. He was so prolific that his work touched almost every theatrical personage of significance during the height of his activity, from 1900 to 1920. Except for a few songs for which he wrote the lyrics, most of the musicals in which he collaborated have deservedly flown from everybody's memory, and only occasionally are *Robin Hood* or *The Fortune Teller* (1898) revived on the light-opera stage. Smith deserves a place in the history of the American musical because his work provided the sturdy foundations for later developments. He was neither an innovator nor an experimenter, but he proved that the musical play had found a real home in America.

Other notable book-writers of the prewar period were Otto Harbach, Rida Johnson Young, Sydney Rosenfeld, and Edgar Smith, and they, too, had long careers. Harbach's first hit, in 1908, was *The Three Twins*, and thereafter he had successes in every decade. His last effort, in 1942, *Hay Foot, Straw Foot*, was not a success but serves as testament to his longevity. These and other writers of the period teamed with composers Herbert, Romberg, Rudolf Friml, Jerome Kern, and Irving Berlin, among others, to turn out such successes as *Naughty Marietta*, *The Firefly*, *Babes in Toyland*, *The Fortune Teller*, *Watch Your Step*, and scores of others. Very often their books depended heavily on European scripts, with only the names and places changed to reflect the Atlantic crossing.

Only one musical-comedy writer during the frivolous prewar years turned away from Europe for inspiration: George M. Cohan, who wrote book, music, and lyrics for shows that he produced and in which he starred. Cohan's books were as American as the Stars and Stripes, which was, incidentally, waved at every performance. He wrote about Americans, set them down in places like New Rochelle, put American slang in their mouths, and involved them in situations in which their Americanism would triumph over all. In *Little Johnny Jones* (1904), an American jockey is vindicated after being accused of throwing an English race, and the hero of *George Washington, Jr.* (1906) changes his name to that of the father of his country in protest against his own father's anglophilism. For as long as he could, Cohan kept musical scripts to a simple formula, and for as long as they could, his audiences kept buying tickets.

Deciding to counter the trend set by Ziegfeld for lavish productions with rapid scene changes, gorgeous costumes, and large choruses of boy and girl dancers, producers F. Ray Comstock and Elisabeth Marbury commissioned Jerome Kern to write the music for small plays for a small New York theater, the Princess, on West Thirty-ninth Street, and they soon discovered that they had an audience. Two young Englishmen, Guy Bolton and P. G. Wodehouse, provided the books and lyrics for most of the Princess musicals from 1915 to 1918. The standard musical comedy of the 1910s had an absurd plot, dealing, most usually, with the love of a prince from an imaginary Middle European country for a poor but beautiful maiden who is eventually discovered to be a long-lost heiress. Taking a fresh tack, Bolton and Wodehouse tried to give a touch of reality to their plots and to create believable people. As Bolton explained, "Americans laugh more naturally at a funny hotel clerk or janitor than a crudely drawn cannibal princess." They dispensed with big choruses, star turns, and

The principal attraction of any of the musical shows in which she starred was Lydia Thompson, who arrived in 1868 to capitalize on the growing popularity of the genre. Here she is, umbrella and all, in Robinson Crusoe, her first production.

L. Frank Baum extended into eternity the life of his popular children's book The Wizard of Oz when he adapted it for the stage in 1903. This fine poster by Russell and Morgan dates from that year. Baum was less than pleased with the first musical based on his classic, a version from which most of the original elements had been dropped. However, in 1939 the book became an enduring movie and in 1975 a successful musical entitled The Wiz.

From the lavish musical spectacles that had overtaken the stage, the Princess Theatre shows, written by Guy Bolton and P. G. Wodehouse, were a refreshing change. Here is a scene from Oh, Lady! Lady!, *with Carl Randall seemingly oblivious of Vivienne Segal and a bevy of chorus ladies.*

irrelevant scenes and made each song contribute to the action. The American musical has traveled long miles down the path of reality since the days of the Princess Theatre experimentations. Compared to the usual Broadway fare of their day, the Comstock-Marbury productions were fresh as paint. Compared to today's musicals, they are quaint trifles.

During the 1920s, New York became the undisputed center of the American theater. The critic Percy Hammond, writing in 1920 for the *Chicago Tribune*, commented ruefully on the new state of affairs: "The drama in America is made by New York, for New York and in New York, and we [the rest of the country as well as Chicago] take the product second hand." Scores, sometimes hundreds of plays debuted in New York each season, and though some flopped, others rolled up hundreds of performances before departing for the hinterlands, or even Hollywood and near-eternal life. Broadway had become the principal supplier of books for filmscripts, and soon the film industry began to pour money into Broadway to finance theatrical productions that might later be transformed into profitable movies. Indeed, for several decades, New York was Hollywood's "road." But despite the welcome prosperity, playwrights regarded the inroads of Hollywood backers with more than a little suspicion, particularly when Broadway producers began to peddle their plays as if they owned them.

In 1925 Fox Films began negotiations with seven Broadway producers over the studio's proposal to back plays, divide the profits, and buy the scripts at fixed fees without competitive bidding. Enraged by the cavalier manner in which producers were treating their work, a group of playwrights met secretly to redress their wrongs. The voice of the playwrights of America was then, and is now, the Dramatists Guild, which was born in 1920 as a subcommittee of the Authors League of America, largely as a result of the successful Actors' Equity Association strike of 1919. At that time, a standard contract was drawn up by the dramatists, but it was nonbinding and was disregarded by both producers and writers. Usually a personal, one-time agreement was struck between playwright and producer on each play. Prevailing practices also included indefinite options on plays, which meant that producers tended to hold scripts for long periods of time before they made their decision to produce or not. Playwrights had very little say about changes in their scripts, about the choice of the cast and director, about the length of the run, and about the duration of the contract. Nor was there any way to force prompt payment of royalties. Subsidiary rights were seldom negotiated ahead of time, and nothing was enforceable except by long and expensive litigation. Early in 1926, the militant playwrights submitted a Minimum Basic Agreement (MBA) to a committee of producers. After a period of five months, when all scripts were withheld from the market, the producers agreed to sign a modified version of the MBA, which endured intact for five years.

From 1926 to 1985, the basic tenets of the MBA have remained in force, with only periodic minor adjustments to reflect changes in the industry. The MBA contract between playwright and producer was predicated on a royalty system that taxed the gross receipts of a production on a weekly basis. When the MBA was written, those terms were consistent with current conditions, but today, with costs inflated beyond anyone's wildest predictions, they have been recognized as unrealistic. A new contract drafted in 1985 lowers the playwright's royalty but provides him a weekly guarantee. Adjustments were also made for playwrights in regional theater, where the rewards have been traditionally smaller than in New York. When the MBA was introduced, there were many more opportunities to place plays for production. Today, unless an occasional show becomes a hit, most playwrights cannot devote themselves exclusively to their craft. As in earlier centuries, they must support themselves by other means. To paraphrase Edward Albee, "Though you can make a killing, you can't make a living."

While the movies were profoundly affecting the livelihood and status of playwrights, by 1920 the artistic tide was again flowing strongly from Europe. No longer was it possible for producers to ignore the work of Ibsen, Shaw, and the German and French realist playwrights. In 1894 Mrs. Fiske slipped a matinee production of *A Doll's House* into Charles Frohman's gem of a theater, the Empire, on Broadway. It eventually became part of her repertory, along with *Hedda Gabler*, *The Pillars of Society*, and Ibsen's grandest shocker of them all, *Ghosts*. She also played in the avant-garde dramas by Hermann Sudermann and Gerhart Hauptmann. Even the Shuberts, those bastions of the trite, the sentimental, and the meretricious, underwrote Ibsen productions to satisfy their stars. Plays by Strindberg, Ostrovsky, Heijermans, Bjørnson, Pinero, Maeterlinck, Wilde, D'Annunzio, Leo Tolstoy, Chekhov, Brieux, and most of the lesser ranks of modern European realists and experimentalists had become respectable enough for the Broadway stage.

But the impact of the new ideas from abroad was felt more significantly away from Broadway than on it, as the European-inspired little-theater movement took hold and spread like an epidemic across the country. Although the mission of most of these early art theaters in the twentieth century was to introduce the works of Ibsen, Strindberg, and the French and German realists or to experiment with the bold new concepts of stagecraft set down by Adolphe Appia and Gordon Craig, some of them were dedicated to providing new American playwrights with a platform to test their dramatic inspirations. To one of them, the Provincetown Players, O'Neill owed his emergence as a playwright. It may be arguable that talent will out and that O'Neill would have achieved recognition in any case, but the Provincetown Players was in existence when he needed it, in 1916, and a few years later the Theatre Guild, which had evolved out of the Washington Square Players, was also in place and able to produce the plays of his mature years.

From 1920 to 1950, American playwrights became themselves the innovators. Few European playwrights could compete with them. Their emergence on the international scene coincided exactly with the establishment of America as a world power—a historical phenomenon that had obvious parallels in the past. As Maxwell Anderson pointed out in 1955, "An era of great plays seems to be something that happens in a country when that country believes itself to be on top of the world—as Athens felt after Marathon, and England felt after the defeat of the Armada; and Ireland after it began to believe that it would be free." The theatrical generation that encompassed Eugene O'Neill at the start of his career and Arthur Miller and Tennessee Williams at the beginning of theirs directed its attention to the country's animating impulses and to an inspection of the national psyche, finding humor and strength in the national

Because the star Richard Bennett took an interest, *Beyond the Horizon* was Eugene O'Neill's first play to reach Broadway, in 1920. In this scene of family conflict, Mary Jeffery as Mrs. Mayo tries to restrain her husband, played by Erville Alderson, from striking his son Robert, played by Richard Bennett. Another son, Andrew, played by Edward Arnold, averts his face, and Mark Mitzel, in the role of Captain Scott, looks on.

Scenic artist Lee Simonson designed posters for the Theatre Guild. In this one, for Eugene O'Neill's *Strange Interlude* (1928), he conveys some of the psychological turbulence of the play.

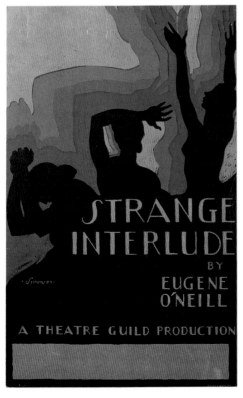

life and native character and flaws and malignancies in the American Dream.

In 1920, at a matinee premiere at the Morosco Theatre, Eugene O'Neill arrived on Broadway with his play *Beyond the Horizon*. His name was not unknown in theatrical circles. Broadway cognoscenti were already aware that he was the son of the romantic actor James O'Neill and that his one-act plays had been produced at the Provincetown Playhouse. One of them, *In the Zone* (1917), which had been given a vaudeville tour, brought him early admirers, including George Jean Nathan, then drama critic for the irreverent, eggheady magazine *The Smart Set*. Nathan was to become O'Neill's lifelong friend and most consistent champion. Before anyone else did, he hailed O'Neill as America's first important playwright and later wrote: "Just as this [current] drama seemed about to be laid low by unremitting stereotyped dullness and preposterous affectation, [O'Neill] jumped upon the scene with a bundle of life and fancy under his arm, hurled it onto the stage, and there let it break open with its hundred smashing hues to confound the drab and desolate boards." Relentlessly despairing, *Beyond the Horizon* unfolds a tale of broken dreams, uncompromising Puritan morality, and Yankee stubbornness, set against a harsh New England landscape. Although it is in the naturalistic mode of Ibsen and Strindberg, its language and its events make it a play that only an American could have written. It won the Pulitzer Prize for drama.

When O'Neill became news on Broadway, he was in his early thirties. He would have preferred to be a poet, but his entire life had been shaped by the theater, and to his dying day he retained a love-hate relationship with it. He had had a troubled childhood and a tortured young adulthood. Only after an enforced stay of a few months at a sanatorium, which cleansed not only his tubercular lungs but his soul, did O'Neill decide that writing for the theater might be his salvation. The year he spent in George Pierce Baker's playwriting class may have convinced him to renounce what he regarded as his father's theater and attempt to invent his own dramatic expression.

Despite a declared debt to Strindberg and a fascination with the ideas of Nietzsche, O'Neill progressed through his own artistic rites of passage and sat at no one's feet. He founded no school, created no new forms, and promulgated no new theories of the drama. At its extraordinary best, his work is intensely personal; at its pretentious worst, it attempts to wrestle prosily with cosmic problems. O'Neill is often quoted as saying he was only interested in man's relationship to God, but his plays belie that. In

In 1931 Robert Edmond Jones designed the set for
Mourning Becomes Electra, *Eugene O'Neill's
transformation of Greek legend into American tragedy.
As this watercolor drawing indicates, Jones evoked the
spirit of classicism with tall, white columns and broad
steps but managed to convey by symmetry and darkness a
sense of mystery behind the facade of the Mannon house.*

fact, he was consumed by man's relationship to himself and by what happens to the
self in its struggle with the world outside. If O'Neill had artistic ancestors, they were
the Greek dramatists of the fifth century B.C. Like their characters, his exist in an
atmosphere permeated by fatality, though O'Neill's fate is existential, not Olympian.
His first plays are based on his adventures as an ordinary seaman in his early twenties.
For O'Neill the sea remained a lifelong metaphor, and he regarded it with mystical
fascination. Resist though they may, many of the characters in these short plays are
drawn to the sea for what O'Neill considered its redemptive power. In *Long Day's
Journey into Night*, young Edmund Tyrone, the play's dramatic counterpart of the
playwright, says that he should have been a gull or a fish, creatures owing their
existence to the sea.

During O'Neill's next period, which lasted about five years, he wrote largely
naturalistic plays about the internal and external forces that shape men's destinies.
The heroine of *Anna Christie* (1922) turns to prostitution out of desperation, a victim
of a society that has unresolved feelings about the place of women. In *Desire under the
Elms* (1924) O'Neill took the stage Yankee and gave the character new and disturbing
dimensions. The flintiness and cunning of the comic Yankee was transformed into
something sinister and forbidding in the personality of Ephraim Cabot. In *The Hairy
Ape* (1922) the playwright depicted a type of primitive man content to exist within
his own environment (the hold of a ship) until the outer world thrusts its way in and
forces him to find a place in a hostile society.

For about ten years, O'Neill departed from realism and produced two novelistic
works, *Strange Interlude* (1927) and *Mourning Becomes Electra* (1931), both reflecting
his further explorations of dramatic technique. In *Strange Interlude*, he created two
levels of expression for his characters, one the real world and the other a stream of
consciousness in which each reveals aloud his inner thoughts in lengthy asides. For
Mourning Becomes Electra, he transformed the house of Atreus into a family of Puritan

Opposite, clockwise from top left:

George Abbott defies precise pigeonholing. He is either a director-playwright or a playwright-director, depending on where the weight of his contribution is felt to lie. Abbott's name is on at least thirty plays and musical books, and his touch lies on easily twice that number. A Harvard "47 Workshop" product, he began his career (after leaving acting behind him) as a play-doctor and collaborator, achieving his first astounding success with Broadway, *written in 1926 with Philip Dunning. Set in a New York nightclub, it is a fast-paced, colorful, and eventful melodrama filled with an array of comic-strip-like characters. Supremely entertaining, it stimulated a host of imitations. Here is Lee Tracy, one of the stars, playing a hoofer, surrounded by his troupe of chorus girls.*

Susan Glaspell began her long literary career as a novelist and short-story writer. In 1915 she founded the Provincetown Players with her husband, George Cram Cook. Beginning in that year, and until she and her husband withdrew from the group, Glaspell wrote plays, mostly one-act in length, for production by the Provincetowners. Her full-length play Alison's House, *which was produced by Eva Le Gallienne and the Civic Repertory Theatre in 1930, brought her belated recognition and a Pulitzer Prize. Set in the Midwest, this fine play deals with the family of a poetess reminiscent of Emily Dickinson and with the effects that closing the house in which she lived and died had upon her survivors. In this photograph of the original production, three members of Alison Stanhope's family—her sister Agatha (Alma Kruger, seated), her nephew Eben (Donald Cameron), and her niece Elsa (Eva Le Gallienne)—gather to burn private papers in the fireplace. The play is suffused with Chekhovian overtones.*

A "47 Workshop" graduate, Philip Barry was still a student at Harvard in 1923, when his first play, You and I, *was produced on Broadway. For the 1938–39 season, he wrote two plays that stand at the opposite poles of his creative achievement.* The Philadelphia Story *deals in scene after sparkling scene with the events of the day before the wedding of a rich, spoiled, headstrong Main Line heiress.* Here Come the Clowns, *foreshadowing O'Neill's* The Iceman Cometh *and Beckett's* Waiting for Godot, *presents a group of seedy vaudevillians whose lives are shaken by the entrance into the back room of a theatrical cafe of a slightly deranged ex-stagehand in search of God. They are manipulated by a satanic magician into personal confession. In this photograph, stagehand Dan Clancy, played by Eddie Dowling, distraught over the death of his child and the desertion of his wife, is shown being comforted by two show-business friends, Eve March (left) as Fay Ferrel and Madge Evans as Connie Ryan.*

The photographer Gjon Mili caught this moment of mutual anguish in the faces of the actors Florence Eldridge and Fredric March in Long Day's Journey into Night *(1956), O'Neill's masterwork.*

Overleaf:

As Mary Tyrone (Florence Eldridge) drags her wedding dress behind her, her sons (Bradford Dillman and Jason Robards) and her husband (Fredric March) react to her return to drug addiction in Eugene O'Neill's masterwork, Long Day's Journey into Night *(1956).*

lineage in postbellum New England and gave a psychological interpretation to the Greek conception of omnipotent fate. O'Neill's interest in Freudian and Jungian teachings is apparent in his dissection of the tortured sexuality of the characters in both plays. Despite his Irish Catholic upbringing, O'Neill manifested in these and his later dramas almost a born-again Puritanism.

After 1931, when *Mourning Becomes Electra* established him as America's greatest living playwright, O'Neill had only one more success, *Ah, Wilderness!* This play, his only comedy, was produced on Broadway in 1933, with George M. Cohan in the leading role. Between 1934 and 1946, O'Neill appeared to have gone into retirement, but in reality he continued to work on a projected cycle of plays that traced an American family from colonial to modern times, and three unconnected plays, *The Iceman Cometh*, *Long Day's Journey into Night*, and *A Moon for the Misbegotten*. Ultimately dissatisfied, O'Neill and his wife, Carlotta Monterey, destroyed all of the manuscripts of the cycle, with the exception of *A Touch of the Poet* and an incomplete draft of *More Stately Mansions*.

In 1946 O'Neill came out of retirement to attend the rehearsals of *The Iceman Cometh*, which was not the critical and popular success he hoped it would be. The last of his plays to appear during his lifetime was the frankly autobiographical *Moon for the Misbegotten*, which opened and closed on the road in 1947, before reaching New York. The obituaries and critical appraisals that flowed into print after the playwright's death, in 1953, necessarily gave an incomplete assessment of his contributions to the world's drama. Shaw had called him the "banshee Shakespeare" and the Swedes had given him a Nobel Prize, but his own country and its theater had interred him long before his actual death.

In 1955 the playwright's widow entered into negotiations with the Swedish Royal Dramatic Theatre, and early in 1956 *Long Day's Journey into Night* received its world premiere in Stockholm and in Swedish. Accustomed to the brooding plays of Strindberg and Ibsen, the Scandinavians were simply astounded by the drama. In an indirect but obvious allusion to Arthur Miller and Tennessee Williams, who were at the height of their powers in the mid-1950s, one Swedish critic praised it above "all the dream-play stagecraft among streetcars and salesmen in late American dramas [which by comparison] become unnecessary trinkets and trifles." He went on to compare O'Neill with Aeschylus and Shakespeare.

Perhaps heartened by its Scandinavian reception, Carlotta allowed José Quintero, whom she had recently permitted to revive *The Iceman Cometh* in New York, to bring *Long Day's Journey into Night* to Broadway. Written, as he described its gestation, in "tears and blood," the play had been dedicated to his wife by O'Neill on the twelfth anniversary of their marriage, in 1941. An early draft of June 1939 shows some irresolution regarding the title and the names of the characters, but the playwright's notes reveal the permutations in the conflicts of the Tyrones that he was to carry forward in the finished work. In 1941 O'Neill deposited the completed play with the publishing firm of Random House, with the instructions that it was not to be published until twenty-five years after his death and was never to be produced. Carlotta's justification for its publication and production in 1956, so soon after her husband's death, was that he had given her the power to dispose of his works as she saw fit. But there is also reason to believe that Carlotta wanted the productions not only to keep O'Neill's name alive but to vindicate the self-sacrificial, compulsive dedication of her life to him. She wanted attention.

Heartrendingly personal in subject, nearly static in action, spread over four acts, and concentrating on only four people, the play simply transcended these limitations, releasing universal harmonics in a masterful exposition of human love and guilt. It reestablished O'Neill as America's first playwright and is generally acclaimed as his best work.

With classical economy, the play runs its course within one day in the house of one family. Each character reveals his or her inner thoughts and makes confessions to the others. The tension among them can be felt as they wait for the results of a test that

will determine whether the younger son, Edmund, has tuberculosis. Impelled by private hurts, each sears the others with scorching accusations, while bitterly turning over family history. As if to bear the pain of the revelations better, the three men—James Tyrone and his sons, Jamie and Edmund—have retreated into alcohol. The mother, Mary Tyrone, begins her redescent into morphine addiction. At the end, the minds of all four are blurred to the inevitable. Mary moves around the motionless men looking for something that she has lost, something they all have lost, the promise of their private dreams.

The play grew out of the calamitous family relationships of the O'Neills. But in the forging, autobiographical details were transmuted into an American tragedy. Certainly, it was no accident that O'Neill interrupted work on his cycle of plays about American society seen through the history of one fictive family to write about his own very real family. Like the O'Neills, the Tyrones were, after all, in the mainstream of the American Dream. In one long scene with Edmund, James tells of his childhood as a poor Irish immigrant, barely educated and apparently condemned to a life at the bottom of the social scale. He tells of changing his own destiny by discovering his talents as an actor and finding his way in an era when the theater offered opportunity to the young and gifted if they persisted. He admits to having been wildly ambitious as a young man until he discovered a play that gave him easy fame and a comfortable living year after year. Lamenting, "I could have been a great Shakespearean actor, if I'd kept on," James nurses this dream as his only solace for selling out.

His sons have shared in the tangible results of their father's success but cannot find their own roots in American life. Envious of established Americans and feeling tainted by their background, they move comfortably only in the class beneath them. Jamie finds release in alcohol and whores, but Edmund's life is being forced into new focus by the discovery of his illness. His is the most incomplete character in the play; he has the most potential for change and is the one whose future is least determined.

The character of Mary Tyrone is the most complex and interesting of all. The daughter of a prosperous Irishman who died of tuberculosis, she describes her dreamlike life as a student in a Catholic girls' school, where she was encouraged in her fantasy of becoming a concert pianist. She believes her true vocation belonged with the nuns of her childhood and that her dream escaped her when she fell in love with James Tyrone and married him. After the birth of Edmund, she became addicted to morphine in an attempt to ease the pain of a difficult delivery and its aftereffects. Although she has just returned from a "cure," she slips easily back into addiction in order to avoid facing Edmund's illness and, more important, to continue her life of

Elmer Rice studied and practiced law, and his first play, On Trial *(1914), reflects his legal background. He received his first practical lessons in playwriting from producer Arthur Hopkins, who took* On Trial *on an option, tore it apart, and then guided Rice as he rewrote it. In 1923 Rice presented the public with* The Adding Machine, *and the critics hailed it as the American form of expressionism, despite the playwright's demurral. The hero, put out of work by an adding machine, kills his boss, goes to heaven, and is taught to operate an adding machine before being returned to earth again. Dudley Digges, as Mr. Zero in the original production, is seen here wrestling with his giant mechanical adversary, which looks almost laughable in the computer age. A marked departure from such experimentation was Rice's* Street Scene *(1929), in which he treated a New York slum tenement as a microcosm of city life.*

Opposite above:
Master of the corrosive wisecrack, George S. Kaufman was a direct theatrical descendant of the writers of comedy who dominated American drama for the first century of its history. Although he wrote several plays alone, he wrote many others in collaboration with other playwrights. He produced his best work in an electric partnership with first Marc Connelly and then Moss Hart. For several years the drama editor of the New York Times, *Kaufman was forced eventually by his success as a playwright to leave journalism and devote his entire attention to directing, writing, and producing plays on Broadway. Though Kaufman was not the originator of the maxim "Plays are not written but rewritten," he was certainly its leading practitioner during his long career as the foremost "play-doctor" of his time.* The Man Who Came to Dinner, *more than slightly based on the life and times of the rapier-tongued but endearing (to some) drama critic Alexander Woollcott, was a Kaufman and Hart hit in 1939. It starred Monty Woolley as Sheridan Whiteside, the Woollcott simulacrum. In this Vandamm photograph of the original production, Whiteside is giving his Christmas broadcast to the nation, surrounded by a boy's choir and his beleaguered nurse, host, and hostess.*

Opposite below:
Marc Connelly was a newspaperman before he was a playwright. He was George S. Kaufman's first collaborator, and their first joint effort, Dulcy, *was a resounding success in 1921. Sharing an antic sense of humor and a passion for pinpricking the pompous, they wrote a half-dozen more plays together before going their separate ways. On his own, Connelly enjoyed a huge and unexpected success in 1930 with a play for an all-black cast,* The Green Pastures, *which interprets the Bible through the eyes of a simple black preacher, who uses the language and experiences of his flock to illuminate scriptural passages and parables. Standing at the gates of heaven, Richard B. Harrison as De Lawd, surrounded by his flock of angels, begins by creating the world. The action proceeded inevitably to the crucifixion of Christ and was broken often by the singing of spirituals.*

unfulfilled dreams. Like her husband, she sold out to society's perception of success—in her case, marriage and motherhood—while avoiding confronting her own sexuality.

Long Day's Journey into Night ends on a note of desolation over lives misspent, dashed dreams and wrong turns, and irreclaimable opportunities and irrevocable decisions. The ending is not forced and the progress to it is unmelodramatic. Although the Tyrones are all articulate Irish, their speech lacks the staginess that flaws some of O'Neill's earlier plays. Scene flows into scene naturally, masking the playwright's art. The Tyrones are doomed, but theirs is not a simple tragedy. It springs not only from what the Greeks called *hamartia*, the fatal personal failing, but from the accident of birth in a society that has forced them down wrong paths and set before them the false gods of success and money and conformity. O'Neill had explored these themes singly in earlier plays, but in *Long Day's Journey into Night* he was able to develop them all.

Tragedy eluded most important twentieth-century playwrights because the findings of Freud had all but obliterated guilt and responsibility for personal behavior and forced dramatists into near-clinical psychoanalysis of their characters. When there are only victims, when unhappy childhoods or traumatic events can be called the wellsprings of human behavior, and when universal truths are supplanted by small personal epiphanies, tragedy cannot make a powerful stand. In this most personal of plays, O'Neill eschewed Freud and created characters buffeted by society, tortured by guilt, and cleansed in public and private confessionals. O'Neill rewrote the formula of tragedy in modern terms.

Although *Long Day's Journey into Night* is replete with symbols and images, they emerge from a central core of realistic circumstances. Despite his earlier experimentations with other modes, O'Neill thought in realistic terms. In this, his greatest play, O'Neill was able to cast realism in a classic form and create a drama of naked truth with classic spareness of technique. Since its introduction in 1956, *Long Day's Journey into Night* has yet to be surpassed by any American play.

O'Neill was the major voice among the American playwrights who emerged from 1920 to 1940, but many talented writers such as Rachel Crothers, Maxwell Anderson, Sidney Howard, Sidney Kingsley, George Abbott, Philip Barry, Thornton Wilder, Robert E. Sherwood, and George S. Kaufman were able to get a hearing on Broadway during that era and establish themselves as important forces in shaping the American theater of the future.

Inevitably, the war and its aftermath wrought enormous changes in American society, and new voices in the theater were caught between the old and the new. Two young playwrights—almost exact contemporaries, one Southern, the other Northern, one a Wasp of old stock, the other sprung from Jewish immigrants—provided the transition. Both Tennessee Williams and Arthur Miller worked comfortably within the realistic tradition in drama and neither broke experimental ground, except Williams, once, in his attempt at a kind of epic, picaresque drama, *Camino Real* (1953). In Williams's works, the gentle postbellum society of his own experience is dragged into the harsh light of industrial and depersonalized America. In Miller's, new and old Americans have lost their way in the northern urban world of rapid subway trains and ungentle and aggressive business tactics. The influence of O'Neill's plays and themes on both these dramatists was subtle, but real nonetheless. And, like O'Neill and earlier playwrights, each continued to examine our Great Divide: the multiple, often incompatible moral codes and perceptions of Americans of different regions and of different degrees of cultural assimilation. Conflict, the stuff of drama, remains a constant in evolving American civilization. The next wave of playwrights would add the battle between generations to this already combustible theme of America's social schisms.

Born Thomas Lanier Williams in 1911 in Mississippi, Tennessee Williams assumed his unusual first name in 1939, giving as his reason a Southern weakness for "climbing the family tree" (his forefathers were prominent in the state of Tennessee). The playwright underwent a ten-year apprenticeship before the initial Broadway production

The most scholarly of men, Thornton Wilder achieved considerable early success as a first-rate novelist. When he turned to writing plays, he liked to tinker with dramatic structure. In 1938 Wilder's Our Town opened in New York. Set on a bare stage and guided by an actor playing "stage manager," it evokes ordinary events in the lives of small-town Americans. This Vandamm photograph of that famous Jed Harris production shows the scene in which Emily and George are married. The play has since become a small American classic. Later in the same year, The Merchant of Yonkers, based on an early nineteenth-century Viennese comedy by Johann Nestroy, failed the first time around; however, in 1954, slightly altered and renamed The Matchmaker, the comedy reappeared with Ruth Gordon in the leading role and achieved a considerable success. The play enjoyed a third incarnation as the book for the musical Hello, Dolly! (1964).

Cast in a small role in the original production of Clifford Odets's Waiting for Lefty was Elia Kazan (third from left), later to become a leading director. Odets began his career in the theater as an actor and was invited to become a charter member of the Group Theatre in 1931. He soon decided his talents lay in writing, and his two earliest plays brought recognition to the Group Theatre and established its political position. In the first, Waiting for Lefty (1934), the right to strike is declared inviolate; in the second, Awake and Sing! (1935), the struggles of a poor Jewish family to survive in the adverse Depression years are depicted in painful detail. In 1936 Odets went to Hollywood as a screenwriter to help finance the Group Theatre's ventures and to raise money for producing his plays, but he was to remain there for most of the rest of his life, while continuing to write for the stage.

Vandamm's stunning photograph shows the operating-room scene in Men in White, Sidney Kingsley's first play (1933). A financial success that brought him a Pulitzer Prize, it was more entertaining than socially significant, making it something of an embarrassment to the directors of the high-minded Group Theatre. A Cornell University graduate, Kingsley was an actor and a screenwriter for Columbia Pictures before he turned to the stage. His best plays, Dead End (1935) and Detective Story (1949), fall within the mainstream of American naturalism. The playwright's photographic eye for detail and his sensitive ear for the cadences of gutter speech helped him create convincing depictions of low life that enrich the simple morality of his themes.

The faint aura of Southern decadence hangs about the late Tennessee Williams in this photograph by Martha Swope.

Left:
In this arresting photograph of Geraldine Page and Rip Torn in Sweet Bird of Youth, photographer Eileen Darby caught the heavy eroticism of Tennessee Williams's hit. By this time in the play's Broadway run, Torn had replaced Paul Newman, who decamped for Hollywood after his contract with the producer expired. Page remained in her role to the end and became one of the leading actresses of the stage for the rest of her life.

of his autobiographical, guilt-ridden *The Glass Menagerie* made him famous in 1945. Two years later his masterwork, *A Streetcar Named Desire*, established Williams as one of the new forces in American theater. A *tour de force*, the drama chronicles the painful descent into madness of Blanche DuBois without allowing the audience to lose its sympathy for her. For a decade the playwright's career remained in the ascendant but then lost momentum when he failed to do more than create variations on the theme of gentility and beauty crushed by a harsh and hostile society. At his best, Williams created a vivid, earthy realism with lyric dialogue delivered by powerful and memorable characters. In his later years, Williams's plays were produced off Broadway and in regional playhouses as they moved away from the theatrical mainstream.

Unlike his near contemporary, Arthur Miller waited until he had gathered nearly a half-century's perspective before he attempted an autobiographical play. *The American Clock*, which appeared in 1980, sprang not, in Miller's case, from unexorcised guilt but from a desire to see unfolded the effects of a larger impersonal social drama, the Depression, on one family, his own. Although it is truthful and incisive, it lacks both the sting of the best social drama and the pain of the confessional. Like Williams, Miller had his greatest success early in his career. His masterpiece, *Death of a Salesman*, which arrived on Broadway in 1949, explores a view of tragedy that, as Miller puts it, develops from "the underlying struggle . . . of the individual attempting to find his 'rightful' place in society." The central character, Willy Loman, has succumbed to popular notions of success as a husband, provider, and father, which have proved false for him and have caused his failure as a human being. Consistently at his best in creating male characters, Miller has repeated the theme of a man who is

In 1939 Tallulah Bankhead, seen here in the role of Regina Hubbard, scored a personal triumph in Lillian Hellman's The Little Foxes, Hellman's second major play, a vision of the American Dream gone corrupt. Although The Little Foxes is highly colored in language and melodramatic in plot, it also draws its life from fascinating characters, whose story Hellman was to trace in Another Part of the Forest (1946). North and South met in Hellman's art and life. Until she was sixteen, her family spent half of each year in New Orleans, her birthplace, and the other half in New York. After a series of jobs connected with the publishing industry, she wrote a play entitled The Children's Hour. Audiences were riveted not only by its sensational subject matter but also by the well-drawn characters. In 1956 Hellman wrote the book for Leonard Bernstein's musical comedy based on Voltaire's Candide.

Starting at the fringes of the theater, Moss Hart tried acting, wrote plays, and contributed to revues and musical comedies before combining his talents with George S. Kaufman's in a collaboration that resulted in a remarkable string of successes in the 1930s. Selz's witty caricature shows Hart "dreaming up a mad situation" for one of the most representative of these Kaufman-Hart comedies, You Can't Take It with You. Written in 1936, before it became fashionable to sound the Bronx cheer at conventional American life, the play paints an unforgettable picture of the unorthodox life-style and family of a superannuated dropout from society. Independent of Kaufman, Hart continued writing and directing plays. In 1941 he devised the literate book for Lady in the Dark, a musical play with a score and lyrics by the formidably talented Kurt Weill and Ira Gershwin.

unable to confront his failures until it is too late in other settings and in other plays, but never more powerfully than in *Death of a Salesman*.

During the 1920s, American playwrights discovered Freud; in the 1930s, they found politics. The shock of the Depression and the realization that Soviet communism had apparently achieved viability led playwrights to an examination of American democracy and its future. The Group Theatre, leftist stepchild of the Theatre Guild, excited audiences into shouting for a strike at the close of Clifford Odets's 1934 play *Waiting for Lefty*, about an uprising of the rank-and-file membership of a taxi union. The Federal Theatre Project introduced the Living Newspaper, a theatrical documentary, to examine such aspects of American life as substandard housing, the rapaciousness of the electric-light-and-power industry, and the subjugation of the farmer by the middleman. Established playwrights like Robert Sherwood, Maxwell Anderson, and Elmer Rice hopped on the wagon of political protest and wrote plays more than slightly tinged with propaganda. The 1940s brought the war, and the theater provided escape. Late in 1939, a small play based on the book by Clarence Day about a New York family living in the 1880s arrived on Broadway. *Life with Father*, by Howard Lindsay and Russel Crouse, so enchanted its audiences that it played right through the war and into the history books as the longest-running nonmusical ever. A few years later, Richard Rodgers and Oscar Hammerstein II created an unpretentious musical, *Oklahoma!*, whose gentle blend of music, story, and dance caught everyone off guard and broke new ground in the long history of musical theater. The rise of the American musical continued unabated in the 1950s as new teams of composers, lyricists, and playwrights joined Rodgers and Hammerstein in producing fresh and imaginative examples of what everyone was calling the national art form of the theater.

Since the writers of the books for American musicals have depended so heavily on source material—novels, biographies, plays, films, short stories, incidents from real life, and, alas, television shows—their work has often been conveniently written off as mere idea-poaching. As a matter of record, they have not only received short shrift from the public and critics but also, until recently, from producers. Their share of the royalty pie has always been smaller than that of the composers and lyricists. Yet without a book there is no musical. The contributions of the expert book-writer are as intricate as they are vital. To begin with, he must know how to pierce the fabric of the story to make room for the songs and the dances. He must sacrifice part of his playwright's ego and surrender golden flights of dialogue to the songwriter, and he must stall the action long enough for dancers to come and go. In the give and take of the collaborative process, he is often the one to give most and take least.

For a long time, the book-writers had an easy job. They followed formulas set down by European librettists and wrote variations, with adjustments for American audiences, on the rich-boy-meets-poor-girl theme. Audiences flocked to musicals not for the stories but for the music, the songs, and the spectacle. Then, after years of playing second fiddle to the composer and lyricist, they were confronted by Oklahoma! (1943), with its stunning choreography by Agnes de Mille. For about a decade thereafter, beginning with On the Town in 1944, they swallowed hard and wrote

Opposite, clockwise from top left:

Although history may grant him a minor place in the annals of American drama, William Inge became, during the 1950s, the voice of the Midwest on the stage. He was born, raised, and educated in Kansas and spent his early career as a teacher and newspaper critic in Missouri. He wrote of small-town Americans who spend their lives trudging ordinary paths in loneliness. Seen here are Shirley Booth as the frowzy housewife and Sidney Blackmer as her alcoholic husband in one of Inge's earliest successes, Come Back, Little Sheba (1950). In the play an ill-matched middle-aged couple confront their misspent lives, forlorn dreams, and each other, finally summoning the courage to make the best of a bad destiny. His career on the decline, Inge returned to Kansas and committed suicide.

Not since Tennessee Williams has a playwright been so enthusiastically received as Edward Albee when his career was launched with a series of one-act plays (several of which were introduced in Berlin before arriving in New York). He was compared to Eugene O'Neill, and his new work was eagerly awaited. There are certain parallels between O'Neill's early life and Albee's. Both were scions of a show-business family, both experienced a painful adolescence, and both achieved first fame with one-act plays. When Albee's Who's Afraid of Virginia Woolf? appeared in 1962, the comparisons were intensified. The play is concerned with a night of violent accusations, retaliations, and painful disclosures between a husband and wife, George and Martha, and another couple who are their guests for the evening. Caught in this photograph are Uta Hagen and Arthur Hill engaged in Albee's version of the eternal battle of the sexes. Though the orgiastic mutilation is not physical, it is as savage and hurtful to the psyche as the revels of the Dionysiacs were to the bodies of their victims. The battle is transfixing in its intensity but it does not quite achieve a clean catharsis for either audience or characters. Albee's recent plays have been criticized for the muddiness of their symbolism and the self-indulgence of their themes, but their author is still regarded as a writer of power and singularity.

Mary Martin sings with Michael DeLeon in a tender scene from Rodgers and Hammerstein's South Pacific (1949). Hammerstein adapted the book from James Michener's Tales of the South Pacific.

LeRoi Jones changed his name to Amiri Baraka as the intensity of his commitment to black nationalism and politics quickened. In 1964 his early one-act plays, Dutchman and The Slave, were produced off Broadway and they fixed critical attention on his gifts as a playwright. Dutchman, here shown in a production starring Robert Hooks and Jennifer West, takes place on a New York subway train and ends with the stabbing of a young black man by a white siren. Baraka's forte has remained the short play in which he rains terrible swift blows on white America. Savage in language, they usually end in violence. Baraka's vision does not admit a communion of the races through forgiveness and love. In recent years he has devoted himself to social causes among the black communities in Newark and has written his autobiography. His plays have yet to appear on Broadway.

books that were little more than an excuse for dancing. Once the dance-musical had run its course, they turned to the adaptation of plays that had enjoyed success on Broadway, or popular biographies, or other sources. Most of the books were far removed in time and concern from the twentieth century and were escapist theater in the true tradition of musical comedy.

Then in 1967, Gerome Ragni and James Rado wrote a book about hippies, drugs, promiscuous lovemaking, and adolescent rebellion against the Middle-Class Ethic. It was turned into the rock musical *Hair* by Galt MacDermot and gave the turbulent 1960s its anthem. It began life at Joseph Papp's New York Public Theater but was later transferred nearly intact to a Broadway theater for a four-year run. *Hair* did not trip an avalanche of musicals of social significance and has remained unique in the annals of American musical theater, although other rock musicals have come and gone in its wake. Certainly, the success of *Hair* made apparent to the producers and book-writers of musicals that almost no subject under the sun could be considered taboo. In the last two decades, this new freedom has launched musicals with startling subject matter along with silly, purposeless claptrap that died an early death.

The best of the book-writers in recent times, Oscar Hammerstein II, cut his teeth writing lyrics for show songs. In 1927 he propelled musical comedy into the future with his adaptation of Edna Ferber's *Show Boat*, in a felicitous collaboration with the composer Jerome Kern. *Show Boat* had something for everyone: a solid story (actually several) that provided natural excuses for songs and dances, entertaining characters, and spectacle. Hammerstein was not to find another sympathetic partner until 1943. Then, beginning with *Oklahoma!*, he wrote or co-wrote the books for six musicals with Richard Rodgers, several of which will endure for the ages. When Hammerstein died, Rodgers turned to other partners but these collaborations never resulted in the same happy blending of talents.

Alan Jay Lerner also found an ideal partner—in Frederick Loewe, with whom he created (among other shows) *My Fair Lady*, which in 1956 set a standard for the musicals that followed it. Betty Comden and Adolph Green have worked with a number of composers, as have such other outstanding book-writers as Michael Stewart, Peter Stone, Joseph Stein, and Arthur Laurents. It is a truism—worthy of mention, nevertheless—that the best musicals also have the strongest books, with well-structured plots, characters with the freshness of life, and themes in which an audience can become involved. The book-writer manifests the same skills and talents as any playwright, and, indeed, such playwrights as Maxwell Anderson, Neil Simon, Abe Burrows, Arthur Kopit, and, most recently, Harvey Fierstein, have ventured into the world of the musical and achieved excellent results. Unfortunately, unless the book is very bad, no one pays much attention to the contribution of the book-writer, and his best efforts tend to be overshadowed by the music and songs and the razzle-dazzle of performance.

As production costs mounted steeply during the 1950s, troupes of young people created a special theatrical turf located outside the hallowed ground of Broadway. At first, Off Broadway was the actors' haven, but it made room for the untried playwright as doors began to slam shut in the bright-lights district. Fewer and fewer plays came to Broadway. From a record high of more than two hundred productions a season during the 1920s, the number of offerings sagged to fewer than one hundred, and then to about fifty during the 1960s. For the theatergoing public, Off Broadway became not merely an adjunct of theater in New York but a necessary lifeline. In 1964 the editor of the annual *Best Plays* series, begun in the early 1920s by the critic Burns Mantle, included Off-Broadway shows among the year's ten best, and in the next decade reached into Off-Off-Broadway, the spawn of the spawn, to make up the required number.

By the 1970s, it almost looked as if the theater was turning against the playwright as Jerzy Grotowski and Peter Brook arrived from Europe to tell us that he was the least important person in the theatrical process. At the end of the decade, Arthur Miller hoped that the alien influences had run their course. "Today, people want to

A native of New York, Neil Simon wrote gags and punch lines for the early TV comedians. When he turned his attention to Broadway, he took few faltering steps after his first success with the comedies Come Blow Your Horn in 1961 and Barefoot in the Park in 1963. A play whose popularity with college and community groups has proved evergreen, Barefoot in the Park confronts the rigors of New York apartment living. The newlyweds were first played by Elizabeth Ashley and Robert Redford. Here shown is their first dinner party, with guests Mildred Natwick as Ashley's mother and Kurt Kasznar as an amorous neighbor. Simon has since then created a small show-business industry with a series of plays that were transformed into movies after their Broadway run and, in the case of The Odd Couple, into an enduring television series. He has written and continues to write comedies, books for musicals, screenplays, and material for TV specials. In his most recent plays, he has turned frankly autobiographical, drawing upon his Brooklyn boyhood and his pilgrim's progress into adolescence in Brighton Beach Memoirs (1982) and in Biloxi Blues (1984). Simon works in the tradition of George S. Kaufman, reveling in rapid one-line verbal blows and building plausible situations that inevitably go haywire.

A recent arrival on Broadway, Big River (1985), adapted by William Hauptman from Mark Twain's The Adventures of Huckleberry Finn, reflects the continuing trend of book-writers to plunder the library shelves for works on which to build a musical. This poster was designed by Doug Johnson.

identify with what they're looking at. In the theatre, younger people want shape again. They want to trace out relationships again." Miller's prophecy has been partially fulfilled by a few of the new playwrights, but it is doubtful whether they will go far enough for him.

In the 1980s Broadway has continued to remain conservative and cautious, with musicals and English imports dominating the boards. For aspiring playwrights, the action has moved to regional theaters and to all the outer rings of Broadway. A few have had the best of both worlds, but the work of the overwhelming number of recent playwrights has remained in the "showcase" stage, from whence it apparently cannot move. But playwrights need Broadway because a success on the Great White Way not only keeps them in business but focuses the spotlight of the world on them in the theater's epicenter. Without a success on Broadway, many playwrights remain in the latent stage, still within the cocoon, waiting with folded wings.

Since 1960 many interesting and provocative playwrights have arisen in America, but few of them have achieved first rank. Like O'Neill, Miller, and Williams, they continue in their own way to dissect the American dream, American town life, and the American family. Unlike their predecessors, they have looked at the American myth as if through distorted lenses, projecting visions of sometimes seething, sometimes tumultuous rage. In their early plays of nightmarish situation and suprahuman characters, Edward Albee and Arthur Kopit looked eastward for inspiration to the playwrights of the absurd (Pinter, Beckett, and Ionesco), but neither has achieved work to equal the best work of his European counterparts. Logic to Albee and Kopit is evanescent in American society and has been replaced by mechanical conformity—the Puritan ethic gone rancid. David Mamet and Robert Wilson have translated their concerns in diametrically opposite ways: Mamet in realistic plays written in bitter gutter vernacular; Wilson through hallucinatory images in forms hovering between opera and architectonic living tableaux. The effect produced by Mamet's violent dialogue and by Wilson's surrealism is the same: an assault on the senses and the soul.

In a civilization that has obsessively pursued a perfected means of human communication, William Inge, Lanford Wilson, and Marsha Norman have written of Americans who cannot connect. Their journeys through time, through ordinary places where ordinary people congregate reveal lonely souls striving hard to reach each other in a loveless world. For the black playwright, exemplified by Amiri Baraka (LeRoi

Jones), the world is not simply loveless, it is hostile, and his rage against white society boils over. In the earliest plays of David Rabe it is the Vietnam War and its aftereffects that dominate. His is a savage indictment of American society for allowing its sons to be sacrificed on the altar of politics.

Of all recent playwrights, Sam Shepard expresses best—if that is the word—the communal rage of the post-1960s generation. His plays bespeak his own life. Born in America's heartland into a scrambled family, he grew up in California, rejected school and the American work ethic, partook of the drug culture of the 1960s, and miraculously survived it all to become a latter-day cultural hero as a movie star. Shepard vents his rage through powerful characters in perplexing, messy plays. The plays are painful yet mesmerizing because they focus at last on an American society that has lost its romanticism, the historical antidote to its violence. The keynote of Shepard's work is brutal realism, which from the beginning has been the American playwrights' mode. Fortunately, realism has never prevented them from discovering and illuming symbols in the real world and slipping the confines into what critic Alan Downer called "the evergreen and limitless fields of poetic truth."

In recent years, the concerns of playwrights have grown smaller and smaller; their world has shrunk to the kitchen table and their talk to labored disarticulateness. No adequate explanation for the drying up of American talent can be found and no reasonable explanation is enough. There is some small consolation in the fact that drama throughout the world has sailed into dead calm. George Bernard Shaw said it best: "From time to time, dramatic art gets a germinal impulse. There follows in the theatre a spring which flourishes into a glorious summer. This becomes stale almost before its arrival is generally recognized; and the sequel is not a new golden age, but a barren winter that may last any time from fifteen years to a hundred and fifty. Then comes a new impulse; and the cycle begins again." After waiting for O'Neill for one hundred and fifty years, we may again face a long journey of expectation.

David Mamet was born in Chicago in 1947, and it was in Chicago's Off Loop—the Windy City equivalent of Off Broadway—that Mamet was introduced as a playwright. There in the 1970s, Mamet founded his own St. Nicholas Theatre, where he tested his abilities as a playwright before attempting Broadway. (It closed in 1981.) His most important work to date is American Buffalo, which has had two Broadway productions, one in 1977 and the other in 1983. Its plot centers on three men who meet briefly in a junk shop to plan a criminal caper that never comes off. Shown here in the 1977 production are (left to right) Robert Duvall, John Savage, and Kenneth McMillan, as the three semiarticulate and inept conspirators. Mamet has recently turned his hand to writing movie scripts. His last play to date, Glen Garry Glen Ross, which won a Pulitzer Prize in 1984, deals with the unscrupulous manipulations of real-estate salesmen in far-off properties.

Opening in the Magic Theater in San Francisco in 1980, Sam Shepard's True West made the rounds of regional theaters before settling down in New York at an Off-Broadway theater for an extended run in 1982. The play was presented by Chicago's heralded Steppenwolf Theatre Company and the roles were developed by (left to right) Sam Schacht, Gary Sinese, and John Malkovich.

Right center:
Critic Richard Gilman has described Sam Shepard as the Jackson Pollock of the American theater. Somewhere in the chaos of his plays there may be an idea, but the spray and sprawl of his words and the eternal shifting of his characters' personalities create a dizzying excitement that has nothing to do with the intellect. Shepard was born in Illinois (in 1943) but brought up in southern California on an anti-intellectual 1960s' diet of rock music, drugs, cars, and science fiction. Arriving in New York at the age of nineteen, he imitated English playwrights Harold Pinter and Edward Bond in several one-act dramas and then turned to longer plays, which reflect a more deliberate control of the rush of dramatic images. Shepard's plays have never reached mainline Broadway and probably never will, although Buried Child received a Pulitzer Prize in 1979. The most autobiographical of his plays, A Lie of the Mind, was not only written but directed by him in the 1985 New York production. Like all of Shepard's plays, its plot resists precise description, but it is mainly concerned with the violent love-hate relationships between two families bound together by a marriage. Left to right: Geraldine Page, Aidan Quinn, Harvey Keitel, and Karen Young.

Opposite above:
The single most important event in the life and development of David Rabe as man and playwright was his tour of duty in Vietnam in 1965. Although he saw no action, he observed its effects as part of a hospital support unit. His observations were collected and given form in three plays: The Basic Training of Pavlo Hummel (1971), Sticks and Bones (1971), and Streamers (1976). Rabe can be counted among Joseph Papp's discoveries and was nurtured early in his career in the protective blanket of the New York Shakespeare Festival. He eventually broke away from Papp and New York, journeying to Hollywood to work as a screenwriter. What came out of that experience was Hurlyburly, a play about the desperate actions of youngish, successful, but unhappy Hollywood types, whose hedonism reflects their moral rootlessness. Under the direction of Mike Nichols, Hurlyburly started its career at the Goodman Theatre in Chicago and in 1984 moved to Broadway. Among the young and vibrant cast were (left to right) Harvey Keitel, Judith Ivey, and William Hurt.

Opposite below:
Seated at the eternal kitchen table are Kathy Bates (left) and Ann Pitoniak in 'night, Mother, by Marsha Norman. The 1983 Pulitzer Prize winner has only two characters, a mother and daughter, who share a perfectly ordinary house in an ordinary small town somewhere in America. Early in the play, the daughter announces that she is going to kill herself and begins to prepare her mother. She is driven to suicide by the colorlessness of her existence—a subject treated recurrently in American dramatic literature. Norman established herself in the mainstream of American realism with her two plays Getting Out and 'night, Mother, both of which were tested at the Actors Theatre in Louisville, Kentucky, before their New York production. Their psychological realism reflects her experiences while working with emotionally disturbed children.

Left:
The career of Lanford Wilson is interesting if for no other reason than that it exemplifies the rites of passage that young American playwrights must undergo today. Wilson's plays were first produced off off Broadway (at the Caffe Cino), then off Broadway (at the Circle Repertory Theatre, of which Wilson was a founder, in 1969), then finally on Broadway itself. He received a Pulitzer Prize in 1980 for Talley's Folly, which began its life at the Circle Repertory Theatre. Most of Wilson's plays are a succession of vivid scenes of interaction between characters rather than intricately constructed dramas. Catching the mood of the 1960s, Balm in Gilead, Wilson's first full-length play, was produced at Cafe La Mama in 1965, revived by Chicago's Steppenwolf Theater Company, and transferred in 1984 to the Circle Rep. It takes place in a cheap all-night coffeeshop with its complement of typically Wilsonian human dregs and misfits, who wander in and out, giving vent to their troubled thoughts and aspirations. This poster was designed by Larry Ashton.

DIRECTORS AND CHOREOGRAPHERS

I N 1965 Whitney Bolton, drama critic of the *New York Morning Telegraph*, did a rare thing. He devoted his usual column of theater commentary to correcting an oversight. He had recently reviewed *Man of La Mancha*, the hit musical of the 1965–66 season, and had failed to mention the director of the show, Albert Marre. Acknowledging his embarrassment publicly, he wrote: "Now, manifestly, no matter how well written the libretto, how exalting and lovely the music, how artful the lyrics and how winning the players, none of these elements could have received their full due without a directorial hand of unusual abilities. Nor could they all have been brought together without that same guiding hand. I feel, in this particular and distinguished case, that a very special director brought all of the elements into balance and perfection." The rest of the article flowed with cascades of compliments and searched out and found the fine hand of the director in every element of the production. Marre, like many of his colleagues, was more than a director. Together with the writer, composer, lyricist, and choreographer, he had helped to develop *Man of La Mancha* during a protracted evolution that had begun many months before the Broadway opening night. For Marre, who relished his work in musical theater and had been perfecting his directorial skills for some twenty years, the show was a triumph. He deserved Bolton's apology.

Reviewers devote few words to the work of a director. They may recognize him in a descriptive word or two—usually a variation on either *expert* or *inept*—or they may extend themselves to a paragraph of praise or blame for the success or failure of a production. If the actors manage not to run into each other onstage, if the scenery stays in place and the curtains go up and down on schedule, his work goes largely unheeded by audiences. Most directors, past and present, agree that the best directing tends to be unobtrusive; so saying, they philosophically accept their lot as the least understood and least appreciated of the theatrical collaborators. Until today, underestimation has been compounded by undercompensation, and the aspiring director still consigns himself to a hazardous occupation. A production may employ several actors, designers and assistants, dancers, and musicians, and a complement of underlings—but usually only one director. When the curtain goes up on the first performance, his work is finished. If it is a hit, he may continue to enjoy the fruits of his labors in the form of a royalty check for each week it runs. If the play fails, his responsibility does not quite end with the final curtain. His producer may remember it as the director's failure and the word goes out. His chances of being hired for another show diminish with each play that does not receive a respectable run. For most Broadway directors, it is a short life and an unhappy one.

Few outside the working theater know much about the function of the director. A writer for the *New York Dramatic Mirror* once attempted to define his role in theatrical production:

There is no branch of stage work so limitless in its responsibility, its difficulties, or the knowledge it requires. Imagination, perception, observation, sympathy and histrionic ability are only the first equipment of the [director]. He requires knowledge. Knowledge of language, human nature, manners, customs, dress, geographical distinctions, historical differences, color, painting, drawing, mechanical construction, architecture, music, refined life, middle-class life, country life, politics, religion, ethics, morals, literature, city life, elocution, and above all a mastering sense of the practical. Further, he must possess moral attributes which are equally rare and indispensable. Patience, the faculty of teaching, of imparting ideas, mental poise, pride, humility, elasticity.

If this sounds like an impossible achievement, add to it the mastery of the complex

stage technology that has evolved in the years since 1902, when it was written.

The history of this Renaissance man and paragon of the theatrical virtues lies almost wholly within the past hundred years. Before his arrival, plays apparently got on the stage without his help or through another agency. On the English stage from the age of Shakespeare onward, the playwright assumed some of his functions. After a playwright's death, his stage directions were passed down from actor to actor and became established tradition. Thomas Betterton, the greatest actor of the Restoration stage, is believed to have been taught how to play Shakespearean roles by the artistic descendants of the playwright, more than forty years after the death of the Bard.

In turn, the great actors of each succeeding age added touches to whatever instructions came from the playwrights, and these, too, were duly recorded in the promptbooks, providing each role with built-in embellishments. This body of tradition constituted the actor's "business," and until another great performer emerged to crack the standard interpretation, actors played their parts according to established custom. The acting companies represented "schools," and actors taught other actors. A contemporary playwright would be expected to instruct the actors in his pieces. Some were more conscientious about this than others. Richard Brinsley Sheridan traveled to Bath in 1777 to supervise personally the production of his play *The School for Scandal*, but such diligence was unusual.

More often than not it was the principal actor of a company who took over a director's functions. He chose the plays, appointed the actors (frequently according to the costumes they possessed), arranged for the scenery, and conducted the rehearsals. Since the actors were supposed to be "up" in their parts, rehearsals involved merely showing them where and when to make their entrances and exits and practicing the traditional business of their roles. Rehearsals of plays already in the repertory were scant and brief. If the actor-manager also happened to be a star, the supporting actors would know enough to give him lots of room so that he could take over the downstage area under the best light. The typical eighteenth-century stage picture shows a group of actors arranged in a semicircle around the star.

In the English theater, the star would rarely conduct or even attend his own rehearsals. It was the prompter who guided the actors through the play. He was the keeper of the promptbook—the bible of the production—which contained notations, underscorings, instructions, descriptions, and technical cues for music and noises offstage. During performances, he perched with the book spread out before him at stage right (the actors' right as they face the audience) and supplied missing lines or words when necessary and followed the performance from cue to cue. Until the demise of the stock company, nothing was allowed to deviate from the promptbook and the established business. When the American actress Anna Cora Mowatt appeared for rehearsals of *The Lady of Lyons* at the Princess's Theatre in London in 1848, she described the experience as walking through a lane of nettles. When one of the supporting English actresses was asked to cross to stage right, her reply was, "Excuse me; I played this part originally with Mrs. Butler, at Drury Lane—I always kept this position—it is *the proper* situation." For generations of actors there was little argument against tradition. With the arrival of Lewis Hallam's troupe in 1752, the English system was introduced in the colonies. American embellishments eventually created a system similar, yet different.

As in England, leadership of the stock companies that sprang up was at first usually assumed by the principal actor; but the increasing complexity of the manager's job led to partnerships in which one member of the team was responsible for scheduling the plays, assigning the parts, and conducting the rehearsals and the other for all of the "front of the house" activities. For example, during the early years of the Park Theatre, William Dunlap held the title of "acting manager with the unusual artistic duties," but so inexperienced was he in the ways of the stage that the "artistic duties" were in fact assigned to John Hodgkinson, one of his partners and also the leading actor of the company. Schooled in the English tradition, Hodgkinson was efficient and expert, often demonstrating by example to his actors when they were uncertain of the business of a part.

Since the actors in early American companies were accustomed to their repertory and to each other, performances of standard plays rolled on relatively well-oiled wheels, even though most troupes could not afford the luxury of appropriate costumes and well-drilled supernumeraries for crowd scenes. When a company presented a new play, however, the result was often organized bedlam. There had probably been time for only a few rehearsals, in which the manager was concerned mainly with getting the characters on and off the stage, and the real star of the first night of a new presentation was usually the prompter. The backs of the scenery were papered with the actors' "sides" (pages of their parts) and the performers winged their way through the lines. It was the wise playgoer who postponed his attendance at a new offering until the company had had time to assimilate it.

Rehearsals were always chaotic. In her memoirs, the actress Olive Logan provided a lively description of one in the mid-nineteenth century. In her day, rehearsals were customarily called by the stage manager (the old acting manager with a new name) during the hours between 10 A.M. and 2 P.M. The notice or "call" for rehearsal was placed in the call box, if the theater had one, or posted conspicuously behind the scenes. Not only the actors but also the "scene shifters, the musicians, and everybody who [had] to do with the production of the piece at night" arrived on stage at the appointed time. Actors came in ordinary street clothing, which, because of their usual perilous financial condition, was of none too good quality or condition. "It seems funny," Logan mused, "to see an actor stalking about the stage in a water-proof overcoat, carrying an umbrella in one hand, and remarking in a very unconcerned tone, 'A horse! a horse! my kingdom for a horse!' Or to behold a well-dressed person kneeling at the feet of a seedy-looking man in a coat out at elbows, and saying, 'Your majesty, I am your slave.'"

Rehearsals were punctuated by backstage hammering and sawing and the general noise and bustle associated with the preparation of scenery. Although the stage manager was in charge, frequent disagreements might spring up between him and the

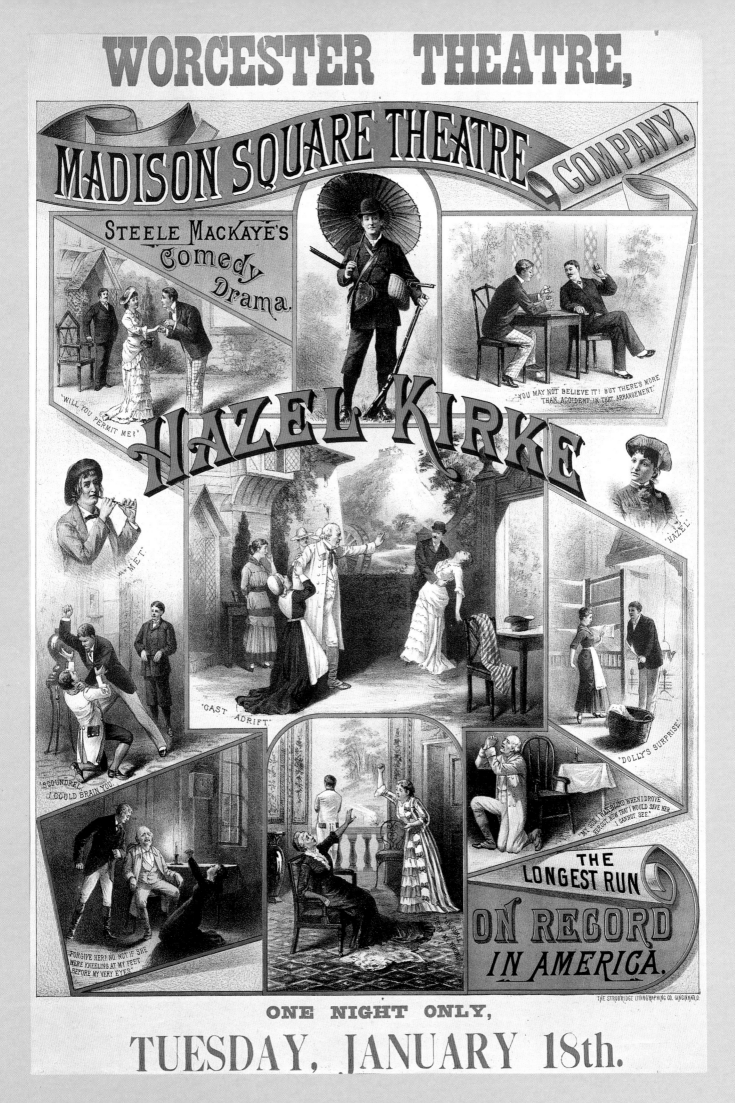

star—male or female—on some point of business. When a resolution seemed elusive, the matter was settled by the oldest member of the troupe, "the patriarch of the company," who would reach into the recesses of his memory and pull out "tradition." Rehearsals were the training ground for the young actors. Logan recalled that one of the great actors of the American stage (whom she did not name) could not refrain from stopping a scene in order to dress down one of the younger players. "My young friend, if you desire to progress in your profession, you should be more attentive. A rehearsal is your *school*, sir, and inattention to what's going on onstage, while you are engaged in the scene, is wrong, sir."

Since the stock companies employed a more or less permanent company of actors, each of whom was in "possession of parts" (that is, versed in certain roles), the casting of plays was largely predetermined. All too frequently, the stage manager had to make the best of a bad situation. Actresses took the roles of young, sweet things long after their faces and figures betrayed them; actors with potbellies and gray hair played less than believable young Hamlets. But giving up the meaty parts was painful for old troupers.

Since the stage manager did not worry about such arcane matters as the interpretation of roles or the psychological nuances of lines, the actors effectively directed themselves. If they conveyed a sense of ensemble—and several companies did—they had their own perseverance and professional pride to thank. The stage manager usually had neither the authority nor the time to accomplish more than to set down the rudimentary business, to move his actors on, around, and off the stage, and to call and conduct rehearsals. The theater waited for someone to seize control of performance and to effect a change in production that was long overdue.

Dion Boucicault, who was introduced earlier as a playwright, was destined to transform the role of the stage manager in America, where he spent only about half of his working theatrical life. Dublin-born, he entered the theater as an actor and later added playwriting, producing, directing, teaching, and lecturing to his accomplishments. His first stunning success took place in London in 1841, when his *London Assurance* was produced by Madame Vestris at the Princess's Theatre. As a mere boy, he revealed an uncanny instinct for the theater and possessed a remarkable confidence in his talents. When the play was accepted, he placed himself at the prompter's table during rehearsals and changed scene after scene to make them more actable, handing to the cast the pages still wet with ink.

Boucicault came to America in 1853, returned to Europe in 1860, and settled permanently in New York City in 1872. He wrote or adapted more than 150 plays, most of them for his own companies or for certain actors. He was able to achieve total control over performances of his scripts by casting them himself, conducting the rehearsals, and eventually acting as his own producer. Supremely surefooted, he could rehearse the first act of a play while he was writing the third. As a stage manager, he dominated rehearsals, which under his aegis became each play's period of gestation. He often changed the script, gave each actor his onstage business, and supervised the scenery and technical details. Frequently, he was also the star. Like a musical conductor, he would roar "Stop!" in the middle of rehearsals while he thought up or changed a bit of business. His comments could be cutting and he drew tears easily from women. Once an actor, smarting under his reprimand, spoke out, "Mr. Boucicault, I have written the directions as you gave them to me yesterday." To which the great man replied sweetly in his Dublin brogue: "Ah! yesterday, certainly, my boy, I told you to do it, but the world is just twenty-four hours older, and we have advanced that much; so do it this way to-day." Described as an "exacting martinet" by his biographer Townsend Walsh, he expected both beginners and seasoned professionals to bend to his will.

Though he lacked some of Boucicault's specific gifts, Augustin Daly was evolving and practicing his own brand of tyranny during the 1870s, when his rival was busily crossing the Atlantic. Apparently from the start, Daly had a clear vision of his role in the theater, and that was total artistic control over all aspects of production. No

Director Augustin Daly was as particular about the settings for his productions as he was attentive to the details of each performance. For the banquet scene in The Taming of the Shrew *(1887), one of his most acclaimed Shakespearean productions, he had his designer paint a backdrop in the manner of Veronese.*

detail was too insignificant to elude his critical gaze. One of the first things he did was to eliminate the system of hiring actors according to their possession of parts or line of business. He told his actors, "There is no line in this theatre; you do everything," and for many years he kept them at the same level. He watched them carefully and, as he once explained, "if one head begins to bob up above the others, I give it a crack and send it down again." (In his mellower years, Daly allowed one or two heads to bob up and remain up as stars of his company.)

The keynote of Daly's rehearsals was discipline. No one was allowed backstage while he was conducting them. Although he hired a succession of stage managers, they were assigned menial tasks and did little more than run and fetch for the master. Actors had to be prompt and attentive, too, and if they did not do what he said, he would jump into their positions and show them what he wanted. He drilled them over and over again in long, agonizing rehearsals until he achieved what he had envisioned. He preplanned everything, reserving the right to make changes when something did not work out as intended. Occasionally, he would listen to actors' suggestions, reflect on them, and incorporate them into his master plan, but generally his ideas prevailed. Even the supers came under his watchful eyes. Clara Morris, who achieved fame in his company before leaving it to pursue stardom, described his effect on actors: "Never had I seen anything so like trick-poodles. They were ready to do 'dead dog,' or jump over a chair, or walk on two legs—ready, too, for either the bone or the blow."

"Acting is action" was Daly's credo but not in the Stanislavskian sense. He simply liked to move his actors around the stage, much as a choreographer moves dancers, and he was occasionally taken to task by the critics for the busyness of his productions. Yet he was careful to provide "motivation" for actors' behavior, as Clara Morris explained, and thus pushed direction a few inches further toward the creation

The great Mrs. Fiske always took an active role in the direction of plays produced by her husband, Harrison Grey Fiske. The equally great French actress Gabrielle Réjane considered her superior to everyone in Europe in the staging of plays. Mrs. Fiske's yearly tours included the Ibsen dramas, which she championed. Here shown is the poster for Ghosts from one of her national tours.

of believable stage behavior. "There were a number of characters on in the scene, and Mr. Daly wanted to get me across the stage, so that I should be out of hearing of two of the gentlemen. Now, in the old days, the stage-director would simply have said: 'Cross to the Right,' and you would have crossed because he told you to; but in Mr. Daly's day you had to have a reason for crossing the drawing room, and so getting out of the two gentlemen's way—and a reason could not be found." After rejecting a number of solutions to the problem and stalling the rehearsal, the director finally accepted one of Morris's suggestions and strategically placed a bottle of smelling salts across the room, adding a line of dialogue to allow her to move to it.

Daly never considered his labors completed even after a show opened. If a play was not a success, he would tinker with it, usually to little avail. Even when he had a hit, he might call in the company after opening night for "cutting and polishing rehearsals." His dedication to the theater was complete. He died in 1899, at sixty-one, after plunging back into a rigorous schedule following a bout of pneumonia. He undoubtedly burned himself out. One of the most respected critics of his time, J. Ranken Towse, said of him: "There can be no doubt that he would have done much more really good work than he did if he had not attempted to do so much. As a stage director he was brilliant, adventurous, prodigal, and catholic, but his knowledge was not universal nor his judgment always sound." Whatever his shortcomings, he succeeded in overturning accepted traditions in the staging of plays and established in their place one man's idea about dramatic production. The cause of director as collaborator took a giant leap forward because of Daly.

Following the lead of Boucicault and Daly, many of the most important and successful playwrights in the last decades of the nineteenth century claimed the right to direct their own plays. One of them, Steele MacKaye, succeeded in out-Dalying Daly. Not only did he write and direct his work, he redesigned theaters, invented a double movable stage, refined the use of stage lighting with incandescent lamps, designed the folding theater seat, experimented with early air conditioning, and introduced a school of acting based on the Delsarte system of facial and physical expression, out of which the American Academy of Dramatic Arts arose, in 1884. He lived a short life, dying in 1894 at fifty-two, but had a frenetic, creative, and protean career, which left its mark on many of his contemporaries.

According to contemporary reports, MacKaye's staging was brilliant. By using lighting for atmospheric beauty, and by toning down dialogue and eliminating stock melodramatic characters, he brought what could be considered the first touch of realism to the American stage. To achieve the effects he wanted, he had to instruct actors schooled in the old stock-company tradition in a quieter, more subtle style; a talented actor himself, he could direct by demonstrating what he intellectualized. He was an intense, nervous, driving, and mercurial director, who appears to have excelled particularly in handling crowds. One of his plays, *Paul Kauvar*, had as its background the French Revolution. He spent three weeks in disciplining the extras for the mob scenes, struggling to fuse it into what he described as "a many-headed character." He began by drilling groups of first two, then four, then eight, until he had trained the entire complement, forcing them all to act instead of going through the motions. MacKaye did not live long enough to influence the course of directing, but David Belasco and others learned from his style.

Clyde Fitch made the right to direct his own plays a stipulation of the contracts he signed once his reputation had become established with producers. Trained as an architect, he designed stage sets for the carpenters and scene painters to execute; not content with that, he sketched costumes for the costumer and selected furniture and props for the property man. His eighteen-hour day led to several breakdowns and illnesses, and his life ended prematurely, in 1909, when he was only forty-four. While he directed his plays, any space would serve as a rehearsal room—home, garden, or hotel suite abroad—until he was ready for his company to move on stage. He gave his actors bits of business, mannerisms, gestures, and vocal intonations to build their roles but never bullied his cast or lost his temper, playing the part of a benevolent despot.

His productions were rich in surface detail, romantically realistic, even though many of the plays were skin deep.

Actors had for centuries conducted rehearsals and performed the dual function of director and producer, but in the late nineteenth century, as the responsibilities of the director grew weightier, only a few performers had the inclination and the talent to interpret a play and control its production. Mrs. Fiske, the greatest American actress of her day, had both the desire and the talent.

Mrs. Fiske's name first appeared as director in the program notes for an 1897 production of *Tess of the d'Urbervilles* in New York. When she and her husband, Harrison Grey Fiske, took over the Manhattan Theatre in 1901, she had the luxury of selecting the plays she wanted to do and commissioning others, of hiring strong supporting players, and of staging plays in her own way. Because she made sure that her actors, from the principals down to the most insignificant walk-on, were first-rate, she allowed them to develop their own characterizations and made suggestions to them privately.

In his autobiography, the English actor George Arliss paid tribute to Mrs. Fiske's talent as a director, which was not as universally known, he thought, as her ability as an actress. During the rehearsals of *Leah Kleschna* her husband fell ill, and Mrs. Fiske had to take over the full responsibility of the production. "The ease with which she piloted the play to success and the brilliancy of her suggestions surprised us all," Arliss remarked. "Personally I have never ceased to regret Mrs. Fiske's advice when I am studying a new part. She had an uncanny capacity for suggesting the tricks of old age, or extreme youth, passion or suffering, in directing others; her character acting was superb and her constant warning to the actors was 'keep it true—keep it true.' Our great difficulty at this time was to prevent her effacing herself. She was so interested in getting the best out of everybody else that she seemed to regard herself as a negligible quantity in the play."

Mrs. Fiske's yearly tours from one end of the country to the other gave her a durable national prominence, and trouping helped to revise her thoughts about staging. In 1914 she wrote to her husband from Texas that out of practicality she was forced to omit some of the scenery and props from her productions. "It was really remarkable, but we all felt that the play had never gone so well! The absence of scenery and properties gave an added spur to the acting and they were never missed. It may be that these new German ideas are right, and if so, it will relieve us of a great

Ralph Barton's caricature of David Belasco at rehearsal amusingly points up the director's concern for the smallest detail.

deal." Throughout her long career, she never lost her joy of discovering new truths about the theater. When the Fiskes gave up the Manhattan, in 1906, the actress appeared under the aegis of different producers, but she and her husband managed to retain artistic control over the plays in which she appeared, even when the producer was the autocratic David Belasco.

In 1907 a cartoon appeared in the *New York Journal* showing David Belasco, with giant leonine head, sprinkling a playscript liberally with a bottle of "Belasco sauce." The message of this cartoon would have been picked up by any playgoer of the period, for the famous Belasco "touch" had brought audiences into his theater year after year. Both during his own lifetime and after his death, in 1931, the Belasco technique was praised and damned. It could achieve heights of theatrical art unapproached by any other director of the day, and it could also be embarrassingly maudlin and transparent as tissue paper. Belasco's popular success was attested by innumerable imitations, but the unseen stage magician was never beaten at his own game. Even today, a critic need say only that a production is Belascoesque and the informed theatergoer will know that the show has a cluttered, realistic set. His achievements and his ideas straddled two centuries: he handled nineteenth-century drama with a twentieth-century approach, and vice versa. When dealing with progressive or risqué subjects, almost without exception he would reduce them to melodrama and claptrap. He kept the apparatus of the stock company and sequestered it in his own theater but produced plays not in repertory but sequentially, always trying for the big Broadway hit.

Although it remains doubtful that Belasco ever wrote a script from start to finish by himself, his name appeared as author or co-author of many of his produced plays. His fine hand also revealed itself in the design of the scenery, lighting, and costumes as well as in the individual performances. No object on the set, no light in the rafters, no extra onstage escaped his attention. Once he became a legend, he never lost an opportunity to expound on his technique or pontificate on his theories, and for more than twenty years, his pronouncements on things theatrical made good copy for the drama pages of the newspapers, Sunday supplements, and popular magazines. Inevitably, he took to contradicting himself in print and idealized methods that existed only in his imagination. The details of his early life and apprenticeship became more and more romanticized and helped to establish him as the grand old man of Broadway, the magnitude of whose mystique was realized when Belasco, a Jew, took to wearing the turned-around collar and black vestments of a priest. His best creation was perhaps himself as the showman without equal. The only man on his staff busier than he was his press agent.

Born in California in 1853, Belasco served his apprenticeship on the road in his native state and in New York, absorbing like a sponge the techniques and practices of professional theater men. From W. T. Porter, the scene painter of the California Theatre in San Francisco, he learned how to achieve realistic effects through scenic details and lighting; from his boss Tom Maguire he received training as a business manager; from Dion Boucicault, for whom he served as amanuensis, he observed how a script is rendered into a playable piece; and watching Steele MacKaye, for whom he worked as a stage manager, he absorbed the ways in which a master director pulls together all the elements of production.

In fact, nothing in Belasco's technique as a director was new or inventive. In his book *Theatre Through Its Stage Door* he set down his idealized method for trimming, cutting, revising, and rewriting plays. But Daly and Boucicault and others before them had done the same. He described how he ceaselessly drove his actors for hours in rehearsal to get a desired intonation, shrug, scream, or other histrionic effect. But long rehearsals and demanding directors had preceded him. He recorded his endeavors to bring a production to life through evocative scenery and flexible lighting, defending himself against the charge that he placed undue emphasis on the external elements of production. MacKaye, the English actor-manager Henry Irving, and others had also striven for realism on the stage through carefully thought-out lighting

and settings—though here it is probably fair to say that Belasco stretched the art to its limits. The "Belasco touch" really consisted in doing everything better than everyone else and in achieving startling theatrical effects that were alone worth the price of a ticket. To achieve all this, Belasco assembled a loyal and hardworking staff, many of whom remained with him for years. In the early years of the twentieth century, when Gordon Craig was expounding the ideal of the super-director who was on top of every aspect of production, David Belasco was enacting the role with near perfect success.

He controlled his actors as few directors have. Although he claimed he gave them latitude in the interpretation of their roles, he rarely did so. Everyone who worked for Belasco had a favorite story about his method of extracting performances from his actors. The famous "watch trick" supposedly was invented during a particularly long and trying rehearsal. Belasco suddenly threw his watch on the floor, smashing it into pieces, as the cast looked on in astonishment. "What have I done?" he whimpered. "My mother's watch. Her last gift to me. Oh, mother, mother!" Then he fell to his knees and gathered the shards of the watch, clutching them to his breast. With tears in his eyes, he piteously asked them to try the scene once more for "a tired, evil old man, so old, so tired." Belasco's performance so electrified the actors that they plunged in anew and turned in a creditable rehearsal. The "trick" worked so well that, according to his biographer, the director later stocked up on two-dollar watches and used them in other rehearsals with other casts.

Unlike Daly, who tried in vain to keep the heads of the individual performers from bobbing up, Belasco believed in star vehicles. Beginning with Mrs. Leslie Carter, he systematically trained a succession of actresses (and an occasional actor), put them into plays with roles tailor-made for them, and converted them into stars. His efforts, as he described them, in transforming his first Galatea into an actress were prodigious:

Mrs. Carter was an amateur and very crude. She was full of mannerisms, a society woman without any knowledge whatever of the stage. I first taught her to walk into a room, showing her for hours how to walk into a room, how to leave a room, how to sit down, to open a book, to turn a page, how to open a letter, how to read a letter and carry on dialogue at the same time.... I taught her how to weep. I would weep myself for hours until I looked like a wet rag. I would tear and scratch myself. I taught her to weep for the different emotions in a different way. So many actresses on stage weep in one way—they only know one way to weep. I instructed her in thirty or forty roles. She was taught boxing, wrestling, fencing and dancing.

About 1920 one of Belasco's stars, Blanche Bates, became the subject of one of photographer Arnold Genthe's arty, slightly out-of-focus portraits.

When I'd get through with her for the day, she'd think she understood. She'd come down the next day and, of course, would be all wrong. She was taught ballet dancing and jig dancing. . . . I taught her to use her muscles and limbs—to be limber. I taught her to become the embodiment of the poetry of motion—a great nerve trial.

On the whole, Belasco received a good press and his shows were eagerly awaited by audiences throughout the country, but they were not without their detractors. George Jean Nathan, who was familiar with the new plays coming out of Europe, gave the typical Belasco production a devastating critical coup de grâce in this parody of a typical script:

Jacques Dupont is a poor artist who lives in an inn with real green shutters. During a Beautiful Belasco Sunlight Effect he and his wife, who is drinking real Vermouth from a glass bought at the Tiffany Studios, have a quarrel. An art-dealer enters through a real door. Jacques shows him one of his paintings, which he places in such a position that the audience may observe it is a real watercolor, but the dealer refuses to buy it as a Gorgeous Belasco Twilight Effect begins to permeate the scene. From her cottage nearby, with a real and completely furnished room visible through the real glass window, the sympathetic little Maria observes poor Jacques' plight and seeks to aid him with some real money she has saved, but Jacques, as a Lovely Belasco Purple Evening Light Effect gets under way, declines. . . .

The second act passes in a studio in New York decorated with real paintings. Jacques, whom everybody believes dead, returns and is discovered by his friend Shepherd after the latter has pulled up the blinds gradually and permitted the studio to be suffused with a Magnificent Belasco Morning Sunlight Effect that is timed exactly to the raising of the blinds. Jacques goes into a room off-stage in which the audience can observe real chairs when the door is opened, and takes a shower-bath, the sound of the flowing water being perfectly life-like. . . .

In the last act, after two beautiful Belasco lamps have been removed from the aisles by the ushers (an act which occurs three years later in a room in Shepherd's house that is furnished with a handsome real baby grand piano and real pictures and a real mantelpiece and real rugs), Jacques confronts his deceitful wife while through the real glass windows one may observe a Surpassing Belasco Daylight Effect. And, in the end, Jacques and the sympathetic Maria—as a real maid retires discreetly from the real room—indulge in a real kiss.

Curtain (real)

Though Belasco revealed how much an effective director could do with an inferior script if it were well cast and well staged—a lesson that would not be lost in later eras of the American theater—his choice of dramatic material frequently came under fire. As if to answer the charges levied against him in this regard, the director produced *The Merchant of Venice* in the season of 1922-23. The event coincided with the visit to New York of the Moscow Art Theatre, headed by Konstantin Stanislavsky. In a letter to his colleague Vladimir Nemirovich-Danchenko, Stanislavsky commented on the Belasco production: "Such an actor as David Warfield, whom I saw in the part of Shylock, we have not got. And Belasco's production of *The Merchant of Venice* exceeds in sheer lavishness anything I ever saw, and as for its technical achievements, the Maly Theatre [Russia's premier, state-supported theater] could envy them." A few years later, Stanislavsky elected Belasco to honorary membership in the Moscow Art Theatre for his contributions to theater art.

No one event or person was responsible for dramatically expanding the role of the director in the late nineteenth century, but certainly the decline of the stock company made his increased importance inevitable. Audiences had not unreasonably become surfeited with the old warhorses, decked out season after season in the same tired scenery and costumes. Big-time managers quickly recognized that by sending their productions to hinterland playhouses they could reap windfall profits of which they had never dreamed, and accordingly they dispatched duplicate companies from New York with a featured star, fresh scenery, beautiful or effective costumes, modern plays—and novelty. When in the 1890s the Theatrical Syndicate streamlined and "industrialized" the theretofore unbusinesslike theatrical art, there were jobs for more and more professionals, one of whom was the stage director, whose home base would remain New York City.

Meanwhile, theaters were becoming smaller as plays centered less and less on

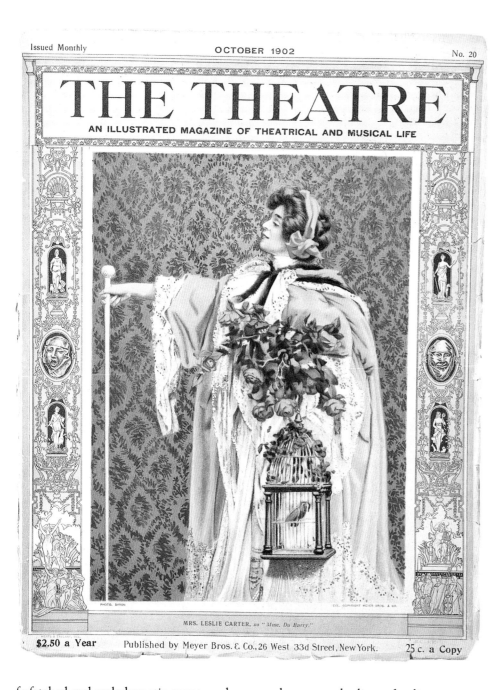

Issued Monthly   OCTOBER 1902   No. 20

THE THEATRE

AN ILLUSTRATED MAGAZINE OF THEATRICAL AND MUSICAL LIFE

PHOTO. BYRON   COL. COPYRIGHT MEYER BROS. & CO.

MRS. LESLIE CARTER, as "Mme. Du Barry."

$2.50 a Year   Published by Meyer Bros. & Co., 26 West 33d Street, New York.   25 c. a Copy

With the beginning of the new century, the theater world received its first important magazine, The Theatre, a chatty, entertaining, and heavily illustrated publication. The early chromolithographed covers featured an actor or actress in a Broadway success. It was only natural that one of them was a Belasco star. Mrs. Leslie Carter, in the director-producer's latest hit, Du Barry, graced the October 1902 issue.

farfetched and melodramatic events and more and more on the lives of ordinary people. (Though spectacles remained popular, they became so expensive to mount that far fewer of them reached the theaters.) Electric lighting literally put the actor in the spotlight, forcing him to exchange the broad gesture for the nuance. The death of the stock company gave actors opportunities to stretch themselves in new roles. Though the new freedom was modified to some extent by typecasting and the personality star, many plays were, for the first time, appropriately cast and played.

After the stock companies disbanded and before the first schools of drama appeared, actors were often ill prepared in all aspects of their craft. The stage itself had to become their training ground. Enter the modern director. The pioneers—they were variously called stage manager, producer, or director—were hirelings of the men who regarded the theater as a business. Naturally, most if not all the successful directors were attached to Klaw and Erlanger, Charles Frohman, the Shuberts, or the important independent producers of the time. For a number of years, the conservative producers sent their directors abroad to observe productions on the English and European stages so that they could later reproduce them intact in America, but as the skill of local directors increased, the practice was largely abandoned. Not surprisingly, the earliest directors were frequently actors, some of whom continued to perform occasionally, most of whom dropped acting because of the greater rewards and security of their new profession. During the four decades that followed 1890, good directors were in constant demand and the best of them worked season in and season out.

The director was the creature of the independent producer, there being few freelance directors at the beginning, and his functions were at first tentatively, then by 1910 definitively, established. He had no choice in the selection of a script, which was the prerogative of the producer. His casting choices were often limited to the stars and performers already in his boss's stable. He had a voice in the casting of extras, but the producer and the playwright could exercise their right of veto if they chose. The interpretation of the script, however, was largely left to him to work out with the stars and supporting actors. He could consult with the playwright whenever necessary and request that lines be rewritten; if he were audacious, he might rewrite them himself or transpose scenes and cut and alter the piece into something akin to the original (this function of the director as play-doctor became increasingly more important).

His duties encompassed the physical production of a play. It was the director who constructed "plots" or working plans for the scenery, costumes, props, and lights, and the person responsible for executing the plots reported to the director in the technical and dress rehearsals. When the curtain went up on the first performance, his responsibility to the show was officially over, except in the event that the play was a success, when he was asked to prepare touring companies for the producer.

The producer created the director, and the director was the paterfamilias of the backstage running crew, the most important of whom was and continues to be the stage manager. This overworked appellation thus finally came to rest on the head of the person who holds the completed promptbook, which contains every morsel of information about the running of the play, from the time the curtain is raised until the last of the curtain calls. After 1910, when they caught their breath, directors would begin to expound on the theories of their "art" in self-conscious mimicry of their European counterparts, but in fact the role of the director was defined and established not philosophically, but through a pragmatic evolution on the American stage.

Before 1900 few directors in the American theater got program credit for what they did. Playbills sometimes carried the line "staged by . . . " in small print at the bottom, but many times the director's name was omitted or placed in the list of the producer's staff. After 1900 the director on the American stage came into his own. He got program credit and a great deal of money, power, and, occasionally, temporary fame. Eventually, to protect himself against the everlasting vicissitudes of the theater, he got his own union.

Among the pioneers was William Seymour, who came out of the old stock-company system. He was born, the child of actors, in New York City in 1855. As he recounted his journey through the ranks:

I began as a child player, was a call-boy, prompter, a utility man, a second comedian, property man, advance agent, baggage assistant, assistant to the stage carpenter, assistant scenic artist, ticket seller, treasurer, business manager, and am now a stage manager [director]. I have never led an orchestra, but have beaten the snare drum for flourishes and marches in the tragedies, have drilled choruses, arranged ballets and taught broad-sword fighting. For all this experience, I have to thank Edwin Booth, Lawrence Barrett and other managers who were more than kind to me.

From 1879 to 1928, Seymour directed plays for the Boston Museum and operas for Henry Abbey and Maurice Grau of the Metropolitan Opera Company, and capped his career in 1901 by becoming the principal stage director for Charles Frohman. In 1912 he was making $250 per week with Frohman—a substantial sum for someone not behind the footlights—directing Maude Adams in the J. M. Barrie plays and Otis Skinner, John Drew, Billie Burke, and other important stars in plays controlled by the producer. From Frohman's employ, he went on to Liebler & Co. in 1919, remaining until 1923. He continued to direct and, occasionally, to act until his retirement in 1927, and was sometimes lured out of retirement to stage a revival of one of his past successes or to speak about directing and the theater.

Considered the dean of Broadway directors during his lifetime, Seymour believed that a good director was born and not made, although he felt anyone "could educate himself to the business." In working with playwrights, he preferred to defer to their judgment. Although he was firm in his handling of actors, he did not believe in cowing them, as did Boucicault, but in treating them with kindness and tact. He felt that more could be accomplished gently than with "a thousand metaphorical kicks." In a career that spanned the age from Edwin Booth to Helen Hayes and from stock company to the hit-or-flop route on Broadway, Seymour made a successful transition from the old system to the new, and he, more than any of his contemporaries, helped to win recognition for the director as the new theater specialist.

Ben Teal was the first of the early directors to strike out on his own and prove that it was possible to make a career and a living by working on a freelance basis. At one time or another, he was employed by Klaw and Erlanger, Charles Frohman, the Shuberts, and the comedy team of Weber and Fields. Born in 1862, he began as a child actor in San Francisco, working up through the theatrical hierarchy until in 1892 he was engaged as the stage director of the Herald Square Theatre in New York, which he left after one season. From then until his death, Teal was possibly the busiest director in New York, and his fame spread as far as London, where he was hired to stage shows for the West End theaters. The stories about Teal's methods are legion. Abusive and tyrannical, he terrorized his actors in rehearsal. Lionel Barrymore recalled that "he frightened everybody, lashed us, derided us, and was particularly astute with cutting remarks about my acting abilities. Some of the people couldn't take it and dropped out, but I reasoned that this experience couldn't be worse than starvation, so I endured." Teal could and did direct dramas, musical shows, and extravaganzas, but he was renowned for spectacles with large casts, with and without music. It was Teal who in 1899 staged *Ben Hur* for Klaw and Erlanger, supervising the enactment of the great chariot race. He was without peer in his ability to move large numbers of extras around onstage, but his particular skill was in his direction of chorus girls. He was notoriously brutal to them and could reduce them easily to tears. Though his methods lacked finesse, the hallmarks of a Teal production were clockwork precision and flawless staging. Because of his energy and thorough professionalism, producers turned to him first with their projects. He never lacked for work.

R. H. Burnside felt that the job of a director was to astonish the audience, and he did not believe that theatrical tricks should be revealed. For many years, Burnside

Overleaf:
R. H. Burnside loved to direct spectacles and to orchestrate the movements of hundreds of performers, both human and animal. In this photograph, he has assembled the entire cast of The Big Show (1916) *on the huge stage of the Hippodrome.*

In this photograph, director Eugene Presbrey and actress Maude Adams are in a Harvard University auditorium watching a rehearsal of Joan of Arc, *in which Adams starred in 1909.*

served as Charles Dillingham's director for the shows on the giant stage of the Hippodrome Theatre. It was he who devised the stunning scene in many Hipp spectacles in which the chorus girls dove into a huge tank of water on the stage, not to reappear for several minutes. The gasping audience was always left wondering how it was achieved—a secret that Burnside did not reveal until years later. Born of a theatrical family in 1870, Burnside left England in 1894, enticed to New York by Lillian Russell, who wanted him to direct her plays. He remained in America to stage more than two hundred shows, the most spectacular of which was the pageant *Freedom* for the Sesquicentennial Exposition in the city of Philadelphia. Five thousand people were employed, of whom half were performers and one hundred were principals. To a man who thought a show without an elephant impossible, the pageant represented the climax of a career. Burnside continued to direct throughout his life and for several years he ran a company that furnished to amateur groups all the makings of shows with which he had been associated, down to the costumes, scenery, and stage business.

Every director worth his salt could serve up any kind of theatrical fare, but several early directors emerged as specialists: like Teal in extravaganzas, like Burnside in large musical shows, or in dramatic pieces. Eugene Presbrey staged his share of musicals but also made his mark with the straight play and the melodrama produced with a wealth of realistic detail. He eschewed flamboyant methods, conducting his rehearsals in a businesslike, methodical, impersonal manner. He cast plays to type and relied upon the talent and resourcefulness of the actors to create convincing characterizations. Like a great many of his contemporaries, he was a skillful play-doctor and finally deserted Broadway for the more lucrative precincts of Hollywood as a director and writer.

According to Presbrey, what the director must seek to create in his productions was "atmosphere." This he defined as "the ingenious arrangement of natural forces to produce convictions; an arrangement that persuades the auditor that what he sees, hears, *and feels*, is real." A director achieved atmosphere by his calculated use of light, color, and sound. In this pallid intellectualization, Presbrey was trying to say something new, but in fact he was merely manufacturing a rationale for the Belasco brand of romanticized realism. In a scene in the third act of *Alabama*, replete with moonlight and twinkling stars, Presbrey's "atmosphere" was attained by pouring a quart of perfume over the stage, so that the smell of the overhanging magnolia trees would waft out into the audience.

Both before and after World War I, the theatrical ferment that had swelled in Europe during the closing decades of the nineteenth century washed up on American shores. The theories of Richard Wagner, Adolphe Appia, and Gordon Craig began to create a greater interest in the role of the theatrical director. Reacting against the cluttered sentimentality of Belasco and his imitators, small groups of thinking amateurs throughout the country were fired by the ideas coming from abroad, and they ignited a small revolution in the American theater. What came to be known as the little-theater movement in America was touched off by Maurice Browne, an English poet married to an aspiring American actress, Ellen Van Volkenburg. In 1912 they founded the Chicago Little Theatre, where they hoped to present a kind of drama that did not depend on the box office and try out ideas and techniques. Beginning with a clean intellectual slate, Browne gradually developed the conception of a theater stripped of everything except movement, light, and sound, fused into a rhythmic evocation of the script. He shaped his company of amateur actors into an ensemble in which no single personality overwhelmed the others. Inevitably, Browne saw the director as the one person within the collaboration who could realize his vision, and he assumed autocratic control over the group. Although he was criticized for not using his theater to stimulate American playwrights, he was content to stage the works of Ibsen, Strindberg, and Shaw and the Gilbert Murray translations of Euripides, which he greatly admired. Only once or twice did he choose original works to illustrate his conception of rhythmic drama. But his experiments were always impressive, and though his theater drew only Chicago's social and intellectual elite (despite the low admission charge), Browne's work as a director immeasurably quickened the cultural life of America's second city and served as a stimulus to other experimental groups nascent in the country.

At about the time Browne was holding sway in his Chicago Little Theatre, Arthur Hopkins was introducing not only unusual plays but startling ideas to establishment theater on Broadway. Short, chubby, and pink-cheeked, he hardly looked the rebel, but in a modest, self-effacing way he was responsible for a new interpretation of the director's functions. Born in 1878, the son of Welsh immigrants in Ohio, he came to New York as a newspaperman, took up press-agentry, and later booked vaudeville acts. In 1913 he produced *Poor Little Rich Girl*, a slight, whimsical play that enjoyed moderate success. It might be said of Hopkins that he became a producer in order to become a director, a route that was to be followed by many of his successors. He produced more than seventy plays, most of which he also directed. Although he had many successes, both critically and financially, he had as many, if not more, notable failures.

Hopkins once said, "Good scripts plus good casts make good directors." He might also have added that hard work (plus a keen intuition) precedeth everything. Before he put a play into rehearsal, he worked for months with the playwright to shape it into an actable script. Once it was ready, he would have the actors read the script over and over for a few days, making corrections only if he felt that their reading revealed a misconception. Then, in an hour or so, he would block out each act and get the cast on their feet for as long as it took to familiarize them with their movements. This accomplished, he felt that the actors needed little instruction. If something was amiss, he would simply take the erring player aside and show him where he had gone wrong. If an actor was on the right track, Hopkins would tell him so in the presence of the company. His rehearsals never lasted more than six hours in order, he said, to preserve the spontaneity of the acting. In his writings on the theater, Hopkins defended his light-handed approach. "When I first came into the theatre," he wrote, "my direction, or absence of direction, was disconcerting to the

Before the curtain rose on The Magnificent Yankee *in 1946, producer-director Arthur Hopkins told the cast of Emmet Lavery's play: "After all, this isn't like the opening of an ordinary play. You are bringing something of your own country to the theatre. It's like bringing a gift—a beautiful present—which is rare." Although the play itself was in no way extraordinary, it was brought to life by the outstanding performances of its stars, Louis Calhern and Dorothy Gish, as Justice Oliver Wendell Holmes and his wife, Fanny.*

actors. They felt lost. Some got the impression that I did not think enough of them to give them my attention. My assurance that they were progressing was sometimes not enough. . . . For some time the myth persisted that I did not really direct at all, a myth for which I was responsible, since that was the effect I sought." He was convinced that the soul of a play was loosed unconsciously through the acting and that the director's function was to allow the actors to explore the emotional recesses of the characters. Here he differed not only from Belasco, who superimposed his own interpretations on his casts, but also from Stanislavsky, who made his actors improvise a before-life for the characters they played.

Hopkins's rehearsals were quiet and orderly, with none of the usual confusion of the typical Broadway production. Maurice Browne recalled that his players loved and respected Hopkins, and that when they teased him, the director responded in kind. Once he and Browne went off to a leisurely lunch in the middle of rehearsals for a show that starred John Barrymore. When they returned, it was nearly four o'clock. " 'Where the devil have you been, Arthur?' yelled Barrymore from the stage. 'We've been in a hell of a mess.' 'Did you get out of it?' asked Hopkins. 'Finally,' said Barrymore. 'Then what the hell are you yelling about?' "

As might be expected, several important directors emerged from the anti-Broadway groups that arose in New York in the teens. One of the founders of the Washington Square Players, Philip Moeller, became the Players' principal director after the original members reorganized as the Theatre Guild in 1919. Moeller did not go the route of the typical director. He was never a callboy or an actor or a producer's general factotum. After graduating from college, he lived the life, in *New York Sun* reporter Helen Ormsbee's words, of a "prosperous dilettante," playing the piano, composing music, and dabbling with writing. Experience gained with the Players lifted him out of the ranks of the amateur, and he became in time a thoroughgoing professional. His entire career was spent with the Theatre Guild, whose productions of O'Neill plays he directed, as well as more than seventy plays by other writers.

In an appreciation of Moeller, Theresa Helburn, one of the officers of the Guild, described his *modus operandi*. He was incapable, she wrote, of planning the details of a

Considered one of Philip Moeller's great triumphs was his direction of Eugene O'Neill's sprawling, novelistic play Strange Interlude (1928), which was interspersed with asides spoken but not heard by the characters onstage. In one of the final scenes of the original production, Lynn Fontanne in the role of Nina Leeds is surrounded, as always, by the three men who love her. Left to right: Earle Larimore, Ethel Westley, Glenn Anders, Lynn Fontanne, and Tom Powers.

production before rehearsals. He went to the first rehearsal "strangely and deliberately unprepared" in order to discover the nuances of the script when the actors began to read it. Once he had a sense of the play and its mood, he would make changes and ask for rewriting, if necessary. He preferred to work only with experienced actors because he did not consider himself a teacher. He gave each actor a conception of his part but left it to him to seek a personal realization of it. His high-water mark as a director came with O'Neill's *Strange Interlude*, a nine-act *tour de force*. In the seven weeks of rehearsals, Moeller had to cope with a fatigued, confused, and often skeptical cast. "Moeller's patience with the worn and jangled nerves of his company was unending; to each rehearsal he had to bring fresh encouragement and new inspiration. It took, also, a great deal of quiet insistence to ultimately gain the confidence of O'Neill's stubborn genius and convince him of the many changes required in the script." *Strange Interlude* exists on two levels. The normal flow of dialogue and reaction among the characters is interrupted by spoken thoughts, the psychological "asides," that convey their secret motivations. Moeller's problem was how to differentiate the overt from the covert action. "After considering and rejecting a number of elaborate and more or less theatrical devices, he finally decided on the extremely simple one used in the production. By allowing the thinker full freedom of motion and expression, while keeping everyone else on the stage in a state of suspended animation during a spoken thought, he succeeded in saving these passages from the taint of monotony and, at the same time preventing the other characters from impinging too strongly on the mental field." The method was proven successful, according to Helburn, by the fact that audiences soon became unaware of it.

The directors who developed their talents in the warm waters of the little theaters enjoyed a sense of security not shared by those who endured a difficult apprenticeship in the hurly-burly of professional theater. By 1920, after the role of the director had been defined through the efforts of the generation of pioneers, the best way to enter the profession was through acting or stage managing. Guthrie McClintic, who was born in Seattle in 1893, tried both routes. Forsaking his conventional middle-class home, he wrested from his parents their reluctant approval to attend the American

Academy of Dramatic Arts in New York—only to find that he could become at best a mediocre actor. An angry letter demanding the attention of the producer Winthrop Ames brought an offer of a job, and McClintic went to work for Ames's director George Foster Platt. Unfamiliar with the duties of a stage manager, he was personally instructed in them by the star of his first show, Julia Dean, who took pity on him. After Platt left Ames, McClintic worked directly under the producer, absorbing everything he could about stage production. During the summer of 1920, while still employed by Ames, he got his first real taste of directing in Jessie Bonstelle's stock company in Detroit, where he also had an opportunity to become reacquainted with a young ingenue by the name of Katharine Cornell, whom he married the following year. Recognizing the talent of his protégé, in 1921 Ames offered to back his first production, *The Dover Road*, and its success launched McClintic professionally. His young wife's star was rising rapidly at the same time and, rather than permit her career to outpace his, she made sure that he directed virtually all of the plays in which she starred. Forty years later, after McClintic's death in 1961, Cornell voluntarily closed her own career on the stage, retreating to her home on Martha's Vineyard.

In addition to his wife's productions, McClintic staged plays for other producers and was one of the busiest directors on Broadway for thirty years. Although he had his detractors, many of the stars with whom he worked felt he was a genuinely brilliant director. Ruth Gordon was especially lavish in her praise of McClintic. She felt that he "induced" performances, making the cast believe they were creating the characters themselves. In his autobiography, McClintic described his directing methods, which he considered unusual for the time, though in fact he had learned much from Ames. He began by having the cast sit around a table and read the play over and over again for a week. He did this to allow the actors to get to know the script and each other, and to convey to them the kind of performance he wanted, trying never to force his own interpretation. When he got them on their feet, he had a diagram placed on the floor indicating the entrances and exits and had the furniture put in place— a technique he had learned from Ames. But unlike Ames, he was high-strung, impatient, and temperamental and could erupt into volcanic rages.

In 1926 he was working for producer A. H. Woods on *The Shanghai Gesture*, a florid melodrama with, as it turned out, one meaty part. Cast in the central role of Mother Goddam, madam of a Chinese brothel, who takes twenty years to wreak her revenge on the man who wronged her and then sold her into prostitution, was Mrs. Leslie Carter, creature of David Belasco long past her prime but thought to have drawing power by Woods. Mrs. Carter would have none of McClintic's methods and, invoking the sacred name of "Mr. Dave," resisted all of his directions. After rehearsals nervewracking for cast and director alike, McClintic grew weary of her excuses and finally shed his affected Ames-like control. "Damn it," he roared, "I am tired of your excuses, I am tired of tables being wrong, people being wrong, business being wrong, when the only thing that's wrong is you. I am tired of you. I refuse any longer to waste my time or my talent on your remembered ineptitudes. Either you go back to your place at the table now and stumble through as best you can, or I am walking out." Unfortunately, his outburst neither turned her into a docile lamb nor improved her performance. Woods was eventually forced to close the show in Atlantic City and open it again with Florence Reed in the leading role. In New York, the play proved to be a triumph, on the strength of Reed's bravura performance and McClintic's showmanship.

Almost the antithesis of McClintic in temperament and method, George S. Kaufman was pronounced to be the "greatest director of his time" by John Steinbeck, whose play *Of Mice and Men* Kaufman staged in 1937. The play represented a dramatic change of pace for the director, who had become known as peerless stager of light comedies with or without music, many of them his own. Before he began his directing career, Kaufman had become a play-doctor and a writer of considerable note. He long resisted impulses to take over the directorial reins. The producer Jed

Harris, possessed of sensitive antennae when it came to talent, recognized Kaufman's latent ability and talked him into directing *The Front Page* by Ben Hecht and Charles MacArthur in 1928. Harris's intuition proved to be flawless, and the success of this first try transformed the playwright into a playwright-director and later into a playwright-director-producer. From 1928 until 1957, only two seasons slipped by on Broadway without a Kaufman-directed play, and they were in the closing years of his career.

Always plagued with self-doubts before and after a play under his direction became a *fait accompli*, Kaufman apparently became the consummate and confident professional while he was actually working on a show, and his good sense led him to place the success or failure of a production where it belonged. "Good plays," he once wrote, in an echo of Arthur Hopkins, "have a way of being well directed." Calmness and consideration for the actors were the hallmarks of his rehearsal techniques. When he had something to say to one of them, he whispered it, and he and the members of his casts addressed each other formally as Mr., Miss, or Mrs. Kaufman tried hard not to give line readings, and he let his actors work out all problems for themselves, gently correcting when he felt that something was wrong. If he did not praise, neither did he scold. He listened for the beat of a script, the inner rhythm, which he tried to sustain throughout. In comedy, where timing is all important, he had the actors underplay and kept the action both economical and on target.

When he began investing money in the plays in which he was involved, he assumed an ever-greater power over the production. He liked to have the sets completed as soon as possible, preferably in time for the second week of rehearsal—and hang the cost! And he was one of the rare directors who revisited his plays after they opened. On returning to *Of Thee I Sing* (1931), he found that William Gaxton, one of its stars, had embellished his role significantly, and promptly sent him a telegram that has become a Broadway legend: "I am watching your performance from the rear of the house. Wish you were here."

Because he was a playwright himself, he never considered the working script inviolate, but once the lines were set, he would not permit the actors to alter a comma. He knew the value of good casting and rarely interfered with an actor or actress whom he knew to be thoroughly professional. When in 1940 he directed Shirley Booth in *My Sister Eileen*, she developed her role in her own way while he watched approvingly. Her co-star, Jo Ann Sayers, had never appeared before on the professional stage, and to cover up her inexperience—painfully apparent to everyone at rehearsals—he gave her bits of business. Jerome Chodorov, one of the playwrights, described Kaufman's technique:

He had her opening ironing boards, taking out the iron, ironing clothes, lifting things, carrying things, cooking, cleaning; she was so damn busy all night long, and she never realized what it was. That was a marvelous way of making an amateur look professional. She had all the personal qualities for the part, a wonderful, fresh innocence, but she really didn't know what to do with her hands or her body. George was the one who solved it.

One of Kaufman's own statements fairly summarizes both his attitude and his approach to directing: "A play is supposed to simulate life, and the best direction is that which is so effortless and natural that it simply isn't noticed at all. Once it begins to call attention to itself, something is wrong."

More than two thousand plays reached Broadway during the 1920s, each of which needed a director. Not surprisingly, directors came from (and returned to) all ranks of the theater. Actors directed; so did designers and producers; and many playwrights either chose to or were asked to direct the products of their imagination. Declaring that "work has no sex," Rachel Crothers agreed with George Bernard Shaw that the playwright was the best director of his own play, "provided," she added, "that the playwright makes it his or her business to learn stagecraft." Some years later, Elmer Rice—who first directed his own play *Street Scene*, and would go on to direct the work of others—would disagree with Crothers's proviso. In an article entitled "The Playwright as Director," he stated that most directors live "too much in a world of their own creation, a sort of self-determined and self-contained microcosm, ruled by the consciousness of kind." On the other hand, the playwright, unsteeped in the world of theater, could approach directing with a tabula rasa. Riding on the crest of his success in *Street Scene*, Rice, in his own amused recollection, "sailed serenely on, profaning I know not what temples, committing I know not what unpardonable sins" of direction.

In 1926 George Abbott directed the productions of his first four plays, and two of them were runaway hits. In 1983 he restaged *On Your Toes*, one of his successes from 1936. Age has not withered him nor staled his infinite variety, and between 1926 and 1983, "Mr. Abbott" has directed four score and more Broadway plays—mostly farces and musicals—many of which he play-doctored, wrote, and produced. His enthusiasm for the theater appears to be unquenchable, but it is not corrupted by sentimentality. To him theater is a business, and his relationships within it in any capacity are

businesslike. His ideas about directing are essentially conventional, but he has consistently put them into practice with such expertness that many critics feel that they can detect his "touch." When he was once asked to define it, Abbott answered that he made the actors pronounce the final syllables of words. Hal Prince once called him the "Calvinist of musical comedy." Since his quite literally Calvinist mother exercised her influence over his conservative, small-town, upstate New York childhood, the description is not far off the mark. Abbott is always punctual, brisk, efficient, economical, and unemotional but not particularly profound, and he expects those qualities in the actors who work for him. In a 1955 Paris production of *The Skin of Our Teeth*, the tables were turned and he was directed in a leading role by Alan Schneider, who was out of a different era and different mold. Schneider made notes for all of the actors, took each aside, and talked privately to them. Abbott's own methods were infinitely more impersonal. When he directed he gave his instructions in front of all of the actors onstage. If he felt an actor was trying to upstage his co-players, he would simply tell him: "Please don't make that move because it hurts so-and-so's effect." The admonition would not only bring the person into line but reinforce the idea that everyone's purpose was to serve the play. Although Abbott was somewhat astonished when Schneider took him aside after the dress rehearsal to tell him that he could not be heard in the auditorium, he did not try to protest, but simply spoke up more loudly and clearly than he had before.

As a director of musicals, Abbott is demanding of his collaborators and expects them to accept his dicta as uncomplainingly as he himself took Schneider's. He threw out so many of the songs written by Mary Rodgers and Marshall Barer for *Once Upon a Mattress* (1959) that they gave him a wastepaper basket papered with them for an opening-night gift. He sees himself as an audience of one; if he is bored, so will be the audience, he thinks. Boredom is the enemy, and Abbott conquers it by keeping the show moving briskly—sometimes to compensate for a lack of logic in the script— by changing the pace, by making the story line clear, by seeing that the dialogue is crackling, by casting to type, and by suffusing the whole with energy. The method has worked for him in the past, and, as a nonagenarian, he continues to practice it.

Jed Harris figured prominently in the careers of Kaufman, Abbott, and many others in the theater. Born in 1900, he was a successful producer by the time he was twenty-six, and everyone had a special name for him, most of them not printable. Noël Coward called him Destiny's Tot, implying, no doubt, that he would go on to a triumphant career as Broadway's leading commercial producer. But Harris chose perversely not to fulfill that particular destiny. Success bored him, and he had the horseplayer's regard for money: it was meant to be put on the next stake. Inevitably, in such a risky business as the theater, too many failures, no matter how noble, put a person out of business. Combined with a studied disregard for fame and money, his wildly eccentric and mercurial behavior, though emanating from a truly brilliant and inventive mentality, was bound to make him more enemies than friends. Both Abbott and Kaufman nurtured a special loathing of Harris despite the fact that he had given them their first employment.

In 1930 Harris decided to become a director, and his choice for a first effort was not one of the fast-paced but lightweight comedies that had become his forte as a producer but a revival of Chekhov's *Uncle Vanya*. He cast Lillian Gish, Walter Connolly, and Osgood Perkins as principals and turned it into a distinguished and memorable production, which paid back an original investment of $9,000 in weeks and played to 200,000 people on the road. Eight years later, Harris finally staged a play that not only gave him new stature but contributed permanently to the literature of the American theater. The play was *Our Town* by Thornton Wilder, who had envisioned it being done, like traditional Chinese dramas, with stylized scenery and props. By the time it reached the out-of-town tryouts, the play had been transformed by Harris into a kind of tone poem of American life, set on a bare stage with the backstage wall radiators in full view, and with simple, evocative elements to serve as the furniture and scenery: a ladder, some stools, a few chairs, and, in the final scene, black umbrellas. It was not typical Broadway fare, and playgoers, though in awe of it, bought tickets and turned it into a success.

At the rehearsals, during which Wilder sat in often unfeigned displeasure at the conduct of the director, Harris worked swiftly to block the action and to instruct the actors gently and quietly in the nuances of their roles. He dredged out of his background all sorts of allusions from literature and art with which he sought to help his cast gain insight in their characterizations. After the first run-through of the play, Wilder was unhappy about Frank Craven's overly sentimental performance as the narrator. Harris explained that the actor had been too busy getting the feel of the stage to act in earnest. At the next rehearsal Craven's performance was flawless, and Wilder was enthusiastic. Harris had whispered something in Craven's ear—what was it? he asked. The director replied, "All I said was, 'Frank, I think that this time you might put away your cello.' "

The stage manager, Edward P. Goodnow, who had never before worked with Harris, initially assumed that the director would be "all temperament and that Wilder would be meek and gentle in the theatre. Both assumptions turned out to be ludicrous. . . . Jed was all coolness and efficiency. He sat in the theatre in Princeton for thirty-eight consecutive hours nibbling on Benzedrine tablets, as he lit the show. Crews of electricians came and went three times while he stayed right on and into opening performance, which he spent backstage."

In 1937 a play that had *not* been offered first to Guthrie McClintic, Jed Harris, or George Abbott was sent to an up-and-coming young director, aged twenty-nine, named Joshua Logan. A relative novice on Broadway, who had begun his career with a talented young group of amateurs who called themselves the University Players, Logan found himself director of *On Borrowed Time*, and his ministrations to the weak script changed it from a probable flop to a real success. Logan's insightful rescue work on scripts was chronicled in his autobiography in profuse detail. Sometimes he received credit for what he did, but often he did not. A leitmotif of the book is the lamentation that a director never gets his full share of the credit for what he does. When he discovered that his contributions to *On Borrowed Time* were ignored by the critics, Logan asked himself:

Why wasn't anyone saying that a discovery had been made, that the theatre had had an amazing stroke of fortune last night when, unannounced and unheralded, a young backwoodsman from Mansfield had blinded the public with his special brand of fireworks? But no one did. In fact, my name appeared in only one review. I decided that I had been paid the highest compliment a theatre director can get. Isn't the final result of a production a knitting together of playwriting, directing and acting? No one element should stand out above the other if it is to be a perfect evening.

That realization would be a consolation, though small, to Logan for the rest of a long and distinguished career.

Although Logan has directed everything from light comedy to serious drama with an even hand and secure professionalism, his name is most often associated with the matured American musical comedy, and particularly with Rodgers and Hammerstein's shows, for it is in handling musicals that he really shines. His technique he feels he learned at the feet of Stanislavsky, with whom he briefly studied on a trip to Moscow during his last year at Princeton. At the time, the great director was staging operas, not plays, and was bringing to them his renowned zeal and inspiration. Logan noticed that Stanislavsky dissolved the formalism of opera by making the arias a natural outgrowth of the action, and he later applied this tactic to musical plays, making each into the emotional peak "of a nervous mood that is started in the dialogue scene preceding the song."

Logan was not the only one in his generation to seek out the great Stanislavsky; the mission to Moscow became *de rigueur* for young Americans interested in the theater during the late 1920s and, more especially, the 1930s, when a decade of unparalleled experimentation was under way. Harold Clurman saw the Moscow Art Theatre productions as a student in Paris before they traveled to America and later, as a small-part actor with the Provincetown Players, he was introduced to the work of Richard Boleslavsky, a Stanislavsky disciple. Those experiences helped to shape Clurman's ideas about the theater, and his association with Lee Strasberg and Stella Adler, both young actors eagerly searching for new and fresh insights, brought him to a state of high excitement that was to create its own channel. The result was the Group Theatre, which was founded by Clurman, Strasberg, and Cheryl Crawford, all working for the Theatre Guild, in 1931. The Guild gave its blessings, and a band of actors and directors assembled, developing their own talents during the next ten years, testing the Stanislavskian principles, formulating their own techniques, finding playwrights to project their own philosophical and political attitudes, and generally producing some of the most stirring and imaginative theater of their generation. Thereafter, Clurman moved into the mainstream of New York's commercial theater as a director and Crawford became a producer. Strasberg continued as the high priest of the Stanislavsky method, eventually dominating the Actors Studio, a workshop founded by Crawford, Robert Lewis, and Elia Kazan in 1947, a few years before Strasberg joined it.

Clurman believed that the Stanislavsky method was never really practiced in the United States, where it had more influence than anywhere else outside Russia. It was a system that flourished where there was time to contemplate, to discover, and to wait upon results during a period of painstaking preparation, analysis, and reexamination. In America, and particularly on Broadway, where time is money and money is synonymous with business and brisk business methods, these ideal conditions could never be achieved. Nonetheless, a modified, Americanized version of Stanislavsky's system opened windows, let in fresh air, and brought about a transformation in both acting and directing.

Clurman, who had a gift for writing, became at once the philosopher-teacher and codifier of the system, or of the Method, as it is known at the Actors Studio. He eventually set the tenets of the Method on paper in his *On Directing*. Interestingly, this book reveals that even Clurman was unable to rely on the Method alone to unloose performance from actors. On one occasion, he experienced great difficulty in eliciting a performance that could be heard beyond the fifth row from a talented but truculent young actor. The use of "affective memory"—an aspect of the Method in which the actor finds in himself the wellspring of the emotion he wishes to portray—

Clurman early recognized the talents of the young Marlon Brando, whom he directed in Truckline Cafe *in 1946. With Brando is Ann Shepherd.*

113

Elia Kazan became the leading exponent of the Method school of directing, probing the depths of each character for every psychological undertone. For more than two decades, from the 1940s to the 1960s, Kazan was offered most of the significant plays on Broadway. In 1959 Sam Norkin, caricaturist for the New York Daily News, *drew director Kazan at rehearsals for* Sweet Bird of Youth.

did not work; nothing worked. Finally, Clurman dismissed all but the young actor from the stage and ordered him to shout his lines. He ordered him to climb a rope hanging from the gridiron above and told him to keep shouting as he climbed. The cast rushed on stage to find out what the commotion was about. The young actor climbed down, and when the rehearsal was resumed he played his scene beautifully. On opening night, according to Clurman, the actor's performance was greeted by a tumultuous ovation. His name was Marlon Brando.

Clurman kept notebooks for himself, which he began before rehearsals and to which he added jottings as the production progressed. In addition to these personal notebooks, he produced detailed working scripts, in which he set down an analysis for each line of dialogue accompanied by the psychological motivations and the physical activities of the actors in their parts. "My working script," Clurman wrote, "is packed with notations for almost every moment of the play, but this does not delude me into believing that the entire direction of a play can be written down or that I, or anybody else, can direct from the written notes alone. The play on the stage is written with and through the actor's being. One works with flesh, blood and spirit much more than with the words one has written or spoken to the actor."

Out of the crucible of the Group Theatre was forged not only a generation of actors but a generation of directors, several of whom, with Clurman, created a Broadway theater dominated by directors in the immediate post–World War II years. One of them, Elia Kazan, has freely admitted his debt to the Group Theatre throughout his life. From Clurman and Strasberg, he learned the Stanislavsky method and he adopted Clurman's method of keeping a private notebook to record his descriptions of characters and subcurrents of the play. Since the Method is actor-oriented, the notebooks of Method directors tend to be deeply analytic of each character's psyche. Kazan has a recognized propensity to cast against type and make it succeed. He calls it spiritual typecasting, attributing it to his ability to intuit a performance in an actor. Known for his interpretations of the texts of Tennessee Williams, for whom he professed a deep spiritual kinship, he several times overrode the playwright's objections to his choice of performer. Because he wanted to work again with Mildred Dunnock, who had played the mother in *Death of a Salesman* so poignantly, he cast her as Big Mama in Williams's *Cat on a Hot Tin Roof* (1955). There is an outward fragility to Dunnock, which the playwright did not visualize for the character, but Kazan knew that the actress would reveal a will of steel in performance. His judgment was correct, and Dunnock played the role brilliantly. For the part of the aging Princess in *Sweet Bird of Youth* (1959), Kazan wanted the young Geraldine Page, and this time even the actress thought she was not right for the role, but under his direction, she was transformed into a believable boozy, decaying Hollywood star and won critical acclaim for her performance. Kazan was also convinced that George M. Cohan would have made a great Willy Loman in *Death of a Salesman*. Kazan's métier is the American realistic play. He admits to having no capacity for directing musicals, and his one attempt at a classic (*The Changeling*) was unsuccessful. His predilection for the plays of Williams and Arthur Miller grew out of his own sympathetic response to the ordinariness of American life, and through the Stanislavsky technique, born of the realistic movement in Europe, he was able to create productions that seemed to throb with honesty. Kazan eventually tired of Broadway. In recent years, he has begun to write novels, but he does not rule out a return to the living theater.

Another graduate of the Group Theatre was Robert Lewis, born the same year as Kazan, in 1909, who joined the company after an apprenticeship with Eva Le Gallienne's Civic Repertory Theatre in the late 1920s. Lewis, as a disciple of the Method, not surprisingly makes the actor the center of the play, but he feels that the technique should be extended to all aspects of the production. In 1957 he delivered eight lectures (later compiled into a book, *Method—or Madness?*), that offered an explanation and a defense of the philosophy and made an attempt to debunk the myths that had grown like a fungus over it. The lectures were witty and erudite and succeeded in throwing much-needed light on the Method's mysterious rites. When in

The Teahouse of the August Moon (1953) was one of Robert Lewis's outstanding successes as a director. The scenery reflected his metaphor for the play's interpretation.

1953 Lewis staged *The Teahouse of the August Moon*, he began, according to accepted Method custom, by framing its theme in the infinitive form:

To "occupy," or force your culture onto anyone is silly—you might get occupied yourself. . . . Now I had to bring out this theme first through all of the theatre elements that would be on the stage. The sets, for example, had to tell that story in their way. They could have just been serviceable or pretty, but then they would not be demonstrating this theme. So we started from the Quonset huts and gradually orientalized them. In the next set we had a bit of an oriental arch which was made of the tail end of a wrecked American plane supported on one side by bamboo poles. Now we could have just had a plain, nice oriental arch which would have served the purpose, but it would not have told this particular story, which was that when this plane had cracked up, the natives had used the remains, and supported it with a bamboo pole. This idea was gradually going to be demonstrated in a deeper sense in the play.

Lewis explained that his assimilation of the Method was so complete that he became unconscious of it while he directed, but that it was there nonetheless feeding his "motor."

The Actors Studio was intended as a place where actors could hone their skills under the direction of Method prophets like Kazan, Lewis, and later Lee Strasberg. In the 1950s some Studio-trained actors developed into directors, and since many directors gratefully assume the role of teacher, the Method became more pervasive than had been foreseen. In 1960 the Studio formally instituted a unit for directors, which has already produced one generation of directors and is training a second.

Between 1948 and 1950, Margaret Webster took to the road in bus and truck to bring her Shakespearean performances to the backwaters of America.

Joseph Anthony represents the first wave. In the mid-1930s he came out of the West and inevitably gravitated toward the Actors Studio. Although he considered himself an actor first, he spent a very busy decade (from 1954 to 1966) directing on Broadway. Like Lewis, he completed his career spreading the Method gospel as a teacher. In 1948 Gene Saks entered the Studio as an actor, and he, too, eventually tried his hand at directing. Producer Morton Gottlieb saw his work, liked his comedic touch, and offered him a play to stage. It was followed by more offers and a call to Hollywood. Saks has found almost steady work directing the plays of Neil Simon.

The actress-manager of the nineteenth century found it hard to be taken seriously as a director, and the situation today is, shockingly, unchanged. Mrs. Fiske was able to direct her own plays, but she was her own producer. Rachel Crothers wrote successful plays and made it clear that her staging came with the package. The talented playwrights who followed her—Sophie Treadwell, Lillian Hellman, Rose Franken, Clare Kummer, and Anne Nichols—were rarely given the opportunity to stage the works of others, despite their obvious talent as directors. Women producers Theresa Helburn and Cheryl Crawford occasionally ventured into staging but they generally hired men to do it for them once they became established. Women's easiest entrée into directing has been stardom. From Fanny Davenport, to Mae West, to Colleen Dewhurst—when a female star has wanted to direct, she has been generally given the opportunity. She has almost always chosen to direct the plays in which she was also the leading lady, but a few stars like Jane Cowl and, more recently, Geraldine Fitzgerald were given a crack at plays in which they did not have an acting role. Today, as in the past, if a woman wants to direct passionately enough, she usually founds her own company or originates her own project so that she can direct it. Success does not guarantee that her phone will immediately ring off the hook with offers for her talents. In 1973, when *The Wager* was moved from the Manhattan Theatre Club into an Off-Broadway theater, the original director, Lynne Meadow, did not go with it. She was replaced by a man, who kept her direction largely intact. Directors Margo Jones, Nina Vance, and Zelda Fichandler carved their careers outside of New York and had to confer upon themselves the grander title of "artistic director" of their theaters to encompass their total contribution.

Women's organizational skills are considered strong enough to run shows backstage but not onstage. Most of the male directors got their start as stage managers, but for women the job apparently has had to serve as an ultimate goal, not an apprenticeship. Men control the theater, and they hesitate to hire women directors, perhaps out of the prejudiced belief that a woman cannot lead or control a cast, cannot obtain the respect of crews and technicians, cannot last the course, and cannot instill the confidence in a male producer that she is competent to protect his and his backers' investment. In recent years, when a woman has been allowed to direct, she has been under intense pressure to come up with a hit since the fate of all womankind appears to be riding on her venture.

Several women in recent history have managed to breach the male bastion directly, without resorting to stratagem, and each did it in her own way. A few years after the death, in 1924, of her wealthy husband, Antoinette Perry decided to resume her career as an actress in New York. She appeared in several Brock Pemberton productions and then realized that acting was not as challenging as assisting the producer in directing the plays. In 1928 Pemberton turned over the directing chores to her. She proved to have a deft touch with comedy and forged a string of successes, culminating with the prizewinning *Harvey* in 1944. She remained Pemberton's partner until her death, in 1947, staging the plays he chose and cast.

Antoinette Perry's wealth gave her financial security; in Brock Pemberton she had a champion as well as an employer; and her background as an actress and natural directorial aptitude supplied her with the necessary tools of the trade—all of which in forceful combination made her able to pursue a career and to achieve a high degree of success as a director. In the case of Margaret Webster, a family history reaching back more than a century in the English theater, solid accomplishment as an actress on both sides of the Atlantic, plus a dual citizenship in the two English-speaking countries became the foundation on which she built a career as a director. According to her own account, Webster drifted into the work of staging plays. "In London," she wrote, "we have many Sunday night performances and plays put on by membership societies, particularly productions which the censor will not pass. I started by directing a little stock company in London and then began to stage larger, more important plays." In 1937 she was asked by the producers Eddie Dowling and Robinson Smith to direct Maurice Evans in Shakespeare's *Richard II* in New York (where she was born in 1905), possibly at the urging of Evans, an old friend. It was an experience that changed her life and deflected her career to the western side of the Atlantic for many years. The play's success prompted other New York producers to offer her plays, some of them "wildly unsuited," she felt, to her talents. In 1937 she wisely resisted directing an "adaptation" of *Antony and Cleopatra* that went on to achieve lasting theatrical distinction as the production in which Tallulah Bankhead barged down the Nile and sank.

Having become renowned as an interpreter of Shakespeare, Webster continued to direct a succession of the Bard's plays, each a memorable event. In 1945, with Eva Le Gallienne and Cheryl Crawford, she established the American Repertory Theatre; chose plays by Shakespeare, Shaw, Ibsen, O'Casey, J. M. Barrie, and Sidney Howard; selected a company; and rented a Broadway auditorium to introduce the first of their productions the following year. Unfortunately, the shows were not a critical success and the costly dream expired in 1948. Out of the ruins, however, emerged the Margaret Webster Shakespeare Company, which traveled the length and breadth of the land in bus and truck to bring live theater to communities that had not seen a professional theater company in thirty-five years. Unfortunately, in 1950 the Marweb Company, too, ran dry of money and passed out of existence.

Still struggling to come into their own on Broadway, women directors have learned to create their own opportunities removed from the auditors' reports and box-office computer printouts of "show business." In 1967 Vinnette Carroll founded the nonprofit Urban Arts Corps and sent black and Puerto Rican youths into ghetto communities to bring minority audiences programs of songs, plays, and poetry readings. The following year, she expanded her activities to include producing Off-Broadway plays on a year-round basis. Although she was educated as a clinical psychologist, Carroll eventually found her true vocation in the theater and became a successful actress, before turning her attention to a special kind of directing. "When I started out, there were no black women directors because there were almost no black playwrights and no black theater to speak of. Now we are getting the playwrights and everything else is bound to follow." Her own method is to "start a play" with an idea or a scene and some music. She then brings in actors and has them improvise on the idea. Micki Grant, a young playwright with the group, described handing the director a show with neither book nor concept and watching her glue it together into a production entitled *Don't Bother Me, I Can't Cope*, which made its way to Broadway in 1972. In the same way, Carroll has brought into existence *But Never Jam Today* (1969), an adaptation of *Alice in Wonderland*, and *Your Arms Too Short to Box with God* (1975), a dazzling "Gospel" version of the Bible. She has a reputation for being a driving force as well as the earth mother of her troupe, and she feels that she has found her mission. "We are bringing to the legitimate stage the sound of black music, soul music, which is far more visceral and not as intellectual as the sound of Broadway." In so doing, she has brought the cause of the woman director a long way.

Harold Prince put himself through a rigorous and practical apprenticeship in his evolution as a director at the feet of George Abbott, whose office he entered in 1948, when he was twenty. Having performed all of the menial backstage jobs from messenger to switchboard operator, he moved on into stage management, becoming a "boy wonder" at twenty-six, when he co-produced his first show, and again at thirty-four, when he directed his first show—the former a hit, the latter a flop. No slavish imitator of Abbott, Prince developed his own style and assembled his own store of

Harold "Hal" Prince learned the art of play production before he became a director. Sometimes he performs both chores. In this photograph, taken at a rehearsal of Merrily We Roll Along *(1981), he is coaxing performances from the young cast. Left to right: James Weissenbach, Ann Morrison, Prince, and Lonny Price.*

techniques. In his book *Contradictions*, he described his usual prerehearsal procedure:

My scripts are a mess by the first day of rehearsal. Covered in squiggles, they document better than anything the changes in tone and detail that inform a project. . . . Perhaps I'll see someone in a restaurant and I'll draw a picture of the hat she wore or tear out an illustration from a magazine. Collecting things on the way to rehearsal, and more and more striking them out with a red pencil, or writing 'No!' meaning awful idea, inconsistent, or no longer valid. I don't have the self-discipline to cram for a play, cram atmosphere, cram character, delve microscopically into each speech to see what the subtext is. Instead, I take my time, and everything collects inside, where I can call on it instinctively.

Prince's technique serves as an accurate metaphor for his maturation as a director. Collecting is his native instinct. At Moscow's Taganka Theatre, he saw a production that gave him the inspiration for the staging of *Cabaret* (1966). At a bouzouki restaurant near Piraeus, he got the idea for handling a group of musicians for *Zorba* (1968). All the filings and shavings of his experiences are placed in mental storage to be summoned up when he needs them.

The route that Hal Prince took to become a director was safe and sane, and it remains the road most heavily traveled by aspiring directors. Polishing the handles of the big front doors of directors and producers may not be glamorous but it can lead to jobs in stage managing. From there the goal is plainly in sight, and accumulated experience and wisdom plus a lucky break can turn a stage manager into a director. What is unusual about Prince's entry into the ranks is that he never aspired to be an actor. Guthrie McClintic's career—from frustrated actor to stage manager to director—represents the more common progression, yesterday and today. But in the case of Mike Nichols the withdrawal from performing was voluntary and the turn to directing was natural for a fertile and inventive theatrical mind. For eight years, Nichols and Elaine May diverted nightclub, television, and, ultimately, theater audiences with their witty, trenchant, and antic animadversions on the social scene in America. In 1961, before he and May went stale, they called it a career and traveled their separate ways. Nichols's first call to directing was fortuitous: in 1963 he was given Neil Simon's *Barefoot in the Park* to stage. The combination of Simon's infectious humor and Nichols's sense of the absurd resulted in a hit that had numerous reverberations on the professional and amateur stages and in motion pictures. Nichols and Simon collaborated in several more successful comedies.

Although he is most often associated with comedy, Nichols has also directed serious plays by such diverse writers as Chekhov, Hellman, and David Rabe. In Nichols's productions there always occurs a moment, sometimes several, when the audience is caught off guard by a swift and incisive physical action that speaks louder than words. Elia Kazan, whom Nichols admires, has called it "turning psychology into behavior." In David Rabe's play *Streamers* (1976), it became necessary to convey the idea that one of the characters wanted his roommate to leave so that he could make love to a homosexual friend. "I wanted to express physically," stated Nichols, "what was going on in their minds, and the solution was to have Richie and Carlyle [the two lovers] start playing an erotic game of footsie with each other." Although these moments pass so quickly that their effect is almost subliminal, they provide a depth of detail and nervous energy that give a subtle richness to a Nichols-directed production.

In 1950, a small group of avid amateurs rented an abandoned nightclub on Sheridan Square in Manhattan's Greenwich Village, raised barely enough capital to set up shop, divided responsibilities, and began producing plays early the following year. Because of the configuration of the nightclub space their stage was three-sided, and they called the venture Circle in the Square. One of the group, José Quintero, became the director by default. Born in Panama in 1924, he had been sent by his family to the States to study medicine but was attracted to the theater, spent a year at the Goodman Theatre School in Chicago studying acting, and came to New York at the suggestion of a friend, Emily Stevens, who like him was to be one of the founders of Circle in the Square. Experience gained both within and outside the theater was Quintero's school for directing. He explained in his autobiography:

Whatever I knew about "directing technique" had found its way to me through people. Most of them had no direct connection with the Circle in the Square or with myself as a director. I believe you learn by being susceptible. You learn about phrasing by being vulnerable to Bessie Smith and old Louis Armstrong and the Bronx-accented telephone operator who tries to sound like Gloria Vanderbilt or Dina Merrill but falls back on her Bronx cadences after a few minutes. Posture, movement, phrasing, speech patterns, you learn all this not only by being vulnerable to everyone you meet, but also by injecting yourself like a guinea pig with the essence of these people.

His production of *Summer and Smoke* in 1952 catapulted Quintero to prominence, and his rapid ascent was given further impetus by his revival of *The Iceman Cometh* in 1956. One of his partners suggested that he direct an O'Neill play, and Carlotta O'Neill, who jealously guarded the playwright's reputation and did not often permit his works to be performed, was charmed by Quintero at their first meeting and acquiesced. The success of the revival prompted her to offer the young director the American premiere of O'Neill's masterwork, and Quintero went on to direct a series of O'Neill plays during the next ten years.

Quintero approached *Long Day's Journey into Night* with a mystical reverence. He wanted it to be the perfect production and selected its cast and his collaborators with infinite care. With Tharon Musser, the lighting director, he held long discussions to try to evoke the atmosphere he wanted to create. The night, he said to Musser, "must have a feeling of a never-ending tunnel that goes deeper and deeper for forever." He wanted the fog to press against the windows and intrude into the room through cracks around them. For the fourth act he asked for a special atmosphere:

You understand . . . that we will have to jail Edmund and his father under a tiny pool of warm light that comes from the electrical bulb from the old dingy chandelier above the table. We have to obliterate all of the familiar objects, sofa, chairs, pictures, posters, vases. In short, deny them access to any props which would remind them of the preconceived relationship of father and son. They are two fighters in a tiny arena. With the dark and the fog pressing in; nailed by the distorted footsteps of the mother, wife, coming from upstairs.

Re-creating the experience in his own mind as he wrote his autobiography, Quintero recounted imaginary conversations with his designers:

And, David, don't forget, think about it—the center table has to be oval. After all, they're

Alan Schneider became the director of choice for Samuel Beckett's plays in the United States. He is shown here (wearing his "lucky cap") directing P. J. Kelly in Endgame (1958).

fighting hard, wounding each other to the point of death, only to achieve the impossible, a wound clean, a scar-clear embrace. They are what they are—two defeated lovers fighting for the last chance. Yes, David, it must be oval. Don't you ever think of oval as a complete embrace?

Quintero's technique, if that is what it can be called, consists in seeking mystical and poetic metaphors rather than psychological motivations for the dramatic action. He has become the primary exponent of O'Neill because he has felt attuned to the playwright's dramatic world of reality fused with unreality. Like O'Neill, he finds poetry in the commonplace, which he views as a thin surface over fantasy; as a director, he has had to develop his own language with actors so that they can release themselves willingly into the fragile world of the play. In rehearsal, he gives the actors an enormous amount of latitude as they work into their roles and he suffers along with them. He does not so much direct as embrace all of the human and nonhuman elements of a play—a process that has tended to deplete him spiritually and has led to personal and emotional difficulties. Recently Quintero has been able to renew himself psychologically, and he remains an active director and teacher.

Quintero directs from the dark center of his soul, but Alan Schneider directed from the mind. He occasionally wrote of the role of the director as he saw it, at times personalizing the definition. "The significant function of the director is to serve the playwright. That's why I veer toward Beckett, Pinter and Brecht. I don't want to spend valuable time dressing up inferior products. I'm not a play-doctor or a cheap popularizer or a prankster." Schneider, who was born in 1917 and died in 1984, came from the university campus and regional theater. For many years his geographical and spiritual home was Washington, D.C.—at the Arena Stage and Catholic University. Ranging the country, he taught and directed in every kind of theater, from large open rooms to traditional prosceniums. Consequently he staged every kind of play, but because he was happier conceiving ideas than reacting emotionally to those of others, Schneider made it his special challenge to bring to life nonrealistic plays of obscure meaning and hidden symbols. The characters in the plays of Beckett, Pinter, and Albee frequently lack a past or present and usually have only an ambiguous future. They are reduced to embodied ideas, which nevertheless have to be given a theatrical presence. There is always the danger that the audience will not understand these plays and, more important, that actors, particularly Americans trained in the Method school, cannot comprehend the characters well enough to act them. A Beckett or a Pinter play needs a director who can slice through the non sequiturs to reach the core and then express it to the actors. In 1956 Schneider took his first plunge into avant-garde drama, the premiere production in America of Beckett's *Waiting for Godot*. The stars were Bert Lahr and Tom Ewell, and the rehearsals became a nightmare for everyone. With his rubber face and burlesque tricks, Lahr not only could not comprehend the character he was to play but became increasingly more hostile to Schneider's methods and his intellectualizing. Instead of tearing down walls, Schneider created new ones between the play and the actor and between himself and the actor. Only occasionally could he penetrate Lahr's defenses and spring his dramatic genius. Lahr had difficulty in learning his part because he saw little meaning in it. During one rehearsal, after he had stumbled over the lines in a scene of quick repartee with Ewell, Schneider said to him, "Bert, that's a ping-pong game." That seemed to strike a chord and Lahr jumped into the scene with new understanding. Although the production was not a success, Schneider had gained important directorial insights. Several years later, Schneider recorded the conclusions he had drawn, which were to serve him in other productions and in the end reward him with success. "But I have long ago discovered that the director's function is not so much to explain the author's meaning to his actors—whose problems of expressing that meaning to the audience is not necessarily helped by intellectually understanding it—but to see that, through whatever theatrical means, the actors are led to *do* those things which will *result* in the author's meaning being expressed."

Like Schneider, Adrian Hall put down his roots in regional theater where, unlike Schneider, he preferred to remain. After spending ten years directing plays around the country and off Broadway, in 1965 he was invited to become director of the newly organized Trinity Square Repertory Theatre in Providence, Rhode Island. There he has directed a profusion of plays from classic to avant-garde, an opportunity that is available to few directors of commercial theater. He sees Trinity Square as serving the community, not as a conduit of talent for New York. Today the company, housed in a made-over vaudeville house in the center of the city, utilizes two experimental theaters, one with a thrust stage and the other with an interior that can accommodate different kinds of staging. Sensitive to the tastes of his audience, Hall routinely schedules and directs Broadway warhorses (*Arsenic and Old Lace*) and crowd-pleasers (*A Christmas Carol*), but he also takes flight into unusual plays and free adaptations of standard ones. A few years ago, he revived *Inherit the Wind,* a fictionalized reworking of the landmark Scopes trial, in which William Jennings Bryan locked horns with Clarence Darrow over the Darwinian theory of evolution. Although the play seemed outrageously dated, Hall found a way to relate its message to a then-current political issue in California: whether the biblical story of creation had a place in the educational curriculum. By freely cutting chunks of dialogue, removing the love story, changing the ending, and interpolating a prologue that included an actual recorded interview with President Reagan, television clips, and other theatrical surprises, Hall gave the play an unexpected afterlife, which he felt was entirely justified. In his program notes for the production, he asked, "Why can't plays and play production be standardized like an auto assembly line? The answer of course is because the elements that constitute the theatre experience: the text, the production values and the audience are all altered by time. And the theatre event always occurs *right now!* That's why a popular play of the 1930s can't be viewed in the same way today as it was then; time has changed the meaning of the text, the production values are not the same but what has been most changed, of course, is the audience!" Away from the battlegrounds of Broadway, Hall is free from time to time to indulge his fancy and create spirited, unorthodox productions for a tolerant audience.

Today's generation of directors moves easily from Broadway to regional theater to films or television and to Off Broadway, completing a full circle. Arthur Penn got his first job in television production and moved into TV directing before his Broadway career began in 1958 with *Two for the Seesaw.* His artistic home is now the Berkshire Theatre Festival in Stockbridge, Massachusetts, and his career calls him more often to Hollywood than to Broadway. Another Method director, Ulu Grosbard reversed the usual procedure by taking a crack at movie directing before making a New York debut, but his first recognition came in 1962 from his staging of an Off-Broadway production, *The Days and Nights of Beebee Fenstermaker.* He has fulfilled his first ambition by directing movies as well as television programs. Wilford Leach is now the principal director of Joseph Papp's New York Shakespeare Festival. Like Adrian Hall, he has the luxury of working within the sheltering arms of an endowed and established theatrical enterprise, some forty blocks south of the organized chaos of New York's theater district, and in relative calm he can reshape classic plays into thought-provoking theatrical events.

Consciously and unconsciously, American directors have selected from the styles, ideas, and methods of European directors as different as Russia's Stanislavsky and England's Peter Brook what could be of use to them. Although they have not created a distinctly American school, with eclecticism and Yankee pragmatism they have tackled every type of play, modern and classic, and come up with workable, sometimes brilliant solutions. Theirs has been a history of solid achievement, if not innovation. The only area where American directors have uniquely excelled and can claim a special dominance is in the staging of musicals. Their spectacular rise in this field has occurred in less than fifty years, following on the heels of an unprecedented interest, bordering on a rage, in serious dance in America. Today theatrical dancing and concert dancing exist in happy symbiosis, with choreographers and dancers moving readily between the two worlds. The importance of theatrical dancing has escalated, and what was once merely a component of musical entertainments has become, on occasion, the structural mainstay for a production's book and songs.

Dance is not new on the American stage. Many of the early English troupers were dancers as well as actors and they might appear between acts to do a hornpipe or an Irish jig. During the early nineteenth century, ballet dancers and troupes from Europe began to arrive regularly in American theaters, where they performed alone, as an exotic delight, separate from any dramatic production. There were also occasional native outcroppings of theatrical dance. John Durang, whom we may call the first native dancer-choreographer on the American stage, developed a kind of native harlequinade, or danced pantomime, on American themes during the last quarter of the eighteenth century. In 1828 T. D. Rice came out in burnt-cork makeup between the acts of a play in the Southern Theatre in Louisville, Kentucky, and did a little shuffling dance while he sang a song, which he said he had picked up from a Negro stableman. At the end of each verse, he did a comic jump or "hitch" to the words "I jump Jim Crow," thus earning himself a place in American theatrical history and coincidentally contributing a term to American idiom. In the early 1840s, a group of men calling themselves the Virginia Minstrels staged in New York the prototype of what became the minstrel show: white men in blackface singing and dancing "Ethiopian" divertissements. They performed jigs, polkas, flings, quadrilles, galops, and what they called plantation dances, which probably bore as strong a resemblance to European as to African antecedents. When the national mania for the minstrel show began to subside in the 1860s, that entertainment was replaced by the variety show, a succession of song-and-dance acts. Neatly deodorized and desexed in the 1880s by Tony Pastor, a music-hall performer himself, it became for a while a national institution called vaudeville. But vaudeville was not a unified entertainment, and musical comedy was not its direct descendant.

An event in 1866 established dance as the natural complement of the musical play. Its genesis was accidental but fortunate. The New York theatrical entrepreneurs Jarrett and Palmer had assembled a large troupe of European dancers under the leadership of the Italian ballet master David Costa, intending to present them in a lavish ballet, *La Biche au Bois*, at the Academy of Music on Fourteenth Street. Practically on the eve of the presentation, the Academy burned down. William Wheatley, the manager of the popular Niblo's Garden theater, conceived the idea of incorporating the troupe, scenery, and costumes into a script in his possession entitled *The Black Crook*. The result was a music and dance extravaganza the likes of which New York had never seen. Costa crowded the stage with thirty ballerinas and fifty "Auxiliary Ladies" from Europe, who became the talk of the town, not because of their skillful dancing but by virtue of their scanty costumes and apparently bare legs. The play was overpowered by the ballet, and it cannot be said that the dancing was fully integrated into the plot or advanced the action, but *The Black Crook* set the foundations for musical comedy, which forevermore included dancing as an important component.

When in 1868, Lydia Thompson arrived in New York with her bevy of buxom, broad-hipped ladies, the public turned its attention to another type of girly show. Though her pantomimes never caught on in America, Thompson's burlesques—light musical satires in which the accent was on the comedy, songs, and dances—were immensely popular. They stimulated a small industry within the entertainment world. Scores of troupes with different headliners were assembled by other theatrical promoters and sent all over North and South America. Undoubtedly, the beefy chorines dressed in tights were the principal attraction of the shows, but several troupes, with Thompson's heading the list, featured artful solo and ensemble dancing. (After describing in careful detail the figure and limbs of a performer in Thompson's burlesque of *Robinson Crusoe*, a critic noted, "In the second act, [Miss Chapman] gave a song-and-dance entitled 'Some Girls Do,' during which her clog-dancing created a furor and she was recalled time and again, until she was compelled from sheer exhaustion to decline repeating her dance.") Each in his own way, David Costa and

Lydia Thompson contributed to the rise of the chorus line as a dazzlingly successful fixture of later musical comedy.

An American producer, George Lederer, gave a significant push to theatrical dancing when he created the prototype of the revue in 1894. His presentation, entitled *The Passing Show,* was a mixture of songs, dances, and comedy sketches, held together by a thread of commentary on the previous theatrical season and current political and social events. In 1900 Lederer imported from England a line of precision dancers trained by John Tiller for the American operetta *The Casino Girl.* Tiller appears to have begun his career in the 1880s in England as the stager of church pageants that became renowned for the precision of their drills and marches. He later moved into dance, opening up a school first in London, then in New York. By adding a few kicks and tap steps, by standardizing the height of the dancers, and by putting them all through rigorous training, he created chorus lines of from twelve to twenty performers that could be inserted easily into any type of theatrical musical entertainment. Tiller claimed to have invented the "pony ballet," a dance number in which petite girls performed a routine imitating horses. Lederer used it in *The Casino*

David Rabe's Streamers (1976) made its way to Broadway from the Long Wharf Theatre in Connecticut under the direction of Mike Nichols. Choosing a predominantly young and unknown cast, Nichols gave the play a fresh, inventive touch, turning inner thoughts into action whenever he could. The original Long Wharf cast included (left to right): Peter Evans, John Heard, Joe Fields, and Herbert Jefferson, Jr.

Opposite above:
Many of the younger generation of directors have struck out for the provinces. By moving his sphere of activities from New York to the Trinity Square Repertory Theatre in Providence, Rhode Island, Adrian Hall has been able to intersperse popular offerings with experimental productions such as a reworked version of Inherit the Wind *for the 1980–81 season.*

Opposite below:
The large cast of Joseph Papp's 1985 hit, The Mystery of Edwin Drood, *was brilliantly directed by Wilford Leach. Leach, who is principal director of the New York Shakespeare Festival, has staged fifteen productions to date for Papp, and they include not only Shakespearean offerings and musicals but avant-garde dramas as well.*

Frequently associated with Florenz Ziegfeld was Ned Wayburn, who had an entrepreneurial instinct of his own and produced and directed his own shows while establishing a school for dancers. In this photograph of 1915, he is showing a neophyte how simple are the steps to a routine in Town Topics.

Right:
Julian Mitchell was Florenz Ziegfeld's favorite director, but he worked for other producers as well. He is shown here instructing the chorus in an unidentified production.

Girl and it became the rage on both continents. The term "pony" still refers to chorus girls, although it is in vogue more on the English than on the American stage.

The Tiller Girls became a fixture in New York and never failed to please the crowd in the revues and shows of Florenz Ziegfeld and Charles B. Dillingham. By 1927 there were seven hundred Tiller-trained girls throughout the world, such was their success. Their triumph immediately sparked American imitations, and each dance director made a personal and innovative contribution to the precision routines. The Tiller technique lives on today in the dancing of Radio City Music Hall's Rockettes, the creation of Russell E. Markert. When Markert retired in 1971, a few months short of his seventy-second birthday, he recalled that his original inspiration for the Rockettes came from the Tiller Girls, whom he had seen in the Ziegfeld *Follies* of 1922. The durability of the high-kicking precision line is attested by its continued presence in such recent presentations as *La Cage aux Folles,* introduced in the 1983–84 season on Broadway. It simply refuses to become a cliché.

The revues and musicals of the 1900–1930 era were filled to overflowing with dancing choruses, and it was no mean feat to get the small armies of performers on and off the stage. The job fell to someone halfway between director and choreographer, who functioned like a general marshaling his troops to music in dance routines. Julian Mitchell began working for producer Florenz Ziegfeld in his pre-*Follies* days and remained to stage thirteen of the nineteen popular revues. When he began to lose his hearing, Mitchell, a dancer and comedian, turned to directing and found his true vocation. Small and dapper, he was adored by his casts from star to lowly chorine and was respected by Ziegfeld and the other producers for whom he worked. He was a master of the comic touch and contributed bits of choreographed drollery to the farces of Charles Hoyt and the burlesques of Weber and Fields. He kept productions moving at a rapid clip and was especially renowned for the routines he devised for the chorus girls.

Despite his deafness, he was able to choreograph by putting his ear to the piano and getting the beat of the music. His disability often created funny moments. Hazel Dawn remembered that a thunderstorm once broke outside the theater where he and the dancers were rehearsing. Dimly hearing the noise of the storm, he asked with some irritation, "Why are you girls shuffling your feet?"

Another of Ziegfeld's directors, Ned Wayburn, staged in his lifetime more than six hundred musical comedies, plays, revues, pantomimes, and dancing-school shows. A big bear of a man, he conducted his rehearsals in an old gray sweater, wearing a whistle around his neck, which he blew to get the attention of the multitude of performers under his command. Wayburn, who had trained in vaudeville as well as worked for his father as a mechanical draftsman, used mathematics to attain precision in his chorus lines. He worked with the number eight and multiples thereof, based on the musical scale. Dividing the stage into eight areas, he built up routines out of simple, basic steps, which he used in various permutations. Like a drill instructor, he put the "ponies" through their paces until they were motion perfect. He made each one learn the steps verbally so that she could "practice" them mentally anywhere. Patient and methodical, he came up each year with hundreds of fresh and different routines for the musicals and revues he directed. The actor Eddie Dowling, who was in the *Follies* of 1919, recalled one of Wayburn's typical scenes. Dressed as a French chef, Dowling had tossed a salad in an enormous papier-mâché salad bowl, singing: "Oooh, zee salade, how you make zee salade, first you take zee peppaire and zee salt . . . " and, as he named them, out of the bowl would step a succession of showgirls dressed up as different ingredients.

In the 1920s two talented ballet choreographers, Albertina Rasch and Chester Hale, founded precision-trained troupes like Tiller's and similar schools to replenish them. (The term *choreographer*, borrowed from ballet, did not replace *dance director* on Broadway and in Hollywood until Russian-trained George Balanchine began to compose dances for musical comedies and films in the mid-1930s.) Rasch, born in Vienna in 1896, and trained as a ballerina at the Royal Opera House School of Ballet, was brought to America at the age of sixteen to dance at the New York Hippodrome, then under the management of R. H. Burnside. After dancing for several years on the concert and vaudeville stage, in the early 1920s she decided to open a school in New York. Out of the school came the Albertina Rasch Dancers, who were sent throughout the country to perform in the presentation houses— theaters combining short vaudeville programs with movies. In 1925 she choreographed *George White's Scandals*, and for the next twenty years she shuttled between Broadway and Hollywood, where she was dance director for MGM. (Her husband, Dmitri Tiomkin, worked as a composer for the same studio and supplied ballet music for her to choreograph.) Rasch used Tiller's rigorous methods to train ballet dancers and to create precision-ballet routines to the music of revues and musical comedies, but in her later work she employed a freer, more eclectic repertoire of dance styles. She was responsible for the memorable choreography for Cole Porter's "Begin the Beguine"—a principal song in *Jubilee* (1935)—giving it an interesting East Indian flavor. Her last notable choreography on Broadway was for the 1943 musical *Lady in the Dark*, in which she followed the trend established by Agnes de Mille toward integrating the dancing with the script.

Like Rasch, Chester Hale started out in ballet, and he had the distinction of working with Nijinsky and the Diaghilev Ballet Russe before turning to vaudeville and the Broadway stage. A year after Rasch launched her dancing troupes, Hale trained and organized the Chester Hale Girls, and by 1930 twenty-two of his companies were dancing throughout America and in Europe. He, too, worked for a chain of movie theaters before staging his first dances for Broadway musicals and revues. Hale was quick to adapt to changes in taste in theatrical dancing, adding jazz-tap, modern, Spanish, and character dancing to classical ballet. "Musical comedy is a land of make-believe, and musical comedy dancing is make-believe, too," he once remarked. Most of the dances he created for a show had nothing to do with the plot, being interpolated as dance for entertainment's sake. One of his famous specialty numbers was the "Under the Sea" ballet for *Delmar's Revels* (1927), which contained a choreographed battle between an octopus and the hero over the life of a maiden and ended with a striking tableau of marine maidens dancing around the bleeding octopus. It stopped the show every time it was performed. Hale ended his career in 1960, after several years of choreographing ice shows.

For a while, tap dancing became the staple of Broadway choreography. Akin to English and Irish clog dancing, which was performed with wooden-soled shoes, the tap dance evolved from minstrel-show "step dancing," which was loosely derived from

Pictured here is Albertina Rasch, who put dancers on their toes, trained them in precision routines, and sent them out in troupes to perform in theaters where live shows alternated with movies. She choreographed Cole Porter's "Begin the Beguine" in Jubilee *(1935).*

Sammy Lee's energetic choreography for No, No, Nanette *in 1925 helped to make it one of the biggest musical successes of the 1920s.*

the plantation dances of Southern slaves. When the shoes of the step dancers were equipped with metal plates, the evolution was complete. The accent was always on footwork and the number of sounds that could be rapidly produced by the dancing feet. Bill "Bojangles" Robinson elevated tap dancing to a high art during the 1930s, the peak of its popularity. Schools to train tap dancers sprang up like weeds throughout the country and untold numbers of children were hustled off to a weekly dance lesson, to prepare them for the bright lights of Broadway.

The specialty created its share of talented choreographers, most of whom, like Busby Berkeley, were inevitably ensnared by the lures of Hollywood in the early 1930s. Among the most innovative and inventive were Sammy Lee and Robert Alton, who came from different backgrounds and left their distinctive stamp on theatrical dance. Lee was a product of the Lower East Side in New York and claimed to have had no formal dance training. As a child he was picked out by Gus Edwards from an amateur vaudeville show on the Bowery to become a member of the "School Days" vaudeville act, which graduated the likes of George Jessel, Eddie Cantor, Groucho Marx, Bert Wheeler, and many others into show business. After dancing from 1912 to 1922, Lee turned to choreography and staged the dances for three Gershwin shows in the 1920s. The high point of his career was his work for *No, No Nanette* in 1925 and *Show Boat* two years later. His choreography transcended the footwork of tap dancing and involved the entire body in fast, complicated, and exuberant routines, which bordered on the violent. An observer compared Lee's dancing artistry to the poetry of Walt Whitman and the music of George Gershwin.

When modern dancing and ballet were beginning to compete with tap dancing during the 1930s, Robert Alton made it contemporary by injecting bits of both into the tap-dance idiom. Trained in ballet, Alton had few illusions about his job in designing theatrical dance. He once said: "I am a commercial man. I have exactly six minutes in which to raise the customer out of his seat. If I cannot do it, I am no good." His career extended from 1933 to 1955, and he often choreographed four to five shows a season. His method was to come to rehearsals without preparation and to work out the routines with the performers. His dances for the 1940 production of *Pal Joey*, generally thought to be ahead of their time, echoed the tawdriness of the setting and the realism of the script. Dance critic John Martin thought the dances were so perfectly unified with the dramatic action that the book could not have existed

Frequently associated with Florenz Ziegfeld was Ned Wayburn, who had an entrepreneurial instinct of his own and produced and directed his own shows while establishing a school for dancers. In this photograph of 1915, he is showing a neophyte how simple are the steps to a routine in Town Topics.

Right:
Julian Mitchell was Florenz Ziegfeld's favorite director, but he worked for other producers as well. He is shown here instructing the chorus in an unidentified production.

Girl and it became the rage on both continents. The term "pony" still refers to chorus girls, although it is in vogue more on the English than on the American stage.

The Tiller Girls became a fixture in New York and never failed to please the crowd in the revues and shows of Florenz Ziegfeld and Charles B. Dillingham. By 1927 there were seven hundred Tiller-trained girls throughout the world, such was their success. Their triumph immediately sparked American imitations, and each dance director made a personal and innovative contribution to the precision routines. The Tiller technique lives on today in the dancing of Radio City Music Hall's Rockettes, the creation of Russell E. Markert. When Markert retired in 1971, a few months short of his seventy-second birthday, he recalled that his original inspiration for the Rockettes came from the Tiller Girls, whom he had seen in the Ziegfeld *Follies* of 1922. The durability of the high-kicking precision line is attested by its continued presence in such recent presentations as *La Cage aux Folles,* introduced in the 1983–84 season on Broadway. It simply refuses to become a cliché.

The revues and musicals of the 1900–1930 era were filled to overflowing with dancing choruses, and it was no mean feat to get the small armies of performers on and off the stage. The job fell to someone halfway between director and choreographer, who functioned like a general marshaling his troops to music in dance routines. Julian Mitchell began working for producer Florenz Ziegfeld in his pre-*Follies* days and remained to stage thirteen of the nineteen popular revues. When he began to lose his hearing, Mitchell, a dancer and comedian, turned to directing and found his true vocation. Small and dapper, he was adored by his casts from star to lowly chorine and was respected by Ziegfeld and the other producers for whom he worked. He was a master of the comic touch and contributed bits of choreographed drollery to the farces of Charles Hoyt and the burlesques of Weber and Fields. He kept productions moving at a rapid clip and was especially renowned for the routines he devised for the chorus girls.

Despite his deafness, he was able to choreograph by putting his ear to the piano and getting the beat of the music. His disability often created funny moments. Hazel Dawn remembered that a thunderstorm once broke outside the theater where he and the dancers were rehearsing. Dimly hearing the noise of the storm, he asked with some irritation, "Why are you girls shuffling your feet?"

Another of Ziegfeld's directors, Ned Wayburn, staged in his lifetime more than six hundred musical comedies, plays, revues, pantomimes, and dancing-school shows. A big bear of a man, he conducted his rehearsals in an old gray sweater, wearing a whistle around his neck, which he blew to get the attention of the multitude of

without them. When the show was revived in 1952, Alton was again the choreographer, but in the intervening years audiences had matured to the point where they could accept an unfunny musical comedy. His "dream" number, in which Joey describes the kind of nightclub he would like to own, mocked brilliantly the standard 1930s musical-comedy choreography: tap dancing, the precision chorus line, the parading chorus, and the ballroom dancing. Alton always returned to the tap dance but he added embellishments as crowd-pleasers. His work was consistently characterized by an ability to work within the confinements of the script, however banal.

As a young man, Oscar Hammerstein II stage-managed his uncle Arthur Hammerstein's musicals. Part of his responsibility was to rehearse the replacements in the chorus. As he recalled, "There were no steps in our dance routines too difficult for me to teach to the newcomers. I had had no training as a dancer. I was twenty-three and normally limber, nimble and rhythmic. That was all you had to be." That was in 1918, when the only purpose of the dance number was to stop the show. In the 1920s the steps became more intricate but the purpose remained the same. No one had yet conceived the idea of integrating the dance with the characters and the action because it was impossible in the prevailing styles of theatrical dance to express ideas and emotions through pure movement. Modern dance had the inherent potential to add a new dimension to theatrical dancing, but its influence was not felt significantly for some time. In the 1930s, the pioneers of the modern-dance movement, Martha Graham, Charles Weidman and Doris Humphrey, Hanya Holm, Jack Cole, and Helen Tamiris, were deeply engrossed in searching to find their own styles and personal idioms, and most of them were not comfortable on the musical-comedy stage either as dancers or choreographers. But as their decade of experimentation drew to a close and their presence could not be ignored, more and more producers urged them to create dances that would enhance and enrich the books of musicals. During the early 1940s, the signal success of two luminaries from the ballet world, George Balanchine and Agnes de Mille, expanded the influence of the choreographer. Soon, Helen Tamiris felt, the necessary and inevitable step would have to be made: the author of the book would conceive of certain scenes in his story in terms of dance, or, if that were not part of his talent, the choreographer would be brought into the collaboration while the project was still in its thinking stages.

When modern dance entered the theater, the nature of stage dancing was

Modern dance inevitably made its way to the Broadway stage. This Edward Steichen photograph of "The Shakers," a dance number by Charles Weidman and Doris Humphrey in Americana, appeared in Vanity Fair early in 1933, a few months after the Shubert revue opened.

In this photograph, dancer-choreographer Jack Cole appears to be defying gravity as he leaps into the air. His exuberant choreography, sparked with ethnic and balletic movements, was dazzling and innovative.

irrevocably altered. No longer did it merely decorate a show. It became an integral part of the fabric of the production, with each episode arising as the natural thing for the characters to do at a particular moment in the action. To achieve this effect, the choreographer had to find the right music to accompany the dancing and open up the stage to accommodate the dancers. Most important of all, the dancers must have been trained not only in ballet and tap but in modern-dance idioms as well.

The contribution to musical-comedy dancing by the early modern-dance choreographers can be measured not so much in terms of individual achievement as in combined impact, for only Helen Tamiris, Jack Cole, and Hanya Holm had more

Helen Tamiris choreographed the dances for the revue Inside U.S.A. *in 1948. In this photograph, the dancers are performing the "Blue Grass" number.*

than a few shows to their credit, and Martha Graham never choreographed a Broadway show. Graham's unseen hand is evident, though, in contemporary stage dancing and her influence will undoubtedly be felt for many years to come. The drama of her concert works, the boundless emotionality of the movements of her dances, and her thrilling technique impressed both the dancers who worked with her and later became choreographers and the dancers who trained with her and later moved on to perform on the Broadway stage.

Although Ruth St. Denis and Martha Graham appeared as specialty dancers in musical shows before 1930, modern dance made its conscious debut on Broadway in that year, when Charles Weidman and Doris Humphrey appeared in a production of *Lysistrata*. They found themselves on a set designed by the avant-garde Norman Bel Geddes, which did not allow room for free movement, making the experience both dangerous and harrowing. In 1932, spurred by the entreaties of Otto Kahn, J. J. Shubert introduced several of their dances in a revue entitled *Americana*. Again the experience was unhappy, this time because of difficulties with Shubert. Although Humphrey was never totally comfortable as a stage choreographer, she and Weidman contributed dances for a few more revues. Weidman worked alone several times, and in *As Thousands Cheer* (1933) he dispensed with big overproduced numbers as well as the chorus line. There was a good deal of humor and satire in his work and he found enjoyment in parodying ballet and the typical Broadway dancing styles. Four years later, in *I'd Rather Be Right*, he had dancers portraying Supreme Court judges turning cartwheels and somersaults.

Helen Tamiris, trained in ballet in both the Italian and Russian modes, turned to modern dance to free her movement from confinements and formalism. Her early career was spent as a concert dancer and choreographer; later, she had an active and remarkable career on Broadway, bringing a fresh approach to stage dancing. After a few false starts, she choreographed *Up in Central Park* (1945), successfully incorporating her modern technique into the dancing, which was hailed for its

131

Alex Gard caricatured the lithe form of choreographer George Balanchine during his Broadway days in the 1930s.

Right:
Combining the talents of Broadway hoofer Ray Bolger and classically trained Tamara Geva, George Balanchine created the routine for Richard Rodgers's "Slaughter on Tenth Avenue" in On Your Toes (1936). Even after her murder, Bolger continued to dance with the lifeless form of his lover, Geva.

originality. Tamiris was always serious about her musical-comedy work. She felt strongly that the choreographer could bring a special point of view to the story. "In the old days," she said, "when musical comedy dancing was just a matter of kick-step-kick, it could be done in four weeks. That kind of dancing didn't demand ideas." She believed that dancing should not be superimposed on a script or interrupt the flow of action, but should become a medium of interpretation. One of her most successful moments was a dance during the scene in *Annie Get Your Gun* (1946) when Ethel Merman as Annie Oakley is ceremonially accepted into the tribe of Sitting Bull. It was full of vibrations, leaps, and frantic motion. The Indians all swirled around Merman, who was transformed by Tamiris momentarily into a real dancer.

Like Weidman, Jack Cole danced in and choreographed Broadway revues relatively early in his career and, like Tamiris, he had training in ballet, which became part of his extensive dance vocabulary. A concert dancer with the Denishawn and the Humphrey-Weidman groups, he was also for years a nightclub hoofer, often startling the patrons with his interpolations of oriental movement and exotic dance patterns. For twenty years, between 1941 and 1960, he choreographed musicals for all of the major Hollywood studios. Cole's work on Broadway combined ethnic, tribal, Eastern, and balletic dancing with modern techniques. His last Broadway contribution was to *Man of La Mancha* in 1965. Cole's choreography for the rape scene—quintessentially his own—was devastating in its wild eroticism and frenetic movement, yet it was disciplined by the techniques of ballet. His modern-dance style has remained one of the most influential in show business. Agnes de Mille believes that all choreographers on Broadway owe a debt to his ground-breaking work.

No one had seriously considered building a show around ballet until the 1936

In 1943 a fresh new ballet, Rodeo, attracted widespread attention. The choreographer was Agnes de Mille, who also danced in the production.

Left:
In 1947 Agnes de Mille choreographed and directed Allegro. This multiple exposure of a photo of Kathryn Lee as the ingenue's best friend, Hazel, suggests the vibrancy of the dance. In the same year, de Mille also choreographed Brigadoon.

Dwight Deere Wiman production *On Your Toes*, which combined the talents of Richard Rodgers, Lorenz Hart, George Abbott, and a recent émigré from the world of the Imperial Russian Ballet, George Balanchine. After leaving Russia in 1924, Balanchine served as ballet master for the Ballet Russe until Diaghilev's death. Catching work where he could, he found himself in London in 1929 as choreographer of a revue, *Wake Up and Dream*, and a year later he composed the dances for another revue for Charles B. Cochran, the English counterpart of Flo Ziegfeld. In 1933 he was invited to the United States by Lincoln Kirstein, and he remained to dance, choreograph, and teach for the rest of his life. From 1936 to 1951, Balanchine devoted at least some of his time to Broadway.

On Your Toes is usually cited with *Oklahoma!* as representing a watershed in the introduction of ballet into theatrical dancing. Of the two musicals, *On Your Toes*, with its revue format, was frankly more in the Broadway mold than *Oklahoma!* It contained two major ballets. "Princess Zenobia," an amusing spoof of familiar Russian ballets, drew enthusiastic applause, but "Slaughter on Tenth Avenue" brought the house down. For this adaptation of ballet to jazz movement, Balanchine chose a classically trained ballerina, Tamara Geva, and a hoofer, Ray Bolger. The dance was sexy and macabre at the same time, as the hero continued to dance with the heroine after she was murdered. The success of the show brought Balanchine into the mainstream of Broadway, where, had he chosen to remain, he probably would have dominated theatrical choreography for the rest of his career, but he preferred to return to the concert stage. His lasting achievement was to give ballet a new expression within musical comedy and to pave the way for other choreographers from the ballet world.

Without Balanchine's example, it is doubtful that Agnes de Mille would have been given the chance to choreograph *Oklahoma!* as she wanted. When in 1942 she was engaged by Theatre Guild directors Lawrence Langner and Theresa Helburn, her career was littered with more failures than successes. Langner and Helburn had been impressed by *Rodeo*, a ballet on a western theme she had just prepared for the Ballet Russe de Monte Carlo, but hiring de Mille called for a singular leap of faith because it was clear that she would never see *Oklahoma!* in conventional musical-comedy terms. On her part, de Mille realized that her approach was risky for an already shaky enterprise. The predictably painful gestation of the choreography was made more difficult still when de Mille discovered that Oscar Hammerstein had definite ideas about the dances with which she disagreed totally. She learned that she had to justify her position, recalling many years later:

The essence of theatre is collaboration, as opposed to the other arts. I really believe this. For instance, the script I was given for *Oklahoma!* is not the script that came into New York City. That happens with every show. The ballet that was outlined by Oscar Hammerstein was a circus. And I was the one who said that it didn't make any sense. Oscar said, "You've got to have a light ballet to end act one with, you can't send them out into the lobby with gloom." I said, "Why not? Just depress the hell out of them." And then I did my spiel and they listened. Now this was so because they were very gifted men. But I absolutely threw out that first ballet.

Many claims have been made for *Oklahoma!* and some of them may have been exaggerated in the cause of producing a legend. The show was a fresh and simple musical based on an American theme; it was laden with lovely songs; and it had dances that extended and amplified the characters and the story. De Mille gave individuality and personality to the dancers, allowing them, almost inadvertently in the tradition of the Method, to express themselves in their dancing. Everything in the production meshed, and the result was a theatrical event that changed the course of the American musical and, particularly, musical-comedy dancing.

De Mille was trained in classical ballet, and until 1929 she considered herself more a dancer than a dance composer. Her early attempts at stage choreography, in New York and later in London in the early 1930s, brought her little satisfaction or applause, but she persevered and learned; on more than one occasion her "spiel" won over a truculent playwright or producer or composer to her conceptions. During rehearsals for *Brigadoon* (1947), which contained her finest work, she persuaded her collaborators to accept a grim and taut funeral dance performed to the sounds of a whining bagpipe in the middle of what was being billed as musical comedy.

De Mille refused to limit herself to the balletic idiom and took what she needed from every dance form to express the characters, the plot, and the music. In *Allegro* (1947), which she not only choreographed but directed, she stripped the stage of elaborate sets and relied on props, curtains, and lights to indicate changes of scene. And she intermingled the singers with the dancers to form a Greek chorus that commented on the action through dance and song. She carefully researched the background of the dances for each script, frequently calling upon experts to provide her with authentic detail. She not only educated audiences to expect more than the usual tap and acrobatic routines but to watch the dancing attentively for the ideas it was expressing. In a tribute to de Mille, Oscar Hammerstein recognized that from the moment the curtain rose on *Oklahoma!* the choreographer in American musical comedy became the peer of the author and composer "in helping to build the very bone and muscle of the story." De Mille arrived at just the right moment in the development of the American musical and contributed to its progress as no one else has done.

Within a few years of *Oklahoma!*, there was so much ballet on Broadway that one reviewer declared he ached to see a "good old-fashioned opening chorus of tap dancers again" (his ache was not assuaged until *42nd Street* opened, some thirty years later). One of the most successful of the choreographers with a ballet background who followed de Mille to Broadway was Michael Kidd, a graduate of Balanchine's School of American Ballet and a first-rate dancer. In 1947 he literally leaped into prominence with his dances for *Finian's Rainbow*, some of which were virtually like

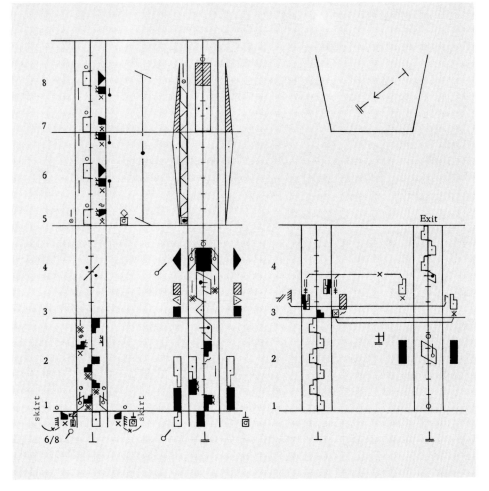

unleashed lightning—the performers flashing across the proscenium until it looked as though they would land in the laps of the patrons in the orchestra. Inevitably, Kidd was handed the reins of choreographer and director, and all his shows after 1956 (Li'l Abner) bore his unmistakable stamp, becoming increasingly dominated by highly energized movement.

In 1952, for the first time in history, the dances for a musical, Kiss Me, Kate, were notated and registered with the Copyright Office in Washington, D.C. Until then, most of the stunning choreography for the musical theater had been irretrievably lost, though a group called the American Dance Machine, under the direction of the dance-choreographer Lee Theodore, has re-created a few for the concert stage. The choreographer for Kiss Me, Kate was Hanya Holm, protégée of Mary Wigman who, with Isadora Duncan, is considered one of the founders of modern dance. Holm arrived in America from Germany in 1931 to spread the dance gospel according to Wigman, though she severed her ties with the Wigman school when she discovered an artistic kinship with the modern-dance movement in the United States. Even before Holm became involved with the theater, at a late stage in her career, there was a certain theatricality in her concert choreography, particularly in her handling of dancers within a stage space. Her first theatrical choreography was a result of a summer's experience on the campus of Colorado College in Colorado Springs. There, beginning in the early 1940s, she began to relate dance to words as well as music. Several of her theater pieces moved to New York, but it was *Kiss Me, Kate* which established her in 1948 as a Broadway choreographer of note. The artistic triumph of her career came in 1956 with her dances for *My Fair Lady*. Under the inspired direction of Moss Hart, the musical fashioned from George Bernard Shaw's *Pygmalion* became an ideal synthesis of song, dance, story, scenery, and costumes. Holm not only designed the dances but suffused the whole show with choreographed movement.

If there were a holy trinity of landmark American musicals, the first would be *On Your Toes* and the second *Oklahoma!* The third would be a version of *Romeo and Juliet* called *West Side Story*, conceived, directed, and choreographed by Jerome Robbins in 1957. Once again, the boundaries of the musical comedy were redefined. *West Side Story* was a stark tragedy erupting out of the tense rivalry between two New York street gangs. Scenes of ugliness and brutality were juxtaposed against love scenes of tenderness and pulsing humanity. Dance critic Walter Terry felt that it was the supreme example of a form that was possibly "the most exciting and potentially fertile development in the theatre since the Greek drama emerged from the danced poetry of the dithyramb. . . . The great wonder of *West Side Story* is that realistic action flows into dancing and out of it again without hitch or break, just as speech swells or snarls its way into poetry and song." From the opening dance, which established the characteristics of the gangs, to the final catastrophic choreographed rumble, the threading of the dance through the music and plot was constant and fluid, a fulfillment of the choreographer's dream of dance movement as the most natural expression of the characters and the action. *West Side Story* was final proof of the effectiveness of combining the roles of director and choreographer, although the dual responsibility would tax the creativity of successful director-choreographers to the limit.

After studying ballet and dancing for several years, Robbins joined the Ballet Theatre, for which he created *Fancy Free* in 1944. Built upon the escapades of three sailors on leave in the city, this theatrical ballet grew logically into a successful dance-musical entitled *On the Town*, which appeared on Broadway later that year. In *Fiddler on the Roof* (1964), his last Broadway triumph, Robbins converted folk dancing into ballet and acting into choreography. This simple tale about a simple man permitted him to use his great talent for transforming elemental emotions into dance gesture. In 1969 he left the Broadway stage to return to the New York City Ballet, of which he is now artistic director. Broadway's tight schedules and budgets and the restrictions imposed by unions and collaborators thwarted Robbins's inspiration. He now has the time to nurse his genius in the relatively gentle, unhurried environment of the concert stage. His defection has constituted a real loss to the American musical, and it is an understatement to say that his career in the commercial theater added significantly to the stature of the director-choreographer.

For the next generations of choreographers and choreographer-directors Broadway was the best training ground. Many of the dancers and assistants of de Mille, Kidd, Balanchine, and Robbins extended and expanded the work of their mentors and created small peaks of fresh and daring choreography for the American musical. When all else failed—book, music, and lyrics—the dancing would often shore up an enterprise and was sometimes sufficient unto itself. In the 1950s and 1960s, young dance directors like Onna White, Donald Saddler, Peter Gennaro, and Patricia Birch thoroughly researched the background of their shows, and whenever possible they

Dancin', *a bookless musical of 1978 that had wide appeal and a long run, presented a synthesis of Bob Fosse's idiosyncratic but exciting choreography.*

reworked American idiomatic dances with intelligence and imagination.

The trend that began with Jerome Robbins has led inescapably to the creation of the super-director, a person who conceives, directs, and choreographs the whole shebang. The first of the type was Bob Fosse, whose career was given its first boost by Robbins. He studied dance and ballet as a child in Chicago and later in New York with Charles Weidman and José Limon and gained experience from playing in nightclubs, variety shows, and burlesque in both cities. His first important choreography was for *The Pajama Game* in 1954, and the sexy, syncopated jazz dance to the music of "Steam Heat" established his style. This, Fosse later claimed, was an extension of his own physique—round-shouldered and pigeon-toed. It is filled with pelvic thrusts, facial grimaces, angular struts, hunching shoulders, and jerking foot gestures, all somehow strung together to create exhilarating and often humorous dance. Fosse's first show as director-choreographer was *Redhead*, a musical of 1959 that starred his wife, Gwen Verdon. But he did not really hit his stride until 1972 with *Pippin*, which has been generally described as the triumph of Fosse over book and music. In it he used what he had picked up from vaudeville, burlesque, striptease, and cheap nightclubs, along with ideas gleaned from operetta, soap opera, movies, and TV. In 1978, after several other successes, Fosse indulged himself in a show containing nothing but dancing. Appropriately named *Dancin'*, the entertainment was an artistic kitchen sink of every kind of theatrical dance filtered through his idiosyncratic style.

Although Gower Champion became periodically disenchanted with Broadway, he was drawn back to it until literally his dying day. When he came to Broadway—after gaining national attention during the early 1940s as an exhibition ballroom dancer with his wife, Marge—Champion fused classical ballet with modern dance (he had trained with Mikhail Fokine and Hanya Holm) in his choreography for such highly

A trademark of Michael Kidd's choreography is the high-stepping, fast-moving, energized routine. In Subways Are for Sleeping, the 1961 musical by Jule Styne, Betty Comden, and Adolph Green, Kidd put a chorus of Santa Clauses through their paces in "Be a Santa."

Opposite above:
"The Ascot Gavotte," devised by Hanya Holm, was a show-stopping dance number in My Fair Lady (1956). The movement was small and stylized, danced almost in place by a large chorus dressed in black, white, and gray.

Opposite below:
Choreographer Onna White guided stars Barbara Cook and Robert Preston (center) with a sure hand through the dances for the folksy, exuberant Meredith Willson musical comedy The Music Man (1957).

successful musicals as *Bye Bye Birdie* (1960), *Hello, Dolly!* (1964), and *42nd Street* (1980). His conception of the role of director-choreographer was very clear:

The choreographer is more dictatorial than the director. The very nature of his work requires him to tell dancers exactly what to do. Yes, you *tell* the dancer. As a director, you *point* the actor in a direction and let him carry it from there and if it doesn't work, you start again or revise or adapt. The choreographer requires that his dancers be expressive in dance terms while the director, in working with actors, tries to elicit the feelings of a character through both speech and gesture. The middle ground—not the dividing line—between choreography and direction is what I call staging. This is what links dancing and acting and I think that the choreographer, in the role of the director, can bring something special to the business of staging.

By assuming complete control, Champion could work directly with the scene designer of a show to create striking spatial images. *Bye Bye Birdie*, for example, opens with a chorus of teenagers cavorting on a gigantic jungle gym as they exchange phone calls. He could also embellish and amplify a script with choreography, as when, in *The Happy Time* (1968), he introduced fantasy in the form of six vaudeville girls in pink tights into a sober middle-class family dinner. In *42nd Street*, he took the old-fashioned Busby Berkeley precision-formation routines and blithely parlayed them into the kind of hokum that modern audiences accept delightedly and unquestioningly. Better than any other modern choreographer-director, he knew how to use stage, costumes, props, performers, and all the other elements of a production to serve his total vision.

Gower Champion's showmanship was in the tradition of Ned Wayburn, two generations before. Michael Bennett has also taken a leaf from Wayburn's book. The pioneer director-choreographer used his school to train his dancers, before moving them into the musicals he was directing; Bennett builds a show in workshops held in his loft on lower Broadway until it can be transferred uptown. A *Chorus Line* (1975), which has broken all existing Broadway records for long runs, was developed in such a workshop. Bennett's initial idea was to present the life stories of a number of chorus boys and girls within the framework of a musical. He interested Joseph Papp in his idea, and the producer underwrote the venture, giving Bennett time to develop his concept with several writers and a composer until, in 1975, it was ready to be showcased in the New York Public Theater. Three months later, it moved to Broadway for its record-breaking run. Each of the performers comes forward and tells his story before breaking into the song and dance that further personalizes him. Awash in sentimentality, without stars and scenery (its simple visual effects are created by upstage mirrors), and without a book in the traditional sense, the show floats upon the surface of significance, yet it clearly has struck a responsive chord in its audiences. The finale, in which the performers leave the stage and then reappear in costume to form a chorus line, is a direct descendant of John Tiller's show-stoppers.

The most recent wunderkind on Broadway is Tommy Tune, a man of Texan proportions (he is six feet six inches tall) and protean talents. As a child he studied tumbling, tap dancing, and ballet and he made up his mind in college that his life would be fulfilled if he could dance in a Broadway chorus. Shortly after arriving in New York, he got a job in the chorus of the road company of *Irma La Douce* and has never been out of work since. He went through the usual apprenticeship and made the necessary contacts along the way until fate and Michael Bennett tapped him on the shoulder. Tune not only assisted Bennett with the choreography of *Seesaw* in 1973, but did a clog dance to the song "It's Not How You Start But How You Finish" and brought down the house. In 1981 he directed *Cloud 9*, a tongue-in-cheek nonmusical play on human sexuality in all of its various permutations, skillfully moving the actors on the stage in dancelike circumambulations. He has returned to the musical stage as a director-choreographer with an unbroken string of successes. Tune's style is characterized by whimsy and inventiveness in using the old idioms in a new way, but its source is pure Broadway. In 1982 he staged "Nine," a musical inspired by Federico Fellini's movie 8 1/2. In the first act he moved dancers and

singers, all clad in black-and-white costumes, in a choreographed stream of consciousness around a stark black-and-white set. The many stunning numbers were connected only by virtue of being aspects of the visualized memory of the central figure. Tune worked on the project for nearly two years and honed it in a six-week workshop for Broadway. The following year, he returned to the stage as a performer in *My One and Only*, a modern version of Gershwin's *Funny Face*, that he also directed and choreographed. The heart of the show's dancing is tap, a nostalgic backward glance at the musicals of the 1930s.

Before the Society of Stage Directors and Choreographers (SSDC) was established, only the star directors were adequately paid; the fledgling or journeyman director found it impossible to make a living from his work. Shepard Traube, a successful director and producer, became the founder of the latest theatrical union. "In the late fifties I realized, based on all my various experiences, that the only unorganized group of workers in the creative aspects of the theatre, were the directors. And I said, 'Why don't I try to organize them? I've got time on my hands.' So I sent out an extensive group of letters to various directors that I knew, inviting them to come to my apartment. . . . This was the beginning of five years of unremitting effort." The immediate results of the meetings, which were eventually moved out of Traube's apartment into a room over Sardi's restaurant, was his dismissal from the League of New York Theatres and Producers (LNYTP) and the inclusion of choreographers in the nascent SSDC, at the insistence of Agnes de Mille. Now a martyr with a cause and a constituency, Traube persisted until the SSDC became a legal entity in 1959. The first real test of the union came about in 1963. Traube asked the producers of *Little Me*, Cy Feuer and Ernest Martin, to agree to recognize the SSDC as the agent for directors and choreographers, and their acquiescence set the stage for negotiations with the LNYTP. Later that year, the SSDC and the LNYTP came to terms. Four years later, directors of Off-Broadway productions came under the protection of the SSDC, which eventually spread its influence throughout the country into regional theater and summer stock. Currently it lists about a thousand members nationwide, of which less than 10 percent are women.

Although they now go into their directing assignments with contracts, assured fees, and fringe benefits, directors and choreographers must still collaborate with producers, stars, authors, and designers. In recent years, the SSDC has been working to copyright the stage directions its members evolve for each production, which eventually appear in printed form. This attempt by directors to treat their work as their own property has pitted them against playwrights, who have traditionally regarded stage directions as belonging to the script. The SSDC has made some recent gains (in Off-Broadway contracts) and will continue to press for recognition of directors as the creators of nonmusical stage directions. (Choreographers have been copyrighting their work since 1952, when Hanya Holm established the precedent for her work in *Kiss Me, Kate*.)

George Kaufman once defied anyone to scare up three people who knew what a director did. At the beginning of this chapter appeared a quote from a turn-of-the-century writer for the *New York Dramatic Mirror* who, in attempting to describe a director's job, fell back on a recital of his qualifications. Seventy years later, Harold Clurman brought the definition up to date but added nothing new: "Direction is a job, a craft, a profession, and at best, an art. The director must be an organizer, a teacher, a politician, a psychic detective, a lay analyst, a technician, a creative being. Ideally, he should know literature (drama), acting, the psychology of the actor, the visual arts, music, history, and above all, he must understand people. He must inspire confidence. All of which means he must be a 'great lover.' " Perhaps, the general inability to define exactly what a director *does* as opposed to what he *is* (or should be) lies in the fact that he deals in something that is seen yet unseen, a conjuring act that lifts printed words from paper and transforms them into actions, conversations, characters, and places as he imagines them. Call him an artist or a creator—in the last analysis he is also a master magician.

ACTORS

NO LONGER the abstracts and brief chronicles of the time, their names no longer writ in water, actors have finally achieved what they had always fruitlessly pursued: immortality. Film and videotape prolong their ephemeral art, making it possible to pass it on to generations yet unborn. A century ago, they played before audiences of a few thousand at most. Now they can reach hundreds of millions of people scattered around the earth via the ethereal waves that reach the television screen. Immortality is within their grasp, but the road to it has not changed in the past four centuries. Acting remains the most difficult and elusive of professions—and the most irresistible.

In America, pursuing the elusive has been both easier and harder than in England and Europe. During the nineteenth century, the great age of American expansionism, opportunities existed for aspirants in all fields. Many a young stagestruck man or woman, as a multitude of stories attest, went to the local stock company and, after a suitable apprenticeship, became an actor as renowned as Edwin Forrest or Charlotte Cushman. Today there are no local stock companies and the competition is fiercer than ever before. The great satisfaction that actors formerly enjoyed in building lifelong careers in the theater more than counterbalanced their modest wages. Today the rewards for the lucky few approach in value King Tut's golden hoard, but the satisfactions have all but vanished for performers who have become corporations and commodities rising and falling on the stock exchange of public opinion. Actors have acquired new fears. The phone may stop ringing, or they may suffer an attack of overexposure, or some new arrival with a fresh face may supplant theirs on the big and little screens. Though more actors are employed today than ever before, it is also more difficult to get that first hearing or that first part. Overnight sensations have often spent ten years in preparation or in obscure apprenticeships in minor theaters in the boondocks. Then they discover that the top rung of the professional ladder is coated with grease and their grasp precarious. The profession continues to breed alcoholics, drug addicts, and neurotics in profusion.

Both in England and on the Continent, theatrical activity has always been more concentrated, more predictable, more balanced, and more rationally handled than in America. The rewards are not so great but the approach is saner and the atmosphere more relaxed. Actors abroad enjoy an esprit de corps, a sense of fraternity, a clubbiness, that is rarely found in America. The size and diversity of this country make it difficult to establish a national theater, and without one there will never be a time when the right actors can be assembled for the best possible production of a play in its own or any other era. From the moment that native-born actors took to the stage, America has produced performers of both sexes who rank with the great theatrical figures of every nation on earth. Most of them rose to the top of their profession both because and in spite of the wasteful and destructive free-enterprise system of American theater.

In 1800 there were about 150 actors and actresses in America, all of them of British descent, trained in English acting styles, playing English plays, and speaking in decidedly English accents. Some of them were the descendants of Lewis Hallam's vagabond players, who reached the shores of Virginia in 1752. Hallam's company had been preceded in the American colonies by a "genteel" band of actors, managed by Thomas Kean and Walter Murray, who established a professional existence in a Philadelphia warehouse in 1749. Whether professional or amateur or a bit of both, this pioneer troupe mounted about two dozen plays, moved to New York, then traveled to the southern colonies, where they eventually disbanded. Along the way, they picked up a young Philadelphian, Nancy George, who may have been our first native thespian.

Enter the Company of Comedians from London, sent by William Hallam, once a player of small parts at Drury Lane but more recently the manager of a theater on the fringes of London put out of business by the great and powerful legitimate houses. The company consisted of William's brother Lewis and his wife, their children, and seven actors and three actresses drawn in all probability from the lesser ranks of performers—those doomed to play small roles at Drury Lane or Covent Garden, if they were lucky, or to travel in the provinces in the bigger roles denied them in London. They were assuredly workmanlike actors, but in any case the colonials had no others with whom to compare them. Since the twelve actors (and children as needed) had to enact all the parts in the plays they put on, they doubled up on roles, danced and sang during the intermissions, and absorbed some of the duties at the business end as well. The company was paid on a share basis, with extra shares going to the Hallams as the managers. The Company of Comedians apparently preferred the hard life of pioneers—trouping over bad roads, scaring up audiences in frequently inhospitable towns, making ends meet as best they could, and strutting their brief hours upon makeshift stages—to the relatively predictable existence of a small-part London actor or a traveling provincial in England's backwaters.

After the war with England was over, once-nomadic troupes like Hallam's company were able to settle down in the larger cities, take up residence in a theater, and limit their travels to a few months of the year. For almost a century, the stationary stock-company system dominated the American theater. Even the players who brought entertainment to the West endured the hardships of barnstorming in order to build audiences that would sustain resident theaters. The stock companies offered actors steady and secure employment and a semblance of a normal life. Rising in the profession meant passing from one stock company to another until the pinnacle was reached: a place in one of the major big-city companies.

With some variations according to size, talent, and relative prosperity, all of the various stock companies were organized on similar lines. There was always a manager, who might also be the principal actor, and a complement of actors and actresses, each of whom was responsible for playing a series of roles. The companies usually had more men than women on the roster simply because most of the plays in the repertory had more male than female parts. The best companies employed actors according to the following lines of business:

1. The Leading Man, who played all major tragic or romantic roles as well as the serious roles in comedy
2. The Leading Lady, who played all the distaff roles opposite the Leading Man
3. The Light Comedian, who played young lovers and juvenile roles
4. The Heavy (often there were two), who played villains and middle-aged men
5. The Eccentric Comedian, who played the farcical and low-comedy roles
6. The Walking Gentleman (often there were several), who played everything from bit roles to leads
7. The Walking Lady (often there were several), who, like the Walking Gentleman, played any role in which she was needed
8. The Old Woman and the Old Man
9. The Singing Chambermaid, known later as the soubrette, who was capable of breaking into song when the occasion demanded
10. Responsible Utilities of both sexes, who played small parts
11. Respectable Utilities of both sexes, who had one or two lines
12. General Utilities of both sexes, who functioned as extras and swept the stage floor

MR. KEAN,
AS
SIR GILES OVERREACH.

Edmund Kean's first appearance on the American stage was at the Park Theatre in New York in 1820. Kean thrilled audiences with his agitated style of acting, never seen before on this side of the Atlantic. He is shown here in one of his most famous and chilling roles, as Sir Giles Overreach in A New Way to Pay Old Debts.

The majority of the great actors and actresses of the nineteenth century progressed through the stock-company ranks, first in utility parts, then as a Walking Lady or Walking Gentleman, and finally in leading roles.

The stock company was the actor's school. Actors learned not only by doing but by observing the older and more practiced members of the company. They also picked up along the way their chosen model's mannerisms and idiosyncrasies. Otis Skinner recalled his own transformation into a mirror image of Lawrence Barrett after spending his formative years in that actor-producer's company; later, as a mature actor, he spent thirty weeks with Edwin Booth and found himself "reading speeches with the Booth cadence, using the Booth gestures, attitudes and facial expression, in short, giving a rank imitation." Some actors, like Skinner, worked to shed their acquired mannerisms, but many were simply content to remain "second" Forrests, Booths, or Cushmans.

Stock-company actors worked hard. Their value to the company depended on their acquisition of parts, and because dramas were performed in repertory, with a change of bill every night or every few nights, they might be required to rehearse a play in the morning, act in another that evening, and memorize lines for a third after the performance. As a Walking Gentleman, Skinner once played six different roles in six nights and by the end of the week ruefully recalled that "all the characters were rattling about within [my mind] simultaneously." By the end of their careers, stock actors were prepared to play several hundred roles on very little notice. The champion was the younger William Warren, who spent all but one of the years between 1847 and 1882 as a stock actor with the Boston Museum company. By the time he retired, he had given 13,345 performances, in 577 roles, 5,799 of them in the same 68 characters!

The nineteenth-century stock-company repertory leaned heavily on Shakespeare, Restoration and eighteenth-century comedies, old standbys (such as Thomas Otway's *The Orphan* and *Venice Preserved* and many others that have since dropped from common ken), attempting newer plays from time to time. Naturally, actors could not handle all of their roles equally well. Countless were the examples of square pegs in round holes: short, thin Falstaffs, barrel-chested Wagnerian Camilles, and overage Romeos. For audiences, who had seen the same plays many times, the sport lay in comparing different performers in the same roles and performances given by the same actor early and late in his career. As long as the stock company remained the only show in town, audiences of apparently saintly disposition seem not to have cared what kind of chaos occurred onstage. Perhaps it is safe to say that they got their money's worth, whether it was an evening of theatrical mayhem or of magic.

Stock-company actors were not well paid. At mid-century, a successful and prestigious company like Wallack's in New York started its salaries at $6 per week for the lower lines, increasing them to between $30 and $60 for the experienced and featured players, and topping them all with $80 for the leading man. Lester Wallack received $100 per week for managing as well as performing. Subtract from these wages the players' makeup and the care and maintenance of their wardrobes as well as their general living expenses, and the residue must have been negligible. Olive Logan had three dresses—a black velvet, a white satin, and a muslin—that served for all parts, from Juliet to Lady Macbeth. When Clara Morris was hired as a Walking Lady, she dreaded being cast in roles that required finery. "I suffered most when I had to play a lady of quality, for what, in heaven's name, had I to dress a lady in? Five dollars a week to live on, to dress myself on, and to provide a stage wardrobe!" Not infrequently, actors were hired on the strength of their wardrobes. Before Francis Courtney Wemyss left England for America, he spent his last pennies on costumes, so that he could land a good spot in a first-rate company.

To add insult to injury, actors were subjected to a long list of rules and regulations. Any infractions brought penalties in the form of deductions from their salaries. In 1872 the management of the Varieties Theatre in New Orleans posted twenty-six conditions of employment. If a performer was still using a script at the last rehearsal of a play, two dollars were deducted from his salary. If he ad-libbed onstage, the charge was one dollar. If he drank, swore, or cut up backstage, he could be discharged or fined five dollars, at the discretion of the manager. If he missed a performance on account of illness, he had to present a doctor's note to the manager. The most serious misdeed of all, refusing a part, could result in the forfeiture of salary while the play was performed, or dismissal, at the discretion of the manager. But despite the restrictions, the low pay, and the rigors of the life, there were compensations, intangible but very real. Clara Morris described a theatrical company as a family. "Our feeling for one another," she wrote, "is generally one of warm good-fellowship. In our manners there is an easy familiarity which we would not dream of using outside our own little company circle. We are socially inclined people, communicative, fond of friendly conversation, and hopelessly given over to jokes, as we put it, 'to guying.'" Alas, the families broke up frequently, as actors moved on to other companies or became stars or simply dropped out of the profession. During its fifty-year history, the Boston Museum employed six hundred actors, three-quarters of whom stayed for only one or two seasons.

One of the stock-company institutions, the actor's benefit, persisted into the nineteenth century. A vestige of Restoration theatrical practice, it was probably created to offset the notoriously low pay. Under the system an actor selected a play and his own role for a performance and was allowed to keep either a share or all of the profits, based upon his importance in the company. He was expected to bring in an audience for the evening through his own efforts. Everything depended upon the popularity of the performer and the willingness of his colleagues to appear for him. A benefit might effectively double his annual salary, if it were a success; if it were not, he might pocket an insignificant sum, or worse, suffer a loss. In 1868 Lester Wallack abolished the system at his theater in New York and other managers quickly followed suit.

Many lamented the passing of the last of the great stock companies at the century's close. The system certainly gave actors versatility, but there was never time to do more than prick the skin of a role. They were able to pick up things gradually through experience, but there was no method or order to their education. "Rules are scattered about the stage," said Dion Boucicault, "and transmitted, gypsy-like in our vagrant life from one generation to another." Mrs. Fiske recalled that it was also a school of bad habits. The last word—and probably the best word—from the actor's point of view came from Otis Skinner. "I am glad," he wrote in his autobiography,

I was able to be in at the death and before the old system had quite passed away; glad that my novitiate was one of hard knocks that compelled me to swallow my technique in great gulps; glad of the vast experience that gave me every sort of character—in two years I had played over one hundred and forty parts; glad of that compulsion of quick study and performance which renders the body supple and the mind obedient; and glad that my dramatic kindergarten was placed among men and women filled with the knowledge of their trade, and with honor for their calling—residents of a true Bohemia since changed for an estate of greater respectability and social recognition and less art.

The stock-company system existed in uneasy and often unhappy alliance with the star system, which was its stepchild. It was inevitable that the bright and shining talent of one member of a company would throw the others into shadow, that these gifted players would attract audiences and fame, and that they would justifiably demand and receive much money and important billing and all the other rewards of their distinction. The star system had its roots in eighteenth-century England, and with the appearance of David Garrick in the 1740s it was set on an uninterrupted course. Stars were not immediately exported to America, for they could hardly be expected to expose themselves to the rigors of the New World and its uncertain rewards. But in the nineteenth century, when the rewards were secured to them by contract and America appeared to be moving out of its "barbarism," stars came in droves—first the English, then the French and representatives of most of the other European nations.

Until actors unionized in the early twentieth century, their contracts were full of restrictive clauses. Clause 10 of this contract signed in 1905 by Bobby Clark and Paul McCullough states that the vaudevillians are not permitted to pick up girls within two blocks of the theater.

Fanfare greeted Edmund Kean when he arrived in the United States in 1820, but Junius Brutus Booth, Kean's rival on the London stage, slipped quietly into America a year later, appearing first in Richmond, Virginia. Booth was painted about 1827 by John Neagle in the title role of Brutus in John Howard Payne's drama.

James E. Murdoch as Petruchio in The Taming of the Shrew strikes the famous "teapot pose," a stance popular with nineteenth-century English actors of the John Philip Kemble school: left hand on hip, left leg slightly extended, right arm raised, and head turned to the right.

Before it received its first fully fledged English star, the American theater created its own in the person of Thomas Abthorpe Cooper. He was lured to America at the age of twenty by Thomas Wignell, who recruited him for the company he had established in Philadelphia. Cooper's special distinction was that he had played at Covent Garden and was considered an up-and-coming talent. He made his debut in Baltimore in 1796 and moved on to Philadelphia with Wignell, but fell out with him and settled into the old American Company in New York two years later. When the Park Theatre opened, Cooper became its star and, but for two trips back to London to appear at Drury Lane, he spent the rest of his life here and for most of it reigned supreme on the stage. His debut in New York was as Hamlet, and William Dunlap, who in his old age wrote a personal history of the American theater, was of the opinion that "never, probably, was the Danish prince so well played in America." Cooper was a graceful and elegant actor, given to posturing to show himself to good advantage. His acting was of the John Philip Kemble school, a style characterized by precision of speech, a tendency to rant, and arm flourishes to punctuate speeches. It was stagy and artificial, declamatory and intellectual, but awesome if done well.

Two established stars followed Cooper to America, George Frederick Cooke in 1810 and Edmund Kean, first in 1820 and again in 1825. When he was sober, Cooke was considered superior to Kemble, the then-reigning god of the English stage. His style was akin to the great Garrick's: quiet, intense, simple, yet exciting. Washington Irving saw his performance in *Macbeth* and considered it among the grandest pieces of acting that he had ever witnessed. But Cooke appeared too often on wobbly legs and with slurred speech and was frequently hooted off the stage by his ungentle American audiences. (Cooke's outspoken contempt for America also did not endear him to its citizens.) Unable to return to England when war broke out between the two nations in 1812, he drew his last breath in America.

Kean had much more influence on contemporary American acting. His style was the antithesis of Kemble's icy grandeur. A highly animated performer, he was also erratic and undependable, but when in fine form he thrilled English audiences as had no actor before him. He played Shakespeare's great villains to perfection, ever on the move around the stage, jabbing the air with convulsive gestures, and working his face into sinister and bloodcurdling expressions. Accustomed to Cooper's stateliness and rigidity, American audiences were fascinated by Kean's emotionality, and American actors also responded to his style and began to assimilate aspects of it into their own. Never overcome by modesty, Kean initiated the practice of appearing before the curtain after a performance to receive his due applause.

The emotional style of acting was still more firmly established on the American stage by yet another Englishman, Junius Brutus Booth, who chose to leave London rather than risk continual comparison with Kean. Short and wiry, the men were strikingly similar in physique, and both threw themselves into their roles with passionate abandon. Arriving without fanfare in 1821, Booth first appeared in Richmond, Virginia, and made his debut in New York shortly after Kean. It was generally conceded that Booth had a better voice than Kean and a greater intellectual grasp of the roles that both of them customarily played. Booth's emotionalism surged from his interpretation of the characters he played, rather than being a conscious display of the art of acting for its own sake, like Kean's. There were moments when Booth became so caught up in a character that he frightened his fellow thespians with his intensity. His dedication to his art was complete. Once when an actor failed to appear at curtain time, Booth ran up to the wardrobe, dressed himself in the absentee's costume, and appeared onstage in his insignificant role to prevent the performance from being cancelled.

Booth's private life was a shambles. Having abandoned his wife in England, he and Mary Ann Holmes, a former London flower girl, raised a family of ten on a Maryland farm and were only able to marry in 1851, a year before Booth's death, a fact that haunted their most famous son, Edwin. Booth was also quite possibly a manic-depressive, subject to great swings of mood complicated by bouts of alcoholism. At times unable to complete performances, he simply disappeared from a theater. He might vary his interpretation of a role from performance to performance, leaving his fellow actors unnerved and floundering in the middle of a scene. But, his career undimmed, Booth traversed the country as a star and died on a Mississippi riverboat, after a tour that had brought him as far as California.

As if on some preconceived timetable, Edwin Forrest appeared in the first quarter of the nineteenth century and launched the cause of native American acting in earnest. Born in 1806 in Philadelphia, poorly educated but stagestruck from childhood, he received training in articulation from the elocutionist Lemuel G. White. When he was only fourteen, he made his debut at the Walnut Street Theatre, which had one of the finest acting companies in America at that time. Young Forrest did not astound anyone by the brilliance of his acting and was not subsequently offered a place with the distinguished company. For several years, he worked as an apprentice actor with stock companies in the South and Midwest. He sought out Cooper for advice and observed Kean during his first visit. During the latter's second visit, Forrest supported him when the star appeared in Albany, playing Iago to Kean's Othello, Richmond to his Richard, and Titus to his Brutus. Kean was impressed with the nineteen-year-old actor and publicly complimented him at a banquet in Philadelphia: "I have met one actor in this country, a young man named Edwin Forrest, who gave proofs of a decided genius for his profession, and will, I believe, rise to great eminence."

Forrest did not become a slavish imitator of Kean. Instead, he fused aspects of both Kean's and Cooper's methods to create his own style. In 1826 he made his debut in *Othello* at the Park Theatre and began his rise to great eminence, which was to endure for most of his long career. His impact on American theater was so forceful and his imitators so numerous that many thought he had created the definitive school of American acting. In 1846 Walt Whitman worried that his "crown of vapid imitators may spread quite all the faults of that style, with none of its excellencies."

At his peak, Forrest was a handsome, imposing man with a barrel chest and bulging biceps and calves. Although only five feet ten inches tall, onstage he appeared to be a giant. From his powerful physique resonated an extraordinary voice that could glide from *pianissimo* to *double forte* with ease. He played only great-souled, morally invincible heroes and, although he appeared to be consumed by his roles, he actually remained coolly detached. Furthermore, he left nothing to chance, preparing his characterizations with painstaking care, researching backgrounds, analyzing the texts, and planning the stage business. But even his sincerest admirers realized that he was always *acting*, no matter how thrillingly he read the lines and how perfectly physically suited he was to his parts. To his credit, Forrest always tried to gather around him excellent supporting players. Once, while rehearsing in Augusta, Georgia, for a performance of *Damon and Pythias*, he refused to continue until a better actor could be found for Pythias. In the company was a young actor named James E. Murdoch, whom Forrest had seen in Philadelphia. He asked that Murdoch take over the part, launching him, incidentally, in his successful career in the theater.

Forrest possessed the quintessential star ego. Not satisfied with his American fame, he decided to conquer English audiences as well. On tour in 1836 and 1845, he won the grudging admiration of frequently hostile British audiences, who especially appreciated his robust "American" interpretation of roles like Metamora, the Indian chief. During his second visit, he and William Charles Macready, the reigning English star, whose ego was a match for Forrest's, began a professional feud that resulted a few years later in a shameful incident in American theatrical history. During Macready's engagement at the Astor Place Opera House in 1849, while Forrest was playing a few blocks away at the Winter Garden Theatre, Forrest's partisans gathered in an attempt to halt the English star's performance. As crowds formed and the mood grew uglier, the city police found that they could not keep order. The appearance of the National Guard exacerbated the situation. The mob turned and attacked the soldiers with a volley of stones. Inexplicably, someone gave the order to fire and, when the smoke had cleared, twenty-two people had been killed and thirty

The tragedian Edwin Forrest introduced John Augustus Stone's Metamora; or, the Last of the Wampanoags at the Park Theatre in 1829. Dressed in the title role of the noble Indian chief, the actor remained a popular subject for drawings and paintings as long as Stone's play was in vogue. He played the part throughout his career and it brought him great riches, but he often intimated to friends that he grew very weary of it.

The English star William Charles Macready became the bitter rival of the American star Edwin Forrest. Like Forrest, he was a great Shakespearean actor. Here he is in the role of King Lear.

An outstanding tragic actress who on occasion starred with Edwin Forrest and Edwin Booth, Charlotte Cushman also enjoyed playing men's roles. She is seen here as Romeo, with her sister Susan as Juliet. In 1849 Susan retired from the stage when she married.

more wounded. Although Forrest was blamed for the incident, political and class feelings and a lingering anglophobia contributed to the tragic insurrection.

The final word on Edwin Forrest was written by William Winter, for sixty years a critic and observer of the American theater:

He could be seen and heard and understood. He had a grand body and a glorious voice, and in moments of simple passion he affected the senses like the blare of trumpets and clash of cymbals, or like the ponderous, slow-moving, crashing, and thundering surges of the sea. In that quality he stood alone. In all others he has been surpassed. That was his charm, and through that he was enabled to render whatever service he did render to the cause of Drama. That service consisted in a widespread, delightful, and improving of the art of acting to the lower order of public intelligence. To the higher order of mind Forrest was superfluous, and of this fact he seemed, in a certain blind way, to be aware—although neither he nor any of his adherents could understand and believe that it was possible for any person, honestly and without hostility or prejudice, to dislike the snorts and grunts, the brays and belches, the gaspings and gurglings, the protracted pauses, the lolling tongue and the stentorian roar, with all of which ornaments it pleased him to overlay his action,—often remarkably fine and sometimes great.

When he began his career, Forrest's flamboyant acting appealed to all segments of the audience, from the boxes to the balconies, but once his star had been eclipsed by the young Edwin Booth, only provincial audiences and the "gallery gods," the ticket-holders seated in the uppermost balconies, found him consistently irresistible. In his later years, Forrest spent most of his time on the road.

The closest thing to a female counterpart of Forrest was Mrs. Mary Ann Duff, who was not reckoned a serious actress until her career was well advanced. Born Mary Ann Dyke in London in 1794, she and two of her sisters became dancers in Dublin while they were all quite young. There she met and married John Duff, an actor at the Theatre Royal, and emigrated with him to America in 1810. For many years, her career was secondary to her husband's, but as his declined, hers began to ascend—perhaps out of necessity, since they had a large family of children. She switched from lighter roles to tragic ones and she began to support the leading actors of her time, Edmund Kean, Junius Brutus Booth, Cooper, and Forrest, whose favorite leading lady she was. Kean once asked her to tone down her acting so that he would not be upstaged, but she refused. At her peak, she possessed beauty, a good figure, and a rich voice. Her acting was graceful and dignified, yet powerful and intense at the same time. Her repertoire listed 220 roles ranging from farce to high tragedy, but tragedy and pathetic roles were her forte. "At Richmond Hill," Horace Greeley recollected, "I saw her personate Lady MacBeth better than it has since been done in this city, though she played for thirty dollars per week and others have since received ten times that amount for a single night. I doubt that any woman has since played in our city... who was the superior of Mrs. Duff in a wide range of tragic characters."

If Mrs. Duff was denied the salaries her leading men were able to demand, Charlotte Cushman reaped recognition and rewards beyond the expectation of other actresses. Born in 1816, the descendant of a *Mayflower* family, Cushman might have lived the life of a proper Bostonian lady had not the death of her father plunged the family into genteel poverty. Possessing a pretty singing voice, she began taking lessons to prepare herself for making a living as a chorister or opera singer. James Maeder, a musician and conductor, and his wife, Clara Fisher, a successful leading lady and singer, prevailed upon Cushman to join them in an engagement at the St. Charles Theatre in New Orleans. The critics in New Orleans were not kind to her, however, and Cushman wisely decided to change careers. She appealed to James H. Caldwell, the manager of the theater, and he recommended that she study acting with James Barton, the tragedian of the St. Charles company. Barton's style was derived from the austere Kemble school of acting and it became the foundation of Cushman's technique. When later in her career she acted with Forrest, his fiery style of acting contrasted memorably with her more intensely controlled interpretations.

After making her acting debut in New Orleans in 1836, Cushman received an offer

Mathew Brady's likeness of Charlotte Cushman as the witch Meg Merrilies in Guy Mannering captures not only the malevolence of the character but the pathos the great actress discerned in the role. This daguerreotype was made about 1844.

from the Bowery Theatre in New York, played there one week, and saw the theater and her contract go up in flames. The next few months she spent in minor stock companies, finally returning to New York City in 1837 for a three-year engagement as a Walking Lady at the Park Theatre. There she learned and played more than a hundred comic and tragic roles, including young ladies and men, old women, chambermaids with a few lines, and important characters with many. Working with perhaps the finest actors of the time, she developed quickly into a first-rate actress.

With her star in the ascendant, Cushman left the Park to establish her reputation in Philadelphia, where she became manager of her own company. In 1843 she was informed that the great English star William Macready had asked that she be engaged during his upcoming tour in Philadelphia. After they had played together, Macready advised her to go to England to polish her art before the more demanding English audiences. She followed his advice, becoming during the next five years in contemporary opinion "the best importation from the New World that we have yet amongst us." She returned triumphantly to America in 1849.

Cushman was a tall, bosomy woman with square shoulders and a commanding presence, fine, intelligent eyes, and an unusual speaking voice. Perhaps as a result of strain during her singing days, it had a woody, veiled quality, but its range and power were awesome. In her maturity she was deeply influenced by Macready, whose acting

Overleaf left:
In the nineteenth century, although good looks could help pave an actress's way to stardom, they were no guarantee of success. The beautiful Mrs. D. P. Bowers became a star because she could assay difficult roles and support stars like Edwin Booth creditably. She is shown here as Lady Macbeth.

Overleaf right:
Edwin Booth succeeded Edwin Forrest (for whom he was named) in public favor and surpassed him in talent. He was the greatest actor of tragedy in the nineteenth century in America and rivaled the best English actors of his time. Here is Booth as Hamlet, perhaps his greatest role.

was more emotional than Kemble's, yet more studied and intellectual than Kean's. The style was best suited to melodrama, in which both Macready and Cushman excelled. As America's greatest actress, she played most of Shakespeare's women, and played them well, but Cushman's greatest triumph was as the sinister Meg Merrilies in the dramatization of Walter Scott's *Guy Mannering*. Her audiences waited breathlessly for Meg's death scene, which was so chilling that the ladies were forced to cover their eyes. Cushman transformed herself for the part into an old, wrinkled hag dressed in rags, but when she took her curtain calls, she kept the audience waiting until she had removed her makeup, returning with a washed and freshly powdered face.

She also appeared often in men's roles—Romeo, Hamlet, Cardinal Wolsey (*Henry VIII*), and Claude Melnotte (*The Lady of Lyons*)—and in private life she liked to wear mannish clothes and surrounded herself with emancipated women. Cushman spent a good deal of her later life in Europe, returning to the American stage in so many self-indulgent "farewell appearances" that she was justifiably ridiculed. When she died of cancer in 1876, her name was a household word throughout the English-speaking world. But because her style was so personal, so embedded in her singularity and yet so absorbed in her characters, there were no Cushman imitators during her life or after her death. Without physical beauty, the usual sine qua non of female stardom, she is a phenomenon of American theatrical history.

Much more typical of the female star were Mrs. D. P. Bowers and Mary Anderson, whose great beauty eased their way to stardom. Mrs. Bowers, born Elizabeth Crocker in 1830, the daughter of a Connecticut clergyman, began her long career at the age of fifteen, became one of the favorite leading ladies of Edwin Booth, and at the end of her career opened a school of dramatic expression in New York. One of her critics described her as the "sort of woman that women rave over and that men fall in love with." As for Mary Anderson, she never even had to endure the rigors of stock-company training. John Ranken Towse, drama critic for the *New York Evening Post* for forty-three years, considered her one of Fortune's darlings: "When as a mere girl she first entered upon the stage, she presented a figure of classic and virginal purity that was almost ideal. Her tall, lithe form was at once stately and graceful, the poise of her head was stag-like, and her face was radiant with health, innocence, and dignified beauty. It was by the spell of her personal charms that she instantly made her way into the heart of the American public." A consummate professional, Mrs. Bowers was undoubtedly the better actress; Mary Anderson simply looked so splendid onstage that she enchanted her audiences. Mrs. Bowers's career extended over five decades; Anderson retired in 1889, at the age of thirty, having spent fewer than fifteen years in the theater.

The "hope of the living drama" in America, the thespian whose name became synonymous with the best native acting in the nineteenth century, was Edwin Booth. Although he was a true star (a memorial service held in 1893 at Madison Square Garden drew thousands of people), Booth never lived a flamboyant life and although he loved to act, he did not like the life of an actor. His only daughter, Edwina, described his "natural melancholy," and among the hundreds, perhaps thousands, of photographs that exist of him, it is almost impossible to find a smiling Edwin Booth. Whether his melancholy was innate or the result of a life punctuated by a series of unhappy, even catastrophic, events can only be surmised. Born in 1833 into an eccentric family, the fourth child of the mercurial Junius Brutus Booth, he endured his father's aberrant behavior, the death of his adored first wife, the assassination of President Lincoln by his brother John Wilkes Booth, the insanity of his second wife, the loss of the dream theater he built in New York, bankruptcy, a bout with alcoholism, and the inevitable stock-actor's burnout. Even by the standards of his time, he was not old when he died, but he looked worn out and aged. In spite of these natural and unnatural adversities, Booth's life was also crowned with triumph. He won the adulation of audiences from coast to coast, honors, and financial success.

He began his acting career almost inadvertently. Traveling while still in his teens as his father's dresser and companion, he was asked to step into a small role (Tressel) in *Richard III* at the Boston Museum in 1849. His father loaned him a pair of spurs, perhaps as a token of parental blessing, though he would not consent to sharing the stage with his son when he was asked on another occasion. For seven years, Booth served a roving apprenticeship in the theater, playing in everything from black-faced minstrel shows to high tragedies and traveling as far as Australia. At the start of his career he imitated his father's restless emotional style but evolved a quieter, more introspective brand of acting, characterized by a controlled intensity.

Booth's best roles were Shakespearean, though he was also successful in contemporary melodramas, and the greatest triumph of his life was playing Hamlet for one hundred consecutive performances at the Winter Garden Theatre in 1865—a record that went unchallenged for more than half a century. His best Shakespearean characterization was universally acknowledged to be Iago, which he played with a surface geniality that made still more horrifying the diabolic machinations of the hero's evil genius. Otis Skinner called Booth's Iago "small, lithe, dangerous and radiant with devilish beauty." To a young actress who once played Jessica to his Shylock, he explained the meaning of a scene and the effect he wanted: "This is a quiet scene. Shylock is speaking to his own flesh and blood here. His mask is off. Each glance of mine to you is significant. My facial expression is important here, but I wish to *do nothing*. Any emphasis in this scene is overemphasis." There were roles, like Shylock and Hamlet, that he continued to explore throughout his career.

Booth created lofty standards and brought an early maturity to American acting that far outdistanced the contributions of the other theatrical collaborators. But because Booth cast a long shadow, many first-rate actors of his day never made it to the very top of the profession, either resigning themselves to second-best status or perfecting and then playing the same special role year after year. In the first camp were actors E. L. Davenport and Lawrence Barrett. Davenport's career spanned the best years of Forrest and Booth and he was eclipsed by both. Forrest called him the best contemporary actor on the American stage, and Davenport's Hamlet was rated second only to Booth's. A native of Boston, where he was born in 1815, he served a ten-year apprenticeship with a number of companies before being chosen by Anna Cora Mowatt as her leading man. He accompanied her to England in 1847 and remained to play with Macready, returning to America to resume his career there in 1854. Considered a polished and skillful actor, Davenport was able to play a variety of roles easily and capably. He founded a family of actors, whose descendants today include John D. Seymour and Anne Seymour. His daughter Fanny Davenport was a stage brat, beginning her career as a child in the 1850s, then graduating into soubrette roles, and finally becoming a leading comedienne with Augustin Daly's company. In 1883 she switched to the melodramatic heroines of Victorien Sardou (Tosca, Fédora, Gismonda, and Cleopatra) and was billed as the American Bernhardt. She died tragically, at the peak of her career, at the age of forty-eight.

Through almost superhuman efforts, Lawrence Barrett, a penniless, illiterate waif on the streets of Paterson, New Jersey, not only rose to stardom but enjoyed a reputation for being the most erudite man on the American stage. Short, not particularly good-looking, Barrett was influenced first by Forrest's acting, then by Booth's. His critics universally condemned him for his singsong method of reading lines, but praised his powerful voice and superb articulation. He played all of the roles in the star repertory of the day. His interpretation of Hamlet was said to be austere (Eugene Field, the poet and critic, called it so cold one should see it only in August or at other times protected by a lap robe), but he played a superb Cassius in support of Booth as Brutus. Most critics believed that no contemporary actor matched him in this role. His early death was considered a tragic loss for the American theater.

In the second camp were actors like Frank Chanfrau, who had stock-company training and could play a large complement of parts in their lines of business but were eclipsed in the classic roles by Booth. Lured by quick fame and attendant riches into playing one or two popular parts, they doomed themselves to the fate of donning the same costume, putting on the same makeup, and repeating the same lines on tour and

Edwin Booth chose not to appear very often with members of his family, though four of them were also notable actors. In 1864 he shared the stage with his brothers John Wilkes Booth (left) as Mark Antony and Junius Brutus Booth, Jr. (right) as Cassius in Julius Caesar. Edwin stands between them in the role of Brutus in this daguerreotype by Mathew Brady.

The talents of Lawrence Barrett were definitely inferior to those of Booth and Forrest, but Barrett carved out a place for himself in American theatrical history by persistence and a lifelong pursuit of self-improvement as an actor. John Singer Sargent painted this portrait of Barrett about 1890, shortly before his death.

Opposite, clockwise from top left:
In the case of Rip Van Winkle and Joseph Jefferson III, role and actor became one. Napoleon Sarony photographed Jefferson in a series of poses from the play, and his prints, of which this is one, were included in an edition of the text published in 1871.

Most of the stars who followed Forrest and Booth on the American stage were not interested in creating a vast repertory of roles. William Gillette—who once declared, "In all the history of the stage no performer has yet been able to simulate or make use of a Personality not his own"—always preferred to play himself. A playwright as well as an actor, Gillette wrote himself the juiciest part of his career in his dramatization of Arthur Conan Doyle's Sherlock Holmes stories. He played the master detective from 1899 until his retirement, in 1932.

During the last quarter of the nineteenth century, Clara Morris was the leading exponent of overblown, emotional acting.

Like Joseph Jefferson III, James O'Neill played one role— Edmond Dante in The Count of Monte Cristo— throughout most of his career because the public clamored to see him. Unlike Jefferson, he grew to hate the part and played it only because it brought him money.

with major and minor companies throughout most of their careers. Unlike Chanfrau, who cheerfully perpetuated the role of Mose, the Bowery B'hoy, for years in a series of plays contrived around the character, were actors like James O'Neill who, according to his famous son, hated playing the Count of Monte Cristo. Specializing, O'Neill felt, had destroyed his career as a serious actor, but the Count remained his money-in-the-bank role throughout his life.

Joseph Jefferson III, the scion of a great family of actors, appears to have enjoyed fully his unparalleled career impersonating one character. It all began when he found a mention of himself and his father in *The Life and Letters of Washington Irving*. Taking this as some sort of sign, he searched out a copy of Irving's *Sketch Book*, which inspired him to write his own version of "The Legend of Sleepy Hollow." In 1859 he tried it onstage, but found it unsatisfactory. Recognizing his limitations as a playwright, he commissioned Dion Boucicault to rewrite the piece while they were both in London. He made his first appearance in the new version at the Adelphi Theatre in London in 1865, where it ran for an unprecedented 170 nights, and introduced it in New York the following year. Until shortly before his death, in 1905, Jefferson played the role sometime, somewhere each year. Rip became his masterpiece as well as his meal ticket. To sustain himself as an artist, he tried telling himself that he was playing the part each time for the first time, and he continued to embellish the role throughout his life.

Few nineteenth-century actresses became closely identified with particular roles. None of those who did specialized in comic types. Fallen or martyred women were these ladies' favored roles, in which they could tear a passion to tatters and drown the stage in floods of tears. The first of the American queens of agony was probably Matilda Heron. She made her debut in 1851, at the age of twenty-one, but hit her stride a few years later with her version of *La Dame aux Camélias* by Dumas *fils*, which she saw in Paris in 1854. The existing English adaptation, renamed *Camille*, had been introduced in New York the same year with another actress, but Heron fashioned her own version from the original play. She tried it out in New Orleans in 1855, but it was not until she played it at Wallack's Theatre in New York two years later that it became the rage. She acted the role a hundred nights, then toured it for several years. Her depiction of the Parisian courtesan spared audiences no realistic detail, and her death from consumption in the last scene was harrowing but fascinating to watch. Heron became the toast of the American theater and inspired a generation of imitators. When she died, "Camille" was engraved on her coffin.

In the next generation, Kate Claxton made a career out of acting the blind waif Louise in an English-language adaptation of Adolphe Philippe d'Ennery's melodrama *The Two Orphans* and never failed to leave her audiences awash in tears as she groped piteously around the stage in her costume of rags. The play was introduced at Daly's Fifth Avenue Theatre, but the actress soon separated herself from the company so that she could tour it under her own management. In 1876 she was playing the role at Conway's Brooklyn Theatre when the house caught fire and nearly three hundred people lost their lives. Far from putting a taint on the star, the incident made her the object of ghoulish curiosity, and she continued to play the part for many years throughout the country. The play had an afterlife when D. W. Griffith adapted it for the movies as *Orphans of the Storm* and starred in it Dorothy and Lillian Gish.

Clara Morris never became closely identified with one particular role. She did become known for her interpretations of a particular type, however, and was dubbed the "queen of spasm" by the frequently acid critic Alan Dale. Rising through the ranks from ballet dancer in Cleveland to a member of Augustin Daly's company in 1870, she tried comedy roles before finding her true métier as a heroine of melodrama. A natural-born actress, she had little technique, was not beautiful or particularly well-proportioned, and became mannered in the limited range of roles she could play. Morris was able to weep at will and simulate a death rattle so well that she could be relied upon to cause several ladies in each audience to faint dead away. But what she did well, she did better than any actress alive. Her preparations were as

A tragedienne of high order, Mrs. Fiske also played comedy with great skill. In the role of the social-climbing Mrs. Bumpstead-Leigh, she charmed the public from 1911 until her retirement some twenty years later. About 1925 Miguel Covarrubias drew her in the role (with Sidney Toler).

painstaking as her finished performances were realistic. When Morris played a woman who lost her mind, she first visited asylums to watch the behavior of the inmates. When her part required a hideous facial scar, she reproduced one that she had noticed while riding in a streetcar. In her autobiography she admitted watching a heart patient run up a flight of stairs so that she could imitate the effects of the exertion in one of her roles. (In "remorseful generosity," she afterward slipped a few dollars in the poor woman's hand.) Onstage, Morris reproduced the woman's look of prostration so realistically that several doctors in the audience wondered whether she would make it to the end of the performance. She developed her gallery of neurotic women in plays that died a natural death in their own era.

When Booth died in 1893, so virtually did Shakespeare on the American stage. When Augustin Daly died in 1899, so finally did the stock-company system. When the melodrama and stage spectacle began to bore audiences, the architecture of the theater was altered to accommodate the small, intimate domestic comedy and the intense, focused play of realism. The new plays also required a different kind of acting: a quieter, more restrained style to point up the nuances and shifting moods of the texts. And audiences of necessity changed, too.

Nineteenth-century audiences had greatness of heart and an inexhaustible supply of patience. They attended the same plays season after season, watched the same actors playing the same roles year after year, tolerated the heavy foreign accents of Helena Modjeska and Fanny Janauschek and, even more admirably, listened to Salvini playing Othello in Italian to Booth's Iago in English. They sat through familiar plays waiting for "points"—those small or large charges of electricity in aria-like moments when actors displayed their skill with bits of stage business or a change of voice. They never questioned the premise that the stage belonged to the actors, not to the playwrights. At the end of the nineteenth century, they accepted a multitude of changes just as readily as they had endorsed the old system. They learned to grasp the subtleties of new plays and attune themselves to small niceties in the acting.

If one performer can be chosen to represent the transition from the old order to the new, from nineteenth-century tradition to twentieth-century innovation, that person is Mrs. Fiske. She was born Marie Augusta Davey in 1864, the child of a theatrical family, and began her career as Minnie Maddern, playing such parts as the little Duke of York in *Richard III*. She spent her adolescence acting in the Boucicault "mellers" and she matured into Ibsen and the realist playwrights: classical to romantic to realistic, all in one lifetime. Apprenticed in the barnlike "opera houses" throughout the country in the years when the stage belonged to the shrieking, clutching, emotion-rending school of acting, she settled easily into the new and intimate theaters that were being built in the closing years of the century. When she was seventeen, Lawrence Barrett, a longtime family friend, gave her a copy of *A Doll's House* and told her to look it over. Baffled by the play, she put it aside, but found it impossible to forget. In time, her mind and her art caught up with it.

In 1890 she married Harrison Grey Fiske, the young editor and publisher of the *New York Dramatic Mirror*, the most influential of the theatrical newspapers, and retired from the stage. When she returned in 1893, it was simply as "Mrs. Fiske." Perhaps with the ghost of Lawrence Barrett looking over her shoulder, she appeared in a single matinee performance of *A Doll's House* in 1894, creating a small stir—not because she was the first American actress to play Nora, but because it was she, Mrs. Fiske, who dared to do it. Her name and reputation imparted a new status and respectability to Ibsen's work. In the ensuing years, Mrs. Fiske added *Hedda Gabler*, *Rosmersholm*, *The Pillars of Society*, and *Ghosts* to her Ibsen repertory. It is doubtful that she really ever approved of Ibsen's plays, but she enjoyed the role of crusader and discovered that she could make it pay. An astute and inquiring actress, she was from the start aware that his plays could not be acted in the usual manner and freely admitted that they had taught her much about the art of acting. Anticipating Stanislavsky, Mrs. Fiske found that she had to "discover and comprehend all that has gone before" in the lives of Ibsen's characters in order to play them effectively.

In her maturity, Mrs. Fiske was described as an intellectual actress. In the usual sense of the term, she was anything but. To her critics and audiences, however, the word signified "reserved" or "restrained." It meant not throwing herself around the stage with violent athleticism. It meant a slight inclination of the head, a barely audible gasp, a delicate movement of the hand. It meant, too, a long stage pause now and then, with her back turned to the audience, a thrown-away phrase or an unintelligible word. Mrs. Fiske's unique style invited both harsh criticism and gentle rebuke, none more on target than a bit of doggerel written in 1910 by Franklin P. Adams in the *New York Evening Mail.*

Staccato, hurried, nervous, brisk
   Cascading, intermittent, choppy.
The brittle voice of Mrs. Fiske
   Shall serve me now as copy.

Time was, when first that voice I heard,
   Despite my close and tense endeavor,
When many an important word
   Was lost and gone forever
Though unlike others at the play,
I never whispered: "Wha'd 'd she say?"

Some words she runstogetherso;
   Some others are distinctly stated
Somecometoofast and s o m e t o o s l o w
   And some are syncopated,
And yet no voice—I am sincere—
Exists that I prefer to hear.

For what is called "intelligence"
   By every Mrs. Fiskeian critic
As usual is just a sense
   Of humor, analytic,
So anytime I'm glad to frisk
Two bones to witness Mrs. Fiske.

Alexander Woollcott, the well-known New York drama critic and Mrs. Fiske's worshipful slave and biographer, was the confidant of her ideas about her work. The essence of acting, she told him, "is the conveyance of certain states of mind and heart, certain spiritual things, certain abstract qualities." To further explain it, she borrowed a term from music. The actor must play each moment, each scene, by deflecting off his "thorough-bass"—by which she meant the motivation for his acting, the key to unlocking the truth of the performance. To accomplish this, an actor must "scientifically" train his voice to be responsive to his every thought, to observe life on every level, and to store it in a lexicon of memorized human emotions. Mrs. Fiske was intelligent enough to realize that the new realistic plays could not be treated as star vehicles. What she strove for eventually came to be known as "ensemble acting," but it is doubtful that the eyes of the audience ever left her own riveting performances.

From 1890 to 1920, the era of Mrs. Fiske's triumphs, the American stage was crowded with the type of actor whose fame depends largely on the appeal of his or her personality in a limited number of roles. Some older actors who remembered the stock companies viewed this breed with contempt. Like E. L. Davenport, who lamented, "There are no actors anymore," they scorned a younger generation that had not been required to endure nine changes of bill a week, master a new part in forty-eight hours, rehearse every day, and perform a wide variety of roles. Other actors who had got their feet wet in the old system were adaptable enough to slip into the new order with only the slightest adjustment of gears.

Otis Skinner, who could play thirty-eight roles in sixteen of Shakespeare's plays, became a matinee idol in 1911, at the peak of his career. Handsome and suave as the

Although he never forgot his training as a stock-company stalwart, Otis Skinner slipped into the new system with ease, playing in several long-running productions, including Kismet (1911), his most notable success. In this portrait by Victor Hecht, Skinner is dressed for the role of Colonel Philippe Bridau in The Honour of the Family.

Opposite:
In the theater world, Charlotte Crabtree was known simply as Lotta. From 1865 to 1891, she sang, danced, and clowned onstage to the delight of her adoring public. In this poster she is pictured in her most popular roles.

MRS. GAMAG.

FIRE FLY.

MARCHIONESS.

PAT MALLOY.

LOTTA.

HARRY RACKET.

LYDDY LARIGAN.

LITTLE NELL.

BEAUTY.

swarthy Hajj in *Kismet*, he made female hearts beat a little faster for many a season. But in 1924, when he wrote his autobiography *Footlights and Spotlights*, he could only agree with old Davenport: "Acting has changed. Versatility, once the choicest possession of the players, is being bred out of the stock. Actors are no longer chosen for their ability to express every and any character, but for their physical and temperamental approximation to one particular character." Yet even Edwin Booth had recognized that the actor's physiognomy is an important part of his stock and refused to assay certain roles because he felt he was physically unsuited to them.

Many actors became stars in this era and stretched their careers through decades. The most famous soubrette of the day was Lotta (born Charlotte Crabtree in 1847), who began her career as a child, singing and dancing in the gold-mining camps of California. Pert and redheaded, she graduated from the barrooms and makeshift playhouses into regular theaters, first in the West and then in the East. Possessed of the most ferocious stage mother in the annals of the theater, she was protected and presided over until the only real life she had was on the stage. Although Lotta appeared in a number of roles, she was never anything but herself—and that was enough for her vast following. In 1891 her career was brought to an abrupt end when she fractured her vertebrae during a routine bit of comic business. Her recovery was slow and painful and she was left with a slight permanent palsy. To insure her future, her mother had her take a course in banking and finance so that she could manage her considerable assets. Lotta was one of the earliest stars to become a millionaire, and on her death she left millions of dollars to charity. Her trust is still in existence.

Throughout the nineteenth century the American stage was overrun with Yankees and other American types. They were all upstaged in the early twentieth century by the brash, bouncy, quick-thinking and even quicker-moving, superpatriotic character created and personified by George M. Cohan. Writing his own plays, he offered his adoring public a series of variations on the same role. Part singer, part dancer, part clown, but in every way a consummate actor and professional, he worked himself out of vaudeville into the kingdom of Broadway. Only two actors in the history of American theater have been honored by having their statues erected in public places. One is of Edwin Booth, placed in the not-so-public environs of Gramercy Park opposite his former home, now the clubhouse for the Players. The other is of George M. Cohan, located smack in the center of Times Square, in a spot that overlooks the site of his many triumphs.

Cohan was the real-life nephew of his old Uncle Sam, but he was also the spiritual godson of Edward Harrigan, who in the 1870s and 1880s began the tradition of writing plays about immigrant life. Cohan focused on the Irish-Americans, and the team of Joe Weber and Lew Fields added their memorable "Dutch act" to this burgeoning branch of theatrical Americana. Both born in 1867, both products of the Lower East Side, Weber and Fields appeared together as children in a blackface, acrobatic song-and-dance act. When a vaudeville manager asked them whether they could do a Dutch act—a standard routine in which the comedy builds on heavily accented German (not Dutch) mispronunciations and misunderstandings of English— they unblinkingly told him they could. "Had we been asked if we could do Antony and Cleopatra or Uncle Tom and Little Eva," explained Weber in later years, "our answer would have been the same. 'Yes' had more possibilities than 'no.' " Their Dutch act brought them to Broadway into their own theater and amassed them a loyal following as well as a fortune. Their shows invariably featured a parody of one of the latest Broadway successes. *Quo Vadis* was transformed into *Quo Vass Ist?*, *The Stubbornness of Geraldine* into *The Stickiness of Gelatine*, *Cyrano* into *Cyranose*, and so on. Their burlesques became such good advertisements for the original plays that producers began to send them their scripts with permission to use them as they pleased. Like most comic teams, the pair eventually broke up and pursued individual careers without ever achieving the success they had had together.

At the peak of their fame, Weber and Fields hired the best available talent. One of their stars had her first job in the chorus of a production of *Pinafore* at the Park Theatre in Brooklyn and was discovered in 1881 by Tony Pastor, who changed her name from Helen Leonard to Lillian Russell and billed her as an English ballad singer. From her start in vaudeville, Russell jumped quickly to the musical-comedy stage and became the queen of Broadway. In a series of autobiographical articles, Russell seems disingenuously unaware of her personal charms as she recalls her triumphs as a chanteuse and actress. Trading almost exclusively on her radiant beauty and personality, she maintained a sense of humor about herself and her stardom.

A number of stars at the turn of the century were the creatures of the producers who took over and nurtured their careers. The undisputed theatrical Pygmalion of the era was Charles Frohman, whose roster listed twenty-eight stars at the peak of his career. His first headliner was John Drew, the son of Mrs. John Drew, progenitress of the Drew-Barrymore family of actors. As the leading man of Augustin Daly's company, Drew was already established in American theater when in 1875 Frohman lured him away. He was a polished, suave, and charming actor who essentially played variations on the same role in light, English-style comedies of manners. For five years Drew was paired with Maude Adams, whose career Frohman had been carefully and lovingly tending.

Like Drew, Adams had the theater in her blood. Her mother had been an actress with the Mormon theater in Salt Lake City, and she herself had appeared as a child in California in such standard roles as Little Eva and as Frank Chanfrau's little lost daughter in *Kit, the Arkansas Traveler*. She graduated into adult roles while working with an itinerant California stock company, and with her mother she made her way east. In 1897 Frohman cast her as Babbie in a dramatization of Barrie's *The Little Minister*, and thereafter she appeared in six other Frohman productions of Barrie plays. *Peter Pan* was her greatest triumph, and she played the role long after she should have. Adams became a cult figure, drawing worshipful female audiences, but no one ever considered her a great actress. In William Winter's words, she was "an actress of amiable personality and respectable talent. Her professional career has been a triumph of incarnate mediocrity." In an inverted publicity stunt that was later brought to perfection by Greta Garbo, Frohman maintained an aura of mystery about his star, keeping her secluded from the prying eyes of the press and public. After his death on the *Lusitania*, Adams's career as an actress virtually ceased, although she made a few scattered appearances until 1934.

Without the stock companies to train actors and actresses and groom some of them into stars, Frohman had to keep himself alert to new faces and fresh, interesting personalities and then wait until he found a play in which he could exploit their

Lillian Russell could hit high C with ease, but it was ultimately her beauty and stage presence that drew audiences to the shows in which she starred. Photographer Benjamin Falk arranged her à la Gainsborough for the camera in 1904.

David Warfield was one of David Belasco's few male discoveries, since that remarkable maker of stars concentrated mainly on actresses. Warfield is shown here as hero of The Music Master (1904), one of Belasco's successful productions.

particular qualities. He did this with Adams and again with Ethel Barrymore. After only a few years of training, first with her famous grandmother, then with Henry Irving's company in London, she joined Frohman's production company in 1898 and was made to take understudy roles before she was given a few parts. Finally in 1901 Frohman found her the right role in the right play and she opened to great acclaim as the vivacious opera singer Madame Trentoni in Clyde Fitch's play *Captain Jinks of the Horse Marines*. A few weeks after the play opened, Frohman put her name in lights and made her a star. Her early triumphs with Frohman were largely attributable to her radiant beauty, her famous theatrical name, her engaging stage manner, and the right parts. After his death, she developed into a polished performer. Ever the leading lady, she then appeared in a series of roles, both on Broadway and in Hollywood, that were suited to her personality. As she grew older, Barrymore played heroines close to her own age, scoring her last great success, in 1940, as the crotchety Miss Moffat in Emlyn Williams's *The Corn Is Green*. She had an enduring career and deserved to be called the First Lady of the American Stage during her lifetime.

Frohman was never above stealing performers from other managements. In 1904 he coupled the careers of Julia Marlowe and E. H. Sothern by offering them a contract they could not refuse. Having noted that there had been no important revivals of the Shakespearean repertory, he proposed to send them around the country for three seasons of forty weeks each under a guarantee of $200,000 per season. He lived up to his promise to spare no expense in mounting the productions, and for two of the three seasons he produced their Shakespearean plays. At the time they were approached by Frohman, Marlowe was under the management of the producer Charles Dillingham and Sothern was appearing for Daniel Frohman, Charles's brother. Son of the actor E. A. Sothern, who had made his name and a fortune playing Lord Dundreary in *Our American Cousin*, E. H. Sothern had developed into a swashbuckling romantic hero and an attractive light comedian. Marlowe, English-born but raised in the Midwest, had made her stage debut in a children's production of *Pinafore* and matured into a series of leading roles in nineteenth-century melodramas. Eventually Sothern and Marlowe formed their own company, and in 1911 their private and professional lives merged when they married. Attractive, intelligent, and competent actors, they played well together and created a chemistry that audiences adored. Marlowe retired in 1916, but Sothern remained active on the stage and as a lecturer and reader until a few years before his death, in 1933.

Second only to Frohman in his star-making genius was David Belasco, who not only trained his stable of stars but frequently wrote the plays they starred in. He alone transformed Mrs. Leslie Carter, a society lady from Chicago, into an actress in the mold of Clara Morris. In a succession of roles, custom-made for her talents, Mrs. Carter gave her audiences their money's worth as she tore up the stage in "athletic anguish." In 1895 Belasco cast her in a Civil War play, *The Heart of Maryland*, in which she had one great scene: to save her lover from capture, she grabbed the clapper of a bell, swinging to and fro to prevent it from sounding and alerting the Southern forces. When the play was performed in London, even Shaw was reluctantly impressed.

Although he was best known for nurturing a string of female stars, Belasco also carved a career for David Warfield, whom he saw first in 1899 in one of the Weber and Fields travesties. Warfield grew up professionally in the variety halls of San Francisco and became respectable acting in the revues at New York's Casino, perfecting his vaudeville turn as a Lower East Side Jew. With Weber and Fields, he reached maturity as a comic performer, but Belasco changed the direction of his career. In his first starring role for "Mr. Dave," Warfield rang a slight variation on the character he had developed on the variety stage, a Jewish auctioneer named Simon Levi. It was a triumph for him and a box-office hit. Later, Belasco gave him other kinds of roles, until in 1922, as Shylock in the producer's one and only Shakespearean production, he managed to impress the great Stanislavsky himself. Warfield and Belasco later became estranged and the actor retired from the stage.

This portrait of Ethel Barrymore in the role of Madame Trentoni, heroine of Captain Jinks of the Horse Marines, *was commissioned about 1901 from Sigismund de Ivanowski by Richard Watson Gilder to be used as a color frontispiece in* Century *magazine.*

In that same year, observing the American theatrical scene, Stanislavsky remarked in a letter to his partner in Moscow: "The whole theatrical business in America is based on the personality of the actor. One actor is a man of talent and the rest are nonentities." He was largely correct in his assessment. The most brilliant of the personality actors was Richard Mansfield, who was temperamental, egotistical, imperious, and a terror to his producers and his fellow actors. He was the son of a German opera diva and his talent overflowed into singing, dancing, painting, writing, and sports. He began his career in England in the operettas of Gilbert and Sullivan,

Collecting photographs of stars became the rage beginning about 1880. Reduced in size, they were slipped into boxes of candy or cigarettes to help boost sales. These samples date from about 1900.

then in 1882 moved into light comic roles and romantic parts in America. In 1898, at the peak of his career, he introduced *Cyrano de Bergerac* in a pirated English version, and it was ecstatically received by his adoring public. Although he excelled in roles like Cyrano, his ambition spurred him to try his hand at Shakespeare and Shaw. His acting was mannered in the extreme and his own eccentric, theatrical personality dominated all the roles he played, but some critics considered him the greatest actor of his time and compared him to Edwin Booth. He lived like a star, surrounding himself with such luxuries as a private railway car and a yacht, a townhouse in New York and a country home in Connecticut, an entourage of flunkies, and all the other trappings of his exalted position. Acting was his compulsion, and he died in 1907, at the age of fifty-three, having pushed himself to the limit of his seemingly limitless energies. Although contemporary critics could and did disagree on the merits of his acting, they joined William Winter in finding him one of the most arresting actors in the annals of American theater.

A Broadway legend was born when Mansfield cast a relative unknown in the part of Roxane, opposite his Cyrano. Having looked her over, he allegedly asked the young actress, who was then appearing in Sothern and Marlowe's company, "Do you think you could make yourself pretty enough to play Roxane?" To which she replied, "Yes, if you could make yourself ugly enough to play Cyrano." He hired her at sixty dollars per week, and after the play opened she was greeted with these words from the reviewer of the *New York Herald*: "An unknown young woman of the name of Margaret Anglin will wake up this morning to find herself famous. She possesses no great personal beauty but in all other ways is lavishly endowed by nature to play an important part in the history of the American stage." Once in a while the hyperbole of Broadway becomes fulfilled, and in this case it was amply fulfilled. By birth Margaret Anglin was Canadian and had the distinction of being born, in 1876, in the House of Parliament at Ottawa because the Speaker of the House, whose daughter she was, had his quarters there. At fifteen she decided she wanted to become a reader of Shakespeare on the lecture circuit and was sent to New York to study elocution. She went first to the American Academy of Dramatic Arts, then to the Stanhope-Wheatcroft School, which was attached to Charles Frohman's Empire Theatre. She caught Frohman's attention during one of the school's performances and he arranged to send her on the road with *Shenandoah*, his perennial success. For the next few years, she played soubrette parts with various companies and was still in her early twenties when she received the call from Mansfield. Anglin eventually became a star in her own right and her own producer. In 1906 she picked up a script to read at bedtime and decided to option it the following day. The play was William Vaughn Moody's *The Great Divide*. With Henry Miller opposite her, Anglin made the play a great success and won for herself a reputation for great daring. When she assembled her own company, she confounded everyone by staging not only the plays of Shakespeare but fresh translations of the Greek tragedies.

When Margaret Anglin made the trek from Ottawa to New York to study elocution at a dramatic school, she was reflecting a historical trend. In earlier years, she would undoubtedly have sought out a respectable stock company, but precious few of those remained in existence in the 1890s. The study of elocution had begun in England in the early eighteenth century and had quickly become *de rigueur* for orators and parliamentarians. Books were written about the dos and don'ts of speaking, and many contained charts describing the correct hand and body positions to accompany each emotion. When he was a Philadelphia schoolboy, Edwin Forrest sought out the elocutionist Lemuel G. White, who also instructed James E. Murdoch. After studying with White, Murdoch became a disciple of Dr. James Rush, whose *The Philosophy of the Human Voice* was published in 1827, and spent much of his own life teaching the Rush method. Rush's book went through six editions and was the most influential text of its kind throughout the nineteenth century in America. When the young Mary Anderson decided to go on the stage, she virtually memorized the book as part of her self-training program.

Cyrano de Bergerac *was introduced in America by Richard Mansfield, an erratic but often brilliant actor. This portrait of Mansfield as the hero of Edmond Rostand's enduring comedy-drama was sketched in 1899 by Howard Chandler Christy.*

Opposite:
Julia Marlowe and E. H. Sothern spent their personal and professional lives together as an acting team and as husband and wife. They are shown together here in the balcony scene from Romeo and Juliet.

Rush's system of disciplining the voice dealt with quality, force, timing, abruptness, and pitch—all of which were meticulously examined and copiously described in his book. He went so far as to invent scales with which he illustrated the rising and falling patterns that would produce the most melodious as well as the most meaningful vocal expression for each utterance. When misused, his technique undoubtedly resulted in mechanical and soulless acting, but Murdoch's talent enabled him to transcend the obvious pitfalls of the system. He was one of the few artists that Joseph Jefferson III could "call to mind who were both professed elocutionists and fine actors."

Throughout the first half of the nineteenth century, actors consciously retained an English accent, although some Americanisms were difficult to avoid. Beginning about 1750, as the colonists drifted away politically from the mother country, differences in life-styles—between England and America and within America itself—the overlay of accents arising from the other-than-English antecedents of many of the colonials, and the absence of a rigid caste system produced gradual but noticeable changes in everyday speech. During the next hundred years, the differences became more and more pronounced. Travelers from England could not refrain from commenting (usually unfavorably) on the "American" language. One visitor predicted that "the dialect of Americans will become utterly unintelligible to an Englishman, and that the nation will be cut off from the advantages arising from their participation in British literature."

For a long while, stage speech was exempted from the universal erosion of the King's English in America. From the start, there was a tacit belief on this side of the Atlantic that British speech was better than American speech, and in some quarters the belief still exists. During nearly every period in our theatrical history, Englishmen have been welcomed on the American stage. From 1752, when the Hallams stepped on shore in Virginia, the English influence has been strongest in American acting, and many English actors resisted assimilation in the nineteenth century. James William Wallack spent the largest portion of his career in America, yet never became a citizen. Nor did his son John Lester (Wallack), who established two theaters in New York that specialized in English drama done in the English style. Born in New York, the younger Wallack never considered himself a native. Once, hearing himself addressed at a dinner party as an American, he interjected, "Don't say that. I'm an Englishman, thank God." In a sense, the theatrical English accent died with the stock company, for it was within the old system that the time-honored way of acting the classic English plays was perpetuated.

The idea of a school for actors as a substitute for the school of experience originated with Steele MacKaye. Intending to prepare himself for a career as an actor, he journeyed to Paris in 1869 to study at the famous Paris Conservatoire, but found himself caught in the spell of François Delsarte, who had been developing a system for teaching acting for thirty years. Delsarte thought of himself as a scientist but was actually a mystic, who interpreted everything in threes. Acting for him was based on a trinity of life, mind, and soul, represented by the actor's limbs, head, and torso. Inspiration came from the heart of the actor, who translated what he felt into speech, gesture, and movement. The young American was instantly attracted to Delsarte and his teacher to him. MacKaye became not only an ardent practitioner of the method but also Delsarte's chief disciple and proselytizer. He returned to America, fired with the dream of founding a school based on Delsarte's system of "psycho-physical training," and after a few false starts did finally succeed, in 1884, in attaching a school to the Lyceum Theatre, of which he was briefly manager. A brilliant but impractical man, MacKaye resigned within months of its establishment, but Franklin Sargent took over the academy and remained with it until 1923. Before becoming a disciple of Delsarte and MacKaye, Sargent had taught elocution and dramatic reading at Harvard. In 1886 he renamed the school the American Academy of Dramatic Arts, and so it has remained.

Unfortunately, the Delsartian system became easy prey to misinterpretation and misapplication since the Master wrote very little about his theories. Eventually it degenerated into a collection of formalized poses and facial expressions to depict emotions, not unlike James Rush's system of elocution.

By 1900 the dramatic school had become established as the primary training ground for actors. Many of the schools were founded by retired actors or by the stage managers of a bygone era. In 1888 Dion Boucicault was engaged by A. M. Palmer to teach at the Madison Square Theatre, and until his death two years later he trained according to stock-company principles, casting the students in actual plays and using rehearsals to teach them the art of acting. Other schools had formal classes in speech training and bodily development, including fencing and dancing, in one- and two-year courses. In 1891 Sargent introduced improvisation at the American Academy of Dramatic Arts, and in 1908 Charles Jehlinger, one of his instructors, began encouraging the students to delve into their own emotional experiences—a Stanislavskian approach antedating by many years the Russian master's influence in this country. It was not long before colleges and universities instituted actor-training in a modest way. At Harvard in 1905, George Pierce Baker turned a basic course in playwriting into the "47 Workshop" and staged the plays written by his students. In 1925 Baker moved to Yale, where he founded the School of Drama, which continues to use the conservatory approach to the teaching of acting within its broad curriculum. In 1914, at the Carnegie Institute of Technology, Thomas Wood Stevens assembled a department of drama that offered the first baccalaureate degree in dramatic arts. Today, there is hardly a college in the country that does not offer some kind of dramatic training, and many now award advanced degrees in acting.

If the English had the first and deepest influence upon American acting, second most influential were the Russians. Alla Nazimova introduced the simplified, unmannered "Russian style" of acting in the early years of the twentieth century, but she quickly became a star and did not attract disciples. Visits by the Moscow Art Theatre in the 1920s, however, profoundly affected American actors and directors, and the schools established by several émigré Russian actors exerted a potent and permanent force upon the continuing search for an American dramatic style. It was Richard Boleslavsky, an actor trained by Stanislavsky, who first carried the torch to American shores. In 1923 he founded the American Laboratory Theatre in New York, where he would teach the principles of Stanislavsky for nine years. He was joined by Maria Ouspenskaya, an actress with the Moscow Art Theatre, who remained in this country after their 1922–23 tour. Their arrival could not have been more opportune. The American plays then being written demanded a freer, truer, and simpler style of acting, and the Russian system of "internal acting," based on the actors' own psychological resources, seemed to provide the key to their interpretation. It was Americanized gradually, at the Group Theatre during the 1930s and after 1947 at the Actors Studio, where it was passed down to an entire generation of performers under the tutelage of Lee Strasberg. Strasberg's Method has been frequently challenged by advocates of "external acting" techniques, which are mastered by training the actor's voice and body. Most American actors today are college-educated and have been exposed to both schools, although the Method has been steadily falling out of favor as the broader conservatory approach has been gaining adherents.

Without the stock company to provide steady employment and a secure, if unspectacular, income, actors' lives were profoundly altered. They found themselves "at liberty" in the closing decades of the nineteenth century, scrambling for jobs in the touring companies and auditioning for parts instead of places at the theaters in the important centers. Since New York was the point of origination for most of the touring shows, performers flocked there during the hot summer months to haunt the producers' offices looking for jobs. Familiarly known as the "slave market," Union Square was thronged daily with actors starting their rounds of visits to the offices of touring-production packagers and with agents keeping a practiced eye on the newcomers, looking over pictures posted at the doors of the talent agencies, and repeating the phrase that struck gloom in the actors' hearts, "Nothing today."

Before he became a playwright, director, and general man-about-theater, Steele MacKaye was on his way to a successful career as an actor. The versatile MacKaye later introduced in America the Delsartian method of training actors and made several attempts to found schools.

When they were lucky enough to land a part in a production on Broadway or in a road company, they could look forward to as many as ten weeks of rehearsals for a dramatic play and eighteen for a musical—without pay. They could be fired at whim and without notice and be forced to take pay cuts if box-office business was bad. They would have to furnish their own costumes, unless they were the stars, and they would have to accept sometimes unspeakable conditions backstage: lack of heat, running water, and adequate toilet facilities; filthy dressing rooms; and, for the members of the chorus, cramped, communal quarters. Young, attractive actresses were often subjected to rights of sexual seigniory by lecherous managers and agents. If they were booked for a tour, actors would have to pay their own way to the place where the production originated and their way home if the show closed out of town. If business was poor, the producer could cancel a tour and strand the company hundreds of miles away from home. Without money for transportation, they would have to walk the railroad ties, carrying their baggage and whatever they could salvage. Unlike the old stock-company manager, who was usually an actor himself, the new breed of producer was often a businessman with, at best, tenuous ties to the profession.

As early as 1849, actors had sought to organize themselves professionally. The main purpose of their first professional association, the Philadelphia-based Actors' Order of Friendship, was to care for the sick and aged performers and arrange funerals when necessary. In 1896, within weeks of the organization of the Theatrical Syndicate, the Actors' Society of America was formed, but it was immediately caught in the riptide of the actions of the monopoly. The society was abandoned in 1912 at a meeting in which a committee was appointed to explore the possibility of founding another organization to represent the actors and to redress their universal wrongs. In 1913, when they met again, the Actors' Equity Association was born. By pricking the tough hide of the producers with lawsuits and union-like tactics, the new association began to receive some attention. In an article in *Equity Magazine*, which was established as the house organ in 1915, one of the council members urged the membership to reappraise the nature of the profession. Is acting really a profession? he asked. "Under present conditions ours is not a profession," was his answer. "It isn't even a trade. It hasn't the dignity of a vocation. *It's only a job.* And half the time we don't get paid for it."

In 1917 Actors' Equity submitted a basic contract to the two associations of producers, the United Managers' Protective Association (UMPA), which principally represented the interests of the Shuberts and Syndicate members Klaw and Erlanger, and the Producing Managers' Association (PMA). The UMPA signed the agreement; the PMA refused. The 1917 contract called for, among other things, a limit of four weeks of rehearsal time (still without pay) for dramatic plays and six weeks for musicals; a minimum of two weeks' employment once a contract had been signed by an actor; eight performances per week (instead of the usual nine or ten); transportation from New York and to New York guaranteed for road shows; costumes for actresses making less than $150 per week, which at that time would have included almost all of them; and an arbitration procedure. No mention was made of minimum pay for members or payment for holiday performances, at which the actors traditionally played for nothing. Within weeks after signing the agreement, the UMPA began to fall apart and the contract was rendered null. The battle between the PMA and Actors' Equity flared anew.

But Actors' Equity continued to increase its membership and to make itself uncomfortably visible to the producers. For two years, the two camps engaged in inconsequential parrying and thrusting. Whenever it appeared that a confrontation was in the offing, the producers would evade and outmaneuver the actors. Finally, its patience strained and its temper sore, Equity staged its first strike, early in August 1919. For the next four weeks, looking and acting very much like a union, it systematically strangled theatrical activity in major theater-active cities throughout the nation. It won the support of the already organized stagehands and musicians, who walked off the job in sympathy. Samuel Gompers, head of the American

The actors' strike of 1919 brought the stars of Broadway out on the streets to man the picket lines. To raise funds, the actors staged an all-star show. Some of the performers posed for this White Studio photograph. Standing (left to right): Lionel and Ethel Barrymore, Conway Tearle, John Charles Thomas, Marilyn Miller, Brendan Tynan, Hassard Short, Louise McIntosh. Seated: Marie Dressler, Ed Wynn, and two unidentified actresses. After the tumultuous applause died down, Lionel Barrymore stepped forward to speak. "We're proud to be here," he said. "We'll be here forever, if necessary."

Federation of Labor, placed his powerful national organization behind the actors.

The strike polarized members of the acting profession. The rank and filers stood with the union because they had little choice, but the great stars who were their own producers—George M. Cohan, Otis Skinner, E. H. Sothern, and Mrs. Fiske— founded their own group, the Actors' Fidelity League (nicknamed the "Fidos" by the opposition), to combat Equity. But Equity took comfort in the financial as well as the moral support of Ethel Barrymore and her uncle John Drew, Marie Dressler, Lillian Russell, Eddie Cantor, Ed Wynn, and many of Broadway's brightest stars. In an atmosphere more of carnival than of desperation, the actors took to the streets to enlist the support of the public. They picketed the theaters, they staged a parade in the rain, and they put on their own shows to raise money for their war chest.

The strike made friends of producers who would barely have acknowledged each other's presence in a closet and forged them into an entente cordiale to break the actors in the courtroom. David Belasco, who thought nothing of keeping performers at twenty-hour rehearsals without a break or pay, ferociously vowed to "starve the actors out." As the strike wore on, both sides became more rigidly fixed in their positions, until the producers realized that the American Federation of Labor through its affiliates could effectively shut down all theatrical activity in the country, not just in the major centers. The actors won the concessions they had originally asked for, with slight modifications, and both parties agreed to a five-year contract. In 1924, following a small and selective strike against several producers, Equity made its first advance toward a closed shop, an agreement that the producers must cast no less than 80 percent of a show with Equity members—a stroke that brought the Actors' Fidelity League to virtual extinction.

In the years that followed, Actors' Equity grew in membership and in muscle. In 1933 the union forged a contract that provided for a minimum wage and, two years later, another that won rehearsal pay for actors. In successive steps, Actors' Equity sought and won control of hiring practices in summer-stock and Off-Broadway productions and in regional theaters, dinner theaters, industrial shows, and other types of professional theaters. The union demanded and received better backstage conditions and improved working practices. Through its dues, it maintains a paid staff and its own counsel and executive director and has established a pension and welfare fund for its members. Today there are more than 36,000 members of Equity, but the perpetual status of the overwhelming number of them is unemployed.

Because their work tends to set them apart from the rest of the population, actors have clung together socially as well as professionally. During the late nineteenth century, actors' clubs and associations arose to fill a need, and they tended to cluster

A leading lady for many years, Jane Cowl chose Juliet for her first venture into Shakespeare, in 1923, and played it for nearly a thousand performances both in New York and on the road.

mainly in New York. The Benevolent and Protective Order of Elks was founded (surprisingly) by entertainers, but by 1895, dominated by nontheatrical folk, it had lost its original purpose of bringing together thespians and vaudevillians for conviviality. In 1875 a dinner was given for Henry Montague, a leading actor of Wallack's company. Everyone had such a good time that the group decided to meet once a month. Montague suggested a name for them, the Lambs, and a club was born. The first members were transplanted English actors but eventually, embracing American actors, the club lost its anglophiliac cast. In 1905 Stanford White designed a clubhouse for them on West Forty-fourth Street and the Lambs flourished under a succession of leaders, called Shepherds, for many years. Dwindling membership forced the Lambs to sell their building in 1974 and move to rented quarters farther uptown.

In 1888 Edwin Booth founded the Players, the most distinguished American actors' club, modeled after the Garrick Club in London, "where actors and men of education and refinement might meet on equal terms." When he died, Booth deeded his Gramercy Park brownstone to the club and left a small endowment to run it. From the beginning, the Players' membership has included men from the worlds of arts, letters, business, and the military. It boasts one of the finest theatrical libraries in the country, which includes Booth's own collection of books and a collection of rare American theatrical memorabilia.

Perhaps as a reaction to the exclusivity of the Players, a group of press agents put together their own organization, the Friars, in 1904. Later, they opened up their ranks to producers, theater owners, and, of course, performers. Their titular leader is called the Abbot, and their clubhouse has stood on West Forty-eighth Street since 1915.

Although women are allowed to enter the sacred halls of the Players, the Lambs, and the Friars on special occasions, they are not now, nor have they ever been, offered membership. The clubs were founded presumably as a haven from the daily pressures of the profession, where the members could be militantly male if they wanted to be, and could drink, cuss, swap jokes and gossip, play billiards or cards, and indulge in other exclusively male pastimes. Actresses of the period quickly founded their own clubs to escape the daily pressures of the profession and to be fiercely female if they wanted to be, and to drink tea, swap jokes and gossip, play cards, tat, knit, and indulge in other exclusively female pastimes. Only two of these clubs, established between 1891 and 1913, survive today.

In 1891 the actresses Alice Fischer and Maida Craigen created the Twelfth Night Club, primarily as a social organization but also to stretch out a helping hand whenever it was needed. Today the club maintains a suite in New York's Hotel Woodward and pursues its original aims. The actress Mary Shaw was instrumental in forming two clubs, the Charlotte Cushman Club in Philadelphia and the Gamut Club in New York, but only the Philadelphia club survives today, in a charming house. Shaw had hoped that a whole chain of Cushman clubs would spring up across the country so that "young actresses might live and avoid the hotel expenses and gain the atmosphere of home." Another institution, known as the Rehearsal Club, but more a boarding house for actresses than a club, occupied a brownstone on West Fifty-third Street until 1980, when it lost its tax-exempt status and was forced to close. The club was immortalized in a 1936 Kaufman and Ferber play, *Stage Door*, which starred Margaret Sullavan on the stage and Katherine Hepburn in the movie version. Sullavan had actually lived at the Rehearsal Club when she was a struggling young actress in New York.

Most of the clubs, both male and female, could be relied upon to come to the aid of a member fallen on hard times, but their principal function continues to be social and recreational. In 1882 a group of actors led by Lester Wallack created a purely philanthropic association, the Actors' Fund of America, to provide relief for needy actors, help for the indigent sick, and burial for the destitute. By an act of the New York State Legislature, the association received status as a formal charity and is able to raise money from the public. The officers expanded their activities to include a

home on Staten Island for aged and indigent actors, which they later transferred to Englewood, New Jersey. Beneficiaries of the charity are not only actors from the legitimate stage but anyone who makes his livelihood in the entertainment world. In 1982 the Actors' Fund of America celebrated its centennial with a benefit performance at Radio City Music Hall, "The Night of 100 Stars," which was later

Ziegfeld discovered Marilyn Miller, fell in love with her, and made her a star. One of the musical comedies Ziegfeld created around her was Sunny (1925). In a niche in a building at Broadway and Forty-sixth Street in New York stands a statue of Miller costumed for the show. Clifton Webb, her co-star, gazes up at her in this photograph.

Like many actors of his generation, Walter Hampden took his successes to the hinterlands to give audiences their first prolonged taste of Shakespearean repertory in almost a generation. Shown here is Hampden as Shylock in The Merchant of Venice.

telecast nationally. The president today is Nedda Harrigan Logan, the first woman to be so honored.

By 1920 very little of the old life of the theater remained unchanged. Paradoxically, unionization brought less, not more, control by the actors over what happened onstage. The shorter rehearsal time mandated by Actors' Equity placed artistic control firmly in the hands of the director, who imposed his own views on casts that he had largely selected. Fewer and fewer playwrights were willing to write "star vehicles," and audiences clamored for new faces. Typecasting reached a kind of apotheosis in the 1920s and brought fame to a number of young, untried actors who were able to step into roles that fit them like a glove. Often, their new fame evaporated just as quickly, when the instant stars could not find parts to fit their special talents or, what was worse, wearied the public by playing variations on the same role.

Still, there were many old familiar faces onstage in the 1920s. Appearing regularly in New York and on the road were such stalwarts of bygone eras as Mrs. Fiske, Mrs. Carter, Robert Mantell, John Drew, Otis Skinner, Sothern and Marlowe, and George M. Cohan. Ethel Barrymore, one of the reigning queens of Broadway, and her brothers, John and Lionel—reluctant stage actors at best—made Barrymore a household name. Lionel, the oldest of the three, made his New York debut with his uncle John Drew in 1901. Attracted by the easy money to be had in the fledgling movie industry, he left the stage for the screen, where he became one of the most enduring character actors in film history. During the early 1920s, he made the last of his stage appearances.

John Barrymore made his stage debut in Chicago in 1903 and was on his way to becoming a peerless farceur when he signed his first movie contract in 1914. For the next ten years, he vacillated between the stage and the screen, sometimes grinding out films in the morning and afternoon and appearing on the stage in the evening. In 1922, at the age of forty, Barrymore played Hamlet in New York with such brilliance that his performance has echoed in the theater world through more than six decades. Having meticulously prepared his performance with his coach, Margaret Carrington, Barrymore conceived and enacted a daring interpretation of the role, filled with Freudian overtones. The critic John Mason Brown recalled his own reaction to the performance some years later: "Although I have sat before many Hamlets, some better read and more solidly conceived, John Barrymore with his slim, proud figure, the lean Russian wolfhound aquilinity of his profile, and the princely beauty of his full face, continues for me to be the ideal embodiment of the Dane. His Hamlet had a withering wit. It had scorn at its command; passion, too. Though undisciplined, it crackled with the lightning of personality." Barrymore's fluid acting style marked a decided break with the old nineteenth-century reverence for the Shakespearean word. He transfixed his audiences, but his cutting of the text to streamline the play did not please George Bernard Shaw, among others. In 1925 Barrymore made his penultimate and greatest stage appearance as the melancholy Dane, returning for a final bow in 1940 in My Dear Children, a travesty of his own life that was not worthy of his efforts.

In the 1920s other actors turned to Shakespeare as a test of real talent, like Barrymore. In the nineteenth century, the Bard's plays were the staple of an actor's repertory; in the twentieth century, they were regarded as the cap to a great many careers. Having come up through the ranks, Jane Cowl was an established star in her thirties when she decided to play Juliet in 1923. Although long out of adolescence, she was considered the best Juliet of her time and in amassing almost one thousand performances in the role, both in New York and on the road, she created a theatrical benchmark. Brooklyn-born Walter Hampden went to England as a young actor to study Shakespeare, picked up an English accent, which he never lost, and in 1925 founded his own company to present the Bard's works in repertory at the Colonial Theatre on upper Broadway. For one of his five seasons there he had Ethel Barrymore as his leading lady, playing Ophelia to his Hamlet and Portia to his Shylock. Like the other stars in his generation, Hampden took his repertory to the hinterlands to give audiences their first prolonged taste of Shakespearean repertory in almost a generation.

The careers of Fanny Brice and Marilyn Miller offer a contrast on many levels. Blue-eyed, golden-haired, Indiana-born Marilyn Miller took to her toes to entrance *Follies* audiences with her beauty, grace, and charm. Ziegfeld adored her and created musical comedies around her talents. Her favorite show, *Sally*, was made into a movie. Her premature death in 1936, at thirty-eight, shocked the theater world. A native of New York with little personal beauty, Fanny Brice graduated from the chorus line into stardom under Ziegfeld's tutelage. She became the reigning comedienne of Broadway, often sharing the stage with Miller, Eddie Cantor, W. C. Fields, and other Ziegfeld headliners. She was a born clown and a brilliant mimic. Her rendition of "My Man" in 1921 was a departure from her usual *Follies* stage antics, revealing a side of her that was hitherto unexplored. She, too, went on to Hollywood and for many years brought a vast audience to the radio to hear her comic routine as Baby Snooks, one of the characters she had originally created on Broadway.

Among the best-known burlesque alumni were Al Jolson and Bert Lahr, who each achieved certain immortality. Born in Lithuania in 1886, descendant of generations of Jewish cantors, Jolson possessed an extraordinary light-tenor singing voice. Discovered by the Shuberts in a minstrel blackface act, he made blackface his standard makeup and it became the hallmark of his act—along with dropping to one knee and spreading his arms to sing, a mannerism he introduced in a Shubert show called *Sinbad*, in 1918. In 1927 Jolson made the first of the important "talking" movies, *The Jazz Singer*, still wearing his familiar blackface and dropping into his familiar stance to render his familiar songs. Nine years younger than Jolson, Lahr went from burlesque to vaudeville to Broadway with his first important revue, *Delmar's Revels*, in 1927, and made his mark in the type of musical revue that eventually passed out of favor in the 1930s. Lahr's special comic brilliance was usually the high point of the show. His mugging, vibrato voice, and physical antics inevitably wrung yet one more laugh from his audiences. With his natural comic impulses held in check, he seemed to play the role of Estragon in Samuel Beckett's *Waiting for Godot* as if his whole career had been in preparation for the part. In 1956 he intuited his way through the abstract portrait without consciously understanding it. His irrepressible comic instinct combined with his personal torment born of a profound insecurity unlocked the interpretation of the character.

For many talented performers who emerged in the 1920s, the theater served as a way station while they chased a greater and more universal fame in movies, radio,

Fanny Brice was a vaudevillian before she became a Follies star. Her singing, dancing, and comic routines entranced her audiences on Broadway, but she reached an even greater public when she went to Hollywood and on the air.

Bert Lahr probably never consciously understood Samuel Beckett's Waiting for Godot *but was able to intuit his way through the play brilliantly. Here with Lahr are some of his fellow players in the 1956 production (left to right): Solito de Soltis, Lahr, Kurt Kasznar, Alvin Epstein, and E. G. Marshall.*

Very few of the players in his dramas pleased Eugene O'Neill, but he approved of Walter Huston as the flinty Yankee farmer in Desire under the Elms (1924).

Opposite:
When G. B. Shaw saw a photograph of Katharine Cornell as the heroine of the New York production of his play Candida in 1937, he was driven to write her, "Fancy my feelings on seeing the photograph of a gorgeous dark lady from the cradle of the human race. If you look like that it doesn't matter a rap if you can act or not. Can you?" This portrait of Cornell as Candida was painted by Eugene Speicher in 1925–26. Oil on canvas over wood panel, 84¼ × 45¼ inches.

and, later, television. Beginning in 1908, Walter Huston toured the country in a vaudeville act before he was spotted by producer Brock Pemberton. In 1924 he won the leading role in *Mr. Pitt*, and thereafter he played in a series of moderate and immoderate successes. Before Hollywood lured him away from the real world completely, he appeared in O'Neill's *Desire under the Elms* in 1924, a dramatic version of Sinclair Lewis's *Dodsworth* in 1934, and Kurt Weill and Maxwell Anderson's musical *Knickerbocker Holiday* (as Pieter Stuyvesant) in 1938. Peggy Wood came out of a chorus line in a Victor Herbert operetta displaying such an unusual versatility that she became a star of both musicals and plays. During the 1920s and 1930s, she was seen almost every season on Broadway, but enduring fame came to her in the age of television. From 1949 to 1957, she appeared as the matriarch in a weekly series called *I Remember Mama*, which recounted the life of a Norwegian family in San Francisco around the turn of the century. Her face became as familiar to millions of viewers as their next-door neighbor.

There were a few actors who did not succumb to the golden blandishments of the movies; others made a quick foray and found it not entirely to their liking. Perhaps sensing that her special look would not travel well from stage to film, Katharine Cornell appeared in only one movie, *Stage Door Canteen*, in 1944 in a brief sequence in which she played herself. Throughout her long career as a star, Cornell remained an actress in the legitimate theater and was the last of the troupers. Coming up through summer stock and a succession of small parts, she graduated into the big time in 1921 with a role in Rachel Crothers's *Nice People*, in which she shared the stage with another newcomer, Tallulah Bankhead, and the star, Francine Larrimore. During the 1930s, Cornell established herself as a star in a series of flashy and mostly forgotten plays. *The Barretts of Wimpole Street*, which she produced and her husband, Guthrie McClintic, directed, gave her at last a perennial vehicle. She went on to play Juliet and Saint Joan and, perhaps her greatest role, Candida, in Shaw's play. Cornell took her stardom seriously. In her autobiography, she somewhat solemnly accepted the responsibilities of being the leading lady. "You can't take cold," she wrote. "You must conserve every ounce of your vitality. You must save yourself entirely for the theatre. You must always be prompt. . . . You are always conscious that you owe a debt to your audiences, your fellow actors, to everyone who may be inconvenienced or thrown out of work if, through your own carelessness or self-indulgence, you are not able to carry on."

In the nineteenth century there were queens of the theater; in the twentieth century there are First Ladies. Cornell was one of the chosen few; Helen Hayes was another, before her voluntary retirement a number of years ago. There was hardly a time in Hayes's life when the theater was not a part of it. Beginning as a child performer, she made her way from small to featured roles and eventually to leading ladies on the strength of a pert stage personality and a virginal quality that was very endearing to her audiences. In 1926 she acted the unlovely but magical Maggie in Barrie's *What Every Woman Knows* and displayed flashes of talent of which everyone had been unaware. Her greatest tour de force was as Queen Victoria in *Victoria Regina* (1938), in which she made her first entrance as the young princess and her last as the dowager queen. Although she appeared in movies in the early 1930s, her first loyalty was to the stage until late in her career, when she turned to films and television to capture a fresh audience who did not know her as a First Lady of the American Theater. She remains the most honored and revered of living stage stars. Her consummate professionalism is indicated in the following anecdote related by the critic Walter Kerr. Attempting to define the director's role in a production, he remembered a striking bit of stage business performed by Miss Hayes in *Harriet*, a play of 1943 about the author of *Uncle Tom's Cabin*. In an important scene, the heroine has a disagreement with her beloved husband, and she reacts uncharacteristically by "shooting out her fist at him." Kerr thought it was an action "shockingly, brilliantly true" and wondered who thought of it, the actor or the director? Later, he was to find out that it was Miss Hayes's invention, not Elia Kazan's.

Although she played many roles during her long career, Helen Hayes will probably be best remembered for her acting in Victoria Regina in 1935.

"Lunt and Fontanne" was normally pronounced as one word, representing as it did for millions an electric combination of talents. Alfred Lunt and British-born Lynn Fontanne shared the same stage throughout most of their careers, retiring in 1960 to their home in Genesee Depot, Wisconsin. In 1958 a theater on Broadway was named for them. They are shown here at the close of Robert E. Sherwood's Idiot's Delight (1936) as bombs exploding outside their hotel light up their faces.

Ruth Gordon was another First Lady who received a new lease on her professional life by making movies. In 1915 she came down from Wollaston, Massachusetts, to study at the American Academy of Dramatic Arts, only to be dropped at the end of the first year for not showing enough promise. Persistence caught her a number of small parts, and there was hardly a season during the next four decades in which Ruth Gordon did not appear on Broadway. Her versatility as an actress is attested by the range of roles that she played in her long career, from the ingenue in *Seventeen* to Nora in *A Doll's House* to a Restoration comedy hoyden in *The Country Wife* to the calculating, likeable Dolly Levi in *The Matchmaker*. In 1944 she turned playwright to provide herself with another set of roles tailored to her talents. In her last years she devoted herself to writing her memoirs, which have proved a lively history of the theater in her own time.

No one had a more fascinating career than Tallulah Bankhead, nor a more loyal following, but no one took her seriously as an actress for many years. As a young woman, during the 1920s, she played variations on herself as a flapper and madcap on the New York and London stages. She had glamor and she had an appealing insouciance, which audiences lapped up like warm milk. When put to the test, she also displayed a rare intelligence and a font of real acting ability. It took the right play, *The Little Foxes*, and the right director, Herman Shumlin, to unleash her talents and to astound the public and critics in 1939. But she found it simply easier to return to her old ways and for the rest of her career, with only an exception or two, her mannerisms and her offstage image dominated every role she played. Only in her early movies, before she settled into her public persona, are revealed glimmers of the talent which she squandered so capriciously in her days as a star.

Laurence Olivier once said that all actors spring from unhappy childhoods. Exaggeration it may be, but history tends to support the fact that few stars come from well-adjusted, middle-class families. Unhappy early lives often gave the spur that propelled people of talent into a life in the theater, but success, riches, and fame did not guarantee a return to emotional balance. Many actors turned to alcohol and drugs to relieve their inner turbulence.

In 1922 Jeanne Eagels electrified Broadway as Sadie Thompson in *Rain*, an adaptation of Somerset Maugham's saga about a prostitute who finds religion only to lose it when her redeemer attempts to seduce her. It was an emotionally overwrought part which had found its actress in Eagels. Born in 1890 in Kansas City of a Spanish father and an Irish mother, and reared in Catholicism against which she rebelled, she worked her way out of a traveling tent show in the Midwest into small parts on Broadway. After *Rain* she had no difficulty in obtaining parts but could not sustain them and was fined by Actors' Equity for abruptly leaving the company of *Her Cardboard Lover* in Milwaukee in 1928. She made a few movies and was for a while one of the highest paid performers in the theater. Alcoholism shattered her health and her reputation, and when she died in 1929 it was discovered that she had been a heroin addict as well. Hailed as a great actress by some, she was unable to quell her private demons and became a victim of them. The personal tragedy of Jeanne Eagels was and continues to be repeated in the special world of the theater.

The decade of the 1920s, when many of the best American playwrights began to emerge, was one of the periods in our theatrical history richest in actable parts. Eugene O'Neill felt that his plays made actors into stars, and to some extent he was right. Though Pauline Lord did not physically match O'Neill's conception for the Nordic heroine of *Anna Christie*, from the moment that she walked on stage in the part she captured its essence, and both she and the play were hailed by the press and the public in 1921. Hers was a quiet, mesmerizing style of acting—magnetic, yet elusive—and through it, Lord was able to bring truth to a distinguished series of tragic heroines. Although Paul Robeson is today associated in the public mind with O'Neill's *Emperor Jones*, it was Charles Gilpin who originated the role, in 1920. Gilpin's portrayal of the unscrupulous Brutus Jones brought him an immediate but short-lived fame that prompted a moment of truth within the theatrical fraternity.

The Drama League wished to honor him at their annual banquet and invited him as a guest. Certain members protested sitting down to dinner with a black man, and the story became front-page news. Equally enraged members rallied to the defense of Gilpin, who found himself cheered not by the usual three hundred or so who customarily attended the dinner but many hundreds more who showed up to prove that art transcends race.

Although O'Neill was pleased with Gilpin's performance, he had already been impressed with the natural ability of the young and dynamic Robeson. When the play was revived and sent to London a few years after its premiere, he was given the part of Brutus Jones and was hailed as a great find for the American theater. In 1924 Robeson appeared, amid threats from the Ku Klux Klan, as the black husband of a white woman in O'Neill's *All God's Chillun Got Wings*. On the basis of his performances in the O'Neill plays, Robeson was destined for a preeminent place in the American theater. Unfortunately, Robeson's politics became his crusade and eventually took him further and further away from his theatrical career, but to him belongs the credit for opening the path to acceptance of the black actor in serious roles on the American stage. In his wake followed Rose McClendon, an actress of great power who became a Broadway star with her portrayal of the tormented Bess in DuBose Heyward's *Porgy* in 1927, and Ethel Waters, whose long career as a singer and actress was capped by her poignant depiction of the black housekeeper in Carson McCullers's *Member of the Wedding* in 1950. After the 1920s, the black performer was an accepted part of the Broadway scene, and with the emergence of the black playwright in the 1950s, the place of all minorities in American theater has been assured.

It is equally fair to say that in several important instances O'Neill's plays were immeasurably helped by the presence of stars or established actors in the cast. But for the interest of Richard Bennett, *Beyond the Horizon*, the first O'Neill play to be presented on Broadway, might never have gone into production. At the age of forty-eight, Bennett, a longtime star, was probably too old for the role of the twenty-three-year-old hero, but he wanted to do it and went to the trouble to assemble a cast and introduce it at a matinee performance in 1920. His act of faith brought O'Neill to the bright lights of Broadway, which he was to dominate for the next twenty-five years. Somewhat against the playwright's wishes, the Theatre Guild lured Alice Brady to accept the leading role in *Mourning Becomes Electra* in 1931, and it became the high point of her career. She realized that the tortured, obsessive Lavinia was nothing like her usual parts, but she became caught up in it and performed it with great distinction. Playing opposite her was another star, Alla Nazimova who, despite her lingering Russian accent, contributed to making the production one of the memorable events in American theatrical history.

The quality of O'Neill's dramatic writing stimulated some stars into giving performances of—for them—unusual depths. While they were under contract to the Theatre Guild, Alfred Lunt and Lynn Fontanne were cast in his plays and won for themselves great critical acclaim. Lunt was given the title role in *Marco Millions* in 1928 and Fontanne played the marathon part of Nina Leeds in *Strange Interlude* in 1931. British by birth, Fontanne caught the attention of Laurette Taylor in London and was invited to join her American company in 1916. Her first venture on her own was a comedy, *Dulcy*, written by Kaufman and Connelly, a feather-light part which she played to perfection in 1921. Alfred Lunt was born in Wisconsin in 1892 and also found his key to stardom in a comedy, Booth Tarkington's *Clarence*. The two actors met in 1919, the year *Clarence* opened on Broadway, and married three years later. From 1923 to 1960, they shared the stage in twenty-seven productions and helped to transform the Theatre Guild from a tentative experimental group into the most potent producing organization in the country during the 1920s and 1930s. Although the Lunts acted in several serious dramas together, their forte was comedy, and many of their plays were stitched together for them.

Throughout this period and later, the American stage remained hospitable to actors

An émigrée from Russia, Alla Nazimova arrived in the United States as a star. Her greatest triumphs were in roles created by O'Neill, Chekhov, and Ibsen. She is shown as Nora in Ibsen's A Doll's House in this drawing of about 1908 by artist Sigismund de Ivanowski.

Ruth Gordon began her career with a small part in Peter Pan (noticed perceptively by critic Alexander Woollcott) and ended it with movie roles. Many believe that she was at the top of her form here, in the Restoration comedy The Country Wife (1935).

Opposite, clockwise from top left:
Jeanne Eagels's escape into drugs and alcohol led to her tragic death soon after her promising career was launched. Her performance as Sadie Thompson in Rain (1922) is always cited as a perfect match of actress and part.

O'Neill's plays proved a test of talent. Pauline Lord turned in a memorable performance in Anna Christie in 1921.

Australian-born Judith Anderson thrilled audiences in 1947 with her interpretation of Medea in a version of Euripedes' play by poet Robinson Jeffers. John Gielgud played Jason in that notable production. Seen here are Anderson with the young actors Gene Lee and Peter Moss.

Charles Gilpin always considered the role of Brutus Jones, the Pullman-car porter turned island despot, in The Emperor Jones (1920) his part. For black actors in the early 1900s significant roles were few and far between. Gilpin never again found its equal.

Tallulah Bankhead may well have squandered her considerable talent as an actress in creating a public persona. This portrait of the actress by Augustus John (1930) is in the collection of the National Portrait Gallery, Washington, D.C.

from other English-speaking countries. Since the eighteenth century, the stream of British actors has never ceased to flow westward, and even in the twentieth century many of them continue to stay on. Maurice Evans appeared in New York as Romeo in 1935, acting opposite Katharine Cornell, and he decided thereafter to make America his home. During the 1930s, Evans made Shakespeare proper Broadway fare and toured an abbreviated version of *Hamlet* to the Allied forces during World War II. In 1962 he and Helen Hayes set out on a bus tour lasting nineteen weeks to sixty-nine cities in a show entitled *Shakespeare Revisited: Program for Two Players.* Evans was also responsible for intelligent productions of the plays of George Bernard Shaw on Broadway, although he enjoyed an occasional outing in less serious drama before his retirement, twenty years ago.

Judith Anderson left her native Australia as a teenager, intending to make her mark in Hollywood, but quickly discovered that movie moguls were not awaiting her arrival with breathless anticipation. She immediately decamped for the East Coast, joined a small stock company, and then got the first of her breaks through the actor William Gillette. She made an auspicious Broadway debut in 1923 and thereafter played to perfection a series of neurotic ladies and tragic regal figures. Her most acclaimed role was as Medea, in 1947, and she returned to Broadway to play the Nurse in the same play more than thirty years later. To cap her long career on the stage, in movies, and on television, she was made Dame Commander of the British Empire in 1960, but has continued to make America her home.

The career of Canadian-born Raymond Massey led him first to England and then to America, where in 1922 he got his first important role in O'Neill's *In the Zone* at the Provincetown Playhouse, because of his English accent. He returned to England and did not reappear in America until ten years later. His most triumphant role was as the

Raymond Massey's career began in Canada, progressed in England, and ended in America. The role in which he made his mark on Broadway was as Abe Lincoln in Robert E. Sherwood's play Abe Lincoln in Illinois *(1938).*

Opposite, clockwise from top left:
In 1936 Lillian Gish played Ophelia to John Gielgud's Hamlet in one of the most memorable productions of the decade.

In Philip Barry's The Philadelphia Story *(1939), Katharine Hepburn played a headstrong Philadelphia Main Line socialite, a role not unlike her own in real life. She is shown here with Vera Allen and Dan Tobin. Looking ravishing in the clothes Valentina designed for her, Hepburn later made a movie of the play.*

Zero Mostel's protean talents were expanded to include singing and dancing. He performed to perfection in Fiddler on the Roof *in 1964 and for many years thereafter on the road.*

Jacob Ben-Ami's path to Broadway was via the Yiddish theater in New York. The actor never forgot his roots, returning periodically to the Lower East Side to appear on the Yiddish-speaking stage. Here is Ben-Ami as he appeared in a modern version of Samson and Delilah *in 1920 on Broadway.*

young Abraham Lincoln in the initial production of Robert Sherwood's *Abe Lincoln in Illinois*, in 1938. Writing in the *New York Times*, Brooks Atkinson described his performance as "rude and lazily humorous on the surface, but lighted from within. He suffuses the simplicity of Mr. Sherwood's writing with the beauty of inspired acting." Massey went on to Hollywood, where he eventually became one of the busiest character actors in the movies.

Yet another dynamic element refreshed the American stage as a succession of performers from the Yiddish theater, a refugee in New York from eastern Europe, were lifted from its ranks into the mainstream. Its greatest star, Jacob Adler, had appeared on Broadway in 1905 as Shylock, speaking his lines in Yiddish while the rest of the players recited the English text. Among the earliest of the Yiddish players to make the transition to Broadway were Jacob Ben-Ami and Paul Muni. Ben-Ami was born in 1890 in Russia, Muni five years later in a part of Austria that later became Polish territory. Both came from theatrical families and spent their early lives as actors within the tightly knit community of the Jewish Lower East Side. In 1919 Ben-Ami was discovered by the producer Arthur Hopkins at the Jewish Art Theatre in a play entitled *Samson and Delilah*, which Hopkins moved to Broadway in an English version. In 1926 Muni was cast as an aged Jewish father in *We Americans*, despite his relative youth. With these right roles, both actors reached stardom. In 1931 Muni gave a brilliant performance in Elmer Rice's *Counsellor-at-Law* and nearly twenty-five years later played another lawyer, a fictionalized Clarence Darrow, in *Inherit the Wind*. Ben-Ami appeared in a variety of roles and was associated with the Theatre Guild and Eva Le Gallienne's Civic Repertory Theatre as actor and director during the heyday of his career. Many other American actors could trace their roots to Yiddish theater: members of the prolific Adler family, Joseph Buloff, Menasha Skulnik, Molly Picon, and Bertha Kalich—and, in more recent times, Herschel Bernardi and Walter Matthau. Yiddish theater exists today, for and of itself, but it continues to send performers into the mainstream of American theater.

In 1929 Wall Street laid an egg, the movies were talking, the road to the provinces had grown shorter and shorter, and the halcyon years were over. Established stars as well as flashy debutantes rushed west with breakneck speed. Some never returned to the legitimate stage; others sampled the sunshine and decided that the malodorous air of Broadway was infinitely preferable. Still others, like the Gish sisters, Lillian and Dorothy, commuted between the two coasts. The new faces on Broadway during the 1930s included the dazzling new ingenue Katharine Hepburn and the bright comedienne Shirley Booth. With her stunning looks and aristocratic air, Hepburn soon had a monopoly on spoiled, rich-girl parts, creating the ultimate representative of the type in Philip Barry's *The Philadelphia Story* in 1939. With her in the same play, Booth delivered her funny lines with her own special verve and timing. Both played many other types of roles during their careers, Hepburn, for example, venturing far from the Main Line into a musical about Coco Chanel (1969), and Booth playing the forlorn and pathetic Lola in William Inge's *Come Back, Little Sheba* (1950). Unable to resist the pull of movies and television, both actresses have appeared on the large and small screens, reaching vast audiences far from Broadway.

With economics dictating the number of productions to reach Broadway, fewer risks were taken on marginal material during the 1930s, and the general quality of the fare improved, particularly in musical theater. The 1930s were the heyday of Rodgers and Hart, Jerome Kern, Irving Berlin, Cole Porter, the Gershwins, and Dietz and Schwartz—and their musical comedies and revues launched the career of many a performer. In 1930 the producer Vinton Freedley caught a singer at the Paramount Theatre in Brooklyn and told George Gershwin about her. When she was asked to sing for him, he was so impressed that he offered her a role in his new show, *Girl Crazy*, and advised her against taking singing lessons. The singer's name was Ethel Merman, and for the next twenty-five years the Broadway season seemed incomplete without her presence in a musical or revue. Outside of early and late vaudeville appearances, her entire career was limited to about fourteen musicals and an equal

number of movies. Although it was different from most of the roles she undertook, Merman considered hard-driving, conniving Rose Havoc in *Gypsy* (1959) the pinnacle of her career. She was accustomed to stopping every show several times during every performance, and *Gypsy* afforded only one such moment, but it remained her favorite. She was the perennial darling of lyricists, who could always count upon her to do justice to their lines.

In 1938 a long-legged twenty-four-year-old Texan named Mary Martin, dressed in a bonnet and short fur coat, with no suggestion of much underneath, perched herself on a steamer trunk and sang "My Heart Belongs to Daddy" in a revue by Cole Porter entitled *Leave It to Me!* She was the proverbial overnight sensation and was quickly whisked off to Hollywood to make movies, but did not become a screen star, as had been expected. Viewing her own lack of success in the movies, Ethel Merman once wrote: "The truth is that I was certain I had things to offer that Hollywood was incapable of using. The qualities that helped me on Broadway limited me in pictures." Merman's analysis applies equally well to Martin, who returned to Broadway, her natural arena. After several musicals of moderate success, she finally hit her stride in 1949 as the quintessential Rodgers and Hammerstein heroine, Nellie Forbush, in *South Pacific*. Like Merman, her successes were so monumental that her career embraced fewer than fifteen musicals and plays. In 1977 Merman and Martin appeared together on the stage of the Broadway Theatre in a benefit for the Theatre Collection of the Museum of the City of New York. Walter Kerr summed up the universal reaction at the beginning of his review of the event: "Ethel Merman was the bonfire and Mary Martin was the smoke. They went very nicely together, if you were in a mood to burn up the town."

Musicals made stars of Merman and Martin, and musicals were then made for them as stars—in the peculiar box-office logic of Broadway. With the arrival in 1943 of *Oklahoma!*—a musical without stars—it almost appeared that a new trend had been set, as a spate of starless musicals quickly followed. But since old habits are difficult to break, new stars emerged and had musicals tailored for them the next time around. After a series of lackluster parts following *Oklahoma!*, Alfred Drake finally hit his stride with *Kiss Me, Kate* in 1948 and *Kismet* in 1953. Another alumna of *Oklahoma!*, Celeste Holm went into a starring role in *Bloomer Girl* the following year. In this same incandescent generation of performers were Carol Channing, who went from featured player in *Gentlemen Prefer Blondes* to star in *Hello, Dolly!*; Gwen Verdon, who went from *Damn Yankees* to *Redhead*; and Richard Kiley, who went from *Kismet* to *No Strings* to *Man of La Mancha*. When Yul Brynner supported the great English star Gertrude Lawrence in *The King and I* in 1951, he was not only unknown but many years younger than the character he portrayed. In recent years he aged into the part, which he transformed into the starring role. Zero Mostel was well on his way to becoming a leading actor of the avant-garde theater when he took the part of the Roman slave Pseudolus in the 1962 musical *A Funny Thing Happened on the Way to the Forum*. The role exposed another facet of his protean talents. In 1964 he received the part of his career as Tevye in *Fiddler on the Roof*, which he continued to play on the road for many years after its run on Broadway.

The new musicals, with their integrated scores and books, demand multifaceted talents, and today's aspirants to the musical stage round out their preparation with singing and dancing training if they consider themselves primarily actors, and with dramatic training if they consider themselves dancers or singers. Although musicals will continue to be custom-made for stars, the starless musical will endure, guaranteeing the survival of the genre on Broadway. The musical is the most expensive type of theatrical production, but without stars its costs remain low enough to encourage some risk-taking. The longest-running musical in the history of the American theater, *A Chorus Line*, opened without stars, has sent companies throughout the country and abroad without stars, and continues without stars—transforming what might have been a liability into its chief asset.

In 1947 Elia Kazan and Robert Lewis, who had begun as apprentices with the

Opposite, clockwise from top left:
Ethel Merman was able to assess her own talents: "As a singer, I do one basic thing. I project. That means that I belt the lyrics over the footlights like a baseball coach belting flys to an outfield." This photograph, with co-star Ray Middleton, shows Merman in top form, projecting as Annie Oakley in the Irving Berlin musical Annie Get Your Gun (1946).

As the irresistible Nellie Forbush, the cockeyed optimist from Little Rock in the Rodgers and Hammerstein musical South Pacific (1949), Mary Martin gave the performance of her career.

Carol Channing progressed from the not-so-dumb blonde of Gentlemen Prefer Blondes in 1949 to a middle-aged matchmaker in the long-running musical Hello, Dolly! in 1964. She continues to play Dolly on the road.

Group Theatre, together with one of its founders, Cheryl Crawford, decided to get talented but out-of-work actors out of that "goddam Walgreen drugstore" on Broadway, where they congregated to pass the time and exchange hard-luck stories, into a healthier, more productive atmosphere. They established the Actors Studio as a workshop where actors could test, improve, expand, and develop their talents. Using their own individualized methods, Lewis trained a class of experienced actors that included Marlon Brando, Montgomery Clift, Mildred Dunnock, Patricia Neal, Maureen Stapleton, Anne Jackson, and Eli Wallach; Kazan preferred to work with younger and more malleable performers, among whom were Julie Harris, Cloris Leachman, Betsy Drake, James Whitmore, and Steven Hill. During the first year, Lewis and Kazan invited prominent people to speak to the Studio actors and provided instructors in speech and movement for those who could benefit by it. After the first year, Lewis resigned over a purely personal contretemps with Kazan, and Kazan, his own career as a director in the ascendant, invited Lee Strasberg to take over some of the classes. Although Kazan remained artistic director from 1951 to 1962, his role in the day-to-day operations of the Studio gradually fell to others and the main burden of training the actors fell to Strasberg.

From the time he arrived until his death in 1982, Lee Strasberg and the Actors Studio have been virtually synonymous. In New York in the early 1920s, Strasberg had discovered theater at the Chrystie Street Settlement House and was profoundly influenced by the Moscow Art Theatre's visit to the city in 1923, when he decided to become an actor in earnest. A brief period of training at Richard Boleslavsky's American Laboratory Theatre gave him more direct experience with Stanislavsky's method, and his own budding acting career led him eventually to the Theatre Guild, where he met Harold Clurman, Stella and Luther Adler, and Cheryl Crawford, who were to join him in the creation of the Group Theatre. By the late 1940s Strasberg had achieved moderate success, first as an actor, then as a director of plays and films, but when he began giving private acting lessons he found his true vocation. Kazan thought him a natural teacher and the right person to assume the chief responsibilities of the Actors Studio. Strasberg read everything in sight and educated himself until he achieved an eclectic erudition in theater, the arts, and psychology.

In a recent book, a "biographer" of the Actors Studio, David Garfield, gave as coherent a description as is possible to find of the Method—inspired by Stanislavsky, nurtured by the Group Theatre, amplified by Strasberg, and subjected to more mysticism, misinterpretation, and criticism than any other aspect of modern American theater: "The publicists' stereotype of the Method-mumbler aside, there is still a distinguishable phenomenon that can be identified as 'Studio acting.' It is a mode of performance readily differentiated from typical English or French acting. It is unconventional, deeply felt, and psychologically detailed. It is more impulsive than calculated and more openly emotional than intellectual. It has idiosyncratic qualities, which at their worst fall into mannerism and at their best create the effect of unique, living individualities." Method-trained actors were exactly what the fresh generation of American realist playwrights had been waiting for. They slipped effortlessly into roles created by Arthur Miller, Tennessee Williams, and William Inge and later by Paddy Chayefsky, Edward Albee, and Arthur Kopit. Like it or not, they constitute the only American School of acting. When he was the reigning director on Broadway, Kazan invariably chose Method actors for his casts: three of the four principals in *A Streetcar Named Desire* (Kim Hunter, Karl Malden, and Marlon Brando) were Studio members. As Kazan and Strasberg both recognized, one of the failures of the Method is that it cannot work with classical plays, which require long periods of intense training. No matter its limitations, for about twenty-five years, Method actors dominated the Broadway stage, movies, and television. If it is not now the force it once was, and if some of the early converts have left the fold, the influence of the Actors Studio has not been eclipsed by any other. Actors Studio West was founded on the West Coast in 1966. Without Lee Strasberg it is difficult to predict what course the studios will take and whether they will survive at all.

Jason Robards and Colleen Dewhurst both began their careers off Broadway, where, in due course, they were directed by José Quintero. In 1973 the three were reunited in A Moon for the Misbegotten, the first successful production of Eugene O'Neill's play. Shown with Robards and Dewhurst in that play is Ed Flanders (left), who, though not forty years of age at the time, played the role of Dewhurst's father convincingly.

What is most striking about the roster of life members of the Actors Studio is that the overwhelming number of them deserted the theater for the movies and television. The two quintessential Method actors, Marlon Brando and James Dean, had the briefest careers on the stage. Considered the most brilliant of the Method actresses, Kim Stanley flashed across Broadway during the 1950s in William Inge's *Picnic* and *Bus Stop* and then left abruptly in 1964 to return home to New Mexico and become a teacher of acting. Her exact contemporary Julie Harris broke into the public's field of vision when, in 1950, at the age of twenty-four, she played a twelve-year-old tomboy in Carson McCullers's *The Member of the Wedding*. Since then, she has become one of the few contemporary actresses who can attract audiences on the strength of her name alone. Her career has included important films and a number of television appearances. A year after Harris, another Method actress, Maureen Stapleton, found fame in Tennessee Williams's *The Rose Tattoo*. From the somberness of the realist playwrights, she turned to roles in comedy and was the star of two Neil Simon plays, *Plaza Suite* and *The Gingerbread Lady*.

Lee Strasberg liked to think of the Method as an individualized approach to acting, since its aim was to enable each performer to confront himself in order to embrace the character of the person he played. Of all the successful members of the Actors Studio, only Geraldine Page seems to have achieved the ideal that Strasberg

envisioned, for all too frequently the reverse occurred as Method actors imposed themselves on the characters they played. After studying at the Goodman Theatre School in Chicago, she gave herself one more year to try for success as an actress. She chanced to meet José Quintero in Greenwich Village and he, remembering her from the Goodman, invited her to come to see a performance at the Circle in the Square. Impressed, Page asked him for a part, any part, before she abandoned her ambitions. Quintero cast her in the 1952 revival of Tennessee Williams's *Summer and Smoke*, a production that brought instant attention to the theater and the director and launched Page's career. After a brief fling in Hollywood on the strength of her Off-

In 1968 James Earl Jones electrified Broadway in The Great White Hope, *playing a prizefighter who throws a championship fight to a white contender. He had originated the role at the Arena Stage in Washington, D.C.*

Opposite, clockwise from top left:
Pairing the talents of José Ferrer as Iago and Paul Robeson as Othello resulted in a once-in-a-lifetime performance: the Margaret Webster production of Othello *for the Theatre Guild in 1942.*

The fragile heroine of Tennessee Williams's tragic A Streetcar Named Desire *was played with unfailing skill and sensitivity by British-born Jessica Tandy in 1947. In a terrifying scene in the play, Marlon Brando as her brutish brother-in-law wreaks his vengeance by raping her.*

Another "graduate" of the New York Shakespeare Festival, Kevin Kline made it to Broadway when a surprise hit of 1981, The Pirates of Penzance, *was moved from the Delacorte Theater in Central Park to Broadway.*

Although he was only thirty-seven at the time, Lee J. Cobb created the role of the over-the-hill salesman Willy Loman in the original production of Death of a Salesman. *In this photograph of 1949, Tom Pedi as the Bartender is standing over the kneeling Cobb.*

Broadway success, Page returned to New York and worked actively with the Actors Studio until 1964, when she and her husband, Rip Torn, became displeased with the handling of the organization's production unit.

Without a trace of offstage glamor, onstage Page is able to project a vast range of characters, from the alluring to the grotesque. The Boston critic Elliot Norton called her the only "subversive" actress on the American stage, "the only one willing—and able—to subvert her own personality, to eliminate her own image, her own personality, her own appearance and to assume that of the character the playwright has created."

Although audiences cheered the stunning performances of the actors who graduated from the Group Theatre and the Actors Studio, they were also electrified by established performers who had taken ways more traveled by. In 1945 Laurette Taylor opened in *The Glass Menagerie* by the then largely unknown playwright Tennessee Williams. For the actress it was an especially poignant triumph. Her career, which had begun with the new century, had been marked by periods of great success and others of failure and despair. She became nationally known through her portrayal of the pert little Irish heroine of the dramatic trifle *Peg o' My Heart*, written for her by her husband, J. Hartley Manners, in 1912. They took the play to London and revived it again on Broadway in 1921. Between those years and after, she appeared in ten more of her husband's plays, none as successful as *Peg*. A period of personal unhappiness plunged Taylor into a long bout with alcoholism and her appearances on the stage became fewer and fewer. In 1938 she was given a small part in *Outward Bound* and made so much of it that Richard Watts, Jr., of the *New York Post* was moved to write, "It merely happens that she is one of the finest actresses in the world." Although Taylor continued to read scripts, she rejected all of them until she received *The Glass Menagerie*. Her portrayal of Amanda Wingfield, the faded Southern belle turned to desperate aging mother, inspired rhapsodies of praise. Critics and public alike concurred with Stark Young's appreciation, "Here is naturalistic acting of the most profound, spontaneous, unbroken continuity and moving life. . . . Technique which is always composed of skill and instinct working together, is in this case so overlaid with warmth, tenderness and wit that any analysis is completely baffled. Only a trained theatre eye and ear can see what is happening, and then only at times." Although the role has been played frequently by other actresses on stage, screen, and television, Laurette Taylor's performance has remained the touchstone.

The prodigious talents of José Ferrer led Oscar Hammerstein II to remark, at the height of the actor's career, "Ferrer is a young man who can scare hell out of you with his Iago, double you up with laughter as Charley's Aunt and choke you with tears as Cyrano—a handy man to have around the American theatre." His parents took Ferrer from Puerto Rico, his birthplace, to New York for his education and later sent him to Princeton, where he met Joshua Logan, James Stewart, Bretaigne Windust, and Myron McCormick and decided, not surprisingly, on a career in the theater. Second only to his skill as an actor is his talent for directing, and for several years in the 1940s and 1950s, he exploited both. As for many of his generation, the lure of Hollywood proved too strong and he spent much of his career on the West Coast before his recent retirement.

In the plays written between 1920 and 1950, when American playwrights were attacking old themes with fresh vigor and dramatizing uniquely national subjects, there was no dearth of challenging parts for actors. In 1949, at the age of thirty-seven, Lee J. Cobb played the battered and defeated Willy Loman in Arthur Miller's *Death of a Salesman*, astounding the public with the truth of his portrayal. Shedding her English accent, Jessica Tandy originated the role of Blanche DuBois in Tennessee Williams's A *Streetcar Named Desire* in an unforgettable performance in 1947. In the revival of O'Neill's *The Iceman Cometh* at the Circle in the Square in 1956, José Quintero cast Jason Robards in the part of the reformed drunkard Hickey, an inspired piece of casting that not only united an actor with a role he could play intuitively but

sparked a new interest in America's greatest playwright. The tide of reawakening interest in the genius of O'Neill, created largely by Quintero, swept Colleen Dewhurst into the public eye. At twenty-six, she had made her Broadway debut in a small part in a 1952 production of *Desire under the Elms*, but more than ten years later she played the leading role in the same play at the Circle in the Square under Quintero's direction. She eventually found for herself the one O'Neill role that had previously defied casting—the hulking Irish romantic Josie Hogan in *Moon for the Misbegotten*. In 1958 at the Circle in the Square and in 1973 on Broadway, Dewhurst *was* Josie in one of the most perfect unions of actress and part.

In the old days, actors made their way by playing bit parts on Broadway and graduating to bigger roles until they became well-known character actors or—the lucky ones—stars. A few fortunates were given roles so suited to their own chemistry that they found themselves stars overnight. When the postwar Off-Broadway movement began, a vast reserve of talented actors wisely decided to create their own opportunities. Off Broadway no longer looked upon Broadway as Mecca and now served its own ends. Inevitably, it became possible to launch an acting career without following the familiar route. Aided and abetted by the original Circle in the Square and Joseph Papp's New York Shakespeare Festival—both cradles of acting talent— actors could go from Off Broadway to Hollywood to television—and to fame—without having ever trod the familiar road to Broadway. A case in point is George C. Scott. Until he was thirty, Scott spent his time acting in regional theater. When he arrived in New York, he auditioned for Joseph Papp in the role of Shakespeare's Richard III, got it, and drew critical praise for his offbeat interpretation. From there he went into a movie, a Broadway play, television, back to Off Broadway (at both the New York Shakespeare Festival and Circle in the Square) until—more than ten years and a few more Broadway sorties later—he was starred on Broadway in Neil Simon's *Plaza Suite*. Throughout his peregrinations, Broadway has been only one whistlestop.

One of the most recent generation of players who commute routinely from the stage to films to television, Kevin Kline spoke for his peers when he declared, "I want to do it all." In its basic pattern, his career has not differed materially from those of Meryl Streep or Michael Moriarty. As representatives of the latest breed of performer, all three are college- or university-educated and all had training of the conservatory type, Streep at the Yale School of Drama, Kline at the Juilliard School, and Moriarty at the London Academy of Music and Dramatic Art. At some point in their careers, early or later, they touched base at the New York Shakespeare Festival. Streep's rise has been meteoric, without the boost of a starring role on Broadway. All three are highly trained, versatile, committed actors, who have shown uncommon intelligence in managing their careers. They adhere to no particular school or style of acting and have not permitted themselves to become typed by any of the parts they have played. They are in the tradition of American actors in their eclecticism—trying new techniques and adapting to the contingencies of their roles—and in so doing, they represent the healthiest development in the continuing evolution of American acting. Both in their formative periods and in their professional lives, they have steadfastly refused to restrict themselves to "safe" roles. If American actors continue to take risks in order to increase their virtuosity, the current generation will keep alive the spirit and vitality that has become part of the acting tradition of this country.

In the beginning, Americans were taught to act by the best teachers—the English—but nearly a hundred years went by before they learned to act themselves. They have always taken what they wanted from all acting styles of all periods and fused it into an essence that became uniquely American. In recent times, they have had the small satisfaction of seeing Method acting usurped by the English, perfected, and returned to the stage in a form that has suited the plays of the postwar crop of English realist playwrights. In the twentieth century they lost the art of performing Shakespeare, in which they had excelled in the previous century. They are peerless in what they do best—the plays of O'Neill, Williams, Miller, Mamet, and the realist tradition. Who could ask for anything more?

Because opportunities to appear on the principal New York stages with any regularity are limited, Glenn Close and Mary Beth Hurt, members of the current generation of actresses, have spread their careers across Broadway, Off Broadway, regional theater, and television. In 1985 they appeared on Broadway in Benefactors, *an English play, to great critical acclaim.*

Opposite above:
Without the usual boost of a starring role on Broadway, Meryl Streep's rise has been meteoric. She returns periodically to the stage where she began, at Joe Papp's New York Shakespeare Festival. In 1980 she appeared as Alice in a version of Alice in Wonderland, *with music by Elizabeth Swados, at Papp's New York Public Theater. Streep is shown here at the Mad Hatter's tea party with (left to right) Mark-Linn Baker, Richard Cox, and Michael Jeter.*

Opposite below:
In the new generation of conservatory- or university-trained actors can be found performers like John Rubenstein, whose versatility allows him to star in both musicals and dramatic fare. In Children of a Lesser God *(1980), by Mark Medoff, he appeared with Phyllis Frelich, a product of the National Theatre of the Deaf.*

DESIGNERS

SCENERY

ON JULY 21, 1786, St. George Tucker, a businessman from Virginia, did what every visitor to New York City has done ever since: he went to the theater. With his wife and a friend, he saw a performance at the John Street Theatre of Nathaniel Lee's *The Rival Queens; or, The Death of Alexander the Great* tricked out (according to the handbill) with new scenery and illuminations. In the second act, they witnessed the "Triumphal Entry of Alexander into Babylon, with a display of Armorial Trophies, Spoils, Ensigns, &c descriptive of his conquest." Tucker duly recorded his reactions to the experience in a letter to his children back home in Williamsburg. He had nothing good to say about the performance, but the evening was made tolerable, he allowed, by the scenery. He was especially struck by "a fall of water [that] was most admirably represented—Your mama and Mr. Peachy declared that they were quite sick at the sight, it was so perfectly natural."

Considering that in 1786 the theater had hardly set roots in America, Tucker's close attention to scenic artistry comes as a surprise. Yet the seasoned company at the John Street Theatre, then under the younger Lewis Hallam, had long recognized the importance of scenic effects. The first professional American company had brought with them some vestiges of the scenery used at William Hallam's old London theater, the Wells on Lemon Street, in Goodman's Field. It probably consisted of a green baize proscenium curtain and some rolled drop curtains depicting a wood and a street and interiors of a palace and a cottage—which together would have had to serve a repertoire that included Shakespeare, Restoration comedies, early melodramas, and several heroic dramas. When in 1758 the Hallam company passed to the management of David Douglass, things improved. A year after he took over, he commissioned a new set of stock scenes from William Williams, an English landscape artist then residing in the colonies, and in 1766 sent to London for scenery from Nicholas Dall, the chief artist at Covent Garden. For a few years, beginning in 1762, he even employed one Jacob Snyder of Providence as company scene painter and generally paid as much attention as his manager's purse would allow to the mounting of his productions.

By the end of the eighteenth century, when new and better-equipped theaters were being built, a scene painter and his staff were added to the regular complement of managers and performers in each stock company in major cities. The inspiration for scenic and lighting effects continued to flow from England and Europe for many generations to come, but the small group of scenic artists working in America during the late eighteenth century learned to create breathtaking effects and to paint splendid scenes for an audience ever hungry for visual novelty, an audience that was coming to the theater with greater expectations than ever before. St. George Tucker would not be the last American playgoer to leave the theater humming the scenery.

The early stage artist did not receive the kind of billing that his twentieth-century counterpart receives. He could console himself, however, with the fact that his salary was well above the average performer's and frequently matched or exceeded that of the principal players of his company. Until about the last quarter of the nineteenth century, he had the luxury of rather handsome budgets for his department, largely as a result of the type of play that the managers, looking into their pockets, felt obliged to produce. William Dunlap at the Park Theatre and his colleagues at theaters of similar standing in Boston, Philadelphia, and Charleston lamented the deteriorating public taste that demanded more spectacle and less cerebration on the stage. Unfortunately, the money spent by the scenic department was responsible for the downfall of more than one manager, with Dunlap being perhaps the first casualty.

The early scene painter's workplace was the stage that had evolved from sixteenth-century Italian Renaissance models. It was "raked," or built to slope upward toward the back wall of the theater, in order to accommodate sets designed in forced perspective, a feat attained by making elements of the scenery in the background smaller than similar elements in the foreground. The scenery consisted of a series of paired flats, or "wings," narrow, tall graduated pieces of painted canvas stretched on frames that could be made to slide in grooves on either side of the proscenium arch, and a background made of two large painted shutters or, alternatively, a rolled drop curtain. To mask the upper part of the proscenium opening, short curtains, or "borders," were hung in sizes gradated to match the wings as they decreased in height from the front to the rear of the stage. (The actors could not venture behind a certain line or they would appear ludicrously disproportionate to the scenery.) An English artist, Philip de Loutherbourg, who worked for the great David Garrick at Drury Lane, introduced several effects that quickly became standard both in America and abroad toward the end of the eighteenth century. Having suspended in front of the upstage wings gauze curtains painted with special scenes, he trained lights on them from behind to give the illusion of moonlight, fire, erupting volcanoes, and moving clouds. He also invented devices to create sounds of thunder, winds, the lapping of waves, and storms of hail and rain.

During the first wave of theater building after the Revolutionary War, it became increasingly common to raise the roof over the stage to accommodate painted curtains, which could be quickly lifted or "flown" out of the sight of the audience while different curtains were dropped in their place. The "fly gallery" became a standard fixture of theater architecture and has endured to the present.

The scene painter's palette included a selection of organic and inorganic pigments more than adequate to satisfy any painted effect he might try for. Bright whites, ochers, siennas, vermilion, oranges, Prussian and indigo blues, and green were among the colors he added to water and size to create distemper, the paint applied to various weights of linen, muslin, or canvas. The cloth was stretched on wooden frames, primed for tautness, and then painted by the scenic artist and his assistants. Throughout most of the nineteenth century, the stretched and primed cloth was hung high up on the back wall of the theater. The scene to be painted was then blocked out in charcoal, square by square, and then colored in by painters, who moved up and down on a scaffolding known as the "flying bridge." Olive Logan recalled that "many an actress has got a good dress covered with drippings of paint which have dropped from above during her rehearsal." The paint-spattered back walls of standing nineteenth-century American theaters bear testimony to this method of creating scenery.

All but the most primitive eighteenth-century stages were equipped with at least one trapdoor so that Hamlet's father or Satan could disappear as if by magic, but the nineteenth-century stage could also boast machines called bridges, which raised or lowered parts of the stage; counterweight systems to fly curtains into the high "stage house," or "stage loft" (the airspace above the stage); multiple trapdoors (each with a special purpose) in the stage floor; and backstage machines to create the sounds and effects of thunder, wind, falling glass or crockery, rain, and snow. The eighteenth- and nineteenth-century scene painter often functioned as his own stage machinist, but the increasing complexity of stage spectacles demanded a specialist. This individual was charged with inventing bigger and better effects, until in 1899 he was allowed to steal the show from everyone in Klaw and Erlanger's famous production of Ben Hur.

Aside from a few names and descriptions in programs or newspapers, nothing is

Not much can be gleaned from this fragment of an early nineteenth-century set design by John Joseph Holland for Adelmorn the Outlaw, *but it is one of the earliest preserved drawings of scenic art in America.*

Using a broad expanse of blue sky on his backdrop, the scene painter Victor Moblard created the setting for Wallack's production of The Merchant of Venice *in 1859. In the foreground of this original watercolor by Moblard are James W. Wallack as Shylock, Lester Wallack as Bassanio, and John Brougham as Gratiano.*

known about the scenery and the men who designed it in the 1700s. When William Dunlap became actively involved in theatrical production in the closing years of the eighteenth century, he hired Charles Ciceri as his scene painter. Noting in his *History of the American Theatre* that scenic decorations up to that time had been "lamentably poor" and that most of the old stock scenes had become "black with age," Dunlap recounted Ciceri's life and contributions to stage art. Born in Milan, Ciceri was dispatched to an uncle in Paris after his father died. There he learned a little landscape drawing and the "rudiments of science" before he embarked upon his life of adventure. He worked at theaters in San Domingo, Paris, Bordeaux, and London, before embarking for America to make his fortune. Though he was shipwrecked with all his worldly goods in the Bahamas, he survived seventeen days on an island and was rescued and taken to Providence. Eventually he made his way to Philadelphia, where he was hired as a scene painter, probably at the Chestnut Street Theatre, then being built by Thomas Wignell. From 1794 until about 1807, Ciceri painted scenery at the old John Street Theatre and at the new Park Theatre under Dunlap. His relationships with the managers were often stormy and complicated somewhat by his imperfect command of the English language. Dunlap reports that there were frequent resignations and rehirings. When Thomas Abthorpe Cooper became the new manager of the Park Theatre, he commissioned John Joseph Holland to redecorate the auditorium. Enraged, Ciceri left the theater, turned exporter of French merchandise to New York and, according to Dunlap, lived out his existence comfortably in France.

Ciceri's scenery for *As You Like It*, which opened the Park Theatre in 1798, was so lavishly praised that he was allowed free rein thereafter. His enthusiasm probably hastened Dunlap's financial downfall, but while he held sway Ciceri created spectacular effects with paint and canvas: vistas of harbors, castles, winter landscapes, dungeons, ancient ruins, picturesque villages, and the like. For *The Constellation; or, American Triumph* (1799), the good ship *Constellation* became in his hands not a two-dimensional cutout but a perfect model of the ship itself! Ciceri was adept at painting lifelike figures on his backdrops, and under his aegis the stage of the Park appeared crowded with actors marching in procession.

Ciceri was at the forefront of his generation of American scenic artists, who during this early period were mostly foreign-born. Many of them worked or trained with each other. J. J. Holland, C. Milbourne, Antony Audin and his son, John Worrall, Joseph Jefferson I and II, Hugh Reinagle, Luke Robbins, and John Evers launched the profession in the early decades of the nineteenth century at the theaters scattered along the eastern seaboard, and the fraternity grew not only in number but in importance.

As the country prospered in the antebellum years, audiences became larger, more democratic, and less sophisticated. They clamored for spectacles and took a fancy to the latest importations from Europe, the melodramas. With unrealistic but moralistic plots, romantically remote settings, and music underscoring the taut emotional scenes, these plays took hold in the late eighteenth century and dominated our stages in the nineteenth century. Melodramas built theaters all over the land—big ones—to accommodate audiences hungry for fresh situations, novel twists of plot, exotic locales, and increasingly inventive stage effects. Whatever else they offered, they provided a field day for the stage designer. One of the most successful of the painters who observed and grasped the opportunity was Russell Smith. Born in Scotland in 1812, he and his parents settled in southwestern Pennsylvania in 1819, moving later to Pittsburgh. When young Smith showed artistic ability he was sent off to study portrait painting. In 1833 actor-manager Francis Courtney Wemyss appeared in Pittsburgh to open a theater and hired Smith, after his first choice had proved unsatisfactory. Smith showed immediate promise and soon became part of Wemyss's company, which traveled through Pennsylvania and West Virginia. When Wemyss leased the Walnut Street Theatre in Philadelphia, Smith was set to redecorating it with a patriotic theme. He also painted a splendid drop curtain representing the battle of Bunker Hill. Though Smith continued to travel for the rest of his career—to Washington, Boston, New York, Wilmington (North Carolina), Savannah, Baltimore, and every other sizable town in the East—he considered the Philadelphia Academy of Music his home base. At one time or another, he painted scenery for Edwin Forrest, Edwin Booth, and Dion Boucicault, and his work was glowingly and often meticulously described by theatrical critics. He was one of the few scene painters in pre–Civil War America who received mention in theatrical handbills.

Smith usually strove for both historical accuracy and originality in design, avoiding, as he wrote, "all false color, glitter and exaggeration of every kind, whilst striving to represent the most beautiful features of Nature. The Material, canvas and color I used were as genuine as the best oil picture." He also observed wryly in his journal that he was forced to make adjustments in his designs "at the behest of managers, who lacked subtlety."

Most of the early nineteenth-century scene painters worked at one time or another for Henry and William Hanington, who specialized in producing panoramas and moving dioramas and toured them throughout the country between 1832 and 1870. It was excellent training since pictures of extraordinary verisimilitude were called for. While these artists were creating trompe-l'oeil scenes of extreme detail and realism, however, the plays they designed were as remote from reality as it is possible to travel.

But at mid-century the winds of change began to blow and, as usual, they blew from England and Europe.

In 1841 Madame Vestris, the actress-manager, introduced a novel setting for her Covent Garden production of Dion Boucicault's fresh comedy of contemporary life, *London Assurance*. It really looked like the interior of a drawing room, with three walls, ceiling, chandeliers, carpets, and furniture. The new "box set" was in tune with the spirit of Boucicault's comedy and his comedy was enhanced by the setting it received. The play and production leaped the ocean quickly, opening at the Park Theatre in New York in October of the same year. Although American scene designers did not immediately scrap the typical wings and drop and border curtains of the period, the echo of the first production of *London Assurance* reverberated throughout the remainder of the century. Inevitably, the box set was established as *the* way to visually interpret the "modern" drama of domestic implosion.

It was Charles Kean, arriving in New York with his English company of actors early in 1846, who infused new ideas into the scenery for Shakespearean productions. Charles lacked the gifts of his father, the great Edmund Kean, but he did have a clear concept of how Shakespeare should be played and displayed. Since the Bard's comedies and tragedies were part of the stock repertory of every theatrical company, most of the time it was the scripts that had to carry the weight of the productions—not the scenery and costumes, which came out of the stockrooms of the theater. Charles Kean changed all that. He tore into old books and musty records to find authentic descriptions and illustrations of early costumes and settings—the minutest details of which he later described at weary length in his playbills. Happily for everyone, Kean's ardor for his own erudition resulted in gorgeous settings and magnificent costumes. His production of *Richard III* at the Park Theatre early in 1846 cost $10,000 and was painted under his supervision by the American scenic artists Henry Hillyard, Peter Grain, and their assistants. Some of the costumes and armor were imported from London, while others were made at the theater. The critic of the *New York Herald* declared it to be "in truth the most splendid, magnificent, and gorgeous spectacle of which theatrical annals have record," and the reporter for the *Albion* rhapsodized about it in prodigious length in his columns:

We confess that even with the magnificent and striking effects of the first four acts...we felt some doubts as to the perfect realization of the almost unapproachable rendering of the battle scene....But the opening scene of the fifth act set the matter at rest. The scene represented a landscape "near Tamworth bridge" a beautiful soft picture of English scenery—over the bridge the army of Richard enters—old English, long bowmen, Norman cross bowmen, with their cumbrous shields—bellmen—soldiers with steel battle axes—Nobles with emblazoned surcoats—and banners bearing the emblem of St. George and other appropriate designs.

Kean took his experiments back to England, and between 1850 and 1860 at the Princess's Theatre in London he treated his audiences to production after production of Shakespeare's plays done in this manner. American scene painters were impressed and theater managers as well, since they could not fail to notice that Kean's productions filled seats. For the next forty or so years—until the arrival of the next boatload of new ideas—American scene painters and stage machinists transported audiences with feats of artistic derring-do, though they continued to utilize the basic equipment and techniques that had prevailed for nearly two hundred years.

In the hands of one native American stage artist, Charles Witham, this stock-in-trade was considerably refined and refurbished. Born in Portland, Maine, in 1842, young Witham found employment in his native city as an assistant to Gaspard Maeder, later the head designer at Niblo's Garden in New York. After a few years of itinerant landscape painting in New England, Witham was hired in 1863 as chief scene painter at the Boston Theatre. There he was to design the settings for the plays acted by America's great tragedians Edwin Booth and Edwin Forrest. So outstanding was his work that Witham was immediately snatched away by Booth to become the principal scene painter at the Winter Garden in New York. For Booth's 1864

Charles Lehr was one of America's most highly respected scene painters during the nineteenth century. His training as a dioramist in the 1830s is evident in this sketch in Harper's Weekly of a scene he created for a production of The Jewess, a melodrama produced in 1853 at the Boston Museum. (The heroine was, of course, saved from the boiling cauldron at the finale.) As was customary at that time, the set consisted of an elaborately painted backdrop, in front of which were placed the props and functional scenery.

An important associate of the nineteenth-century scene painter was the stage machinist, who was called upon to create props of great complexity. The chariot for Klaw and Erlanger's spectacle of 1899, Ben Hur, was so cleverly constructed that it could ride over treadmills, lose a wheel, yet carry the driver to victory.

production of *Hamlet*, Witham was asked to paint three new scenes. The rest of the scenery was to have been supplied from the storeroom, but in cahoots with Joseph Hanley, Booth's stage manager, Witham decided to redesign the entire production after discovering that there was enough canvas and paint on hand to do the job. Largely abandoning the old wing-and-drop system, Witham designed a series of architectural settings strongly influenced by the box set. Whatever reservations Booth might have had about the new look of *Hamlet*, they disappeared instantly when the public received the production with acclaim.

In 1869 Witham followed Booth into his new theater at Sixth Avenue and Twenty-third Street in New York. There he created a more flexible stage than had been devised to that time and was probably instrumental in making a real break with the past. He eliminated the traditional raked stage, grooves in the stage floor to hold the wings, doors in the proscenium, and thrusting apron, or forestage, in front of the proscenium arch. He raised the stage house to a height of seventy-six feet to make room to fly backdrops and for hydraulic elevators to raise and lower heavy pieces of scenery from the basement. Wings or flats could now be individually braced to the stage floor and, what was more important, could be randomly scattered across the stage area. Although these improvements in stagecraft had already been made,

Witham was probably the first to include them all in one theater.

Booth's financial difficulties and his inability to pay anyone a decent salary probably led Witham to seek greener pastures with Augustin Daly. Witham remained as one of the scene designers on Daly's payroll from 1873 to about 1880. During that time, Mark Twain selected him to design the Daly production of his play *Ah Sin* in 1877, and Witham stayed with the production as it toured the country. Witham's career and the subject of his designs changed completely when in 1881 he became the scene designer for Edward Harrigan, the great chronicler of street life in New York. Starting with Harrigan's basic ideas, Witham first drew detailed scenes of Manhattan, from which were created the models, then the designs, and finally the sets for the productions. Harrigan could occasionally churn out his plays in short order and once he wagered Witham and Witham's stage mechanic, William Vail, that he could write a play faster than they could build the sets for it. A month later the script was finished but the set was missing a few strokes of the paintbrush and Harrigan won two hundred dollars.

Witham remained with Harrigan until 1890, and from then until he retired, in 1909, he worked for a number of New York managers on a freelance basis. He died in 1913. Unlike the great body of original nineteenth-century stage art, Witham's carefully wrought scene renderings were preserved and presented by his family to the Theatre Collection of the Museum of the City of New York. Since representative examples of the work of his contemporaries is lacking, it is difficult to ascertain just how typical of the era Witham's stage art was. But certainly it reflects the nineteenth-century obsession with historic detail and reveals an expanded use of color, due no doubt to improvements in stage lighting, and a full-bodied architectural quality that was the result of abandoning the wing-drop-and-border system. As designer for men of the theater as different as Booth and Harrigan, Witham had ample opportunity to expand and try his talents, as his preserved art attests.

Because of the forceful presence of the manager in the last decades of the nineteenth century, the scene designer continued to play a subservient role in theatrical production. His job, after all, was to provide backgrounds for plays, musicals, and melodramas—not to use his art for comment or to advance or enhance a message. Once in a while, something would stir the American scene painter out of his well-paid complacency, as when Henry Irving and his English troupe arrived for the first of several tours of the States. In the fall of 1883, Irving moved into the Star Theatre for his first production, *The Bells*, a psychological melodrama with an unusually realistic edge. Although it took them a while to get used to his mannered acting style, New York audiences appreciated the completeness of the production: the sense of ensemble, the realism of the setting, and the atmospheric lighting. Irving personally set the tone for all of his productions but chose his associates carefully. His scene designer was Hawes Craven, a stage artist who had apprenticed at Dublin's Theatre Royal, where he had attracted attention by the originality of his scenic designs. He had a painterly style, which gave the effect of fine watercolor drawings, and his settings were considerably enhanced by a deft use of lighting. The designer bathed the stage in soft, colored lights, which heightened the three-dimensionality of the papier-mâché detail.

From the end of the Civil War to the turn of the century, about four thousand theaters were built from coast to coast. Only the major houses in the principal cities could afford to employ a resident scene designer; the rest made do with scenery purchased from one of the manufactories that had sprung into existence to satisfy their demands. In 1875 Mathias Armbruster, a young scene painter from Germany, settled in Columbus, Ohio. There he set up the Armbruster Scenic Studios, which in its heyday became one of the largest manufacturers of stock scenery in the country. Armbruster furnished settings for plays starring Tomasso Salvini, Sarah Bernhardt, Helena Modjeska, James O'Neill, and Robert Mantell, as well as for the hundreds of small "opera houses" and school and community theaters throughout the Midwest. Among the backgrounds stocked by the studio were Victorian hotel lobbies, southern

Charles Witham was scene painter at Edwin Booth's New York theater, where he produced sets of breathtaking beauty. Shown here is a watercolor drawing of act 1, scene 2 from Booth's 1869 production of Hamlet (the audience room in the palace). The influence of the box set is clearly evident.

Most theaters in the nineteenth century contained workrooms. Charles Witham painted this watercolor of the interior of the paint room at Edwin Booth's theater between 1869 and 1873, while he was the star's chief scenic artist.

swamps, South Sea islands, Atlantic City, deserts in Arizona and the Holy Land, and a Japanese garden. The Armbruster craftsmen worked with pure-color aniline dyes and distemper on several weights of muslin, using small, feathery brushstrokes. The aniline-dye drops could be folded or rolled, but the distemper pieces had to be sent flat. The studio continued in business, with Armbruster's sons at the helm, until 1958, when there was no longer a market for their business. In order to hang on for so many years, the Armbrusters shrewdly altered their artistic course to follow new trends in theatrical production.

The studio that advertised itself as the world's largest came into existence several years after Armbruster's. In 1891, fresh from an eight-year Parisian sojourn, a young painter named Lee Lash got work in San Francisco as the designer of an advertising olio curtain, a concept dreamed up by P. T. Barnum. Never one to let a revenue-producing opportunity slip by, Barnum had hit upon the idea of selling advertising space on a theater curtain to be rolled down in front of the stage during scene changes and sometimes at the beginning or end of a show. His artists painted the names and sales pitches of advertisers in bold, bright colors on these curtains, patchwork-style, until Lash conceived the idea of incorporating the names of the advertisers in natural places within a street scene. Lee's brother Sam offered to hang such a curtain at the Tivoli Opera House without charge as long as he could sell the advertising space. The combination of Lee's talent and Sam's business acumen gave birth to Lee Lash Studios, which quickly expanded its operations throughout the country. In 1893 the Lash brothers outgrew San Francisco, moved east to Philadelphia, and came to rest on Broadway in 1898. For thirty years, their studio produced backdrops, curtains, and sets for the Shuberts, Klaw and Erlanger, Sam Harris (George M. Cohan's producer), and David Belasco as well as hundreds, perhaps thousands, of large and small theaters throughout the country. The studio distributed a stock book showing plain and fancy interiors and street, horizon and forest drops, as well as special pieces. All could be ordered by submitting measurements of stage and proscenium, supplemented as necessary with little diagrams. In 1926 Lee Lash sold out his interest in the company to H. J. Kuckuck, the firm's treasurer, and returned to the easel to paint landscapes and street scenes for the rest of his days. Kuckuck continued to run the company until his death, in 1945.

In 1894 Richard Marston, one of New York's leading and busiest scene painters, attacked the "scenery factories," which he said produced theatrical settings "on the same principle as teaboard workshops." Marston decried the use of "cheap colors, cheap materials and the imitated art of established scene painters." But since the business had proven successful, it was to endure despite the bitterness of the old guard. In several cases, scene painters themselves set up scenery shops.

With the decline of the Lee Lash Studios in the 1920s, other firms arose to supplant it, and one of them, Nolan Scenic Studios, still exists today. In the 1920s Joseph Urban established the Triangle Studios, introducing European stagecraft techniques to America, and in the 1930s Cleon Throckmorton, one of the New Movement designers, published a series of catalogs for college, school, community, and little-theater groups, offering not only a full range of equipment down to the smallest stage screw but copious advice gleaned from his experience as a designer and builder of many Broadway stage settings. At first, the shops were clustered in and around the theater district, but as New York real estate became more and more valuable, they moved to Brooklyn, New Jersey, the Bronx, and Westchester County. Today, the studios work out the technical engineering conceived by ever-inventive scene designers.

Catching the tailwind of the exploding labor unionization movement, the scene painters formed their own association in 1892, the American Society of Scene Painters, in order "to promote the artistic and practical efficiency of the profession." Twenty years later, edging into the mainstream of the labor movement, they established the United Scenic Artists to protect their professional interests. Gone was the era when scene painters like Mitchell Cirker would work for five days on the complicated sets for Maurice Maeterlinck's *The Blue Bird* without leaving the workshed set up outside St. Louis. They began by asking for and getting more money, fewer hours, and better working conditions and ended in 1918 by formally joining the Brotherhood of Painters, Decorators and Paper-hangers of the American Federation of Labor, Local 829. Contracts were and continue to be periodically negotiated to regulate all aspects of the scene painter's professional life.

At this period, the union included the men (and a few women) who wielded the paintbrushes in shops or at theaters, but not the rising generation of designers who worked at the drawing board in their own studios. Men like Joseph Urban, Norman Bel Geddes, Robert Edmond Jones, and Lee Simonson initially balked at joining the union. Their job, they felt, was to furnish the inspiration *first,* to supervise the drafting of plans *second,* and to consult with the painters, carpenters, and electricians when the set was being installed onstage *last.* In 1923, sensing that hostility between the artists and the craftsmen might result in sets not getting built or painted, the designers agreed to join, provided that they could negotiate fees and terms for their own group. Under the umbrella of the union, for the first time designers received full recognition for their contribution to a theatrical production; their names now appear on the program under the title and above the enumeration of the cast, no longer lost in the fine print of the credits at the end. Today, designers are bound by rigid requirements and must pass an examination given to prospective union members. Beginning with Aline Bernstein in 1926, women began to join the "brothers"; the costume designers followed in 1938, and the lighting designers were admitted in 1962.

Fooling and feasting the eye had been the main concerns of the nineteenth-century scene painter. But in the waning years of the century, a new type of play was pushing sprawling melodramas off the boards. Labeled "well-made" by a later generation, it was tightly constructed, had fewer characters, and was modest in scope. Such plays demanded a realistic setting—the interior of a room complete with three walls, a ceiling, and real furniture, or part of a garden—and the box set offered the best means of achieving it.

The man who raised the realistic box set to its highest form in America (and perhaps in the world) was David Belasco. The canvas never flapped on a Belasco set, the windows moved up and down, the doors were made of wood, the rocks of plaster, real flowers bloomed in the window boxes, and real wheatcakes sizzled on the grill. Belasco had served his theatrical apprenticeship on the West Coast, moved to the East in his journeyman years, and then struck out on his own in 1895, putting into practice all that he had picked up along the way, from the innovative stage work of W. T. Porter in San Francisco to the visionary experimentations of Steele MacKaye at the Madison Square Theatre in New York. Filled with exquisitely irrelevant detail, Belasco's box sets were alone worth the price of admission. His technique won the highest praise of James Gibbons Huneker, New York's most influential dramatic critic in the 1890s and early 1900s: "In all the theatres I visited at London and on the Continent, I saw nothing that had not been foreshadowed by the genius of Belasco; not the startling lighting effects of Gordon Craig, not the atmospheric innovations of Reinhardt, nor the resonant decorations of Bakst were novel to me, for I had watched the experiments at the several Belasco theatres, had heard the discoverer himself discourse his theme."

Although not a scene designer in the literal sense, Belasco worked closely with his principal designers, Wilfred Buckland and Ernest Gros. Gros once described Belasco's *modus operandi:* "When a play is to be put on at the Belasco theatres, Mr. Belasco sends for me, and he literally acts the entire play for me himself. Then he tells me what he desires. I am at liberty to make suggestions. Perhaps these are accepted; perhaps they are not. But the consultation is exhaustive. Mr. Belasco is exacting. He wants results, and these are only obtained by hard work on his part and that of everybody else. Plenty of time is given. We spend from six to seven months in preparing a play." Gros and Louis Hartmann, Belasco's lighting designer, remained with him for more than twenty years—something like a lifetime then and now in the

For David Belasco's production of Zaza (1900), Ernest Gros split the stage into two areas. Loading each with realistic and romantic details, he created an on-stage, off-stage environment.

theater—and they always received program credit for their work, which approached genuine artistic collaboration.

Realistic box sets of the type Belasco popularized dominated the stage for about twenty years, and the theater has never really outlived them. Whenever the curtain is rung up and a perfectly livable room or dazzlingly lifelike outdoor scene is revealed, the scene designer should be somewhere quietly tipping his hat to David Belasco. But the upcoming generation of American scene designers would reject Belasco's approach and travel to Europe to learn more about the craft of Adolphe Appia and Gordon Craig. The new theater that Appia and Craig were separately but eloquently expounding required neither visual pyrotechnics nor skillful but artificial realism, but simple, suggestive, symbolic or abstract scenery that would place the focus on the actor and, through him, on the drama. One column would suffice to suggest a Greek temple, and one tree a forest, for the play of light and the skill of the actors would charge the atmosphere with emotion and meaning. Yet theatrical settings were not to be mere backdrops for the actors. They would assume an almost metaphysical role, becoming, in the words of Donald Oenslager, a disciple of the new stagecraft, "the silent characters of the designer—the realization of all that is in the mind's eye of the dramatist."

The first of these travelers abroad to bring back in his theatrical trunk the new look in stagecraft was Livingston Platt. Born in Plattsburg, New York, in 1874, Platt originally intended to be an artist, but study in Paris brought him in contact with the world of the theater and altered the course of his career. In 1903 be took over a small theater in Bruges and began to experiment with scenery and lighting. His work caught the attention of the local minister of fine arts, who induced him to design the sets for several operas.

In 1911 Platt returned to the United States at the invitation of Mrs. Lyman Gale, the manager of the experimental Toy Theatre in Boston. On a tiny twelve-by-twenty-foot stage, he created impressionistic scenery stripped of all but the most necessary architectural elements. Opting for pale monotones and subtle, diffused, even minimal lighting, Platt set his stage in planes against a blue cyclorama, making no attempt to create false perspective.

In his early, experimental period, Platt relied heavily on mass and line and flexible, fluid lighting schemes. As he said, "It seems to me that the next step in theatrical art is toward a more imaginative stage. All superfluous details should be eliminated and the settings should stimulate the audience to create in their own imaginations the dominant features of the play." Margaret Anglin saw a set of this type—"a cyclorama lit with hot yellow, a single sail showing above a low wall of yellow"—which Platt designed during his Boston sojourn for a production of *The Comedy of Errors* at the Castle Square Theatre. The actress liked it and asked Platt to design four of her Shakespearean productions in the same manner. For these plays, which have rapid changes of scene, Platt increased the stage apron to allow action to take place before the curtain while interchangeable units were slipped into place behind.

Success inevitably led Platt to New York, where he became a much-sought-after designer. For Kaufman and Ferber's *Dinner at Eight*, he designed a most stylish set, all done in Art Deco. A turntable stage used almost cinematically effected rapid changes of scene. From 1923 to 1933, Platt designed six or seven plays a year. His career ended abruptly after he was charged with impairing the morals of a minor. The designer disappeared, a presumed suicide.

The second strong push toward modernism in American scene design was made by the Viennese architect–book illustrator–interior decorator Joseph Urban, whose bold and unusual settings for the opera house startled conservative Bostonians during the 1911–12 season. By 1911 Urban had carved a successful and award-laden career in his own country and elsewhere on the Continent. Lighter, simpler, more suggestive and impressionistic than traditional opera scenery, his Boston sets were painted in vivid and varied color and lighted exquisitely, at times achieving a special fairytale quality. Introducing American scene painters to the French technique of pointillism, he covered a base color with flecks of paint in built-up layers. When white light was played on the canvas, the surface took on a textured feeling; when colored light was used, one of the flecked layers was made to appear dominant. In order to achieve the

The rebellion against the busy Belasco type of box set was led by Livingston Platt, who designed simple, evocative scenery that depended heavily for effect on atmospheric light. Shown is his 1913 design for the priory scene in The Comedy of Errors at Boston's Castle Square Theatre, in which he used light to create depth on a shallow stage.

Joseph Urban created breathtakingly beautiful scenes with colored light. Here is his rendering for the opening scene of Ziegfeld's Follies of 1916.

203

kinds of effects he wanted, Urban set up his own scenic studio and hired European craftsmen, who introduced the technique of painting large expanses of canvas resting on the floor, rather than hung on the back walls of a theater or studio.

Urban treated the stage as an architectural environment with many invisible planes, rather than as a floor surmounted by an expanse of air. He included platforms in his settings and used narrow walls and solid horizontal borders to alter the dimensions of the stage. After two seasons in Boston, Urban was engaged by none other than Florenz Ziegfeld, who was searching for someone to give his productions a distinctive look. For years the stage designer produced scenes of incredible beauty and versatility to complement the flamboyant theater manager's lavish spectacles. Then in 1917 Giulio Gatti-Casazza, a master from a different theatrical world, called upon his prodigious stagecraft. The manager of the notoriously conservative Metropolitan Opera House, who was accustomed to having his sets shipped from Italy, asked Urban to design a production of *Faust*. The result so pleased him that he engaged the designer to revamp a number of the productions in the repertory. From then until his death, in 1933, Urban functioned as artistic director of the Met. He was once asked to design a new opera house, then envisioned in the environs of Columbus Circle, but the project was postponed out of existence.

Urban worked with Thomas Lamb on the design for Ziegfeld's theater, which did become a reality, in 1927, on the corner of Fifty-fourth Street and Sixth Avenue. He decorated the interior, uniting stage and auditorium through what he described as "animated detail" but what might be better termed high Art Deco. Urban worked for other producers but continued to design Ziegfeld's shows. One of the highlights of his career was his collaboration in the ground-breaking musical *Show Boat,* produced by Ziegfeld in his new theater in 1927.

Livingston Platt and Joseph Urban assimilated the strong new European currents but did not transform them into a distinctively American expression. That revolution awaited the passionate and articulate voice of Robert Edmond Jones. On the very eve of his long and illustrious career, Jones predicted, "I am distinctly pro-American and I believe that in a few years we will lead the world in stagecraft." The man who wrote these words in 1917 had not seen a professional stage production until he left the family farm in New Hampshire to begin his college career at Harvard, in 1906. While at the university, Jones visited the theaters and vaudeville houses of Boston and quietly enrolled in "English 47: The Technique of the Drama," the course taught by Professor George Pierce Baker that was to propel many a future designer, director, and playwright into the mainstream of American theater. After graduation, Jones remained at Harvard for two years as an instructor in the fine-arts department before trying his luck in New York. There he became part of a circle of young, educated free thinkers that included John Reed and Kenneth Macgowan. His friends decided to send him to Europe for a *Wanderjahr* and set up "The Robert Edmond Jones Transportation and Development Company" to finance the grand tour. Jones made a beeline to Florence, but for some reason did not succeed in getting into the atelier that had been organized by Gordon Craig for the promulgation of his ideas. Instead, he made his way to Berlin, via Paris and a few other stops. Enormously impressed by Max Reinhardt's concept of total theater and his painstaking attention to every aspect of production, Jones worked with the Austrian producer's designers and began to formulate his own credo.

In 1914, within a few months of returning to New York, he received an assignment that not only elevated his career into the theatrical stratosphere but won playgoers over to a concept of stage design at the antipodes of Belascoism and inspired a generation of stage artists to shake the theater free of the conventions of the past. Harley Granville-Barker, the English producer-director, working under the auspices of the Stage Society of New York, asked Jones to design a one-act play by Anatole France, *The Man Who Married a Dumb Wife,* limiting him to "a door, two windows and a room." What he received was a setting of geometric simplicity in silvery gray tones and black outlines. Touches of color were provided by the props and costumes,

which Jones also designed. The setting drew the kind of attention that Jones was later to condemn. "Scenery isn't there to be looked at, it's really there to be forgotten. The drama is the fire, the scenery is the air that lifts the fire and makes it bright."

For the next forty years, Jones had the rare privilege of living exactly the kind of artistic life he had envisioned and putting into execution all of the ideas that crowded into his lively imagination. He became the high priest and principal spokesman of the new stagecraft, or New Movement, in America. He turned the ideas of his European mentors into something quite unique and American because he reached toward his own roots and the national cultural experience for his stimuli. His lectures and writings about what he was trying to achieve were frequently hortatory and highfalutin, but his colleagues knew him to be an intensely practical Yankee when it came to working with paints, canvas, and lighting.

Jones designed for experimental groups such as the Provincetown Players, the Washington Square Players, the Neighborhood Playhouse, and the American Laboratory Theatre under Richard Boleslavsky; for the Metropolitan Opera Association, the Philadelphia Grand Opera Company, the Chicago Opera Association, Sergei Diaghilev, the Theatre Guild, and the Playwrights' Company; for producers Arthur Hopkins, Brock Pemberton, Flo Ziegfeld, William A. Brady, Dwight Deere Wiman, Jed Harris, and Max Gordon; for Radio City Music Hall (briefly, as art director); and for the City of New York during the Shakespeare Tercentenary Celebration in 1916; and sets for plays by William Shakespeare, William Congreve, Eugene O'Neill, Edward Sheldon, Clare Kummer, Sidney Howard, Sean O'Casey, Anton Chekhov, August Strindberg, Philip Barry, S. N. Behrman, Sophie Treadwell, and Henrik Ibsen. Within his settings appeared some of the most talented performers on the English-speaking stage. Without the least exaggeration Jones could write in the foreword to *The Dramatic Imagination,* a compilation of his thoughts and ideas in essay form, "I have had the good fortune to be associated with the foremost artists of my time."

Jones had no fixed style; his was an inspired eclecticism. He believed that every play has its own characteristic quality and that his task was to "enhance and intensify this characteristic by every means in his power." He thought of settings as "a kind of symphonic accompaniment or obbligato to the play" with no independent life of their own. Everything must be directed toward the performance; as soon as the actors entered, the background should disappear. In actual practice, his settings did not disappear; they were frequently striking and gloriously effective.

Jones's unit setting for the 1922 production of *Hamlet* with John Barrymore in the

In the early 1920s, Norman Bel Geddes's fierce drive brought him several commissions from the Metropolitan Opera, the Chicago Ballet, and producers William A. Brady, Morris Gest, and Winthrop Ames. His name was firmly established in 1924, when he designed the scenery for Max Reinhardt's morality play The Miracle, for which he transformed the entire Century Theatre in New York into a giant cathedral-like ambience. Shown above is the Inquisition scene from that famous production. Escaping the confinements of the proscenium arch became an obsession; Geddes's massively sculptural sets encroached insistently upon auditorium spaces. Geddes is considered by his peers to have been a designer of uncompromising genius. His stage sets were comparatively few in number, but together they transformed the concepts of Adolphe Appia, Gordon Craig, and Reinhardt into an assured American idiom.

Jo Mielziner enrolled at the Art Students League in New York and later at the Pennsylvania Academy of the Fine Arts in Philadelphia. In 1921 he got a job with Jessie Bonstelle's stock company in Detroit and worked as an actor, scene designer, and stage manager. Two years later, he joined the Theatre Guild, where he would learn the significance of stage lighting from co-designer Lee Simonson. In 1924 Mielziner designed The Guardsman. From that point on, Mielziner was represented on Broadway by as many as a dozen shows a year, for which he also preferred to design the lighting and costumes whenever he could. Of all American stage artists' renderings, his most closely approach fine art. They are also notable in that they approximate the actual stage picture in mood as well as physical detail. Shown here is Mielziner's superb set rendering for Death of a Salesman (1949).

leading role, which consisted of a simple center stairway leading up to a high, vaulted archway, was so skillfully lighted that it produced the effect of many scene changes. But he had no patience with the "suggestive" settings of some of his American and European colleagues. A single Gothic column did not represent a cathedral for him. It made him feel as if he "had been invited to some important ceremony and had been given a poor seat behind a post." He reiterated over and over his belief that a setting should not be a self-conscious and self-indulgent expression of an aloof designer, but a thing inspired by the playwright and brought to life by performers. The element that lifted it into existence was light. He often quoted Max Reinhardt: "I am told that the art of lighting a stage consists of putting light where you want it and taking it

For The Fabulous Invalid, *a play of 1938 that chronicles the deterioration of a theater from its opening night to its end as a derelict building,* Donald Oenslager *designed four scenes, of which this is the first. Oenslager was one of the lucky theater men whose lives are characterized by goals achieved, conceptions brought to actualization, and zeal rewarded. He studied at Harvard, then went to Europe to absorb Continental stagecraft. Back in America, he became Robert Edmond Jones's assistant at the Provincetown Playhouse. He debuted as a stage designer in New York in 1925 at the Neighborhood Playhouse on Grand Street, with a production of* Sooner or Later, *a dance satire. The career that stretched before him was to include more than 250 productions, associations with the Metropolitan Opera, the New York City Opera, and the Central City (Colorado) Opera Festival, and forty-five years of teaching stage design at the Yale School of Drama. He had opportunities to design in every conceivable mode of expression and to experiment in revitalizing musical theater through innovative staging. He lived to see scores of his students succeed in the commercial, university, and nonprofit theater throughout the country.*

Cleon Throckmorton *was educated as an engineer at the Carnegie Institute of Technology and at George Washington University, and the training he received there he later applied creatively to the theater. He was invited to join the Provincetown Players when it was under the artistic control of George Cram Cook. In 1920 he designed the setting for the original production of Eugene O'Neill's* The Emperor Jones, *and he went on to design nine more of O'Neill's plays. Shown here is his set for* SS Glencairn, *a 1924 production of four of O'Neill's early sea dramas. Throckmorton became one of the most prolific American scene designers, producing hundreds of settings for Broadway and for theaters throughout the country. Because of his engineering background, he had an ability to solve thorny construction problems that was legendary, and his advice was frequently sought by other designers.*

away where you don't want it." Although simple in principle, the precept was monumentally difficult to put into practice. But Jones cajoled his lighting experts into accomplishing what he wanted and his sets were washed in constantly moving and shifting lights, which gave them a special luster.

Very few contemporary American designers or those who came after him escaped the touch of Jones's work or his credo. But he did not dominate in the same way as did Appia and Craig in Europe. His Dutch colleague Herman Rosse summed up the history of the New Movement in the United States as "a communal creation, one man adding to what another man has already done." Jones left another legacy, possibly more profound than his philosophy of design. His colleague and admirer Lee

Mordecai Gorelik served his theatrical apprenticeship under Robert Edmond Jones, Norman Bel Geddes, and Sergei Soudeikine. He launched his professional career in the ground-breaking 1925 Theatre Guild production of John Howard Lawson's Processional, for which he designed both the sets and the costumes. A founding member and designer for the Group Theatre in the 1930s, Gorelik was drawn to dramas of social conflict, and he consistently championed the kind of theater propounded by Bertolt Brecht and Erwin Piscator. Speaking about his own technique, Gorelik once said: "Some stage designers begin with a sketch, others with a ground plan or a preliminary model. It may be notorious by now that I start with a metaphor." He asserts that a setting need not be closely coordinated with other components of a production—a belief that sounds very much like a reading from the dogma of Brecht and Piscator. He likes to use discordant elements: projections on screens, film sequences, and fragmentary settings. Here is a sketch of his original set for Clifford Odets's The Flowering Peach (1954), a retelling of the biblical story of Noah. Gorelik has designed a homey ark, the kind of boat a simple peasant farmer might have imagined.

Lee Simonson was determined as a boy to become an artist. Acquaintance during his youth with George Pierce Baker and George Santayana at Harvard and with Max Reinhardt and Sergei Diaghilev in Paris, and in his later years with George Bernard Shaw turned him into a profoundly perceptive and thoughtful man, whose personal ambition was divided between the worlds of art and letters. Eventually, he became an artist who wrote. In 1915 he joined the experimental Washington Square Players, which regrouped after World War I as the Theatre Guild, and remained a director and principal designer of the organization for twenty years. In the Guild's early, less affluent years, he worked magic onstage with very little money, relying for the most part on projected scenery, permanent units, screens, and neutral curtains. His work was usually bounded by the proscenium arch because, according to Donald Oenslager, he designed as a director. But for the Guild's production in 1930 of Roar China, Simonson designed the set shown here, which is dominated by menacing guns that loom out from the proscenium toward the auditorium. Simonson, who designed the costumes and occasionally the lights for many of his productions, in 1948 completely recast the settings and costumes for the Ring cycle for the Metropolitan Opera.

Opposite above:
Watson Barratt learned and practiced illustration before he turned to scene design. His chance on Broadway came in 1918. The show was Sinbad, and it marked the beginning of Barratt's long association with The Shubert Organization. He worked on hundreds of shows for his employers, sometimes slavishly reproducing the sets of other designers to please them. Occasionally he slipped out from under the umbrella of the Shuberts, acting for a decade as principal designer for the St. Louis Municipal Opera Company, running his own summer theater in Spring Lake, New Jersey, and designing for the Brussels World's Fair. The mark of the illustrator shines through his projects for the theater but, like this characteristic setting for a Shubert revue—brash, brightly colored, and pictorial—they invariably transcend slickness and reveal a versatility of style.

Simonson stated it simply: "He was the first to win recognition in this century for the scenic designer as an indispensable collaborator in the interpretation of a script." Since Jones's time, the designer has taken a seat at the conference table when a play begins to germinate into a production. He sits at the right hand of the director, listening, digesting, visualizing, and at last shapes the physical interpretation of the play out of all he has seen, thought, and heard. He may have to do battle to preserve his original concept; he may agree to a compromise on this point or that; but when the curtain rises, it is he who has established the look of the play. With Robert Edmond Jones, American stage art came of age. His early prediction that Americans would lead the world in stagecraft has been fulfilled, not by one man alone but by several generations of designers who caught his original inspiration to slip from the confinements of realism into the free air of imagination and style.

The "communal creation" that Rosse described exists to this day. Each new wave of designers has become the practical as well as the spiritual godchild of the last. Most of them have served apprenticeships with established designers or studied in the university classes that they taught. Unlike the majority of artists, whose work

Howard Bay reached Broadway via a route that took him to the Carnegie Institute of Technology, the Chappell School of Art in Denver, and, in the mid-1930s, the Federal Theatre Project. One-Third of a Nation (1938), one of the most powerful of the FTP's Living Newspapers, was designed by Bay. Bay's first important Broadway set was for Lillian Hellman's The Little Foxes in 1939. He prefers to design shows that stimulate him intellectually, but he is never self-indulgent in his visual interpretations. The style he chooses varies from realism to surrealism, depending on the nature of the assignment. Currently president of the United Scenic Artists, the designers' union, he is recently retired from Brandeis University. Bay's Stage Design has become the standard college textbook on the subject. Shown here is Bay's buoyant, gaily colored garden scene for Up in Central Park, a hit musical about New York in the 1870s, produced in 1945.

Oliver Smith has scores of productions to his credit, notably some of Broadway's most successful musicals, including My Fair Lady, Candide, West Side Story, and Hello Dolly! Shown here is the translucent muslin drop for the chapel in a convent cloister in The Sound of Music (1961). After studying architecture at Pennsylvania State University, Smith decided to try his luck in the New York theater. In 1941 the Ballet Russe de Monte Carlo offered him his first design job, for the ballet Saratoga. He went on to design Agnes de Mille's Rodeo (1942) and has remained closely identified with the ballet world as co-director of the American Ballet Theatre. He is known among designers as a precise and meticulous craftsman, who pares his sets of every extraneous detail.

George Jenkins designed this double-decker unit for The Miracle Worker, a play of 1959 about Helen Keller and Anne Sullivan. It could be rotated to reveal different rooms within the Keller house. Jenkins studied architecture at the University of Pennsylvania, receiving his training as a set and lighting designer under Jo Mielziner between 1937 and 1941. In 1943, he designed his first Broadway show, Early to Bed, and has followed those sets with set or lighting designs for more than fifty productions. He has also been in demand as a motion-picture art director. Jenkins uses realistic detail selectively to convey an overall impression rather than for its own sake.

In designs like this one for Legend of Lovers (1951), an impressionistically rendered railway station in an imaginary provincial town in southern France before World War II, Eldon Elder has shown an acute sense of the practical as well as great style and artistry. Like many designers of his generation, Elder has made New York City and Broadway the base for far-ranging activities. Among the regional theaters for which he has created sets, costumes, and lighting are the Santa Fe Opera, the St. Louis Municipal Opera, the American Shakespeare Festival in Stratford, Connecticut, and the Pittsburgh Playhouse. He has also accepted assignments in London. After gaining some experience off Broadway, he debuted on Broadway in 1951 with The Long Days. In 1958 he began a long association with the New York Shakespeare Festival; it was Elder who in 1961 designed the Delacorte Theater in Central Park for the company.

By placing the monumental doors of the palace of Creon before a vista of the sea, set designer Ben Edwards was able to suggest both the primitivism and the epic scope of Euripides' drama Medea (1947). Edwards had received training at the Feagin School of Dramatic Arts and at the Kane School of Art. He received early experience as a set, costume, and lighting designer at the Barter Theatre in Abingdon, Virginia, and with the Federal Theatre Project in New York during the mid-1930s. His first Broadway credit was Another Sun (1940), and he has since designed for Broadway producers, for the Repertory Theater of Lincoln Center, and for summer stock, regional theater, television, and films.

Top:
Born in 1900 in Kiev and trained at the state art school, Boris Aronson reached New York in 1923. There, for the Yiddish theater he designed such intriguingly futuristic settings that word eventually reached Broadway. His first important assignment came in 1932—for S. J. Perelman's Walk a Little Faster. Then, for nearly five decades, Aronson turned down more shows than he designed. Working in no particular style, he looked for and captured through his designs the essence of a play. Shown here is Aronson's model for the American warship that arrives in Tokyo Bay during the early scenes of Pacific Overtures, a musical of 1976.

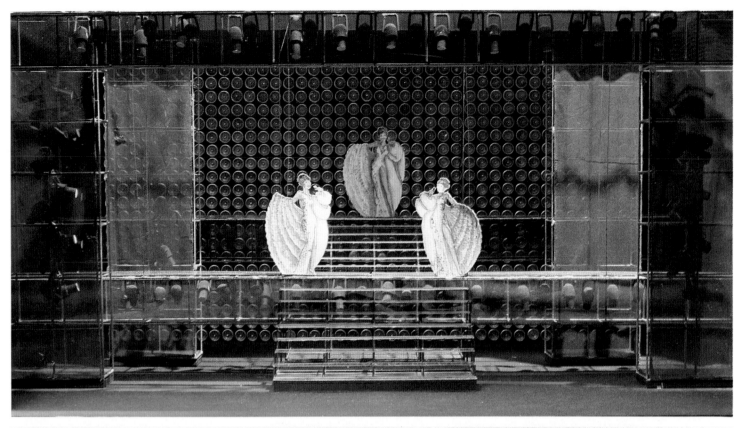

After receiving an M.F.A. degree from the Yale School of Drama, John Lee Beatty planned to obtain experience in regional theaters before assaulting New York. When he discovered that regional theaters wanted New York designers, he altered his course and found work as a design assistant and as a painter and scene builder with the leading New York studios. In 1976 he entered the Broadway scene with *The Innocents,* and today he is among the busiest of the younger generation of scene designers, working in what is best described as a style of romantic or poetic realism, exemplified by this rendering of the old boathouse at Talley's farm, near Lebanon, Missouri, for *Talley's Folly* (1980).

At the suggestion of playwright-director Sidney Kingsley, who wanted to take a cinematic approach to the action of Darkness at Noon (1951), Frederick Fox created a basic set that could be altered quickly to create different scenes. Shown here is his rendering for the Cafe Marseille set, which was mounted on a turntable. Fox began his career as a theatrical designer but moved into television in the 1940s as lighting and scenic designer for Max Liebman's landmark series Your Show of Shows. Educated at Yale and the National Academy of Design, Fox was apprenticed at the Ward and Harvey Scenic Studios. He accumulated experience at the Ivoryton Theatre in Connecticut, before his New York debut with Farewell Summer in 1937. He has since divided his time between Broadway and Metropolitan Opera Company productions, television, and industrial design.

During the 1970s, the last decade of his life, Ralph Alswang turned from scene design to the fields of theater design and theater technology. Earlier he had developed a sophisticated system of projection called Living Screen whereby live and filmed action could be integrated on the stage. A native of Chicago, Alswang studied at the Art Institute of Chicago and at the Goodman Theatre, later becoming Robert Edmond Jones's assistant in New York. His first Broadway assignment was Comes the Revelation (1942). While on military duty, Alswang designed Moss Hart's Winged Victory (1943). After the war, he continued his career, lighting and designing nearly one hundred shows, which ranged from spectacles to one-person performances. Shown here is a rendering for the scene in Sunrise at Campobello (1958) in which Ralph Bellamy as Franklin D. Roosevelt accepts the nomination for president at the Democratic convention.

Opposite above:
Robin Wagner studied at the California School of Fine Arts and spent his early professional years as a busy designer in and around the San Francisco area. When he reached New York, he assisted Ben Edwards and Oliver Smith in a number of Broadway productions, all the while piling up Off-Broadway and regional credits. His first Broadway ventures, The Trial of Lee Harvey Oswald and the much-acclaimed The Great White Hope, were both produced in 1968. Every season since then, Wagner has designed several productions. He relies heavily on architectonic elements, with strikingly effective results. In A Chorus Line (1975), he used mirrored panels to give the impression of a stage crowded with dancers. In the basic set for Dreamgirls (1981), seen in the photograph above, two light-towers on each side of the stage marked changes of time and scene when pivoted. Wagner has worked for the New York Shakespeare Festival, for regional theaters throughout the country, and for theaters abroad.

frequently constitutes their only voice, stage designers are on the whole an articulate lot—the result, no doubt, of many wearying hours of arguing points with their collaborators in the theatrical process. The greatest of them have become teachers and writers, building a significant literature of the profession. It is testimony of their respect for their art that some of them have become collectors of each other's scenic "renderings," those preliminary drawings of evolving visual ideas. Many renderings display magnificent draftsmanship; a few approach fine art; others look crude and amateurish. Sometimes the stage designer makes no formal rendering, merely scribbling sketches on paper napkins, the backs of envelopes, or whatever else is

Ming Cho Lee is one of the most inventive of the current generation of American designers. Born and brought up in Shanghai, he studied Chinese landscape painting before emigrating to the United States. After hearing a lecture by theatrical lighting expert Edward Kook, he decided to make his way as a scene designer. Through Kook, he got a job as Jo Mielziner's assistant. He also worked for Boris Aronson. His first important assignment was for the Phoenix Theatre's production of The Infernal Machine in 1958. Lee then worked for the New York Shakespeare Festival for more than ten years, designing about thirty plays for the company. He has also designed for ballet and opera companies in and outside New York and Europe. Like this sole set for K–2 (1983)—which the artist has modestly described as a hunk of styrofoam made to look like an ice mountain through the magic of Allen Lee Hughes's lighting—Lee's settings usually consist of sculptural or skeletal pieces, which can be manipulated to give the impression of different scenic environments. To translate Lee's design in model form into reality was a triumph of theater technology. The basic set for K–2 was built in the scene shop of Arena Stage in Washington, D.C., and shipped to New York for the Broadway opening. Only a few changes were made to satisfy local union requirements.

After attending the Yale School of Drama, and before assaulting Broadway, Peter Larkin accumulated summer-stock experience at four East Coast playhouses. In 1951 he was hired by the New York City Center to design Ibsen's The Wild Duck, and a year later he created the scenery for the Broadway thriller Dial M for Murder. His award-winning set for The Teahouse of the August Moon (1953) received its inspiration, according to his own account, from a split-bamboo placemat bought at a five-and-dime store. Larkin has also designed for the New York City Ballet Company, the American Shakespeare Festival in Stratford, Connecticut, and the touring National Repertory Theatre. His style, characterized by a highly imaginative blend of realistic detail and impressionistic passages, is exemplified here by the evocative scenery for The Rink (1984), which manages to evoke the cavernous space of a roller rink without encroaching on the stage area required by dancers on roller skates.

Like most American designers today, Santo Loquasto resists working in any one style, but many of his designs are characterized by strong lines and angles. For Richard II, which he designed in 1982 for the outdoor Delacorte Theater in Central Park, the setting soared to a height of forty feet and was broken by jutting elements and materials—matching the play's theme of an orderly English court gone awry. As a young man, Loquasto studied acting and appeared in summer stock. Turning to scene design, he worked for the Yale Repertory Theatre, the Hartford Stage Company, the Long Wharf Theatre in New Haven, Connecticut, the Arena Stage in Washington, D.C., and, beginning in 1969, the New York Shakespeare Festival. He was responsible for the set for Sticks and Bones, a production that moved in 1972 from the Public Theater in downtown New York to a Broadway playhouse, giving him his first important exposure as a designer. Since then, Loquasto's talents have been in great demand, but he has maintained his association with the New York Shakespeare Festival. He also designs for opera, ballet, and an occasional movie.

Since the beginning of the twentieth century, when Aline Bernstein virtually created her own opportunities, many women set designers have looked for work on Broadway, but only Marjorie Bradley Kellogg has achieved assignments with any regularity, and she must depend upon Off-Broadway and regional theater work for survival. Like John Lee Beatty, Kellogg counts Ming Cho Lee as the most influential teacher in her life. She has worked as an assistant to Lee as well as to Robin Wagner and David Mitchell, among others. Her designs are generally realistic and superficially cluttered, but every detail is relevant to the script. Characteristic of her recent work is this rendering for the junk-shop setting of American Buffalo in its second Broadway incarnation, in 1983.

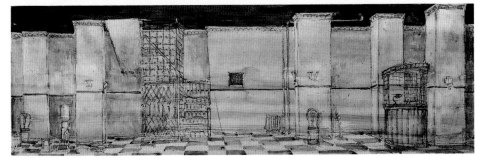

David Hays, who in 1964 designed this long, lonely, and shabby lobby to underscore the feeling of isolation in Eugene O'Neill's Hughie, received a Fulbright scholarship to study with Roger Furse and Leslie Hurry, two of the leading designers on the London stage. His first solo experience came with the Circle in the Square's production of The Cradle Song in 1955. During the next twenty-five years, he designed a number of successful Broadway shows, and his sets have invariably been singled out by the critics for special acclaim. He has also worked in opera and ballet and for regional and Off-Broadway theater. He prefers to light his own sets.

David Mitchell studied with Horace Armistead and Raymond Sovey in Boston before coming to New York, where he became assistant to Ming Cho Lee during the period when Lee was principal designer for the New York Shakespeare Festival. In 1965 producer Joseph Papp gave Mitchell the first of several independent assignments, which led to a long and continuing association. When Papp took over the Vivian Beaumont Theater in Lincoln Center, Mitchell became the principal designer there. His first Broadway show was How the Other Half Loves, and since 1972 he has been one of the most active designers in New York, working on and off Broadway and for the New York City Ballet and the New York City Opera. He has also designed opera productions for the Berlin and Paris opera companies and worked extensively in regional theaters. His is an eclectic and bold style, which relies upon broad strokes and literalism in the best sense. Pictured here is Mitchell's model for Barnum (1980).

Of necessity, designers must adapt the sets they create for Broadway productions to withstand the rigors of the traveling show. For his imaginative set for Pippin (1972) on Broadway, Walton split the stage in half, front to back, to allow his "soft scenery" to emerge unseen by the audience. To compensate for the loss of this effect for the touring version of the set, he relied mostly on the soft scenery, much of it constructed of rope and painted canvas, which could be flown up and down or moved sideways from the wings. For the scene shown here (from the touring version), near the beginning of the musical, the figures in the mural were equipped with moving eyes that seemed to follow the progress of the conspiracy occurring on the forestage. Born and educated in England, Walton moves between two worlds of theater, London's West End and Broadway. His admiration for the American designers Jo Mielziner, Robert Edmond Jones, and Oliver Smith drew him inevitably to New York. His design renderings approach fine art, as do Mielziner's. His sets are often witty and contain the atmosphere of the play. Walton is also a talented caricaturist and poster designer.

handy. Howard Bay produced a "preliminary sketch" for *Man of La Mancha* four months after the opening because the *Saturday Review* wanted it for a cover. The sum total of sketches, renderings, ground plans, and blueprints representing intense historical and psychological research for a show can never evoke the actual stage pictures, washed in their special light and straining against the theater's inherent artificiality to become for a few hours the environment in which a special kind of life will throb and flicker. The illustrations in this chapter—be they reproductions from the artists' hands or photographs of the sets they designed—are merely shadows of a splendid reality and are intended to indicate the versatility and the multifaceted talents of the communal creation that is American stage art.

COSTUMES

IN EVERY AGE, it has been the responsibility of the manager or producer or theater owner to provide some sort of scenery for the plays and musical dramas presented under his aegis. But until recent times, theatrical costumes were more often than not supplied by the performers. This casual arrangement produced startling, often extraordinary, visual moments in the theater. In 1873 a writer for the *New Orleans Picayune* described the costumes of a production of *Macbeth* in that city as being "of every age and nation except the right ones." The statement could have been made of many productions throughout the land. Although they must certainly have recognized the importance of costumes in a theatrical spectacle, managers and producers tended either to look the other way to spare themselves additional expense or to depend on the stars to dress themselves attractively out of vanity. They could justify spending great sums of money for the construction of gorgeous and elaborate scenery, but they were reluctant to grant more than a trifling supplement to each player's salary to cover the purchase of costumes.

The established London houses, Drury Lane and Covent Garden, had wardrobe collections from which they supplied costumes for the actors, though the provincial theaters did not, and many English stars bought their own costumes or, like David Garrick, had wealthy patrons who supplied their stage clothes. When the first professional companies arrived in America, they reflected the practices of the provincial English playhouses rather than the London theaters. If Lewis Hallam took trunks of costumes on board the *Charming Sally*, bound for the New World, very little is known of their contents. The plays he produced ranged the centuries, the globe, and the strata of society, yet all were probably played in contemporary dress, fleshed out with some symbolic accoutrements. The kings wore crowns, the heroes sported feather headdresses, Arabs and Turks wore turbans. Since no pictorial records exist for the early theater in America, everything is a matter of conjecture. English engravings of the time show Juliets and Cleopatras in hoopskirts and Macbeth in eighteenth-century military uniform, and the transplanted English performers were probably similarly dressed, perhaps not so well.

After the Revolutionary War, managers like Thomas Wignell in Philadelphia began to build wardrobes for their resident companies. John Henry went to England in 1792 to buy theatrical supplies, among which were costumes, and he and his co-manager, Lewis Hallam, had already employed a master tailor for the company at the John Street Theatre. Under Wignell, the Chestnut Street Theatre opened its doors in 1794 with a brand-new wardrobe, which was, according to John Durang, the chronicler of theater in Philadelphia, "capable of equipping any comedy in the English language with dresses for all the females in the cast." William Dunlap's accounts for the Park Theatre in 1798 list the munificent sum of fifteen dollars for wardrobe and seven dollars to "Martin who [is] to superintend the stage & prompter, take charge of the Wardrobe & Armoury and make the necessary ornaments, armour &c devoting his whole time to it." In 1786 Harmony Hall opened in Charleston, ushering in an era of elegance: even the stage chambermaids dressed in rich silk.

For the part of King Lear, David Garrick wore an ermine-trimmed coat to signify his royal status and a scarf around his neck to denote wintry weather. The costuming traditions of his era in England were carried to the New World by the first emigrant troupe of actors.

By the nineteenth century, managers knew that in order to create an adequate
effect they had to provide at least some costumes and supplement the meager salaries
of their employees so that they could purchase stage clothes, but the choice of
costume still rested with the actors and actresses. The results were not always
predictable. When Fanny Kemble played Juliet in 1833, she appeared in a white satin
ball gown only to discover that her Romeo "looked like a magical figure growing out
of a monstrous, strange colored melon, beneath which descended his unfortunate legs,
thrust in a pair of red slippers." Most of the repertory was still played in contemporary
dress, but there were glancing attempts to define some characters by their costumes.
Hamlet was usually played in black velvet, Shylock in a long cassock-like gown, and
Ophelia and Juliet in virginal white. These were essentially English conventions;
others were established for the quintessential American characters. Edwin Forrest's
fringed leather tunic and trousers for Metamora defined Indian dress; T. D. Rice's
outfit for the role of plantation black included an undersized jacket and old shoes and
hat, all ragged and patched; Frank Chanfrau's costume for the city tough consisted of
black turned-up trousers with a red double-breasted shirt, topped by a black plug hat
with a narrow black band. So many actors played variations on the stage Yankee that
his costume was never clearly defined, but some elements remained constant: a long-
tailed coat, a brightly colored vest over a white shirt, and striped trousers. These
costumes were not consciously designed; they gradually evolved, with the taste and
preferences of the stars serving as the strongest influence on their creation.

The role of the costume designer developed rather more slowly than that of the
scene designer. Obviously, the costumes for companies like the Chestnut Street in

Philadelphia or the Park or the Bowery in New York had to be made by somebody, but since most stage clothes were contemporary in style they were probably made by tailors and seamstresses of the city and then altered to fit by either the performers themselves or by their dressers, before being returned to the storeroom.

Beginning in the 1820s, now and then a name would appear among the credits on the handbills: "dresses by Lewis," or "by Harbaugh," or by one of a half-dozen others who are known only by their names. But the very appearance of these names in print signifies a shift in the attitude of the managers, many of whom were (or had been) performers themselves. Their recognition of the importance of accurate, appropriate, effective costuming was given a strong boost by events (again) in England.

In 1823 James Robinson Planché, a minor playwright and man-about-the-theater, talked (he claimed) Charles Kemble into allowing him to design the costumes for a Covent Garden production of *King John* that were historically accurate. After consulting "indisputable" authorities, Planché outfitted the actors in the clothes of the correct period—to their displeasure, for they were much more at ease in conventional dress. Though he later professed he had been very nervous about the audience's reaction to the new look, Planché basked in "a roar of approbation, accompanied by four distinct rounds of applause" for the costumes and was convinced that "a complete reformation of dramatic costume became from that moment inevitable upon the English stage."

The reformation received further assists from two other English stars, William Charles Macready and Charles Kean, both of whom played in America in the 1830s and 1840s. The success of their authentically costumed productions sent actors scurrying to historical treatises and works of art in pursuit of historical accuracy. In the latter half of the nineteenth century, they were assisted in their research by the publication of great tomes devoted to the history of dress, all of which were elaborately illustrated and hand-colored. Planché's *Cyclopaedia of Costume or Dictionary of Dress* covered the subject from the Christian era to the accession of George III. In France, Albert Racinet compiled a book on historical costume, and in Germany a number of historians collaborated on a monumental history of dress. Period costumes would have been only partially effective without period scenery, however, and by the end of the nineteenth century, the scene painter and costume designer were working together to produce a harmonious ambience in American productions of Shakespearean and period plays.

The great stars and enlightened managers of the nineteenth century were largely responsible for the rise of the costume designer. In 1831 Andrew Jackson Allen, a minor actor, was commissioned to make Edwin Forrest's costumes for *The Gladiator*, and several years later he was asked by manager Francis Courtney Wemyss to produce the "dresses" for the Walnut Street Theatre run of Forrest's *Richelieu*, at a cost to Wemyss of $600, not an inconsiderable sum at that time. Unable to sustain himself as a costumer, Allen continued acting bit parts for the rest of his life. Another actor, Thomas Joyce, became Edwin Booth's costumer in 1869, when Booth was planning to open his own theater. Joyce had served an apprenticeship in the wardrobe department of the Boston Museum for about ten years before getting the appointment with Booth. He remained in charge of Booth's costume department until his untimely death in 1873, at the age of fifty-two. During his tenure there, he produced historically accurate and impressive costumes, which were rarely accorded the notice by the critics that they deserved.

In the last decades of the nineteenth century, the names of costume designers began to appear more regularly in the playbills, particularly those printed for the New York productions of Augustin Daly and A. M Palmer and for Henry Irving's American tours. Daly was sometimes criticized for the undue sumptuousness of his productions. In 1883 he hired the English costume designer E. Hamilton Bell to dress Ada Rehan and Virginia Dreher as Mistress Ford and Mistress Page in *The Merry Wives of Windsor*. The inappropriateness of their costumes—rich silks dripping with lace—was not lost upon the critics. Whenever he had a long run, such as *Divorce* or *Pique*, both

One of Fanny Janauschek's greatest roles was Medea. Here she is as the tragic heroine of ancient times, dressed in faux Greek dress with a hoop!

Right:
English designer E. Hamilton Bell dressed Ada Rehan and Virginia Dreher in sumptuous costumes of no recognizable time or period for Augustin Daly's production of The Merry Wives of Windsor *in 1883.*

of which were set in contemporary times, Daly insisted that the actors recostume themselves in order to attract audiences for a second visit to see the new gowns. Although he and Palmer provided the period costumes for their shows, their performers had to supply their own contemporary suits and dresses.

For these, actors had various sources. Some, hoping to improve their chances of being hired, would take a financial plunge and have their wardrobe tailor-made. Others would buy ready-made clothing or go to secondhand costume dealers or to the clothes brokers who bought up the castoffs of society folk. Most of the bit players made their own or remodeled what they had to suit a role. Many a young actress would sit, needle and thread in hand, on the train carrying her to a one-night or one-week stand, altering a costume for the performance.

Charles Frohman, who began his career in 1883, was the first producer to choose and purchase contemporary costumes for his actors. He indulged the female stars of his legendary Empire Theatre company—Maude Adams, Ethel Barrymore, Julia Marlowe, Elsie Ferguson, and Billie Burke, whose careers were launched under his aegis—in costumes made in London or Paris, where he could get them for about one-third the going American price. Ethel Barrymore remembered in her autobiography that as a fledgling actress she was forced to pay for her costumes out of a salary of thirty-five dollars per week, but when she became a star and could afford to spend the money, producers rushed to provide her with expensive gowns.

Because American society at the turn of the century was particularly fashion-conscious, producers recognized the wisdom of dressing their female stars in the latest styles, especially if they had a weak play. Elsie de Wolfe, who had the briefest of careers onstage, took care to step before the footlights in elegant gowns, sometimes paid for from her own purse. Billie Burke wore clothing beautifully and was a fashion trend setter. Whatever styles she wore onstage would usually appear offstage on the backs of her female admirers. John Drew was a dandy who attracted both men and women to the theater to see what he was wearing and how he parted his hair. One of the most perceptive critics of his day, Alan Dale, took many a journalistic swipe at costuming excesses. "The average play," he wrote, "impresses you with the idea that it has been written for and around the clothes." Most play-reviewers and critics, however, rarely expended more than an adjective or two on the costume designer's achievements.

Several stars of the era liked to research or assist in the design of their own stage clothes. When Maude Adams was engaged to play in Barrie's *Peter Pan,* she asked her summer neighbors, the artist John Alexander and his wife, Elizabeth, for help. In the course of the collaboration, the Peter Pan collar was born.

The costume designer was the creation of the enlightened theatrical producer, who became, almost inevitably—at least in his eyes—the thrall of his own creature. Although even the most successful designers never received more than a thousand dollars for their work on a production, the cost of the costumes could be staggering, especially if they were executed by the French or English high-fashion houses—Callot Soeurs, Worth, Paquin, or Lucille—or by one of the American costumers. On occasion, they were more costly than the scenery. Many of the leading producers of the early twentieth century set up their own costume workrooms to reduce costs and, as a result, eventually built up large inventories that could be used to costume touring shows and future productions.

By 1900 the specialty was universally acknowledged, and the costume designer became still more firmly entrenched after the dawn of the age of electricity, which exposed patched-up costumes relentlessly. He or she might work freelance, in which case the commission would be by the show. Charles Frohman preferred to hire a number of freelance costume designers. Other producers hired one or two designers on a permanent basis and assembled a staff to serve current and future productions as well as touring shows. Belasco hired Albertine Randall Wheelan and Elmer Traflinger to supervise the costuming of his productions, although he never surrendered his authority over any detail. With costuming, he went to the same outrageous lengths to achieve realism as he did with scenery. For *The Music Master,* which starred David Warfield, he bought out the ready-made and secondhand clothing stores on the Lower East Side, and for *The Darling of the Gods* he sent to Japan for the costumes of the principal performers. He admitted that his bills for contemporary dresses from the fashionable modistes "would stagger a rich society woman."

Freelancer or staff member, the designer would submit sketches to the producer which, if approved, would be given to the costumer, who would provide a cost estimate. A muslin mock-up of each costume was generally shown to the designer before it was converted into the actual fabrics he or she had chosen. All of this was subject to the final approval of the producer—and occasionally of the star. The most professional of the producers would schedule a "dress parade," a ritual in which all of the performers would march across the stage so that the designer, producer, and (later) director could catch the effect of the costumes against the scenery, under the lighting, and with each other. At this point, critical decisions and changes could be made, up to and including scrapping what had been designed and starting all over again. The costume parade was followed by one or more "dress rehearsals" to allow the actors to get the feel of the costumes before the opening performance.

Another source of employment for the costume designer was the costume house. The oldest was Dazian's, which had been established by a young Bavarian immigrant,

A trained painter, E. H. Sothern sometimes sketched ideas for costumes for Sothern and Marlowe productions—but never his wife's, which were usually handled by E. Hamilton Bell or another prominent designer. Here is Sothern's costume for Part I of Henry IV.

Theatrical costume has and continues to set trends in the larger world. Maude Adams's costume as Peter Pan was adorned by a round collar that became part of the lexicon of dress, beginning in 1905.

H. A. Ogden's career intersected the theatrical world at a number of points. During his early years as a professional artist and illustrator, he made sketches for theatrical posters and worked for Frank Leslie's publications, where his artwork appeared on the cultural pages. With his meticulous eye for detail, it was inevitable that Ogden would turn to costume designing. He was given early program credit for designing The Irish Artists in 1894, E. H. Sothern's If I Were King in 1901, and Viola Allen's Twelfth Night in 1904. Shown is an Ogden drawing for an unsuccessful play of 1899, Peter Stuyvesant, by Bronson Howard and Brander Matthews. The marginal notes specify the fabrics and colors for the finished costumes.

To reflect the primitive passions of the play, English-born Jane Greenwood designed a swirling, voluptuous dress for Zoe Caldwell as the queen of Colchis and rough-textured robes for Judith Anderson as the Nurse in the 1982 Broadway revival of Robinson Jeffers's translation of Euripides' Medea. Greenwood frequently collaborates with her husband, Ben Edwards, who designed the set. Since The Ballad of the Sad Cafe opened in 1963, Greenwood's work has been on display at least once a year. She has costumed shows of nearly every description—from Shakespeare, to musical comedy, to avant-garde theater, to ballet and opera. She has also taught costume design in New York.

Wolf Dazian, in 1842. Starting out with a dry-goods store on what is now Lafayette Street in lower Manhattan, Dazian became supplier of fabrics to P. T. Barnum during his first year in business and had the additional good fortune to expand his activities to include costume-making shortly after the invention of the industrial sewing machine, at mid-century. The company moved uptown with the theaters, from the Bowery to Union Square, and finally to Times Square, before abandoning the costume-making business in 1919, having won many outstanding credits, including the costumes for The Black Crook, and having dominated the competition for fifty years.

Although by the late nineteenth century every major city in America that could boast a theater or two also had a costume house, the principal costumers were located in the East. Albert R. Van Horn came down from Bucks County to seek his fortune in Philadelphia and found it in the embroidery business. After working all day at his machines, some of which he invented, he spent his evenings at the Arch Street Theatre, where he was a member of the acting company. Skilled with needle and thread, he made his own costumes, which were evidently so superior to the average stage dress that actors and managers came to him with orders to make their costumes. In 1852 Van Horn established his costume-making business on North Ninth Street, next door to the house where Ethel and Lionel Barrymore were born. The company waxed prosperous and began supplying costumes for Broadway and touring shows and

to the repertory companies. In 1901 Frank Van Horn opened a New York office, which subsequently separated from the family firm. The Philadelphia company eventually opened its own New York office, which remained in business until 1981. The Philadelphia branch closed down its operations in 1969.

Another actor, Albert G. Eaves, founded the Eaves Costume Company at 63 East Twelfth Street in Manhattan in 1867. Like the Van Horns, Eaves not only made costumes for all the important stars and producers, but established a thriving rental business as well. In 1897 the firm was bought by Charles Geoly, an early Eaves employee, and it still remains in the hands of his family. Merged with the amalgamated Brooks and Van Horn costumers in 1981, the company continues in business today. Their inventory stands at something over a million costumes, stored in

The daughter of Joseph Frankau, an actor and trouper, Aline Bernstein remained within the orbit of the theater throughout most of her life. She studied art in Manhattan, first at the School of Applied Design, then at the New School of Art, where she attracted the interest of the painter Robert Henri, who encouraged her to turn her attention to costume and scene design. Bernstein became involved in the activities of the Henry Street Settlement House on the Lower East Side and costumed a pageant to commemorate the twentieth anniversary of its founding. The costume illustrated above for The Little Clay Cart, produced in 1924, was one of Bernstein's earliest assignments for the Neighborhood Playhouse, which she had helped to create and where she later taught design. In the same year, she assisted Norman Bel Geddes in his production of The Miracle. When the productions at the Neighborhood Playhouse began to move to Broadway, her talents gained wider exposure and she was engaged by the Theatre Guild, the Civic Repertory Theatre, Herman Shumlin, Gilbert Miller, and Elmer Rice. She was one of the founders of the costume collection at the Metropolitan Museum of Art.

a warehouse in Long Island City that now serves as the firm's office-headquarters.

In the early years of the twentieth century, there were probably more than a hundred costume-making companies in the United States, of which about three-quarters were located in New York. Most passed out of existence during the Depression, but a few hung on. In 1906 Ely Stroock bought out a small uniform manufactory and piled up a fortune dealing with South American governments, which changed so quickly that armies had to be reuniformed practically overnight. As the Brooks Costume Company, Stroock's firm began to make and rent theatrical costumes after buying up the stock of Charles Frohman's warehouses in 1919. Like its competitors, Brooks moved uptown along with the theater district, but as the activity along Broadway and on the road diminished, so did business. In 1962 the company was bought by the Van Horn Costume Company and in 1981, the three major companies—Eaves's, Van Horn's, and Brooks's—came under Eaves's administrative umbrella.

There have always been a handful of small costumers that employ a few people to do highly specialized work, based on the extravagant and complex conceptions of certain costume designers. During the 1920s the costuming house of Madame Elise Freisinger was the particular favorite of Robert Edmond Jones. Since Jones liked to drape and pin cloth on his actors so that he would know from the start what the costumes would do for the actors and what the actors would do for the costumes, he kept Madame Freisinger with him from the moment he conceived his ideas for their construction. She would take his mock-ups back to her shop and translate them into finished stage clothes. Like Madame Freisinger, Helene Pons operated a small, high-quality costume house, but this White Russian expatriate was a designer as well as a fabricator. Her husband had been a member of the Moscow Art Theatre and of the Chauve-Souris company under Nikita Balieff, and Pons began by making costumes in her New York apartment for Chauve-Souris. Her business received its first real boost in 1928, when she was commissioned to costume *Marco Millions*. Thereafter, Pons dressed all of the Theatre Guild productions during its peak years. One of her last productions was *Camelot*, in 1961.

Many small New York costume houses have come and gone since the turn of the century, bespeaking the precariousness of such an intensely specialized, competitive business. Among the welter of small firms, two stand out. The Grace Costume Company was founded in the early 1960s by Maria Brizzi and her sister Grace Miceli, formerly head draper for Madame Karinska, the principal costumer for the New York City Ballet. Although it employs a resident designer, the company also works from the sketches of theater professionals, costuming about three Broadway shows a year. English-born Barbara Matera received her apprenticeship with Van Horn and in 1967 began costuming, like Helene Pons, in her own apartment. Today, Barbara Matera Ltd. has its own quarters and employs as many as eighty people, in a good season, to make the costumes for about ten Broadway shows, the American Ballet Theatre, and opera. The costumes produced by these two firms are among the finest in the West.

During the boom years, from 1890 to 1930, theatrical costuming departments specializing in contemporary clothes were established in the major department stores in New York and in the large repertory cities. Many of them hired an expert to work as a liaison between Fifth Avenue and Broadway. Margaret McCoy Pemberton, wife of producer Brock Pemberton, during her association with Saks was responsible for choosing the famous slouch hat that Katharine Cornell wore in *The Green Hat*.

The event that made the costume designer an indispensable member of the theatrical team was the actors' strike of 1919. One of the hotly contested issues was the requirement, still made by the small producers and company managers, that performers supply some of their own costumes. In the contract forged by Actors' Equity was a clause obliging every producer or manager to provide costumes or the wherewithal to purchase them, down to and including an actor's underwear if it was visible to the audience. The effect of the clause was to give increased stature to the costume designer and more work to the costumer, stylist, and couturier. The theatrical garment workers were unionized much earlier than the costume designers, who did not carry cards until 1938, when they were taken into the United Scenic Artists. Not until 1966 were they allowed to vote. Today, the union negotiates their contracts and oversees examination of candidates for admission as it does for the scenic and lighting wings of the organization. The costume designers tend to complain that they are not sufficiently respected by producers or honored by critics, and in fact their contribution to a theatrical production is as immeasurable as it is subtle. Their names appear in program credits, and if they are lucky enough to achieve special eminence they are rewarded with a small percentage of the production profits, waxing wealthy as well as famous.

Today's costume designer is a highly trained and educated professional, who has served an apprenticeship in a costume house or with an established costume or fashion designer. The best of them know how to sew, cut and drape, choose fabrics, dye and distress textiles, supervise costume shops and, if most producers are to be believed, spend money. Because, like scenic artists, they consume much of their lives communicating their ideas to other people, they have all also become highly articulate. One of the great twentieth-century costume designers, Lucinda Ballard, said somewhat disingenuously that her work as a designer was not as creative as a writer's, that she *did* what he had no time to do. She explained: A playwright might say that a character was "a lovely girl, poor, but with good taste and she wore an attractive dress"; in the play, the costume designer would have to say it for him.

Before costume designers sit down at their drawing tables, they have usually read the play they are to dress until they practically know the lines by heart; they have researched the period in which the play is set until they become part of it, sometimes

The cloche that Katharine Cornell wore in The Green Hat (1925) created a small industry. Women rushed to their milliners to order duplicates.

During the "Take Back Your Mink" number in Guys and Dolls (1950), the chorines did a striptease from dress and furs down to black lace underwear—all designed by Alvin Colt. Like most costumers of his generation, Colt has of necessity divided his attention among the theater, ballet, opera, films, and television. After study at the Yale School of Drama with master teachers Donald Oenslager and Frank Bevan, Colt began his career in 1940 designing ballet costumes. He then moved quickly to Broadway with On the Town (1944) and became principal designer for the New York City Center and the Phoenix Theatre during the 1940s and 1950s. He has made a specialty of designing fluid yet stylish costumes that move easily with a dancer's body.

Opposite below:
Florence Klotz, a native New Yorker, attended the Parsons School of Design and received valuable training in costume building at Brooks's. She also assisted Lucinda Ballard and Irene Sharaff, before becoming a designer in her own right. Her first solo work on Broadway came in 1961, when both A Call on Kuprin and Take Her, She's Mine went into production. In recent years, she has been part of Harold Prince's team, costuming most of his shows. Like most successful designers, she has also worked in motion pictures and ballet. Because the cast of Pacific Overtures (1976) was so large, Klotz designed many of the costumes, including the one shown here, to be reversible so that they could be changed rapidly.

Clockwise from top left:

A stagestruck teenager, Charles LeMaire tried his luck briefly as a performer with a song-and-dance act in Salt Lake City. After the act broke up, he went to New York to join the ranks of unemployed dancers and found a job as a theatrical costumer. He circulated his own designs among the leading producers and landed his first important assignment with Arthur Hammerstein in 1923. In 1925 he became house designer for Brooks's, but left to form his own costume house. During the 1920s, LeMaire designed hundreds of costumes for musicals and revues produced by George White, Earl Carroll, and Florenz Ziegfeld, for whose production Rio Rita in 1927 he executed the costume sketch shown here, for a ballet sequence performed by the Albertina Rasch troupe. He also changed the course of circus costuming with his designs for "Nepal," an oriental spectacle introducing Frank "Bring-em-back-alive" Buck, who was traveling with the Ringling Brothers Circus in the early 1930s. In 1943 LeMaire became executive designer for the 20th-Century Fox studio. He remained in Hollywood for the rest of his active designing career.

Irene Sharaff was still in her teens when she began an unpaid apprenticeship under Aline Bernstein, who in 1928 was head designer for the New York Civic Repertory Theatre. In 1932, Sharaff designed both the sets and the costumes after John Tenniel for the landmark production of Alice in Wonderland at the Civic Rep. Sharaff attended the School of Fine and Applied Arts and the Art Students League in New York. She has been a force not only in the theater but also in motion pictures, ballet, and television. Her first Broadway show was As Thousands Cheer (1933), and since then she has costumed more than sixty productions. She claims to have started a number of fashion trends, including mesh stockings, which she chose for Tamara Geva's costume in the 1936 production of On Your Toes. For West Side Story (1960), Sharaff had to design costumes both appropriate to the play and tailored to the exuberant choreography of Jerome Robbins. Shown is her sketch for members of one of the street gangs, the Sharks.

Freddy Wittop has had a double career: as dancer and partner of the famous Argentinita (under the name of Federico Rey), and as a well-known designer of theatrical costumes. He started his second career designing for the Folies-Bergère before emigrating to the United States. Wittop has never learned to cut a costume, although he studies fabrics so that he can match them to the movement of a performer. In 1942 he designed two Broadway shows, Count Me In and Beat the Band, and for the rest of his long career specialized in musicals and, while they were in vogue, nightclub shows. Wittop's sketch for Anna Maria Alberghetti's costume in Carnival (1961) is testimony to his belief that "a costume should never look like a costume but like the person it portrays."

Miles White's double forte has been costuming for the musical theater, where he has had to provide designs for dancers, and for the circus, where he has had to be inventive and showy. His costumes are constructed to move with the performer's body—not an easy feat. Like the illustrated dress for Josephine Premice in the musical Jamaica (1957), they are characterized by a sense of humor, which shines through the designer's renderings. After his success with the costumes for Oklahoma! in 1943, White dominated musical-comedy costuming for more than twenty-five years.

after traveling around the world for inspiration; and they have worked closely with the scene designer to insure that the clothes are in harmony with his conceptions and colors. Their costumes must fit the actors' bodies as well as their roles and they must, in designer parlance, "work." Unfortunately, when their creations are most successful, they also go unnoticed. Frustration is part of the costume designer's psychological profile.

Like the lighting designer, the costume designer has become an important figure backstage only within the last fifty years. About 1900 the producers grudgingly gave them some status, and unionization later won them recognition, but their acceptance as creative partners was ultimately the gift of the scene designers. New Movement designers chose to handle all the visual aspects of a production, but when the technology to achieve the ideal became too monstrously complex for one person to handle, enlightened designers like Jo Mielziner and Donald Oenslager began to relinquish control over the costuming to people whose special talents and insights they could trust. Today costume designers have joined their colleagues at the conference table as full participating members of the theatrical collaboration.

LIGHTING

DURING THE 1981 Broadway production of *Dreamgirls*, a large and spectacular musical show, two immense towers, one on each side of the stage, pivoted and flashed bright lights directly into the eyes of the audience. Seconds after eyes adjusted to the change of light, another episode was in progress onstage. Shining lights in the direction of the audience is an effect that lighting designers have conscientiously avoided for years; in *Dreamgirls*, it provided transitions that the book frequently could not give. The bursts of light acted like "curtains," a brilliantly imaginative effect, achieved by the lighting designer, Tharon Musser, and the scene designer, Robin Wagner, working in tandem.

Lighting design is the youngest of all of the theatrical arts, its history lying almost wholly within the twentieth century. When theatrical productions moved permanently indoors in the late sixteenth century, stage managers had to grapple immediately with the problem of providing enough illumination so that theatergoers could see both what was happening onstage and each other, for in the English and Continental court theaters the audience was frequently more a cynosure than the show. Since the only artificial source of light was the candle, huge chandeliers were hung above the stage and the auditorium. High rear windows provided natural light during daylight performances, and sconces and brackets were hung on entrance, lobby, and auditorium walls. Wax candles were expensive and used sparingly over the stage. Tallow candles dripped hot animal or vegetable fats over the audience in the pit. Smokeless and dripless spermaceti candles, made from whale oil, were many times the price of wax and tallow candles and were burned in only the most prosperous theaters. Candles emit a soft glow and create a halo-like effect. They also flicker with gusts of air and sputter as the wick burns down. By the end of the seventeenth century, when footlights were introduced to provide greater illumination onstage, the candle-snuffer, a member of the theatrical company, man or boy, would trim wicks and replace candles in full view of the audience. His chief qualification was to be able to walk quietly and do his job deftly and quickly.

Candlepower was supplemented by the light of oil lamps, which could be fitted with one or two wicks and placed in troughs at the foot of the stage and hung above the stage behind the pieces of scenery known as borders. Lights in vertical or horizontal rows were placed behind the wings. The three types of lights—footlights, borderlights, and striplights—became established in the late eighteenth century as the principal system for lighting a stage. In England at this time, David Garrick banished chandeliers from the stage area, and his scene designer, Philip de Loutherbourg, experimented with special lighting effects. Reflectors and mirrors were attached to the candleholders and oil lamps, but even these improvements in equipment can have produced nothing more than a hazy, smoky, malodorous illumination. The actors confined themselves to the first ten feet of stage area and had to be wary of the flames. Fires were a common and inevitable occurrence in that age of the candle and oil lamp, during which professional theater in America was introduced.

Experiments with creating a flammable air from a distillation of soft coal or some other fuel began in the late eighteenth century in England, and by the early nineteenth century manufactured "gas" had made its first serious appearance in the industrial age. But a whole new technology had to be created to allow it to become a common source of illumination. Gasworks had to be built, mains had to be laid in streets, and networks of pipes attached to meters had to be installed in buildings to be served by the new energy source. Theater managers were quick to see its advantages and did not wait upon the industry, preferring instead to install their own generating equipment. Gas was brought into the Drury Lane and Lyceum theaters in London in 1817 and used to light both stage and auditorium. Other English theaters quickly followed their lead.

In the early years of the nineteenth century, actor-manager William Warren saw a demonstration by Benjamin Henfrey in Baltimore, Maryland, where the first gasworks were to be built in 1817. Warren introduced gas to light the auditorium of the Chestnut Street Theatre in 1816, only to see the playhouse consumed by flames four years later, one of the first casualties of the new illuminant. From Philadelphia, the use of gaslight in theaters spread to New Orleans, Boston, Baltimore, and New York. The changes wrought were incalculable. On the plus side, gas was bright and more easily controlled than candlelight or oil light. By varying the amount of the illuminant fed to the flame, it became eventually possible to dim the auditorium while increasing the light on the actors. By directing the attention of their audiences to the stage, managers inadvertently brought about a change in audience etiquette. Theatergoers began watching the plays, not each other, and consequently expected more and more in the way of spectacle onstage.

Gaslight made scenery more visible, and scene painters reduced their broad brushstrokes to fine brushstrokes. Actors had to adapt their dramatic styles as well as their makeup and costumes to the more powerful illuminant, which exposed artificiality mercilessly in its glare. They also had to begin to act to each other rather than to a visible audience. Gaslight was responsible for the shortening of the forestage, the area jutting into the auditorium that had been reserved for great dramatic moments and feats of acting bravura. New theaters were designed without windows in the auditorium; instead, ventilation through the ceilings was provided to cleanse the air of carbon dioxide and accumulated odors. The flickering gas lamps were covered with colored glass mantles to change mood and with wire screens to prevent accidents if costumes brushed close by. By the end of the nineteenth century, the gas table, a sophisticated means of controlling individual jets, had been developed; on cue, lights could be varied in intensity and in color to suit the onstage action. By placing a gaslight in a drum covered by transparent paper and raising or lowering it—usually to the sound of squeaking pulleys—a stagehand could achieve the effect of the moon or sun rising or setting. On occasion things went awry. During a performance of *Won at Last* in 1877 at Wallack's Theatre, the audience began laughing uproariously just as the love scene began. The actor playing the hero looked over his shoulder to discover the moon "going up and down like a jig saw." It eventually leaped out of the canvas background and rolled across the stage. Nothing was reported of the fate of the "moon-man" after the performance.

In 1816 Thomas Drummond, the Scottish inventor, created a light of great brilliance by heating a stick of pure lime to a high temperature with an oxygen-hydrogen flame. Developed in the early 1820s as an aid to land surveyors because it was visible at great distances, limelight was introduced into the theater sometime between 1826 and 1837, though it did not come into general use until later. The cylinder of lime was contained inside a box fitted with a lens so that the light could be directed upon an actor or a special part of the stage. Eventually, colored silk or

glass was placed in front of the lens to ameliorate the greenish glare. The actor Charles Fechter and, later, David Belasco mounted limelight lamps in the auditorium in front of the stage to provide better overall illumination. Because of its intensity, the use of the limelight persisted into the age of electricity. But it always required special handling and a technician trained to control it.

In the hands of Steele MacKaye, theatrical gas lighting achieved its apogee. But though MacKaye's technicians at the Madison Square Theatre in New York created subtle and beautiful effects with gaslight, there were always persistent and inherent difficulties. It was cumbersome and dangerous to use, and the degree of control that could be maintained over it was limited. Although gaslight was many times brighter than candlelight, it was incapable of producing more than a murky, misty effect onstage in a dimmed but not completely darkened auditorium. It also produced an odor, to which, perhaps, audiences had become accustomed since their homes were also lighted by gas.

The invention of the electric incandescent lamp in 1879 brought changes in both the science and the philosophy of stage lighting, and this time the transformations were truly revolutionary. Thomas Edison's first lamps were dim and short-lived, but his incipient technology promised much and would deliver more than gaslight ever could. Twenty years later, as the means to control it were being developed, Gordon Craig and Adolphe Appia issued lyric pronouncements about the qualities of electric light. These influential stage designers found in light a potential for conveying emotion and for uniting scenery and actors that had only been dreamed of by past theatrical designers.

The reverberations of Appia's and Craig's philosophies of stage lighting were felt both abroad and in America. Many American scene designers put their theories into practice. More than that, they kept abreast of the developing technology in the world outside the theater in order to expand their theories. In the early years of the twentieth century, the man who followed the scene designer in lockstep around the theater was the stage electrician, his invaluable accomplice in creating lighting magic.

According to David Belasco, the California Theatre in San Francisco was the first American playhouse to use electric lamps, in 1879; if so, it must have generated its own power because electrical plants did not start to rise until the 1880s. Edison personally supervised the installation of the first electrical system in a New York theater, Steele MacKaye's Lyceum, and planned and tested some of the instruments in his laboratories in Menlo Park, New Jersey. When the theater opened in 1885, it contained the last word in sophisticated electrical equipment.

As power plants were built and wires strung from pole to pole across America, electricity was brought into the old theaters, but, surprisingly, some of the new theaters installed gas as well as electricity, just in case the new power failed. Ultimately, the reliability of electricity and its cheapness won over even the most diehard managers. The miles of tubing through which gas was conducted to jets throughout a theater were replaced by wires that could be snaked through walls and narrow spaces. The bulky gas table backstage was supplanted by an equally bulky electric lightboard, which became smaller and smaller as technology progressed, until in the computer age it has come to rest on an inconspicuous table at the rear of the orchestra floor or in a raised booth above the seats.

The New Movement scene designers in America exercised near total control of the lighting of their sets. Livingston Platt, Joseph Urban, and Robert Edmond Jones all exploited the interpretative properties of light and made it an integral part of their designs. Their scene renderings often show shadows and misty and moody effects, which were brought to life onstage via colored lights, transparent curtains known as scrims, and lights placed to provide special angles of illumination. But even before the masters of the New Movement, Belasco pioneered the field. With Louis Hartmann, his longtime associate, he developed techniques for creating the refined effects he wanted for his dramas. Hartmann wrote a short book, a kind of manual of stage lighting, and in it he pointed out that although the same equipment was available to everyone, only Belasco had succeeded in achieving the plasticity with light that Appia had set as an objective just a few years before. In the dome of his first Belasco Theatre he created a small laboratory in 1902, and there, working with Hartmann on a model, devised all of the lighting cues for each production before devoting a week to lighting rehearsals in the theater below.

Belasco considered the lighting for a production of *Madame Butterfly* in 1900 his crowning achievement. He kept the audience spellbound by subtle changes of illumination, accompanied by mood music, as the heroine, Cho Cho San, was seen waiting out the night from dusk till dawn for her lover's return. Hartmann described how the effects were accomplished in three minutes:

Several colors of silk... in long strips... were attached to tin rollers; the rollers were set into bearings fastened to a wooden frame that slid into the color groove of the lamp. The turning of the rollers passed the colors in front of the light and they were projected on the windows in a series of soft blends. As the orange deepened into blue, floor lanterns were brought on the scene and lighted; as the pink of the morning light was seen the lanterns flickered out one by one.

No wonder that Puccini was so enraptured by the play that he decided to set it to music.

Belasco dreamed of dispensing entirely with footlights for many years and dared to do so in 1917. The harshness of direct upward light was replaced by the softness of reflected and angled light so that his sets and the contours of the faces and bodies of his actors were gently illuminated, not sharply outlined. Belasco's detractors, many of whom were the young Turks of the New Movement, grudgingly admired his flair for lighting design, although they declared it was wasted on the trivial productions he mounted and was fettered by his obsessive literalism.

Belasco was not alone in the early years of the century in experimenting with lighting. Livingston Platt eliminated footlights in his Shakespearean productions for Margaret Anglin before Belasco did. In Boston, Monroe Pevear studied the components of light and its action on pigments. In 1911 he broke stage light into its own primary colors of red, green, and blue and recombined them as "white" light. Using colored gelatin in thin sheets in front of a lamp, he achieved an almost limitless spectrum of colored illuminations. He also devised instruments for special effects. The actress Maude Adams eagerly welcomed each new invention that provided greater flexibility in illumination. She experimented with stains on incandescent lamps, seeking through colored light to give greater definition to actors' faces so that they could dispense with exaggerated facial contortions and to prevent makeup from appearing artificial. She prevailed upon Charles Frohman, her producer,

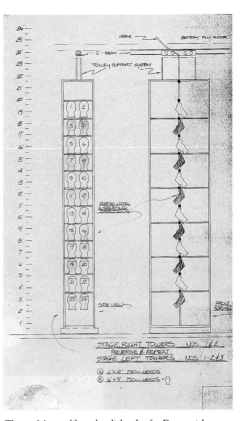

Tharon Musser likens her light plot for Dreamgirls *to a piece of written music, whose symbols can be understood by both designers and electricians who translate them into moving, form-giving, and atmospheric light. (Shown is a section for the pivoted light towers.)*

Stanley McCandless wrote the bible for modern stage lighting and taught for many years at Yale's School of Drama. Here he is shown, about 1950, at the American Theatre Wing addressing students on the mysteries of light and the capabilities of instruments.

to bring from Germany special lamps that had the intensity of arc lights, a substitute for limelight that to Adams was a torment: "If a scene needed quiet and concentrated attention, the arc took that moment to chitter and sizzle, hum a little tune and—go out." The new lamps, safely transported to New York in Frohman's private stateroom, were installed on the balcony rail in the Empire Theatre and were a great success, much to her delight.

Adams was one of the first theater people to insist that the controls for the lighting—the dimmer box—be placed in front of the stage so that the electrician could see the actors as he worked the lights. Lionel Barrymore remembered that, much to everyone's surprise, Adams "came forward to supervise the lights" in a production of *Peter Ibbetson* in which he starred in 1917. In 1921 General Electric invited Adams to help in developing lighting powerful enough to make color cinematography a possibility. She spent two years in Schenectady in a small laboratory, hoping for a breakthrough so that her performance in *Peter Pan* could be filmed in color and sound. Unfortunately, all the elements of the nascent technology did not coalesce in time.

Prior to World War I, European designers had the luxury of working in state-supported theaters and could install permanent equipment with which to conduct their experiments. American designers had to think in terms of portable equipment, since shows, with rare exception, had to be packed up and taken on the road. Large scenic structures like the curved plaster cyclorama, a neutral background upon which lights could be played, were not feasible in America; however, the cyclorama adapted in cloth by Adolphe Linnebach, the German technical designer, which could be hung on a curved track, was successfully used in American theatrical productions. Linnebach also invented a projector with a lamp that could be used to cast, through a transparent painted slide or cutout design, a powerful beam of light at the cyclorama to create the effect of skies or silhouetted scenes. This early version of projected scenery has undergone several generations of improvement, until today it is part of both the scene and the lighting designer's stock of effects.

In the decades after World War I, great strides were made in developing lighting instruments with a variety of shapes, sizes, and functions; in miniaturizing lamps; and in compacting control boards, all of which extended the use of light onstage. Because the college and university theaters, like the European repertory theaters, can afford to install complex permanent equipment, it has been on the American campus rather than on the commercial stage that most new techniques have been launched. At the Yale School of Drama, George Izenour and Stanley McCandless taught and invented lighting technology, and, beginning in the mid-1930s, Yale graduated scores of young men and women grounded in the latest lighting techniques and approaches to the new art. As authors and as consultants for theaters and auditoriums throughout the country, both McCandless and Izenour personally extended their influence beyond academia. Theodore Fuchs at Northwestern University has played a similar role in the Midwest. Other professionally oriented schools, such as the Carnegie Institute of Technology (now Carnegie Mellon University), the universities of Iowa, Indiana, and Illinois, and other major universities with established drama departments, offer instruction in lighting design with very sophisticated facilities.

During the twentieth century, companies specializing in stage lighting have sprung up to meet the increasing needs of commercial, academic, and community theaters. In 1896 two immigrant Austrians founded Kliegl Brothers, a firm that designed and manufactured the special housing for the incandescent lamps used in theaters throughout the country, and other companies followed in their wake. During the era of the New Movement, when the emphasis on lighting and special effects created new demands, and when community and "little" theaters became experimental in their use of scenery and lighting, specialty lighting companies proliferated. Today, using sophisticated electronics technology, companies both large and small create complex lighting-control systems tailored to the needs of theaters and scenic designers.

If it can be said that one person created the role of lighting designer in the modern

American theater, that person is Abe Feder. Born in Milwaukee in 1909, he became fascinated with light at age fourteen, when he happened to catch a performance of the Great Thurston at a Milwaukee theater. Feder was entranced by the magician's ability to manipulate light to create his effects and decided then and there that his life would be dedicated to exploring its possibilities. At the Carnegie Institute of Technology, where he intended to study architecture and engineering, Feder spent most of his time lighting shows for the drama department. He left school after two years and made his way to Chicago, where he became lighting designer for the Goodman Theatre in 1928. In 1930 he struck out for New York and began by lighting Yiddish theater productions, summer stock, and anything else he could find to work on. His first Broadway show was *Trick for Trick,* which opened in 1932, when he was just twenty-three. During the next few years, he worked in the Broadway milieu while designing for the Group Theatre and the Federal Theatre Project (FTP)—shuttling back and forth between the commercial and the avant-garde. He became Orson Welles's technical director for the New York branch of the FTP and was ecstatic with the million-dollars' worth of equipment placed at his disposal by the government. His contribution to Welles's landmark production of *Doctor Faustus* in 1937 was to move the characters on and off stage by means of light and nothing more: the usual stage gimmickry of trapdoors and manufactured smoke was banished in favor of pools, curtains, and walls of light, all of which must have had its roots in Feder's first visit to the Great Thurston.

His delight in the mystique of light is tempered by his cool appraisal of its function in a play: "The slightest mistake shows up and the whole character of the show may be changed by the lights. Stage lighting is a mixture of science and art. Scene follows scene. You must rely on speed, flexibility and a minimum of machinery." He ran afoul of George M. Cohan when he failed to produce the customary spotlight on the star during a rehearsal. When he told George M. it was unnecessary, Cohan got the word to him that Abe Feder was likewise, and fired him. In the course of his career, he designed the lighting for hundreds of plays and sometimes the sets as well.

When in 1934 "Lighting by Abe Feder" began to appear below the title of plays, it marked the arrival of a new type of theatrical collaborator. In 1962 the United Scenic Artists recognized lighting as a distinct and separate specialty and expanded its membership to include lighting designers. Abe Feder's contribution has been more than giving his profession new status; he has given it new techniques. When the equipment he needed in order to achieve the effects he wanted was not available, he invented it. Inevitably, Feder moved in other directions, although he never entirely abandoned the theatre. He set up a consulting and engineering firm, Lighting by Feder, which has designed industrial and architectural lighting. He has also lectured extensively and conducted workshops at colleges and universities throughout the country. His life continues to be lighting.

Abe Feder's one-time assistant, Jean Rosenthal, made stage lighting an art and gave it a vocabulary. To her, light was not something ethereal, it was real and palpable. Her colleague the late Boris Aronson remembered how in rehearsal "she would put her hand up into the light, and it was like a flower." During her lifetime, Rosenthal lighted hundreds of Broadway shows, ballets, and operas. She became a theater and lighting consultant, the foremost expert in the field. Because she was a woman in men's territory, she knew from the start of her career that she had to be better than good, she had to be the best. Standing barely four feet six inches tall, she worked with electricians and stagehands who towered over her but, unintimidated, she remained invariably courteous, knowledgeable, and firm. Since most scene designers prefer to light their own sets, if Rosenthal was called in to handle the lighting of a show, she strove with tact and respect to gain their confidence. She invariably did.

She was born in New York City in 1912. Her well-to-do, cultured family sent her to a series of progressive schools, and instead of attending a conventional college she went to the Neighborhood Playhouse School of the Theatre in New York, learning a great deal from the theatrical professionals who taught there. From the beginning, she

That light has plastic qualities was demonstrated by Jules Fisher in Jesus Christ Superstar (1971). Note how it curves over the actor's head and how the color projects a mood.

gravitated toward the backstage side of theater. She was accepted as a student at the Yale School of Drama and spent three years there absorbing all she could from Donald Oenslager and Stanley McCandless. In 1933 she was ready to assault Broadway, but jobs were not plentiful during the early Depression years. She eventually landed a job as technical assistant with the FTP in New York through John Houseman, the co-director. Abe Feder was the lighting designer, Nat Karson the scene designer, and Orson Welles the artistic director. It was an exciting time for her, and it extended her theatrical education. When Houseman produced Leslie Howard's Hamlet in 1936, she became the assistant stage manager in charge of light cues.

In the same year, she participated in the historic production of Marc Blitzstein's The Cradle Will Rock. Because of its agitprop nature, she and everyone else associated with it were fired from the FTP, and almost immediately Welles and Houseman formed the Mercury Theatre company and invited Rosenthal to become the technical and lighting director. At the same time, she continued to work as a technical assistant to Martha Graham, whom she had met at the Neighborhood Playhouse, and began an eighteen-year professional relationship with Lincoln Kirstein's Ballet Society, which was to evolve into the New York City Ballet. Rosenthal received her first Broadway credit as lighting designer in the 1943 production of Richard III, which she also produced for John Houseman and the remnants of the old Mercury Theatre company. Thereafter, she became Broadway's leading lighting designer. Her contributions were many and enduring, but her principal legacy was to make theatrical lighting a more precise and flexible art. She invented symbols for instruments and colors and formulated light plots on paper so that nothing was left to chance. She insisted on lighting rehearsals, at which errors could be quickly caught and changes made. For her, light had shape, color, and movement—and these qualities she played upon unerringly to catch shifting moods within an evolving drama. Angela Lansbury recalled how Rosenthal's lighting transformed her from an old crone into a young woman without a change of makeup or costume, as she sang of a youthful love in the musical Dear World. Rosenthal died on May 1, 1969, a few weeks after lighting her final ballet for Martha Graham, Archaic Hours, at New York City Center, an event that marked thirty-seven years of collaboration.

During the decades following World War II, largely in emulation of Rosenthal, women have dominated the field of lighting on Broadway. Peggy Clark began her career as a costume and scene designer but switched to lighting design in 1946, with Beggar's Holiday. Born in Baltimore in 1915, she began her theatrical career as a costume designer shortly after leaving Yale's drama school. While working for Oliver Smith, she decided to specialize in lighting design. He concentrated on the sets and costumes, she on designing the lights. The two collaborated on a number of musicals, and Clark soon made lighting musicals her particular forte.

Tharon Musser, who dominates the field of lighting design on Broadway today, introduced the computerized lightboard into the commercial theater, a prodigious feat. After working closely with its inventor, she won concessions from the theatrical employees' unions and persuaded theater owners to change the wiring of their auditoriums to AC current. Musser, in fact, achieved the impossible, and in so doing she revolutionized her profession. A small, portable lightboard can be controlled by one or two electricians who follow the action onstage and make subtle adjustments in the pre-set, stored lighting cues, as the audience reacts to the play. Musser first used the computerized controls in A Chorus Line at the Shubert Theatre and has acknowledged that the swift changes of light could not have been achieved without them. Cues can be set in less time, and they never vary unless an operator adjusts them. Best of all, the controls extend the range of possible effects. And as the electronic age progresses, doubtless the lightboard of the 1990s will reflect improvements in engineering made in the world outside the theater.

Born in 1925, Musser was another graduate of the Yale School of Drama. She became Rosenthal's assistant and, like her mentor, she began her career outside Broadway's precincts. Her atmospheric and evocative lighting for Long Day's Journey

In his lighting for Hair (1967), Jules Fisher deliberately exposed the instruments to the audience and used spotlights and colors to intensify the theatricality of the event.

into Night in 1956 drew critical acclaim, and from that moment on she has worked on Broadway every season, usually walking off with any and all available awards.

Lighting design is not a totally female province. Martin Aronstein, John Gleason, and Jules Fisher have been highly regarded and in demand on Broadway for two decades. Of the three, Fisher most closely resembles Abe Feder in his total dedication to the art. Fisher's interest in lighting began in his high-school days. After undergraduate study in the drama department of the Carnegie Institute of Technology, he came up through the ranks of regional theater, summer stock, and Off-Broadway theater until, in 1963, at the age of twenty-six, he reached Broadway with *Spoon River Anthology*. He proceeded to collect a prodigious number of Broadway credits, while establishing a consulting firm that has expanded its sphere of activities into industrial lighting, architectural design, and, recently, motion-picture production. Fisher's theatrical lighting is often daring and innovative. It reflects the bold and exaggerated look of the rock concert, tending to call attention to itself. His style has often been imitated, but it works best in his own hands.

American lighting designers are probably the most inventive on earth, and they are in some danger today of being swallowed up by the welter of gadgetry and space-age equipment they have devised. In roughly fifty years, their job has become preeminently important. Lighting designers also attend the first production conferences, even though they do not begin their practical work until the sets have been installed and the costumes have been prepared. Six designers can light an entire season of plays on Broadway, and each major American resident theater company requires only one, aided by an assistant or two. If they are good, lighting designers enjoy long careers in the theater, but they remain and will continue to remain a small group of dedicated wizards who have plumbed the secrets of light, only to reaffirm its mysteries each time the curtain rises.

ARCHITECTS

THAT the drama has achieved its finest moments in casual, undesigned, or, worse, incidental structures, most of which were left open to the elements, must give pause to any architect who is commissioned to design a theater. Until relatively recently, the building that houses theatrical performance has undergone its own special evolution with a blithe disregard for architectural art, actors and producers having had the greatest say in the development of its design. Pragmatic people, they realized early on that it was simply a place where people gathered to see other people perform for their entertainment. When performance took on other dimensions—specifically, architectural scenery and artificial light—they adapted the basic structure to fit the new arrangements. When the public would no longer put up with having their heads scorched by the sun or their bottoms numbed by hard seats, the professionals began to provide greater comfort for their audiences, too. But rarely have they lost sight of the fact, first, that the theater building, reduced to its essentials, is a special room for a special event and, second, that if the event works the magic it should, the encompassing structure will simply fade from the audience's consciousness. If any building embodies Louis Sullivan's principle that form follows function, it is the theater.

Though architects have never achieved the status of full-fledged collaborator in the theatrical event, there have always been specialists who were responsible for planning and constructing auditoriums, and since like everything else, building has become a complex technological, social, and economic undertaking, the theatrical profession today allows architects into its private circle to help solve increasingly knotty problems and to lend guidance in its quest for the perfect playhouse. So far, the ideal theater has eluded everyone—as well it should. If it is to continue to survive, the theater should not be shackled by a structure that would prevent it from moving on. The playhouse must change not only when the play changes but when the method of presenting it changes. The theater architect should simply be on board for the ride.

Though in the past theater people have created their own playhouses, they have also had to abide by the rules of the society they served. American history proves the point. The English men and women who braved life and limb to settle North America began arriving at the close of the greatest era in English theatrical history, but their religious scruples would not allow them to build playhouses. Besides, survival was uppermost in everyone's minds. When the colonies became established and life was gentler, there was time to contemplate sophisticated pleasures and to ease the moral code accordingly.

That time arrived in Williamsburg, Virginia, at some point between 1716 and 1718, when a simple wooden theater was erected by the merchant and sometime dancing master William Levingston. The foundations of the building lie on the east side of the Palace Green, but how it looked or what merry performances took place on its stage may perhaps never be known. The records show that in 1745 it was converted into a court of hustings, its day as America's first theater over.

Living was easier in the South, and the Puritans never settled there. It was not until the middle of the eighteenth century that professional troupes began to appear in the northern cities. In 1749 a band of players headed by Walter Murray and Thomas Kean were offered a room in a sturdy brick warehouse owned by William Plumstead of Philadelphia. A renegade Quaker, Plumstead must have enjoyed certain personal satisfactions in allowing the actors to play under the very noses of his uncompromising former brethren. Murray and Kean were not sufficiently encouraged by their reception to tarry long in Philadelphia, and within a few months they took the road to New York. What they found there was a makeshift vestige of a former period, when amateurs had first begun to tread the boards, a theater in a building on the Nassau Street estate of former mayor Rip Van Dam that may have been either a warehouse or a brewery (or both). The Plumstead and Van Dam "theaters" were probably fitted up with a stage at one end, benches in front of it, and a raised gallery at the rear for the common folk. Murray and Kean made a significant addition to their New York playhouse: they added boxes along the side walls, not only to increase the seating (a sign that they attained a moderate success) but also to provide a special place for the elite of the city.

After their encouraging reception in New York, Murray and Kean turned south toward Williamsburg. There they found a playhouse that had been especially erected for them by Alexander Finnie, the proprietor of the Raleigh Tavern. Built in two months, it may have resembled a rough English country theater, with a pit (orchestra), boxes ringing the pit, and a gallery (balcony) hanging from the wall opposite the stage. Unlike Plumstead's and Van Dam's, Finnie's playhouse was located at the edge of town, not in its busy center. Before Murray and Kean and their troupe disappeared into history, they visited other southern towns, playing in courthouses and warehouses, or whatever available space they could find. If they performed no other service, they at least broke ground for their successors by lulling the suspicions of the entertainment-starved colonials.

Murray and Kean appear to have materialized from nowhere, but the troupes that followed theirs, from England and Jamaica, had appeared on the English provincial stage and occasionally in London. They brought with them the theater architecture with which they were familiar, just as the early settlers had quickly built the kinds of structures they remembered in their homelands. When Lewis Hallam arrived in Williamsburg in 1752, he bought Finnie's theater, remodeled it to increase the stage area and seating capacity, and presented his plays against the scenery he had brought from London. He did the same to Plumstead's warehouse, but in New York, in his own words, "having been promised a very fine Playhouse Building," he found instead the old makeshift Van Dam theater, which he promptly gutted and rebuilt.

His successor, David Douglass, not only improved Hallam's playhouses but made his own significant contributions. By 1774, when he returned to Jamaica after sixteen years of wandering with his troupe, Douglass had not only wooed public opinion but erected a string of theaters in the towns and cities on his itinerary. A bold manager and a canny entrepreneur, he was also America's first, if inadvertent, theater architect. His first theaters were little more than facsimiles of the simple English country playhouse, but success in New York and Philadelphia prompted him to build two substantial and permanent theaters. In 1766 Douglass constructed the Southwark Theatre in Philadelphia, just outside the city limits and out of reach of religious zealots. The theater was two-and-a-half stories high, topped with a cupola. The foundation and the first story were built of brick and the rest of wood. The front facade was broken by three large windows with a painted arch above them in the pseudo-Palladian style. A year after building the Southwark, Douglass erected a theater on John Street in New York. It was not outside the city limits but certainly stood a brisk walk from the southernmost residential section. It may have been an exact duplicate of the Southwark, though a contemporary account describes it as entirely of wood. Both theaters were painted with the mixture of red brick dust or ocher and skim milk commonly used for barns. Douglass would have had neither the money to use expensive imported lead paint nor the audacity to allow his structure to compete with churches and other public buildings.

We have maddeningly little information about the interiors of the American

In one of these two warehouses in 1749, William Plumstead of Philadelphia allowed the actors assembled by Walter Murray and Thomas Kean to use a storeroom for their activities, much to the chagrin of his neighbors.

This view of the Southwark Theatre in Philadelphia is a conjectural reconstruction drawn by Edwin P. Durang for his History of the Philadelphia Stage (1868).

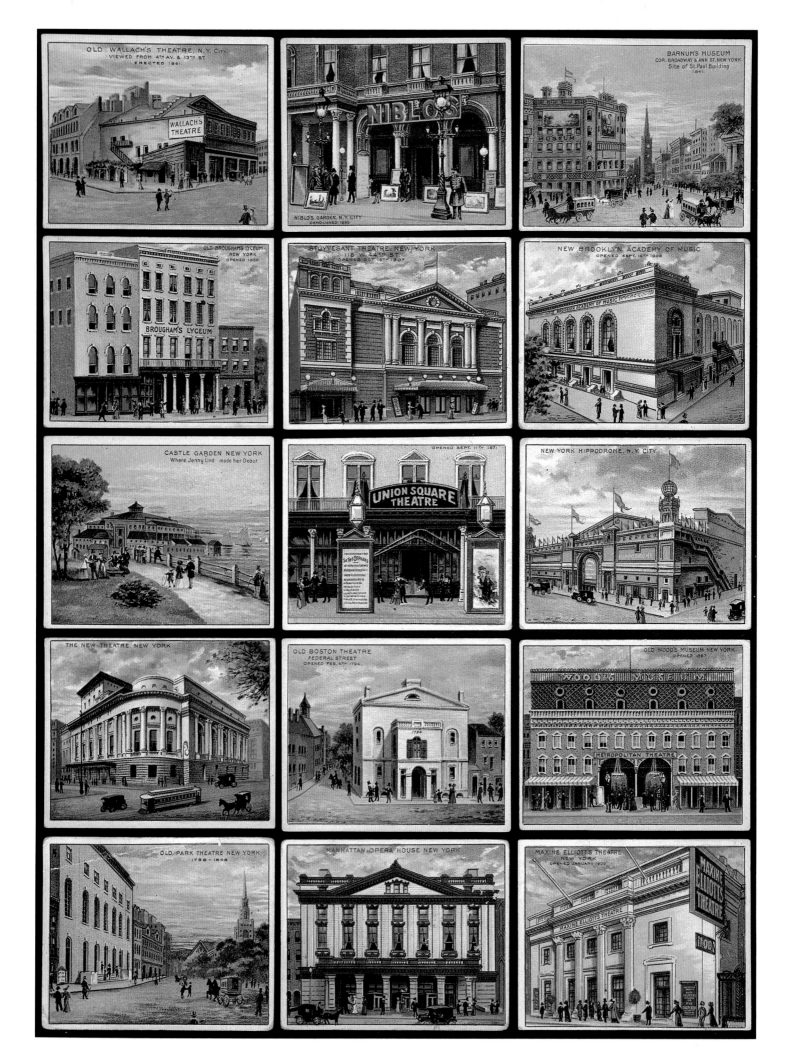

OLD WALLACH'S THEATRE, N.Y. City.
VIEWED FROM 4TH AV. & 13TH ST.
ERECTED 1861.

NIBLO'S
NIBLO'S GARDEN, N.Y. CITY
DEMOLISHED 1895

BARNUM'S MUSEUM
COR. BROADWAY & ANN ST. NEW YORK
Site of St. Paul Building
1841.

OLD BROUGHAM'S LYCEUM
NEW YORK
OPENED 1850
BROUGHAM'S LYCEUM

STUYVESANT THEATRE, NEW YORK
118 W. 44TH ST.
OPENED OCT. 16TH 1907

NEW BROOKLYN ACADEMY OF MUSIC
OPENED SEPT. 14TH 1908
BROOKLYN ACADEMY OF MUSIC

CASTLE GARDEN NEW YORK
Where Jenny Lind made her Debut

OPENED SEPT. 11TH 1871
UNION SQUARE THEATRE

NEW YORK HIPPODROME, N.Y. CITY
HIPPODROME

THE NEW THEATRE, NEW YORK

OLD BOSTON THEATRE
FEDERAL STREET
OPENED FEB. 4TH 1794
1794

OLD WOOD'S MUSEUM NEW YORK
OPENED 1867
WOOD'S MUSEUM
METROPOLITAN THEATRE

OLD PARK THEATRE NEW YORK
1798 – 1848

MANHATTAN OPERA HOUSE NEW YORK

MAXINE ELLIOTT'S THEATRE
NEW YORK
OPENED JANUARY 1909
MAXINE ELLIOTT'S THEATRE

238

Company's theaters and only nineteenth-century conjectural drawings of their exteriors. A description of their New York theater was incorporated in Royall Tyler's play *The Contrast,* which was first presented in John Street. In the third act, the hero's valet, Jonathan, joins a crowd and is swept into a long entryway "clean up to the garret, just like a meetinghouse gallery." He sees "a power of topping folks, all sitting round in little cabbins, just like father's corn-cribs." A "great green cloth" is raised to allow the congregation to look "right into the next neighbor's house." Another glimpse into the interior of the John Street has been left to us by Grant Thorburn, whose feed-and-grain store was located near the "synagogue of Satan." He reported seeing the respectable women of the town in boxes; men, women, and children in the pit; and "Blacksmiths' apprentices and Canvastown girls in the gallery." The new republicans obviously clung to the social divisions of pit, box, and gallery that had been introduced by the English managers.

The rest is conjecture. The stages in Douglass's two theaters may have been as large as any in the English provinces, since they accommodated the scenery that he ordered from London. As in contemporary English theaters, they were probably raked and may have been separated from the pit by a row of spikes to discourage rowdies from intruding on the actors' space. People having box seats may have entered by way of the stage, those in the pit through passageways under the first tier of boxes, and those who bought the cheapest seats by a special stairway to the gallery. Lighting was supplied by sconces on the box fronts and a chandelier above the pit. There was no heating, and such fresh air as entered came from the windows and perhaps a vent concealed by the cupola. People sat on hard benches, and interior adornment was minimal—perhaps green paint over lightly plastered walls and some wallpaper in the boxes.

Although they were still primitive by any standards, the John Street and Southwark theaters not only represented a significant improvement over the large converted rooms of the previous era, they reflected the acceptance of the playhouse by the public. Ministers still raged from the pulpit about the devilish allurements of the theater, but the townspeople appeared to be willing to risk eternal damnation for a few hours of entertainment. The prosperity of the colonials, their growing sophistication, and their desire to be amused in their free time caused Douglass to build his theaters. They were the best he could afford and were designed on the playhouse form he knew best. They served their purpose.

When the Revolutionary War was over, the professional companies returned to the mainland with fresh recruits from England to begin a new period of theater building (religious opposition had not disappeared, but only the diehard fundamentalists were paying any attention to it). The three major playhouses that rose in the early years of the Republic were larger, better designed, more accessible, and more comfortable for audiences. All three were designed by architects, not by a company manager, and all reflected a swing away from the simple English country playhouse and toward more graceful Continental models. While these early American architects leaned heavily on Old World traditions, they adapted them to suit the New World. They were also influenced by such mundane matters as availability of materials, craftsmen, and money.

The plain, uninteresting exteriors of the prewar theaters were superseded by more imposing, ornamented facades, and, if their exteriors were more attractive and inviting, so were their auditoriums. The pit, boxes, and gallery arrangement remained unchanged but was now encompassed within a graceful curve—either a semicircle or a flattened ellipse—which improved the visibility of the stage from just about all points in the house. Although the young Republic was fiercely democratic in most of its civic functions, tradition in the theater fostered an unspoken plutocracy. But inequality was only reflected in the price of the seats. In 1793, when Thomas Wignell was building a new theater on Chestnut Street in Philadelphia, he was approached by a society matron who offered to buy one of the boxes at any price if she could use it exclusively and keep it locked when she could not attend. "With many expressions of polite address," Wignell declined the offer and reported that the lady rarely ever

With St. Paul's spire in the background, this drawing shows the John Street Theatre in New York. The sketch, another conjectural reconstruction, was possibly the work of Abraham Hosier, an artist-contributor to the History of the City of New York *by Mrs. Martha J. Lamb and Mrs. Burton Harrison (1877–80). Note the long covered entryway to the theater.*

Opposite:
In the early years of the twentieth century, P. Lorillard, the tobacco company, inserted colored cards, about three inches square, of American theaters past and present in the tin boxes containing their Between the Acts Little Cigars.

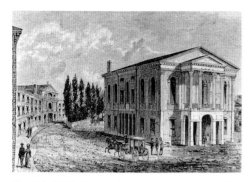

Like Philadelphia, Boston also got a theater in 1794—its first ever. The Federal Street was designed by native-born Charles Bulfinch in a vaguely classic revival style and executed in red brick.

visited the theater thereafter. Warren and Wood continued Wignell's policy and advised every wise manager in America to "set his face like flint" against selling exclusive rights to boxes to the wealthy. Seating continued to be on a first-come-first-served basis until around the middle of the nineteenth century, when an early version of the reserved-seat system was introduced in New Orleans and Boston.

In 1791 Wignell and Alexander Reinagle, a musician and conductor, had joined forces to build the first postwar American playhouse, on a centrally located lot near Sixth Street in Philadelphia. Wignell sent to London for a plan from his brother-in-law, the noted scene designer Inigo Richards, and raised the construction money through subscription among the well-to-do. The subscribers were the actual owners of the theater, which was leased back to Wignell and Reinagle. Looking very much like a proper English theater designed on a Continental model, the Chestnut Street playhouse was completed, more or less, in 1793, but an outbreak of yellow fever prevented the manager from opening it for more than a year. The facade, which featured a colonnaded entrance and a central Palladian window surmounted by a decorative pediment, was still not completed when the doors were finally opened in 1794. The gray and gold auditorium, seating more than a thousand people, was pronounced handsome by most contemporary observers. The exterior continued to be worked on from drawings furnished by Benjamin Latrobe, the first important architect in America, who would plan many of the buildings in Washington, the new capital of the nation.

In 1805 the Chestnut Street was finally finished, both inside and out, and was rated the finest theater in America. In 1816 it assumed the added distinction of being the first playhouse in America to experiment with gas lighting. The story of the Chestnut Street provides a pattern for the histories of other early theaters. A succession of managers redecorated the interior, added improvements to increase seating or safety, and made so many other alterations that the modified building bore little resemblance to the original. In 1820 the Chestnut Street burned down and two years later was rebuilt with a marble facade and redecorated with William Rush's two sculptures of Comedy and Tragedy, rescued from the fire. In 1855, now too small and in a neighborhood that had substantially changed in character, the theater closed its doors and was demolished. A new Chestnut Street Theatre was built six blocks away, but it bore no physical relationship to the old. It, too, went the way of old playhouses when it was pulled down in the name of progress in 1917.

A few weeks before the Chestnut Street was scheduled to open in 1794, Boston, the impregnable bastion of conservatism during the prewar period, made ready to introduce its citizens to the first professional theatrical season in the history of the city. Their new playhouse was the work of Charles Bulfinch, the first important native-born architect. Located at the corner of Federal and Franklin streets, it was known in its early years simply as the Federal Street Theatre; later it was referred to as the Old Boston, to differentiate it from the Boston Theatre of greater fame, which was erected in 1854. The Federal Street was a sizable building measuring 140 feet long by 61 feet wide by 40 feet high that also contained an elegant ballroom. Two tiers of boxes ringed the semicircular pit; pit and gallery together held more than a thousand patrons. By no means the architect's finest work, the Federal Street contained one advanced structural element not found in English playhouses of the same era. Instead of supporting the first tier of boxes with the usual columns that obstructed the view of many of those sitting in the pit, Bulfinch made use of the cantilever principle. The interior was decorated by the carvers John and Simeon Skilling, who created decorative moldings, columns, pilasters, and medallions within a color scheme of crimson and gold. Damaged by fire in 1798, the theater was reconstructed by Bulfinch within a few months. In 1852, when it burned again, no thought was given to its reconstruction.

By far the most important theater to be built in the final years of the eighteenth century was the new playhouse in New York. It was referred to as the New Theatre or the New-York Theatre at first, but became known everlastingly as the Park Theatre shortly after it opened. In 1795 a group of prominent New Yorkers had wanted to replace the aging and decrepit John Street playhouse with a theater that would reflect the aspirations of the city. They chose a site in the northern reaches (at the time) of Manhattan that was promising to become the center of the municipality and its cultural life. At a point where Broadway was moving toward merging with the Bowery, the road to Boston, there was a triangle of land that had been used as a commons. Along the eastern side of this open site was a short street that came to be known as Park Row. After the theater was built, on a lot midway through the block, the commons was turned into a park and, just above it, City Hall was erected in 1811.

In an early precedent for the construction lags and cost overruns that have become so permanent a part of the city's legend, it took two-and-a-half years and $90,000 more than the sum originally estimated to complete the theater, which was still unfinished when it finally opened in 1798. The architect was probably Joseph Mangin, a Frenchman, who with his brother founded an architectural firm in the early Republic.

No one liked the Park's facade, in either the original or the rebuilt versions. Mangin may have envisioned an Italian marble or a smooth-cut stone exterior, but the Indiana limestone quarries had yet to be opened, and marble was still too expensive to import from Europe for an American playhouse. What he apparently settled for was a plain stucco finish painted to look like marble. In 1821, when the theater was rebuilt after a disastrous fire, architect Hugh Reinagle applied a brown-oil cement finish to the exterior, which only served to make matters worse. One English visitor to New York gave sarcastic utterance to the general disapproval:

The beauty of the outside is a matter of serious astonishment, consisting of the best quality of colored plaster variegated by straight lines, which are ingeniously intended to imitate cracks. This gives it an appearance of venerable grandeur, calculated to strike the beholder with silent awe. Indeed, the munificence of its owners has spared neither plaster nor brown paint to impart to it a sombre cast, and anxious for improvement, they have changed it from its former color, which was yellow, here and there blackened with smoke, to one of becoming and unvaried brown.

The interior was a different matter. Larger than its sister houses in Philadelphia and Boston, the Park could seat two thousand and was later enlarged to accommodate almost five hundred more. The auditorium was U-shaped, with three tiers of boxes surrounding the capacious pit and with a gallery set above the highest tier of boxes at the back of the house. Although the ceiling was flat, it was painted in trompe l'oeil to look like a dome. Originally, the first tier of boxes was cantilevered, as at the Federal Street Theatre, but when the house was enlarged, a fourth tier of boxes was added and pillars were inserted for support. The color scheme and decorations were changed often, but the interior of the Park was generally considered handsome in its variations by most visitors.

The Chestnut Street, the Federal Street, and the Park theaters were erected at the beginning of a great explosion in theater construction that lasted for more than a hundred years to accommodate an expanding audience. The population was growing by leaps and bounds, fed by a trickle of immigration in the early decades of the nineteenth century and by a gigantic tide at the end. The new immigrants were for the most part Europeans who were accustomed to having a theater or opera house in their communities, and even before they had completely mastered the language, they were climbing up to the galleries and balconies of the urban theaters. Playhouses not only got larger but also proliferated, until by mid-century New York, Boston, and Philadelphia were supporting a half-dozen or more theaters and a variety of entertainments from grand opera to minstrel shows. By 1875 New York had its first "theater district," around Union Square, and other eastern cities also had clusters of playhouses in their downtowns.

Theaters followed the settlers west, developing from large rooms in standing

The first proper theater built in Philadelphia after the Southwark was the Chestnut Street Theatre, created from plans probably by the English designer Inigo Richards and built by Thomas Wignell. It opened in 1794.

Manhattan's Park Theatre was opened to the public in 1798. Forty-eight years later it was still part of the City Hall Park streetscape. It appears on the right at midblock, flag marking the entrance, in this print of 1846 by Currier and Ives. Two years later, the theater burned down and was replaced by commercial buildings.

buildings, to simple freestanding structures, and finally to large edifices rivaling their eastern counterparts in splendor. After the Civil War they became a symbol of affluence and cultural pretensions. Instead of theaters, they were called opera houses, town halls, athenaeums, and academies of music by the people of the towns and villages that barely had the population to sustain them. A theater was included in the master plan of Pullman, Illinois—one of the prototypical company towns of the nineteenth century—smack in the central core of public buildings. Throughout the century, ticket prices remained the same—from ten cents to two dollars—and were within the means of practically everyone. When the playhouse provided the only show in town, it loomed very large in the lives of the townspeople.

Although the first generation of native-born architects continued to depend on Europe for technology and styles, they modified the ideas they imported to conform with American materials, the American environment, and the native spirit. Most started from the ground up. Ithiel Town, the Connecticut-born designer of New York's first Bowery Theatre (1826), first worked as a carpenter. Isaiah Rogers, who also began as a carpenter, was only twenty-six when he opened his Boston office and received the assignment to design the Tremont Theatre (1827). The Philadelphian

William Strickland was apprenticed at the start of his career to Benjamin Latrobe. It was he who designed the reconstructed Chestnut Street Theatre in 1822. As the century wore on, most of America's leading architects would receive at least one commission during their careers to plan theaters, and several made it a specialty.

Most of the early nineteenth-century playhouses were brick-and-masonry structures that took a long time to erect. With the widespread introduction of iron joists in the 1820s, and the manufacture of cheap nails in the 1830s, theaters could be built quickly—sometimes in months—with wood frames and iron supports. Fire was the greatest threat to nineteenth-century theaters. Many went up in flames, some with a loss of life, and a number burned several times during their histories. In 1811 the first of the theater fires to rock the nation occurred at the Richmond Theatre, in Richmond, Virginia. Although it was a brick building, it had a wooden roof and the interior walls were covered with canvas. A candle in a chandelier hanging above the stage ignited the scenery, which was suspended on wood rods, and turned the playhouse into an inferno in minutes as flames crept up the walls to the roof. At least seventy people died—no one knows the exact number—and many more were injured. As an immediate consequence, theatrical activity throughout the country was curtailed and a few necessary reforms instituted, but to no real avail.

New York, which had the greatest concentration of theaters, suffered thirty theater fires during the century. The worst conflagration occurred at Conway's Brooklyn Theatre in 1876, during a performance of *The Two Orphans,* a melodrama that the star, Kate Claxton, was to play for many years. A small fire broke out backstage when a piece of scenery brushed against an open gas jet and started to burn. Aware of what had happened, the actors went on with the play until the flames were in sight of the audience. From that moment on, pandemonium reigned as theatergoers rushed to reach safety. The dry timbers burned rapidly, sending smoke and deadly gases into the auditorium. Nearly three hundred people died in the fire: those who were not burned died from suffocation or from being trampled to death on stairways or in front of the four doors leading to the streets. Remembering the Brooklyn fire, manager-designer Steele MacKaye had a pump installed in the basement of his Madison Square Theatre in New York to supply water to several hydrants on stage, and he instructed and drilled his stagehands in fire-emergency procedures. His precautions prevented a disaster, on the evening of February 26, 1880. The act curtain at the Madison Square caught fire, but was quickly doused with water by the stage crew.

In 1903 the Iroquois Theatre in Chicago was advertised as being absolutely fireproof. Within five weeks of its building, it was a burnt-out ruin, despite the curtain made of asbestos installed, as in many theaters, as a result of the Brooklyn fire, to serve as a last defense against the spread of flames. Eddie Foy was playing to a house of two thousand packed into an auditorium that contained 1,719 seats. A spark from an arc lamp or an electrical wire ignited a portion of the grand drapery valence, which sent flames up into the stage loft. Within minutes, the entire loft was ablaze. Foy rushed from his dressing room to order the asbestos curtain lowered. About two-thirds of the way down it stuck on a wire stretched across the stage for an aerial act. The lights went off and people could not find the adequate but unmarked exit doors. Although the fire was confined to the stage area and front orchestra, panic, combined with smoke and gases, resulted in a death toll of more than six hundred.

In the aftermath of the Brooklyn fire, stringent building codes were enacted throughout the country to prevent similar catastrophes. After the Iroquois fire, the codes were tightened to provide for periodic inspection by fire authorities. The new regulations not only controlled the number and placement of exits, fire escapes, and stairwells, but stipulated that all remain lighted, even during performance. All materials used either in the fabric of a theater or backstage were required to be flameproof, and instructions for vacating a theater in a fire emergency had to be printed in its programs.

Municipal fire and building codes were additions to the many requirements and considerations that already guided the hand of the nineteenth-century theater architect. Managers and producers began to pay increased attention to creature comforts in order to keep audiences coming to their shows. They began to add lobbies, lounges, and foyers within their theaters for socializing before and between acts. Early amenities like fireplaces in the lobbies, carpets in the boxes, and refreshment stands had been augmented by outdoor balconies and primitive forms of air conditioning by the end of the century. All tended to increase the bulk of the building. Within the auditorium, hard benches were replaced by more comfortable seating. By 1833 the National Theatre in New York had upgraded the back of the old pit into the Frenchified "parterre" and provided mahogany chairs upholstered in blue damask to hasten the trend toward acceptance by the respectable folk. The floor of the parterre (also called the parquet) was built to slope up toward the back of the auditorium to increase visibility of the stage.

The boxes were another matter with which the nineteenth-century manager and

architect wrestled. Increasingly anachronistic in militantly democratic nineteenth-century America, they had also come to be recognized for what they were: bad seats, except in the center section. Their purpose had been to allow the denizens of the boxes to look at each other before, after, and during the dull patches of plays. By the end of the nineteenth century, the auditorium was dark and people were perforce watching the show. The tiers of boxes metamorphosed into dress circles and first balconies or mezzanines.

The proscenium boxes were moved into the auditorium, victims less of changing social structure than of alterations in stagecraft and playcraft. As long as wing-and-drop scenery remained in common use, the stage had great depth and included a proscenium stage, or forestage. Actors entered from doors on both sides of the proscenium, above which was room for one or two sets of boxes. As plays began to be presented with less artifice, they required realistic scenery that could be integrated into the dramatic action. Actors performed not merely in front of the scenery but within it, and this necessitated an adjustment in the entire stage to accommodate the new trends. Once the dominion of the star, the forestage retreated to a point where it

became an "apron," a slip of stage projecting beyond the curtain. The proscenium boxes had nowhere to go except to the lateral walls of the auditorium. Why they were preserved at all is a mystery, because they offer a very restricted view. Perhaps the idea of boxes as the correct place for honored guests or heads of state died hard; perhaps architects could find nothing else to dress what would have become unadorned and uninteresting side walls.

At the back of the nineteenth-century auditorium, above the tiers of boxes, loomed the gallery, the domain of the poor. Filled to capacity with servants, blacks, and workingmen and their apprentices, it could become rowdy, noisy, and disruptive. When prostitutes joined the general melee, it became wicked as well. Because they were high up and out of view of the respectable folk, the "gallery gods" were silently endured by audience and management alike. Washington Irving was once warned by a neighbor in the pit not to pay attention to the gallery folk when they began to rain down "apples, nuts, and gingerbread." Sit down quietly, he was told, and bend your back to it. The wisdom of this advice was quickly demonstrated when another playgoer decided to lash back. Jumping up on his seat, he remonstrated by shaking his fist and swearing at the gods, who rewarded him by making him their favorite target for the rest of the evening. Attacked as a place of corruption by the press everywhere, the gallery had all but disappeared as such by mid-century, gentrified into the balcony or sometimes, euphemistically, the family circle.

Until the twentieth century, the theater always adhered to two distinct divisions, the auditorium, which was the world of the patron, and the stage, which was the working place of the theater professionals. The worlds met at the proscenium arch but did not merge. Behind the curtain was a factory-like rabbit warren of dressing rooms, prop rooms, storerooms, and shops for making and painting scenery. The area below the stage was the province of the stage machinist and his crew, who could whisk away Hamlet's Ghost or pop up Macbeth's witches out of fake mist through trapdoors cut into the stage floor. The area above the stage rose higher and higher during the course of the century so that scenery and curtains could be lifted out of sight and stored until they were ready to be used again. In order to make it move easily, each curtain and piece of scenery was counterweighted by a sandbag or a lead bar hung on ropes and then tied to rails along the theater's side walls or "wings." When gas and then electric lighting arrived, the lamps and fixtures were fastened to heavy iron pipes, which were reached by catwalks or bridges above the stage. The stage house held the structural framework—known as the gridiron—for all of the scenery and lights plus the ropes, pulleys, and the rest of the gear that was kept out of sight of the audience. It protruded from the roof of the theater, giving the building an awkward and unlovely exterior profile. Many architects worked diligently to soften it; some simply raised the roof to the level of the stage house.

The theaters that were being built about 1800 in the rapidly developing centers of the burgeoning cities stood on what gradually became the most expensive urban real estate. As the century wore on, architects were faced with a double conundrum: how to build larger theaters on smaller midtown sites and still include what the actors and stage crews required and what audiences had come to expect by way of amenities. To compound matters, by mid-century architects were being asked to add offices and stores to the theater complex so that the owners and managers could survive on rental revenues in the likely event that their playhouses would experience nonprofitable periods. Even in smaller cities and towns, where the pressure on real estate was not so acute, theaters did not always remain free of the clutter of commercial enterprises. In 1895, the tiny hamlet of Norway, Maine, built an "opera house" containing stores on street level, below the auditorium—an object lesson in Yankee thrift.

Actors' comfort was given short shrift in the nineteenth-century playhouse. Dressing rooms were tucked away in subterranean passages or reached by steep or winding backstage staircases. One actress described them as "bare and beggarly little cubbyholes, ill-lighted, damp, and foul-smelling." The green room, the "time-honored rallying ground of the players," also fell victim to progress. For more than a hundred years, actors had assembled in this backstage oasis to learn their lines, wait for their cues, receive a few friends, or relax quietly before or after a performance. By the end of the century, the green room was just a warm memory shared by the oldest members of the profession.

As the theaters were abuilding, American architecture passed through a succession of styles, each of which dominated for a while and was never entirely discarded. From the beginning of one century to the start of the next, the pendulum swung from one classic revival to another. Between the return to Greek and Roman models about 1810 and the birth of the Beaux-Arts style in the early twentieth century, there were excursions into Italian Renaissance, Second Empire, Near Eastern, Oriental and Gothic, Romanesque (from the drawing board of Henry Hobson Richardson), and Victorian. Since most of the architects who became exponents of the various styles got a chance to design a theater, nineteenth-century playhouses reflect the gamut of architectural predilections. But because their purpose prevailed over everything, theaters could never be built with any purity of style. They became and remained eclectic. Often the exterior of a theater was different from the interior. A classic revival theater might well have an ornate Italian Renaissance auditorium. No American architect, not even Louis Sullivan, was predisposed to experiment with the interior arrangement of the playhouse. Those developments awaited a later age.

Many theaters burned and rose from their own ashes. Sometimes a rebuilt theater looked like its antecedent; often it was very different. Interiors changed as frequently as money would permit. A manager often gave his auditorium a facelift when he could ill afford it, on the time-honored American merchandising principle that new is better. Only one theater, the Walnut Street in Philadelphia, survives from the early nineteenth century, and how it managed to elude destruction is a saga of periodic renovations. When it was built, late in 1808, it was intended for a circus and had a central dirt arena surrounded by seats and was roofed over with an eighty-foot dome. Two years later, enlarged and fitted with a conventional stage and orchestra pit, it became the Olympic Theatre. In 1820 the dome was removed and the theater assumed its original name. In 1828 the architect John Haviland gave it a classic revival facade, which subsequent designers "improved" upon. In 1919, when the old and dilapidated theater was finally doomed to be demolished, the owner discovered that new building ordinances would restrict him to a smaller theater than the one he had planned. He chose instead to rebuild, and the old Walnut Street reopened in 1920. In 1968 the theater was declared a national landmark, and restoration was begun the following year. Workers peeled off layers of accretions to reveal John Haviland's 1828 facade, which the architects wisely chose to conserve. Unfortunately, no records of its nineteenth-century interior existed, and they created a starkly simple and anachronistic stage and auditorium.

Built in 1826, the Bowery Theatre, known as the Thalia at its demise, rose above elevated tracks in the last of its many reincarnations, before it burned in 1929 for the last time. Among its neighbors about the year 1879 were the Atlantic Garden, a popular concert saloon, and a photographic gallery.

From the outset New York, Philadelphia, and Boston were established as the country's centers of theatrical activity, and these cities competed to build the most elegant playhouses, which in turn became models for the rest of the country. In 1826 a group of New York's prominent and respected citizens indulged themselves in a repetition of history. Believing that Manhattan needed a newer and better theater than the Park, they selected a site on the Bowery where Henry Astor owned a tavern and where, at that very moment, some of New York's fashionable were deciding to build houses. The tavern was torn down and Ithiel Town was hired to design a splendid new theater. When it was completed, it resembled a Greek temple, with massive columns supporting an impressive pediment and with many classical details. The handsome auditorium held 3,000 seats, many with backs, and it was lighted with gas. Two years later, it burned to the ground and was rebuilt. During its 103-year history, the Bowery was destroyed by fire again and again, in 1836, 1838, 1845, and for the last time in 1929. It was first known as the New York Theatre and ended its existence as the Thalia, but for most of its life it was the Bowery. When the neighborhood was abandoned by people of quality, its managers turned to the poor immigrants who were flocking into the area. For many years it was renowned as the house of melodramas and spectacles, the only theater that retained the old-fashioned pit for the young bucks, the Bowery boys, who had their own special argot. Later it became a German-language theater, then a Yiddish theater, an Italian vaudeville house, and, before its demise, a Chinese opera house. Every time it burned down, the rebuilt version looked a little less like Town's theater. John Trimble designed its final incarnation with antebellum New Orleans in mind, including exterior balconies between the pillars and omitting the pediment. In 1862 the Mormons turned back the clock when they designed their Salt Lake Theatre to look very much like the first Bowery.

Sometimes, two popular styles met in one building. The facade of the first St. Charles Theatre, built in New Orleans in 1835, incorporated aspects of both Renaissance Italy and classical Greece. Rounded Palladian windows joined a classical colonnade, and the Grecian pediment was surmounted by a balconied upper story in an elegant hodgepodge of several styles. Elegance extended into the interior, which was decorated sumptuously in a vaguely classical motif. For the comfort of the ladies,

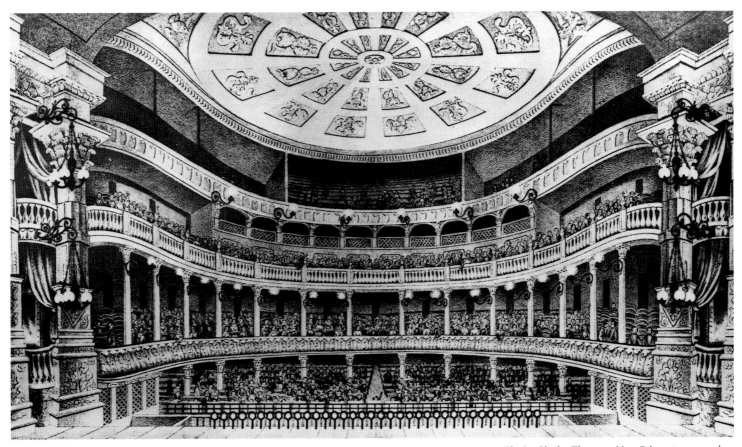

The St. Charles Theatre in New Orleans incorporated a hodgepodge of architectural styles but was declared the handsomest theater in America when it first opened, in 1835.

each box in the first tier was provided with a "boudoir," where they could dress or relax as they desired. Designed by Antoine Mondelli, who doubled as scene painter for the owner, James Caldwell, and erected at an unheard-of cost of $350,000, the house seated 4,000 people and was considered more than a match for any theater in the East. Alas, it burned to the ground in 1842 and was replaced by a pallid version of its former self.

Another influential style, imported from France, was the Second Empire, which embraced Gothic and classical details. The mansard roof, which had begun as a circumvention of Parisian building-height regulations, became the style's most notable architectural feature. A mansard roof topped several important theaters in New York, notably Wallack's on Thirteenth Street, Booth's new theater on Twenty-third Street, and Harrigan's Theatre on Thirty-fifth Street, and many more rose throughout the country. In its several variants, the Second Empire was sometimes known as General Grant Gothic, since so many public buildings during the 1870s were erected in the style. One of its most striking adaptations is the Goodspeed Opera House, a six-story wood-frame building, erected and still standing on a ferry landing in East Haddam, Connecticut. Designed in 1876 by Jabez Comstock and paid for by William R. Goodspeed, a prosperous banking and shipping entrepreneur, it was restored in the early 1960s and opened its doors again as a theater in 1963. Its most arresting feature is a tall mansard roof, which is pierced by dormers and broken up, front and back, by two ungainly towers. Although artfully preserved, the theater is not a museum. It houses a professional company that specializes in musical theater.

The Goodspeed was one of many theaters built as a monument to a wealthy founder and benefactor in the post–Civil War boom years. Samuel N. Pike and Jacob Pabst, both of whom made their money as brewers of alcoholic beverages, erected theaters bearing their names in Cincinnati and Milwaukee. John Collingwood, the owner of a prosperous coal and lumber business in Poughkeepsie, New York, built a 2,000-seat theater that could hold 10 percent of his hometown's population! Lumber baron Thomas Ramsdell put up an opera house in Manistee, now a small village in the western reaches of Michigan, and quick-rich, quick-poor Horace Tabor erected another in Leadville, Colorado. When an economic boom had cooled, many small towns were left with large, fancy playhouses that they could not support. Some were

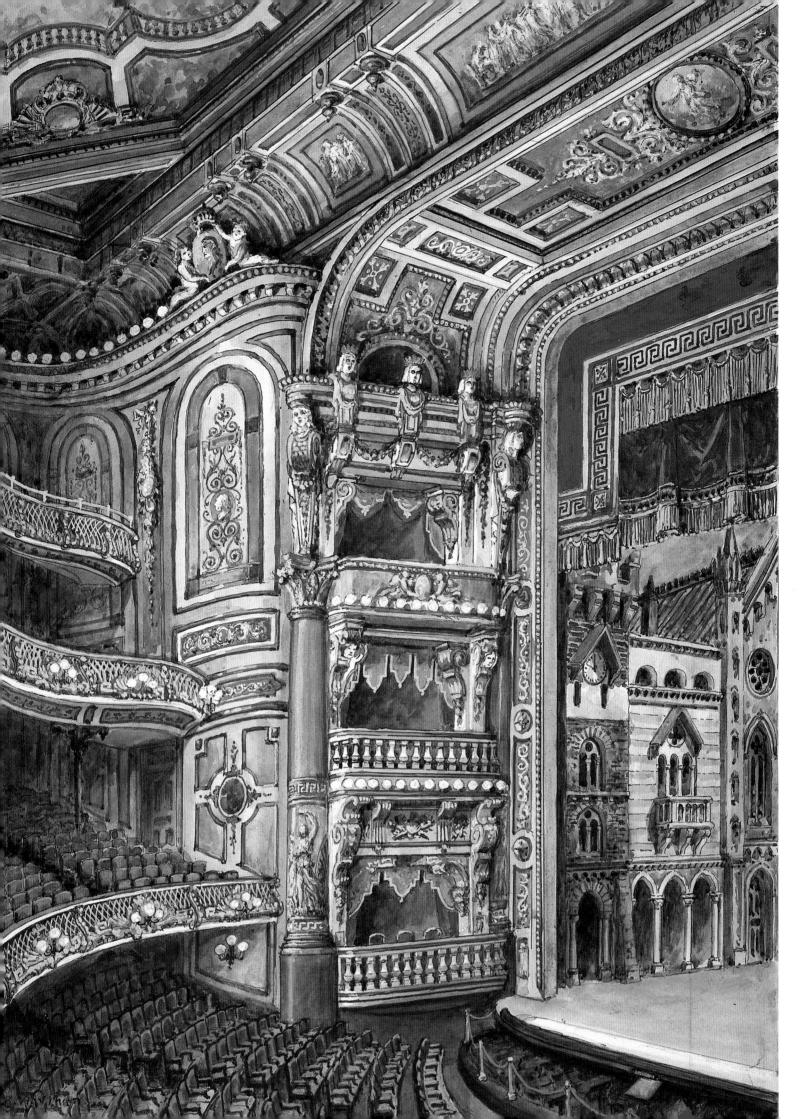

Booth's Theatre

C.W. Witham 1918

Opposite and above:
Edwin Booth's dream of the "perfect theater" became a financial nightmare after he opened his New York house in 1869 at great personal cost. A handsome building, with a mansard roof in the French Second Empire style, Booth's was beautifully decorated within, and the stage was equipped with every up-to-date device for set designers and stage machinists. The scenic artist Charles Witham painted these two views of the theater at its opening.

By the close of the nineteenth century, many prosperous citizens across America had established theaters in their names. Shown here is the Goodspeed Opera House, in East Haddam, Connecticut, built in 1876 for William Goodspeed. It was restored and reopened as a theater by Michael Price in 1963.

The photographer Paul Elson, Herbert J. Krapp's grandson, took this picture of the interior of the Majestic Theatre while standing in the balcony facing the stage. Built in 1927 by Krapp for the Chanin Construction Company, the Majestic remains one of Broadway's premier houses for musical plays. The theater has recently been completely refurbished by its owners, The Shubert Organization.

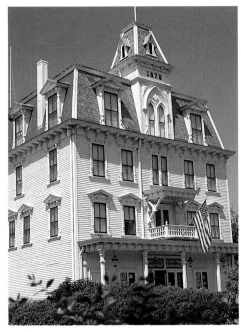

The actor James McVicker named his Chicago theater for himself. It was designed in 1857, by Otis Wheelock, to look like a clapboard palazzo. Rebuilt four times, McVicker's was in use as a legitimate house until 1913, when it was turned over to vaudeville and the movies. Here shown is the second version, in the Victorian mode.

In 1882, on the southeast corner of Broadway and Thirty-ninth Street in New York, arose the exotic Casino Theatre. Designers Francis Kimball and Thomas Wisedell carried the Moorish theme into the interior. Anthony F. Dumas sketched the Casino and its Broadway setting in 1918. Though his rendering is remarkably accurate in its detail, the artist made one slip—misspelling the name of producer Arthur Hammerstein.

torn down, and new owners converted others into vaudeville, burlesque, and movie houses. A few of the survivors have been restored and taken over by civic groups with the support of public and private funds. Federal, state, and local governments have added some of the most architecturally distinctive to the rolls of landmark buildings. Of the several thousand theaters built from coast to coast during the nineteenth century, probably fewer than three hundred have been spared demolition in the twentieth century.

In 1849 a playhouse was built in California whose only claim to distinction was that it had no style at all. The first theater to be built at the beginning of the Gold Rush, the Eagle cost the people of Sacramento $75,000, a very high price tag for the day. Consisting of a 30-by-90-foot frame, with canvas walls, a dirt floor, a tin roof, and a stage made from the wood salvaged from packing crates, it was erected by one Z. Hubbard, who had performed a similar service for the town of Houston, Texas. The "parquet" was entered through a makeshift saloon, and the "dress circle," a rough balcony at the far end, by means of a stepladder, to which canvas was nailed on the underside in deference to the modesty of the "ladies" who ascended to their seats. The Eagle Theatre had a brief life of three months. When the floodwaters of 1850 rose above the parquet seats, the manager and his company decamped for San Francisco and higher ground.

In the last decades of the nineteenth century, an era of unrestrained eclecticism, architects made forays into fresh styles. Francis Kimball and Thomas Wisedell designed the Casino Theatre on Broadway in Moorish Gothic, both inside and out. Atop the theater, they built New York's first roof garden, an inspiration of the proprietor, Rudolph Aronson. It became a popular after-theater rendezvous, serving light refreshments along with light musical entertainment, a precursor of the modern nightclub. Richardsonian Romanesque influenced the design of the Criterion Theatre in Brooklyn and the Auditorium Theatre in Chicago. But the architecture that predominated in those years issued from the drawing boards of J. B. McElfatrick and Sons, a firm that was responsible in whole or in part for about three hundred theaters in the United States and Canada between, roughly, 1870 and 1920. Arriving in New York in 1883 by way of Indiana and Kentucky, J. B. McElfatrick became, in the opinion of Hugh Tallant, no mean theater architect himself, the Father of the American Theater. In 1896 J. B. and his sons advertised themselves as theater specialists, having evolved their own serviceable style vaguely reminiscent of Italian Renaissance. Their theaters, preferably settled on corner lots, and including stores, restaurants, and offices, were apt to be squarish structures with heavily ornamented facades of Indiana or Bedford limestone, brick, and wrought-iron work. Interiors were ornate and in a variety of styles ranging from Victorian to Persian. The firm favored shades of red, green, or olive, with gilt and ivory. The auditoriums held an average of 1,800 seats, mirroring a trend toward smaller theaters at the end of the century.

In 1906 the New York Dramatic Mirror stated that McElfatrick's "designed the acoustics and lines of vision upon which the construction of all other theatres is based." The firm prided itself on their ability to build theaters with no bad seats. The compact design of their auditoriums and their use of wood paneling may have been responsible for the excellent quality of the acoustics. McElfatrick's did not alter the basic plan of the nineteenth-century theater but brought modern technology to bear on its construction in order to enhance its strengths and to make it safe.

One of the firms of interior decorators that worked closely with McElfatrick's was Leo Sielke and Son. After his death in 1938, the elder Leo Sielke, who had learned mural painting in the theaters and opera houses of Germany, was credited in his obituary with the decoration of 60 percent of the theaters in the United States, presumably during the heyday of theater building. Marks on his extant drawings indicate that he would submit watercolor paintings or pencil sketches of walls, ceilings, panels, prosceniums, and friezes for approval by either the architect or the client. Most of Sielke's work, reflecting the nineteenth-century penchant for sentimental, fanciful, or allegorical subjects, abounded in nymphs, cupids, and

Responsible for the design of several hundred American theaters, J. B. McElfatrick and Sons was the firm of Oscar Hammerstein's choice. Looking somewhat like an Italian Renaissance palace, the Olympia, which was intended to be Hammerstein's crowning glory, arose on Broadway from the firm's drawing board in 1895. Within three years, Hammerstein declared bankruptcy and moved on to other projects.

chariots pulled by snow-white horses, all emerging out of fluffy clouds—but some of it had contemporary touches. Much of the decoration done by the Sielkes and other artists of their generation was lost forever in recent years, when owners painted it over in a zealous attempt to clean and freshen their theaters.

Of the nearly forty theaters that McElfatrick's designed in New York City, not one is still a playhouse. Those few left standing have been converted to other uses, but most of them have been demolished. Although the movies prolonged the life of some, the simplified movie house eventually rendered them superfluous. The firm went out of business in 1922, just a few years before the Depression brought an end to the theater-building boom that had spilled into the early decades of the twentieth century.

If theaters did not change in their essentials between 1800 and 1900, everything else in American society was moving toward a twentieth-century consciousness of what it meant to be American. In architecture the skyscraper, made possible by the invention of the elevator and the development of skeleton-steel framing, became the quintessential American urban building beginning in the 1880s. But even though the only plausible way to utilize dwindling urban land was to find it in the air, for many years the skyscraper bore no relationship to the earthbound theater. Even Steele MacKaye, who is always described as our visionary Renaissance man of the theater, did not consider such an eventuality. Nor did he alter the basic relationship between stage and auditorium in the giant "spectatorium" he planned for the 1893 World's Columbian Exposition, though he did provide for a gigantic "scenitorium" behind the proscenium that could produce all manner of special effects. A victim of the financial panic of 1893, the building was never completed and what had been erected was carted off for scrap.

The architectural activity following the fire of 1871 and the competitive spirit engendered by the 1893 exposition contributed to making Chicago, not New York, the center for new ideas and experimentation in architecture. Working in the city at this time was a young architect, Louis H. Sullivan, who entered the firm of Dankmar Adler in 1879, when he was not quite twenty-four. Adler was an established engineer and architect known for his expertise in acoustics, while Sullivan was just beginning his career.

In 1885 F. W. Peck, a wealthy Chicagoan, conceived the idea of including a theater, a hotel, offices, and stores under one roof, with the commercial enterprises underwriting and supporting the entire cost of the theater. It was to be a theater for

everyone, where, from every seat in the house, everything onstage could be seen and heard. Adler and Sullivan were engaged as architects, and in 1889, with President Benjamin Harrison in attendance, the most advanced theater in America was introduced. The Auditorium Theatre was constructed of solid masonry and was strongly redolent of Richardsonian Romanesque in the heavy stone arches breaking its facade. The motif of arches was continued in the auditorium, where the curve of the proscenium was repeated in the structure and decoration. The backstage area was equipped with the latest devices to raise and lower sections of the stage and with the most advanced lighting system yet devised.

The theater could serve as a convention hall, ballroom, concert hall, opera house, or playhouse. The seating capacity could be raised to 7,000 or reduced to 2,500 through the use of hinged ceiling plates, which could be lowered to close off two upper balconies. The proscenium opening could be made smaller by a curtain of decorative plaster on an iron frame, which was suspended above the stage when not in use. Adler's acoustics became architectural legend and Sullivan's sightlines allowed everyone an excellent view of the stage. Many considered it a triumph to provide a feeling of intimacy in so large a hall.

Although a marvel—one that has happily been preserved and restored—the Auditorium did not represent a break with the past, nor did its architects include anything substantially innovative, not even the skeleton-steel framing that they were to pioneer so successfully in future ventures, but it did represent the nineteenth-century theater at its architectural and technological zenith. If it was a precursor of anything, the Auditorium anticipated a time, some ninety years in the future, when theaters would be components of large, tall, multipurpose buildings.

Although Sullivan eventually renounced what he called "the violent outbreak of the Classic and Renaissance in the East," he himself had attended the famous Ecole des Beaux-Arts in Paris, along with John Merven Carrère, Thomas Hastings, Henry Herts, Charles McKim, and many other exponents of the Beaux-Arts style. The conservative institution based its teachings on the study of Greek and Roman architecture and was highly influential through its graduates in America. Led by Carrère and Hastings, the Beaux-Arts movement was a return to the classic and Renaissance models that had been popular early in the past century. Very few public buildings of the time escaped its heavy touch.

In 1906 Carrère and Hastings won a competition for the design of a theater, which its organizers hoped would be a people's playhouse subsidized by the wealthy citizens of New York. They raised the money and found a site on Central Park West between Sixty-second and Sixty-third streets, far from the din of the new theater district taking shape twenty blocks to the south. The enterprise was plagued by a series of mishaps, but when in 1909 it was finished, the New Theatre, built of clear gray Indiana limestone, was something to behold. Its inspiration was Sansovino's Library of San Marco in Venice. The color scheme of the interior was driftwood-gray and gold, and the draperies were in rich cerise. Connemara marble was used liberally in the lobby and on the sweeping twin staircases. The Baudry ceilings were dotted with crystal chandeliers, and the floors were thickly carpeted.

The auditorium was in the form of an ellipse, the long axis of which was parallel to the proscenium arch, thus guaranteeing good visibility. It accommodated twenty-three hundred patrons in twenty-three boxes, an orchestra floor, and two balconies. The stage was equipped with a turntable and a complex lighting system. The rest of the massive building contained workshops, public rooms, restaurants, offices, a library, and a roof garden, which was later converted into another theater. But the venture was not a success either practically or economically. The house was too large for the repertory for which it was intended, its acoustics were terrible, and it was located in the wrong place. After two years, it was abandoned by its founders, and as a "national theater" was leased to Broadway producers for spectacles and big musicals under the name Century Theatre.

The New–Century Theatre did not represent the last stand of traditional styles in theater architecture. Playhouses continue to be designed to this very day in what Ada Louise Huxtable whimsically dubbed Caricature Classicism. But the interiors of the proscenium theaters built in the early decades of the twentieth century changed profoundly. The new plays being written and produced were set in small rooms or gardens and demanded an intimacy that could only be achieved in a scaled-down theater with fewer seats. Economic and practical changes were taking place in theater and show business that could not fail to touch the playhouse. Since scenery and costumes were now being made off the premises, there was no need for a honeycomb of workshops and storerooms. As real estate in the largest cities became scarcer and more expensive, theaters were built on smaller sites and could no longer include commercial enterprises. Sometimes playhouses had to conform to sites with strange configurations, and in New York many were erected without any lobbies to speak of, so that patrons simply spilled out into the sidewalks and streets to smoke or chat during intermissions. The rise of the theatrical unions led to further adjustments in the structure. Technicians demanded better working conditions and actors clamored for such simple amenities as heat, toilets, and running water, all of which were eventually written into contractual agreements with producers. With the demise of the resident stock company, theaters in New York and on the road were transformed into rented space for packaged shows and lost much of their individual identities. As a consequence, many playhouses were poorly cared for.

Theater building after 1900 received an artificial stimulus from the rivalry between the monopolistic Theatrical Syndicate and the Shubert brothers. To break the Syndicate's control, the Shuberts built a theater in cities across the country whenever they were unable to take over the standing house. The result was an unnecessary proliferation of outlets in a business that rested in the best of times on shifting sands. In the worst of times (the Depression), the excess theatrical baggage was quickly wiped off the books by bankrupt owners, including the Shuberts, and playhouses reverted to mortgage-holders, who sold them off to movie chains or converted them to other uses.

During their years of greatest activity, the Shuberts probably built more theaters than any other organization before or since in America. Their principal architect was a man with the unfortunate name (in light of future connotations) of Herbert J. Krapp. In 1913, when they built their flagship theaters—the Sam S. Shubert and the Booth, together forming the western wall of Shubert Alley—they employed Henry Herts, who with his partner, Hugh Tallant, had been a theater architect since the early years of the new century. Among their impressive credits were the Brooklyn Academy of Music, the Lyceum on Forty-fifth Street, and the Folies-Bergère (which was renamed the Helen Hayes at a later date). Krapp had been Herts's assistant, but when the architect's personal problems eroded his ability to function, the young draftsman-architect struck out on his own. He came to the attention of Edward Margolies, the leading theater contractor-builder in New York, who recommended him to the Shuberts. In 1917, when he was just thirty, Krapp became their "house architect," even though he was never in their direct employ and continued to accept commissions from others. In that year he designed three Shubert houses, the Bijou,

In 1909 public-spirited citizens raised the necessary funds to build the New Theatre on Central Park West in New York. After just two seasons as a people's theater in search of a purpose, the great pile of Indiana limestone in Beaux-Arts style passed to commercial producers of Broadway-type fare.

The heavy-arched Romanesque style of H. H. Richardson influenced several American theaters, none more important than the Auditorium in Chicago, designed by Dankmar Adler and Louis Sullivan in 1889. The Auditorium continued in use until 1942, when it was allowed to fall into disrepair. A restoration campaign was launched, and it reopened in 1967.

This section of Herbert J. Krapp's blueprint for the Forrest Theatre in Philadelphia, a typical proscenium theater of the 1920s, shows the fine detail of the architect's planning.

the Broadhurst, and the Plymouth. Krapp remained with the Shuberts until 1928, designing their theaters not only in New York but around the country.

Krapp quickly won favor with the Shuberts because of his ability to crowd as many seats as possible into a theater, even if public amenities had to be sacrificed. Often he had to work with odd-shaped sites, but he always came up with a workable solution. A Krapp-designed house is compact, intimate, and economical; its acoustics are generally excellent; and its sightlines range from satisfactory to very good. The facades are generally eclectic in a style that might best be described as Krapp Conservative. Of the forty theaters built in the immediate Times Square area, Krapp's playhouses have proven to be the most enduring. Most of them still fly the Shubert flag and have undergone periodic renovations that prolonged their existence.

From 1893, the year Charles Frohman jumped to Fortieth Street and Broadway to build his Empire Theatre, until 1928, when the Ethel Barrymore and the Craig were erected, within the small area bounded by Thirty-ninth Street and Fifty-ninth Street, Eighth Avenue and Sixth Avenue, eighty theaters were compressed into New York's newest theater district. During the 1920s, it enjoyed its headiest days, but even then there were ominous signs that it was overbuilt. When the Depression hit the theater district, the number of legitimate playhouses was reduced by more than half, and those that survived are now under siege by developers. Forces are at work to preserve the best of them for posterity, but their future is tied to the health of live theater in

New York. When the firm of Hardy Holzman Pfeiffer in 1983 completed their study of thirty of the Times Square theaters, they came to an inevitable conclusion: "Their stages are severely limited, their dressing rooms cramped, their support areas inadequate, their technology outmoded, yet they are the best performance halls known." These Broadway playhouses and their facsimiles around the country continue to cast their own special spell, which has nothing and everything to do with architecture, their style or lack of it, and their outmoded proscenium stages. No one can or will ever be able to reproduce them as they are now. If nothing else, modern building codes would prevent it, even if the economics were propitious.

In building these anachronistic playhouses, producers and theater owners reaffirmed their faith in the durability of the dramatic fare that was being presented on their stages, stubbornly refusing to acknowledge the ominous presence of the movies in their midst or possessed of short sight in heroic but foolish proportions. Many of them were openly contemptuous of the small young experimental groups that, beginning in the 1910s, were challenging established theater and doggedly pursuing theatrical "art" in living rooms, fish houses, abandoned mills, office and factory buildings, or wherever they could find large spaces that were free or cheap to rent. The leaders of the little-theater groups unconsciously assumed the role of architects in arranging the space for their ingeniously but modestly produced plays. Understandably, most chose to work within the architectural configuration they knew best: the proscenium stage. Of necessity, these stages were often shallow, cramped platforms at one end of a room, in front of which, on the level floor, producers arranged benches or seats for their patrons. But because the space enveloped both spectators and performers, these makeshift theaters created an enviable intimacy that often could not be recaptured when prosperity propelled the groups into larger, grander quarters. The amateur and improvisational quality of the ambience became part of the charm of the little-theater experience. Many of the leaders in the movement exploited this psychological factor when they chose unusual or unlikely spaces for their experiments.

Although these avant-garde American groups were adventurous in their choice of dramatic material and resourceful and imaginative in their use of lighting and scenery, on the whole they were more pragmatic than innovative in their architecture. But gradually they became aware of the work of Max Reinhardt in Germany, Harley Granville-Barker in England, and Jacques Copeau in France. Many of the designers in the little-theater movement went off to Europe to see for themselves, and a very few, like Robert Edmond Jones, worked with the Europeans to digest their ideas. Reinhardt's use of theater-in-the-round as early as 1910, and Barker's and Copeau's translations of the proscenium stage into a three-sided neo-Elizabethan platform a few years later were to have lasting and influential but delayed effects on new American theater architecture. All three men eventually re-created their new-old ideas for American audiences. The first to experiment with the new stages were college and university groups. In 1914 the young designer Raymond Sovey set up a theater-in-the-round in the middle of the gym at Columbia University's Teachers College. Other academic groups seized upon the idea as a solution to their perpetual problem of finding space on campus for dramatic activities without having to build a conventional and expensive theater building.

According to Margo Jones's chronicle of the theater-in-the-round, Gilmor Brown was next to use it, in 1924, before he built his Playbox as an adjunct to his conventional proscenium stage in the Pasadena Playhouse. But it was not until 1947, when Jones established her own theater-in-the-round in Dallas, that it became a seriously regarded architectural form. Her stage, actually trapezoidal in shape, stood within a theater created out of an exhibition hall originally used by an oil company. Jones placed her first row of seats on the playing level (the floor of the building) and raised the rest on platforms in tiers of from three to five rows. Seating only 198, Jones's theater had a magical intimacy, and her staging convinced, among other savants, *New York Times* critic Brooks Atkinson of its theatrical integrity. Jones considered theater-in-the-round the "theater of tomorrow." She transformed its

The Ziegfeld Theatre, built at the northwest corner of Sixth Avenue and Fifty-fourth Street in 1927, was not the typical Broadway playhouse. First, it was east and uptown of the great concentration of Broadway theaters; second, it was designed by the distinguished scenic artist Joseph Urban in cooperation with architect Thomas Lamb, who was best known for sumptuous movie palaces; and third, it was designed in Art Deco throughout.

The Arena Stage has become an established part of the cultural life of Washington, D.C. Shown here is the main theater, designed by Harry Weese in 1961. It seats about eight hundred people, in four sections of eight rows surrounding and rising from a rectangular stage.

weaknesses and difficulties into its virtues. The absence of scenery, she felt, gave the audience a chance to exercise its imagination, and because the actors were exposed on every side she believed the audience could more readily catch their every nuance of movement and expression. She was convinced that its possibilities were limitless and proved it by staging both the classics and new realistic plays successfully. Lighting was all-important, she thought, and should be used daringly and ingeniously—for example, as a substitute for a curtain, plunging the theater into darkness to begin and end a play and to signal changes of scene and mood. No matter that there was no way to hide the lighting paraphernalia: it was all part of the new look of the theater and the new psychology of theatergoing. It all seemed to work.

Nowhere did it work more successfully than at the Arena Stage in Washington, D.C. In 1961, after eleven years of playing in theaters slipped first into an old movie house and then into a brewery, the company under the leadership of Zelda Fichandler moved into a brand-new playhouse, which utilized "everything it had learned... about the artistic possibilities of the arena staging form, the total experience of theatre-going from the point-of-view of the audience, and the work requirements of staff, acting company and technical personnel." The success of the new building was attributable not only to the pooled experience of the company but also to the sensitivity of the architect, Harry Weese, who was able to grasp and express that experience in the structure.

About the same time that the Arena Stage company was introducing Washingtonians to theater-in-the-round, a group in New York was cleaning up an abandoned nightclub and transforming it into the Circle in the Square. A decade later, success bought the group a new theater in a subterranean space in a modern skyscraper on Broadway, an updated version of its original quarters. The artistic director, Ted Mann, made the decision to hold to the original configuration; the architectural translation was made by Alan Robert Sayles in collaboration with the lighting designer Jules Fisher. The theater was completed in 1972.

Despite their particular success, one wonders whether the new theaters of the Arena Stage and the Circle in the Square were built not so much with the intent of releasing a newer, freer architectural form as in an act of nostalgia. Certainly there was no rush to imitate them. So easy is it to set up a theater-in-the-round in a large space—a gym or banquet hall or warehouse—with portable bleachers and folding chairs on platforms that many directors treat it as merely another alternative in staging. In the late 1950s the form became popular for summer theaters presenting musicals, ushering in an era of "music circuses" built at the outskirts of large cities. The first were erected economically—a concrete dish surrounded by tiers of folding chairs was covered with a canvas tent. Later, several were made more permanent with the addition of solid walls, a roof, and fixed seating.

The type of stage used most frequently by the first little-theater groups and then again during the renascence of the movement after World War II was the end stage: a flat or raised platform that could be assembled and disassembled within a large room, or "black box," as it commonly came to be called. The absence of a proscenium arch insured that there would be no psychological separation between performers and spectators. Because there frequently was no curtain, and because the lighting equipment often lay open to view, the end stage rivaled in intimacy, immediacy, and theatricality the theater-in-the-round. Still popular today, end stages proliferated on campuses during the 1960s. A few were built from the ground up. One of them, the Kalita Humphreys Theater of the Dallas Theater Center, was designed by Frank Lloyd Wright, the only theater he ever built. The exterior is dominated by a cylindrical white concrete tower rising forty feet above a nest of geometric concrete masses. Inside Wright designed a stage with seventy feet of frontage, spanning the auditorium. A thirty-two-foot central turntable was flanked by two side stages. Roughly five hundred seats rose in a 180-degree arc in front of it, an arrangement in which a large part of the audience was brought closer to the players. (Since 1959, when it was built, the stage has been modified into a thrust platform stage.)

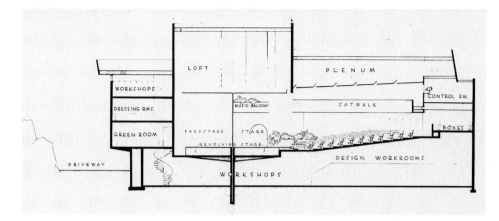

By far the most popular stage that emerged from postwar experimentations was the open or thrust stage, which combines aspects of both the end and the arena stage. The whirlwind behind its rapid rise to popularity was the late English director Tyrone Guthrie. For his presentations of Shakespearean plays, Guthrie pioneered a return to the kind of three-sided open stage prevalent in the Bard's day—with the addition of some personal refinements. His efforts were first realized in 1957, when the Shakespearean Festival Theatre opened in Stratford, Ontario. Later, working with architect Ralph Rapson, Guthrie brought another version of the neo-Shakespearean stage to Minneapolis, in a theater that was eventually named for him. Guthrie argued for the open stage for the following reasons:

First, our intended program is of a classical nature, and we believe that the classics are better suited to an open stage than to a proscenium one. Second, the aim of our performances is not to create an illusion, but to present a ritual of sufficient interest to hold the attention of, even to delight, an adult audience. Third, an auditorium grouped *around* a stage rather than placed in front of a stage enables a larger number of people to be closer to the actors. Fourth, in an age when movies and TV are offering dramatic entertainment from breakfast to supper, from cradle to grave, it seemed important to stress the differences between their offering and ours.

The Tyrone Guthrie Theater, contiguous to the Walker Art Center, has formed part of the cultural heart of Minneapolis since 1963, when it first opened. The architect devised an asymmetrical stage within an asymmetrical auditorium, which has the feel of an amphitheater. The rising rows of confetti-colored seats—none more than fifty-eight feet from the stage—and the acoustical "clouds" set into the ceiling add architectural drama to the stage event. Before it was recently removed, the exterior was enveloped by a stuccoed screen that created a rhythmic pattern around the concrete building. The most recent director, Liviu Ciulei, has also enlarged the thrust stage to bring it in line with his own artistic vision.

The new stages and theaters have not been without problems. Because of the bonding effect they create between audience and actors, they quickly won public acceptance, but though the patrons could see from everywhere in the house, they often could not hear. The early architects or planners of proscenium theaters used wood for their construction, chose curved shapes for box fronts and ceilings, and covered walls with fabric hangings—without at first recognizing the sound-enhancing qualities of these elements. They continued to use them, not only in deference to tradition but because they had learned their practical value. When they did away with the proscenium arch, modern architects knew that they were also depriving the theater of its principal sounding board, for whose loss they would have to compensate. In revising the relationship of stage to auditorium, they have also been inadvertently responsible for creating a new specialist, the acoustician, who has resorted to movable panels, discs or "clouds" in the ceiling, and as a last recourse, electrical sound amplification. Today, acousticians are routinely called in when a theater is to be built. Despite their ingenuity, however, very few of the new theaters have matched the acoustical perfection of old halls like La Scala in Milan and Carnegie Hall in New York or even the small houses in New York's theater district.

259

The spurt of postwar theater-building reached its height during the 1960s and was over by 1980. Rather than build from scratch, regional and community groups have taken over standing buildings and have converted them into workable and flexible theaters. Many municipalities, finding themselves saddled with derelict theaters in their downtowns, some dating from the nineteenth century, have bought them up with public and private funds and renovated them from roof to basement to spark cultural activities within their communities.

The most spectacular conversions have been of buildings other than theaters. In 1966 Joseph Papp took over the Astor Place Branch of the New York Public Library and transformed it into the New York Public Theater. To date, he has created six small theaters plus a small movie house within its interior. Because mercury runs in his veins, it is likely that Papp will continue to arrange and rearrange the space to serve the purposes of his experiments. Already he has achieved double success: a fine nineteenth-century building has been preserved and he has demonstrated that audiences will seek out entertainment no matter where it is located.

Just west of Manhattan's theater district, ingenuity and grit turned a row of tenements that once housed massage parlors, pornographic theaters, and peep shows into a mini-theater district for Off-Off-Broadway companies. Aided and abetted by public and private agencies determined to redevelop the area, it was officially dedicated as Theatre Row in 1978. Today it houses fourteen companies, extending from Ninth Avenue to Tenth Avenue. The second phase of the project has already begun: to reclaim buildings in the next blocks on West Forty-second Street and turn them into studios and theaters for performing-arts organizations. Theatre Row has provided many lessons, not the least of which is that small miracles can occur when the community cooperates with imaginative and resourceful young people.

The postwar merchandising concept of putting everything anyone could possibly want under one big roof has afflicted the arts in America. City after city in an almost juggernaut trend has built omnibus performing-arts centers where one can sample a variety of events, much as one can now park and shop for everything from a hairpin to a household in a lushly landscaped suburban marketplace. The concept has given birth to elephantine ventures like Washington's Kennedy Center, New York's Lincoln Center, and Los Angeles's Center for the Performing Arts. Occasionally, as at Atlanta's Memorial Arts Center, which includes the fine as well as the performing arts, such schemes have gone off the rails. Within these giant complexes, monumental buildings have been erected, some by America's most respected architects—Edward Durrell Stone (Kennedy Center), Wallace K. Harrison, Max Abramovitz, Philip Johnson, and Eero Saarinen (Lincoln Center)—others by firms known only within the communities they serve. Some are built in the lean International style, highlighted by vast expanses of glass and mirrored in reflecting pools; others display marble-faced facades and vaulting colonnades in a style Ada Louise Huxtable dubbed Running Scared Modern. Interiors range from the high-tech of Denver's Boettcher Hall to the traditional red-gold–crystal-chandeliered decor of the Metropolitan Opera House at Lincoln Center. The proscenium stage dominates, with some notable exceptions such as Hardy Holzman Pfeiffer's Boettcher Hall, which is a "surround" or open-stage auditorium; the three Denver Theatre Center playhouses devised by John Dinkeloo and Kevin Roche; and the Vivian Beaumont Theater at Lincoln Center, built to the specifications of Jo Mielziner, who envisioned a stage that could be converted from proscenium to thrust by means of a below-floor lift.

Most, if not all, performing-arts centers need constant financial buttressing, for costs outrun revenues even when the audiences warmly support them. In most cases, the role of the architect was to design something impressive but not necessarily innovative or imaginative, something that made a statement about the community's respect for the past and its commitment to the future; something that was also safe, well-lighted, and reachable by car. Culture centers tend not to please the critics on any artistic level, but on the other hand they appear to fulfill a need in American society today. If they go the way of the nineteenth-century theaters, future generations may one day decide to recycle the old plants, or raise money to restore them to their day of glory.

During the past hundred or so years—from the McElfatricks, whose look-alike theaters could be erected quickly anywhere, to Herbert Krapp, who got the most theater into the least plot, to the current generation of builders, who have to deal with the complex problems of acoustics and sightlines in open-stage theaters—architects have gradually become indispensable to the theatrical profession. The best of them work closely with their clients to shape buildings that must be responsive to the ideas and needs of producers, players, and designers. Theaters have changed not only because the events upon their stages have changed but because events in life around them have changed. When the movies and television began to do things that live entertainment was incapable of doing, theater people had to try something different. What they did architecturally was to knock down the proscenium arch to bring the performance closer to the spectator. The earliest theaters created for this experience were indescribably makeshift and uncomfortable, but since then architects have made them interesting places with their own integrity. Their work as collaborators is tempered by a fact best expressed by the late Brooks Atkinson: "For there is one basic principle in the design and decor of theatres: nothing is really important except the performances on stage. The sole function of a theatre is to provide a place where people can assemble and enjoy a show." No matter how marvelous a theater he designs, the architect's role is forever limited by this single fact.

The spacious glassed foyer of the Denver Theatre Center, designed by Kevin Roche and John Dinkeloo in 1980, serves three auditoriums: the Stage, seating about 650; the Space, seating about 400; and the Lab, a flexible area seating about 100.

Beginning in 1966, with the help of an adventurous and talented staff of designers and architects, Joseph Papp created on Astor Place in New York City a beehive of equally adventurous theatrical activity in what he has appropriately named the New York Public Theater.

BEYOND BROADWAY

EACH OF THE MANY observers of the American theatrical landscape during the last fifty years has gently but firmly reminded us that Broadway is *not* the American theater: that beyond the irregular rectangle of forty square blocks in the midsection of the isle of Manhattan there occurs at any given time more theatrical activity than ever takes place on Broadway—excluding, perhaps, the brief period from about 1890 to 1910. This activity beyond the bright-lights district arose as a natural and spontaneous expression of dissatisfaction on the part of the public with the vast amounts of theatrical junk it was being force-fed as the theater evolved into the brave new world of modern fast-buck industrialization. The citizens lured to the theater by the multicolor, large-type announcements of shows "Direct from Broadway" were too smart not to become disillusioned by the shoddy performances, the tatterdemalion scenery, the tired plays, and the general lethargy of the productions touring west of the Hudson River and at all points off Broadway during the early years of the twentieth century. The first waves of rebellion occurred, of course, among the intelligentsia, but they were followed by later, greater waves within the ranks of ordinary folk, who showed their displeasure by going to the movies or turning on the radio or, finally, switching on the television set. But the middle class, which has traditionally formed the backbone of theater audiences, was and continues to be lured back by the other kind of theater. Zelda Fichandler, one of its important dispensers in our time, has called it the "whaddaya-call-it" theater; historians have called it the little-theater movement. At first it was dedicated to art, experiment, and the new. Some of its purposes were educational, recreational, and social. At various times and places it might espouse and promote native, folk, rural, local, and grass-roots art. Its plays could be realistic, symbolic, poetic, fantastic, or Freudian. A little theater might start as amateur in the classic sense of the word and move by steps into the professional in the narrow sense that its members began being paid. Such a company might have the word *community*, *civic*, or *municipal* in its title. Support could come from subscriptions, donations, or philanthropic grants, but many groups apparently lived on air. They considered themselves laboratories or workshops and were housed in theaters described as "little," "toy," "intimate," "bandbox," or "portmanteau." Repertory was much on the minds of their founders and they all strove for it. The movement was (and continues to be) characterized by an abundance of youthful zeal and idealism. Its only permanent aspect has been impermanence. Above all, these individual groups and theaters arose because of a driving force, in the form of a man or woman who was determined to bring a little theater to life. The history of the movement, from the boondocks to Off Off Broadway, is as much a history of these obsessed, uncompromising human whirlwinds as it is of anything else.

Because so many of these groups fell soundlessly through the historical sieve into oblivion, it is not easy to assign an exact time or place to the birth of the movement. Even during the nineteenth century, there were faint rumblings of dissatisfaction with establishment theater. As early as 1799 there was an informal theater in New York, at 242 Water Street—not a likely place to start a venture—which briefly presented a type of variety entertainment. A few years later, another challenge was made to the newly established Park Theatre when a small group of thespians began to present plays on the Park's off nights. It expired early in 1805, within months of its inauspicious beginnings. These early ventures were fueled by little more than bravado and appear not to have offered serious challenges to the only show in town. More than likely, having failed to find employment with the principal theaters in New York, or later in Philadelphia or Boston, performers simply created their own jobs—an act that has engendered many little theaters to this very day.

Stimulus other than necessity was provided toward the end of the nineteenth century by the revolutionary currents in European drama represented by Henrik Ibsen, August Strindberg, and later the Irishman-turned-Englishman George Bernard Shaw. Their plays needed a special forum, which arrived when a young clerk for the Paris gasworks, André Antoine, nursing a grudge against the Conservatoire for not accepting him as a student actor, set up his own little theater at 37 Elysée des Beaux-Arts. He named it the Théâtre Libre and dedicated it to the new naturalistic plays. In 1890, three years after it was founded, Antoine produced Ibsen's *Ghosts*. His theater of amateurs became the talk of Europe and England and gave the spur to the creation of similar little theaters in most of the great capitals of the western world.

The progress of the little-theater movement in Europe and England was avidly followed by American intellectuals. In Boston, William Dean Howells and Hamlin Garland urged the establishment of an experimental theater. Garland had found a playwright, James A. Herne, to champion, and Herne happened to have a play, *Margaret Fleming,* that dealt with the damaging results of marital infidelity—too controversial a subject for the ordinary producer to accept. In 1891 Herne rented Boston's Chickering Hall, which was used for concerts and had only five hundred seats, and went to work to transform the stage to accommodate the necessary settings. Garland became his unpaid press agent and began to beat the drums for *Margaret Fleming.* He sent letters to the Boston intelligentsia and promised that Chickering Hall would be "our théâtre libre for a week at least." Though the play failed to draw sufficient audiences to sustain a run, after it closed prematurely Garland remained stimulated enough to try to found the First Independent Theatre Association, "to encourage truth and progress in American Dramatic Art" and "to secure and maintain a stage whereon the best and most unconventional studies of modern life and distinctively American life" could be presented. Plans for such a theater were discussed and a Boston architect was commissioned to design it, but the entire project came to naught. In the American theater, things tend to be more evolutionary than revolutionary, but when the moment came for the little-theater movement to spread its wings, it outdid its European prototypes in true Yankee fashion.

The productions at Hull House in Chicago grew more and more polished under the direction of Laura Dainty Pelham, who took over in 1899 and began to present plays by Shaw, Ibsen, and Pinero. Seen here is one of her amateur actors in an unidentified play.

Opposite:
La Mama E.T.C., the quintessential Off-Off-Broadway theater, has been sustained by the tenacity of the extraordinary Ellen Stewart, who benevolently presides over her theater while giving her artists free rein. Shown here is a moment during the 1981 revival production of Why Hanna's Skirt Won't Stay Down with Helen Hanft, written and directed by Tom Eyen. It was first produced at La Mama in 1965.

Before experiment became the rallying cry of the little-theater movement, the idea that dramatic activity could become a force for social good began to gain ground. In 1889, to combat the evils engendered by poverty, Jane Addams and Ellen Gates Starr founded a settlement house in the slums of Chicago to bring rays of cultural light into the lives of the poor. Ground down by low-paying, repetitive jobs, they needed to experience the restorative power of arts and crafts as participants, not observers, reasoned the two women, who set about establishing programs at Hull House in which to involve the community. Noting that the boys and girls spent their pennies on trashy melodramas at low-class theaters, Addams decided that dramatic activities could be used to keep young people off the streets. In 1893 her Dramatic Section planned its first full-scale production and a few years later it had its own resident director. In 1897 a production of As You Like It presented by high-school-age members of the club was so successful that it toured two of the wealthy Chicago suburbs. In 1899, through the fund-raising efforts of Addams, Hull House auditorium was built and a year later a former actress with a name sounding like a confection, Mrs. Laura Dainty Pelham, took over the dramatic association. With advice from the great Joseph Jefferson, she transformed the little band of amateurs painstakingly into a well-organized ensemble troupe. She gradually weaned them from light comedies, and by 1911 the Hull House Players had achieved national prominence and renown for their repertory of modern plays by Ibsen, Shaw, and Pinero. Though the Hull House Players looked and acted for a while like a European little theater, they were not permitted to outgrow their social mission. For as long as they existed, they remained amateur and dedicated to the aspirations of the settlement house.

Several years after the founding of Hull House, Lillian Wald established the Henry Street Settlement House on New York's Lower East Side and created a dramatic club, which presented its first productions at Clinton Hall, once the notorious Astor Place Opera House. In 1915, the dramatic activities were transferred to the Neighborhood Playhouse on Grand Street, designed and built under the sponsorship of Alice and Irene Lewisohn, who gathered around them a professional and often talented amateur staff. In addition to running the repertory company and establishing their own costume and scenery workshops, the Misses Lewisohn set up classes in the performing arts for the community. When the enterprise expired from natural causes in 1927, out of its ashes arose the Neighborhood Playhouse School of the Theatre, which eventually transferred its activities to East Fifty-fourth Street. The school remains in existence today and offers a tuition-supported two-year program. For many years, the acting department has been headed by Sanford Meisner.

The little theaters dedicated to art for art's sake—and not for society's—arrived shortly after the turn of the century. Within twenty years there were a thousand little theaters across the nation, of varying size, stability, and effectiveness. They had been carved out of stables, barns, Masonic temples, storefronts, saloons, churches, abandoned factories, warehouses, lofts, private dwellings, office buildings, and at least one abandoned fish house. They sprang up not merely in large cities but also in the unlikeliest suburbs, seashore villages, prairie towns, and farming areas. In the metropolises, the little theaters eventually found their own special audiences, but in the outlying regions they had to invent themselves and their audiences at the same time. Collectively, they tried everything. They often began by presenting original plays, the modern Europeans, and the classics and sometimes at their final gasps they offered warmed-over Broadway. They lasted anywhere from a few months, to a few years, to a decade or more. If they were able to hang on for more than five years, they were accounted successful. A few of the pioneers are still in existence, but with their policies altered by changing times and new leaderships. When they began they had no money, but they made up for it in hard work and imagination. Most of the little theaters reflected the artistic ideas of their leaders, and when the energy, patience, or interest of these enthusiasts faltered, or when they decided that they had accomplished their goals, their enterprises simply expired.

The little theaters were hailed as the hope of the American stage. Playwright Percy MacKaye considered them no less than the hope of American civilization. Waxing almost poetic, he prophesied that the locally supported "civic theatre" would extirpate "the most baneful habit of mature beings—the habit of 'killing time.' Its object is to fill time, not kill it, to refill it to overflowing with that quality of charmed eternity...." Even David Belasco, who condemned them as a menace to the theater, did a complete about-face during the 1920s, when he awarded a cup to the winner of the Little Theatre Play Tournament. The audiences that became the foundation of the little-theater movement were asked to sacrifice in extremis. They more often than not coped with hard benches, cramped, airless (or drafty) auditoriums, overheated (or heatless) theaters, bad acting, poor plays, hastily designed and constructed scenery and costumes, and rudimentary lighting. Occasionally, they were present at a splendid, shining moment in the theater—and one of these made all of the rest worthwhile.

In 1912 English-born Maurice Browne and his American bride, Ellen Van Volkenburg, took over the fourth floor back of the Fine Arts Building on Michigan Avenue and founded the Chicago Little Theatre. The Fine Arts Building was a beehive of cultural activity, sheltering under the same roof the Baldwin Piano Company, two poetry magazines, the Cliff Dwellers Club, and a number of art schools and singing studios. Out of their unprepossessing space, the Brownes fashioned a theater with a tiny stage (fourteen feet across by twenty feet deep by eight feet high) and an auditorium that seated ninety-one people. It was so small that when the single toilet in the outer area was flushed, the entire theater reverberated with the sound of rushing water. Admission was by subscription only, ten dollars for the entire season. In his manifesto—all little theaters from that moment on had one—Browne dedicated his venture to the "creation of a new plastic and rhythmic drama in America."

Browne had the good fortune to command the services of a young designer, C. Raymond Johnson, who was inspired by the ideas of Craig and Appia to perform small miracles of stagecraft, mainly through color and light, on the diminutive stage. Browne opened his theater in November with two short Irish plays, and then moved on to more ambitious productions during the five years his experiment endured. Browne's players were mostly amateurs, whom he trained in his own theories of acting and who received a salary of ten dollars a week after two years of service with the company. Browne eventually won converts to his cause and built up a loyal following among the Chicago intelligentsia, but his project seemed doomed from the start. Beginning with a $10,000 debt that kept getting bigger, he was finally forced to declare personal bankruptcy and retire from the fray, but while his little theater lasted it enjoyed a special fame that spread beyond Chicago. Lawrence Langner, who was later to help found the Washington Square Players and the Theatre Guild, and other visitors took away vivid impressions of Browne's graceful and imaginative productions. Though he was credited with launching the little-theater movement in America,

Browne generously awarded the distinction to Mrs. Pelham of the Hull House Players.

Two little theaters that arose almost simultaneously in New York took heart from Browne's Chicago experiment, and where Browne failed they succeeded. Both groups took shape within the artistic ferment of Manhattan's Greenwich Village. Before it became bohemian chic in the 1920s and 1930s, the Village lured young writers, painters, and performers with its cheap and plentiful apartments and rooms, its restaurants offering wholesome food at low prices, and its gentle and friendly ambience. Many of the Village inhabitants came to MacDougal Street, off Washington Square, to the rooms in a brownstone rented by the Liberal Club, whose motto, A Meeting Place for Those Interested in New Ideas, attracted the poets Edna St. Vincent Millay and Vachel Lindsay; the writers Upton Sinclair, Max Eastman, Sinclair Lewis, Hutchins Hapgood and Neith Boyce, his wife; political activists John Reed and Alexander Berkman; lawyers Lawrence Langner and Justus Sheffield; the sculptor Jo Davidson; and the photographer Nickolas Muray. In the group were a number of people who were interested in the theater, including George Cram "Jig" Cook and Susan Glaspell, his wife, Gilbert Seldes, Helen Westley, and Bennett Cerf. Of course, attention was centered on politics (liberal to left), sex according to the Freudian gospel, and the arts in general.

Several members of the club brought the Washington Square Bookshop into existence next to the Liberal Club as an amenity for the members. In its back rooms the idea for the Washington Square Players was born in 1914. The founders, Liberal Club members all, felt that the time was ripe to launch the venture. They included on their roster Albert Boni; Edward Goodman and his wife, Lucy Huffaker; Philip Moeller; Eastman; Langner; Westley; and, for a short time, Cook and Glaspell. It was early decided that the entire enterprise was to be guided by strict democracy, with everyone down to the office boy exercising his right of opinion in play selection and casting. The system was often chaotic but never boring.

Armed with a manifesto that emblazoned their purpose—"The Washington Square Players believe that a higher standard can be reached only as the outcome of experiment and initiative"—the group rented the little Bandbox Theatre on East Fifty-seventh Street and presented their first program in February 1915. Two years later they moved to the larger Comedy Theatre on West Forty-first Street, in the Broadway bright-lights area. Their plan was to produce one-act plays—by themselves and others, foreign and domestic—and to practice the new European stagecraft. Within three years, they had produced sixty-two plays, which included *In the Zone* (Eugene O'Neill), *The Magical City* (Zoe Akins), *The Girl in the Coffin* (Theodore Dreiser), *Suppressed Desires* (Cook and Glaspell), and *Neighbors* (Zona Gale). They introduced Philip Moeller as a director of exceptional promise and launched the careers of Frank Conroy, Katharine Cornell, Elizabeth Patterson, Glenn Hunter, Mary Morris, Roland Young, and Helen Westley. They existed on subscriptions of five dollars per season, on loans from their own members, and on an occasional benefaction of the philanthropist Otto Kahn. When the war came, many of the members enlisted and others drifted away, but they had accomplished their purpose in awakening interest in plays of social comment and in proving that scrupulous realism was not the only way to convey a play's message. Although of short duration, their experiment turned earnest amateurs into adventurous professionals, and when three of the group met after the war to form the Theatre Guild they were sure of themselves and confident of their purpose. In its way, the Theatre Guild was also an experiment, but from its inception it was intended as a commercial organization and its productions were shaped by committee. Although in its early years, the Guild swam upstream of the Broadway currents, it eventually came ashore during the late 1920s and 1930s as the single most important producer on Broadway. Its nursery was the Washington Square Players, whose existence was, if for no other reason, thereby justified.

In the summer of 1915, while vacationing on Cape Cod, some of the same Greenwich Village intellectuals who belonged to the Liberal Club and who had

In this 1939 drawing, Mary Bicknell recalled the old Wharf Theatre in Provincetown, Massachusetts, which once rang with the words of Eugene O'Neill. The theater that housed the Provincetown Players beginning in the summer of 1916 was destroyed during a storm in the early 1920s.

helped to found the Washington Square Players presented a bill of four short plays by Cook and Glaspell, Neith Boyce, and Wilbur Daniel Steele at Hutchins Hapgood's house in Provincetown. With the sea as backdrop, Robert Edmond Jones set the "stage" in the house and proved that things done simply can be effective. Another participant in the proceedings, Mary Heaton Vorse, offered an abandoned fish house to the group, who transformed it into the Wharf Theatre. They produced two more short plays and returned the following summer with greater ambition and vigor to present a dozen more plays, some carry-overs from the previous summer. Since they had decided to produce nothing but original works, they listened with interest to tales told about the young Eugene O'Neill and his legendary "trunkful of plays." The first of his plays they presented was *Bound East for Cardiff,* and Susan Glaspell remembered it in later years as the most moving production she had ever seen.

In the fall of 1916, under the aegis of Jig Cook, the Provincetown Players rented the parlor floor of a brownstone at 139 MacDougal Street and turned it into a theater fifteen feet wide by forty-four feet deep, into which they crammed a little stage and, grandstand-style, 150 seats that became universally renowned for their extreme discomfort. The twenty-nine members included John Reed, Louise Bryant, Max Eastman, William Zorach and his wife, O'Neill, and Cook and Glaspell. Eight members chipped in thirty dollars each to start things going, and subscriptions were sold to augment the production capital. After the group had established its reputation, tickets were difficult to come by and became all the more desirable, in a reverse box-office psychology. After the first season, the original group was diminished by half, and after their second season, they moved to larger quarters nearby (at 133 MacDougal), taking over a four-story building that had served in the past as a storehouse, bottling works, and stable. Not only were they able to expand into a large theater, but they now had workshops, dressing rooms, and a proper box office. Otto Kahn, who in his era functioned as a one-man Ford Foundation, donated money to establish a restaurant on the second floor, which dispensed wholesome, if not fancy, meals to the Provincetowners and their friends at a cost of sixty cents per person. The playhouse at 133 MacDougal served as their artistic home for the next ten years.

Largely as a result of O'Neill's association with it, the Provincetown group over the years became suffused with mystique and legend. In the published memoirs of some of the founders, there is frequent disagreement. Jig Cook has been described as the guiding spirit and inspiration but has also been remembered for his disorganization and impracticality. Some recall the activities as ablaze with rebellion and political radicalism; others thought of them as just so much recreation. Many were the talents tested over the years, but by comparison very few were the successes. Because O'Neill insisted that it be known as the Playwrights Theatre, the emphasis at 133 MacDougal tended to rest more strongly on the play than on the players, and the quality of the acting rarely matched the strength of the words. Before 1924, when O'Neill, Robert Edmond Jones, and Kenneth Macgowan took over the larger, more orthodox Greenwich Village Playhouse on Sheridan Square as an adjunct theater, stage space was too cramped to allow for much experimentation with scenery, although Jones, Millia Davenport, and the other Provincetown designers seem to have accomplished small miracles on even smaller budgets.

As long as the group was alive with ideas and excitement, Jig Cook was in his element, but as it settled down into a kind of experimental orthodoxy, his interest and enthusiasm seemed to flag. After a sabbatical year, Cook and Glaspell left the theater permanently in 1922. Although he eschewed any sort of managerial role, O'Neill was prominent in setting artistic policy, but his involvement became increasingly attenuated as he was pulled into the orbit of Broadway after the success of *Beyond the Horizon* and *The Emperor Jones* in 1920. When the Provincetown quietly folded its tent in 1929, it left a legacy unparalleled in the history of American theater. O'Neill remains the crowning achievement of the Provincetown Players, but as his friend and associate during those years Kenneth Macgowan has pointed out, they "found their justification, outside of O'Neill, in the creative spirit which their

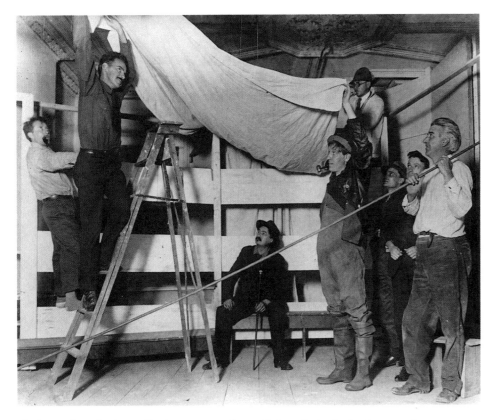

During the early days of the Provincetown Players, the tasks of presenting plays were shared by all members of the group. Putting up the scenery for Eugene O'Neill's Bound East for Cardiff in 1916 are the playwright himself, standing on a ladder, and his associates (left to right) Francis Burrell, Hippolyte Havel, William Stuart, B. J. Nordfeldt, Frank Jones, Henry M. Hall, and George Cram Cook.

playhouse breathed on all who came within it." For all the little theaters that came after it, both in New York and abroad in the land, it represented, and continues to represent, the apogee of what can be achieved by an inspired band of amateurs.

During these same years, little theaters were nursed into existence in Boston, Philadelphia, and Chicago, and even more heroically in smaller cities like Detroit, Los Angeles, Duluth, St. Louis, Kansas City, Minneapolis, Pittsburgh, and New Orleans. No matter how well-intentioned or hard-working their founders, most flickered out for lack of a sustaining audience. There were a few notable exceptions, several of which remain miraculously in existence today because of something akin to an urban ego. The stronger a city's sense of itself, the easier it is for a little theater to grow there into a permanent institution—as is demonstrated by the city of Cleveland and its Cleveland Play House.

The idea of the Cleveland Play House germinated in the drawing room of Charles S. Brooks, one of the city's prominent citizens, where on Sunday evenings in 1915 plays were performed under the direction of Raymond O'Neil, a newspaper drama and music critic who had fallen under the spell of Gordon Craig and the modern European theater during his travels abroad. When the group outgrew the homes of the members, they took over an empty Lutheran church, made it over into a theater, and drew up a manifesto with such noble aims as encouraging native artists and native art and cultivating folk art. In 1921 Frederic McConnell took over the direction of the theater and transformed it from an amateur into a predominantly professional organization with a permanent company of actors, nightly performances in an eight-month season, and a paid administrative staff. Trained at the drama department at Carnegie Institute of Technology, McConnell had served his apprenticeship at the Arts and Crafts Theatre of Detroit and at Pittsburgh's Guild Theatre before taking on the job. He reported to a board of trustees made up of people from the cultural, social, and business communities of the city. Under his management, the theater presented eight hundred productions and moved into a new complex of two theaters and offices in 1927. McConnell remained at the helm until 1958. His assistant K. Elmo Lowe took over the job until in 1969 he, too, retired. Since the early 1970s, the director has been Richard Oberlin, a longtime member of the company. In 1983 a new building designed by Philip Johnson consolidated the activities of the Play House, encompassing under one roof three theaters, rehearsal rooms, storage spaces and workshops, and the administrative offices. The enterprise has mushroomed into a

The Cleveland Play House, a potent force in the cultural life of the Ohio capital since the 1920s, expanded in 1983 into this new theater complex designed by architect Philip Johnson.

Gilmor Brown's successors at the Pasadena Playhouse could not keep afloat the theater and school he founded. Plans are in progress to revitalize them in the 1980s.

nonprofit resident theater with a $3 million yearly budget, a peak-season staff of 160, and a subscription list of 11,000 names. It is no longer a little theater.

The secret of its longevity is the sensitivity of its leaders to the care and feeding of the patrons. If the Play House began in a spirit of innovation, it soon rushed to mix its avant-garde offerings with the classics to please its audiences. Undaunted and untouched by the radical theater of the 1960s, it has continued on its merry course with generally the same diet of plays. Now and then, it has introduced something by a playwright of promise, but the enduring policy has been to hug the middle ground. If the Play House today presents a play by Slawomir Mrozek, it will not forget to include *A Funny Thing Happened on the Way to the Forum* in the same season. In order to insure that there will be future offerings, the Play House runs programs in the schools and a "Youtheatre" as well as acting classes and discussions about the productions in the complex. The management offers discounts to students and senior citizens and a host of other services and activities as an integral part of its campaign to reach out into the community. McConnell and his successors were canny enough to include a restaurant on the premises to complete their patrons' evening-on-the-town.

At about the time that the Cleveland Play House was coming into existence, another little theater more than two thousand miles to the west was beginning to bloom, but its story has no happy ending. In the fall of 1916, the young actor Gilmor Brown and his small stock company traveled to California on the assurance of one of the city's club women that Pasadena was fertile ground for a little theater. Brown liked what he saw and set himself to organizing the Pasadena Community Playhouse Association, made up of amateurs, with a sprinkling of professionals like himself. Starting out with a bill of one-act plays at the Shakespeare Club, they moved later to the Savoy Theatre, which had previously presented burlesque, and finally, in 1925, to a handsome mission-style building with a theater that seated more than seven hundred people, office space, a library, and workshops. In 1928, in a move that changed the purpose of his organization, Brown opened the Pasadena Playhouse School of the Theatre, later adding two little theaters and a classroom building to the complex. The school became renowned for its program and its graduates, and as long as Brown was around and in good form the Playhouse flourished, but as his health began to fail, the health of the enterprise began to deteriorate, too. Brown retired in 1959 and died a year later. During the next ten years, the Playhouse ran out of steam, money, and local support, until it was declared bankrupt in 1969. In 1975 the complex was bought by the city of Pasadena, which then leased it to a developer for restoration and revitalization. In 1980 a small step was taken toward a second life when one of the small auditoriums was opened with the appropriate hopeful name of Interim Theatre. Work continues on the other theaters, and there is optimism that the Playhouse will return to some of its former glory.

Not to be outdone by their big-city brethren, several entrepreneurial wizards brought the little-theater movement to rural America. Although the sparsely populated agricultural states were not the most hospitable terrain for theater, wonders were accomplished through the drive of men imbued with native pioneering spirit. When Alfred G. Arvold joined the faculty of North Dakota Agricultural College (now the State University) at Fargo in 1907, most of his students and their families had never seen a play. (North Dakota was then a no-man's land even for the traveling troupes.) In 1914 Arvold took over an old, unused chapel on the second floor of the administration building and remodeled it into the Little Country Theatre. His stated aim was to put "culture into agriculture" and he remained until 1953, proving that a one-man dynamo could do it. Not only did he produce and direct plays, stimulate students to write folk dramas drawn from their Scandinavian background, and bring concert and opera stars to the campus, but he went out into the field himself to spread drama like Johnny Appleseed. He staged outdoor festivals and pageants, he got farmers to put on plays and start their own theaters, and he kept a lending library of plays with instructions on how to put them on that could be ordered from the campus. Did it work? Perhaps the best assessment of Arvold's contributions is reflected in the comment of one of the farmers who had just seen his production of a play by Bjørnstjerne Bjørnson: "This show has got the movies skun a mile."

Arvold's successors kept the Little Country Theatre as a symbol of past glories but have since moved into a new campus theater. Since 1980 the old theater has been used for a repertory company that has ambitions to become a professional resident company. In bringing the little-theater movement to North Dakota, Arvold felt he was achieving the real purpose of drama, which he saw as "getting people together and acquainted with one another." He was interested in social, not theatrical, experiment and he was content to keep it all on the amateur level. He sensed that the campus was the best and the right place from which to launch his mission, and subsequent history proved the wisdom of his thinking.

Before he received the call to go to the University of North Carolina in 1918, Frederick Koch also tilled the theatrical soil of North Dakota, at the University at Grand Forks, setting up the Dakota Playmakers as he was later to set up the Carolina Playmakers. Using the campus as his base, "Proff" Koch succeeded in enlivening the backwoods culture of the state by loading his dedicated group of players into a truck and bringing the theater to the country. He hoped not only to make the rural folk appreciate the living stage but to arouse their consciousness of their own dramatic heritage. He wanted everyone to write a play about his life, his work, and his background in order to create folk plays representative of the American experience. Many did, but Paul Green remains the only outstanding product of the experiment, though, to give Koch his due, many of the Carolina Playmakers fanned out to campuses across the country to spread the word. The result has been several dozen folk and historical pageants in as many states.

The same seasons of discontent that gave rise to the little-theater movement also brought forth an organization that appeared for a brief moment in history to look, sound, and act like an audience collective or union of theater patrons. In 1910 a group of club women in Evanston, who had been studying the plays of the Chicago season, decided instead of merely talking about the bad plays they had all seen to found the Drama League of America, which would rate plays and make recommendations to the members. Its guiding force and first president was a woman with the almost incredibly appropriate name of Mrs. A. Starr Best. Within a year, the league had organized 165 clubs and boasted 12,000 members. With its national office now in Chicago, it expanded its activities to include an annual convention, the publication of bulletins and outline courses, and an information bureau for members. Some chapters launched little theaters on their own or supported the work of local community groups. The membership was predominantly female, but it could and did wield considerable influence. Although theatrical managers and producers began to pay attention, the league had to brook a fair share of waggishness from the press—Heywood Broun of the *New York World* even going so far as to say that most producers dreaded a Drama League endorsement.

The Drama League evaporated from the national scene during the hectic years of World War I, but a few of the chapters managed to hang on independently. Currently the most active, New York's Drama League continues to recommend plays to a constituent body of about a thousand and to hold panel discussions and lectures about current theater on Broadway. In addition, the New York group raises money for scholarships to train young professionals and bestows a Distinguished Performance Award, of which Katharine Cornell was the first recipient, in 1935. What started in 1910 as an exciting, innovative experiment, one that might have altered the course of American drama and theater, has all but vanished.

The little-theater movement engendered a modicum of aberrations, antics, and eccentricities. In 1915 a young refugee from Belasco's production organization decided to build a little theater that could be set up in a few hours and carted about from place to place. Stuart Walker's Portmanteau Theater, billed as "The Theater That

Paul Green was the most important of the American playwrights who heeded the call of Professor Frederick H. Koch of the University of North Carolina to seek drama in the life of the country, its history, and its people. Before accepting the mission, however, Green won a Pulitzer Prize in 1927 for In Abraham's Bosom and launched New York's Group Theatre with the initial production of his The House of Connelly (1931). Returning then to North Carolina, Green wrote the first and most important of his regional "symphonic dramas," The Lost Colony, which has been presented each summer on Roanoke Island since 1937. In later years, Green created symphonic dramas for the states of Virginia, Kentucky, Florida, and Texas and for Washington, D.C. Several of his other plays have reached New York, but Green preferred to remain near his roots, in North Carolina. The actors shown here are members of the cast of the third-season production of The Lost Colony.

Between 1915 and 1917, Stuart Walker literally took drama to the people. His portable Portmanteau Theater (above assembled, below folded and boxed) could be set up in three hours and packed into ten large crates.

Comes to You," began its history at the Christadora Settlement House on the Lower East Side of Manhattan, where it was first assembled and tried out. Thereafter, it received amazing press coverage and was heralded as a latter-day cart of Thespis. The stage was twenty-five feet wide by sixteen feet high by eighteen feet deep and was packed with its own lighting system, cyclorama, and scenery in ten cartons, weighing in at 1,500 pounds. It fit very nicely into a railway car and could be assembled in any large room or out-of-doors. Walker wrote most of the plays himself and presented them in fanciful or period decor at admission prices ranging from fifty cents to two dollars. He and his company trouped with the Portmanteau for two years before they moved on to other pursuits. Perhaps the Portmanteau's most triumphant moment occurred on the snowy Christmas night of 1916, when Walker set up in Madison Square and gave a free performance of his play *The Seven Gifts* for the homeless and destitute sitting on the park benches.

Also in 1915 in New York, Butler Davenport founded the tiny Bramhall Theatre on East Twenty-seventh Street, in a building which had at various times served as a private home, Baptist tabernacle, and Knights of Columbus Hall. Originally an actor, Davenport had left the theater for real estate to try to recoup his family fortune, before receiving a psychic "call" in the middle of a night to return to his own profession. Not only did he star in the productions at Bramhall but he also wrote all of his own plays. Somehow he managed to hang on until 1923, when he changed the name of the theater to the Davenport and announced that it would be the first free theater in the world and would produce classical dramas and untried plays with amateur casts. During one of his performances, Mayor Fiorello La Guardia happened to be in the area, strolled in out of curiosity, and discovered that the performance was gratis. Thereafter, he exempted the theater from taxes. Although Davenport's theater did not survive him, by 1958 it had become a haven for grocery clerks, office boys, salesgirls—all those with humdrum lives who wished to strut a brief hour upon the stage. It even produced a couple of famous alumni in Gene Raymond and John Ireland.

The little-theater movement settled down into a kind of middle age during the 1920s. By the end of the decade, there were about four hundred theaters in existence, some venerable (like the Cleveland and Pasadena playhouses), some new entries on the list. Then as now, the mortality rate was high. Many of them seated a hundred patrons or fewer and subsisted on subscriptions, which hardly ever covered the costs of production. If staff and acting company were paid at all, their salaries were minuscule, and many had to moonlight or simply give up. When they first had issued their thrilling manifestos, they declared themselves dedicated to producing the work of new playwrights, but the supply of plays inevitably gave out. Out of the thousands of these devoted followers of Melpomene and Thalia, the best were absorbed into the mainstream of American theater. One estimate of the period places their number at about 5 percent of all those who aspired to professional status. The little-theater movement was their crucible as well as their creator.

The little theaters that arose during the 1920s followed the general pattern established in the previous decade, with notable exceptions. In 1925 the parents of Kenneth Sawyer Goodman, a promising young playwright who died in the 1918 flu epidemic, built one in his memory as a part of the Art Institute of Chicago. Located on Chicago's lake shore, the theater was built entirely below ground (except for the box office and business office) to comply with the city's building code, which prohibited structures of more than one story in the area. Thomas Wood Stevens, the creator of the first drama department at Carnegie Tech, was the first director of the Goodman, and for the next five years it flourished. The Depression forced the Art Institute to convert the theater into a drama school, when the resident company could no longer support itself. Stevens departed and Maurice Gnesin took over and developed the Goodman into one of the finest institutions of its type in the country. With its excellent facilities and an uncompromisingly professional approach, it attracted students of exceptional talent and graduated many people directly into the mainstream theater. In 1957 John Reich took over from the ailing Gnesin and began to bring guest stars into the student productions. Finally he asked the board of the Art Institute for permission to return the Goodman to professional resident-theater status and they agreed. In 1969 the school was shunted into a small studio and was gradually deemphasized. In 1978 what was left was absorbed by De Paul University. The Goodman, until 1986 under the aegis of Gregory Mosher and his Chicago Theatre Group, no longer reports to the Art Institute. As an independent regional theater, it encompasses two producing units, one for the main stage and the other for the presentation of new plays by resident playwrights. The Goodman is now back where it began.

Lacking all of the advantages enjoyed by the big-city little theaters, the Hedgerow Theatre in the tiny community of Moyan–Rose Valley, Pennsylvania, seemed to thrive on adversity. In 1923 Rose Valley had eighty-two registered voters, some of whom presented amateur offerings at an old stone mill, which had become a center of sorts for the village. Jasper Deeter, who had both acted and directed for the Provincetown Players, discovered the mill playhouse and decided to found a theater there based on his own personal vision. For a number of years, Deeter changed the bill nightly for audiences drawn from Philadelphia and its environs to the only true repertory theater in the country. To make the Hedgerow financially viable, the seating capacity was increased over the years from just under 100 to about 165 seats.

Deeter did not pay himself or his company, and everyone lived communally, with free room, board, and cigarettes. Three years later, he was evicted from the playhouse, but he returned in 1927, bringing with him the New York production of Paul Green's *In Abraham's Bosom*, which he had just directed. An iconoclast without a scintilla of talent for public relations, Deeter displayed such fierce dedication that O'Neill gave up his customary royalties to help him, Ann Harding, Rose McClendon, and Eva Le Gallienne (among others) performed at the Hedgerow during some of his many eleventh-hour crises, and young actors gravitated there as to a well of inspiration, staying for an average of six years. For Deeter, keeping the little theater alive was a daily struggle, and in 1956 the battle was lost and the theater closed. It reopened as a drama school, and in 1959 a community theater group was installed, with Deeter acting as sometime director of the troupe and teacher for the school. Shortly after Deeter died, in 1972, the theater entered another precarious period while other groups have tried to make it go. The Hedgerow serves as a classic example of the little theater that lives and dies as an extension of its creator.

Among the noble ventures that went aglimmering during the 1920s was Eva Le Gallienne's Civic Repertory Theatre in New York. The Civic Rep was especially notable because Le Gallienne was a star on Broadway who was willing to gamble on an experiment that was historically chancy. In 1926 the actress took over the old, battered, but still standing Fourteenth Street Theatre, far removed from the Elysian Fields of Broadway, and brought audiences down to see cherished revivals of Shakespeare, Chekhov, J. M. Barrie, Molière, Ibsen, and many others. She established a permanent company of actors and apprentices, she opened up the theater's workrooms to make costumes and scenery, she sold season memberships for a dollar a year to make her plays available to everybody, and she cajoled such stars as Alla Nazimova, Burgess Meredith, Joseph Schildkraut, and Jacob Ben-Ami to appear as guest artists. With Florida Friebus she adapted Lewis Carroll's *Alice in Wonderland* and *Through the Looking Glass* and herself played the White Queen in a performance that still stirs many happy memories in those who were around to see it. Worn down by the immensity of the enterprise, harried by increasing financial difficulties, and faced with constantly eroding audience support in the darkest days of the Depression, Le Gallienne closed her big little theater in 1933 and returned to Broadway the following year. In many ways, the Civic Rep presaged the coming of the Off-Broadway movement a generation in advance.

Like most little theaters, the Civic Rep was the brainchild of a single person; the Group Theatre was breathed into existence by a committee of three. The history of

The Hedgerow Theatre, a small playhouse established in an old stone mill in Moylan–Rose Valley, Pennsylvania, was destroyed by fire late in November 1985, but the Hedgerow company intends to rebuild it with the help of the community.

Perhaps the most memorable production at Eva Le Gallienne's Civic Repertory Theatre was Alice in Wonderland. *It opened in 1932 with Josephine Hutchinson as Alice, Donald Cameron as the White Rabbit, Burgess Meredith as the Dormouse, and Theodore Tenley as the Mad Hatter.*

the Group Theatre as recounted con brio by one of its founders, Harold Clurman, has been subjected of late to a small amount of revisionism, reevaluation, and reinterpretation, after some of those present at its creation took to the printed page with their version. Most of them agreed that it grew out of weekly discussions led by Clurman, who was in despair over the state of the American theater and had ideas on how to reform it. After a short career as an actor, Clurman had accepted the job of play reader for the Theatre Guild, where he met Cheryl Crawford, the casting director, and Lee Strasberg, an actor in Theatre Guild productions. All three were dissatisfied with the policies of the Theatre Guild, and Clurman proposed a venture that would lead them out of the wilderness of commerce into the promised land of art. Floated by a gift of a thousand dollars from the Theatre Guild and whatever donations the considerable persuasive skills of Crawford had been able to elicit, a band of twenty-eight actors, three directors, and assorted spouses and children decamped for Brookfield, Connecticut, in June of 1931, to put into practice what the triumvirate preached.

They came together to try out a new-old idea, imitating the Moscow Art Theatre: that a group of actors, living as well as working together, could perform with such perfect fusion of personalities that the players and the play would become inseparably entwined. Strasberg, who had been briefly introduced to Stanislavsky's method by Richard Boleslavsky, was to act as director-teacher, while Crawford's job was to keep the whole enterprise afloat. Clurman was both prophet and proselytizer, and remained throughout its existence the guiding spirit.

From the beginning, the Group Theatre manifested a hodgepodge of ideals, aims, and purposes. It was true to the little-theater movement in that its directors intended to experiment with fresh ideas imported from Europe and to apply them to new and original plays written by, for, and about Americans. But they were not interested in playing to an elitist audience of precious few. They wanted a Broadway audience and a Broadway playhouse for their experiments, since they knew that in any case they would have to stand the test of Broadway standards and would draw the criticism of Broadway reviewers. Very shortly after the Group Theatre was launched, they also realized that they needed the kind of success that would insure a long run and money in the bank to finance their next ventures. They later learned how to swallow the bitter pill of compromise to survive.

The Group Theatre came into existence during a stressful period in the nation's history and, given the youth of the members and their predilection to experiment, inevitably they were drawn into the liberal-to-left political currents. Their greatest critical success was Clifford Odets's frankly agitprop *Waiting for Lefty*. Because it was tough and gutsy and magnificently acted, the audiences paid less attention to its Marxist message than to its essential theatricality. Of the twenty-three plays produced by the Group Theatre, only four could be labeled clearly leftist, and ten were basically apolitical. Among the latter was Sidney Kingsley's *Men in White*, the Group Theatre's greatest box-office success; among the former was *1931*, its resounding failure.

Although Clurman did not intend the Group Theatre to be a school, it perforce became one. Rehearsals took on the aspect of a classroom as Strasberg interrupted the proceedings to give one actor or another specific instructions on how to approach his or her role. Eventually, Helen Tamiris was brought in to teach dancing and fencing, and instruction was offered in speech, singing, gymnastics, and acrobatics. For a season, the Group set up a recognized school under Robert Lewis and enrolled about thirty students, most tuition-paying, the others on scholarships.

The Group Theatre never tried to build an audience by subscription, since all three of the directors remembered too well the difficulties the Theatre Guild encountered in providing a season of plays that would completely satisfy its subscribers. As with all little theaters, lack of money loomed as the ever-present Problem Number One. A succession of hits insured financial independence; a failure or two meant looking for backing like any other producing organization. The Theatre Guild remained its offspring's principal font of money, but when it, too, encountered vicissitudes the Guild was forced to turn its back on its artistic protégé. The Shuberts helped finance one Group Theatre production, and Eugene O'Neill, Maxwell Anderson, and Franchot Tone, a founding Group Theatre member, all gave support when they were asked. But no Otto Kahn stepped permanently into the breach, and the Group Theatre eventually ran out of steam and money at the same time.

In its later years, it began to experience a talent drain as well. Strasberg and Crawford left in 1937 to pursue their own destinies in the theater: he as a director and, later, as a teacher at the Actors Studio; she as a Broadway producer. Odets went to Hollywood, although he maintained his ties with Clurman until the very end, and some of the most prominent actors—Franchot Tone, Frances Farmer, John Garfield, Stella and Luther Adler, and Lee J. Cobb—went to Hollywood or back to Broadway at its own level. The principal designers, Mordecai Gorelik and Boris Aronson, for whom the "poor" theater had provided the ultimate test of talent, rose to become two of the finest scenic artists in America. Judged by little-theater standards, the Group Theatre must be reckoned a success. It endured for a decade and had notable artistic triumphs. Judged by every other standard, its failures must weigh more heavily, but it remains a symbol of the best kind of experimental theater.

The political position of the Group Theatre was middle-of-the-road by comparison with the radicalism of some little theaters. Intellectual converts to Marxism watched with avid interest as the Communist experiment in Russia began to unfold before the eyes of the world. The party line "drama is a weapon" spurred the formation of amateur groups in the 1920s, but it was during the cataclysmic years of the 1930s that the American radical theater movement took shape and made some strides. In 1933 the Theatre Union was established by a coalition of liberals who ranged from socialist to communist to pro-labor. From 1933 to 1937, these enthusiasts presented anti-fascist, pro-labor, antiwar plays in an all-out effort to reach the masses. Because the amateurishness of early radical theater groups had scuttled their own efforts, the Theatre Union brought in professional actors and directors, leased the old Fourteenth Street Theatre (vacated by the Civic Rep), and studied Stanislavsky. The proletarian audience they were addressing persisted in staying away, and the Theatre Union decided to try Broadway. The middle-class Broadway audiences also resisted their message, and the Theatre Union expired after its final production of John Howard Lawson's *Marching Song*.

On a summer's day in 1931, Cheryl Crawford, Lee Strasberg, and Harold Clurman, founding members of the Group Theatre, conferred on the grass at Brookfield, Connecticut, as they began their grand experiment in group acting inspired by Stanislavsky.

Although groups coalesced in Boston, Philadelphia, Chicago, Los Angeles, and random pockets across the country, New York remained the most active center of the radical little-theater movement. In 1936 the New Theatre League was set up to unify and stimulate socially oriented theaters throughout the country. Unfortunately, the national organization never got off the ground and the office in New York served chiefly as a clearinghouse for plays, books, and various other kinds of publications, though it did set up a short-lived school in an attempt to control the direction of the movement. But there were never enough plays to feed to the group and the coming of World War II put an end to the Theatre League's activities.

The most successful of the political little theaters was organized by the International Ladies Garment Workers Union in 1936. Made up entirely of amateur performers drawn from the shop workers' ranks, Labor Stage presented an edition of *Pins and Needles* soon after the group was assembled. In 1937 the show reopened at the little Princess Theatre, on West Thirty-ninth Street, in the Broadway milieu. Singing their songs of social significance, the cast satirized Mussolini, American advertising, the DAR, war, censorship, radical plays, and most aspects of American society. The revue ran through several editions and moved to the Windsor Theatre, a larger Broadway playhouse, before closing in 1940. Because of its success, it was the only show ever produced by the Labor Stage and has been revived from time to time.

In the summer of 1935, a colossal social and artistic experiment was launched in America. When the Works Progress Administration was established by the executive order of President Franklin Delano Roosevelt, four special units were set up to take musicians, writers, artists, and theater people off the welfare rolls and put them into meaningful jobs. Put in charge of these units was Harry Hopkins, special assistant and advisor to the president. Hopkins had gone to Grinnell College, where he met Hallie Flanagan Davis, a classmate, whose main interest was the stage. For ten years Davis had served as director of the Vassar College Experimental Theatre, where the accent had been on original plays done in an assortment of fresh and exciting styles. It was she to whom Hopkins turned when he needed a day-to-day director for the new Federal Theatre Project (FTP).

In one fell swoop, Uncle Sam was not merely in show business but the creator of an entirely new and different little-theater movement. Mrs. Davis was to try to put back to work about 13,000 theater people, who were to earn from $21 to $55 a week (an upper limit of $105.40 was established in New York City only) and to play before audiences who would be admitted free of charge, if possible, or at admission fees ranging from ten cents to a dollar. With the surprising exception of Lee Shubert, theatrical management was frankly against the project or believed that it would never

work. Mrs. Davis tried to overcome their opposition and the suspicions of the theatrical unions and never really succeeded in doing either. Units of the project were set up under regional directors in all sections of the country. During the four years of its existence, the dramas that were played before public audiences never equaled in intensity, pitch, polemics, or theatrics the dramas that took place behind closed doors, on the telephone, by mail, and in forums as Mrs. Davis dealt with the unions, answered to the politicians, tried to find the right people for the right jobs and persuade them to stay on, found the money for some projects, and justified the existence of the FTP ad infinitum.

Because the greatest concentration of unemployed theater professionals was in New York and Los Angeles, the most serious pitfall Mrs. Davis had to avoid was to focus too much attention on these centers. Eventually, she organized a system of lend-lease, whereby actors, directors, and writers would be sent to regions that needed them. Many attempts were made to bring FTP workers into local, community, or amateur theaters, but the successes were few because the established groups resented the newcomers, whom they considered interlopers. Whenever there was a sufficient number of unemployed theater people on the relief rolls, some sort of theatrical activity was coaxed into existence. When it was ended by Congress in 1939, the FTP had spread its activities into thirty-one states in addition to New York City and the District of Columbia, had played to 25 million people, and had cost the federal government approximately $46 million. It had also assumed some familiar characteristics: it was regionally oriented; it was experimental; it was nonprofit; it existed in every kind of theater, from makeshift to conventional; it relied upon repertory; it embraced traditional stock companies; it inspired playwrights; it gave jobs to actors, directors, and designers; and it graduated its successes into the mainstream of American theater. While it lasted, it represented the little-theater movement on a grand scale.

Out of the fallout from the FTP emerged a well-named experimental theater, the Mercury, under the leadership of the mercurial Orson Welles and the steadier John Houseman, both of whom had created some of the most significant productions of the FTP. Their departure from the project was hastened by their defiance of Washington in presenting and continuing under their own auspices the FTP production of *The Cradle Will Rock,* Marc Blitzstein's brilliant anticapitalistic opera. In 1937, with a windfall of $10,000 from an unsolicited backer, they took over the little Comedy Theatre on West Forty-first Street in New York, renamed it, and prepared a modern-dress version of *Julius Caesar,* which made unmistakable references to Mussolini and his Fascist empire. The production stunned both critics and audiences with its genius and originality. Welles was just twenty-two years old at the time, Houseman ten years older. They went on to produce four more plays at the Mercury, none of which matched the success of *Julius Caesar,* before Hollywood hired Welles away.

There are always the ingenious few who do not wait for help to arrive but who create their own opportunities. One such was Robert Porterfield, a lanky young Virginia farmboy turned actor, who found himself in New York, down on his luck, during the bleakest days of the Depression. With a number of fellow unemployed actors, Porterfield returned to his hometown, the tiny Virginia hamlet of Abingdon, in the spring of 1933 to start a theater. He hit upon the masterful idea of charging thirty cents for admission or its equivalent in "vittles or work" and named his enterprise, appropriately, the Barter Theatre. At the end of the first season the actors had earned no money but had gained a collective 305 pounds, and news of the theater began to spread beyond the borders of the remote village. Later invited to appear on Fred Allen's nationally syndicated radio show, Porterfield was asked by the comedian how he made change: "Suppose I bring in a turkey worth four dollars. Do you give me ten pounds of string beans and a rabbit in change? Or does your cashier chew off thirty-five-cents-worth of white meat?" In 1939, his promotional abilities still intact, Porterfield began dispensing the National Barter Theatre Award to show-business celebrities. The award consisted of an (unreachable) acre of farmland, a

Hallie Flanagan Davis stewarded the Federal Theatre Project during its brief and beleaguered existence in the 1930s. Although she waged a fierce battle for its survival, she and the project were undone finally by an act of Congress in 1939.

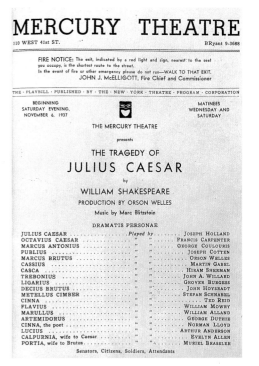

With music by Marc Blitzstein, the Mercury Theatre production of Julius Caesar *(1937) had a cast of then-unknowns, many of whom graduated into the ranks of Broadway and Hollywood stars.*

Calling itself with pride the oldest summer theater in the land, Elitch's Gardens Theatre, set in a pleasure park outside of Denver, Colorado, has remained active since 1893.

Virginia ham, and a platter to put it on. Until 1962, with only one three-year interruption during the war, Porterfield returned annually to Abingdon with a fresh set of recruits. In 1947 the state of Virginia granted him an outright subsidy and named his playhouse the State Theatre, for which in 1953 Porterfield salvaged some of the furnishings of the about-to-be-demolished Empire Theatre in New York. Finally, in 1962 the Barter Theatre became a year-round professional theater. Porterfield remained with it until his death, in 1972. He was succeeded by Rex Partington, who still remains in the post.

Although a few summer theaters, like the Barter, have developed into genuine little theaters, they have not always arisen from the same serious artistic impulses. Until the age of air conditioning, the urban playhouses closed down during the summer months, throwing actors and other stage people out of work. Most of the theatergoing population retreated from the heat of the city to summer cottages in resorts by the sea or in the mountains. In the early nineteenth century, several enterprising men of business established pleasure gardens after the European model on the outskirts of towns, fencing the grounds, planting gardens and trees, arranging footpaths amid the greenery, and charging admission. In time, light refreshments followed by open-air concerts lured the public into the small parks. One of the earliest American summer theaters was located in New York City beyond City Hall on Chatham Street. The manager, a Frenchman named Hippolite Barrière, in 1823 opened a tent theater, where he began to present light dramatic fare in addition to concerts. In the following year, he built a proper theater where he could produce full-scale plays year round.

Summer theaters like Barrière's proved very popular, and during the next hundred years many temporary playhouses were established in cities, under canvas, or in public parks. At the same time the thought occurred to other entrepreneurs to follow the crowds to the seashore and mountain retreats, find a large old building, and transform it into a theater of rustic charm and individuality, if they were lucky. Those movies about a strawhat theater—with budding Judy Garlands and Mickey Rooneys running about, painting the big barn red, setting up a stage at one end, cleaning out the hay, and getting up a show—were not far off the mark. Summer stock had its heyday from the 1920s to the 1940s, when the war restricted travel and many of the strawhat theaters closed, never to reopen.

From 1925 to 1941, the Lakewood Summer Theatre in Skowhegan, Maine—as far from Broadway as was possible to get during the early years of the twentieth century—became a tryout theater for Broadway. As soon as the ice was off the pond, producers, playwrights, and actors beat a path to the north woods to showcase their productions. The Lakewood began in 1901 as an open pavilion in a small amusement park at the end of a trolley line. The manager of the line, Herbert Swett, developed the pavilion into a theater in hopes of luring patrons to ride the trolley to its terminus at the park. Included in the fare was part-admission to the theater. He hired managers and directors to furnish entertainment, which got better and more professional as the years went by. Eventually, Broadway actors were attracted by the prospect of being kept busy while enjoying the delights of the Maine woods and lakes. In 1925 Howard Lindsay, then at the beginning of his career, took over as director-actor and brought Broadway tryouts as well as shows fresh from New York to fill out the summer season. Robert Sparks, manager and publicity agent, got the Lakewood into the national spotlight by arranging for such newsworthy events as a production of *Hamlet* designed and directed by Norman Bel Geddes, which wended its way to Broadway a few years later. Under the management of Melville Burke, who took over after Lindsay and Sparks departed, the reputation of Skowhegan remained undiminished. In 1939 Lindsay and his wife, Dorothy Stickney (who had met at Skowhegan), showed their loyalty by presenting the premiere of *Life with Father* there. Hundreds of actors appeared at Lakewood during their careers, some, like Stickney, appearing first as a fresh young ingenue or juvenile and returning later as a star. In 1950 the Lakewood went the way of most summer theaters when it began to present stars in prepackaged

touring shows. As its lure as a vacation resort diminished, so did the theater. The glory years behind it, it has been recently operated as a nonprofit state theater.

One of the most famous summer theaters in history was hatched by a junior from Harvard and a junior from Princeton at a tea given in 1928 for the Moscow Art Theatre actors. The eager young men were Charles Crane Leatherbee from the Harvard Dramatic Club and Bretaigne Windust from Princeton's Theatre Intime. They formed a University Players Guild, which took over a movie house at Falmouth on Cape Cod to present plays during the summer. The following year, they built their own theater, paid themselves five dollars a week, plus room and board, and showed off their talents. The world soon began to hear of James Stewart, Henry Fonda, Margaret Sullavan, Joshua Logan, Myron McCormick, Mildred Natwick, Kent Smith, and Barbara O'Neil—all members of the guild. Their theater burned down in 1936, after they had all departed to greater fame and fortune, but it was eventually replaced, and Falmouth is still a stop on the summer circuit.

Rollo Peters, Sam Wren, Dorothy Gish, and Romney Brent are pictured, from left to right, in a scene from The Streets of New York, the production that opened the Westport (Connecticut) Country Playhouse in 1931. In 1980–81, the play was repeated with a modern cast during the playhouse's golden anniversary season.

Opposite, top to bottom:
Established like most 1930s summer theaters in a rural community populated by exurbanites and vacationers from nearby cities, the Bucks County Playhouse began life with a ready-made audience for its mostly warmed-over-Broadway fare. Alas, time has wrought its changes, and the theater struggles today to keep afloat with the support of a diminished summer population.

For thirty-seven summer seasons, Lucille Lortel's White Barn Theatre in Westport, Connecticut, has been a haven for new plays, untried and veteran performers, and fresh ideas in any form.

The remoteness of many strawhat playhouses is vividly conveyed by this aerial photograph of the Barn Theatre in Augusta, Michigan, which shows ribbons of roads amidst flat farmland leading to the box office.

All the survivors of the strawhat era have had their vicissitudes. Most have abandoned the resident stock-company system in favor of packaged productions, and many of them have become nonprofit enterprises. Notable exceptions are the Berkshire Theatre in Stockbridge, Massachusetts, which still maintains a resident company, and, more recently, Lucille Lortel's White Barn Theatre in Westport, Connecticut, which tests untried plays or works-in-progress. The old-fashioned summer-stock theater is best represented today by Jack Rogotzy's Barn Theatre in Augusta, Michigan, which has for almost forty years maintained a resident stock company and shows a profit each season.

No one is able to give an accurate count of the summer theaters in existence at any one time. Every winter ambitious plans are announced by eager entrepreneurs of all ages, who somehow run out of steam as the warm weather approaches. There are (perhaps) between 200 and 250 summer theaters now in existence in about forty states, most in the East. Although many are located in well-known resort areas and in the suburbs, several can be found only through assiduous use of map and compass. The major summer theaters constitute a circuit for star-laden touring musicals and plays, while the minor ones remain amateur and are usually attached to a college campus. Many have sophisticated physical plants, and a few operate out of steamboats, outdoor theaters, and makeshift playhouses. In Maryville, Tennessee, the Smoky Mountain Passion Play Association presents (you guessed it) a passion play, while at Manteo, North Carolina, Paul Green's *Lost Colony* has been attracting audiences since 1937. Sooner or later, everyone who wants to get into show business serves time at a summer theater, if only to acquire a union card, since many now operate under contract with the theatrical unions. The movement has progressed from the "Hey, kids, let's put on a show in the barn" stage to a highly organized, frequently professional, and apparently indestructible national institution.

While summer stock was developing into a mostly eastern, mostly Broadway-in-the-boondocks, mostly city-oriented affair, the rural Midwest and South were not without summer entertainment. There, too, the provincial theaters closed down during the summer in the late nineteenth and early twentieth centuries. Noting that summer was the season for traveling circuses, managers with empty theaters on their hands began to explore the possibility of sending their troupes out to tent theaters in the rural communities. With the arrival of the automobile and the expansion of the railroad, the traveling tent show blossomed into a major theatrical industry in the geographical center of the country. Known in the trade as "tent rep" (tent repertoire) shows, hundreds of companies took to the road every summer, each carving a slice of the vast territory, cultivating audiences with a ten-cent admission fee, offering a different program each night in one-week stands, and presenting the kind of plays (with vaudeville acts during intermission) that would have been scorned by big-city audiences. At first, the tent-rep companies relied on such nineteenth-century staples as *East Lynne, Camille, The Two Orphans,* and *Kathleen Mavourneen;* later they relied for novelty on pirated and altered versions of new plays shown at the urban theaters. Dialogue and stage business would be surreptitiously recorded by stenographers, transcribed and typed in the office, and sent out in mimeograph. The most notorious of the play pirates was the Chicago Manuscript Company, which had to switch tactics when the owner began spending more time in court than in his office. He then began to hire writers to grind out plays for the tent-rep companies, and these came to be known as "rube dramas." All extolled the homely virtues and the good rural life.

In 1911 Fred Wilson, an actor with Murphy's Comedians, was playing in *Out of the Fold* by Langdon McCormick in a little town in Louisiana. The character he was acting, Toby Tompkins, caught the fancy of the audience. Very soon Toby was taken up by comedians of other companies and became the central figure in dozens of plays written by the hack playwrights of the Chicago Manuscript Company, among others. Red-haired, freckle-faced, dressed in farmboy clothing, Toby was a blend of Huckleberry Finn and Peck's Bad Boy. He was at once lazy and stupid and quick-acting and shrewd. He talked in the dialect of the back country and was frequently boastful and brash, yet was also the self-appointed champion of maidens, mother, home, country, and God—almost in that order. First and foremost, he was a lovable clown, and so he remained, in the hands of the many actors who played him. Virtually unknown to eastern audiences, Toby was by far the most important contribution of tent repertoire to the American theater.

The 1930s dealt several harsh blows to tent rep. Not only were the times bad and money scarce but the federal government was assiduous in bringing electricity to the nation's outback, which put remote country households in touch with the outside world through radio and phonograph. The shows that endured to the end of the decade were decimated by gas rationing during the war years, and one by one the rest disappeared in the age of television. Today tent rep exists only in the minds of those old enough to remember when the bills were posted in town and Toby was joyfully anticipated by his admirers.

After World War II, a new kind of grass-roots theater arose in America. Unlike tent rep, it relied on the growing sophistication of American audiences and their increasing involvement in the world beyond American borders. A not inconsequential factor in its emergence was the flood of would-be actors, directors, and writers out of the nation's colleges, universities, dramatic schools, and conservatories, courtesy of the United States government under the GI Bill of Rights. Anxious to gain theatrical experience, most of them gravitated to New York or to the three or four major theater centers outside New York to look for work. But by that time, Broadway was feeling the pinch of television, and theaters along the Great White Way were tumbling down like tenpins or were being converted to movie houses. The "road" was limited to the few legitimate theaters still standing in the cities that had the audiences to support live entertainment. The postwar commercial theater could not assimilate the vast reservoir of talent fast collecting in the 1950s. All the conditions necessary for the second coming of the little-theater movement were in order, and arrive it did, first in New York, soon after in the big cities across the nation, and finally in the not-so-big cities in a network of regional theaters. Like the first little theaters, these out-of-the-way playhouses sent and send their best products on to Broadway, but they avow that they did and do not today consider themselves mere tributaries. They have a lively sense of their own destiny. The new movement does not show signs of abating. When little theaters die others arise to take their place.

At the turn of the century, Harvey Havestock, who trouped his tent-rep company in the Southwest, played his version of the Toby character in an ill-fitting checked suit.

The first groups to form after the war were composed mainly of actors who had gone to school together or had played together in summer stock. They had no objection to the theatrical status quo except that it prevented them from working. They were content to revive classics, with Shakespeare high on the list, and plays of more recent memory. In the sense that they paid themselves very little or not at all, they were amateurs, and for a while, the theatrical unions were content to look the other way.

The term *Off Broadway* was first used by Burns Mantle in a modest listing in the back pages of *Best Plays of 1934–35*. Even during the darkest years of World War II, the tiny Cherry Lane Theatre and the Provincetown Playhouse, both in Greenwich Village, opened their doors to troupes and groups. But the postwar movement spread beyond the established little theaters. Then as in earlier decades, the newcomers went out and looked for spaces, and with a minimum of expenditure and a major commitment of time, effort, energy, and hard work, they turned unlikely places into little theaters. During the first twenty years after the war, the little theaters served as the springboard for actors who were developing and acquiring an American acting style. Then, slowly, Off Broadway also began to pull in playwrights—new voices in the American theater who refused to speak in acceptable Broadway language. It was at this point that Off Broadway became genuinely experimental and more at one with its historical tradition.

It is generally conceded that the theatrical moment that launched the theater that launched the Off-Broadway movement in earnest occurred when the last lines of Tennessee Williams's *Summer and Smoke* were spoken in a revival performance late in April 1952. The theater was the Circle in the Square, the young actress speaking the lines was Geraldine Page, and the equally young director who had chosen the play and the players for it was José Quintero. The small, dedicated band of young people who founded the Circle in 1951—Quintero, Emily Stevens, Jason Wingreen, Aileen Cramer, Ted Mann, and Edward Mann—had not set out to make history or money. They wanted desperately to work in the theater and could find no better way of beginning than to create their own playhouse as an extension of the shared dream. Naive and inexperienced, they formed a tight circle within their Circle, sharing responsibilities, doing the dirty work, alternately hating and loving each other, wrangling and fighting and eventually breaking away until only one of the original group was left to continue the theater.

The group at the Circle in the Square was not the first in Greenwich Village to spring up after the war. Preceding them, in the late 1940s, was a little theater named New Stages that prided itself on presenting plays considered untouchable by Broadway producers and surprised itself when one of their productions, Jean-Paul Sartre's *The Respectful Prostitute*, made it to Broadway for an eight-month run. Nor was the Circle to follow the historical course of most Off-Broadway groups. For one thing, it has had a charmed life. The idea to present plays within an "alternative" space, not quite in-the-round, not quite proscenium, proved to be inspired. Quintero took great pains to choose plays that were suited to the space, plays that were small and intimate in scope.

Within a few years, four of the original group departed, leaving Ted Mann, Quintero, and a new partner, Leigh Connell, in charge. In 1959 they were evicted from their Sheridan Square theater and reopened the following year in a small Bleecker Street movie theater previously remodeled into a playhouse by New Stages. In 1961, in the best tradition of the little-theater movement, they opened a school. In 1964, beset by enormous personal difficulties, Quintero left, following Leigh Connell, and Ted Mann became artistic director. Paul Libin, a Broadway and Off-Broadway producer who had joined the year before, became the managing director.

In the 1960s various New York mayors made it part of their municipal responsibility to encourage the building of theaters within and on the fringes of the theater district. They offered concessions, the most important of which was to allow the inclusion of theaters within high-rise office buildings. Because of their track record, the directors

Its prior life as a nightclub is evident in this photograph of the first Circle in the Square, at 5 Sheridan Square, New York. (The production shown is unidentified.)

of Circle in the Square were approached, and in 1972 the Circle in the Square took up new quarters in a 650-seat theater in the bowels of the Uris Building, on West Fiftieth Street. In one fell swoop, it became part of mainstream Broadway, perhaps completing its metamorphosis. It also managed to retain its Downtown Circle, which is operated as a typical Off-Broadway theater.

The Circle wintered in an era of "poor theater," when each production was scratched together by hard work and no money, unobserved by the theatrical unions. It has summered in an era of large grants—by foundations, by corporations, and by wealthy sponsors. It has been sustained by a subscription audience and it has been trammeled by union regulations. It has been envied by many a similar group that has since disappeared without a trace, and it has settled into a kind of respectability that many of its early supporters deplore. But it is impossible to underestimate the achievements of the Circle in the Square, among which must be counted the renewal of interest it sparked in the plays of Eugene O'Neill. The Circle introduced many talented actors into the mainstream of American theater and films and gave directors like Quintero, Stephen Porter, and William Ball a chance to polish their talents and establish themselves. Although it never lived up to its promise of discovering new playwrights, it revived some important neglected works by older Americans and introduced plays by Europeans that would not have had a Broadway airing. Mainly it has endured as a house of revivals—sometimes brilliant, insightful, and tasteful—and occasionally it has been able to move them to Broadway. It continues its policy of short runs, but is not averse to extending the run of a particularly strong revival. Its financial battles are by no means over, but the Circle management probably has yet another card up its sleeve to play in case of dire emergency. The Circle just keeps spinning along.

As a study in contrast, the Phoenix Theatre, founded in 1953, shortly after the

Circle in the Square, groped for its *raison d'être* throughout its existence and passed through several metamorphoses in an unwitting exemplification of its name, before expiring in the late 1970s. Two theater-wise and experienced men, Norris Houghton and T. Edward Hambleton, tried at first to establish the theater along the lines of the Old Vic, presenting unusual plays with stars and strong casts outside the commercial mills of Broadway. They planned to do it in an Off-Broadway setting but expected that their audience would consist of regular Broadway theatergoers. Because they were known and respected on Broadway and in social circles, they quickly raised the money for the first season, found a 1,200-seat theater at Second Avenue and Twelfth Street that had been built during the heyday of the Yiddish theater movement, got their first play, a revival of Sidney Howard's *Madam, Will You Walk?*, and were on their way. Despite early critical successes, the Phoenix directors could never change the red ink to black. They tried everything. They became nonprofit to attract foundation money and charitable donations. They moved to a small theater. They transferred their hits to Broadway. They brought in big names (Tyrone Guthrie) and gave a home to wayward productions *(Once Upon a Mattress)*. They established a permanent acting company, dissolved it, then teamed with the Association of Producing Artists (APA) from the University of Michigan to reestablish a permanent company in repertory for several seasons. They took over the Lyceum Theatre in the theater district to swim in the Broadway currents. Houghton left, other people came aboard, but Hambleton remained as the anchor. Because of its checkered career, there will always be a lurking hope that the Phoenix will arise out of its ashes once again, off or on Broadway, and that T. Edward will be there fanning the flames.

The greatest success of the Off-Broadway movement and the little-theater movement in general remains the New York Shakespeare Festival. It has resisted going "legitimate" like the Circle in the Square and has turned deficit spending into a high art, something to which the cool-headed Hambleton could never adjust. The New York Shakespeare Festival owes its existence and persistence to one man, Joseph Papp, whose manifesto, if he ever stood still long enough to think one through, would consist of one simple, direct, and unwavering statement: everybody needs theater. The rich should bear the costs and, in Papp's mind, the rich includes government at any and all levels. Throughout his long career with the festival, he has been the author of no set policy or philosophy. He has issued contradictory statements, but he sees contradiction as part of his personal growth and of the theater's growth. Along the way, he has turned one little theater into the largest arts organization of its kind in the country. In the 1976–77 season, his budget of more than $30 million exceeded that of the Metropolitan Opera. During that season, he not only operated out of the New York Public Theater on Lafayette Street, but managed two theaters at Lincoln Center, had two shows running on Broadway, presented free Shakespearean performances in Central Park and in his mobile unit throughout greater New York, and had television projects hanging fire. Not only has Papp been the guiding and sometimes devilish genius of the entire enterprise, he has become in its promotion the latter-day incarnation of P. T. Barnum, if on a higher, more genteel level. He takes to the air in singing commercials to exhort the many to see his plays. He takes to the streets to fight battles on behalf of his theater or of any cause that attracts him. He has gone into the breach so often that it has become his second home. He chooses the plays, selects the important personnel, and determines how the money is to be spent and from whom it is to be raised. He has apotheosized the little-theater leader into a cultural head of state without portfolio. He is unique.

Papp began modestly. He found space in the basement of the Emanuel Presbyterian Church on East Sixth Street, on the Lower East Side, and began presenting Shakespearean plays free of charge. In 1956, two-and-a-half years later, he persuaded the Parks Department to let him take over an old amphitheater standing in East River Park and give free open-air performances. He formed a mobile unit to present the shows in New York's boroughs, but the trailer-truck stage began to disintegrate and came to rest in Central Park. He next moved to a little theater tucked into the

Heckscher Building at Fifth Avenue and One Hundred Fourth Street, but during the summer of 1958 he returned to Central Park. The following summer, he accomplished the impossible: he won a battle against Parks Commissioner Robert Moses, long considered invincible in city politics, and was allowed not only to continue presenting free Shakespearean performances but to construct a permanent theater through a gift of George Delacorte.

In 1966 Papp bought the old Astor Library, on Lafayette Street, which had been owned by the Hebrew Immigrant Aid Society, and a few years later moved to have it declared a landmark and coaxed the city into buying it from him and leasing it back to the festival for one dollar. Papp named it the New York Public Theater and fashioned six theaters out of its innards. From 1973 to 1977, he ran the Vivian Beaumont Theater at Lincoln Center and also the little subterranean playhouse there, for which he had found a donor and a new name, the Mitzi E. Newhouse Theater. He has brought other companies under the Public Theater umbrella, underwritten experimental shows like *Hair* and *A Chorus Line,* and has teetered on the brink of insolvency through much of his tenure with the giant theatrical octopus he has created. He regularly turns adversity into celebration, as at the twelve-hour marathon of Shakespearean plays at Central Park in 1970, held to point up the financial difficulties of the Shakespeare Festival. He is a restless, nervous, highly charged man who functions best when challenged.

Papp's one significant defeat, as steward of the Lincoln Center theaters, can be explained by his spiritual discomfort in residing among the swells and catering to audiences that resist his kind of theater, whatever it is at any given time. As a public persona who has worn the poor robes of populism, he has been attacked by some critics for his autocratic decisions. Some of the many plays that he has produced have been considered not worth doing, and quite a few of his experiments died an early and blessed death. The sum of his contributions was succinctly and aptly assessed by the late Brooks Atkinson: "A lot of people who had never before seen Shakespeare had a chance to see it free in the park. Downtown, he created a new theatre civilization. It owes nothing to other theatres. It does not borrow or imitate." Whatever his artistic prejudices or personal petulances, Joe Papp has emerged as the towering figure of America's other theater in the twentieth century.

Inevitably, the prosperity of the little theaters brought them to the attention of the unions, particularly Actors' Equity, which demanded a share of the box-office take for

During his tenure at Lincoln Center, Joseph Papp tried presenting the kind of plays he would have produced at the New York Public Theater downtown. In 1976, he put Streamers, David Rabe's harrowing drama of military life, in the Mitzi E. Newhouse Theater, a small, experimental space in the depths of the complex. Papp's poster designer Paul Davis caught the mood of the piece in this stylish poster.

Opposite:
A fine example of the capacity of regional theater to infuse new blood into the mainstream is the musical Annie, which was tried out at the Goodspeed Opera House in East Haddam, Connecticut, and then moved to Broadway in 1977. It remained in New York for more than two thousand performances and generated four road companies and a movie. Shown here are Andrea McArdle (Annie) and Sandy, photographed from the wings of the theater.

its members. Eventually, formulas based on the number of seats in a theater were arrived at, and contracts were negotiated between Equity and the Off-Broadway managers, who were forced into forming the League of Resident Theatres to deal with the business of their collective enterprises. Slowly, Off Broadway found itself slouching toward Establishment. The stage was set for another return to innocence and poverty, and soon a different little-theater movement swelled in New York, one that reflected the drug-oriented, sexually liberated, and politically radical subculture of a new generation.

It had its start in the coffeehouses that began to proliferate in the late 1950s in New York. The most prominent were located in Greenwich Village, of course, but they also sprang up in other sections of the city where rents were low and the inhabitants were young and restless, searching for an outlet for their creative energies. The cafes started by dispensing coffee and cappuccino, progressed toward allowing patrons to read their own (or others') poetry, and ended by presenting tatterdemalion actors in plays staged on makeshift platforms. Usually operating without a license, the coffeehouse owners permitted the hat to be passed after each performance to sustain the writers and actors or to provide a few dollars to float the next production.

The people who emerged from the Caffe Cino, which is considered by most to be the birthplace of the Off-Off-Broadway movement, suffuse it today with a holy glow. Joe Cino founded it in 1958 on Cornelia Street, in Greenwich Village, and began the following year to allow (nearly) spontaneous entertainment within its walls, which eventually escalated into mini-productions on a tiny stage. After Cino committed suicide, in 1967, his friends tried to keep it going, but without him it had lost its nerve center, and the cafe closed in 1968. Recalling its glories, Robert Patrick, a playwright who got his start at the Cino, ended his memorial: "The Cino was grubby, glorious, historical, hysterical, dazzling, dirty, creative, destructive, the top, the bottom, the beginning."

Unlike the Caffe Cino, most of the coffeehouses expired quickly, but they had served a purpose. They had brought theatrical activity back to its beginnings: two boards, a passion, and an audience. Inspired by the intimacy of the coffeehouse, where actors establish immediate rapport with an audience, young theater people found themselves cheap, affordable spaces and, at first, gave away their talents. Working by day at low-paying jobs, they performed by night in out-of-the-way aeries and basements and, incredible to say, found their own audiences without advertisement. The new groups made the entire city a theater district and eventually created a new theatrical identity in New York. No one quite remembers how the term *Off Off Broadway* got started, but it crept into the vocabulary to remain. Newspapers now list Off-Off-Broadway productions as a service to their readers. Off-Off-Broadway plays have been published in anthologies and have been designated best plays of the year. In 1966 Actors' Equity set up a code to protect its members from exploitation in Off Off Broadway and has kept a wary eye on the activities of producers there. More than eighty Off- and Off-Off-Broadway groups are members of a professional organization, the Alliance of Resident Theatres/New York, which functions as a trade and service organization, dispensing advice, aid, publicity, and information and speaking out in their collective cause. In the 1983–84 season, Off Broadway and Off Off Broadway together represented a $45 million industry. More than seven hundred productions were presented, before an audience of nearly three million people. New York's little theaters have become big business.

Joe Cino helped to invent Off Off Broadway and Ellen Stewart built it into the Universal Better Mousetrap. Knowing nothing about the theater, she came to New York from Louisiana to try her luck as a clothes designer in the early 1950s. After deciding that her real vocation was to help aspiring playwrights like her brother, she opened the Cafe La Mama in 1962, a Greenwich Village coffeehouse that was really a front for her theater. Harried by city inspectors for dispensing entertainment without a license, she had to break and move several times before settling down, without a coffeehouse ruse, on East Fourth Street, near the Bowery. Foundation grants enabled

The founder of La Mama Experimental Theatre Club company and its ambassador-at-large around the world is the dynamic and ageless Ellen Stewart.

her to buy a building, in which she has housed two theaters, each seating ninety-nine people, and later to add close by a larger annex with other performing spaces. Stewart makes her theaters available to playwrights, directors, and troupes—mostly amateurs—who must function as their own producers. Like Cino, she rarely reads scripts left with her, simply relying on her impressions of the people who come to her with their projects. Incorporated as La Mama Experimental Theatre Club, Stewart's theaters epitomize the Off-Off-Broadway movement at its experimental best. Now booked months in advance, they keep churning on a year-round basis. Stewart has mothered many aspiring playwrights on the first wobbly legs of their careers. More important, she has taken troupes abroad and has encouraged the founding of theaters similar to hers in all the places to which her troupes have traveled. La Mama has become its own message.

During the 1960s, Off Off Broadway became the natural staging area for Americans stirred by the artistic and political explosions that were rocking the foundations of their society. In an era of plenty, peace seemed an illusion. In an era of peace, plenty was elusive for black Americans. Homosexuals were emboldened by new psychological studies attesting to their normality to come out of their closets. Somehow, drugs and rock music entered into the mixture and became synonymous with the events. John Kennedy's assassination burst the balloon and enforced a period of national introspection. Americans coming of age found little that they liked or respected in their society, which they were being asked to defend in a far-off place named Vietnam. Meeting these currents head on were trickles of fresh, anarchic ideas from abroad. The new theatrical generation began to question established norms and forms, inspired by the work of Antonin Artaud, the French visionary of the 1930s.

Artaud had wanted nothing less than a total and uncompromising destruction of the theatrical order and, in its place, a new theater inducing mystical, trancelike reactions through powerful blows to the senses. He believed in an audience that thought with its senses and sensed what it thought. Music, dance, symbols, and visual imagery were to be combined in stunning theatrical spectacle. He called it the theater of cruelty. No sooner was Artaud digested than the theories of another visionary, Jerzy Grotowski, began to seep out of Poland. In place of conventional plays, Grotowski pressed for communal creations. In place of psychologically realistic acting, he wanted ritualistic and symbolic movement. In place of actor and spectator, he proposed intermingling performers and audience in a shared experience, without the conventional barriers of stage and aesthetic distance. The theories of Artaud and Grotowski were heady stuff for a generation primed for protest.

The American group that first fused politics with theatrical theory was the Living Theatre, founded by Julian Beck and Judith Malina, husband and wife, in 1947. Already confirmed pacifists and anarchists, they spent their first ten years forming an outer-limits experimental group, a living and collective embodiment of Grotowski's "poor" theater, laced with Artaudian theories of surrealistic drama. From producing avant-garde but recognizable plays in their living room, they progressed to the Cherry Lane Theatre, then to an uptown loft, finally coming to rest in 1957 in a building on Fourteenth Street and Sixth Avenue. Sitting through an early Living Theatre production was not easy but it *was* arresting, and the Becks built up a following drawn mostly from the intellectual theatergoing middle class (they professed an ambition to reach ordinary, non-theatergoing people and looked to the day when they could perform in the streets). Always on the brink of bankruptcy, they were arrested by Treasury agents in 1963 for nonpayment of admissions income and social security taxes, which the Becks had in fact withheld—but for the use of the company. At the time, the troupe was performing Kenneth H. Brown's *The Brig,* a scathing indictment of the dehumanization of men confined to an American military prison. The Becks' supporters cried foul and saw political implications in the event. If the Becks were victims of anything, they were victims of the slowly grinding bureaucratic mills, but overnight they became a *cause célèbre.* They drew short jail terms, after which they elected to go into self-imposed exile in France, where they were not only welcomed

Julian Beck, with hands in prayer-like position, and his wife, Judith Malina, are surrounded in this picture by members of the Living Theatre. Beck died in 1985. Malina is writing about the experiences of the company.

but financially buttressed and given their own theater. They began a second and more potent round of experimentation, returning in 1968 to America. Their new creations, called "theater pieces," startled audiences to their hair follicles. They included seminudity, symbolic scenery, choreographed acting (or acted choreography), audience-touching interspersed with spoken political pontifications and chanted exhortations—all presented in a nonlinear, formless style calculated to assault the senses and rouse the consciousness. Wherever they went, comment and controversy followed. After their tour they returned to Europe, to reappear in 1984 with some of their usual repertory, plus a few new pieces. This time, their reception was not so enthusiastic and they were forced prematurely to end their short engagement at the Joyce Theatre, an Off-Broadway playhouse. They had found their real moment in the turbulent 1960s, and it could not be re-created nearly twenty years later.

The Living Theatre created a powerful after-tide of theatrical experimentation, which continues today. Since 1968 Richard Foreman, the founder of the Ontological Hysteric Theatre in a SoHo loft, south of Greenwich Village, has fragmented conventional theater into its component parts—acting, music, lighting, scenery—and allowed them to exist independently in one of his many original theater pieces. He creates a theatrical dadaism, upsetting all of the familiar relationships between actor and actor, actor and scenery, play and audience, and word and image. Like the Becks, he, too, finds a more comfortable artistic ambience in France, but one of his more recent iconoclasms startled even the tolerant French. In a production of Johann Strauss's *Die Fledermaus,* he had twelve nude couples dance to the famous waltzes but

In this photograph, taken at the Center for American Studies in Paris in 1966, founding members of the Mabou Mines—JoAnne Akalaitis, David Warrilow, and Ruth Maleczech—perform in Play *by Samuel Beckett.*

had to bend to public outrage and clothe them in later performances.

Although Foreman likes to mix media, the troupe that has made the process its hallmark is the Mabou Mines, which has performed just as frequently in art galleries and museums as in theaters. Currently residing under the umbrella of Joseph Papp's Public Theater, the Mabou Mines is a theatrical collective rather than the brainchild of one person. Some of the group met in California in the late 1950s and were part of San Francisco's Actor's Workshop, under the artistic leadership of Jules Irving and Herbert Blau. They eventually drifted east and were invited by Ellen Stewart to perform at La Mama. Collectively, they have developed a way of interpreting (rather than presenting) the works of Samuel Beckett through mime, puppetry, surrealistic scenery and lighting, and synthesized electronic music. In 1969 they took the name Mabou Mines from a dilapidated, abandoned mining village in Nova Scotia, and originated pieces they call "animations," which are visualizations of verbal or intellectual images. They create surrealistic tableaux vivants in a blend of visual and performance art that is often astonishing to the eye and stunning to the mind.

One of the few experimental groups that strives for comedy, the Ridiculous Theatrical Company, received its first important notice in 1973 with a production of *Camille*, the nineteenth-century melodramatic warhorse. The part of the Parisian courtesan was played by a man, Charles Ludlam, the founder of the company, its principal star and playwright, and the director of its artistic destiny. Having been ejected from a group called the Play-House of the Ridiculous, which specialized in a surrealistic zaniness, Ludlam organized his own company in 1967 and gave midnight performances on weekends in a series of loaned spaces (including La Mama's) until he and his troupe were able to settle down in their own theater at One Sheridan Square. Audacity is the emblem of the company—whether Ludlam is playing Camille in low décolleté, revealing a hairy chest, or impersonating the opera queen Maria Callas in a semi-travesty entitled *Galas* that won an award in 1983. With its grotesque mixture of sex and scatology, with its blurring of gender as men play women and women play men, and with its dramatic horn of plenty from which flow literary allusions and evocations of old movies, Ludlam's form of humor is not everyone's cup of tea. He believes, however, that he is working directly in the theatrical mainstream— presenting stereotypical age-old comic types with his brand of crazyhouse campiness. Of his style he says, "It's Elizabethan, it's Restoration, it's soap operas." Ludlam has become a cult figure among the homosexual population in New York, but his work has achieved sufficient renown to enable him to tour the country and Europe.

Since their beginnings, the Off-Broadway and Off-Off-Broadway movements have undergone familiar cycles, the highs and lows characteristic of theater in a historical context, which are caused not only by shifts in the economy but by dry and fertile spells of artistic creativity. Admittedly, a disproportionate amount of their activity has been wildly self-indulgent, but in a city as large as New York audiences somehow materialize for the most unlikely presentations. The city has lived up to its reputation for providing aid and comfort to the exotic and unusual and has sheltered all forms of artistic diversity.

But if Broadway is not America, neither is New York. Many young people after the war gravitated to the large provincial cities, particularly the university centers, and carved their own theaters out of architectural refuse and with the same high goals as their big-city sisters and brothers. But geography enforced significant differences in their approach. For one thing, they had to draw upon smaller populations for their audiences and, compounding the problem, by the late 1940s most Americans living west of the Hudson had lost the habit of going to the theater. It was not easy, and the lesson learned was to make little-theater spaces as attractive and inviting as possible and to get into better quarters as soon as it was financially feasible.

Another solution was to get the community involved in the theatrical enterprise as quickly as possible. Business and government leaders were invited to sit on boards of directors as a means of getting respectability and, in its wake, money. Unfortunately, the tactic has been a double-edged sword. The more thoroughly the community has become enmeshed in an enterprise, the louder the voice it has wished to raise in its councils. A strong artistic director or founder (the two are frequently the same person) makes for a stable enterprise, but he or she is ultimately answerable to the constituency of the theater, either directly or through representatives sitting on the board. As a result, there has been experimentation in regional theaters, but experimentation has never been allowed to dominate the artistic policy of any of them.

Finally, the regional theaters have found that they cannot afford to ignore Broadway. On the minus side, this means they are forced to produce plays that have finished their Broadway run just to please the crowds who have heard about them through the media. On the plus side, they can point with pride to the playwrights whom they have nurtured (usually on some kind of private or government grant) and the plays they have sent to New York. Their physical plants are often of such technical sophistication that Broadway designers and technicians accept out-of-town assignments just for the pleasure of working within them. All of the regional theaters must send for actors from New York when they are unable to fill their ranks with local talent of sufficiently high professional caliber. None of them can hold the best of their personnel, who, when the tide inevitably reverses itself, must seek their fortunes in New York.

The postwar regional theater movement was launched in Dallas, Texas, by Margo Jones, who had tried and failed to set up a unit of the Federal Theatre Project in Houston. (Hallie Flanagan Davis recalled that Texas was so hard a nut that no one succeeded in cracking it.) During the next ten years, Jones learned her trade both in her home state and on Broadway. Then, in 1947 she established Theatre 47 in an air-conditioned building once used by the Gulf Oil Corporation as part of an exposition. She borrowed seats from a movie theater and arranged them around a trapezoidal playing area, thus making extensive and expensive scenery unnecessary. She hoped to make up in the acting, directing, costuming, and substance of her plays what she lost in visual marvels. Her policy was to do new plays or plays that were at least fifty years old, and with rare exception she stuck to it. On all accounts she gambled and she won.

During the next eight years, Jones presented more than a hundred plays in the round and established that kind of staging as an alternative and viable mode of production. She introduced plays by Tennessee Williams, William Inge, Joseph Hayes, and Jerome Lawrence and Robert Lee and she broke in many an actor and actress. Although she changed the name of the theater each new year, to her audience it was simply "Margo's," and she annually increased her subscribers by personalizing the entire operation. She greeted patrons at the door and made speeches at intermission. She hired the staff, made all of the decisions, spent the money, and supervised every detail. In July 1955, she accidentally inhaled chemical fumes as she sat on a freshly cleaned rug reading scripts and she died as a result of it. Her theater died with her. Jones's dream had been to give over the stage to playwrights. "If we succeed in inspiring the operation of thirty theatres like ours," she once said, "the playwright won't need Broadway." To honor her memory, in 1961 playwrights Lawrence and Lee set up an award in her name to be given to the theater and its producer "whose policy of presenting new dramatic works continues most faithfully in the tradition of Margo Jones."

Margo Jones's torch was carried all over America by men and women like her. In Houston, Nina Vance, her former assistant, founded an amateur group in 1947 who performed at the end of a long brick alley. She called it the Alley Theatre, then had misgivings about the name because "it smacked of bohemianism." But the playhouse caught on, turned professional a few seasons later, and through the beneficence of the Ford Foundation moved into a modern two-theater complex in downtown Houston. By the time Mrs. Vance died, in 1980, the theater was entrenched in the cultural life of the city, and it continues to flourish today under new leadership.

Three years after Mrs. Vance set up shop in Houston, six people affiliated with

In 1973 Charles Ludlam audaciously adapted a nineteenth-century tearjerker to his own special talents. Here he is as Camille with company member Bill Vehr.

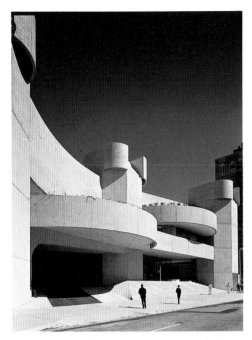

Nina Vance saw a dream come true in 1968, when her new Alley Theatre, a modern poured-concrete complex (300-seat arena-style auditorium, 800-seat fan-shaped playhouse, plus offices and workrooms) opened at the north end of Civic Center Plaza in downtown Houston. Architect Ulrich Franzen described it: "as ancient as stone and as modern as Houston."

In 1964 Richard Block and Ewel Cornett mounted their productions in an old Louisville bank building, which they had converted into a playhouse, launching the Actors Theatre.

Washington University founded the Arena Stage, under the artistic leadership of Edward Mangum, a university professor, and opened their first season in an old Washington, D.C., movie house. After Mangum departed and four of the remaining group drifted away, Zelda Fichandler was left to carry on the dream. She reassembled the company in 1956 in an old brewery, which was immediately and piquantly dubbed "the Old Vat" and had the aroma to go with it. Gradually she built both an audience and a reputation for excellence. In 1961 the Arena, too, was tapped by the golden wand of the Ford Foundation. The company moved into a new complex with a modern theater-in-the-round plus ancillary spaces. In recent years, Mrs. Fichandler, with her husband as co-director, has added a second theater with a modified thrust stage and a small cabaret, nostalgically named the Old Vat Room, to provide entertainment for a quarter of a million Washingtonians. The Arena has fulfilled Margo Jones's dream of providing a home for playwrights, as Mrs. Fichandler has sent the cream of her crop to New York.

Most regional theaters started as small seedlings that were tended with love, care, and hard work by steel-spined dreamers such as Zelda Fichandler, but one of them sprang full-grown from its creators' heads in 1963. Oliver Rea and Peter Zeisler, both living and working in New York, wanted to start a regional theater devoted to the classics in a hospitable American city. They had the good sense to enlist the aid of Tyrone Guthrie, the eminent British director, who became an equal partner in the enterprise. In a stroke of brave and brilliant press-agentry, they prevailed upon Brooks Atkinson to insert a paragraph in his *New York Times* column announcing the plan and asking if there were any takers. Seven cities responded and Rea, Guthrie, and Guthrie's wife took to the air "equipped with spears and blowpipes, with pretty beads, bright shells and jews' harps to bribe the native chieftains" in Boston, San Francisco, Cleveland, Detroit, Minneapolis, and Milwaukee. The denizens of Minneapolis allowed themselves to be bribed, and four-and-a-half years of back-breaking fund raising and planning brought forth a splendid theater and an equally splendid company in their city. After several peerless four-month seasons, the original luster began to wear thin and the enthusiastic subscribers slowly dropped away. Subsequent directors lengthened the season, but costs outran receipts. At the end of the 1983 season, the Guthrie had a huge deficit and had to suspend the resident actors from the company for the first time. Under the direction of the Rumanian-born director Liviu Ciulei, who took over in 1981, it began to bounce back. Ciulei made alterations in the theater and launched an aggressive campaign to return the theater to experimentation, but his resignation effective at the close of the 1986 season may signal another period of change.

Founded in 1964, the Actors Theatre of Louisville was also conceived as a repertory theater. Initially, the company presented well-acted, carefully mounted productions of revivals in a made-over bank building on Main Street. In 1969 Jon Jory, fresh from some pioneering work at the Long Wharf Theatre in New Haven, took over as artistic director and energized the company. In 1977 he began to deemphasize the classics and Broadway retreads in favor of original plays by American authors. The festival he staged in April of that year has now blossomed into an annual rite of spring that attracts agents from Broadway and Hollywood as well as interested visitors from all over the world. Unfortunately, its organizers have become self-conscious about its mission. A brochure proclaims that the "Louisville Festival gives you a chance to pick the big winners first and let New Yorkers pay triple prices later." Jory claims that the Actors Theatre has discovered a hundred new American playwrights and points to the three Pulitzer Prizes won by writers who began with his company. Operating with a staff of one hundred, a budget of nearly $2.5 million, hundreds of volunteers, and a well-oiled promotional campaign, the Actors Theatre flourishes in a medium-sized American city but has developed a big-city profile. It has become the essential American theatrical success story.

In the last twenty years or so, perhaps following the lead of Lincoln Center in New York and Kennedy Center in Washington, a number of regional cities have chosen to group their performing-arts activities downtown in a clump of buildings. The most stunning of these massive architectural-cultural statements is the Denver Center for the Performing Arts, which includes among its constituent parts the Denver Theatre Center. The dream of one man, Donald Seawell—a Broadway producer who has moved his sphere to the Mile High City—and the beneficiary of a trust fund from the Helen G. Bonfils Foundation, the Denver Theatre Center is housed in a magnificent tentlike structure of steel and glass with a large lobby that enwraps three theaters: the Stage, the Space, and the Lab, each of which has a separate function. Opened in 1980, the center has operated on a rotating repertory system, offering as many as seven or eight plays in its two main theaters and a number of experimental plays, free to the public, in its laboratory theater. Triply blessed with sound management, a state-of-the-art physical facility, and adequate funds, the Denver company is struggling to find an identity and an audience.

Private subsidy has been a constant factor in the survival of little theaters. The Otto Kahns of the first wave have been supplanted by foundations and corporations, who have been spurred into giving away their excess cash through adjustments in the Internal Revenue laws. For many years, wealthy citizens and corporations used tax-exempt foundations to hide their embarrassment of riches from the prying eyes of the government, but in 1950 Congress made it illegal for foundations to hoard income. This came as a blow to the directors, who quickly had to find ways of giving away their money. It was no longer enough just to support the pet charity and, forced to explore other fields, they found that they could not completely neglect the arts. Trickles of money began flowing into the little theaters during the 1950s and 1960s. Then in 1969 the government, having begun to tax the income of the foundations, issued a mandate that 6 percent of the market value of their assets must be given away. Education, health, science, and welfare agencies remain the favored beneficiaries of the foundations, but about 10 percent of their money finds its way to the arts and humanities, the part of the pie that the theaters must share.

As a result of these events, the theaters beyond and off Broadway had a decision to make: whether to struggle to find a niche in the profit-making world of the commercial theater or to become not-for-profit enterprises, sharing in the golden pot created by government regulations. It was apparently not a difficult decision to make, and one by one they traded in their artistic manifestos for legal corporate charters attesting to their nonprofit status and started to apply to foundations for funds. Soon staid and stiff-backed conservative foundations found themselves making out checks to little-theater groups around the country, many of which they had never heard of and, in less enlightened times, would never have approved of.

Without a whisper of a doubt, the foundation that has been most generous to the postwar little-theater movement is the Ford Foundation. It was set up in 1936 as a small, family-dominated organization "to receive and administer funds for scientific, educational and charitable purposes, all for the public welfare and for no other purpose"—a statement of generality at its sublimest. In 1956 the foundation received a bonanza when Henry Ford II began to divest himself of his stock in the Ford Motor Company, a percentage of which was dedicated to the trust. Since that time, the foundation has sold off its Ford holdings, making it effectively free of family influence. The Ford Foundation has been sensitive to swings in the economic cycle and has been subject to the usual directorial idiosyncrasies, but it survives today as the richest foundation in the world, with assets of nearly $3.5 billion.

From 1957 to 1975, the division of the humanities and the arts was under the aegis of E. MacNeil Lowry, to the happy providence of the nonprofit little theaters. During his reign, the Ford Foundation nursed, cosseted, and supported them: it gave them money to build theaters or to expand and modernize their facilities; it provided funds to raise actors' salaries in order to strengthen the professionalism of the companies; it made grants to develop audiences, particularly among the young; and it financed a host of projects and experiments to keep the movement alive, responsive, and vital. From 1962 to 1968 alone, it allotted more than $10 million to the regional theaters

Zelda Fichandler, artistic director of Arena Stage in Washington, D.C., has given a hearing to new and untried playwrights, many of whom later moved on to greater glory in New York. She is seen here at a rehearsal for Screenplay early in 1983.

and in 1961 it set up the independent Theatre Communications Group, Inc., to function as a clearinghouse and service agency for the widespread groups. Headquartered in New York, this organization keeps the member theaters in touch with each other and creates a sense of unity and continuity among and within them. The director of the agency, Peter Zeisler, has credited Lowry with changing the face of American theater through the support of his office, and he may be right. Since Lowry's retirement from the foundation, there has been a marked diminution in the attention given to the regional-theater movement. Today, the Ford Foundation funnels grants to all arts organizations through an offshoot, the National Arts Stabilization Fund, to help them achieve greater financial stability through better management of their resources.

There are more than two thousand foundations in America with assets of more than $1 million, and there is an even greater number of smaller, localized trusts and corporate funds. The share of the more than $2 billion that is currently dispensed annually by the foundations to the arts organizations is minuscule compared to the share given to educational, scientific, and welfare interests, but it is very visible because the theater is very visible, particularly at the small or medium-sized city level. The fact, for instance, that the Humana Corporation sponsors the annual play festival of the Actors Theatre in Louisville is widely advertised in all of the publicity generated by the event. Undoubtedly, foundations and corporations enjoy basking in the reflected glory of the successful groups they sponsor. It is simply the American way of doing things, part of the system, good business and public relations—and if any real artistic benefits accrue, well, it is to the good of everyone concerned.

In 1964 a dream of the liberal politicians came into being with the establishment of the National Council for the Arts and the Humanities. A year later the first funds, a modest 2.5 million tax dollars, were dedicated to strengthening the cultural life of the country through the National Endowment for the Arts (NEA) and the National Endowment for the Humanities. Today, federal support of both endowments has climbed to more then $300 million. The nonprofit theaters must compete with all other arts groups for NEA dollars, but they have received their fair share of help and it has made a difference in their ability to survive in difficult times. In 1978 NEA support of the theaters came to about $9.5 million, but it has dropped sharply in recent years under administrations with different policies. Although in its support of the arts the United States suffers in any superficial comparison with the European countries, the hidden role of our government is generally overlooked. By regulating the foundations and by providing significant tax reductions to private citizens in all brackets who contribute to the nonprofit arts organizations, the federal government sweetens the pot considerably. In 1973, a year for which complete data are available, the government supported the arts to the tune of $650 million, of which $200 million came in direct grants and $450 million in indirect aid via tax regulations. It is highly likely that direct and indirect funding of the arts today may be approaching $1 billion, which is still not quite the cost of one superweapon in the nation's defense arsenal, but which represents a much greater commitment than anyone could have predicted when the government slowly and painfully lurched into its policy of supporting the arts in the postwar years.

Even the commercial theater in New York has taken a somewhat avuncular role toward the nonprofit groups. In 1967 the Theatre Development Fund (TDF), created by the League of New York Theatres and Producers, was established to develop audiences for the commercial theater, but it has since expanded its activities to include support of the Off-Broadway and Off-Off-Broadway groups as well. In the years since it was set up, the TDF has accumulated a huge mailing list of theatergoers within the city and in neighboring states, to whom it sends notices of reduced-price tickets and offers of low-cost vouchers that can be redeemed for tickets at the box offices of little theaters (sometimes with an additional charge). The vouchers cashed in by the groups are an additional source of revenue but, more important, they represent an audience that would have remained untapped but for the far-reaching

activities of the TDF. The agency also maintains a collection from which nonprofit, educational, and community theaters may rent costumes at rates much lower than those of the established commercial rental companies.

With help forthcoming from the commercial theater, from the NEA and the foundations, from corporations and individuals, the little theaters need not feel quite so abandoned as they did in the early years after the war. The fact that the Arena Stage in Washington, the New York Shakespeare Festival, the Cleveland Play House, the Actors Theatre of Louisville, the Barter Theatre in Virginia, the Dallas Theater Center, and the Alley Theatre in Texas, plus a score or two others, now have histories that span more than several decades attests to the permanence of the little-theater movement. In a variety of forms, with a variety of policies, established in a

With Oliver Rea and Peter Zeisler, Tyrone Guthrie created the theater that bears his name in Minneapolis. In this picture, he is shown striding across the structural framework of the stage.

Lonne Elder's exuberant Ceremonies in Dark Old Men *was a wise choice for a subsidized national tour in 1984. Seen here, from left to right, are members of the Negro Ensemble Company in a performance on the road: Walter Allen Bonnett, Jr., Ruben Hudson, Patty Holly, and Douglas Turner Ward.*

variety of spaces, the little theater is here to stay.

Yet, many insist that there is still something missing, a federally subsidized institution that would represent the best theater in America, much as the Comédie-Française and the National Theatre of Britain represent the best theater in their respective countries. They forget that Congress did indeed create a national theater in 1935, when it enacted the charter of the American National Theatre and Academy (ANTA) without appropriating any money to support it. In the days immediately following its establishment, ANTA was eclipsed by the Federal Theatre Project, sat out the war, was resuscitated in 1945 and headquartered in New York under different leadership, acquired a theater (the old Guild) in 1950, set up a school and closed it, experienced periods of dormancy followed by small explosions of rekindled interest, and has generally had a hard time of it. Without funds or recognition through most of its history, ANTA has had to rely on the efforts of interested theater people, most of whom have had to devote their time and energy on a volunteer basis (and, sometimes, support it financially). Although chapters were formed outside New York, the lion's share of its activities took place in New York, which was its nerve center as well as its heart and head. After another long sleep, ANTA appeared in the news again in 1981, when its board sold off the Guild Theatre for $5 million, which it intends to use to launch productions from the government-built and government-buttressed Kennedy Center in the nation's capital to other theatrical centers. Roger Stevens, who runs Kennedy Center, and Donald Seawell, chairman of the board of ANTA, together head the joint venture, and they have appointed the first artistic director, Peter Sellars, who is noted for his unconventional dramatic and operatic productions, and hope to take what they have described as the "first steps toward the foundation of an American national theater company." ANTA appears to have been born again, but only time will tell whether it can fulfill its mission as the duly legislated National Theatre.

While all of this was going on in Washington, Joseph Papp in New York formulated an audacious proposal that would include commercial theater in New York as part of a grand plan for a national theater. Citing the widespread destruction of theater buildings since World War II, and arguing that nothing but lavish musicals can succeed profitably on Broadway, he predicts that the time will one day arrive when all New York theaters will be publicly administered with money from a trust fund established by grants from the city, state, and federal governments and augmented by the sale to real-estate developers of "air rights" above the buildings themselves. Visionary in its current form, Papp's plan recognizes without apology the importance of Broadway as a stimulant to all theatrical activity in the country and speaks forcefully for its continuance as the nation's theatrical showcase.

Throughout the centuries, there have been attempts at private subsidy of "national" theaters. The Park Theatre in New York and the Chestnut Street Theatre in Philadelphia would not have come into existence without the interest and financial support of the wealthy classes. More than a century later, in 1909, another generation of New York patricians tried again, erecting a splendid, subsidized edifice on Central Park West, which they named the New Theatre. This national theater of sorts lasted only two seasons and was brought down by the grandeur of the productions and by its millionaire backers' pretentious perceptions of what comprised theatrical art—both of which were regarded suspiciously by the audiences which the New Theatre was intended to attract. In strong contrast was the publicly supported City Center of Music and Drama in New York, which was created a generation later, under the administration of Fiorello La Guardia in 1943, and was housed in the dilapidated and cavernous Mecca Temple on West Fifty-fifth Street. Perceived from the beginning as a no-frills and low-priced theater, popular in the best sense of the word, the City Center lived up to expectations, and only the New York City Theatre Company, created by Jean Dalrymple, the profit-making constituent of the center, did not survive the trip to the new quarters of the ballet and opera companies at Lincoln Center.

Why a National Theater, when a national theater has slipped quietly into place? With the North, South, East, and West served by professional regional theaters, decentralization has already occurred. Now that the important regional theaters send their best to Broadway, the flow of plays and professional talent has been reversed significantly for the first time in American history. With Off Broadway and Off Off Broadway harboring experimental, black, Oriental, Hispanic, Shakespearean, gay and lesbian, repertory, and mime troupes, cultural and ethnic diversity has been achieved without fanfare. America's other theater is underwritten by a friendly partnership of private citizens, foundations, corporations, and government agencies, and this way of paying for it has been accepted by Americans of nearly every political persuasion. What better example of the nationalization of American theater can be given than the sponsorship by a New York bank of a 1984 revival of *Ceremonies in Dark Old Men* by the Negro Ensemble Company, which will tour fifteen or twenty cities in the country nationwide and, perhaps, the major cities of Europe? The little-theater movement, which began tentatively in the last years of the nineteenth century and blossomed in the twentieth century as the fountainhead of American theatrical genius, has assumed its rightful role as America's national theater.

Overleaf:
Under the direction of Joseph Papp, free performances of Shakespeare's plays attracted great crowds to the New York Shakespeare Festival at the Delacorte Theater in Central Park beginning in the late 1950s. This photograph dates from the early 1960s.

THEATER IN AMERICA:
PAST, PRESENT, AND FUTURE

I t is not surprising that the American theater came of age when the country came of age. Global events pushed America into finding its political and ideological identity on the world stage in the early years of the twentieth century and, at same time, prodded the country to define its cultural identity at home. The theater did not react so quickly as the other arts to changing conditions, probably because it was shedding century-old practices and evolving a new system of production. Although the theater would continue to be star-driven well into the twentieth century, the star was becoming an employee of others, entrepreneurs with artistic pretensions. By 1900 the old stock company, resident in its own playhouse, with a sheaf of plays in its repertory, and headed by one of its own—most often a star-manager or a playwright-manager—had become obsolete. The system that begat stars and trained each successive generation of actors was a thing of the past despite sporadic attempts to revive it. Increasingly, shows were assembled one by one by men and women (the producers), who formed companies customized to the play or musical. They assembled the personnel to whip a show into shape (the director) and set it into its own scenic environment and dress the actors (the scene and costume designers), and, last but not least, a complement of actors cast to perfection for the roles they were to assay. Each show needed its own special style and look, and the producer made sure that it got it. Everyone was striving for a long run.

Although the script remained (and continues to remain) the raw material of theatrical performance, playwrights in the newly evolved system began to "sell" their original plays to producers in return for a monetary advance and royalties on future performances. More important, they demanded—and got—an expanded role in the collaborative process. When the new century dawned, all the pieces were coming together. With periodic adjustments as a result of changing conditions both within and without the world of the theater, the collaborative system was established and has endured. One notable break in the tradition has been the absence since the 1970s of new stars exclusively of the stage, whose attachment to certain producers would ensure them a constant flow of "vehicles" for their talents.

Early in the new century, collaborations were almost always dominated by the producer, and a few producers, like David Belasco and Charles Frohman, often functioned as their own directors. Belasco, a one man theatrical band, also had a hand in writing scripts and controlling the design of the shows he produced. In the 1920s, with the emergence of designers of extraordinary talent and imagination, such as Robert Edmond Jones, Norman Bel Geddes, and Lee Simonson, producers frequently saw the wisdom of allying themselves with one designer to ensure fully coordinated and seamless productions. Jones was the early favorite of producer-director Arthur Hopkins, while Simonson dedicated his work almost exclusively to the Theatre Guild. Later in the century, Jo Mielziner joined producer Dwight Deere Wiman's team and later was allied with Rodgers and Hammerstein in their musicals and with Elia Kazan in the production of Tennessee Williams's plays. In more recent times, collaborations became even more

Editor's note: This chapter brings *Theater in America* into the late 1990s. Some statements and predictions made in earlier chapters are reexamined here; new trends and new talents are explored. For a description of changes and additions that have been made elsewhere in the book, the reader should consult the Preface.

extended. George Abbott was among the first producer-directors to assemble complete teams from the 1930s on. During his lifetime, Michael Bennett surrounded himself with designers Robin Wagner (scenery), Theoni V. Aldredge (costumes), and Tharon Musser (lighting) for his most successful ventures. Harold Prince is another producer-director who has continued to use the same people again and again. What has been learned from the collaborative process is that individual members of the team can spark each other's imaginations and thus, by the generated electricity, each contributes to the success of a show. Although in past years playwrights maintained loyalties to certain producers—Eugene O'Neill to the Theatre Guild, Lillian Hellman to John Golden, and George S. Kaufman to Max Gordon—today the author of a script sells it to the highest bidder. In recent memory, only Neil Simon has continued his association with a single Broadway producer, Emanuel Azenberg.

In resident or regional theaters both in and out of New York, collaboration among administrators, directors, and designers is the foundation of most companies. As on Broadway, the only stable elements missing are the actor, who remains peripatetic, and the playwright, who occasionally aligns himself with a regional company, as has Terrence McNally with the Manhattan Theatre Club. Then, the artistic net also encloses the writer of the scripts. Outside talents, and even whole productions from sister regionals, are brought in to augment the resident artistic company and to vary the menu from time to time. Collaboration emerged at the beginning of the century as a pragmatic solution to reorganizing the theater from the ashes of the old stock-company repertory system, primarily to enable entrepreneurs to make the theater profitable for themselves. Happily, it has resulted in the frequent creation of perfectly realized theatrical productions with all elements meshing into an artistic whole. There appears to be no system emerging that is better and will take its place.

Today, the death of the theater is predicted almost on a daily basis and, to paraphrase Mark Twain, the reports are always greatly exaggerated. True, Broadway and the American theater have seen much better days. A backward glance attests to this. In the year 1900, Broadway audiences had their pick of nearly 120 different productions in dozens of theaters located from Fourteenth to Forty-fifth Street, an area that encompassed the dying theater district and the new one abuilding farther uptown. Running were 80 plays (not counting Shakespearean productions), and these embraced dramas, comedies, and farces from the pens of writers both foreign and domestic, including Henrik Ibsen, Alexander Ostrovsky, Gerhart Hauptmann, George Bernard Shaw, Arthur Wing Pinero, William Butler Yeats, and Georges Feydeau from abroad and the home-bred dramatists Augustus Thomas, Clyde Fitch, Edward Sheldon, George Broadhurst, James A. Herne, and Israel Zangwill. (Fitch, then at the height of his career,

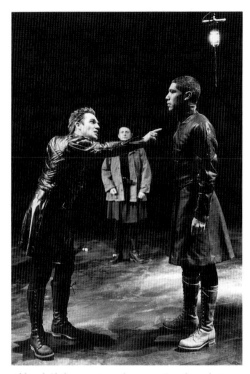

Although Shakespeare is rarely seen on Broadway, he is alive and well in America, thanks to regional theaters from coast to coast, where his plays continue to outstrip every other playwright's, alive or dead. Regional theater is also the place where actors of note from the stage and films can go to stretch themselves in classical roles. At the Hartford Stage in 1994, Richard Thomas (left) appeared as the dark and evil Richard III under the direction of Mark Lamos. Seen with him here are Peter Von Berg (center) and Peter Francis James.

had ten plays running both in New York and on the road in one season.) In bright lights, marquees writ large the names of the stars: John Drew, Richard Mansfield, William Gillette (as Sherlock Holmes), Otis Skinner (in a play he wrote himself), James O'Neill (in his old warhorse *The Count of Monte Cristo*), Maude Adams, Marie Dressler, Olga Nethersole, Mrs. Leslie Carter, and Henry Miller. The year 1900 was notable in other ways. In the same season, two rival productions of *Quo Vadis* opened on the same evening, which kept the critics hopping and schizophrenic.

In those days, actors sometimes unjustly bore the brunt of censure for the productions in which they were appearing. (Although as Helen Hayes once somewhat impatiently observed, actors don't write the lines they speak, the public and their unelected representatives—the critics—often choose to believe otherwise.) On March 5, the police padlocked Wallack's Theatre, which was showing Fitch's *Sapho*, to prevent Olga Nethersole, the heroine, from being carried by her leading man up the stage steps to a night of (imagined) illicit love. (Miss Nethersole was later acquitted of charges of public immorality and resumed the role.) Best of all, two dollars got theatergoers the best seats in the house to see this daring scene, and as little as twenty-five cents got them through the door.

In that year 1900, when several productions of Shakespeare were on the boards, theatergoers could choose between E. H. Sothern in his first appearance as Hamlet or Sarah Bernhardt in breeches in the same role at the beginning of another of her lucrative tours of the American provinces. In addition to the serious stuff, there were more than twenty new musical comedies and almost a dozen musical novelties billed as "extravaganzas" or "fantasies" or "vaudevilles" or "burlesques." Musicals by John Philip Sousa, Victor Herbert, and Reginald De Koven were among the offerings, but the biggest success was achieved by *Florodora*, which began its run on November 10, 1900, and finally rang down the curtain after the Florodora Sextet, a bevy of demurely dressed chorus girls, had answered for the 505th time the ardent question pressed by six top-hatted chorus boys: "Tell Me, Pretty Maiden, Are There Any More at Home Like You?"

Beyond Broadway, more than 300 companies fanned out across the country performing spin-offs from popular Broadway successes of previous seasons as well as the standard repertory fare. Sometimes they lingered a week in a town or city, but most of the time the productions were up and down after one night. The price of tickets ranged from fifteen cents to a dollar in the 3,000 or more provincial theaters. Most of the major cities had multiple theaters and productions with standing and, often, long-running companies. The entire country bristled with theatrical activity.

A century later, all that has changed. Although theatrical activity from coast to coast may not have lessened in quantity and may, in many instances, have improved in quality, theater in America has undergone enormous upheaval. Gone are the commercial playhouses in every town and city, organized in "circuits" and controlled by a few powerful men in New York. (With them went the audiences of ordinary people who bought tickets to the many "direct-from-Broadway" offerings.) In their place are regional theaters, both large and small, which provide live entertainment that may range from a production of the latest Broadway hit to Shakespearean drama or a work in progress, either play or musical, on its way to New York. Gone are the legendary producers of Broadway, who put together teams of collaborators to prepare promising scripts and who raised the money from investors eager to take their chances on another *Oklahoma!* or *Life with Father*. In their place are General Managers, who take their orders from the investors, from producing organizations, and from theater owners, who put up the money but have little creative role in the development of a show. Gone is the crop of new plays each season from American playwrights, who routinely contributed one or more works to make the rounds of theaters from Broadway to Spokane during an era that lasted from the 1920s to the 1950s. Playwriting has become a precarious profession, but that fact does not appear to have discouraged men and women from attempting the impossible.

In the intervening years, from the 1960s to the present, critics and observers of the theatrical scene bemoaned the lack of fresh writing talent in the American theater, particularly on Broadway, and asked with prickly persistence: Where are the new

David Henry Hwang's M. Butterfly was given a spectacular production on Broadway after moving from the National Theater in Washington, D.C., in 1988. Hwang, the son of first-generation Americans, grew up in California and was educated at Stanford University and the Yale School of Drama, all the while developing his talents as a playwright. In M. Butterfly, he successfully fused traditions of the East and West as he told the saga of a French diplomat Rene Gallimard (John Lithgow, below) in love with Song Liling, a Beijing Opera singer (B. D. Wong, above), who is really a man disguised as a woman—and a spy in the bargain. The play was staged in a semi–Chinese-opera style with the strains of Giacomo Puccini's Madame Butterfly as background music.

O'Neills and Williamses? In a piece he wrote in 1988 for the *New York Times*, the dean of American theater critics, Walter Kerr, stated unequivocally: "The American theater does not lack for playwrights. It has playwrights, plenty of them, mostly young ones. They are all over the place, and when I say playwrights I mean that they have not only written plays, they have had at least one produced professionally and they have stood there and watched it *succeed*." In a sense, Kerr is correct in his assessment, but the American theater traditionally has rejoiced and flourished when one of them—the Master Playwright—stood out from the rest and pulled in audiences at the mere mention of his (and occasionally *her*) name. Until the 1960s, the Master Playwright was able to cast a glow over the efforts of his lesser contemporaries. For many years, Eugene O'Neill did just that. He was followed by Arthur Miller and Tennessee Williams, who enjoyed their moment of glory under Broadway's sun. No longer first among many, Miller continues to write but has been badly buffeted by the critics every time a new play of his has appeared. Unlike the Miller of old, his plays are likely to be presented away from rather than on Broadway. When Williams died in 1983, he was a has-been, a playwright everyone remembered but considered sadly out of touch with present-day issues. Certainly the 1960s and 1970s engendered a new wave of playwrights, the young ones that Kerr alludes to, but not one of them has emerged as the hope of the American theater, nor is it likely that there will be a single powerful voice that will dominate all the rest very soon.

The Reagan policies of the 1980s chilled many creative impulses by producing an atmosphere that deemphasized the arts at the same time it promoted materialism in its most virulent form. Reforms in the income taxes paid by the rich no longer encouraged donors to contribute to not-for-profit arts organizations to receive tax deductions. This significant loss of revenue led to widespread retrenchment among all of them. In the more temperate climate of the early 1990s, playwrights chose to raise the flag of artistic multiculturalism, dumping out the melting pot and demystifying it. The chorus of voices includes Luis Valdez, who has written and rewritten (as time and circumstance changed) the drama of the Chicano in California, and David Henry Hwang, who sometimes uses a technique reminiscent of Chinese opera to describe the schizophrenia of the Chinese American, faced with the American immigrant's eternal dilemma of choosing between heritage and assimilation. For August Wilson, the stage is a platform to elucidate what it has been like being black in America in each decade since 1900. The apostate Catholic Christopher Durang does not hesitate to satirize authority in any of its forms, religious, secular, or psychological. Plays by the late Miguel Piñero depict the world of the macho Puerto Rican male and his almost inevitable brushes with the law. On other fronts, Wendy Wasserstein continues to explore the ambivalence of the liberated woman toward her own hard-won and imperfect liberation, and A. R. Gurney scrutinizes the morbidity of WASPdom in America. Tony Kushner and William Finn have written wrenchingly about the ordeal of gay men as they struggle to survive under the shadow of AIDS, the disease that has preyed on homosexual men in disproportionate numbers. The concerns of playwrights have both enlarged and contracted. Many still write their own

Because he had a play written expressly for his particular talents, Charles S. Dutton can count himself among the most fortunate actors in recent Broadway history. He is here shown as a dreamer-drifter in August Wilson's The Piano Lesson (1990), which the playwright wrote for him after seeing what he could do in two of his previous plays, Ma Rainey's Black Bottom and Joe Turner's Come and Gone. At the start of his career, Dutton was an unlikely candidate for such an honor. A product of Baltimore's Latrobe Housing Project, growing up poor and black, he spent his formative years in and out of reform school and prison. While in prison, he began reading plays and was encouraged by a teacher to write and perform. Once out of prison, Dutton earned a college degree and was accepted at the Yale School of Drama. An instinctual actor, he needed the polish that he received at Yale. His career has enlarged to include films and television.

Wendy Wasserstein's peregrinations from fledgling to Broadway Pulitzer-Prize–winning playwright follow the typical story of most of the writers of her generation. First produced at the Yale School of Drama during the 1970s, moving on to Off Broadway and regional theater with her first successes in the 1980s, and then invading Broadway with The Heidi Chronicles, Wasserstein has been sustained along the way with grants and the encouragement of nonprofit producing groups. Like her previous plays, The Sisters Rosensweig (1992), about three sisters from Brooklyn whose lives have taken vastly divergent paths, mixed comedy with serious overtones. In a cheerful scene, the sisters toast each other (left to right): Madeline Kahn as Gorgeous, Jane Alexander as Sara, and Frances McDormand as Pfeni.

Several things are different about Mercedes Ruehl, who is shown here as Bella, the slow-witted daughter of Grandma Kurnitz (actress Irene Worth) in Lost in Yonkers. First, she is five feet ten inches tall and was told by everyone along the way that she would never make it as an actress because she would tower over leading men. Second, she received both a Tony Award (for Lost in Yonkers) and an Oscar (for the movie The Fisher King) in 1991, the first performer to be doubly honored in one year. Her preparation included the College of New Rochelle and studying acting in New York, plus about fifteen years of work in regional theater and off Broadway. She returned to New York in 1995 in a revival of Tennessee Williams's The Rose Tattoo, as the earthy Italian widow.

Although she made her Broadway debut in 1971, in Two Gentlemen of Verona, Stockard Channing began her career fresh out of Radcliffe College, acting with a Boston theater company. Hollywood was her next stop, then television, then more work on the stage in Los Angeles. Returning to the East, she has picked up plum roles along with awards. Her role as Ouisa Kittridge in Six Degrees of Separation (1990), the Park Avenue matron who befriends a young black man posing as Sidney Poitier's son (played by James McDaniel and seen with her in this picture) and is thereby led to self-revelation, came naturally to her. Her own Park Avenue upbringing resonated in her Tony-Award–winning performance.

private memoirs and of worlds bounded by the kitchen table. Others have used explosive theatrics to strike out against an American society torn by brutality and violence, a culture gone awry.

In the past, enjoying a hit on Broadway could bring almost instant wealth—and it still does occasionally to one or two—but almost all playwrights presently produced throughout America have been supported, but just barely, by a thin stream of funds coming from many directions. Securing grants from the National Endowment for the Arts, the John Simon Guggenheim Foundation, and scores of other foundations, and commissions from theater companies both east and west of the Hudson River and professional producing organizations has become a way of life for writers showing a glimmer of ability. As a showcase for their talents, producer George White founded the

Eugene O'Neill Theater Center, which since 1964 has produced readings of their plays-in-progress on indoor and outdoor stages in an informal summer-camp setting in Waterford, Connecticut. Professional actors, who read the scripts, and a covey of critics, who observe the proceedings, enable the emerging playwrights to see what they have wrought and how their work can be improved. Many of the O'Neill's "alumni" have moved into the mainstream of the country's theatrical life.

Without a commanding figure to lead it into the next millennium, the American theater relies on the cumulative impact of a generation of playwrights—some nurtured and some *born* in the 1960s, and some now approaching the edges of deep middle age—who all continue to write. They have much in common. Although most began their writing heavily influenced by English and European models, principally Pinter, Brecht, Chekhov, and Beckett, they now cross-pollinate, looking to each other for inspiration, which is a healthy sign. They have won Pulitzer Prizes and Tony Awards and now regard New York, once the center of the playwrights' universe, as a way station, albeit an important one, in their careers. A few of them, like Megan Terry, have all but abandoned New York to work in regional theater, while the rest commute from company to company to show their dramatic wares. It is both a bad time and a good time for American playwrights. Tina Howe, who has received some measure of success but not soaring fame as a playwright, believes it to be a remarkable time for writers: "There's a tremendous ache out there for what is daring and heartfelt. . . . I think the theater needs us more than ever. And it's pining for the outrageous part of us, not the cautious part." Perhaps that says it all.

Gone are the great stars of former eras. No one can expect dazzlingly talented actors to be satisfied with the comparatively meager rewards of live performing, both in the limited audiences they reach and in the relatively small financial gains they receive, when they can play to millions of people on big screens in movie theaters or on small screens in their own homes and make millions while doing it. The fact that a movie or television star may on occasion appear in New York or tour with a summer-stock company or even join a regional theater for a short spell is cause for rejoicing. Lloyd Richards, the longtime artistic director of the prestigious Yale Repertory Theatre, explains the absence of stars as a result of the rise of the regional theaters. Because these playhouses are scattered around the country, it has become almost impossible for actors to gain national fame if they work only in the regionals. For this, Richards also blames the popular perception that only Broadway can make stars and because of it, he suggests, "one of the things we have lost is our capacity to make or attract what are called stars" in the traditional name-in-lights-on-the-marquee sense. Once we have regional theater productions that routinely traverse the country, Richards would like to see engendered "a *national* perception of what has been a *regional* event." Actors can then gracefully ply their profession in the regionals without regarding them as a springboard to Broadway, always allowing for the bit of luck that will find them cast in a production headed to New York, still the country's ultimate showcase for talent. Whether one or more of them will achieve a special kind of stardom unknown in the twentieth century is anyone's guess.

Today's players prepare themselves for all eventualities. Having shucked off Lee Strasberg's Method, they adhere to no particular school or style of acting and many refuse to become typed by any of the parts they have played. Although the classical style perfected by English performers continues to elude them, they have remained faithful to the American tradition of eclecticism—trying new techniques and adapting to the contingencies of their roles—and in so doing they assure the ongoing healthy development of American acting. Although there are no Cornells or Lunt-and-Fontannes or Barrymores or Bankheads or Mermans, there are fine actors all over the place equal to every challenge. Actors learn how to sing and dance (Nathan Lane); dancers how to act (Bernadette Peters); and singer-dancers how to act (Gregory Hines). If American theater lacks stars in the old sense, it more than makes up for this lack with a generation of immensely talented and versatile actors who go everywhere, explore all forms of entertainment, and do everything extremely well.

Regional theater has not only become the informal training ground for actors, it is now an incubator for directors, who are given a chance to initiate the long apprenticeship necessary to achieve a place in the theatrical sun—away from the pressurized atmosphere of Broadway. Most contemporary directors began as actors, then experienced mid-life epiphanies that turned their lives around to the other side of the footlights. After making the switch, they have had to wait for at least one major successful production before they themselves and the world began to take them seriously as directors. More often than not in recent times, the process has run more smoothly when they have hitched their wagons to young, untried playwrights and have been pulled into the spotlight by these lucky associations. A case in point is the career of Lloyd Richards, whose work with not one but two playwrights has helped establish him as a director and also brought him the skills necessary to compete in the traditionally all-white theatrical world. Richards was the first African American to direct on Broadway. His big chance came in 1959 with a production of A Raisin in the Sun by Lorraine Hansberry. Although the success of the play opened up other opportunities for him, he was not offered plays by Tennessee Williams, Arthur Miller, William Inge, or any of the other important American (white) playwrights dominating the stage at the time. But in 1968, he found his niche out of New York as artistic director of the Eugene O'Neill Theater Center, a position that gave him access to the work of young, untried playwrights. A decade later, he became dean of the Yale School of Drama and artistic director of the Yale Repertory Theatre. In these capacities, he could produce plays by new writing talents and develop them in a way that could not be achieved in the unpressured atmosphere of the O'Neill Theater Center. As head of Yale Rep, he nurtured the careers of many playwrights, most notably August Wilson, whose work Richards introduced in the early 1980s and eventually took to Broadway. Replaying the most influential event in his own life but with a role change, Richards was able to do for Wilson what Hansberry had done for him: allow a latent talent to blossom. Richards summoned up Wilson's talent by letting him work unconstrained by playwriting conventions. In fact, he positively encouraged Wilson to listen to himself rather than others and to make mistakes if necessary. In Wilson's case, this risky director's technique worked and led to the creation of a series of dramas that were inexpertly crafted, yet powerful in their message.

This kind of creative partnership between director and playwright has been repeated again and again in recent memory. The artistic symbiosis between director Marshall Mason and playwright Lanford Wilson resembles the sympathetic bond between Elia Kazan and Tennessee Williams. Hearing the music in Wilson's lines, Mason evokes gently flowing yet deeply probing performances from the actors who create Wilson's characters. Founders of the Circle Repertory Theatre in New York in 1969, Mason and Wilson had the opportunity to develop their theatrical skills before being subjected to Broadway's limelight. Another near perfect melding of sensibilities has been achieved by director Gregory Mosher and playwright David Mamet. Mosher uses Mamet's language as the plays' action because Mamet's works are almost devoid of plot and physical action in the traditional stage sense. In Glen Garry, Glen Ross, Mosher had the actors speak Mamet's lines as drumbeats, which assaulted the ears of the audience but served the playwright's intent to make the real-estate hustlers appear without conscience or a shred of humanity. Both Mosher and Mamet served their apprenticeship at the Goodman Theatre in Chicago. Both were pulled into the mainstream in New York and have become the mainstream in New York.

Although Jerry Zaks found "his" playwright in Christopher Durang, he, too, has fanned out in other directions, moving past but not forgetting Durang. After directing several of the young playwright's comic satires, beginning in 1979 with the irreverent Off-Broadway hit Sister Mary Ignatius Explains It All for You, Zaks began to flourish as a director of comedies. A dynamic and voluble man, Zaks has for years zigzagged off and on Broadway and out into the regionals, gradually gathering speed in the 1990s. Now he can choose to direct any comedy by any writer in America. In the 1991–92 Broadway season, he branched out into musical comedy, directing a fast-paced revival of Guys and Dolls in

Not many actors can say that they began their careers as Jesus Christ, but Victor Garber did just that, playing the part in Godspell in a production in Toronto. The young Canadian, a high-school dropout still in his teens, expected his musical talents to take him into musical comedy or into rock music, but a part on Broadway in the long-running mystery melodrama Deathtrap (1978) revealed the actor in Garber. From that point on, he has been one of the most sought-after actors in the theater. In 1993, he returned to musical comedy as the Faustian devil Applegate (pictured here) in a revival of Damn Yankees, for which he received critical acclaim for singing, dancing, and acting.

The "overnight success" of Faith Prince in the 1992 revival of the musical Guys and Dolls had a twelve-year prelude of hard work and modest successes in shows both off Broadway and on the road. A graduate of the Cincinnati Conservatory of Music, Prince landed a part in the Boston company of Scrambled Feet and then began a long run in the Off-Broadway success Little Shop of Horrors (1982). A gifted comedienne, she delights audiences with her deft portrayals in the tradition of Nancy Walker, Judy Holliday, Edie Adams, and Carol Channing. Playing the eternal fiancé to Prince's sassy and brassy stripper (left) in the 1992 revival of Guys and Dolls is Nathan Lane (right), who grew up across the Hudson River from New York in Jersey City. Like Prince, he accumulated a long list of credits before making it into the Big Time. A favorite actor of playwright Terrence McNally, Lane appeared in a number of his plays off Broadway as well as in summer stock, dinner theater, and movies. Beginning in Los Angeles as half of the comedy team Stack and Lane, he has exercised his comedic talents in TV commercials and as one of the voices heard in Disney's animated film The Lion King.

his position as director-on-retainer for the Jujamcyn Theatre Organization. What approximates the comedy of manners in America has become the province of director John Tillinger, whose associations with playwrights A. R. Gurney and Terrence McNally at the prestigious regional Long Wharf Theatre in New Haven and the Manhattan Theatre Club in New York have not been the short road to Broadway but have led to a rich career all over the place, with an occasional sortie on Broadway. Zaks and Tillinger, who have been able to capture the special antic spirit of American comedy, are, surprisingly, not born-and-bred Americans. Both agree that their backgrounds in other traditions have given them a special insight in allowing them to step back, observe, and peel to the core of the plays that they were fortunate enough to direct.

Unlike Tillinger and Zaks, directors Mark Lamos, Jack O'Brien, and Daniel Sullivan have remained happily tied to a home base in regional theater after flings with the 1960s and 1970s Off-Broadway action in New York. They have sent some of their most successful productions to Broadway and could have used their achievements as a springboard to a career in New York theater. All serve as artistic directors of their theaters—Lamos at Hartford Stage, O'Brien at the Old Globe in San Diego, and Sullivan at Seattle Repertory—and all have directed plays of their choice year after year, governed only by what their subscribers would accept. In any given season they may direct Shakespeare, a recent Broadway hit, or a brand-new play. Lamos has become noted for giving an American twist to his Shakespearean productions, arguing convincingly that because American actors are not trained in a classical technique, they are from the start closer to the raw emotions of the texts than English interpreters of the

One of the busiest directors in the country, Jack O'Brien often moves productions that he has directed from his own venue, the Old Globe Theatre in San Diego, to niches on Broadway or off Broadway—winning acclaim and awards. His repertory consists of Shakespeare and the classics along with contemporary plays, which are mounted in any of three theaters comprising the Simon Edison Center for the Performing Arts. All costumes, sets, and props are constructed by resident artisans within the complex. O'Brien is seen here directing actors in William Congreve's The Way of the World at the Old Globe.

Bard. O'Brien's output has been prodigious. Directing at a furious pace at the Old Globe since 1981, he considers himself a "rep baby," born and brought up within the regional theater movement. Nonetheless, he has developed productions in San Diego with an eye to New York. Several have gone east as "packages" with the cast and scenery intact—like the 1993 revival of the musical *Damn Yankees*. Sullivan, whose tenure as artistic director of the Seattle Repertory began in the same year as O'Brien's at the Old Globe, travels to New York regularly to direct, scoring successes *on* Broadway with Herb Gardner's *Conversations with My Father* and *off* Broadway with Jon Robin Baitz's *Substance of Fire* at the Mitzi E. Newhouse Theater. But he always returns to Seattle. During his absences, he has made his home theater hospitable to plays-in-progress from other theatrical venues, each arriving complete with cast and director.

Unlike most of his colleagues, Des McAnuff, who has headed the La Jolla Playhouse in California since 1987, follows a highly personal agenda. He looks for a social or political message in the plays he directs and sets the style of the production accordingly. With the classics, he searches the text analytically until he finds a political or moral nuance that for him gives the play a special life. Overseeing the playhouse only half of each year, McAnuff is free in the other half to roam, taking directorial assignments as he chooses. In 1992, he and his team of collaborators in La Jolla reworked a rock musical, *The Who's Tommy*, and brought it to New York, where it enjoyed critical acclaim and a long run. In 1995, he advanced another step in his career by directing a revival of the 1961 musical *How to Succeed in Business Without Really Trying*, which also began in his nursery in La Jolla. McAnuff tailored it for 1990s audiences and succeeded in impressing Broadway critics.

It is impossible to pigeonhole Peter Sellars in any category or put one's finger on just who he is or what he is doing at any specific time. Sellars was the *enfant terrible* of the 1980s. With his prestigious MacArthur "genius" fellowship tucked under his arm, Sellars interpreted the classics in renditions that either scared people out of their wits and sent them running out of the theaters or kept them rooted in their seats. His work is explosive, outrageous, irreverent, and very personal. Sellars justifies his technique by what he sees in the text. Each play for him is like a Pandora's box: open the lid and all kinds of ideas fly out, each demanding to be heard. He will accompany spoken dialogue from the text, mixing it with video images and sound. He will dislocate scenery and costumes, create contemporary metaphors for the characters, move everything and everybody out of their time and place, and generally confuse the audiences. Sellars has said, "Art exists to be chewy." His brand of art has given indigestion to some of his critics but nourishment to his supporters. In 1984, Sellars received the surprise of his life when he was asked to head the American National Theatre at Washington's Kennedy Center. His tenure lasted two years, and then he was off and running to other projects. During the 1990s, Sellars has been involved in staging operas both here and abroad, employing his surrealist approach to fracture traditional methods and interpretations. He promises to return to the theater one day soon because he believes that he is a man for the new century.

A similar artistic ideology helped to bring to a quick end the tenure of JoAnne Akalaitis as artistic director and successor to Joseph Papp at the New York Shakespeare Festival. Although Akalaitis had been at the center of avant-gardist theater since the 1960s, she did not become a director until her late thirties. At that point, she looked around and discovered that the American theater did not abound in women directors and that she was an even rarer bird, a woman director *and* experimentalist. No one has expected her productions to be accessible to a wide audience. They always reflect her point of view, which is antitraditionalist and abstract. They are memorable to the right audiences because they can bring to light nuances in scripts that few thought existed. In 1983, she directed a production of *Endgame* by Samuel Beckett for the American Repertory Theatre in Cambridge, Massachusetts, setting it in a dank and littered subway station. Her choice of environment brought loud objections from the playwright himself from across the Atlantic, but she defended her right to interpret it through her own sensibilities. Before Papp tapped her as his artistic heir at the New York Shakespeare

Peter Sellars's theatrical iconoclasm thrives better in regional than in establishment theater. In 1994, when he attacked (and that is the appropriate verb to describe his directorial technique) Shakespeare's Merchant of Venice for the Goodman Theatre in Chicago, the unexpected was expected and audiences were not disappointed. Setting an empty stage with only tables and chairs as props, he conjured up a southern California beach town and peopled it with black, white, Asian, and Hispanic actors. He employed nine television monitors onstage and in the auditorium to promote his message that society has fallen into a state of decay. Paul Butler as Shylock (on the TV monitor) is black; Jessica (Portia Johnson) at right is black; and Launcelot (Philip Seymour Hoffman) and Old Gobbo (Del Close) are white. Old Gobbo wears a sandwich board that displays biblical graffiti.

JoAnne Akalaitis, the avant-gardist director, presented a controversial version of Samuel Beckett's Endgame at the American Repertory Theatre in Cambridge, Massachusetts, during its 1984–85 season. She set the play in a littered and dirty subway and directed a multiracial cast, even though Beckett's original stage directions did not call for either of these things. When the playwright objected, Akalaitis defended her right as a director to interpret the play as she saw it. Who controls the destiny of a script in production continues to be a tug-of-war between living playwrights and the interpreters of their work. Pictured are John Bottoms as Clov and Ben Halley, Jr., as Hamm.

Festival, she had tackled Shakespeare and the classics, staging a production of 'Tis Pity She's a Whore in 1992 that had about as many staunch supporters as outraged detractors. Like Sellars's, hers is a personal vision, and her productions display a seemingly scattershot and unpredictable technique, but are actually deliberate. She aims to shock, not to please. When the Shakespeare Festival began to lose subscribers and financial support and when her productions failed to garner critical acclaim, the board of directors refused to renew her contract.

Singer, dancer, film director, stage choreographer, film actor, TV performer, band leader, nightclub entertainer, Gregory Hines effortlessly meets every challenge to his wide-ranging talents. After growing up backstage at the Apollo Theatre in Harlem, he appeared on Broadway in the late 1970s, gaining considerable attention in Eubie *as an outstanding singer and dancer. A few seasons later, he headed the cast of the hit show* Sophisticated Ladies, *but then left the stage to pursue many other careers. Hines returned to Broadway triumphantly in 1992 to star in* Jelly's Last Jam, *winning a Tony Award for his portrayal of the jazz musician Jelly Roll Morton. He is shown here (center) executing one of his lively dances in* Jelly's Last Jam *surrounded by the dancing-singing chorus.*

A sprawling and dazzling dramatic display spread over two plays and lasting seven hours, Tony Kushner's Angels in America, *subtitled* A Gay Fantasia on National Themes, *cannot be adequately summarized. What it does convey is the angst of a gay playwright over the cultural and social milieu of the 1980s. Homosexuality with its joys and terrors is the leitmotiv of the dramas, which interweave at least three story lines involving heterosexual and homosexual couples and the last agonies of Joseph McCarthy's counsel Roy Cohn. The plays range without respect to chronology over the political landscape, summoning up the McCarthy anticommunist witch hunts along with the era of AIDS. Depending on one's reading of the symbolism, the "angels" in the title may mean either hope or death in a culturally arid America. Developed with grants to the playwright by the National Endowment for the Arts, the plays eventually made it to New York after a long tryout period in regional theater and in London and were showered with awards in 1993 and 1994. Pictured is Stephen Spinella, as the character dying of AIDS, being ministered to by the Angel (who has crashed through the ceiling), played by Ellen McLaughlin.*

When Akalaitis took over at the Shakespeare Festival, one of the resident directors was George C. Wolfe, an African-American writer whose star had begun to rise in the mid-1980s. At the Public Theater, under Papp's approving gaze, he was allowed to write and direct, but it was not until 1992, when he reached Broadway with a musical production of *Jelly's Last Jam*, that his full force was felt. The show, a dramatic biography of Jelly Roll Morton, a 1930s jazz musician who never came to terms with his African roots, was both written and directed by Wolfe. In his cool, intellectual appraisal of Morton's life, a few critics divined a Brechtian approach. Since Wolfe had recently directed Brecht's *The Caucasian Chalk Circle* at the Public, he may still have been under the influence of the famed *Verfremdungseffekt*, Brecht's artistic credo of distancing the audience from the drama. Yet it is clear that Wolfe's own preference as a director is for a conscious theatricality, a cerebral approach, that may rob his productions of some emotional impact. When Tony Kushner's *Angels in America* was brought to Broadway after its break-in period in 1992 at the Mark Taper Forum in Los Angeles, Wolfe replaced Oskar Eustis, the original director. He transformed a sprawling play into a pageant, a visual smorgasbord, as well as an assault on the mind and sensibilities of his audiences. Perhaps it is too early to make pronouncements about Wolfe's place in the American theater, but he is riding the crest of his 1990s successes, which may well propel him into the new century as a formidable figure.

The "new" generation of directors is not young in age because the making of a director takes at least a decade and becoming practiced in the profession takes almost that long. Few directors are at their top speed until they reach their forties. Once they have achieved success in New York or in the regionals, their longevity is almost assured. They can take heart from the career of George Abbott, who continued to direct well into his eighties. To all of them, directing has become a very personal journey of discovery. All say that they rely on the script for inspiration, all say that they depend on actors to fill out the blank check that is the essence of their characters, all agree that every play is open to interpretation. Each has his or her own method of reaching the goal. Loud voice or gentle coaxing, analytical rehearsal preparation or off-the-top-of-the-head improvisations, creation of a nurturing or a deliberately tense atmosphere, articulate verbalization of the action or grunts and body language to convey direction—all generations of directors use a variety of techniques to achieve their goals. Directing is a "customized job" and derives its methods from each script, each actor, each scenic environment, and every other element in a play. Occasionally the seams can be visible, particularly when the director opts for self-conscious theatricality *à la* Sellars and Akalaitis, but most of the time good directing remains invisible to the audience. Ask any director: the greatest rewards of the job remain in the actual creation.

In 1993, The Who's Tommy came to Broadway from the La Jolla Playhouse with designer John Arnone's set virtually intact. Arnone, who started out as an actor, became a designer by accident. When assignments were being made for a production of Vanities (1976) by the Lion Theatre Company, of which he was a founder, the job of designing the scenery was all that was left and fell to him. When the production turned into a hit and became an Off-Broadway legend (it still holds the record as the longest-running nonmusical production off Broadway), Arnone's life was changed. Design jobs were offered to him and, to fill in the gaps of his knowledge about his new calling, he enrolled in the Parsons School of Design and Lester Polakov's Studio. Thereafter, he found his services much in demand in regional theaters throughout the country, and this eventually led him to Broadway. Arnone's work is characterized by a self-conscious theatricality. His set for The Who's Tommy was a display of lighting pyrotechnics wedded to scenery that flashed across the stage in quick-moving segments. At center: Michael Cerveris as Tommy.

Billed as a full-length musical in one act, Once on This Island (with book and lyrics by Lynn Ahrens and music by Stephen Flaherty) was a "small" show by any standards. Without the stars and the trappings of the typical big Broadway musical, and beautifully directed and choreographed by Graciela Daniele, it enacted a folktale from an island in the French Antilles about the love of a black peasant girl for a light-skinned "grand homme" and its sad consequences. Performed entirely in song and dance by a talented group of performers, it managed to charm its way from Playwrights Horizons and Off Broadway into a niche on Broadway in 1990. Left to right: Ellis E. Williams, Sheila Gibbs, Gerry McIntyre, Andrea Frierson, Kecia Lewis-Evans, Milton Craig Nealy, Nikki Rene, and Eric Riley.

An example of what can be done with good old songs and a bad old book, Crazy for You became a success in 1992 largely on the strength of lively staging, marvelous scenery and costumes and, most important, the brilliance of Susan Stroman's choreography, which was rewarded with a Tony Award. With songs by George and Ira Gershwin, borrowed from several of their greatest shows, and the book inspired by the Guy Bolton–John McGowan original, Girl Crazy, this modern pastiche benefited from the best elements of both. The show also gave heart to audiences long accustomed to having dancing de-emphasized in musicals during the 1970s and 1980s, and who believed that American inventiveness in dance was past its prime. Now a sought-after choreographer, Stroman moved on to Harold Prince's revival of Show Boat in the season of 1994–95 and the second of her Tony Awards. Left to right: Tripp Hanson, Jeffrey Broadhurst, and Ray Roderick, part of the dancing-singing chorus in one of the lively routines of Crazy for You.

311

Like directors, choreographers usually started out in the theater as performers in a tradition that began with the fabled careers of George Balanchine, Agnes de Mille, and Jerome Robbins. Age takes its toll earlier on dancers than on any of the other theater professionals and becomes a compelling reason for some of them to change direction. Many of the current crop have moved from the dancing chorus of Broadway musicals into assistantships with the leading choreographers of the day. Bob Avian, who first appeared as a Broadway dancer in *West Side Story*, a Robbins creation, became the chief assistant to Michael Bennett during that director-choreographer's most productive years. After Bennett's death, Avian came out of the shadows and established his own career. He has stayed close to home, choreographing a number of mega-musicals, notably *Miss Saigon* (1990) and *Sunset Boulevard* (1994). At its best, his choreography is solid and professional but has not thrown off the sparks sent across the footlights by the work of Robbins, Fosse, or Bennett.

Wayne Cilento, one of the many "graduates" of *A Chorus Line*, began his dancing career at a comparatively late age but rose quickly through the ranks of Broadway chorus dancers (known as "gypsies") to become a sought-after dancer-singer-actor. In 1983, he turned his sights on choreography with the musical *Baby*, which had as its central theme a celebration of pregnancy and childbirth, not the usual stuff of a Broadway musical. His breathless and athletic dances placed him in a direct line from Michael Kidd. Deserting Broadway for a while, Cilento turned to television and choreographed song renditions known as MTVs, quickly adapting his style to suit the largely rock-and-roll music. In 1993, he was the natural choice for the Broadway production of *The Who's Tommy*, a reprise of a rock musical, which Cilento had helped to develop during the previous year at the La Jolla Playhouse with Des McAnuff. His work on the show won him a Tony Award. He and McAnuff collaborated anew on the fresh production of *How to Succeed in Business Without Really Trying* that arrived on Broadway in 1995.

One of the busier choreographers of the past decade has been Graciela Daniele, who began as a ballerina in Buenos Aires and Paris but made an abrupt career turn after she saw a production of *West Side Story* abroad. Arriving in New York in 1963, she studied jazz dancing so that she could dance on Broadway, then served an apprenticeship in choreography with Michael Bennett. In 1976, she choreographed "The Millikin Show," an annual industrial extravaganza, which traditionally utilizes the talents of big stars. From there, it was a short jump to big musicals. In the 1980s, she worked on *The Pirates of Penzance* and *The Mystery of Edwin Drood*, both of which went from Joe Papp's Public Theater to Broadway, and *The Rink*, which starred Liza Minnelli and Chita Rivera, both established stars of the stage whose talents encompass acting, singing, and dancing. In the 1990s, she added directing to her activities, serving as both director and choreographer for *Once on This Island* in 1990. Given her diverse background, it is not surprising that Daniele is an eclectic choreographer. She prefers not to set an individual stamp on her productions but to work out from the core of the music and script. She has been very good at turning actors into dancers, styling their movements to take advantage of their particular strengths and/or idiosyncrasies.

Before his untimely death from AIDS in 1995, Christopher Chadman danced in a dozen Broadway musicals and assisted Bob Fosse in the assembling of the anthology of Fosse's choreography known as *Dancin'* in 1978. For the most part, his list of credits as a choreographer was accumulated less in theater than in cabaret acts staged for performers like Michael Feinstein, the pianist-singer, and the dancer-singer Chita Rivera, and creating the dances for the Rockettes at Radio City Music Hall. From the start, he was Broadway bound, and he hit his mark in the 1992 revival of *Guys and Dolls*. Reminiscent of the leaping, bounding, no-holds-barred style of dancing designed by Michael Kidd for the original 1950 production, Chapman nonetheless brought a contemporary look to the dancing, a result, no doubt, of his choreography styled to the age of rock and roll.

Of the recent crop of choreographers, none has been so impressive as Susan Stroman. A small, blond ex-dancer, she vibrates with ideas and innovations. Behind her lies a career as a Broadway gypsy and a choreographer of Las Vegas–type shows, and ahead of her looms a career as the top designer of dance both on Broadway and in such venues as the New York City Opera. For *Crazy for You* (1992), a pastiche of Gershwin songs scattered through a musical fashioned tongue-in-cheek from a flimsy 1920s-ish musical-comedy model, she created dances that were the freshest element of the production. She delighted audiences with "prop" dancing, in which the chorus grabbed any available items—clothesline, pickaxes, tire pumps, washboards, and a toilet plunger—and launched into spirited movement to accompany "Slap That Bass" and "I've Got Rhythm." Stroman won the Tony Award hands down for her choreography for the show. In 1994, for the Harold Prince reworking of *Show Boat*, she designed a subtle segue of dances from the can-can to the cakewalk to the Charleston to convey the passage of a half-century, confirming her promise as the most talented choreographer to appear in years.

With the pickings in musical productions on Broadway getting slimmer each year, American choreographers—even the most experienced and best known—cannot keep busy in New York alone, and many take jobs with the regional and summer theaters or ply their talents in television, particularly in choreographing MTVs, and big traveling shows (like the "Millikin") created as good public relations by large industries. The importation of musicals from England has also compounded their difficulties in finding outlets for their specialty because the productions arrive with the dancing prearranged by English choreographers as part of the package. Given a chance and the shows in which to create their innovative work, promising choreographers can revitalize an art that has, for want of the proper stimulus, been sliding into the doldrums for almost a decade. Near perfect conditions abound for a second blooming. All of today's choreographers are blessed in having their pick of a pool of highly trained and resourceful dancers, many of whom danced with the people who now design their movements. But the field has remained open not only to relative newcomers but also to people from the world of serious dance and ballet. In the wake of a tradition that began with George Balanchine, such classical and modern-dance choreographers as Peter Martins, Twyla Tharp, and Michael Smuin have occasionally brought their talents to musical comedy in recent years, blending their special strengths with the bounce of the form. Such American popular dances as jazz and tap never seem to go out of style and remain a source of ideas for choreographers. Since the revival of tap dancing in *42nd Street* in 1980, there has hardly been a season when a stage has not reverberated to the sound of metal taps on wood. In the 1991–92 season, Broadway offered three excellent examples of the art: *Crazy for You, Five Guys Named Moe,* and *Jelly's Last Jam*—the last with tap dances choreographed by the star of the show, Gregory Hines. In a tradition of extraordinary show dancing from Agnes de Mille to Stroman, someone will predictably step out of the chorus or from some other corner of the dance world brimming with ideas and extend the succession into the next century.

If the movies and television have exerted a baleful effect on the American theater in terms of shrinking its core in New York and luring talented actors and writers into their well-cushioned nets, they have had an entirely different and, it would seem, healthier effect on the scenic art of the stage. As movies and television have pushed realism to the extreme bounds of possibility, designers for the stage have been liberated from the responsibility of creating the perfectly realistic set. Audiences both in and out of New York have been more than indulgent in allowing them to explore how to convey in visual terms the meaning of the play, even when that has meant imperfect perspective or architectural anomalies that would not happen in the real world. Rather than provide a beautiful scenic display, the current generation of designers tends to want to astonish audiences by juxtaposing mixed images, much as an abstract or surrealist painter might, or to present them with less-than-pretty environments for the plays. What they have been doing seems to deepen the theatrical experience rather than detract from it.

Musicals, of course, are a different matter for designers of both scenery and costumes. For too many years, Broadway designers have been influenced by musicals brought over from England, which have been almost quaint in their fussiness. Persuaded that people who buy tickets to musicals like that sort of thing, producers have allowed directors and designers to talk them into paying for the kind of intricate sets and spectacular costumes

that first accompanied importations from London. From *Cats* (1982) to *Sunset Boulevard* (1994)—notably Andrew Lloyd Webber works—almost every second musical that has come to Broadway has relied heavily on special and highly mechanized scenic effects. The lavish scenery does not come cheap and is now part of the (very high) price of the ticket for all musicals. All of the 1980s and 1990s musicals have been a far cry from *A Chorus Line*, designed in 1975 by Robin Wagner with pivoting mirrors as its one and only effect. Although it seemingly set a high-water mark for what could be accomplished *without* rising, twirling, shifting, and rolling stages, its relatively simple stagecraft was all but ignored when the imported English scenic hocus-pocus became established as part of the choreography of each show. Scenic spectacle will probably remain with musicals, if only because audiences can find it in no other place.

If nothing else, the spectacular musicals of Broadway have stimulated astounding developments in stagecraft and lighting. Whatever the nature of the dramatic or musical presentations at any given time in history, theater technicians have been on the cutting edge of technology, transforming the mechanics of stage production by adapting each new development to their specialty. They have been hampered only by the restraints placed upon them by producers, who historically have not been happy about spending money in the cause of experimentation. Yet there has always been an inevitability about each improvement. When new materials or machines or techniques are introduced in the world outside theater, technicians demonstrate how costs could be cut by adapting them for use in the theater. Producers have been forced to relent when confronted by hard proof that everyone would benefit from the saving of time and effort. Scenery-making studios, bolstered by designers clamoring for more intricate and mutable scenery, have added computers to aid in cutting and shaping set pieces with the kind of automated tools used in industry. Machines controlled by computers that are programmed to scan original artwork can spray tiny jets of colored ink onto large surfaces of canvas and muslin to create backdrops and special pieces with a fidelity to the designers' original conceptions that could not be achieved by human hand. New materials have also been introduced in the fabrication of props and scenery, subject only to rigid regulations governing fireproofing and environmental safety.

Since the first computerized-memory lighting-control board arrived on Broadway with *A Chorus Line* in 1975, lighting designers have been swift to exploit the potentialities of this liberating instrument. Where once they were straining the limits to include a hundred light changes, they now program hundreds of subtle alterations in intensity and movement. Where once they might order a few hundred instruments to light the show (to the consternation of producers), now they routinely require one thousand and more

Heidi Landesman, the first woman designer to win a Tony Award, describes her style as anti-architectural. The Yale School of Drama graduate won the award for her sets for Big River (1985), a musical evocation of Mark Twain's Adventures of Huckleberry Finn. She prefers to pictorialize the productions to which she has been assigned—but always with a touch of the poetic. Her work has been seen almost exclusively in New York, both on and off Broadway. Her scenery for The Secret Garden (1992), pictured here, was inspired by images from the Victorian era, as the evocation of a lush valentine in its inner proscenium suggests. The topiary garden art actually moved, marking transitions from scene to scene, in this tale of spiritual blooming of two children as they brought an old, tangled, and weed-infested garden back to life.

Tony Straiges found his true vocation in stage design at the Library of Congress in Washington, D.C. He and a group of his coworkers founded a puppet theater in their off-hours and his job was to design the costumes and sets. Self-educated, he later filled in the gaps by studying with Eldon Elder and then with Ming Cho Lee at the Yale School of Drama. In the mid-1970s, he began branching out into regional theater, designing not only for Yale Rep but for the Arena Stage in Washington, D.C., the Guthrie Theater in Minneapolis, the Williamstown (Massachusetts) Theatre Festival, and eventually for productions both on and off Broadway. There is always a neat geometry in his designs whether they are realistic or abstract, and they exude a sense of completeness and logic. Pictured is his set for Shimada, the office of a small bicycle factory in Australia. The play had a short run on Broadway in 1992.

A graduate of La Mama's Third World Theatre Arts Studies program (associated with Ellen Stewart's famed La Mama E.T.C.), Loy Arcenas best represents a contemporary scene designer's pilgrimage from Off Off Broadway to Off Broadway to Broadway and thereafter to regional theaters from coast to coast. He has worked with budgets so small that he has had to use junkyard or "found" materials to create a set. His designs can sometimes be spare to the point of nonexistence in terms of three-dimensional elements, but he can also make them lush in texture and architecture. He has successfully designed for various types of stages (arena, end, proscenium). His set shown here—for the 1994 revival at Hartford Stage of Clare Boothe Luce's 1936 Broadway hit, The Women—is somewhat typical of his geometrical, flat-planed approach.

In 1900, it took a gang of strong-muscled men to hoist, secure, move, and fly scenery on and off stage for big spectacles like Ben Hur. A century later, an abbreviated cadre of highly trained technicians still performs some of the manual labor on the stage floor and in the flies, but one person in the basement of any theater can run the cues and move the scenery once it is in place. Seated at the console of a computer, stylus in hand, in voice communication with the stage manager onstage, the technician follows the progress of the show as it is programmed. Shown is Peter Feller, Jr., testing the equipment that was shipped to Toronto to run an edition of Sunset Boulevard (1995).

Like many young designers in contemporary theater, Charles McClennahan is a disciple of Ming Cho Lee, his teacher at the Yale School of Drama, and does not hesitate to admit that he emulates his mentor with his highly architectural sets. McClennahan is one of several black designers to come to prominence in the 1980s, designing productions for the Hartford Stage, the Manhattan Theatre Club, and Yale Rep, as well as for African-American companies. Like many in the current generation, he has discovered CAD (computer-assisted designing), which obviates drafting by hand while still maintaining the designer's intent. His setting for the backyard of August Wilson's Fences (1985) is shown as it was developed by computer.

instruments to be hung above the stage, on the side walls and in front of the curtain in the auditorium, and around the perimeter of the balcony (to the even greater consternation of producers). In the late 1970s, technology was developed to automate individual lighting instruments. First used at rock-and-roll concerts, the new technique was applied in the Broadway production of *Will Rogers' Follies* in 1990 and is growing in use. The computer-controlled automated instruments, known commercially as Vari-Lites, are capable of changing the intensity, color, shape, focus, and patterns of light and can rotate in place when programmed for the course of the show. But although they do the work of many conventional lighting instruments, they are not designed so much to replace as to augment them. Because they can accept slides for projections, there has been a vast improvement in the quality and definition of projected scenery since the introduction of Vari-Lites.

The only effect, so far, that has not been automated is the "follow spot," a bright light focused on one or more moving performers, most often in a musical. This continues to be controlled by stagehands perched on small platforms at the rear of the auditorium, high above the heads of the audience. In a few years, this effect, too, will be automated, as experimentation-in-progress seeks to make the performers the controllers of the light that shines on them. A small radio transmitter worn by the performers will accurately signal the automated spotlight to follow their movements on the stage.

The success of automation in lighting has been duplicated backstage in the handling of scenery. In the year 1900, all the moving parts of the scenery were lifted, shifted, and pulled by the strong muscles of a small army of stagehands. With the curtain down for changes in locale in the course of the play, the stagehands had to set up new scenes, bracing flats to the stage floor, pulling down backdrops from the fly gallery, placing furniture and props in their correct positions, and making everything ready as swiftly as they could so as not to tax the patience of the audience during long "stage waits." The centuries-old counterweight system, whereby scenery is lifted from the stage, was controlled by men pulling ropes attached to scenery, the weight of which was carefully counterbalanced by sandbags. Lead weights eventually replaced the sandbags, and later manually operated winches were attached to the ropes as a time- and labor-saving device. Through the work of engineer-inventor George Izenour, which was carried out at Yale University in the postwar years, the winches became motorized and synchronized and, consequently, more versatile in the control of scenery.

The moment that motors were introduced backstage, it was a relatively short jump to developing a computer-driven system that could manipulate the winches automatically and, more important, that could be tied into a central console to be placed under the guidance of the stage manager, a step in the direction toward which lighting control had been rapidly moving. The driving force was the demand by stage directors for a more responsive and mutable scenic environment for increasingly complex plays and musicals. With the audience already "educated" to accept scene changes in full view, scenery

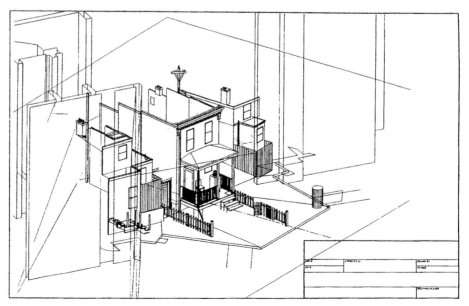

studios went to their drawing boards to devise the mechanics and electronics to accomplish another technical miracle. This they did. In 1983, Feller Precision in New York introduced an automated system to control the movement of scenery in a Broadway production, *The Tap Dance Kid*. From that moment on, automated scenery became a way of life backstage. Reduced to modular essentials so that it is compact and space-saving, the equipment can be packed up and moved to different theaters on road tours and installed and reinstalled on location. Although the customized technology is complex and each motion must be precisely programmed into a computer, once it is up and running the system has elegance in performance and handling—and it has evolved into one of the aesthetics of show production. While research continues to refine the technology, there is no longer any doubt that it will get better and better.

If there has been a small revolution going on backstage, what has been happening onstage all over America reflects a sharp turn toward conservatism. The rebels of the 1960s are now middle-aged and enjoying retrospectives of their early work, which serve to remind present-day audiences of the turbulence that they could *once* expect when they bought tickets to makeshift theaters in strange places. In the 1990s, the few whiffs of the avant-garde have come from what has become known as "performance art," which is difficult to define because it can be anything and performed anywhere. Its spiritual ancestry is rooted in the 1960s, but its artistic impulses come from philosophical antecedents centered on visual art as exemplified by the work of Marcel Duchamp, the Surrealists, the Cubists, and the Expressionists. If anything, it is antitheater. More often than not, performance artists work alone, using their bodies (or parts thereof) as their means of artistic communication. They also use electronic devices—slides, amplifiers, synthesized music, and videotapes with or without scenery and props—in an interdisciplinary approach, or simply perform on a bare stage. Their art is subjective in the extreme, always unpredictable and often spontaneous, and it can also be scatological, sexually explicit, and politically oriented. Because they aim to shock and to redefine (or destroy) the boundaries between performer and viewers, their performances have appealed to small, like-minded audiences. In the early 1990s, certain performance artists achieved a special notoriety when they and other controversial artists became the target of conservative senators, who objected to having government funds awarded to them by the National Endowment for the Arts. Their objections smacked of government censorship and set off a national debate about the role of the NEA in defining what is and what is not art that promises to continue *ad infinitum*. When the fires of controversy were finally damped, the artists quietly received their grants. It is doubtful that performance art will ever enter mainstream American theater, but it burns with a spirit of experimentalism that will certainly never be extinguished.

The world plague that surfaced in the early 1980s and came to be known as AIDS has enveloped the community of performing artists with especial severity. The theater has been particularly hard hit as actors, dancers, singers, choreographers, stage managers, and designers, as well as support personnel in theatrical press-agentry, make-up art, and hair and wig dressing have died from the infection. The very public and poignant deaths of Rock Hudson of the movies in 1985 and Michael Bennett of the stage in 1987 led to the creation of organizations throughout the country to help combat the scourge and to care for the afflicted. Shortly after Hudson's death, the American Foundation for AIDS Research (AmFAR) was set up, with movie star Elizabeth Taylor as its chief spokesperson and fund raiser. In 1987, Broadway Cares, an organization with a similar mission, was founded by and for the New York theatrical community. Hundreds of thousands of dollars are raised each year by these and other groups, but the plague continues unabated. Among its victims have been the playwrights-directors-actors Charles Ludlam, Paul Shyre, and Donald Driver; playwright Harry Kondoleon; directors Wilford Leach and John Hirsch; choreographer Christopher Chadman; singer-actor Larry Kert; and many, many more whose names are less familiar to the general public.

Inevitably the AIDS epidemic created its own dramatic literature. Homosexuality, long accepted within the theatrical profession but rarely alluded to onstage, finally became a subject fit for public airing in theater during the sexually liberated period of

Although Anna Deavere Smith filled the stage with many characters in her 1994 production of Twilight: Los Angeles, 1992, *a play about the riots that followed the racially charged Rodney King trial, she was working her magic onstage alone. She evokes rather than emotes, penetrating the souls of her multitude of characters. She does not mimic them. They become her, and she them. Like most so-called performance artists, she uses electronic technology to assist her, but her "characters" transcend the show-business aspects of her productions.*

What to call Bill Irwin? Actor? Acrobat? Baggy-pants hoofer? Post-modern clown? Satirist? Writer? Modern dancer? Choreographer? He does not easily slide into a slot but seems to be all of those things and more. Born in southern California, educated at UCLA and Oberlin College, he discovered his real calling at Clown College, operated by Ringling Brothers and Barnum & Bailey Circus. When he took his own brand of clowning to audiences, they were delighted. So was the MacArthur Foundation, whose board awarded him their first "genius" grant in 1984. Irwin's clowning has a depth of meaning rare in the art. He satirizes the inept, butts heads with the electronic civilization, and shows how important is the role a clown must play in the hurly-burly of life. He is seen here in Largely New York, *his 1989 one-man show.*

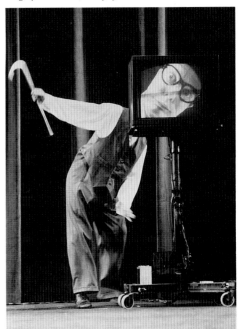

Although Terrence McNally has been a working and produced playwright since the mid-1960s, the 1990s have seen him "edging into fame" with a series of plays that show his talents and perspective continually enlarging. He has been lucky in his association with the Manhattan Theatre Club, his artistic home and the showcase for his plays. In 1995, McNally's Love! Valour! Compassion! moved to Broadway from the MTC under the auspices of the Broadway Alliance, a special arrangement with theatrical unions that pares all costs of production in order to allow a play to reach greater audiences in a Broadway theater. The play, a wry comedy about four gay couples who interact during three holiday weekends at a summer house, turned a profit after just six weeks. Left to right: John Glover, Nathan Lane, and Randy Becker.

Founded in 1976 in Minneapolis, and dedicated to the promotion of cultural pluralism, the Mixed Blood Theatre Company is staffed by a multiracial group of administrators and artists. The company presents a varied menu of original works and a standard repertory of contemporary and classic plays. Following a trend in regional theater, the company sends its productions to fifteen states each year and maintains a training program. In 1994, the group produced Eastern Parade, an anthology of the Asian-American experience, with (left to right) Damus Jian, Miriam Laube, and Lia Rivamonte.

the 1960s. Before that, the best a playwright could do to recognize its existence publicly was to allude to it by innuendo. Lillian Hellman's The Children's Hour never came openly to grips with the unspeakable, although it was a thread running through the relationship of the two women protagonists. In 1944, a play titled Trio, which made a forthright attempt to portray lesbianism, met with such a barrage of protests by self-appointed protectors of public morality that it was withdrawn by its producer, Lee Sabinson, after the Commissioner of Public Licenses threatened to revoke the license of the Belasco Theatre, where it was playing. In 1968, the taboo was broken by The Boys in the Band, a play that openly depicted the secret tensions of being a closet homosexual not only in a heterosexual society but in the gay world as well. It was the most successful of a series of plays on the subject. In the mid-1980s, the subject of AIDS inevitably coalesced with the theme of gay life. From the groundbreaking The Normal Heart by Larry Kramer and As Is by William M. Hoffmann, which played off and on Broadway, respectively, in 1985, to Tony Kushner's prize-winning Angels in America (subtitled A Gay Fantasia on National

Themes) and Terrence McNally's *Love! Valour! Compassion!* both produced ten years later, AIDS has remained the center of attention for many young and not-so-young playwrights. Whether everyone can or will agree with George C. Wolfe, the director of *Angels in America*, who believes "the fringe is now the center" of American life, everyone can appreciate that the public drama of AIDS and homosexuality has opened a window on *all* aspects of American society. From this and other social ills, playwrights extract metaphors for ailments of the country's soul.

The current celebration of multiculturalism has also touched the theater. There are those who will continue to herald cultural diversity as a healthy sign and to see its various manifestations in the theater as a cause for rejoicing. Long before his death in 1991, Joe Papp introduced "color-blind casting" at the New York Shakespeare Festival, meaning that roles were assigned on the basis of the talent of the performers rather than the colors of their skins, and many theaters followed his example soon after. A Broadway musical now routinely features black, white, and Asian chorus gypsies, and the practice makes sense. But even color-blind casting has not been enough to catch all the diversity of America. Black, Asian, and Latino theater companies, encouraged by foundation grants and applauded by their communities, now have histories that reach back decades, not just a few years. Like the century-old Yiddish theater, they glorify their individual cultural identities and have generated plays and playwrights, hoping to attract and retain audiences from their own ethnic and national groups. Unsurprisingly, all this experimentation takes place away from Broadway, which has rarely functioned as the natural habitat of avant-gardist theater. It prefers to wait until what has been tried elsewhere captures the public imagination. Then it leaps into action and embraces the astounding new playwright or designer or performer.

At the turn of the twentieth century, New York was the wellspring of most of the country's theatrical activity. Since the 1980s, Broadway has been able to muster a meager thirty or forty attractions each season for its public. The celebrated theater district, which passed its centennial in 1993 and still clusters around Times Square, now has fewer than forty playhouses, half of which are usually dark at the end of each season in June. The era after World War II, when theaters were chopped down like so many Christmas trees, was ended permanently, it is devoutly hoped, by the action taken by the New York Landmarks Commission, the quasi-governmental agency that was set up to preserve the cultural heritage of the city as it is reflected in architecture. Overcoming the objections of the major theater owners, the agency began to demark the unique aspects of the extant Broadway playhouses for preservation. One by one, the landmark designation began to be applied to the theaters in the late 1980s, and the destruction has been halted. To placate theater owners, who declared themselves injured by the loss of control over their holdings, the agency had to grant them certain concessions. Establishing a principle that buildings in the various zones of the city could have been built to uniform heights, the municipal government gave theater owners the right to sell the imaginary unbuilt space (known fancifully as "air rights") above their short and squat freestanding theaters to developers seeking to erect in close proximity buildings higher than the code allowed. (The Palace Theatre on Broadway now is surmounted by several stories, which are attached to the hotel next door.) These concessions have already begun to change the character of the Broadway theater district, as skyscrapers have increasingly invaded an area long recognized for its close-to-human scale. Only time will tell whether the city-owner resolution will prove to be a deal made in heaven or in hell.

After a long sleep as a movie house, the old Republic Theatre on Forty-second Street, built in 1900, has been the first of the old playhouses to be restored to its former legitimacy. In July 1995, the giant Walt Disney Company took over the renovation of the deteriorating New Amsterdam Theatre, once the lodestar of Forty-second Street, to make it their anchor in the city. Other entertainment enterprises have expressed interest in reclaiming more of the decaying theaters on the street, and the city government expects that a planned hotel and other new buildings will intensify the groundswell of interest in revitalizing the theater district in the twenty-first century.

What has kept New York's theater district from falling apart in the last decades has

The new look for Broadway in the twenty-first century will include a number of the familiar, short playhouses surmounted by a newer high-rise building with another function—a hotel or office building. The Broadway Theatre (shown here) is one example of the trend. The value of the "air rights," those imaginary stories above the small, freestanding theaters, is translated into extra money for the theater owner, but the price is a denser and closed-in theater district, which is less oriented to the public.

When the Walt Disney Company brought its first offering, Beauty and the Beast, to Broadway in 1993, it spared no expense to make it the most sumptuous production seen onstage for many decades. The task of designing the 200-plus costumes fell to Ann Hould-Ward, who was given two and one-half years to complete the job. Reveling in unusual textures and custom-dyed colors, she often treats the surfaces of the costumes as paintings to achieve her effects. For her efforts in Beauty and the Beast, she received a Tony in 1994. Hould-Ward studied at Mills College in California and the University of Virginia, always intending to devote her talents to theatrical costume design. For many years she assisted Patricia Zipprodt, eventually codesigning Sunday in the Park with George in 1984. She is now an established designer on call both in New York and in regional theater throughout the country. Pictured is Beth Fowler in one of Hould-Ward's spectacular costume creations for Beauty and the Beast.

It was probably as much a surprise to William Finn and James Lapine that their musical Falsettos made it to Broadway in 1992 as it was to the theatrical world. Beginning off Broadway as two separate musicals, March of the Falsettos *and* Falsettoland, Falsettos *is the saga of a family torn apart first by the husband and father's revelation of his homosexuality, later by complications of his life with his lover, who has developed AIDS. With the simplest of scenery, the musical had no spoken dialogue and was propelled by lively music sung by its spirited cast. Mirroring the exuberance of the musical, the cast of* Falsettoland *(shown) jumps à là Richard Avedon. Left to right: Danny Gerard, Lonny Price, Faith Prince, Michael Rupert, Stephen Bogardus, Janet Metz, and Heather MacRae.*

been the spectacular musical—or the spectacle with music, depending on one's viewpoint—which continues to be long on scenic effects and short on musical substance. The carefree musical of the past, with or without a message but with wonderful songs and melodies, has been replaced by serious musicals, frequently portraying the dark side of human existence with aria-like songs that have little or no afterlife if lifted from the musical fabric of the work. Most of the newer-style musicals incorporate very little of the dancing that during the 1950s and 1960s became almost the center of attraction. Some of the new musicals have been brilliant in concept. Stephen Sondheim, who launched the trend in 1979 with *Sweeney Todd*, a show about misanthropy gone mad, has continued to write daring musicals that fit into no known mold. In 1994, his *Passion*, a relentlessly dark tale about obsessive love, was a *succès d'estime*, opening and closing after eight months without being profitable for its investors despite garnering several Tony Awards. Like many of Sondheim's musicals, *Passion* advances the musical form a notch further in its continuing development.

One of Sondheim's earlier creations, *Assassins* (1991), began its life in a "workshop," a money- and face-saving system for developing new shows that has replaced the costly and risky out-of-town tryouts that dominated in the first half of the century. Sondheim's musical, which follows the lives of notorious assassins (or would-be assassins) of American presidents through history, was deemed so unconventional that it begged to be tried out before a launching on Broadway. After a gestation period in a rehearsal space, it finally opened to the public at Playwrights Horizon, an Off-Broadway theater. New works are also developed in regional theaters, where they can flourish or quietly fail before being exposed to New York's public and critics. If they succeed with regional audiences, chances are they will hit the high road to Broadway or Off Broadway under the aegis of New York producers. The system has proved practical in saving time and money. *Assassins*, again to cite this celebrated example, did not die after it ended its Off-Broadway run. It has been taken up by regional theaters, where it will probably continue to be revived from time to time.

In addition to the original works written by Sondheim and Lloyd Webber, American theater resounds to the music and tunes of tried-and-true musicals from the past. Each year brings fresh productions—everywhere—of works by Rodgers and Hammerstein, Frank Loesser, Jule Styne, or the Gershwins. Occasionally, a pastiche of a past work is put together, updated or retitled, with songs lifted from several musicals, to be packaged as something new. Although the trend represents a step backward in the continuum of the American musical, it serves to keep theaters lighted and audiences delighted.

When the twentieth century opened, there were about 3,000 American playhouses accepting the more than 300 commercial shows that flowed across the country each year in a steady stream, mostly from Broadway but also from large theatrical centers like

Chicago and San Francisco, where shows were also originated. The number of commercial for-profit theaters with the technical ability to accept a full-blown legitimate stage production has dwindled to about 250. Many of these are multipurpose auditoriums with seating capacities of 2,000 and more, better suited to house symphony concerts, operas, and big musicals than plays. At the end of 1994, there were only eight shows traveling on the road, and of these six were musicals, one was a play (Wendy Wasserstein's *The Sisters Rosensweig*), and one was a theatrical novelty from Britain called *Stomp*. Last rites are periodically administered to "the road." As a sign of its seemingly eternal life, however, several new theaters have been built in places like Fort Lauderdale (Florida), Denver (Colorado), Stamford (Connecticut), and Lincoln (Nebraska) to accommodate Broadway shows. The most successful of Broadway's hits often settle down in cities like Chicago or Los Angeles or Toronto for extended runs.

Most everyone in the American theater today would agree—some with reluctance—that the action has shifted to the not-for-profit regional theaters both in and outside of New York. Not that they have an easy time of it. Regional theaters have worked hardest of all to survive by preparing a diverse menu to tempt all palates: ethnic plays and performers; children's projects (early childhood to late teens); accessibility to their theaters for senior citizens and the handicapped; Saturday classes in acting and what-have-you. All are geared to keep up the perception that they are institutions that belong to the communities. The object is to develop audiences and keep them coming in fair weather and foul. Consequently, they have become more self-reliant and resourceful. Although they continue to hold out their hands to the NEA and national foundations, they do so more to legitimatize their efforts than to succor them significantly. There are hundreds of theaters across the country, ranging from the largely amateur community theaters with limited resources to the impressive regional theaters with multimillion-dollar operating budgets and professional staffs.

The eleventh edition of *Profiles* (1994), the Theatre Communications Group guide to the country's regional theaters, includes the activities of 238 theaters in 131 communities in 39 states across the country and is compelling testimony to the continuing growth of the regional movement and the staying power of the most ambitious groups. With histories now reaching back almost fifty years, several of them have become an incontrovertible part of the American cultural scene. When 182 of those theater companies participated in a recent TCG survey, some important statistics were uncovered: their collective budgets amount to $366 million; they staged 2,300

productions and played 46,184 performances to more than 16 million people. Even more astounding is that they employed 27,600 actors, directors, designers, playwrights, technicians, and administrators throughout the country. Their theater plants range from sophisticated, high-tech, state-of-the-art buildings to simple spaces known as "black boxes" that would never have been called theaters in another age. No longer assured of the kind of support doled out to them in the 1960s by the giant Ford Foundation, they are still building theaters and launching massive campaigns to foot the bills—and they are being successful at it. In short, wherever they are and whatever they do, they have become a substantial industry—and a significant part of American life. To impress their local patrons and board members, many of whom are solid businessmen and businesswomen in the community, they have put themselves on budgets and worked out marketing strategies to keep their subscribers and audiences happy.

Artistically, they often represent the very best in American theater. Pulitzer Prizes for drama, previously locked up by plays premiering on Broadway, are now routinely awarded to plays which open in regional venues before appearing in New York—if they do at all. Performers of yesteryear, who would not have dreamed of appearing anywhere but Broadway or in a first-class road house in the major cities, have been succeeded by a generation of theater professionals who will go anywhere and do any play that interests them. The pay is not good, but if the production *is*, so what? Playwrights not only get their start beyond Broadway but also remain loyal to the theaters that took a chance on them and will return with other plays. Designers and directors routinely commute from theater to theater to stay invigorated in their respective professions and make something like a respectable living.

The clamor for a National Theater that began more than a century ago has all but died out, now that Broadway and the regionals together satisfy the appetite for live-performance theater for Americans who are still doggedly devoted to the art. What has been created is a *de facto* diverse and informal "national theater," with tributaries branching out throughout the country. The sad chronicle of the American National Theatre and Academy (ANTA), which has again slipped into the doldrums, illustrates the impossibility of establishing a permanent temple to the dramatic muses of Melpomene and Thalia in America. There is something about the American spirit that does not like it.

Fifty years ago, Joseph Papp proclaimed in his own way that people could not do without theater. But can we? The movies and television are far more consumable than

Michael Yeargan has long been one of the busiest scene (and sometimes costume) designers in the country, but little of his work has been seen in New York. Working in regional theaters from coast to coast, Yeargan has acquired a reputation for designing scenery that connects with the inner meaning of the play in subtle and often astonishing ways. His ability to divine a visual image for a play has made him a special favorite of regional directors like Robert Brustein, Andrei Serban, Arvin Brown, and Mark Lamos. His home base remains the Yale Rep, and he also teaches design at the Yale School of Drama. His set (shown) for George Bernard Shaw's Misalliance at the Long Wharf Theatre in New Haven, Connecticut, conveys the mood of the play without being literal

the theater. They cost less and we all have easier access to them. And most of the time they offer such an array of entertainment that we can find something to see week after week, night after night, whatever our tastes or interests. Occasionally, a movie or TV program will stir the soul, but, alas, rarely do they leave a lasting resonance, the "flash upon that inward eye" that the writer Roger Angell described in a nostalgic piece in the *New Yorker* about Broadway's "grand era." He can summon up, he says, a scene from Maxwell Anderson's *Winterset* in which the actor Eduardo Ciannelli dies in a doorway, delivering "whispered maledictions," or, in a lighter vein, a scene from *Simple Simon*, in which the now un-famous baggy-pants comic Ed Wynn crosses his eyes and lisps his line: "I'm tho exthited!" "Only the theater," he thinks, "conserves movements and snatches of talk and music in this family-album fashion." Maybe he is right and inadvertently gives the key to the Theater Eternal. There will always be something magical about the lifting of a curtain in the theater, about sharing a special place with strangers who become partners in the unfolding experience, about the enveloping darkness that precedes the increasing glow of stage lights, about the moment when three-dimensional actors begin to speak their lines, and about bits of acting or snippets of dialogue that take the breath away. There is always the expectation and the hope that we will see our collective selves truthfully for the first time. How many—or few—of us get this feeling from the plethora of electronic entertainment products?

Although America elected a movie star as president in the twentieth century, it may never convey that honor on one of its playwrights, as the Czech Republic did when its citizens selected Vaclav Havel, the world-renowned playwright, as its first president some years ago. In his address on World Theatre Day in March 1994, he told the world that he did not believe that theater was dwindling in importance; rather he thought that it is better suited than any of the electronic entertainment media to reveal the light and dark forces of present-day existence. He went on to say:

Yes, theater is not just another genre, one among many. It is the only genre in which, today and every day, now and always, living human beings address and speak to other human beings. Because of that, theatre is more than just the performance of stories or tales. It is a place for human encounter, a space for authentic human existence, above all the kind of existence that transcends itself in order to give an account of the world and of itself. It is a place of living, specific, inimitable conversation about society and its tragedies, about man, his love and anger and hatred. Theatre is a point at which the intellectual and spiritual life of the human community crystallizes. It is a space in which it can exercise its freedom and come to understanding.

As to its future, theater in America will continue to experience hard knocks, but it will absorb changes and make all necessary adjustments. It may be forced to reinvent itself from time to time, but it will endure.

CHRONOLOGY

	PRODUCERS	PLAYWRIGHTS	DIRECTORS AND CHOREOGRAPHERS
1750	David Douglass Lewis Hallam the Elder	Thomas Godfrey	David Douglass Lewis Hallam the Elder
1775	Lewis Hallam the Younger John Hodgkinson Charles Stuart Powell Thomas Wignell	Royall Tyler	John Hodgkinson
1800	James H. Caldwell William Dunlap Noah M. Ludlow Stephen Price Edmund Simpson Sol Smith William Warren the Elder William B. Wood	James Nelson Barker William Dunlap John Howard Payne	John Durang (ch)
1825	P. T. Barnum William E. Burton Moses and David Kimball William Mitchell James W. Wallack	Robert Montgomery Bird Anna Cora Mowatt John Augustus Stone	
1850	Augustin Daly Mrs. John Drew (Louisa Lane) Laura Keene John Lester (Wallack) James H. McVicker Tom Maguire	George Henry Boker Dion Boucicault Augustin Daly	Dion Boucicault David Costa (ch) Augustin Daly

1875	David Belasco
	First Independent Theatre Association
	   (Hamlin Garland)
	Daniel Frohman
	Hull House Players
	Steele MacKaye
	A. M. Palmer
	Theatrical Syndicate (Charles Frohman, Hayman,
	   Klaw, Erlanger, Nixon, and Zimmerman)
		David Belasco
		Clyde Fitch
		William Gillette
		Edward Harrigan
		James A. Herne
		Bronson Howard
		William Dean Howells
		Charles Hoyt
		Steele MacKaye
		Augustus Thomas
			David Belasco
			Mrs. Fiske
			Steele MacKaye
			Eugene Presbrey
			William Seymour
			Ben Teal

1900	Winthrop Ames William A. Brady Carolina Playmakers (Frederick Koch) Chicago Little Theatre (Maurice Browne) Cleveland Play House (Frederic McConnell) Charles B. Dillingham Henry Street Settlement House	George Broadhurst George M. Cohan Rachel Crothers William Vaughn Moody Edward Sheldon Harry B. Smith Eugene Walter	Maurice Browne (Chicago Little Theatre) R. H. Burnside Rachel Crothers Arthur Hopkins Julian Mitchell (ch) Laura Dainty Pelham (Hull House Players) John Tiller (ch)

American theater is the product of an ongoing creative collaboration between producers (and producing organizations), playwrights, directors, choreographers, actors, designers, and architects. This chart is designed to show at a glance which key theatrical professionals were at work during the same years. The reader should bear in mind that many of these men and women and the institutions they founded remained active for several decades. Abbreviations are as follows: ch (choreographer), co (costumes), l (lighting), s (sets).

ACTORS		DESIGNERS	ARCHITECTS
David Douglass Nancy George (first American actress) Lewis Hallam the Elder Lewis Hallam the Younger Nancy Hallam Mrs. Hallam-Douglass John Henry Thomas Kean Mr. and Mrs. Owen Morris Walter Murray Maria Storer		Jacob Snyder (s) William Williams (s)	David Douglass Lewis Hallam the Elder
Thomas Abthorpe Cooper John Hodgkinson John Martin (first American actor) Ann Merry Dennis Ryan Miss Tuke William Warren the Elder Thomas Wignell		Antony Audin (s) Charles Ciceri (s)	Charles Bulfinch Benjamin Latrobe Joseph Mangin
Junius Brutus Booth Mary Ann Duff Edwin Forrest William Mitchell Thomas D. Rice Francis C. Wemyss		John Evers (s) John Joseph Holland (s) Joseph Jefferson II (s) C. Milbourne (s) Antoine Mondelli (s) Hugh Reinagle (s) Luke Robbins (s) John Worrall (s)	William Strickland
John Brougham William E. Burton Caroline Chapman William Chapman Charlotte Cushman Anna Cora Mowatt James E. Murdoch James W. Wallack William Warren the Younger		Andrew Jackson Allen (co) Richard Bengough (s) Peter Grain (s) Henry Hillyard (s) Thomas Joyce (co) Charles Lehr (s) Minard Lewis (s) Russell Smith (s)	John Haviland Antoine Mondelli Calvin Pollard Isaiah Rogers Ithiel Town John Trimble
Lawrence Barrett Edwin Booth Dion Boucicault Mrs. D. P. Bowers Frank Chanfrau E. L. Davenport Mrs. John Drew (Louisa Lane) Matilda Heron	Cordelia Howard Joseph Jefferson III Olive Logan Lotta (Charlotte Crabtree) Adah Isaacs Menken Lydia Thompson Lester Wallack	Albert G. Eaves (co) Victor Moblard (s) Albert R. Van Horn (co) Charles Witham (s)	J. B. McElfatrick and Sons Otis Wheelock
Maude Adams Mary Anderson Maurice Barrymore Mrs. Leslie Carter Kate Claxton Fanny Davenport John Drew Mrs. Fiske (Minnie Maddern) William Gillette Edward Harrigan Tony Hart James A. Herne Elsie Leslie	Steele MacKaye Richard Mansfield Julia Marlowe Frank Mayo Helena Modjeska Clara Morris James O'Neill Ada Rehan Lillian Russell Otis Skinner E. A. Sothern E. H. Sothern	Mathias Armbruster (s) Lee Lash (s) Steele MacKaye (l) Richard Marston (s)	Jabez Comstock Francis Kimball Louis Sullivan Thomas Wisedell
Margaret Anglin Frank Bacon Ethel Barrymore John Barrymore Lionel Barrymore Richard Bennett Fanny Brice	Billie Burke George M. Cohan Jane Cowl Maxine Elliott Dorothy Gish Lillian Gish Al Jolson	Elizabeth Alexander (co) Watson Barratt (s) Wilfred Buckland (s) Ernest Gros (s) Louis Hartmann (l) Robert Edmond Jones (s,co,l) Monroe Pevear (l)	John M. Carrère Thomas Hastings Henry Herts Herbert J. Krapp Hugh Tallant

	PRODUCERS		PLAYWRIGHTS		DIRECTORS AND CHOREOGRAPHERS	
1900 (cont.)	Little Country Theatre of Fargo, North Dakota (Alfred G. Arvold) Oliver Morosco Neighborhood Playhouse Pasadena Playhouse (Gilmor Brown) Provincetown Players	Henry W. Savage Sam, Lee, and J. J. Shubert Theatre Guild Washington Square Players A. H. Woods Florenz Ziegfeld, Jr.			Ned Wayburn (ch)	
1920	Civic Repertory Theatre (Eva Le Gallienne) John Golden Goodman Theatre Hedgerow Theatre (Jasper Deeter)	Gilbert Miller Brock Pemberton Herman Shumlin University Players Guild	George Abbott Maxwell Anderson Philip Barry Susan Glaspell Paul Green Oscar Hammerstein Sidney Howard	George S. Kaufman (with Edna Ferber and Marc Connelly) George Kelly Eugene O'Neill Paul Osborn Elmer Rice Robert E. Sherwood	Chester Hale (ch) George S. Kaufman Sammy Lee (ch) Guthrie McClintic Russell Markert (ch) Philip Moeller Antoinette Perry Albertina Rasch (ch)	
1930	George Abbott Barter Theatre (Robert Porterfield) Bucks County Playhouse Cheryl Crawford Federal Theatre Project Max Gordon Group Theatre Jed Harris	Lakewood Summer Theatre Mercury Theatre (Orson Welles and John Houseman) Playwrights' Co. Westport Country Playhouse	S. N. Behrman Moss Hart Lillian Hellman Sidney Kingsley Howard Lindsay and Russel Crouse Clifford Odets Thornton Wilder		Robert Alton (ch) George Balanchine (ch) Harold Clurman Agnes de Mille (ch) Jed Harris Doris Humphrey (ch) Joshua Logan Lee Strasberg Helen Tamiris (ch) Margaret Webster Charles Weidman (ch)	
1940	Alley Theatre (Nina Vance) Kermit Bloomgarden Living Theatre (Julian Beck and Judith Malina) New York City Theatre Co. (Jean Dalrymple)	Richard Rodgers and Oscar Hammerstein Theatre 47 (Margo Jones) White Barn Theatre (Lucille Lortel) Robert Whitehead	William Inge Arthur Laurents Alan Jay Lerner Arthur Miller Tennessee Williams		Joseph Anthony Gower Champion (ch) Jack Cole (ch) Morton Da Costa Hanya Holm (ch)	Margo Jones (Theatre 47) Elia Kazan Michael Kidd (ch) Robert Lewis Jerome Robbins (ch)
1950	Arena Stage (Zelda Fichandler) Caffe Cino Circle in the Square (Greenwich Village) Alexander Cohen Morton Gottlieb David Merrick	New York Shakespeare Festival (summer theater; Joseph Papp) Phoenix Theatre (T. Edward Hambleton and Norris Houghton) Hal Prince Roger L. Stevens	Robert Anderson William Gibson Lorraine Hansberry		Bob Fosse (ch) Adrian Hall Arthur Penn José Quintero Alan Schneider	
1960	Actors Theatre of Louisville Cafe La Mama (Ellen Stewart) Arthur Cantor Lincoln Center Repertory Co. Negro Ensemble Company Tyrone Guthrie Theater		Edward Albee Amiri Baraka (LeRoi Jones) Arthur Kopit	Sam Shepard Neil Simon Joseph Stein Lanford Wilson	Vinnette Carroll Ulu Grosbard Michael Kahn Mike Nichols Gene Saks	
1970	Emanuel Azenberg Roger Berlind Circle in the Square (West Fiftieth Street) Elizabeth McCann Cameron Mackintosh	Nederlander Organization New York Shakespeare Festival (Joseph Papp) Playwrights Horizons The Shubert Organization	Thomas Babe David Rabe David Mamet		Wilford Leach Richard Maltby, Jr. Tom Moore Tommy Tune (ch)	
1980	Denver Theatre Center		Christopher Durang Harvey Fierstein Wendy Wasserstein		Wayne Cilento (ch) Graciela Daniele (ch) George Faison (ch) Peter Sellars Jerry Zaks	
1990	Dodger Productions Garth H. Drabinsky Jujamcyn Theatre Organization Lincoln Center Theater National Actors Theater	Producers Circle Company Barry Weissler and Fran Weissler Frederick Zollo	William Finn Herb Gardner John Guare A. R. Gurney	Tony Kushner Craig Lucas Terrence McNally August Wilson	Christopher Chadman (ch) Mark Lamos James Lapine Joe Mantello	Gregory Mosher Jack O'Brien Susan Stroman (ch) Daniel Sullivan Jerry Zaks

ACTORS	DESIGNERS	ARCHITECTS
Doris Keane, Bert Lahr, Robert Mantell, Henry Miller, Marilyn Miller, Alla Nazimova, Fritzi Scheff, Edgar Selwyn, Laurette Taylor, David Warfield, Joe Weber and Lew Fields, Bert Williams	Livingston Platt (s,l), Lee Simonson (s,co), Elmer Traflinger (co), Joseph Urban (s,l), Albertine Randall Wheelan (co)	
Judith Anderson, Tallulah Bankhead, Jacob Ben-Ami, Alice Brady, Katharine Cornell, Jeanne Eagels, Lynn Fontanne, Charles Gilpin, Ruth Gordon, Walter Hampden, Helen Hayes, Walter Huston, Eva Le Gallienne, Pauline Lord, Alfred Lunt, Rose McClendon, Fredric March, Raymond Massey, Paul Muni, Florence Reed, Paul Robeson, Joseph Schildkraut, Cornelia Otis Skinner, Ethel Waters, Peggy Wood	Boris Aronson (s), Norman Bel Geddes (s), Aline Bernstein (s,co), Abe Feder (l), Elise Freisinger (co), Mordecai Gorelik (s), Charles LeMaire (co), Jo Mielziner (s,l), Donald Oenslager (s,l), Margaret McCoy Pemberton (co), Helene Pons (co), Cleon Throckmorton (s)	Thomas Lamb, Joseph Urban
Shirley Booth, Maurice Evans, José Ferrer, Katharine Hepburn, Mary Martin, Ethel Merman, Dorothy Stickney, Margaret Sullavan	Lucinda Ballard (co), Howard Bay (s), Frederick Fox (s), Stanley McCandless (l), Jean Rosenthal (l), Irene Sharaff (co)	
Barbara Bel Geddes, Carol Channing, Hume Cronyn, Alfred Drake, Mildred Dunnock, Judy Holliday, Celeste Holm, Danny Kaye, Jessica Tandy	Ralph Alswang (s,l), Peggy Clark (l), Ben Edwards (s), George Jenkins (s), Oliver Smith (s), Miles White (co), Freddy Wittop (co)	
Yul Brynner, Art Carney, Lee J. Cobb, Colleen Dewhurst, Ben Gazzara, Tammy Grimes, Julie Harris, Richard Kiley, Karl Malden, Zero Mostel, Geraldine Page, Christopher Plummer, Tony Randall, Jason Robards, George C. Scott, Kim Stanley, Maureen Stapleton, Gwen Verdon, Eli Wallach, David Wayne	Theoni V. Aldredge (co), Alvin Colt (co), Eldon Elder (s), David Hays (s,l), Peter Larkin (s), Ming Cho Lee (s), Tharon Musser (l), Tony Walton (s,l), Patricia Zipprodt (co)	Frank Lloyd Wright
Jane Alexander, Beatrice Arthur, Sandy Duncan, Judd Hirsch, Raul Julia, Frank Langella, Hal Linden, Cleavon Little, Liza Minnelli, Rita Moreno, Douglas Turner Ward	Martin Aronstein (l), Jules Fisher (l), John Gleason (l), Jane Greenwood (co), Willa Kim (co), Florence Klotz (co), Eugene Lee (s), Jo Mielziner (s), David Mitchell (s), Robin Wagner (s)	Max Abramovitz, Welton Becket, Hugh Hardy, Ralph Rapson, Edward Durrell Stone, Harry Weese
Glenn Close, Mary Beth Hurt, William Hurt, Kevin Kline, Patti Lupone, Michael Moriarty, Meryl Streep	John Lee Beatty (s), Marjorie Bradley Kellogg (s), Santo Loquasto (s), Jennifer Tipton (l)	Ralph Alswang, Robert Allan Jacobs, Alan Robert Sayles
Matthew Broderick, Betty Buckley, Patti Cohenour, Ed Harris, Edward Herrmann, Dana Ivey, Judith Ivey, John Malkovich, Amanda Plummer	Allen Lee Hughes (l), Heidi Landesmann (s,co), Jennifer von Mayrhauser (co), Richard Nelson (l), Tony Straiges (s)	Roger Morgan, John C. Portman, Jr., Kevin Roche and John Dinkeloo
Stockard Channing, Charles S. Dutton, Peter Frechette, Peter Gallagher, Victor Garber, Joanna Gleason, Harry Groener, Gregory Hines, Jonathan Hogan, Bill Irwin, Zeljko Ivanek, Nathan Lane, Stephen Lang, Maryann Plunkett, Faith Prince, Mercedes Ruehl, Courtney B. Vance	Loy Arcenas (s), John Arnone (s), Pat Collins (l), Paul Gallo (l), Natasha Katz (l), Heidi Landesman (s), William Ivey Long (c), Charles McClennahan (s), Michael Yeargan (s)	

BIBLIOGRAPHY

Considerations of space do not permit me to list every source used in the preparation of this book. Most of my research was centered on the exhaustive clipping files and scrapbooks of the Billy Rose Theatre Collection of the New York Public Library at Lincoln Center and the personality and production files of the Theatre Collection of the Museum of the City of New York. Regretfully omitted are most biographies, autobiographies, and original and personal documents consulted in my research. What follows is a list of readily available general reference works and the most important citations for each chapter.

GENERAL REFERENCE WORKS

BOOKS

The American Theatre: A Sum of Its Parts. New York: Sam French, 1971.

Atkinson, Brooks. *Broadway.* New York: Macmillan, 1974.

Bernheim, Alfred L. *The Business of the Theatre.* New York: Actors' Equity Association, 1932.

Best Plays series, various editors. Boston: Small, Maynard, 1920–25; New York: Dodd, Mead, 1916–.

Bordman, Gerald. *American Musical Theatre.* New York: Oxford University Press, 1978.

———, ed. *The Oxford Companion to American Theatre.* New York: Oxford University Press, 1984.

Brown, John Mason. *Dramatis Personae.* New York: Viking, 1963.

Brown, Thomas Allston. *History of the American Stage.* New York: Dick & Fitzgerald, 1870.

Browne, Walter, and F. A. Austin, eds. *Who's Who on the Stage: The Dramatic Reference Book and Biographical Dictionary of the Theatre Containing Records of the Careers of Actors, Actresses, Managers, and Playwrights.* N.p.: Dodge & Co., 1908.

Coad, Oral S., and Edwin Mims, Jr. *The American Stage.* Vol. 14 of *The Pageant of America.* New Haven, Conn.: Yale University Press, 1929.

Cohen-Stratyner, Barbara Naomi. *Biographical Dictionary of Dance.* New York: Schirmer, 1982.

Crawford, Mary Caroline. *The Romance of the American Theatre.* New York: Halcyon House, 1940.

Dunlap, William. *Diary of William Dunlap (1766–1839).* First published 1930. Reprinted New York: Benjamin Blom, 1969.

———. *History of the American Theatre.* New York: J.& J. Harper, 1832.

Goldman, William. *The Season.* New York: Harcourt, Brace and World, 1969.

Green, Abel, and Joe Laurie, Jr. *Show Biz from Vaude to Video.* New York: Henry Holt, 1951.

Herbert, Ian, ed. *Who's Who in the Theatre.* Detroit: Gale Research, 1981.

Hornblow, Arthur. *A History of the Theatre in America.* 2 vols. Philadelphia: J. B. Lippincott, 1919.

Hughes, Glenn. *A History of the American Theatre 1700–1950.* New York: Sam French, 1951.

Hutton, Laurence. *Curiosities of the American Stage.* New York: Harper and Brothers, 1891.

———. *Plays and Players.* New York: Hurd and Houghton, 1875.

Jefferson, Joseph [III]. *The Autobiography of Joseph Jefferson.* New York: The Century Co., 1889.

Mates, Julian. *America's Musical Stage: Two Hundred Years of Musical Theatre.* Westport, Conn.: Greenwood Press, 1985.

Meserve, Walter J. *An Emerging Entertainment: The Drama of the American People to 1828.* Bloomington: Indiana University Press, 1977.

Moody, Richard. *America Takes the Stage.* Bloomington: Indiana University Press, 1955.

Mordden, Ethan. *The American Theatre.* New York: Oxford University Press, 1981.

Morehouse, Ward. *Matinee Tomorrow: Fifty Years of Our Theatre.* New York: Whittlesey House, 1949.

Morris, Lloyd. *Curtain Time: The Story of the American Theatre.* New York: Random House, 1953.

Moses, Montrose, and John Mason Brown. *American Theatre as Seen by Its Critics.* New York: W. W. Norton, 1934.

New York Times Directory of the Theater. New York: Arno Press, 1973.

Notable Names in the American Theatre. Clifton, N.J.: James T. White, 1976.

Odell, George C. D. *Annals of the New York Stage.* 15 vols. New York: Columbia University Press, 1927–49.

Poggi, Jack. *Theater in America: The Impact of Economic Forces, 1870–1967.* Ithaca, N.Y.: Cornell University Press, 1968.

Rankin, Hugh F. *The Theatre in Colonial America.* Chapel Hill: University of North Carolina Press, 1960.

Seilhamer, George O. *History of the American Theatre before the Revolution.* First published 1888–91. Reprinted New York: Benjamin Blom, 1968.

Spritz, Kenneth. *Theatrical Evolution: 1776–1976.* Yonkers, N.Y.: Hudson River Museum, 1976.

Taubman, Howard. *The Making of the American Theatre.* New York: Coward, McCann & Geoghegan, 1965.

Vinson, James, ed. *Contemporary Dramatists.* New York: St. Martin's Press, 1982.

Wilson, Garff B. *Three Hundred Years of American Drama and Theatre.* Englewood Cliffs, N.J.: Prentice-Hall, 1973.

PERIODICALS

American Theatre
The Broadway
Dance Magazine
Dramatists Quarterly
New York Clipper
New York Dramatic Mirror
Other Stages
Playbill
Stage
Stages
The Theatre (1886–93)

The Theatre (and *Theatre Magazine*)
Theatre Annual
Theatre Arts Magazine (and *Theatre Arts Monthly*)
Theatre Crafts
Theatre Design & Technology
Theatre Guild Magazine
Theatre Journal (and *Educational Theatre Journal*)
Theatre News
Theatre Survey
Variety

PRODUCERS

Alpert, Hollis. "Broadway's Abominable Showman." *Esquire,* January 1960.

Booth, John E. "Producer's Changing Role." *New York Times,* 13 December 1959.

Bost, James S. *Monarchs of the Mimic World.* Orono: University of Maine Press, 1977.

Brady, William A. "In the Spotlight for Forty Years." Parts 1–3. *Pictorial Review,* September–November 1924.

Candidus [pseud.]. Letter. In *The British Magazine,* June 1760.

Carson, William G. B. *Managers in Distress.* St. Louis, Mo.: St. Louis Historical Documents Foundation, 1949.

———. *The Theatre on the Frontier.* Chicago: University of Chicago Press, 1932.

Carter, Randolph. *The World of Flo Ziegfeld.* New York: Praeger, 1974.

"Charles Dillingham." *New York Herald Tribune,* 18 March 1934.

Cibber, Colley [pseud.]. "Old Playbills." *Philadelphia Sunday Mercury,* c. 1860.

Coad, Oral S. *William Dunlap.* First published 1917. Reprinted New York: Russell & Russell, 1962.

Cowell, Joseph. *Thirty Years among the Players.* New York: Harper and Brothers, 1844.

Crawford, Cheryl. *One Naked Individual.* New York: Bobbs-Merrill, 1977.

Dalrymple, Jean. *From the Last Row.* Clifton, N.J.: James T. White, 1975.

Donohue, Joseph W., ed. *The Theatrical Manager in England and America.* Princeton, N.J.: Princeton University Press, 1971.

Dudar, Helen. "He Just May Be Today's Barnum," *New York Times,* 7 March 1982.

Eaton, Walter Pritchard. *The Theatre Guild, the First Ten Years.* New York: Brentano's, 1929.

Freedman, Samuel. "Last of the Red Hot Producers." *New York Times Magazine,* 2 June 1985.

Frohman, Daniel. *Daniel Frohman Presents.* New York: Claude Kendall and Willoughby Sharp, 1935.

Gagey, Edmond M. *The San Francisco Stage.* New York: Columbia University Press, 1950.

Golden, John, and Viola Brothers Shore. *Stage-Struck John Golden.* New York: Sam French, 1930.

Harriman, Margaret Case. "Gilbert Miller." Parts 1–2. *New Yorker,* 29 May and 5 June 1943.

Hatton, Mr. and Mrs. Frederick. Series of articles on producers, random dates. *Chicago Herald,* c. August 1914–January 1915.

Hewitt, Barnard. "The Producer's Many Roles." In *The American Theatre: A Sum of Its Parts.* New York: Sam French, 1971.

Highfill, Philip, Jr. "The British Background of the American Hallams." *Theatre Survey,* May 1970.

Hodgkinson, John. "A Narrative of His Connection with the Old American Company 1792–1797." First published 1797. Reprinted in *History of the American Theatre,* by William Dunlap. New York: J. & J. Harper, 1832.

Hollingshead, John. "Theatrical Management." *The Broadway,* April 1868.

Hutchens, John K. "Arthur Hopkins Presents," *New York Times Magazine,* 7 April 1946.

Jennings, John J. "Winthrop Ames' Notes for the Perfect Theatre." *Educational Theatre Journal,* March 1960.

Kakutani, Michiko. "The Public and Private Joe Papp." *New York Times Magazine,* 23 June 1985.

Kissel, Howard. "Kermit Bloomgarden." *Women's Wear Daily,* 28 January 1974.

Langley, Stephen, ed. *Producers on Producing.* New York: Drama Book Specialists, 1976.

Leavitt, M. B. *Fifty Years in Theatrical Management.* New York: Broadway Publishing, 1912.

Levin, Herman. "The Producer's Lot." *Theatre Arts,* October 1958.

Little, Stuart. *Enter Joseph Papp.* New York: Coward, McCann & Geoghegan, 1974.

Little, Stuart, and Arthur Cantor. *The Playmakers.* New York: W. W. Norton, 1970.

Ludlow, Noah. *Dramatic Life as I Found It.* St. Louis, Mo.: G. I. Jones, 1880.

Ludwig, Jay. "McVicker's Theatre, 1875–1896." Ph.D. diss., University of Illinois, 1958.

Malone, John. "The Actor, the Manager, and the Public." *Forum,* October 1895.

"Men Who Produce Plays." *New York Sun,* 10 March 1895.

Morosco, Helen M., and Leonard Dugger. *Life of Oliver Morosco: The Oracle of Broadway.* Caldwell, Idaho: Caxton Printing, 1944.

Odell, George C. D. *Some Theatrical Stock Companies of New York.* New York: Brander Matthews Dramatic Museum, Columbia University, 1951.

Pemberton, Brock. "Winthrop Ames." *New York Times,* 7 November 1939.

"Private Merrick and Major Hater." *St. Louis Post-Dispatch,* 8 August 1976.

Ryan, Pat M., Jr. "A. M. Palmer: A Study of Management, Dramaturgy and Stagecraft in the American Theatre, 1872–96." Ph.D. diss., Yale University, 1959.

Sabinson, Harvey. *Darling, You Were Wonderful.* Chicago: Henry Regnery, 1977.

St. John, Molyneux. "New York Theatres." *The Broadway,* February 1868.

Savage, Henry W. "The Dilemma of the Theatre." *Saturday Evening Post,* 11 May 1912.

Smith, Sol F. *Theatrical Management in the West and South.* New York: Harper and Brothers, 1868.

Smither, Nelle. *A History of the English Theatre in New Orleans.* New York: Benjamin Blom, 1967.

Stagg, Jerry. *The Brothers Shubert.* New York: Random House, 1968.

Strickland, Dorothy Jean. "Laura Keene: Nineteenth Century American Actress-Manager." Master's thesis, University of Arizona, 1961.

Waldau, Roy S. *Vintage Years of the Theatre Guild 1928–1939.* Cleveland, Ohio: Case Western Reserve University Press, 1972.

Wallack, Lester. *Memories of Fifty Years.* New York: Charles Scribner's Sons, 1889.

Wood, William B. *Personal Recollections of the Stage.* Philadelphia: Henry Carey Bird, 1855.

PLAYWRIGHTS

"American Playwrights Self-appraised." *Saturday Review,* 3 September 1955.

American Theatre. New York: St. Martin's Press, 1967.

"Benjamin Baker." *Spirit of the Times,* 10 September 1890.

Birdoff, Harry. *The World's Greatest Hit—Uncle Tom's Cabin.* New York: S. F. Vanni, 1947.

Bogard, Travis. *Contour in Time.* New York: Oxford University Press, 1972.

Bogard, Travis, Richard Moody, and Walter J. Meserve. *American Drama.* Vol. 7 of *The Revels History of Drama in English.* London: Methuen, 1977.

Boucicault, Dion. "Points for Playwrights." *New York Herald,* 28 June 1888.

Bradley, Edward S. *George Henry Boker.* First published 1927. Reprinted New York: Benjamin Blom, 1972.

Brown, John Mason. "New Voices and Old." *Saturday Review,* 13 January 1951.

Cohn, Ruby. *New American Dramatists 1960–1980.* New York: Grove Press, 1982.

"The Craft of the Playwright: A Conversation between Neil Simon and David Rabe." *New York Times Magazine,* 26 May 1985.

Crothers, Rachel. Lecture given at The White House, dated 25 April 1939. Theatre Collection, Museum of the City of New York.

Downer, Alan. *American Drama and Its Critics.* Chicago: University of Chicago Press, 1965.

———. *Fifty Years of American Drama, 1900–1950.* Chicago: Henry Regnery, 1951.

Engel, Lehman. *The American Musical Theatre.* New York: Macmillan, 1975.

Frenz, Horst, ed. *American Playwrights on Drama.* New York: Hill and Wang, 1965.

Freser, Lloyd A. "Bronson Howard: Dean of American Dramatists." Ph.D. diss., University of Iowa, 1971.

Gagliano, Frank. "The American Theater Today: From the Eyes of a Practicing Playwright." *The O'Neill Quarterly,* February 1982.

Garland, Hamlin. *Crumbling Idols.* First published 1894. Reprinted Cambridge, Mass.: Harvard University Press, 1960.

Gassner, John. "The Winter of Our Discontent." *Theatre Arts,* August 1955.

Gilman, Richard. Introduction to *Seven Plays,* by Sam Shepard. New York: Bantam Books, 1981.

Goldstein, Malcolm. *George S. Kaufman.* New York: Oxford University Press, 1974.

———. *The Political Stage.* New York: Oxford University Press, 1979.

Gramsted, David. *Melodrama Unveiled: American Theater and Culture 1800–1850.* Chicago: University of Chicago Press, 1968.

Green, Stanley. *Broadway Musicals.* Milwaukee: Hal Leonard Books, 1985.

———. *The World of Musical Comedy.* San Diego, Calif.: A. S. Barnes, 1980.

Guernsey, Otis L., Jr., ed. *Playwrights, Lyricists, Composers on Theater.* New York: Dodd, Mead, 1964.

Hodge, Francis. *Yankee Theatre.* Austin: University of Texas Press, 1964.

Kahn, E. J., Jr. *The Merry Partners, the Age and Stage of Harrigan & Hart.* New York: Random House, 1955.

Kakutani, Michiko. "Myths, Dreams, Realities—Sam Shepard's America." *New York Times*, 29 January 1984.

Kaye, Phyllis Johnson, ed. *The National Playwrights Directory*. Waterford, Conn.: O'Neill Theater Center, 1977.

Kinne, Wisner Payne. *George Pierce Baker and the American Theatre*. Cambridge, Mass.: Harvard University Press, 1954.

Klein, Charles. "Vicissitudes of a Playwright." *The Theatre*, June 1915.

Krutch, Joseph Wood. *The American Drama Since 1918*. New York: G. Braziller, 1957.

MacNicholas, John. *Twentieth Century American Dramatists*. Detroit: Gale Research, 1981.

Marranca, Bonnie, and Gautam Dasgupta. *American Playwrights: A Critical Survey*. Vol. 1. New York: Drama Book Specialists, 1981.

Middleton, George. "The Dramatists Guild: What It Is and Does. How It Happened and Why." *Authors' League Bulletin*, January 1939.

Moody, Richard. *Edward Harrigan*. Chicago: Nelson-Hall, 1980.

Moses, Montrose. *The American Dramatist*. Boston: Little, Brown, 1925.

Moses, Montrose, and Virginia Gerson. *Clyde Fitch and His Letters*. Boston: Little, Brown, 1924.

Mowatt, Anna Cora. *Autobiography of an Actress*. Boston: Ticknor, Reed, and Fields, 1853.

Nathan, George Jean. "A Brief History of the American Stage." *Puck*, August 1918.

Perry, John A. *James A. Herne: The American Ibsen*. Chicago: Nelson-Hall, 1978.

Quinn, Arthur Hobson. *A History of the American Drama from the Beginning to the Present Day*. 2 vols. New York: Appleton-Century-Crofts, 1936–44.

Rahill, Frank. *The World of Melodrama*. University Park: Pennsylvania State University Press, 1967.

Rees, James. *The Dramatic Authors of America*. Philadelphia: G. B. Zieber, 1845.

Shewey, Don. "Arthur Kopit: A Life on Broadway." *New York Times Magazine*, 29 April 1984.

Smith, Cecil, and Glenn Litton. *Musical Comedy in America*. New York: Theatre Arts Books, 1981.

"Some Playwright Biographies: A Cross-section of the American Theatre." *Theatre Arts*, July 1927.

Spoto, Donald. *The Kindness of Strangers: The Life of Tennessee Williams*. Boston: Little, Brown, 1985.

Tanselle, G. Thomas. *Royall Tyler*. Cambridge, Mass.: Harvard University Press, 1967.

Vaughn, Jack A. *Early American Dramatists*. New York: Frederick Ungar, 1981.

Weales, Gerald. *American Drama Since World War II*. New York: Harcourt, Brace and World, 1962.

Wharton, John F. *Life among the Playwrights*. New York: Quadrangle, 1974.

DIRECTORS AND CHOREOGRAPHERS

Abbott, George. "A Director's Lot." *New York Times*, 15 April 1951.

Arliss, George. *Up the Years from Bloomsbury*. New York: Blue Ribbon Books, 1927.

Aronson, Harvey. "He's Directed Himself Right off the Stage" [Gene Saks]. *Newsday*, 15 February 1966.

Barnes, Howard. "The Power Behind the Showshop Thrones." *Theatre Magazine*, December 1929.

Belasco, David. *The Theatre Through the Stage Door*. Edited by Louis V. DeFoe. New York: Harper, 1919.

Bennetts, Leslie. "Women Directing More Plays But Broadway Is Still Elusive." *New York Times*, 16 January 1984.

Berkvist, Robert. "How Nichols and Rabe Shaped 'Streamers'." *New York Times*, 25 April 1976.

Binns, Archie. *Mrs. Fiske and the American Theatre*. New York: Crown, 1955.

Bolton, Whitney. "Belated Nod to Director of 'Man of La Mancha'." *New York Morning Telegraph*, 4 December 1965.

Brustein, Robert. "The Strategies of Adrian Hall." *New Republic*, 25 April 1981.

Chinoy, Helen. "The Impact of the Stage Director on American Plays, Playwrights, and Theatres 1860–1930." Ph.D. diss., Columbia University, 1963.

Ciment, Michael. *Kazan on Kazan*. New York: Viking, 1974.

Clurman, Harold. *On Directing*. New York: Macmillan, 1972.

Cochran, James Preston. "The Development of the Professional Stage Director: A Critical-Historical Examination of Representative Professional Directors on the New York Stage, 1896–1916." Ph.D. diss., State University of Iowa, 1958.

Cole, Toby, and Helen Chinoy. *Directors on Directing*. New York: Bobbs-Merrill, 1963.

Coley, Thomas. *"Our Town" Remembered*. New York: Hudson Rudd Co., 1982.

Coward, Edward Fales. "The Men Who Direct the Destinies of the Stage." *The Theatre*, July 1906.

Crothers, Rachel. "The Producing Playwright." *Theatre Magazine*, January 1918.

Dale, Alan. "Alan Dale Says: Mme. Butterfly Is a Gem and Advises Everybody to See It." *New York Journal*, 8 March 1900.

Daly, Joseph Francis. *The Life of Augustin Daly*. New York: Macmillan, 1917.

Felheim, Marvin. *The Theater of Augustin Daly*. Cambridge, Mass.: Harvard University Press, 1956.

Gelb, Barbara. "The Creative Mind of Mike Nichols." *New York Times Magazine*, 27 May 1984.

Gent, George. "Black Women Take Roles as Directors." *New York Times*, 17 November 1971.

Gottfried, Martin. "Bennett's Workshop for a New Breed of Musicals." *New York Post*, 8 October 1977.

Gussow, Mel. "Alan Schneider, Pioneering Director, Is Dead," *New York Times*, 4 May 1984.

Harris, Jed. *Watchman, What of the Night?* Garden City, N.Y.: Doubleday, 1963.

Helburn, Theresa. "Raising the Curtain on a Director" [Philip Moeller]. *New York Sun*, 30 November 1929.

Hopkins, Arthur. *Reference Point*. New York: Sam French, 1948.

"The Improving Status of the Stage Manager." *New York Dramatic Mirror*, 20 December 1902.

Lewis, Robert. *Method—or Madness?* New York: Sam French, 1958.

Logan, Joshua. *Josh*. New York: Delacorte, 1976.

McClintic, Guthrie. *Me and Kit*. Boston: Little, Brown, 1955.

MacKaye, Percy. *Epoch: The Life of Steele MacKaye*. 2 vols. New York: Boni & Liveright, 1927.

Metten, Charles L. "The Development of Theories of Directing as Found in American Writings, 1914–1930." Ph.D. diss., State University of Iowa, 1960.

Morris, Clara. *Life on the Stage*. New York: McClure, Phillips, 1902.

Moulton, Robert D. "Choreography in Musical Comedy and Revue on the New York Stage from 1925 through 1950." Ph.D. diss., University of Minnesota, 1957.

O'Haire, Patricia. "She Came a Long Way" [Vinnette Carroll]. *New York Daily Mirror*, 10 May 1976.

O'Malley, Frank Ward. "Zipp—A Remarkable Judge of Human Nature" [R. H. Burnside]. *American Magazine*, March 1920.

Perron, Wendy. "The New Broadway: Dance Takes Center Stage." *Village Voice*, 8 May 1978.

Prince, Hal. *Contradictions: Notes on Twenty-six Years in the Theatre*. New York: Dodd, Mead, 1974.

Quintero, José. *If You Don't Dance, They Beat You*. Boston: Little, Brown, 1974.

Ranous, Dora K. *The Diary of a Daly Debutante*. New York: Duffield, 1910.

Rice, Elmer L. "The Playwright as Director." *Theatre Arts*, May 1929.

"Robbins Weighs the Future—Ballet or Broadway?" *New York Times*, 12 July 1981..

Schaal, David G. "Rehearsal-Direction and Actor-Director Relationships in the American Theatre from the Hallams to Actors' Equity." Ph.D. diss., University of Illinois, 1956.

Schneider, Alan. "What Does a Director Do?" *New York Theatre Review*, Spring–Summer 1977.

Shapiro, Herman. "Jed Harris as a Director." In *Watchman, What of the Night?*, by Jed Harris. Garden City, N.Y.: Doubleday, 1963.

Teichmann, Howard. *George S. Kaufman, An Intimate Portrait*. New York: Atheneum, 1972.

Terry, Walter. "Broadway Choreographer" [Gower Champion]. *New York Herald Tribune*, 1 March 1964.

———. *I Was There*. Reviews compiled and edited by Andrew Mark Wentink. New York: Marcel Dekker, 1978.

Timberlake, Craig. *The Life and Work of David Belasco, the Bishop of Broadway*. New York: Library Publishers, 1954.

Walsh, Townsend. *The Career of Dion Boucicault*. New York: Dunlap Society, 1915.

Watts, Richard, Jr. "Musical Comedy and Revue Dancing—How Did It Develop." *Dance Magazine*, January 1929.

Wayburn, Ned. *The Art of Stage Dancing*. New York: The Ned Wayburn Studios of Stage Dancing, Inc., 1925.

———. "Realizing Musical Shows." *Saturday Evening Post*, 9 February 1913.

Webster, Margaret. "Credo of a Director." *Theatre Arts*, May 1938.

Wetzsteon, Ross. "Broadway's Triple Threat" [Tommy Tune]. *Saturday Review*, May 1982.

"Wilford Leach." *New York Magazine*, 23 February 1981.

"William Seymour, Veteran among Stage Managers." *New York Sunday Telegraph*, 24 April 1904.

ACTORS

"The American on Stage." *Scribner's*, July 1879.

Archer, Stephen, ed. *American Actors and Actresses*. Detroit: Gale Research, 1983.

Ashby, Clifford C. "Realistic Acting and the Advent of the Group in America 1889–1922." Ph.D. diss., Stanford University, 1963.

Ayres, Alfred. *Acting and Actors, Elocution and Elocutionists*. New York: D. Appleton, 1894.

Brown, John Mason. *Two on the Aisle*. New York: W. W. Norton, 1938.

Brumm, Beverly. "Preparation in Private: The Professional Acting School in New York City from 1870 to 1970." Ph.D. diss., New York University, n.d.

Clapp, Henry Austin. *Reminiscences of a Dramatic Critic*. New York: Houghton Mifflin, 1902.

Cole, Toby, and Helen Chinoy. *Actors on Acting*. New York: Crown, 1970.

Downer, Alan S. "Early American Professional Acting." *Theatre Survey*, November 1971.

Duerr, Edwin. *The Length and Depth of Acting*. New York: Holt, Rinehart and Winston, 1962.

Dunning, Jennifer. "The New American Actor." *New York Times Magazine*, 2 October 1983.

Eaton, Walter Pritchard. *Plays and Players*. Cincinnati: Stewart & Kidd, 1916.

Funke, Lewis, and John E. Booth, eds. *Actors Talk about Acting*. New York: Random House, 1961.

Garfield, David. *A Player's Place: The Story of the Actors Studio*. New York: Macmillan, 1980.

Gillette, William. *The Illusion of the First Time in Acting*. New York: Dramatic Museum of Columbia University, 1915.

Goodale, Katherine. *Behind the Scenes with Edwin Booth*. Boston: Houghton Mifflin, 1931.

Hamilton, Thomas. *Men and Manners in America.* Philadelphia: Carey, Lea & Blanchard, 1833.

Harding, Alfred. *Revolt of the Actors.* New York: William Morrow, 1929.

Hethmon, Robert H., ed. *Strasberg at The Actors Studio.* New York: Viking, 1965.

Izard, Forrest. *Heroines of the Modern Stage.* New York: Sturgis & Walton, 1915.

Kakutani, Michiko. "When Great Actors Put Their Stamp on a Role." *New York Times,* 20 May 1984.

Krapp, George P. *The English Language in America.* 2 vols. New York: The Century Co., 1925.

Leman, Walter M. *Memories of an Old Actor.* San Francisco: A. Roman Co., 1886.

Lewes, George H. *On Actors and the Art of Acting.* New York: Henry Holt, 1878.

Logan, Olive. *The Mimic World.* Philadelphia: New-world Publishing Co., 1871.

McArthur, Benjamin. "Theatrical Clubs of the Nineteenth Century: Tradition versus Assimilation in the Acting Community." *Theatre Survey,* November 1982.

Mammen, Edward W. *The Old Stock Company School of Acting.* Boston: Trustees of the Public Library, 1945.

Matthews, Brander, ed. *Papers on Acting.* New York: Hill and Wang, 1958.

Moody, Richard. "American Actors and Acting before 1900: The Making of a Tradition." In *The American Theatre: A Sum of Its Parts.* New York: Sam French, 1971.

Morris, Clara. *Stage Confidences: Talks about Players and Play Acting.* Boston: Lothrop, 1902.

Moses, Montrose J. *Famous Actor-Families in America.* New York: Thomas Y. Crowell, 1906.

Murdoch, James E. *The Stage: Recollections of Actors and Acting from an Experience of Fifty Years.* Philadelphia: J. M. Stoddart, 1880.

Nightingale, Benedict. "Great Acting Must Touch the Heart." *New York Times,* 2 October 1983.

"On Actors and Acting." *Theatre Arts* (special issue), September 1931.

Oppenheimer, George, ed. *The Passionate Playgoer.* New York: Viking, 1958.

Ormsbee, Helen. *Backstage with Actors.* First published 1938. Reprinted New York: Benjamin Blom, 1969.

Patterson, Ada. "Actresses' Clubs in America." *The Theatre,* October 1914.

Rush, James. *The Philosophy of the Human Voice.* Philadelphia: J. Maxwell, 1827.

Skinner, Otis. *Footlights and Spotlights.* Indianapolis: Bobbs-Merrill, 1923.

West, E. J. "Revolution in the American Theatre: Glimpses of Acting Conditions on the American Stage 1855–1870." *Theatre Survey,* 1960.

Wilson, Garff. *A History of American Acting.* Bloomington: Indiana University Press, 1966.

Winter, William. *The Wallet of Time.* New York: Moffat, Yard and Co., 1913.

Woodbury, Lael J. "Styles of Acting in Serious Drama on the Nineteenth Century Stage." Ph.D. diss., University of Illinois, 1954.

Zorn, John W. *The Essential Delsarte.* Metuchen, N.J.: The Scarecrow Press, 1968.

DESIGNERS

Alexander, Elizabeth. "Designing Costumes for the Theatre." Manuscript, c. 1910. Theatre Collection, Museum of the City of New York.

American Stage Designs. Catalogue of an exhibition at the Bourgeois Galleries, New York. New York: Theatre Arts Magazine, 1919.

Aronson, Arnold. *American Scene Design.* New York: Theatre Communications Group, 1985.

Bay, Howard. Keynote address on stage design, 15th International Congress of Société Internationale des Bibliothèques et Musées des Arts du Spectacle. In *Performing Arts Resources* (Theatre Library Association, New York) 8, 1983.

Bentham, Frederick. *The Art of Stage Lighting.* London: Pitman, 1968.

Brown, Frank C. "Lighting in Early Playhouses." *Theatre Magazine,* July 1918.

Brown, John Mason. "The American Theatre and Its Designers." In *American Stage Designs.* New York: Theatre Arts Magazine, 1919.

"A Century of Costumes" [Dazian's]. *New York Times,* 23 March 1941.

Clurman, Harold. "Master of Visual Art" [Boris Aronson]. *New York World Journal Tribune,* 16 April 1967.

Croce, George C., and David H. Wallace. *The New-York Historical Society's Dictionary of Artists in America, 1564–1860.* New Haven, Conn.: Yale University Press, 1957.

Davids, Edith. "Modern Stage Effects." *Munsey's Magazine,* July 1901.

Duerr, Edwin. "Charles Ciceri and the Background of American Scene Design." *Theatre Arts,* December 1932.

Fuchs, Theodore. *Stage Lighting.* Boston: Little, Brown, 1929.

Gelb, Arthur. "Cost-Saving Project." *New York Times,* 3 December 1950.

Gerdts, William H. "William Williams: New American Discoveries." *Winterthur Portfolio* 4, 1968.

Gilbert, Douglas. "Cloth of Gold." *New York World-Telegram,* 1 May 1941.

Gillette, Arnold S. "American Scenography 1716–1969." In *The American Theatre: A Sum of Its Parts.* New York: Sam French, 1971.

Gray, Beverly. "A Conversation with Tharon Musser." *Performing Arts* (California), August 1984.

Haggin, Ben Ali. "A Glance Back at Stage Costuming." *Theatre Magazine,* May 1920.

Hamar, Clifford E. "Scenery on the Early American Stage." *Theatre Annual,* 1948–49.

Harrison, Eelin Stewart. "The Rise of the Costume Designer: A Critical History of Costume on the New York Stage from 1934 to 1950." Ph.D. diss., Louisiana State University, 1968.

Hartmann, Louis. *Theatre Lighting.* New York: D. Appleton, 1930.

Hewes, Henry. "Scene Designers: Their Art and Their Impact." *Saturday Review,* 12 December 1964.

Houghton, Norris. "The Designer Sets the Stage." *Theatre Arts,* October 1936.

Humphreys, Mary Gay. "Stage Scenery and the Men Who Paint It." *The Theatre,* August 1908.

International Theatre Institute. *Stage Design Throughout the World Since 1935.* New York: Theatre Arts Books, 1956.

————. *Stage Design Throughout the World Since 1950.* London: G. G. Harrap, 1964.

Joyce, Robert S. "The Ambruster Scenic Studio," *The OSU Theatre Collection Bulletin,* no. 12, 1965.

Krows, Arthur Edwin. *Play Production in America.* New York: Henry Holt, 1916.

Larson, Orville K. "A Commentary on the 'Historical Development of the Box Set' (*Theatre Annual,* 1945)." *Theatre Annual,* 1954.

Lawrence, William J. "Early American Scene Painters." *New York Dramatic Mirror,* 13 January 1917.

Leverton, Garrett H. *The Production of Later Nineteenth Century Drama.* New York: Teachers College, Columbia University, 1936.

Lewis, Virginia. *Russell Smith: Romantic Realist.* Pittsburgh: University of Pittsburgh Press, 1956.

Loring, Janet. "Costuming on the New York Stage from 1895 to 1915, with Particular Emphasis on Charles Frohman's Companies." Ph.D. diss., State University of Iowa, 1960.

Lounsbury, Warren C. *Theatre Backstage from A to Z.* Seattle: University of Washington Press, 1967.

McCandless, Stanley. *A Method of Lighting the Stage.* New York: Theatre Arts Books, 1958.

McDowell, John H. "Historical Development of the Box Set." *Theatre Annual,* 1945.

MacKay, Patricia. "*A Chorus Line:* Computerized Lighting Control Comes to Broadway." *Theatre Crafts,* November–December 1975.

Marshall, Thomas F. "Charles W. Witham: Scenic Artist to the Nineteenth Century American Stage." In *Anatomy of an Illusion: Studies in Nineteenth Century Theatre Design.* Amsterdam: Scheltema & Holkema, 1969.

Marston, Richard. "Art in the Theatre: The Decline of Scenic Art." *Magazine of Art* 17, 1894.

Moderwell, Hiram K. *The Theatre of Today.* New York: Lane Publishing, 1914.

Oenslager, Donald M. *Stage Design: Four Centuries of Scenic Invention.* New York: Viking, 1975.

Paterek, Josephine. "Costuming on the New York Commercial Stage from 1914 to 1934." Ph.D. diss., University of Minnesota, 1961.

Pendleton, Ralph, ed. *The Theatre of Robert Edmond Jones.* Middletown, Conn.: Wesleyan University Press, 1958.

Penzel, Frederick. *Theatre Lighting before Electricity.* Middletown, Conn.: Wesleyan University Press, 1978.

Pilbrow, Richard. *Stage Lighting.* New York: Van Nostrand, 1970.

Ranck, Edwin Carty. "An American Stage Wizard." *The Theatre,* August 1915.

Richardson, Genevieve. "Costuming on the American Stage 1751–1901: A Study of Major Developments in Wardrobe Practice and Costume Style." Ph.D. diss., University of Illinois, 1953.

Ritter, John P. "Scene Painting as a Fine Art." *Cosmopolitan,* November 1889.

Rosenthal, Jean, and Lael Wertenbaker. *The Magic of Light.* Boston: Little, Brown, 1972.

Rubin, Joel, and Leland H. Watson. *Theatrical Lighting Practice.* New York: Theatre Arts Books, 1954.

Simonson, Lee. *Part of a Lifetime.* New York: Duell, Sloan & Pearce, 1953.

Smith, Russell. "Autobiographical Recollections of Russell Smith." Undated manuscript. Vose Galleries, Boston.

"Stage Effects in Ben-Hur." *Scientific American.* 25 August 1900.

Stoddard, Richard. "Notes on John Joseph Holland, with a Design for the Baltimore Theatre, 1802." *Theatre Survey,* 1971.

————. "Stock Scenery in 1798." *Theatre Survey,* 1972.

————. "Thomas Joyce, Edwin Booth's Costumer." *Educational Theatre Journal,* March 1970.

Stowell, Donald C., Jr. "The New Costuming in America: The Ideas and Practices of Robert Edmond Jones, Norman Bel Geddes, Lee Simonson and Aline Bernstein, 1915–1935." Ph.D. diss., University of Texas at Austin, 1972.

————. "Unionization of the Stage Designer—Male and Female." *Theatre Design & Technology,* October 1974.

Topor, Tom. "Confessions of a Costume Designer" [Patricia Zipprodt]. *New York Post,* 15 October 1978.

Twiggar, Beth. "Veteran Scene Designers Scoff at New 'Overdressed' Theater." *New York Herald Tribune,* 3 August 1941.

Wechsberg, Joseph. "Lighting by Feder." *New Yorker,* 22 October 1960.

Worden, Helen. "Lee Lash Gives Credit to Tariff Bill in Success as Theater Curtain Painter." *New York World-Telegram,* 20 December 1937.

Zolotow, Maurice. "How to Dress a Broadway Show." *Saturday Evening Post,* 24 June 1944.

ARCHITECTS

Atkinson, Brooks. "The Theatre Is *Not* the Thing." *New York Times Magazine,* 31 October 1954.

Birkmire, William H. *The Planning and Construction of American Theatres.* New York: John Wiley & Sons, 1901.

Blackwood, Byrne David. "The Theatres of J. B. McElfatrick and Sons, Architects, 1855–1922." Ph.D. diss., University of Kansas, 1966.

Botto, Louis. *At This Theatre.* New York: Dodd, Mead, 1984.

Bowman, Ned A. "American Theatre Architecture: The Concrete Mirror Held up to Yankee Nature." In *The American Theatre: A Sum of Its Parts.* New York: Sam French, 1971.

Burris-Meyer, Harold, and Edward C. Cole. *Theatres and Auditoriums.* New York: Reinhold, 1964.

"A Charming Folly Restored" [Goodspeed Opera House]. *Architectural Forum,* August 1963.

Dimmick, Ruth Crosby. *Our Theatres To-Day and Yesterday.* New York: H. K. Fly Co., 1913.

Duis, Perry R., and Glen E. Holt. "Curtains for the McVicker's." *Chicago,* December 1979.

Edwards, John C. "A History of Nineteenth Century Theatre Architecture in the United States." Ph.D. diss., Northwestern University, 1963.

Furnas, J. C. *The Americans: A Social History of the United States 1587–1914.* New York: G. P. Putnam's Sons, 1969.

Gardner, Paul. "Central Park's Shakespeare Amphitheatre Dedicated." *New York Times,* 19 June 1962.

Gutheim, Frederick. "Arena Is Bold Step in Design." *Washington Post,* 29 October 1961.

Hardy, Holzman, Pfeiffer Associates. *Broadway Theater Study.* New York: privately printed, 1983.

Henderson, Mary C. *The City and the Theatre.* Clifton, N.J.: James T. White, 1973.

Huxtable, Ada Louise. "All of the Arts but Architecture." *New York Times,* 13 October 1968.

Isaacs, Edith J., ed. *Architecture for the New Theatre.* New York: Theatre Arts Magazine, 1935.

Jenner, Cynthia Lee. "Reclaiming a Neighborhood." *Other Stages* (special issue), 1980.

Jones, Margo. *Theatre-in-the-Round.* New York: Rinehart, 1951.

King, Donald C. "Theatre Disasters." *Marquee,* no. 3, 1976.

Kroll, Jack. "Denver's Crown Jewel." *Newsweek,* 14 January 1980.

Leacroft, Richard and Helen. *Theatre and Playhouse.* London: Methuen, 1984.

Lee, Ming Cho. "Rebuilding a Landmark" [New York Public Theater]. *Theatre Crafts,* July–August 1967.

Lewis, Stanley T. "The New York Theatre; Its Background and Architectural Development: 1750–1853." Ph.D. diss., Ohio State University, 1953.

McDermott, William F. "The Cleveland Playhouse." *Theatre Guild Magazine,* September 1930.

MacKay, Patricia. "Theatre Architecture in the Seventies." *Theatre Crafts,* September 1974.

McNamara, Brooks. *The American Playhouse in the Eighteenth Century.* Cambridge, Mass.: Harvard University Press, 1969.

————. "David Douglass and the Beginning of American Theatre Architecture." *Winterthur Portfolio* 3, 1967.

Mayer, Martin. "Bricks, Mortar and the Performing Arts." In *Report of the Twentieth Century Fund.* New York: Twentieth Century Fund, 1970.

Meersman, Roger. "The National Theatre Lives!" *Theatre News,* no. 2, 1984.

Mielziner, Jo. *The Shapes of Our Theatre.* New York: Clarkson Potter, 1970.

Mullin, Donald C. *The Development of the Playhouse.* Berkeley: University of California Press, 1970.

Nicoll, Allardyce. *The Development of the Theatre.* New York: Harcourt, Brace, 1917.

Pollock, Thomas C. *The Philadelphia Theatre in the Eighteenth Century.* Philadelphia: University of Pennsylvania Press, 1933.

Poppeliers, John, S. Allen Chambers, and Nancy B. Schwartz. *What Style Is It?* Washington, D.C.: The Preservation Press, 1978.

Power, Tyrone. *Impressions of America.* 2 vols. First published 1836. Reprinted New York: Benjamin Blom, 1971.

"Rites Held for Leo Sielke, Decorator of New York Theaters." *Bergen Record,* 19 August 1938.

Sexton, R. W., and B. F. Betts, eds. *American Theatres of Today.* New York: Architectural Book Publishing Co., 1927.

Shafer, Yvonne. "The Auditorium Theatre." *Educational Theatre Journal,* March 1965.

Stewart, H. Michael, ed. *American Architecture for the Arts.* Vol. 1. Dallas, Tex.: Handel & Sons, 1978.

Stoddard, Richard. "The Architecture and Technology of Boston Theatres 1794–1854." Ph.D. diss., Yale University, 1971.

Tallant, Hugh. "The American Theater." *The Brickbuilder,* December 1914.

Tidworth, Simon. *Theatres: An Architectural and Cultural History.* New York: Praeger, 1973.

Ward, Carlton, comp. *National List of Historic Theatre Buildings.* Washington, D.C.: League of Historic American Theatres, 1983.

Wolcott, John R. "The Scene Painter's Palette: 1750–1835." *Theatre Journal,* December 1981.

"Wright Theater for Dallas." *Life,* 18 January 1960.

Young, William, ed. *Famous American Playhouses, 1716–1971.* 2 vols. Chicago: American Library Association, 1973.

"ANTA Steps Out." *Cue,* 20 January 1951.

Arvold, Alfred G. *The Little Country Theatre.* New York: Macmillan, 1923.

Berkowitz, Gerald M. *New Broadways.* Totowa, N.J.: Rowman and Littlefield, 1982.

Blau, Herbert. *The Impossible Theatre: A Manifesto.* New York: Macmillan, 1964.

Browne, Maurice. *Too Late to Lament.* London: Victor Gollancz, 1955.

Burch, Sallie. "The Barter Theatre: A Stage in Virginia History." *GMU Today* (George Mason University), Winter 1982.

Buttitta, Tony, and Barry Witham. *Uncle Sam Presents.* Philadelphia: University of Pennsylvania Press, 1982.

Cheney, Sheldon. *The Art Theatre.* New York: Alfred A. Knopf, 1925.

Chinoy, Helen, ed. "Reunion: A Self-Portrait of the Group Theatre." *Educational Theatre Journal,* December 1976.

Coe, Robert, and Don Shewey. "Q.: Is Mabou Mines Plural or Singular? A.: Both." *Soho News,* 29 April 1981.

Colander, Pat. "Chicago Theater Comes into Its Own." *New York Times,* 27 May 1984.

Davy, Kate. "Richard Foreman's Scenography." *Theatre Crafts,* May–June 1978.

Deutsch, Helen, and Stella Hanau. *The Provincetown: A Story of the Theatre.* First published 1931. Reprinted New York: Russell & Russell, 1972.

DeVries, Hillary. "Actors Theatre of Louisville." *Christian Science Monitor,* 14 July 1983.

Dickinson, Thomas H. *The Insurgent Theatre.* New York: B. W. Huebsch, 1917.

"The Drama League of America." *The Theatre,* August 1911.

Epstein, Helen. "The New York Shakespeare Festival—Does Biggest Mean Best?" *New York Times,* 27 February 1977.

Flanagan, Hallie. *Arena: The History of the Federal Theatre.* First published 1940. Reprinted New York: Limelight Editions, 1985.

Freedman, Samuel G. "As Off Broadway Thrives, Its Problems Mount." *New York Times,* 9 October 1983.

———. "Theatrical Gambles Pay Off for the Guthrie." *New York Times,* 5 July 1984.

———. "Will Success Spoil Nonprofit Theater?" *New York Times,* 22 July 1984.

Garland, Robert. "Jasper Deeter Alone Impels His Theatre." *New York Evening Post,* 29 May 1934.

Gerard, Jeremy. "The Changing Face of Summer Theater." *New York Times,* 16 June 1985.

———. "Regional Theater Shows Its Best." *New York Times,* 2 June 1985.

Glueck, Grace. "A Federal Benefactor of the Arts Comes of Age." *New York Times,* 10 November 1985.

"The Goodman Theatre." *Chicago Daily News,* 4 October 1975.

Gottfried, Martin. *A Theater Divided.* Boston: Little, Brown, 1967.

Green, Harriet L. *Gilmor Brown: Portrait of a Man and an Idea.* Pasadena, Calif.: Burns Printing Co., n.d.

Gussow, Mel. "The Living Theater Returns to Its Birthplace." *New York Times,* 15 January 1984.

Guthrie, Tyrone. *A New Theatre.* New York: McGraw-Hill, 1964.

Henderson, Archibald. *Pioneering a People's Theatre.* Chapel Hill: University of North Carolina Press, 1945.

Houghton, Norris. *Advance from Broadway.* New York: Harcourt, Brace, 1941.

Houseman, John. "The Birth of the Mercury Theatre." *Educational Theatre Journal,* March 1972.

Kakutani, Michiko. "Ellen Stewart Works Hard to Keep LaMama Going." *New York Times,* 5 April 1980.

———. "Nina Vance, Leader of Alley Theater." *New York Times,* 19 February 1980.

Langner, Lawrence. *The Magic Curtain.* New York: E. P. Dutton, 1951.

Little, Stuart. *Off-Broadway: The Prophetic Theatre.* New York: Dell, 1972.

Lynes, Russell. "The Case against Government Aid to the Arts." *New York Times Magazine,* 25 March 1962.

McCleery, Albert, and Carl Glick. *Curtains Going Up.* New York: Pitman, 1939.

McDowell, Edwin. "Tax Laws Aiding Arts Faulted by Foundation." *New York Times,* 28 July 1983.

Macgowan, Kenneth. *Footlights Across America.* New York: Harcourt, Brace, 1923.

MacKaye, Constance D. *The Little Theatre in the United States.* New York: Henry Holt, 1917.

MacKaye, Percy. *Civic Theatre.* New York: Mitchell Kennerley, 1912.

Mathews, Jane De Hart. *The Federal Theatre, 1935–1939.* Princeton, N.J.: Princeton University Press, 1967.

Matz, Mary Jane. *The Many Lives of Otto Kahn.* New York: Macmillan, 1963.

Moderwell, Hiram K. "The Drama Leagues in Annual Convention." *Boston Transcript,* 29 April 1915.

Monroe, John G. "Charles Gilpin and the Drama League Controversy." *Black American Literature Forum,* Winter 1982.

Netzer, Dick. *The Subsidized Muse: Public Support for the Arts in the United States.* New York: Cambridge University Press, 1978.

Noble, Peter. *The Fabulous Orson Welles.* London: Hutchinson, 1950.

Novick, Julius. *Beyond Broadway.* New York: Hill and Wang, 1968.

Papp, Joseph. "What the American Theater Needs Most." *Christian Science Monitor,* 14 September 1978.

Parone, Edward, ed. *New Theatre in America*. New York: Dell, 1965.

Patrick, Robert. "The Other Brick Road." *Other Stages*, 8–11 February 1979.

Perry, Clarence A. *The Work of the Little Theatres*. New York: Russell Sage Foundation, 1933.

Pollock, Channing. "Giant Oaks from Little Theatres." *Green Book*, February 1917.

Ranney, Omar. "Forever Toby." *Theatre Arts*, August 1953.

Rosenfield, John. "Margo Jones: Theatre Pioneer." *New York Times*, 31 July 1955.

Ross, Don. "Ten Years of Circle in the Square." *New York Herald Tribune*, 26 February 1971.

Ross, Laura. *Theatre Profiles 6*. New York: Theatre Communications Group, 1984.

Shafer, Yvonne. "The Guthrie Revisited: Minneapolis Celebrates 20 Years of Theatre Achievement." *Theatre News*, Summer 1983.

Shalett, Sidney M. "B. Davenport Et Cie." *New York Times*, 31 March 1940.

Shank, Theodore. *American Alternative Theater*. New York: Grove Press, 1982.

Sherakawa, Sam H. "The Eccentric World of Charles Ludlam." *New York Times*, 3 July 1983.

Shewey, Don. "Has Regional Theater Fulfilled Its Promise?" *New York Times*, 7 August 1983.

———. "Repertory Takes Root—and Feeds Broadway." *New York Times*, 11 March 1984.

Simon, John. "Who Calls That Living?" *New York Magazine*, 30 January 1984.

Slout, William L. *Theatre in a Tent*. Bowling Green, Ohio: Bowling Green University Popular Press, 1972.

Steinberg, Mollie B. *The History of the Fourteenth Street Theatre*. New York: Dial Press, 1931.

Sterling, Wallace. "Cleveland Play House Unveils New Theatre Complex." *Theatre News*, December 1983.

"The Theatre That Comes to You." *The Theatre*, July 1916.

Wetzsteon, Ross. "Theatre Journal: The Living Theatre." *Village Voice*, 3 October 1968.

Ziegler, Joseph W. *Regional Theatre: The Revolutionary Stage*. Minneapolis: University of Minnesota Press, 1973.

THEATER IN AMERICA: PAST, PRESENT, AND FUTURE

Angell, Roger. "My Old Flame." *New Yorker*, 31 May 1993.

Bartow, Arthur. *The Director's Voice: Twenty-One Interviews*. New York: Theatre Communications Group, 1988.

Bennett, James. "Vibrancy to Vacancy: Remaking the Deuce." *New York Times*, 6 August 1992.

Bernstein, Richard. "Why the Cutting Edge Has Lost Its Bite." *New York Times*, 30 September 1990.

Blumenthal, Ellen. "The Avant-Garde Is Taking a Look Backward." *New York Times*, 1 February 1987.

Bly, Mark, and Mark M. Bocek. "Seattle and Broadway." In *Prologue* (program of the Seattle Repertory Theatre), January 1992.

"Broadway Box Office Hits Five-Year High." *New York Times*, 2 June 1994.

Brustein, Robert. "Culture by Coercion." *New York Times* (Op-Ed page), 29 November 1994.

———. *Reimagining American Theatre*. New York: Hill and Wang, 1991.

Canby, Vincent. "Is Broadway Fogbound in a Special-Effects Age?" *New York Times*, 16 January 1994.

Cohn, Ruby. *New American Dramatists 1960–1990*. 2d ed. New York: St. Martin's Press, 1991.

Collins, Glenn. "The Play Is Just Not the Thing." *New York Times*, 3 January 1994.

"Directors on Comedy." *Back Stage*, 20 June 1986.

Dunning, Jennifer. "Crazy for Dance, a Broadway Gypsy [Susan Stroman] Creates Her Own." *New York Times*, 10 February 1992.

Epstein, Hal. "An Actor's Odyssey: From Prison to Broadway [Charles S. Dutton]." *Washington Times*, 15 January 1985.

———. "Christopher Chadman, Dancer and Stage Choreographer" (obituary), *New York Times*, 3 May 1995.

Goldstein, Michael. "Re-Inventing Broadway." *New York Magazine*, 29 May 1995.

Gordy, Molly. "A Role to Live By [Mercedes Ruehl]." *New York Newsday*, 12 May 1993.

Guernsey, Otis, Jr. *Curtain Times: The New York Theater 1965–1987*. New York: Applause, 1987.

Gussow, Mel. "500 in the Theater Gather at the Altar of Diversity." *New York Times*, 30 June 1994.

Havel, Vaclav. "World Theatre Day Message—27 March 1994." *The Newsletter of the International Theatre Institute of the United States, Inc.*, Summer 1994.

Horwitz, Simi. "Inside the Secret Garden: Women Directors Make Inroads on Broadway." *TheaterWeek*, 10 February 1992.

———. "Tackling Two Shakespearean Actors." *TheaterWeek*, 20 January 1992.

Ingram, Bruce. "Steppenwolf Opens $8 Mil, 2-Stage Theater." *Variety*, 4 March 1991.

Isenberg, Barbara. "Covering All the Bases." *Los Angeles Times* (Calendar), 26 September 1994.

Kerr, Walter. "A Net to Catch Playwrights before They Fall Away." *New York Times*, 3 April 1988.

King, Bruce, ed. *Contemporary American Theatre*. New York: St. Martin's Press, 1991.

Kisselgoff, Anna. "Broadway's Dance: At Play with the Past." *New York Times*, 20 January 1995.

Kramer, Richard. "A Play of Words about a Play." *New York Times*, 31 October 1993.

Lahr, John. "Angels on Broadway." *New Yorker*, 31 May 1993.

Lubow, Arthur. "George Wolfe in Progress." *New Yorker*, 20 September 1993.

———. "Tony Kushner's Paradise Lost." *New Yorker*, 30 November 1992.

McGee, Celia. "To the Manner Born [Stockard Channing]." *New York Magazine*, 22 October 1990.

McNeil, Donald G., Jr. " 'Love! Valour! Compassion!' Recoups Six Weeks After Opening." *New York Times*, 24 April 1995.

Mantle, Burns, and Garrison P. Sherwood, eds. *The Best Plays of 1899–1909*. New York: Dodd, Mead, 1944.

Merkling, Frank. "The Director [John Tillinger] in Residence." *Danbury News Times*, 19 March 1988.

O'Haire, Patricia. "Choreographer's Dancing Feat [Wayne Cilento]." *New York Daily News*, 28 June 1993.

Pacheco, Patrick. "Ready for the Opener [Victor Garber]." *New York Newsday* (Fan Fare), 27 February 1994.

Pottlitzer, Joanne. "Cultural Diversity in U.S. Theatre." *The Newsletter of the International Theatre Institute of the United States, Inc.*, Fall–Winter, 1994.

Rich, Frank. "A New Generation on Old Broadway." *New York Times*, 6 June 1993.

Richards, David. "Counting Down to the Year 2000." *New York Times*, 27 June 1993.

———. "Faith Prince, How Does Your Garden Grow?" *New York Times*, 31 March 1992.

———. "A One-Woman Riot Conjures Character Amid the Chaos." *New York Times*, 24 February 1994.

———. "Sellars's Merchant of Venice Beach." *New York Times*, 18 October 1994.

———. "A Working Playwright Edges into Fame [Terrence McNally]. *New York Times*, 29 August 1993.

Riedel, Michael. "A Renaissance in Cleveland." *TheaterWeek*, 12 July 1992.

Saffian, Sarah. "Performance Art's Outrageous Mosaic." *New York Daily News*, 2 December 1993.

Samuels, Steven, ed. *Theatre Profiles 11*. New York: Theatre Communications Group, 1994.

Savran, David. *In Their Own Words: Contemporary American Playwrights*. New York: Theatre Communications Group, 1988.

Shapiro, Laura. "Send in the Clown [Bill Irwin]." *Newsweek*, 15 May 1989.

"Six Directors." *Back Stage*, March 4–10, 1994.

Smith, Ronn. *American Set Design 2*. New York: Theatre Communications Group, 1991.

Stayton, Richard. "Nathan's Famous (Almost) [Nathan Lane]." *Los Angeles Times* (Calendar), 1 August 1993.

Sullivan, Daniel. "Confessions of an Onstage Director." *American Theatre*, June 1985.

Weber, Bruce. "Broadway's Role on the Stages of the Nation." *New York Times*, 29 August 1994.

———. "Just Clowning Around with Intellect [Bill Irwin]." *New York Times*, 3 March 1993.

Wetzsteon, Ross. "Up from Solitary." *New York Magazine*, 5 May 1990.

White, Bruce N. "The Warehouse and the Church [Theatre de la Jeune Lune]." *Theatre Crafts*, May 1992.

Winer, Linda. "Dancing's Talented Newcomers." *New York Newsday* (Fan Fare), 3 May 1992.

Witchel, Alex. "Find the Ginger! It's Anxiety Time for an Original [William Finn]." *New York Times*, 26 April 1992.

Wontorek, Paul. "A Murder, a Marriage, and Two Musicals." *TheaterWeek* 13 April 1992.

Zesch, Lindy. "Harris Poll Is at Odds with Arts Statistics." *American Theatre*, May 1988.

INDEX

Whenever possible, the birth and death dates of important figures in the American theater have been included in this index. *Italicized* page numbers refer to illustrations.

347

PHOTOGRAPH CREDITS

Mary C. Henderson and Harry N. Abrams, Inc., wish to express their appreciation to Phil Pocock, who with skill and patience did a vast amount of copy work and original photography of artwork, and to Kenneth Taranto, Lynton Gardiner, Otto Nelson, Scott Hyde, and Robert Baldridge, all of whom contributed much to the quality of the photographic work in this volume. The author and the publisher would also like to convey their special thanks to Martha Swope and her associates for consistently providing superb photographs.

Actors Theatre of Louisville, courtesy of: 292 below. Albright-Knox Art Gallery, Gift of Julia and Estelle L. Foundation: 175. Alda, Arlene: 287. Aldredge, Theoni V., courtesy of: 227 above and below left. Andrews, Bert: 296. AP/Wide World Photos: 277. Arena Stage, courtesy of: 258; 293 (Annalisa Kraft). Aronson, Mrs. Boris, courtesy of: 211 above. Ashton, Larry, courtesy of: 86. Beatty, John Lee, courtesy of: 212 below. Beinecke Rare Book and Manuscript Lib., Yale Univ.: 42. Boston Public Lib.: 17 above. © Bryan-Brown, Marc: 311 above, 315 above. Cherney, Lawrence/FPG Internat.: 297. Chicago Historical Soc.: 19, 243 below, 252 above, 265. Cleveland Playhouse, courtesy of: 270 above. Columbia Univ. Rare Book and Manuscript Lib., Joseph Urban Coll.: 203 below. Culver Pictures: 171 above. Dance Collection, New York Public Library at Lincoln Center: 127 (White), 133 right. Darby, Eileen/New York Public Library at Lincoln Center, Billy Rose Theatre Coll.: 119, 189 above left, 189 below left. Darby, Eileen/Museum of the City of New York Theatre Coll.: 1, 79 left, 115, 189 above right, 223 above. Davis, Paul: 286. Denver Theatre Center, courtesy of: 261 above. Elder, Eldon, courtesy of: 210 below. Elitch's Gardens Company Theatre, courtesy of: 278. Elson, Paul, courtesy of: 251 below left. © Erickson, T. Charles: 302, 315 center, 323. © Feldman, Richard: 309 below. Feller Precision, courtesy of: 316 above. Fisher, Jules, courtesy of: 234, 235. Fox & Fowle Architects, P. C., © Andrew Gordon, photographer: 319 above. Frank Lloyd Wright Foundation: 259. Gibson, William, © Martha Swope Assoc.: 317 above. Goodspeed Opera House, courtesy of: 251 below right (Wilson Brownell). Hampden-Booth Theatre Lib. at the Players: 15, 154. Harry Ransom Humanities Research Ctr. Art Coll., Univ. of Texas at Austin: 32 below, 156. Harry Ransom Research Ctr., Univ. of Texas at Austin: 206 above. Harvard Theatre Collection: 13, 16, 48, 51 below, 55 below, 91, 147 below, 167, 237 above, 239, 263. Hays, David, courtesy of: 215 below. Heller, Michael: 187 above. Henderson, Mary C., courtesy of: 12, 15 above, 50, 96, 143, 146 below, 148, 150, 202 above, 217, 218, 220 right, 237 below, 240, 242 above, 243 above, 245, 261. Hirschfeld, Al: 81 center. Holm, Hanya, and the Dance Notation Bureau, courtesy of: 135 below. Image by View by View: 321 above. © Jeffry, Alix, Harvard Theatre Coll.: 38 above, 288. Johnson, Doug: 84 below. Judd, *History of the American Theatre*, 1919: 20. Katvan, Rifka: 118. Kauffman, M., Life Magazine © 1967 Time Inc.: 41. Kauffman, M., Life Magazine © Time Inc.: 182 below. Kellogg, Marjorie, courtesy of: 215 center. Kim, Willa, courtesy of: 227 below right. Klotz, Florence, courtesy of: 224 below. Kook, Edward, courtesy of: 206 below. Kravis Center, courtesy of: 321 below. Larkin, Peter, courtesy of: 214 below. © Lauren, Liz : 309 above. © Lester, Jennifer: 315 below. Library of Congress: 27 above left and right, 149, 151, 153, 161, 249. Lortel, Lucille, courtesy of: 281 center. © Marcus, Joan: 303 below, 310 below, 311 below, 314, 317 below. McClennahan, Charles, courtesy of: 316 below. Metropolitan Museum of Art, New York: 193. Metzer, W./ H. Armstrong Roberts: 246. Mili, Gjon, Life Magazine © Time Inc.: 71 below left. Mitchell, David, courtesy of: 216 center. Moiseiwitsch, Tanya, courtesy of: 295. Morath, Inga, © Magnum: 81 above. Museum of the City of New York, Print Dept.: 242 below. Museum of the City of New York, Theatre Coll.: 11; 12; 13; 14; 15 above; 17 below; 21; 22; 23–25; 26 above; 26 below (Byron); 27 below left and below right; 28 below; 29; 30 above; 30 below (D. Barnes); 31 center (White); 31 below (Vandamm); 32 above; 33; 34 above; 34 below left (Vandamm); 35 below; 36–37; 38 center (Vandamm); 39 above; 43; 44; 47; 51 above; 53 (Byron); 54; 55 above; 56–60; 62 (Byron); 63; 64 above (White); 64 below; 65; 64 above (White); 68 above (White); 68 below; 69; 71 above left (Vandamm); 71 below left (Lucas and Monroe); 74 (Lucas and Monroe); 75; 76 (Vandamm); 77 above (Vandamm); 77 below (Look Coll.); 78 (Vandamm); 80 above; 81 below; 83 above left and right (Vandamm); 84 above; 89 (Bob Goldby); 93; 94; 95 (Byron); 97 (Byron); 98 (Arnold Genthe); 99; 100; 104 (Byron); 106 (Vandamm); 107 (Vandamm); 109; 110 (PM, Mary Morris); 111 (Vandamm); 116 (Vandamm); 124 above; 126 (Byron); 129; 130 below (M. Seymour); 132 right (Vandamm); 132 left; 133 (Look Coll.); 135 above (Van William); 139 above (Friedman-Abeles); 139 below; 145; 146 above; 147 above; 155 above left (Sarony); 155 above right (Byron); 155 below left; 155 below right; 158; 159; 160 (Byron); 162 (Sarony); 163; 164 (White); 165; 169 (White); 170 (White); 171 below; 172 above; 172 below (White); 173 below; 176 (Vandamm); 177; 178 above left (White); 178 above right and below right; 179 above (Vandamm); 180 (B. Pinchot); 181 above left and right (Vandamm); 181 below right (Friedman-Abeles); 182 above left and right; 185 above right (Arthur Zinn); 187 below; 194; 195; 199; 202 below (Byron); 207; 210 above; 213 above; 220 left; 221; 222 above; 225 below; 226 above left, below left, and below right; 238; 248; 250; 251 above; 252 below; 253; 254; 255 above; 257; 267; 269; 274. Musser, Tharon, courtesy of: 231. National Portrait Gallery, Smithsonian Institution, Wash., D.C.: 179 below. New York Public Library at Lincoln Center, Billy Rose Theatre Coll.: 4–5 (Vandamm), 16, 17 below, 29, 31 above (Byron), 34 center (George Karger PIX), 35 above (Vandamm), 71 above right, 83 below left, 83 below right (Vandamm), 84 above, 85 (Roger Greenawalt), 102–3 (White), 113 (Alfredo Valenti), 128, 131 (Friedman-Abeles), 138 (Friedman-Abeles), 174, 178 below left, 181 below left, 185 below (Alfredo Valenti), 188 (Friedman-Abeles), 197, 208 above, 208 below (Vandamm), 209 below, 210 center, 211 below, 213 below (courtesy of the Alswang Family), 222 below (Jack Buxbaum), 224 above, 225 above (White), 232, 255 below, 270 below, 271–73, 276 above (Harriet Arnold), 276 below, 277 below, 279 above, 281 below, 283, 285 (James Gossage), 289, 290 (Tony Kent). New York Shakespeare Festival, courtesy of: 39, 215 above, 298, 299. Norkin, Sam: 114. © Paul, Michael: 318 below. Phototeque/Daily News: 72–73. Pond, Helen, and Herbert Senn, courtesy of: 322. Ridiculous Theatrical Co.: 291 (John Stern). Roberts, H. Armstrong: 281 above. © Rosegg, Carol: 320. Selz, Irene, by permission of Tom Engelhardt: 80 below. Sharaff, Irene, courtesy of: 226 above right. Shubert Archive: 28 above, 209 above, 256. Southwestern Coll., Texas Tech Univ.: 282. Steiner, Ralph: 275. Stickney, Dorothy: 279 below. Stiga, Paul, courtesy of: 205. Stoller, Ezra © ESTO: 292 above. © Swope, Martha: endpapers, 40, 79 right, 86 above and center, 87, 121, 124 below, 125 below, 137, 141, 185 above left, 186, 189 below right, 190, 191, 214 above, 216 above, 230, 301, 303 above, 304, 306 below, 307 above, 310 above, 311 center, 318 above. Theatre Magazine: 203 above. Thompson, Jay: 38. Trinity Square Repertory Company, courtesy of: 125 above (Robert Emerson). © Tucker, David A., II: 307 below. Tyrone Guthrie Theater, courtesy of: 260 above. Vanity Fair © 1933 (renewed 1961) by the Condé Nast Pubs. Inc.: 130 above (Edward Steichen). Vezzuso, Jerry: 264. Wagner, Robin, courtesy of: 212 above. The Walt Disney Company, courtesy of, photo © Joan Marcus: 319 below. Walton, Tony, courtesy of: 216 below. Watts, Ron/West Light: 260 below. Westport Country Playhouse, courtesy of: 280. Wisconsin Center for Theatre Research: 173 above. Zipprodt, Patricia, courtesy of: 2–3, 223 below.